Dementia and the Law

Dementia and the Law

Tony Harrop-Griffiths

Jonathan Cowen

Christine Cooper

Rhys Hadden

Angela Hodes

Victoria Flowers

All Barristers at Field Court Chambers

Steven Fuller

Barrister

JORDANS

Published by
Jordan Publishing Limited
21 St Thomas Street
Bristol BS1 6JS

British Library Cataloguing-in-Publication Data

A catalogue record for this book is available from the British Library.

ISBN 978 1 84661 756 0

Typeset by Letterpart Limited, Caterham on the Hill, Surrey CR3 5XL

Printed in Great Britain by CPI Antony Rowe, Chippenham and Eastbourne

FOREWORD

As the Introduction to this book records, a significant number of people in the UK have dementia; one in three people over 65 will develop it.

This invaluable book will greatly assist practitioners who specialise in this field of work as well as the increasing number of people who are not lawyers, but want to understand the many complex legal and practical issues that arise when someone has this challenging progressive condition.

The structure of the book is extremely well laid out and combines a clear and authoritative exposition of the law, with guidance on practice and procedure. It provides readily accessible help on all the issues which are likely to arise. I have no doubt it will provide a welcome safe port of call for all those who seek guidance or need answers in this area of work. Each of the authors is to be congratulated on pooling their knowledge, and utilising their considerable expertise, to produce this excellent book.

Lucy Theis
High Court Judge, Family Division
December 2013

INTRODUCTION

Dementia, more than any other condition, is set to shape our view of later life, challenge our health and social care system, frame our elder law. The future for our ageing population is stark: there are already over 800,000 people in the UK living with dementia, many still undiagnosed, and there are projected to be a million by 2021 (Alzheimer's Society; 2007, 2012).

The issues that dementia presents – medical, psychological, social; philosophical, ethical, legal – are complex and distinctive. Each person's lived experience of dementia is unique. Legal considerations must sit within a framework that recognises, values and supports the individual living with dementia: 'the person comes first' (Kitwood; 1997). Yet achieving true person-centredness means going further than legal considerations as to what is in a person's best interests.

Dementia is an umbrella term (a 'syndrome') which is characterised by memory loss and difficulties with thinking, problem-solving or language. It predominantly affects people over the age of 65, particularly those in their 80s, 90s or above. The most common causes of dementia as listed below are incurable and the condition is gradually progressive. In spite of this, with support many people can remain independent for a long time and live well with dementia at all stages (Alzheimer's Society; 2007).

There are more than 100 different causes of dementia, but over 95% is due to (Alzheimer's Society; 2007):

- Alzheimer's disease
- Vascular disease (sometimes together with Alzheimer's – 'mixed dementia')
- Lewy bodies
- Parkinson's disease
- Frontotemporal lobe degeneration (including Pick's disease).

The symptoms of these different dementias overlap to varying degrees. People with dementia in the earlier stages will often have:

- Loss of memory – this particularly affects short-term memory, such as forgetting messages, forgetting routes or names, and asking questions repetitively. Long-term memory is usually still quite good.
- Difficulties with language – people may not follow a conversation or they might struggle to find the right word for something.

- Disorientation – people with dementia can become confused about time or place, especially in unfamiliar surroundings.
- Problems carrying out everyday tasks – people need increasing levels of support from other individuals or organisations.
- Changes in mood or behaviour – people with dementia may become withdrawn or easily upset, or they may behave out of character.

Whatever the cause, dementia presents challenges for legal professionals that are distinct from those of the older client in general. These are primarily challenges of capacity, consent and communication.

The progressive nature of dementia means that, while someone with the condition may vary from day to day, over a period of several years their ability to make different decisions will at different points be lost. Legal considerations of capacity and consent are necessarily set against this trajectory of cognitive decline.

The second challenge is that communicating with the person will, from quite an early stage, require consideration and empathy so that they are supported to make or take part in a decision. Seeing the person – not the dementia – is paramount. Some practical tips on communication are:

- Talk to the person not their partner or carer. Listen carefully and give the person your full attention.
- Don't make assumptions about the person's level of understanding.
- Speak clearly in short sentences, allowing more time for the person to process information. Give the person extra time to respond.
- Break complicated decisions into smaller steps, and check the person's understanding at each stage.
- Make sure your body language and facial expressions match what you are saying.
- Provide written supporting information which people can read at their leisure. Make it succinct and accessible.

Whatever the dementia type, this book addresses many of the complex legal issues that arise from the time of diagnosis to the time when the dementia has a significant impact on a person's life.

The first section of the book covers issues concerning the diagnosis and assessment of a person who may have dementia that can give rise to particularly complex problems. Chapter 1 discusses why data protection and best interests need to be considered on balance and who has permission to access the information. It also considers some circumstances when a duty to report a diagnosis of dementia may arise.

Chapter 2 then considers the interaction between the regime under the Mental Capacity Act 2005 (MCA 2005) and that under the Mental Health Act 1983 (MHA 1983), both of which are likely to affect a person with dementia at some point in time. The criteria by which a person with dementia can be hospitalised and sectioned and when a section can be challenged are discussed. The powers in relation to the assessment and treatment of those detained are explained in this chapter which also looks at what happens when the section expires.

The final chapter in the first section covers the three different types of assessment that are commonly applicable to a person with dementia which are:

(1) capacity assessments under the MCA 2005;
(2) continuing healthcare assessments; and
(3) assessment for local authority services.

The second section goes on to consider the issues surrounding the provision of care for the person with dementia. To understand the legal issues surrounding the care provided to a person with dementia it is important to have an understanding of the concept of a person's best interests which permeates all decisions about their welfare. Also important is an appreciation of the principles of deprivation of liberty along with the legal approach under the MCA 2005. Chapter 4 covers the issues involved around welfare and best interests and deprivation of liberty and discusses what needs to be put in place when making such welfare and best interests decisions for the person with dementia.

People with dementia require increasing and complex forms of care and treatment and Chapter 5 considers the legal implications surrounding the National Health Service's responsibilities and duties in the treatment of people with dementia. Do they have the right to refuse medical treatment and care at any time? The rights to receive healthcare and to refuse treatment are set out in Chapter 5 along with the most important legal issues concerning these provisions. The care services provided by local authorities and the criteria by which decisions as to what care services will be provided are covered in Chapter 6. The various statutes and regulations that govern both care services in the home and those provided in residential care homes are covered here as well as when a person is no longer eligible for after care support under s 117 of the MHA 1983.

Chapter 7 sets out the rights of those caring for the person with dementia. This is a subject about which the leading care charities receive thousands of enquiries every year. What are the assessment duties and rights under the Carers (Recognition and Services) Act 1995?

The third section is concerned with the property and affairs of the person who has dementia. Although it is a feature of the law in England and Wales that individuals should always enjoy the freedom to manage their own affairs, once an individual becomes incapacitated with dementia, how can their affairs be managed in their best interests? This section begins with a chapter considering the powers of attorneys, their obligations and duties and the legal processes involved.

The property and financial issues affecting those with dementia are of major concern for many reasons, especially as funding is required for on-going care. Chapter 9 explains the role of the Court of Protection in making decisions about the financial affairs of those who have dementia and the significant changes brought about by the MCA 2005. Section 3 concludes with a chapter covering issues concerning the funding of care at home and in a residential care or nursing home. These include aftercare under the MHA 1983, continuing health care, individual budgets and direct payments and self-funding.

The final section of the book covers remedies available when disputes arise applying to a person with dementia. Chapter 11 deals with the informal processes available when challenging decisions made and making complaints to the relevant authorities. Alternative methods of dispute resolution can be particular important where there is a need for on-going care services and these are explained in Chapter 12 before turning in Chapter 13 to the substantive remedies available through proceedings in the Court of Protection and then in Chapter 14 to applications for judicial review. The section concludes with a chapter on other court proceedings that may be relevant to a person who has dementia such as the use of the inherent jurisdiction of the High Court, damages claims for personal injuries and professional negligence claims. This chapter also covers damages arising from a breach of human rights as well as remedies for discrimination and those arising out of contractual disputes.

The legal issues surrounding dementia are of increasing concern to current and future generations who are caring for and supporting those who have this illness. It is hoped this book will provide guidance on how to deal with many of the legal issues involved in the daily life of a person with dementia, his family and carers.

References

- Alzheimer's Society (2007). *Dementia UK; a report to the Alzheimer's Society on the prevalence and economic cost of dementia in the UK produced by King's College London and the London School of Economics*. Alzheimer's Society, London.
- Alzheimer's Society (2012). *Dementia 2012: a national challenge*. Alzheimer's Society, London.
- Kitwood (1976). *Dementia reconsidered*. Open University Press, Buckingham.

ACKNOWLEDGEMENTS

The authors would like to thank Sabina Smith, Dr Andrew J Hartle, John Crosfill, Jacqueline Lefton and David Brounger for their assistance in producing this book and to thank their families and partners, whose patient support has made this book possible.

CONTENTS

TABLE OF CASES

References are to paragraph numbers.

TABLE OF STATUTES

References are to paragraph numbers.

TABLE OF STATUTORY INSTRUMENTS

References are to paragraph numbers.

CHAPTER 1

ACCESS AND RIGHTS TO PERSONAL INFORMATION

1.1 This chapter is concerned with personal information relating to a person who has been diagnosed with dementia. The individual concerned may wish to have access to their own records in order to make plans for the future. Alternatively, people caring for or managing the finances of someone who lacks capacity may need information to assess the person's capacity to make a specific decision, determine that person's best interests or make appropriate decisions on the person's behalf.

1.2 Firstly, this chapter will consider how the law strikes a balance between ensuring a right of access to personal information and the right to keep personal information confidential. Secondly, it will look at how personal information can be requested on behalf of others, particularly if that individual lacks capacity. Finally, it will consider certain specific situations when a person may have a duty to report a diagnosis of dementia.

ACCESS TO PERSONAL INFORMATION

1.3 The right of access to information is not an absolute right. It is a qualified right and requires a balance to be struck between competing interests and principles. For example, the right of access to personal information can potentially conflict with the right to keep such information confidential.

1.4 There are a number of different laws that relate to the processing, holding and sharing of personal information, including health and social care records. The three most important areas of law are:

(i) the common law duty of confidence;

(ii) the Human Rights Act ('HRA 1998') and European Convention on Human Rights ('ECHR'), in particular Article 8 (the right to respect for private and family life); and

(iii) the Data Protection Act 1998 ('DPA 1998').

The common law duty of confidence

1.5 The common law has long recognised that a person has a right to expect that personal information about him or her will be kept confidential.[1] Information will be protected if it has 'the necessary quality of confidence about it' and has been imparted in circumstances importing an obligation of confidence.[2] The general duty is based upon a presumption against disclosure to third parties.[3]

1.6 For information to have a quality of confidence it is generally accepted that: it is not trivial in its nature; not in the public domain or easily available from another source; it has a degree of sensitivity; and it has been communicated for a limited purpose and in circumstances where the recipient is likely to assume an obligation of confidence. For example, information given to a doctor, social worker or lawyer would normally be considered to have this quality of confidence, but a conversation with an acquaintance would not. A duty of confidentiality may also arise as a result of a contract where one party agrees to keep confidential information provided by the other party.

1.7 In certain circumstances an individual may lack the capacity to be aware of their rights in relation to confidential information but this does not diminish the duty of confidence.

1.8 As a general principle, personal information may only be disclosed by its recipient with the consent of the person who has divulged this information, even to close relatives. However, there are circumstances when disclosure may be permissible in the absence of consent. As with the HRA 1998, confidentiality is a qualified right. A public authority is able to override a duty of confidence when it is required by law to do so or if it is in the public interest to do so. The disclosure of confidential information is, in any particular circumstances, about balancing the private and public interests of confidentiality against the private and public interests of disclosure. The courts have generally expected the recipient to carry out a 'pressing need' test before any disclosure is made.[4]

Human rights and confidentiality

1.9 Whereas the common law duty of confidence protects confidential information, the enactment of the HRA 1998 has led to the development of the principle of privacy, by incorporating the ECHR into English law.

1.10 In a number of cases, the European Court of Human Rights has confirmed that Article 8 ECHR is concerned both with the duty on the state to

---

1 *Prince Albert v Strange* [1849] EWHC Ch J20.
2 *Coco v AN Clark (Engineers) Ltd* [1968] FSR 415 per Megarry J at [47].
3 *R v Mid Glamorgan FHSA ex p Martin* [1995] 1 All ER 356 per Nourse LJ at [363j].
4 See, for example, *R v Chief Constable of North Wales ex p AB* [1997] 4 All ER 691.

protect individuals from the unreasonable disclosure of publicly held confidential information[5] as well as with the right of individuals to access such information.

1.11 Section 6 of the HRA 1998 requires public authorities, such as NHS organisations and social services, to act in conformity with the ECHR. An individual's rights under the ECHR may be extended to independent sector providers where they provide publicly funded care through contractual arrangements. Legislation generally must also be compatible with the HRA 1998.

1.12 Article 8(1) ECHR provides that 'Everyone has the right to respect for his private and family life, his home and his correspondence.' This right covers health and social care records.

1.13 As with the common law, the right to privacy in the ECHR is qualified. This means that interferences by the State can be permissible, but such interferences must be justified and satisfy certain conditions set out in Article 8(2). Any interference with Article 8 must be:

(i) in accordance with the law; and
(ii) necessary and proportionate; and
(iii) in the interests of the legitimate objectives identified in Article 8(2) (including the protection of health or the protection of rights and freedoms of others).

1.14 Disclosure of private information will only be 'necessary in a democratic society' where it is justified by a pressing social need, and is proportionate to the legitimate aim pursued.[6]

1.15 Proportionality involves two concepts. First, whether the means employed are proportionate to the legitimate aim pursued. Second, whether a fair balance has been struck between the interests of the community and the protection of the individual's rights.[7] In *R (L) v Commissioner of Police of the Metropolis*,[8] Lord Hope stated at [42]:

> '...the issue is essentially one of proportionality. On the one hand there is a pressing social need that children and vulnerable adults should be protected against the risk of harm. On the other hand there is the Applicant's right to respect

---

5 See, for example, *Z v Finland* (1997) 25 EHRR 371 and *MS v Sweden* (1997) BHRC 248.

6 According to the ECtHR settled case-law, the notion of 'necessity' implies that the interference corresponds to a pressing social need and, in particular, that it is proportionate to one of the legitimate aims pursued by the authorities (see, among other authorities, *Olsson v Sweden* (1988) 11 EHRR 259, para 67).

7 See *Huang v Secretary of State for the Home Department* [2007] UKHL 11, per Lord Bingham at [19].

8 [2009] UKSC 3.

for her private life. It is of the greatest importance that the balance between these two considerations is struck in the right place.'

1.16 In general, compliance with the DPA 1998 (see below) and the common law of confidentiality will satisfy the requirements of the HRA 1998. However, this is a complex area of law that is open to interpretation by the courts and specific legal advice may sometimes be required to ensure compliance with a request or to challenge a refusal not to release information.

Data Protection Act 1998

1.17 The DPA 1998 is the main piece of legislation that governs the protection of personal data in England and Wales. It establishes a framework of rights and duties that is designed to safeguard personal data[9] in balance with the legitimate needs of organisations to collect and use these data.[10]

1.18 The structure and provisions of the DPA 1998 are complex and can be hard to navigate. Guidance on how the DPA 1998 works has been issued by the Information Commissioner's Office ('ICO').[11] The Department of Health has also issued specific guidance to the NHS ('NHS Guidance')[12] and local authorities' social services departments ('Social Services Guidance').[13]

Data protection principles

1.19 A data controller[14] must comply with the data protection principles established by the DPA 1998. The eight basic principles are set out in Schedule 1 to the DPA 1998. In summary, these require that information must be:

- processed[15] fairly and lawfully;
- processed for limited, specifically stated purposes;

---

9 Data that relate to a living individual who can be identified from those data or from those data and other information that is in the possession of, or is likely to come into possession of the holder of the data – see DPA 1998, s 1(1).

10 Para 1, *Guide to Data Protection*, Information Commissioner's Office, http://www.ico.org.uk/for_organisations/data_protection/the_guide.

11 Information Commissioner, *Guide to Data Protection.*

12 *Guidance for access to health records and requests* (2010) and *Confidentiality NHS Code of Practice* (2003).

13 *Data Protection Act 1998 Guidance for Social Services* (2000).

14 A person who (either alone or jointly or in common with other persons) determines the purposes for which and the manner in which any personal date are used – see DPA 1998, s 1(1).

15 'Processing', in relation to information or data, means obtaining, recording or holding the information or data or carrying out any operation or set of operations on the information or data, including: (1) organisation, adaptation or alteration of the information or data; (2) retrieval, consultation or use of the information or data; (3) disclosure of the information or data by transmission, dissemination or otherwise making it available; or (4) alignment, combination, blocking, erasure or destruction of the information or data – see DPA 1998, s 1(1).

- processed in a way that is adequate, relevant and not excessive;
- accurate;
- kept for no longer than is absolutely necessary;
- handled according to people's data protection rights;
- kept safe and secure; and
- not transferred outside the UK without adequate protection.

1.20 In addition, personal data cannot be used unless at least one of the conditions in Schedule 2 to the DPA 1998 is met and, moreover, sensitive personal data[16] cannot be used unless at least one of the conditions in Schedule 3 is met. One such condition, common to both schedules, is that the data subject[17] has given his consent to the data being used. Another condition under Schedule 3 is that the processing is necessary for medical purposes and is undertaken by a health professional.

1.21 An individual who suffers damage following a breach of the requirements of the DPA 1998 is entitled to compensation from the data controller for that damage.[18] An individual who suffers distress following a breach is entitled to compensation from the data controller for that distress if the individual also suffers damage by reason of the contravention.

What information does the DPA 1998 apply to?

1.22 The DPA 1998 gives a data subject a right of access to any personal information held by a data controller about them. The DPA 1998 applies to all 'accessible public records' no matter when they were compiled and includes electronic and manual data.

1.23 The DPA 1998 does not apply to information relating to a person who is dead, since within the meaning of the Act, personal data only relate to a living person.[19] However, issues of confidentiality would still apply to a request for information about a dead person. Requests to public bodies of this nature would be handled under the Freedom of Information Act 2000, or in certain circumstances, the Access to Health Records Act 1990.[20]

---

16 Personal data consisting of information as to the racial or ethnic origin of the data subject, his political opinions, his religious (or similar) beliefs, whether he is a member of a trade union, his physical or mental health or condition, his sexual life, the commission or alleged commission by him of any offence or any proceedings for any offence committed or alleged to have been committed by him, the disposal of such proceedings or the sentence of any court in such proceedings – see DPA 1998, s 2.

17 The individual who is the subject of personal data – see DPA 1998, s 1(1).

18 DPA 1998, s 13.

19 DPA 1998, s 1.

20 A doctor's obligation of confidence is not necessarily ended by the death of his patient but will depend on all the circumstances, including the nature of the information, the extent to which it is already available and the length of time since death. Where an application for access to the health records of a deceased patient is made by the patient's personal representatives or any person who may have a claim arising out of the patient's death, access must not be given if the

1.24 Section 68 of the DPA 1998 defines an 'accessible public record' as a record that contains any personal information held by the health body or social services department for the purposes of their health/social services functions, irrespective of when the information was recorded.

1.25 Special rules apply to health and social work records. Access to health records may be refused on medical advice by the data controller where disclosure would be, 'likely to cause serious harm to the physical or mental health or condition of the data subject or another person'.[21] However, the data controller can only refuse access after consulting the 'appropriate health professional' (meaning the person most recently responsible for the patient's clinical care in connection with the subject matter of the request). There is a similar provision in relation to social work records.[22] In this case, however, the decision rests with the social services authority alone, with no obligation to consult any other professional.

Subject Access Requests

1.26 Section 7 of the DPA 1998 creates the right of access to personal information. It is commonly referred to as 'subject access'. It is most often used by individuals who want to see a copy of the information an organisation holds about them.

1.27 Section 7(2)(a) of the DPA 1998 requires all requests for access to information to be in writing and accompanied by such fee as may be required.[23] Section 7(8) of the DPA 1998 stipulates that a request for information shall be complied with 'promptly' and in any event within 40 days, starting from the day they receive both the fee and the information required to identify the personal data requested.

1.28 Where joint records are held (eg by social services and a CCG), a request for subject access can be made to either body.[24]

1.29 All information must be disclosed, unless it is subject to a statutory exemption (see below) or where the data includes information about another person. The information should not be altered in any way and should be the information that the authority held at the time of the request.

---

record includes a note, made at the patient's request, that he did not wish access to be given on such an application (Access to Health Records 1990, ss 3(1)(f) and 4(3)). Where such an application is made, access must not be given to any part of the record which, in the opinion of the holder of the record, would disclose information which is not relevant to any claim which may arise out of the patient's death (Access to Health Records 1990, s 5(4)).

21 Data Protection (Subject Access Modification) (Health) Order 2000, SI 2000/413, art 5(1).

22 Data Protection (Subject Access Modification) (Social) Order 2000, SI 2000/415 (as amended), art 5(1).

23 At the time of writing the statutory maximum authorities are permitted to charge is £10, including the cost of supplying copies. Special rules apply to access to manual health records for which the current maximum fee is £50.

24 Social Services Guidance, para 5.2.

1.30 Section 8(2) of the DPA 1998 provides that the information requested should be provided in the form of a permanent copy to the applicant, although a copy need not be provided if it is not possible or would involve disproportionate effort.

1.31 A public authority is not obliged to comply with a subject access request in relation to any 'unstructured' personal data unless the request also contains a description of the data.[25]

1.32 Even if the data are described in the request, a public authority is not obliged to comply with such a request in relation to unstructured personal data if the authority estimates that the cost of complying with the request would exceed the appropriate limit.[26] The appropriate limit for the purposes of the DPA 1998 is: (1) £600 for public authorities listed in Schedule 1, Pt 1 of the Freedom of Information Act 2000; and (2) £450 for other public authorities. Local authorities and CCGs presently fall into the latter category.

1.33 If a disabled person finds it impossible or unreasonably difficult to make a subject access request in writing, the organisation may have to make a reasonable adjustment for them under the Equality Act 2010 ('EqA 2010'). This could include treating a verbal request for information as though it were a valid subject access request. The organisation might also have to respond in a particular format that is accessible to the disabled person, such as Braille, large print, email or audio formats.

Third party information

1.34 Section 7(4) of the DPA 1998 provides that where an organisation cannot comply with a request without disclosing information relating to another individual who can be identified from that information (eg a family member or another service user), it is not obliged to comply with the request unless: (a) the other individual has consented to the disclosure of the information to the person making the request; or (b) it is reasonable in all the circumstances to comply with the request without the consent of the other individual.

1.35 In determining whether it is 'reasonable in all the circumstances' to disclose the information requested without the consent of the third party, the organisation is required to have particular regard to: (a) any duty of confidentiality owed to that other individual; (b) any steps taken with a view to

---

25 By DPA 1998, s 9A(1), 'unstructured personal data' means any information that is not recorded as part of any set of information structured by reference to individuals or criteria relating to individuals. In other words, files which are not about the data subject, or are not about subjects that indicate that information about the data subject is held in the file (eg files relating to general subjects like 'finance'.

26 By DPA 1998, s 9A(5), 'the appropriate limit' means such amounts as may be prescribed by the Secretary of State by regulations, and different amounts may be prescribed in relation to different cases.

seeking the consent of the other individual; (c) whether the other individual is capable of giving consent; and (d) any express refusal of consent by the other individual.[27]

Exemptions from disclosure

1.36 Part IV of the DPA 1998 creates a number of statutory exemptions that mean that information does not have to be disclosed in certain situations. For the purposes of this chapter, the most notable exemption is in relation to health, education and social work.[28] In particular, information about physical or mental health conditions. Social services are prohibited from disclosing any information without first consulting an appropriate health professional[29] (normally the person responsible for the person's clinical care, eg a GP or psychiatrist).

1.37 In the event that any of the statutory exemptions are relied upon, the Social Services Guidance recommends that the applicant must be notified as soon as practicable and in writing, even where the decision has also been given in person. Reasons should also be given.[30]

What if disclosure is refused?

1.38 In the event a request for personal information is refused, the person who has made a request under the provisions of the DPA 1998 may either make a complaint to the ICO[31] or apply to court. The ICO can give the organisation advice and ask it to resolve the issue. In the most serious cases it can order disclosure of the information. However, it cannot award a person compensation.

1.39 If a court is satisfied on the application of any person who has made a request under the DPA 1998 that the data controller in question has failed to comply with the request in contravention of these provisions, the court may order him to comply with the request.[32]

Stevens v Plymouth City Council

1.40 The interplay between the DPA 1998, the HRA 1998 and the common law was considered in the case of *R (on the application of Stevens) v Plymouth City Council.*[33] This case concerned 'C', an adult with learning and behavioural difficulties who had been assessed as lacking mental capacity to consent to the

---

27 DPA 1998, s 7(6).
28 DPA 1998, s 30.
29 As defined by art 2 of the Data Protection (Subject Access Modification) (Health) Order 2000, SI 2000/413 (as amended).
30 Social Services Guidance, para 5.39.
31 See http://www.ico.org.uk/complaints.
32 DPA 1998, s 7(9).
33 [2002] EWCA Civ 388.

disclosure of information in his health and social services to his mother (his nearest relative for the purposes of the Mental Health Act 1983). The local authority obtained a guardianship order in relation to C as it considered that it was not in his best interests to live with his mother.

1.41 The local authority initially refused to disclose to the mother the information and evidence on which the guardianship order had been made on the basis that it could not disclose the information because it was confidential. It subsequently shifted its position, accepting that it had power to disclose but that this could not occur without very good reasons.

1.42 The Court of Appeal allowed the appeal and rejected the revised approach of the local authority. In the circumstances, the DPA 1998 provided little assistance. Giving the lead judgment, Hale LJ noted that under the DPA 1998, all the information that the mother was seeking was 'sensitive personal data' within the meaning of s 2(e) of the DPA 1998. However, this did not mean it could not be disclosed to third parties since the DPA 1998 permitted this when at least one condition in Schedule 3 to the DPA 1998 is met (per Hale LJ at [27]). Instead, the final decision on the disclosure of confidential information depended on a careful analysis of the relevant common law and HRA 1998 principles.

1.43 Hale LJ held that both the common law and Arts 6 and 8 of the ECHR required that a balance be struck between the various interests involved.[34] These were: confidentiality of the information sought; the proper administration of justice; and the mother's right of access to legal advice to enable her to decide whether or not to exercise a right which was likely to lead to legal proceedings against her if she did so. The right of both C and his mother to respect for their family life, including adequate involvement in decision-making processes about it, and the right of C to respect for his private life and the protection of his health and welfare were also to be considered. The balance would not lead in every case to disclosure of all the information a relative might possibly want, still less to a 'fishing exercise' amongst the local authority's files, but in most cases it would lead to the disclosure of the basic statutory guardianship documentation.

1.44 In light of this decision, public bodies need to consider specifically the reasons for asserting information is confidential and have regard to whether a refusal to disclose truly promotes the best interests of the person concerned. Confidentiality may be claimed as a reason to protect themselves, rather than the person who lacks capacity. This point is reinforced in the *No Secrets* guidance, where the Department of Health recommends that:

> '...principles of confidentiality designed to safeguard and promote the interests of service users and patients should not be confused with those designed to protect

---

34 [2002] EWCA Civ 388 per Hale LJ at [32], [48]–[50].

> the management interests of the organisation. These have a legitimate role but must never be allowed to conflict with the interests of service users and parents...'[35]

Caldicott Guardians

1.45 In 1997 a review was commissioned by the Chief Medical Officer of England concerning the use of patient-identifiable information by the NHS in England and Wales after serious doubts were expressed about the way in which the NHS and other statutory bodies treat confidential information. The review was chaired by Dame Fiona Caldicott.

1.46 The Caldicott Report[36] made a number of recommendations that the government has sought to implement in a series of initiatives. One of the most important of these was the recommendation that all NHS organisations appoint a senior person, now known as a 'Caldicott Guardian', to be responsible for protecting the confidentiality of patient and service user information and enabling appropriate information-sharing by providing advice to professionals and staff, particularly in respect of the requirements of the DPA 1998. Initially Caldicott Guardians were restricted to the NHS only.[37] However, the process has now been extended to cover all English social services departments.[38]

REQUESTING PERSONAL INFORMATION ON BEHALF OF OTHERS

1.47 Individuals with sufficient mental capacity may authorise someone else (an agent) to request information on their behalf under the DPA 1998 (eg a family member, carer or lawyer). The person or organisation holding the information has a legal duty to release it.

1.48 Paragraph 5.13 of the Social Services Guidance states that agents should provide evidence (normally in writing) of their authority and confirm their identity and relationship to the individual. If satisfied that the agent is duly authorised, the organisation must treat the request as if it had been made by the individual concerned.[39]

1.49 It should also be borne in mind that a person may have the capacity to agree to someone seeing their personal information, even if they lack capacity to make other decisions (eg in relation to financial matters). Furthermore, in

---

35 *No Secrets: Guidance on developing and implementing multi-agency policies and procedures to protect vulnerable adults from abuse* (2000), para 5.8. This can be found at: https://www.gov.uk/government/publications/no-secrets-guidance-on-protecting-vulnerable-adults-in-care.

36 The original report can be found here: http://confidential.oxfordradcliffe.net/caldicott/report/.

37 This was mandated for the NHS by Health Service Circular HSC 1999/012.

38 This was mandated by Local Authority Circular LAC 2002/2.

39 Department of Health, *Data Protection Act 1998 – guidance to social services* (2000), para 5.13.

some situations, a person may have previously given consent (while they still had capacity) for someone to see their personal information in the future.

Requests for information on behalf of someone who lacks capacity

1.50 There are no special provisions in the DPA 1998 in relation to requests for access made on behalf of an adult who lacks the capacity to make the request in his own name. This glaring defect has been compensated to an extent by the approach adopted by the courts in relation to the common law and, in particular, the HRA 1998.[40]

1.51 Chapter 16 of the Mental Capacity Act 2005 Code of Practice ('the MCA Code of Practice')[41] explains the legal position in relation to access to information on behalf of a person who lacks capacity. It provides useful guidance for people such as family members, carers, deputies and attorneys who care for or represent someone who lacks capacity.

When can attorneys and deputies ask to see personal information?

1.52 In the case of a person lacking capacity, a person with a Lasting Power of Attorney ('LPA'), Enduring Power of Attorney ('EPA') or a deputy[42] appointed by the Court of Protection can request to see information under the subject access provisions in s 7 of the DPA 1998, so long as the information relates to the decisions that the nominated representative has the legal power to make.

1.53 There are no specific statutory provisions in the DPA 1998 enabling a third party to exercise subject access rights on such a person's behalf. However, guidance published by the ICO confirms that, 'it is reasonable to assume that an attorney with authority to manage the individual's property and affairs, or a Deputy appointed by the Court of Protection to make decisions about such matters, will have the appropriate authority'.[43] It is the third party's responsibility to provide evidence of this entitlement. This might be in the form of specific written authority to make the request or it might be a more general power of attorney.

1.54 Paragraph 7.21 of the MCA Code of Practice details the types of decisions that a personal welfare LPA may be required to make. Paragraph 7.36 sets out what decisions may be covered by a property and affairs LPA. Many of

---

40 For example, see *R (Stevens) v Plymouth City Council* [2002] EWCA Civ 388.

41 This can be found at: http://www.justice.gov.uk/downloads/protecting-the-vulnerable/mca/mca-code-practice-0509.pdf.

42 For further information about Deputies appointed by the Court of Protection please see Chapter 8.

43 See *Subject Access Code of Practice: Dealing with requests for personal* information, pp 10–11. This can be found at: http://www.ico.org.uk/for_organisations/data_protection/the_guide/principle_6/access_to_personal_data#others.

the examples cited require access to personal information in order to make a best interests decision. For example, a son responsible for his father's personal welfare under an LPA may need to request access to his father's records from his residential care home to assess whether or not that care home is still able to meet his needs.

1.55 Attorneys and deputies should only request information that will assist them to make a decision they need to make on behalf of the person who lacks capacity. For example, a family member who has an LPA in relation to the financial affairs of an individual would not then be necessarily entitled to request information in relation to their health.

1.56 When asking to see personal information, attorneys and deputies need also to bear in mind that their decision must always be in the best interests of the person who lacks capacity to make that decision. An attorney or deputy must treat the information confidentially and be extremely careful to protect it. In the event they fail to do so, the Court of Protection could, in an extreme case, cancel the LPA or deputyship.

Information about healthcare and social care

1.57 If someone lacks the capacity to give consent and they have not given anyone else legal authority to do so by way of a power of attorney, disclosure can still be made in a person's best interests if they lack capacity to give consent and they have not given else legal authority to make such a request on their behalf.[44] The MCA Code of Practice expressly states that in consulting about a person's best interests, health and social care staff may need to disclose information about the person lacking capacity in order to make the consultation meaningful.[45]

1.58 Sometimes a person's right to confidentiality will conflict with broader public concerns. In exceptional circumstances information can be released if it is in the public interest, even if it is not in the best interests of the person who lacks capacity. The NHS Code on Confidentiality gives examples of when such disclosure may be in the public interest.[46] For example, where disclosing information could prevent, or aid investigation of, serious crimes, or to prevent serious harm, such as to spread of an infectious disease.

1.59 For disclosure to be in the public interest, it must be proportionate and limited to the relevant details. It is not just things for 'the public's benefit' that are in the public interest. Disclosure for the benefit of the person who lacks capacity can also be in the public interest (eg to stop a person who lacks capacity suffering physical or mental harm). Each request ought to be considered on its merits.

---

44 For further detail in relation to 'best interests' decisions on behalf of an incapacitated adult please see Chapter 4.

45 MCA 2005 Code of Practice, para 16.20.

46 See Confidentiality NHS Code of Practice (2003), paras 30–34.

Financial information

1.60 It can often be more difficult to obtain personal financial information than it is to get information in relation to a person's welfare. For example, a bank manager is less likely to know the person concerned, be able to make an assessment of their person's capacity to consent to disclosure and be aware of the carer's relationship to the person. As such, they are less likely than a doctor or social worker to be able to judge what is in a person's best interests and are bound by duties to keep clients' affairs confidential.

1.61 In the absence of any EPA, LPA or deputyship authorising access to financial information, it is more likely than not that someone will need to apply to the Court of Protection for access to such information.[47]

DUTY TO REPORT INFORMATION

1.62 In certain circumstances where a person has been diagnosed with dementia he or she may be obliged to notify others of the diagnosis.

Driving

1.63 A person who has been diagnosed with dementia has a legal obligation to notify the DVLA immediately of this information.

1.64 The Secretary of State for Transport, acting through medical advisers at the Driver and Vehicle Licensing Agency ('DVLA'), has the responsibility to ensure that all licence holders are fit to drive[48]. This means the DVLA needs to know if a licence-holder has a condition or is undergoing treatment that may now, or in the future, affect their safety as a driver.

1.65 The medical standards are applicable to both Group 1 and Group 2 licence holders. Group 1 licence holders, include those who drive motor cars and motor cycles. Group 2 licence holders refer to large lorries (Category C) and Buses (Category D). The medical standards for Group 2 drivers are much higher than those of Group 1 due to the size and weight of the vehicle, as well as the amount of time spent on the road behind the wheel.

1.66 Section 94(1) of the Road Traffic Act 1988 ('RTA 1988') requires that if a person with a valid driving licence becomes aware that he is suffering from a 'relevant' or 'prospective' disability[49] or that a disability or medical condition which they have previously disclosed has got worse since the licence was

---

[47] For further details about applying to be appointed a property and affairs deputy, please see Chapter 9.

[48] The legal basis of fitness to drive is derived from the EC Directive on driving licences (91/439/EEC) as amended by Directive 2009/112/EC, the Road Traffic Act 1988 and the Motor Vehicles (Driving Licences) Regulations 1999.

[49] For the purposes of the RTA 1988, the term 'disability' also includes various medical conditions.

granted the licence, then he or she must notify the DVLA immediately in writing of the nature and extent of their disability. Failure to do so is a criminal offence.[50]

1.67 Section 92(2) of the RTA 1988 sets out the definition of 'prescribed', 'relevant' and 'prospective' disabilities (also known as 'notifiable' medical conditions or disabilities). In summary they are as follows:

- A prescribed disability is one that is a legal bar to the holding of a licence. The regulations state that certain conditions bar a person from being medically fit enough to drive.[51] An example of this is epilepsy.
- A relevant disability is any medical condition that is likely to render the person a source of danger while driving. An example of this is a visual field defect.
- A prospective disability is any medical condition, which, because of its progressive or intermittent nature may develop into a prescribed or relevant disability in the course of time. An example of this is dementia. A driver with a prospective disability may normally only hold a driving licence subject to medical review in one, two or three years.

1.68 Once a person has informed the DVLA of their condition and provided consent, medical enquiries will be made and they may also be required to take a driving assessment. The DVLA will then use this information to determine whether or not he or she can still drive. It can be a relatively lengthy process to obtain all the necessary reports and, during this period, the licence holder normally retains a legal entitlement to drive under s 88 of the RTA 1988. However, where a licence has been previously revoked for medical reasons and an application is in process for the restoration of the licence, then the entitlement under s 88 of the RTA 1988 does not apply.

1.69 On receipt of all the required medical evidence, the DVLA will then decide whether or not the driver can satisfy the national medical guidelines and the requirements of the law. The range of decisions that can be taken by the DVLA are:

- the driving licence is retained or a new driving licence is issued;
- a driving licence may be issued for a period of one, two or three years if the medical adviser decides that a review of medical fitness is required in the future;

---

[50] Section 94(3) RTA 1988. A person can be fined up to £1,000 if they fail to notify the DVLA about a medical condition that affects their driving.

[51] Regulation 71(1) of the Motor Vehicles (Driving Licences) Regulations 1999 identifies certain prescribed disabilities: (a) epilepsy; (b) severe mental disorder; (c) liability to sudden attacks of disabling giddiness or fainting; (d) liability to sudden attacks of disabling giddiness or fainting which are caused by any disorder or defect of the heart which has caused the applicant for the licence or the licence holder to have a device, such as a pacemaker implanted; (e) persistent misuse of drugs or alcohol whether or not such misuse amounts to dependency; (f) any other disability likely to cause the driver to be a danger to the public when driving a vehicle.

- a driving licence may be issued which indicates that special controls need to be fitted to the vehicle to enable the driver to overcome the effects of a physical disability; or
- the DVLA will tell the person to stop driving if medical enquiries confirm that they are not fit to drive until their condition improves.

1.70 Drivers who have their driving entitlement revoked or refused on medical grounds have the right to appeal to the magistrates' court under s 100 of RTA 1988.

Duties upon medical professionals

1.71 If a doctor suspects that a patient has not informed the DVLA of a medical condition then he or she must inform the patient of their legal duty to do so.

1.72 The doctor in charge of a person's care should also be able to advise them whether or not it is appropriate for them to continue to drive. Patients may be reminded that if they choose to ignore medical advice to cease driving, there could be consequences with respect to their insurance cover. Doctors are advised to document formally and clearly in the notes the advice that has been given.

1.73 Driving ability can be very difficult to assess in a patient with any degree of memory impairment or dementia. The DVLA issues guidance to the medical profession on how to interpret the relevant provisions of the RTA 1988.[52] The most recent version of the guidance, states in relation to dementia:

> **'Group 1 entitlement ODL – car, motorcycle**
>
> It is extremely difficult to assess driving ability in those with dementia. Those who have poor short-term memory, disorientation, lack of insight and judgement are almost certainly not fit to drive.
>
> The variable presentations and rates of progression are acknowledged. Disorders of attention will also cause impairment. A decision regarding fitness to drive is usually based on medical reports.
>
> In early dementia when sufficient skills are retained and progression is slow, a licence may be issued subject to annual review. A formal driving assessment may be necessary
>
> [...]

---

52 *At a glance: Guide to the current Medical Standards of Fitness to Drive* (April, 2013), p 39. This can be found at: https://www.gov.uk/government/publications/at-a-glance.

Group 2 entitlement vocational – lorries, buses

Refuse or revoke licence'

1.74 A diagnosis of dementia in a Group 1 licence holder does not necessarily mean that they will have to stop driving immediately but will be subject to further assessment. The more stringent medical requirements on Group 2 licence holders means that a diagnosis of dementia (or any organic brain syndrome) will lead to a licence being refused or revoked.

1.75 The General Medical Council ('GMC') has issued helpful guidelines to medical professionals about what they should do in this type of situation:[53]

> '4. The driver is legally responsible for informing the DVLA about such a condition or treatment. However, if a patient has such a condition, you should explain to the patient:
>
> (a) that the condition may affect their ability to drive (if the patient is incapable of understanding this advice, for example, because of dementia, you should inform the DVLA immediately), and
> (b) that they have a legal duty to inform the DVLA about the condition.
>
> 5. If a patient refuses to accept the diagnosis, or the effect of the condition on their ability to drive, you can suggest that they seek a second opinion, and help arrange for them to do so. You should advise the patient not to drive in the meantime.
>
> 6. If a patient continues to drive when they may not be fit to do so, you should make every reasonable effort to persuade them to stop. As long as the patient agrees, you may discuss your concerns with their relatives, friends or carers.
>
> 7. If you do not manage to persuade the patient to stop driving, or you discover that they are continuing to drive against your advice, you should contact the DVLA immediately and disclose any relevant medical information, in confidence, to the medical adviser.
>
> 8. Before contacting the DVLA you should try to inform the patient of your decision to disclose personal information. You should then also inform the patient in writing once you have done so.'

Duty to notify an employer

1.76 According to the Alzheimer's Society[54] as many as 18% of people diagnosed with dementia under the age of 65 continue to work after a diagnosis of dementia. 27% of carers diagnosed with dementia also continue

---

[53] This can be found at: http://www.gmc-uk.org/Confidentiality_reporting_concerns_DVLA_2009.pdf_27494214.pdf.

[54] Alzheimer's Society, *Employment and Dementia*: http://www.alzheimers.org.uk/site/scripts/documents_info.php?documentID=1836.

to work. As numbers of people with dementia rise, this will mean that there are likely to be increasing number of carers and people with dementia in the workforce.

1.77 In many professions there is no legal obligation to notify an employer about a diagnosis of dementia. However, in certain jobs there is likely to be a contractual obligation do so, eg if that person works on a plane or ship or is in the armed forces. In all circumstances it is advisable to check the terms of the particular employment contract in question.

1.78 Irrespective of any contractual obligation to inform an employer about a diagnosis of dementia, it is still strongly advisable to do so, otherwise they may not have any legal duty to provide assistance under the EqA 2010.

1.79 The EqA 2010 protects anyone who has a disability, including people with dementia. It imposes a duty upon employers to make reasonable adjustments for employees with a disability so that they are not disadvantaged at work.[55] For example, by adjusting his or her working hours or providing them with a special piece of equipment to help them do the job.

1.80 Furthermore, the EqA 2010 prohibits any discrimination in relation to all aspects of employment, including: (i) the recruitment process (eg application forms, interview arrangements, aptitude or proficiency tests, job offers etc); (ii) the terms of employment, including pay, conditions and benefits; (iii) promotion, transfer and training opportunities; (iv) treatment compared to other workers, such as dismissal, harassment and victimisation.

1.81 The EqA 2010 also protects people who experience discrimination because they are associated with someone who has a disability, such as their carer. Carers have the right to request flexible working, and the right to request time off to look after dependents in an emergency.

1.82 For further information in relation to the statutory protection provided by the EqA 2010 please refer to the section on Discrimination in Chapter 15 below.

---

55 For the duties owed by employers to make reasonable adjustments for disabled persons see s.20 and Sch. 8 of EqA 2010.

CHAPTER 2

HOSPITALISATION AND SECTIONING

2.1 This chapter focuses on the compulsory admission to, and detention in, hospital for assessment or treatment (the process commonly known as 'sectioning') of people with dementia. First, it outlines the different ways in which people with dementia might be admitted to hospital for assessment or treatment: voluntarily or 'informally'; formally under the Deprivation of Liberty (DoL) procedures in the Mental Capacity Act 2005 (MCA) (Schs 1A and A1); or, in the absence of a suitable alternative, under the compulsory detention provisions of the Mental Health Act 1983 (MHA) (ss 2, 3 and 4). The chapter seeks to outline how the decision should be taken as to which is the appropriate route. The chapter then proceeds to summarise the thresholds and procedures for compulsory admission under MHA 1983, the bases and procedures for challenging such detention and what happens when a period of detention ends. It concludes by considering the role of guardianship under the MHA 1983. The chapter considers the role of the 'nearest relative' throughout.

POWERS UNDER THE MHA 1983 AND MCA 2005

2.2 The MHA 1983 includes formal, compulsory powers of detention in hospital for mentally disordered people for either assessment (ss 2 and 4) or treatment (s 3). The powers are to be used for the purpose of securing the health or safety of the patient or for the protection of others. However, the Act is based on the principle that the compulsory powers should not be used unless the care and treatment required can be provided in no other less restrictive way. This is clear from the fact that one of the express preconditions of detention for treatment under the Act is that the treatment cannot be provided except under the section.[1] It is therefore important for those involved to consider, before the decision to admit to hospital under MHA 1983 is taken, whether alternative means exist of providing the care and treatment.

2.3 For people with dementia, alternatives to detention under MHA 1983 may be either voluntary admission to hospital (or a residential care home) or admission to or detention in a hospital or residential care home pursuant to the DoL authorisation safeguards in the MCA 2005. Indeed, it will often be the case that an alternative setting, under an alternative regime, is more appropriate for those with dementia than compulsory hospital detention under MHA 1983.

1 MHA 1983, s 3(2)(c).

As observed by Lady Hale: 'It is now unusual for people with those disabilities [severe dementia and learning disabilities] to be formally admitted to hospital under the 1983 Act.'[2]

2.4 In addition to the need to be conscious of the different statutory regimes which might be used and the importance of adopting the least restrictive possible approach, all those involved in making decisions about hospitalisation and treatment need to have regard to the Codes of Practice which accompany the MHA 1983 and MCA 2005. While the Codes do not impose specific legal duties, those involved in making decisions must have regard to the Codes and failing to follow the guidance can be taken into account when determining the lawfulness of decisions. Departure from the Codes without good reason is likely to be considered unlawful. The MCA code is dealt with in detail below (see Chapter 4). As for the MHA, there is a MHA Code for England,[3] published by the Department of Health, and a separate Code for Wales,[4] published by the Welsh Minister for Health and Social Services. Both codes give detailed guidance, and have slightly different emphases, but both underline certain key general principles, which it is important to bear in mind. These are that the least restrictive possible approach to treatment should be taken, that patients' views should be listened to and followed where possible and that patients should be as involved as possible in planning their own treatment.

Voluntary admission to hospital

2.5 The first alternative to formal detention under MHA 1983 is informal, voluntary admission. Informal admission to hospital is expressly provided for in s 131 of the MHA 1983, which makes clear that nothing in the Act 'shall be construed as preventing a patient who requires treatment for mental disorder from being admitted to any hospital or registered establishment and in pursuance of arrangements made in that behalf and without any application, order or direction rendering him liable to be detained under this Act'. People admitted voluntarily are free to discharge themselves, subject to the possibility (see below) that the holding power[5] will be used by the treating staff in the hospital pending a formal detention pursuant to an application under s 2 or s 3.

2.6 Informal admission may happen in circumstances both where the person with dementia has the mental capacity (within the meaning of MCA 2005) to make a decision as to their admission and treatment in hospital and where they lack such capacity. In circumstances where they lack capacity, however, it is crucial to distinguish between an admission where the hospitalisation will involve a DoL and circumstances where it will not. The circumstances which will amount to a DoL are considered below in Chapter 4. If a DoL is necessary,

---

2 *MH v Secretary of State for the Department of Health* [2005] UKHL 60.
3 *Code of Practice: Mental Health Act 1983* (2008).
4 *Mental Health Act 1983: Code of Practice for Wales.*
5 MHA 1983, s 5 (see further below).

then a specific procedure prescribed by law will need to be followed whether compulsory detention pursuant to MHA 1983 or DoL authorisation under MCA 2005.

2.7 If a DoL is not necessary, and the person lacks capacity, then the process defined by the MCA 2005 for assessment of best interests will need to be followed (see Chapter 4), but the DoL safeguards under Schedule A1 will not be relevant. If the conditions in s 5 of the MCA 2005 are fulfilled – the person carrying out the act of care or treatment has taken reasonable steps to assess the patient's capacity, reasonably believes that the patient lacks capacity and reasonably believes the act is in the patient's best interests – then the person carrying out the care or treatment is provided with a defence. This can extend to situations where the patient is subject to restraint ('the use or threat of force to secure the doing of any act which P resists, or the placing of any restriction of P's liberty of movement, whether or not P resists') which does not amount to a DoL. Under s 6 of the MCA 2005, restraint is lawful where (a) the person carrying out the act reasonably believes that it is necessary to prevent harm to the patient and (b) the act is a proportionate response both to the likelihood of the patient suffering harm and the seriousness of that harm.

Where a DoL is necessary and the patient lacks capacity: use of the DoL authorisation under MCA 2005 or the MHA 1983

2.8 If the admission to hospital of a person with dementia requires a DoL, the first question is whether or not the appropriate legal regime is the MCA 2005 or MHA 1983. As noted above, the starting point is that the MCA 2005 is to be preferred over MHA 1983 where possible, since MHA 1983 is only to be used where there is no appropriate alternative. In certain circumstances this will plainly be a question of clinical or professional judgment. The authorisation process under MCA 2005 is considered in detail below in Chapter 4. The following sections focus on the circumstances where it will not be possible for MCA 2005 to be used, such that MHA 1983 will be the only option if detention is required.

2.9 There are legal restrictions on the circumstances where MCA 2005 can be used. These fall into three principal categories of case:

(a) patients already subject to MHA 1983;
(b) patients who have made a valid advance decision to refuse the particular form of treatment or whose attorney or deputy refuses the authorisation of a DoL;
(c) patients who are 'within the scope' of MHA 1983, where the proposed DoL authorisation would authorise the detention of a patient being a mental health patient and the patient objects.

Patients already subject to MHA 1983

2.10 The scheme of MCA 2005 ensures that where a person is already subject to MHA 1983, then decisions taken under MHA 1983 and the process under that Act take precedence. Thus, if a person is already subject to a hospital treatment obligation under MHA 1983 and continues to be detained under that obligation then they cannot be deprived of their liberty pursuant to MCA 2005.[6]

2.11 The MCA 2005 also precludes its own use for a deprivation of liberty where that deprivation of liberty would be inconsistent with any obligation placed on a patient (such as an obligation as to where to reside) who is: (a) subject to a hospital treatment regime, but is not currently detained in a hospital (ie is on a leave of absence); (b) subject to a community treatment regime; or (c) subject to guardianship.[7]

2.12 Additionally, if the proposed DoL authorisation would involve hospitalisation and the patient is on a leave of absence or subject to a community treatment regime under MHA 1983 already, MCA 2005 cannot be used to deprive that patient's liberty. This is to ensure that, insofar as a patient needs to be recalled to hospital, it is the MHA 1983 procedures which take precedence.

Valid refusals of treatment

2.13 Where a patient has made a valid advance refusal of treatment (or a refusal of a necessary component of the treatment) which is proposed to be provided under the DoL, then the MCA procedure cannot be used. Similarly, it will not be possible to use the Schedule A1 procedure under MCA 2005 where an attorney or deputy (see Chapter 4) refuses the proposed DoL.

A patient within the scope of MHA who objects to mental health treatment

2.14 The final category of patient who may not be subject to a DoL authorisation under MCA 2005 is one who falls 'within the scope of MHA', but is not yet subject to it, who objects to becoming a 'mental health patient' and whose attorney or deputy has not consented.

2.15 Falling within the scope of MHA means that an application under s 2 or 3 MHA 1983 could be made and the patient could be detained under either of those sections if the application were made (the qualifying tests for these sections are outlined below). In essence, if the DoL which is proposed is for mental health treatment in a hospital and this is objected to by the patient, then the MCA cannot be used.

---

6 MCA 2005, Sch 1A. The relevant hospital treatment obligations are ss 2, 3, 4, 35, 36, 37, 38, 44, 45A, 47, 48 and 51 of the MCHA 1983.

7 MCA 1983, Sch 1A.

2.16 Whether or not the patient is objecting is to be determined by having regard to all the circumstances (insofar as they are reasonable ascertainable), including their behaviour, their wishes and feelings and their beliefs and values, regard is to be had to past circumstances only insofar as reasonable to continue to have regard to them.

2.17 Whether a person is intended to be a 'mental health patient' depends on whether the proposed authorisation will see them being 'accommodated in a hospital for the purpose of being given medical treatment for mental disorder'. The issue arose in a case involving a patient with dementia, *GJ v The Foundation Trust*.[8] GJ had dementia and, as a consequence, did not manage to control his diabetes, frequently experiencing dangerous hypoglycaemic episodes. It was evident that the episodes were connected to the dementia, in that the condition led him not to understand the need to take the medication and to eat. The question for the court was whether in those circumstances, a deprivation of liberty was permissible under MCA or whether GJ was properly considered to be a 'mental health patient'. Adopting a 'but for' test, the court held that the MCA route was permissible: but for the diabetes, GJ would not have been detained and was not therefore a 'mental health patient'.

DETENTION FOR ASSESSMENT IN HOSPITAL UNDER MHA 1983

2.18 MHA 1983 provides two routes for non-offender patients to be admitted to and detained in hospital for the purposes of assessment. They are s 2, the primary route which provides for a non-renewable period of assessment for up to 28 days and s 4, which provides for emergency admission for up to 72 hours.

The threshold for admission for assessment under s 2

2.19 The grounds for admission for assessment under s 2 are that the patient:

(a) is suffering from mental disorder of a nature or degree which warrants the detention of the patient in a hospital for assessment (or for assessment followed by medical treatment) for at least a limited period; and
(b) ought to be so detained in the interests of his own health or safety or with a view to the protection of other persons.

2.20 The definition of 'mental disorder' is broad: 'any disorder or disability of the mind'.[9] It is plain that dementia can fall within this definition and this is recognised in the Code of Practice published by the Department of Health, which includes a non-exhaustive list of clinically recognised conditions which are likely to be considered disorders or disabilities of the mind.

---

8 [2009] EWHC 2972 (Fam).
9 MHA 1983, s 1(2).

2.21 The 'nature or degree' qualification in s 2 involves consideration of 'the particular mental disorder from which the patient suffers, its chronicity, its prognosis, and the patient's previous response to … treatment. The word degree refers to the current manifestation of the patient's order'.[10]

2.22 In order for detention to be permitted, it is important to note that, contrary perhaps to popular perceptions of the legislation, the detention does not need to be necessary for the protection of others or even for the safety of the patient. It can be either the health or safety of the patient or the protection of others which requires detention. However, the wording of the section and the requirements of human rights law, particularly Article 5(1) of the European Convention on Human Rights, mean that the detention must be a proportionate response to the risks identified and be the least restrictive setting in which the risk can be managed.

The procedure for an application under s 2

2.23 An application for admission and detention for assessment can be made by either an Approved Mental Health Professional ('AMHP') or the patient's 'nearest relative'. Both of these are legal 'terms of art' with specific legal meanings, which it is convenient to set out first. Most applications in practice are made by AMHPs.

The nearest relative

2.24 The 'nearest relative' is the relative who is given powers under the MHA 1983 to apply for compulsory admission, seek discharge and challenge detention before a Mental Health Tribunal. Which relative qualifies is determined by a statutory hierarchy.[11] In descending order the relative may be:

(a) husband or wife or civil partner (this includes cohabiting couples living together as if married or in a civil partnership who having been living together for no less than 6 months);
(b) son or daughter;
(c) father or mother;
(d) brother or sister;
(e) grandparent;
(f) grandchild;
(g) uncle or aunt;
(h) nephew or niece.

2.25 Half-blood relatives are to be treated as whole blood for these purposes. Relatives also include any person with whom the patient has been ordinarily

10 *R v Mental Health Review Tribunal for the South Thames Region, ex parte Smith* [1999] COD 148.

11 See MHA 1983, s 26 for definition of nearest relative.

residing for a period of at least 5 years, although such a person would be placed at the end of the hierarchy defined above and could not take precedence over a spouse or civil partner unless there was a permanent separation or the patient or spouse/civil partner had been deserted. If a relative is ordinarily residing with or caring for the patient, then that relative will take precedence in the list above all others. Where there is more than one person who would qualify as the nearest relative according to the criteria outlined, then as appropriate the list above is applied, whole blood relatives come ahead of half-blood relatives and older relatives come ahead of younger, regardless of gender.

2.26 It is important to note that the nearest relative is capable of 'displacement' under s 29 of the MHA 1983, in a procedure intended to comply with a court decision[12] that a patient must be able on reasonable grounds to remove a person from acting as their nearest relative. Section 29 enables the patient, any relative, a person with whom the patient resides or was residing prior to admission, or an AMHP to make an application for displacement to the county court. The bases for substituting an alternative person (or simply identifying a person to act in the role) are that: there is no nearest relative, or it is impracticable to identify to ascertain whether there is a nearest relative or who it is; that the nearest relative is incapable of acting, such as for reason of their own mental disorder; the nearest relative is unreasonably objecting to an application for admission for treatment or for guardianship; the nearest relative is exercising their powers without regard for the welfare of the patient or the interests of the public; and that the person is otherwise unsuitable to act.

The AMHP

2.27 An AMHP is a person, approved by a local social services authority ('LSSA'), with expertise in dealing with people suffering from mental disorder who is a social worker, nurse with relevant qualifications, occupational therapist or chartered psychologist.[13]

2.28 AMHPs cannot be medical practitioners (that is, doctors), as this is specifically excluded by the Act. The purpose of this restriction is to ensure that there is an independent and professionally distinct social judgment made as to the need for admission which is separate from the perspective of a treating clinician.

Applications made by AMHPs

2.29 If a LSSA has reason to believe that an application under s 2 might need to be made in relation to a person in the LSSA's area then an AMHP has to be identified to address the particular person's case and consider whether an application should be made.[14]

---

[12] *JT v United Kingdom* [2000] 30 EHRR CD 77.

[13] The Mental Health (Approved Mental Health Professionals) (Approval) (England) Regulations 2008 and MHA 1983, s 114.

[14] MHA 1983, s 13.

2.30 The AMHP, if directed to consider a case, must make an independent professional judgment as to the need for admission, based on social and medical evidence, taking into account not only the statutory threshold, but the wishes expressed by relatives or carers, as well as the patient themselves.

2.31 The Code of Practice indicates that the following factors should be considered:

- the patient's wishes and view of their own needs;
- the patient's age and physical health;
- any past wishes or feelings expressed by the patient;
- the patient's cultural background;
- the patient's social and family circumstances;
- the impact that any future deterioration or lack of improvement in the patient's condition would have on their children, other relatives or carers, especially those living with the patient, including an assessment of these people's ability and willingness to cope; and
- the effect on the patient, and those close to the patient, of a decision to admit or not to admit under the Act.

2.32 As part of the process of assessment, the AMHP must interview the patient in a 'suitable manner' in order to be satisfied that the use of the section is in 'all the circumstances of the case, the most appropriate way of providing the care and treatment which the patient needs'. What constitutes a suitable manner for these purposes is principally a question of professional judgment, and the requirement for an interview can be satisfied even where the AMHP is unable to obtain responses (or only inadequate responses) from the patient if the patient's manner is indicative of the need that they do require treatment.

2.33 The medical evidence and recommendation for admission which the AMHP must take into account must come from two doctors fully registered under the Medical Act 1983. One of these doctors must be approved as having special experience in the diagnosis and treatment of mental disorder ('a s 12 approved doctor'). The other must, if practicable, have previous acquaintance with the patient, unless the s 12 approved doctor himself or herself has that acquaintance. The reports must be signed on or before the date of any application pursuant to the section and the reporting doctors must both have seen the patient personally, whether together or separately. In cases where the doctors do not see the patient together, then they must see the patient within 5 days of one another.

2.34 If the AMHP considers that an application for assessment pursuant to s 2 ought to be made, taking into account the above considerations, then the AMHP is under a duty to make the application. The application must be made to the managers of the hospital in which detention is sought. The AMHP must also inform the person appearing to be the nearest relative, either before the application has been made or within a reasonable time afterwards, that the application for an assessment has been or will be made. The AMHP also has to inform the nearest relative that he or she has the power to discharge the section (see further below).

Applications made by nearest relative

2.35 An application which is made by the nearest relative must be supported by the same medical recommendations outlined above and similarly be addressed to the hospital managers. However, there are no other statutory procedural requirements or considerations which have to be taken into account by the nearest relative beyond obtaining the medical recommendations.

After the application is made

2.36 A duly made application is sufficient authorisation for whoever made the application – whether the AMHP or the nearest relative – to take and convey the patient to the hospital, or to authorise another person to do so on their behalf. This must happen within 14 days of the last examination by a medical practitioner for the purposes of the application. The patient is to be considered in legal custody and any person authorised to take and convey the patient has all the powers of a constable in that respect.

2.37 A properly made application addressed to the hospital managers, who serve as the detaining authority, is, without more, sufficient authority for the managers to detain the patient.

2.38 Once the patient is admitted it is the responsibility of the hospital managers to ensure that the requirements of the Act are followed. In particular they must continue to ensure that patients are detained only as the Act permits, that patients' care and treatment accords with the provisions of the Act and that patients are fully informed of their rights.

Admission under s 4

2.39 Section 4 of the MHA 1983 provides an emergency power, to be exercised only in cases of urgent necessity, to admit a patient compulsorily for a period of no longer than 72 hours. As with admissions under s 2, the application can, in theory, be made by either an AMHP or a nearest relative. Although, as with s 2, the overwhelming number of applications in practice will be made by an AMHP.

2.40 The purpose of s 4 is to enable rapid admission where the delay caused by obtaining a second medical opinion under s 2 will be undesirable. The section therefore enables detention on the basis of a sole medical recommendation, which should be from a practitioner who is familiar with the patient, if possible. This recommendation does not have to come from a practitioner who is approved under s 12. The same threshold conditions as outlined above for s 2 have to be met, of course, and the AMHP must undertake the same process outlined above, save obtaining the second opinion, where the AMHP is making the application.

2.41 To underline the emergency nature of the power under s 4, an application is possible only where the person making the application has personally seen the patient within the previous 24 hours and the detention in hospital must commence within 24 hours of the earlier of the time the application was made or when the patient was last medically examined.

2.42 Because the patient has not necessarily had the protection of the opinion of a person approved under s 12, the admission may last for only 72 hours, after which it lapses, unless the second medical recommendation required under s 2 is furnished to the managers within that period. If that is done then the detention for the purposes of assessment may be extended to 28 days from the time of the initial admission under s 4.

DETENTION FOR TREATMENT IN HOSPITAL UNDER MHA 1983

2.43 Compulsory admission for treatment is provided for by s 3 of the MHA 1983. This can be for up to 6 months and is renewable initially for a further 6 months and thereafter for 12 months at a time. Again, as with compulsory admission for assessment, an application may be made by either the nearest relative or an AMHP and must be supported by the recommendations of two medical practitioners of which at least one must be approved under s 12. The procedural requirements placed on an AMHP making the application – such as to interview of the patient and the considerations to be taken into account – are as discussed above in relation to admission under s 2.

The threshold for admission for treatment under s 3

2.44 Section 3 provides that in order for an application to be made:

(a) the patient must be suffering from mental disorder of a nature or degree which makes it appropriate for the patient to receive medical treatment in a hospital; and
(b) it must be necessary in the interests of his health or safety or for the protection of other persons that he should receive such treatment and that it must be the case that the treatment cannot be provided unless he is detained under this section; and
(c) appropriate medical treatment must be available, the appropriateness taking into account the nature and degree of the mental disorder and all the other circumstances of the case.

2.45 Insofar as question of 'nature or degree' is concerned, it has been held that, in respect of the need for treatment, this can include circumstances where the patient may not currently be showing severe symptoms, but has stopped adhering to their medication regime and there is evidence both that the patient will deteriorate if the medication is not taken and that the medication will not be taken unless detention is sought.

2.46 For the necessary treatment to fall within the section it must be treatment the purpose of which is to alleviate, or prevent a worsening of, the mental disorder or one or more its symptoms or manifestations. However, it is not confined to medication and includes 'psychological intervention and specialist mental health habilitation, rehabilitation and care'. This means that it is important to be aware of the relatively difficult line to define between what is described in the Code of Practice as qualifying care which 'consists only of nursing and specialist day-to-day care under the clinical supervision of an approved clinician, in a safe and secure therapeutic environment' and mere preventive detention.

The regulation of mental health treatment when a patient is detained for treatment

2.47 With the exception of certain treatments, MHA 1983 enables mental health treatment to be given to patients for up to 3 months without their consent, on the basis of the clinical judgment of those treating the patient and subject to the authorisation of the approved clinician in charge of the patient's care. After the 3-month period has expired, either consent on the part of the patient or the approval of a second registered medical practitioner (the second opinion appointed doctor or 'SOAD') is required for mental health treatment to continue. Even if the patient has capacity to consent to treatment, but has decided not to, the opinion of two registered medical practitioners is sufficient to override the absence of consent.

2.48 For electro-convulsive therapy (ECT), consent or a second opinion is required from the outset. Further, if the patient has the capacity to consent and refuses to do so, then the medical practitioners cannot overrule that decision. It is only in the case of patients who lack capacity that the two medical practitioners can make the decision on behalf of the patient.

2.49 For certain treatments with likely long-term and irreversible effects, and which are perhaps less likely to be considered appropriate in patients with dementia – such as implants of hormones to reduce male sex drive – only consent *and* a second opinion are sufficient for the treatment to be lawful.

Section 117 after care

2.50 Section 117 of the MHA 1983 imposes a duty on clinical commissioning groups ('CCGs') and social services authorities to provide after-care services for patients who have been detained in hospital for treatment under s 3. The duty commences once the patient is no longer subject to detention and has left the hospital. It continues until the patient is no longer in need of the services, in the opinion of the CCG and local authority. The responsible authority has been held by the courts to be that where the person was resident (where they lived and had a settled intention to remain for the time being) *prior* to being detained under MHA 1983. If, however, they did not have a residence prior to being detained, then the responsible authority will be that for the area where they are sent on discharge from hospital.

2.51 Further detail about the duties on the relevant authorities as to the carrying out of assessments for the purposes of s 117 and as to the nature of the services they should provide are set out below in Chapter 6.

Challenging a section

2.52 Given the draconian nature of the powers under the MHA to detain on mental health grounds, the existence of adequate means of redress and challenge is crucial to the operation of the system. There are therefore a number of safeguards and routes to challenge detention under MHA 1983 designed to ensure that powers to detain or treat compulsorily are being used only when necessary and that patients' human right not to be subject to arbitrary detention[15] is being protected. This section considers, first, the ability of the nearest relative to object to and block the use of the power to detain for treatment[16] and to discharge a patient[17] (subject to being overridden by the responsible clinician), second the role of the hospital managers and, in particular 'managers' hearings' in reviewing patients' ongoing detention and, third, the crucial role of the Mental Health Tribunal.

The nearest relative's powers

2.53 The nearest relative has the ability to block an application for detention for treatment under s 11(4) of the MHA 1983. This power is not exercisable in relation to admission for assessment, but is otherwise a significant check on the system of MHA detention. The nearest relative is able to stop the application for treatment even where it is the clear view of all the professionals involved that the admission is necessary. Of course, this power is exercisable only if the nearest relative is aware of the application, which is one of the reasons why the nearest relative must be consulted (except where impracticable or the circumstances mean that there would be unreasonable delay) about the exercise of the power to detain for treatment. It should be remembered therefore that the nearest relative can be displaced by the county court and that one basis for doing so is the unreasonable objection on his or her part to the use of MHA detention.

2.54 The second significant power of the nearest relative is to discharge the patient from detention. So long as the nearest relative gives 72 hours' written notice to the hospital managers of their intention to use the discharge power,

---

15 Article 5(1) of the Convention.

16 MHA 1983, s 11(4).

17 MHA 1983, s 23.

the patient may be discharged from detention by the nearest relative communicating in writing to the hospital managers that they are ordering the patient to be discharged.

2.55 The reason for the 72-hour notice period, however, is that this provides time for the responsible clinician to consider whether they wish to exercise their power to override the wishes of the nearest relative. Section 25 of the MHA 1983 gives the responsible clinician the ability to do this where they consider that, if released, the patient would be likely to act in a manner dangerous to themselves or others. If the responsible clinician furnishes a report, known as a barring certificate, to the hospital managers to that effect then two consequences flow: the first is that the discharge by the nearest relative is rendered void; the second is that the nearest relative is unable to make a further order for discharge until 6 months have passed; see also **2.74**.

The hospital managers and hospital managers' hearings

2.56 Section 23 of the MHA 1983 also gives the hospital managers the power to discharge patients from detention. There is detailed guidance in the Code of Practice as to the managers' power of discharge and their duty to ensure that all patients are aware of the fact that they may seek discharge in this way.

2.57 Managers are able to review the ongoing detention of a patient at any time. However, they must specifically consider whether it is appropriate to hold a review when a patient requests one or when the responsible clinician overrules the intention of the patent's nearest relative to discharge a section. If the detention has been recently considered on a review then the managers may take the view that, without evidence demonstrating a change in the patient's circumstances, they will not hold a further review. Where the patient's detention is liable to be renewed, however, after the responsible clinician has furnished a report to that effect, then the managers must hold a review, even if the patient is not objecting.

2.58 The procedure adopted by the managers may well vary depending on whether or not the patient has expressed objections. In the case of an uncontested renewal, the Code of Practice recognises that it can be appropriate for the case to be considered on the papers, without an oral hearing. However, if the patient wishes, it is advised that he or she is interviewed by a single member of the panel. Additionally, the panel may take the view that it would be appropriate for the patient to be interviewed after they have considered the papers. In circumstances where the panel form the view that there appear to be reasons to think that the patient's continuing detention is not lawful, then they should proceed to hold a full hearing.

2.59 In the case of contested hearings, the procedure which is recommended by the Code broadly follows the structure of a Mental Health Tribunal, with the significant difference that the managers themselves do not have a medically qualified member as part of their panel. This has the consequence that the panels are advised that they are not qualified to arrive at their own clinical assessments and that, if they consider there is reason to question the view of the responsible clinician as to the clinical basis for a patient's ongoing detention, they should consider seeking further medical advice and adjourning for that reason.

2.60 The panel should have written reports from the responsible clinician providing a history of any self-harm or violence, a history of the patient's treatment, a risk assessment and a care plan. These reports should normally be made available to the patient unless the managers are of the view that such disclosure would be liable seriously to harm the health of the patient or any other person.

2.61 There is no detailed set procedure laid down in statute or in the Code, but the panel has to adopt a procedure which is fair. The major features of such a fair procedure and which are advised by the Code are:

- giving the patient a proper opportunity, and appropriate assistance, to set out why he or she wants to be discharged from detention;
- allowing the patient to be assisted by a friend or representative, often a legal representative, in advocating his or her case;
- seeking the views of the responsible clinician and other appropriate professionals on whether the detention continues to be justified and the reasons they hold those views;
- giving the various parties the opportunity to hear each other's case and to put questions to each other;
- giving reasons for the decision.

2.62 The key question for the panel to consider is evidently whether the patient's ongoing detention continues to meet the statutory criteria. The panel therefore has to address:

- Does the patient continue to suffer from a mental disorder?
- Does the disorder continue to be of a nature and degree which means that treatment in a hospital is appropriate?
- Is the continuing detention of the patient still necessary for the health or safety of the patient or for the protection of others?
- In relation to patients being detained under s 3, is appropriate medical treatment available?

2.63 In cases where the managers' hearing is brought about by the responsible clinician having blocked the nearest relative's discharge of the patient the threshold is slightly higher. The focus is on the probability of dangerous acts such as causing serious physical injury rather than on the broader question of whether the detention is necessary for the patient's general health and safety or the general need for protection of others.

REVIEW OF DETENTION BY THE MENTAL HEALTH TRIBUNALS (ENGLAND) AND MENTAL HEALTH REVIEW TRIBUNALS (WALES)

The tribunal system

2.64 The original mental health tribunals (Mental Health Review Tribunals, MHRTs) were created by the Mental Health Act 1959 in order to review detention and direct the patient's discharge where ongoing detention was unlawful. After reform of the tribunal system there are now separate tribunals for England and for Wales, with slightly different, albeit very similar, procedural rules. The function of the tribunals is to provide patients with an opportunity to have their ongoing detention on mental health grounds considered speedily by an independent, impartial judicial body, in accordance with Article 5(4) of the European Convention on Human Rights.

2.65 Following the general reform of the wider tribunal system in England in the Tribunals, Courts and Enforcement Act 2007, a two-tier tribunal system was created in England. The English tribunal system now has a First-tier Tribunal ('FTT') and an Upper Tribunal. The FTT consists of a number of separate specialist chambers which hear cases in the first instance and which accordingly hear all the evidence and make the necessary factual decisions involved in adjudicating on cases. The jurisdiction of the MHRTs to decide on mental health cases accordingly moved to the Health, Education and Social Care Chamber of the FTT. Where this tribunal is considering mental health cases, it is referred to as the Mental Health Tribunal ('MHT'). The procedure in the tribunal is governed by the First-tier Tribunal (Health, Education and Social Care Chamber) Rules 2008 ('FTTHESC Rules 2008'). The Upper Tribunal is the first appellate court which hears appeals on points of law. Its function is not to reconsider the factual material, only to decide whether the First-tier Tribunal made an error of law.

2.66 The MHT in England has two Regional Tribunal Judges, based in London and in Preston. Judges and members of the tribunal are appointed by the Lord Chancellor. The tribunal's duties must be performed by three or more of its members. At least one must be a 'legal member', one a 'medical member' and one a member who is neither a legal member or a medical member. The legal members in England are known as judges and are appointed from people with suitable legal experience. Ordinarily this will mean people who have held the right of audience before county courts and magistrates' courts for a period of at least 7 years. The medical members will ordinarily be psychiatrists who have held an appointment as a consultant psychiatrist for at least 3 years. The other members of the tribunal will be people with experience of social services or having other suitable experience and qualifications.

2.67 In Wales, the tribunal is known as the Mental Health Review Tribunal for Wales (MHRT), which is based in (and administered from) Cardiff. Again, the tribunal's duties must be performed by three or more members, one of whom is legally qualified, one who is medically qualified and one who is neither a legal nor a medical member. The legal member of the panel of the MHRT in Wales is known as the President. The procedure rules applicable to the MHRT are the Mental Health Review Tribunal Wales Rules 2008 ('MHRT Wales Rules 2008').

2.68 In both England and in Wales the legally qualified member presides over the hearings and has the responsibility for ensuring that proceedings are conducted fairly, in accordance with the relevant tribunal rules and the MHA 1983. The function of the medical member in both tribunals is first, to carry out an examination of the patient prior to the hearing so as to form as opinion of their mental condition, and second, to advise the tribunal on medical matters. The function of the 'lay member' is to provide balance by offering a separate 'social' view distinct from the particular professional expertise provided by the medical and legal members.

2.69 The Upper Tribunal serves as the first appeal court from both the First-tier Tribunal in England and the MHRT in Wales.

The function and powers of the Tribunals

2.70 The principal role of the Tribunals is to determine whether, at the time of the hearing, the statutory criteria for mental health detention continue to be met. In light of the findings of the Tribunal as to whether the statutory criteria continue to be met, the Tribunal can: direct that the patient be discharged as of right (that is to say, the Tribunal must discharge, because the continued detention would be unlawful); direct discharge in the exercise of its discretion (because the continued detention would not be unlawful according to the statutory criteria, but nonetheless the Tribunal considers in all the circumstances it is appropriate to discharge); or not direct discharge because the detention continues to be lawful and appropriate in the circumstances. The criteria to be addressed by the Tribunal in considering the lawfulness of the detention (and accordingly whether to order discharge as of right) are set out in s 72 of the MHA 1983 and are effectively a mirror of the relevant thresholds for admission in s 2 and s 3. It is important to bear in mind that it is for the detaining authority to establish that the detention meets all the necessary legal thresholds on the balance of probabilities. Thus if the Tribunal is not satisfied on the balance of probabilities that any element is met, then it must order discharge. The burden of proof is not on the patient to demonstrate the unlawfulness of their detention.

2.71 In cases where there is no discharge as of right (because the legal thresholds for detention continue to be met), but the tribunal is considering discharge in any event, the tribunal will need to consider and explain what treatment is necessary and be satisfied that it would otherwise be available without ongoing detention before the discretion to discharge could properly be exercised. It should be noted that in practice tribunals very rarely exercise their discretionary right to discharge a patient. If the tribunal is considering a discharge, it will also need to address the possibility of delayed discharge under s 72(3). This section empowers the tribunal to direct discharge on a future date specified by the tribunal. The tribunal might, for example, consider that it is appropriate to delay discharge until a date when certain community support will be available.

Who is entitled to apply for a Tribunal hearing and when

2.72 In order to comply with the European Convention on Human Rights, the MHA 1983 makes provision for all detained patients – whether detained for assessment or for treatment – to be able to make an application for a tribunal hearing to assess the validity of their detention. The Act also provides for automatic referrals in cases where patients themselves have not exercised the right for whatever reason. There is also an entitlement for nearest relatives to apply to the tribunal in certain circumstances. Further, the Secretary of State for Health (or, in Wales, the Welsh Ministers) can make references to the tribunal at any time, although, in practice, there will be limited circumstances where this is likely to be appropriate or necessary.

Patients detained under Part II MHA 1983

2.73 A patient admitted for assessment under s 2 may apply once to the tribunal within the first 14 days of detention. A patient who has been detained for treatment under s 3 may apply once in the first 6 months of detention and thereafter once in every period for which the detention is renewed. Where a patient makes an application to the tribunal to challenge his detention under s 2 and is then detained under s 3 before the hearing to consider the detention under s 2, the tribunal will proceed to hear the case as if it were a challenge to detention under s 3. However, this will not affect the patient's right to apply for a further tribunal hearing in the first period of 6 months' detention after the change in status to s 3.

Nearest relatives

2.74 Where the nearest relative has sought to exercise their power to discharge the patient from detention, but the responsible clinician has issued a barring certificate, then the nearest relative may apply to the tribunal within 28 days. If the nearest relative has been displaced by the county court on the basis of unreasonable objection to admission for treatment or having exercised the power of discharge without due regard to the welfare of the patient or the public interest, then the nearest relative is entitled to apply to the tribunal once in every 12 month period during which the order displacing them applies.

Automatic references to the tribunal where the patient himself or herself does not appeal

2.75 If a patient has not made an application to the tribunal within 6 months of the date on which they were first detained, then the hospital managers must refer that patient's case to the tribunal. Further, if a tribunal has not considered a patient's case in 3 years then, again, the hospital managers must make a reference to the tribunal.

References by the Secretary of State for Health and the Welsh Ministers

2.76 The Secretary of State or, in Wales, the Welsh Ministers have the power pursuant to s 67 of the MHA 1983 to refer the case of any patient detained under MHA 1983 Part II (non-offender patients detained for assessment or treatment) to the MHT or MHRT at any time.

2.77 The Code produced by the Department of Health makes clear that anyone may request a referral by the Secretary of State at any time and that it will be considered by the Secretary of State on its merits. If making a request of the Secretary of State, it will be appropriate to explain in writing the reasons for the request, the last time the patient's detention was considered by the tribunal, the length of time that will elapse before a further tribunal application or referral can be made under the MHA 1983 and the basis for the issue sought to be referred by the Secretary of State falling within the jurisdiction of the tribunal.

2.78 The circumstances where such an application to the Secretary of State may be particularly appropriate include the case where a patient is detained pursuant to s 2 for assessment and this detention is then extended pending the determination of an application to displace the nearest relative. Since an application to displace automatically extends the period of detention under s 2 until the county court hears the case, there can be circumstances where a patient who has not applied to the MHT or MHRT within 14 days of their initial detention has no right to seek a consideration of the lawfulness of their ongoing detention from the tribunal. In those circumstances, the Code of Practice emphasises that the hospital managers should always consider making an application to the Secretary of State for a reference. In particular the code recommends that hospital managers should ask the Secretary of State to consider making a reference where:

- a patient's detention under s 2 has been extended under s 29, MHA 1983 pending the determination of an application to displace the nearest relative before the county court;
- the patient him – or herself lacks capacity to request a reference from the Secretary of State; and
- the patient's case has never been considered by the tribunal, or a substantial period of time has elapsed since the tribunal last considered the case.

Procedure in the MHT and MHRT

2.79 As noted above the procedural rules in the English MHT and the Welsh MHRT are slightly different, albeit with very little practical distinction. However, if making an application, it is nonetheless important to have regard to the particular set of relevant rules which apply to the jurisdiction in which the application is made.

Applications

2.80 The application must be made in writing to the tribunal and be signed either by the person who is making the application or by a person authorised on their behalf to do so. The application should set out certain information required by the procedural rules including the patient's name and address, and the name and address of the responsible authority (the hospital managers). The tribunals provide forms – labelled T110 in the English MHT – which should be used to make the application. Notice of the application must be sent by the tribunal on receipt to the patient (where they are not the applicant themselves) and to the responsible authority for the patient.

2.81 The patient, the person making the application (if someone other than the patient), and the responsible authority are the parties to the case. The following people also must be given notice by the tribunal of the application once the responsible authority has given its response (see below): the private guardian of a guardianship patient; the Court of Protection if there is an order in force in relation to the patient from that court; any person or body who has the power to discharge the patient under MHA 1983, s 23; and any other person who the tribunal considers should have the opportunity to be heard. The tribunal may allow such of these people as it considers appropriate to make written or oral representations to the extent the tribunal considers proper.

Response by the responsible authority

2.82 The requirements as to a response to the application from the responsible authority are mandated by different sets of rules in England and in Wales. The English rules are the FTTHESC Rules 2008 read with the Practice Direction on Statements and Reports in Mental Health Cases (April 2012). In Wales, the rules are the MHRT Wales Rules 2008 and, in particular, the Schedule to the Rules on 'Statements by the Responsible Authority and the Secretary of State'.

2.83 In England, for patients who are detained otherwise than simply for assessment (ie detained for treatment), the statement provided by the responsible authority must include the following:

- a statement of biographical detail about the patient;
- a clinical report signed or countersigned by the responsible clinician;
- a nursing report;
- a social circumstances report.

2.84 In Wales, the equivalent response from the responsible authority must contain a similar set of biographical information as set out above in relation to the English tribunal as well as:

- an up-to-date clinical report;
- an up-to-date social circumstances report;
- the views of the responsible authority on the suitability of the patient for discharge;
- where the provisions of s 117 of the MHA 1983 may apply to the patient, a proposed after care plan in respect of the patient; and
- any other information or observations on the application which the responsible authority wishes to make.

2.85 In relation to s 2 patients detained for assessment, the responsible authority must provide a copy of the application authorising detention, the medical reports which supported that detention and such of the other information detailed above as is reasonably practical in the circumstances. The hearing in relation to a patient detained under s 2 must be within 7 days of receipt of the application by the tribunal.

Access to information

2.86 Historically the reports produced by the responsible authority as to the patient's condition were often withheld on the basis of alleged potential damage to the patient/doctor relationship were they to be disclosed. This meant that in certain circumstances the patient might be at a considerable disadvantage in bringing their case, since they may not have been able fully to challenge the detail of the reports.

2.87 The rules now provide, in effect, for a presumption of full disclosure. The FTTHESC Rules 2008 and MHRT Rules 2008 both provide that the reports should be disclosed unless the tribunal is satisfied both that:

- the disclosure would be likely to cause that person (to whom the document was disclosed) or some other person serious harm; and
- having regard to the interests of justice, it is proportionate for the tribunal to direct that the documents should not be disclosed.

2.88 In England the tribunal is left with a discretion as to whether it orders that documents be withheld even where it considers the above tests are met. In Wales, the tribunal must order non-disclosure if the thresholds are crossed.

Medical examination of the patient

2.89 Both the English and Welsh rules require a medical member of the tribunal, so far as practicable, to examine the patient and take such other steps as necessary to form an opinion of the patient's mental condition before any hearing takes place. The medical member will examine the patient before the hearing and either provide a written report or a verbal report, discussing his or her opinion with the other members; in practice it is almost invariably a verbal report that is provided. Where a tribunal makes a decision on the basis of something in the opinion of the tribunal medical member on which there has been no evidence put before the tribunal, the tribunal will have to ensure that the applicant or the applicant's representative are aware of the views of the medical member and have the chance to deal with them. Normally the tribunal would be expected, as a matter of course, to explain the medical view of the medical member in adequate detail and in adequate time so that the parties have the opportunity to respond.

Representation, evidence and hearings

2.90 Any party to proceedings before the MHT or MHRT may be represented by any person (except by a person themselves subject to the provisions of MHA 1983), whether that person is legally qualified or not. In order to notify the tribunal of the fact that there is a representative acting, the party or their representative must give the tribunal written notice of the representative's name and address.

2.91 The tribunal itself has the power to appoint a legal representative for the patient if the patient has not exercised his or her right to do so and either: (i) the patient has indicated that they do not wish to present their own case; or (ii) the patient lacks capacity to appoint a representative and the tribunal considers it is in the best interests of the patient to be legally represented.

2.92 The tribunal rules in both England and Wales provide for wide direction-making and case management powers for the tribunal. These can be exercised on the motion of the tribunal itself or on the application of any party. The direction-making powers of the tribunal extend to considerable discretion over the evidence the tribunal considers necessary to dispense with the application fairly. This includes: the question of whether the parties are permitted or required to provide additional expert evidence on any issue and whether that expert should be a single, jointly appointed expert; the possibility for the tribunal to limit the number of witnesses who may be put forward; and whether the evidence will be given orally at a hearing.

2.93 Hearings in both England and Wales must be in private unless the tribunal orders otherwise. In England, the tribunal can order a public hearing if it considers to do so would be in the interests of justice. In Wales, the tribunal may only order a public hearing if there is an application for such a hearing by the patient and the tribunal considers that such a hearing would be in the interests of the patient. The tribunal may decide who is allowed to attend the hearing and has the power to exclude any person, including a party, where that person's presence is disruptive or where the exclusion is necessary in order to give effect to a direction withholding information which is likely to cause harm.

2.94 Subject to that power of exclusion on the part of the tribunal, all parties may attend the hearing and are entitled to see copies of all documents put before the tribunal by the other parties in the case (again, subject to the tribunal's power to withhold documents from disclosure should it consider that such disclosure would cause harm). Hearings will typically follow a relatively standard pattern for legal proceedings of the evidence being heard first, followed by the opportunity to address submissions to the tribunal, emphasising the key arguments.

The MHT or MHRT decision and its consequences

2.95 The tribunal usually gives its decision immediately and orally at the end of a hearing. Very rarely it may take further time to consider its decision. In any event, the rules provide for strict deadlines for the tribunal to reach decisions and to provide written reasons for the decision. In a s 2 case, the tribunal must provide a written decision within 3 working days and in other cases must do so within 7 days. The decision notice stating the decision must be accompanied by a statement of reasons. As with disclosure, there is an exception to the duty to provide written reasons where the tribunal considers that the provision of full reasons would be likely to cause serious harm to the patient or to another person. If the tribunal considers this to be the case, it may, for example, elect to provide reasons to the patient's representative on the condition that the sensitive part of the reasoning is not disclosed.

2.96 The reasons given by the tribunal must be more than simply restatements of the statutory criteria which apply. The tribunal must engage with any dispute as to evidence and explain why it prefers the account of one party rather than another. Similarly, the tribunal must provide sufficient explanation as to why it prefers the view of one expert over another insofar as there is such a dispute.

2.97 A decision of the tribunal to end detention means that any further detention pursuant to the particular application or other authority for detention which applied at the time of the tribunal hearing would be unlawful. However, it is important to be aware that this does not in itself prevent a further, fresh application for detention being made. Obviously if the circumstances change compared with those that applied at the time of the tribunal then another application might properly be made. But the courts have also decided that if the applicant for a fresh detention has formed a reasonable and genuine opinion that he or she has information which was not known to the tribunal when it made its decision, then another application can properly be made. This means that, although probably quite rarely, it will sometimes be possible for new applications for detention to be made, even where circumstances have not in fact changed after a tribunal has discharged a patient from detention.

WHAT HAPPENS WHEN A SECTION EXPIRES

2.98 If a section expires and has not been renewed then a patient is, in principle, free to leave hospital and can no longer be detained under MHA 1983. However, this is subject to the power of a registered medical practitioner or nurse to use their 'holding powers' where they consider that a fresh application may need to be made.

The holding powers – where someone is already an inpatient, but not subject to detention

2.99 If a voluntary or informal patient, having consented to admission, is already in hospital but then wishes to leave and a registered medical practitioner, approved clinician or nurse in the hospital consider there may be a need to detain, there is a temporary holding power provided for in s 5 of MHA 1983. There are two distinct legal frameworks: one relating to the power of a registered medical practitioner or the approved clinician in charge of an in-patient's treatment and one relating to the power of the nurse.

The holding power of the doctor or the approved clinician

2.100 Under s 5(2) the registered medical practitioner or approved clinician in charge of an in-patient's treatment in *any* hospital, regardless of whether it is a psychiatric hospital or whether the patient is receiving mental health treatment, may exercise a temporary holding power.

2.101 If the doctor or approved clinician is of the view that an application for compulsory admission will need to be made they may provide a report to the hospital managers confirming their view. Upon this being completed, the patient is liable to be detained in the hospital for a period of up to 72 hours from the point at which the report was presented to the managers.

2.102 It is important to note that the power may not be used, nor would be necessary, where someone is already detained pursuant to the MHA 1983. However, the power may be used in relation to someone who is currently being held in hospital pursuant to a DoL under MCA 2005.

2.103 Of course, the purpose of the holding power is to provide time for the application under s 2 or s 3 to be made. The s 5(2) power should not be deployed as a separate species of short-term detention. Rather, the process of putting together the application for either assessment or treatment under s 2 or s 3 should be made immediately. It is also plain that if it becomes clear that no detention is, in fact, required then the detention pursuant to the s 5(2) power must be ceased immediately. The patient should be informed straight away that the s 5(2) power no longer applies and that they are accordingly free to leave.

The nurse's holding power

2.104 Under s 5(4) a nurse with certain experience may hold an inpatient in a psychiatric hospital or ward (and not any other form of hospital), and who is receiving treatment for mental disorder, for a maximum of 6 hours. This power is designed to give the registered medical practitioner or approved clinician the time to consider whether to exercise their own, longer, holding power under s 5(2) as described above.

2.105 Currently, the legislation prescribes that the class of nurse able to exercise the power is: 'a nurse registered in sub-part 1 or 2 of the register maintained by the Nursing and Midwifery Council whose entry in the register indicates that their field of practice is either mental health nursing or learning disability nursing.'

2.106 As with the s 5(2) power, the s 5(4) power may not be used, nor would be necessary, where a patient is already liable to detention under MHA 1983. The thresholds for the nurse to be able to exercise the power are that both: (a) the patient is suffering from mental disorder to such a degree that it is necessary for his or her health and safety or for the protection of others that he or she is immediately restrained from leaving hospital, and (b) that it is not practicable to secure the immediate attendance of a practitioner or approved clinician in order to provide a report to the hospital managers pursuant to s 5(1).

2.107 The procedure for the nurse to use the s 5(4) power is that he or she must record in writing on a statutory form the fact that the statutory threshold is met. The patient may be detained from that point onwards and the hospital managers must be furnished with the form immediately. If the registered medical practitioner or approved clinician exercises their s 5(2) power within the 6-hour period, then the 72-hour detention under s 5(2) will be treated as having started at the point the nurse first recorded the fact that the statutory conditions in s 5(2) were met.

GUARDIANSHIP

The powers of the guardian and the application

2.108 Guardianship provides an alternative regime for the protection of people with mental disorder to formal detention under MHA 1983. The regime is intended to provide patients with a degree of supervision and control, but to enable to them to live in the community as independently as possible. Guardians can be the local social services authority for the person or any person approved by that authority to carry out the function. The guardian has certain powers to make decisions on behalf of the mentally disordered person, such as requiring them to live in particular places or attend for treatment.

2.109 In order for a person to qualify for guardianship, it is necessary that he or she is suffering from mental disorder of a nature or degree which warrants his or her reception in guardianship and that it is necessary in the interests of the welfare of the person or for the protection of others that he or she should become subject to guardianship.

2.110 An application for guardianship is made pursuant to s 7 of the MHA 1983. It can be made by either an AMHP or the nearest relative. As with detention for treatment under s 3, the Act requires that the application be supported by the opinion of two medical practitioners. Similarly, an application made by an AMHP can be blocked by the nearest relative. The procedural requirements are essentially the same as set out above in relation to formal detention.

2.111 Guardians have the power to:

- require the person subject to guardianship to reside at a place specified by the authority or person named as the guardian;
- require the person to attend at places and times specified for the purpose of medical treatment, occupation, education or training; and
- require access to the person to be given at any place where the patient is residing, to any registered medical practitioner, AMHP or other specified person.

2.112 If a person absents himself or herself without leave from the place where he is required to reside by the guardian or does not go to such place in the first instance, then any officer of the local social services authority, any constable or a person authorised in writing by the guardian or the local authority may take the person into custody and return him to the appropriate place.

2.113 While the MHA 1983 does not expressly state that guardianship cannot authorise such steps as amount to a deprivation of a person's liberty, the MCA Code is very clear that guardians are not able to deprive a person of their liberty separately from the procedures under MHA 1983 or MCA 2005.

2.114 The Code also suggests particular circumstances in which an application for guardianship might be thought especially appropriate:

- where it is thought to be important that decisions about where the person is to live are placed in the hands of a single person or authority over a continuing period – for example where there have been long-running or particularly difficult disputes about where the person should live;
- where the person is thought likely to be respond well to the authority and attention of a guardian, and so be more willing to comply with the necessary treatment and care for their mental disorder;
- where there is a particular need to have explicit authority for the person to be returned to the place the person is to live (for example, a care home).

Objecting to guardianship

2.115 As noted above, the nearest relative has the power to block a guardianship application simply by notifying the AMHP or the local social services authority on whose behalf the AMHP is acting. This is of course subject to the possibility of that relative being displaced under s 29 of the MHA 1983.

2.116 If a person is already subject to guardianship, the nearest relative has the power to discharge the guardianship by making an order for discharge in writing. Again, the nearest relative may be displaced if they exercise the power of discharge unreasonably.

2.117 Applications may also be made to the MHT or MHRT for discharge from guardianship. The tribunals have a general discretion to discharge and must do so if they consider that the person is not suffering from mental disorder and/or that it is not necessary in the interests of the welfare of the person, or the protection of others, that the person should remain under guardianship. The procedural aspects of an application before the tribunal challenging guardianship – and the governing procedural rules – are effectively the same as those for an application challenging compulsory detention.

CHAPTER 3

RIGHTS TO ASSESSMENTS

3.1 This chapter considers the various assessments available to an individual following a diagnosis of dementia. The purpose of such assessments are myriad, ranging from safeguarding and promoting the best interests of an incapacitated individual to ensuring that his or her health and social care needs are being met by the appropriate statutory body.

3.2 Three types of assessments are considered that may commonly apply to an individual with dementia. These are:

(1) an assessment of mental capacity;

(2) an assessment of community care needs; and

(3) an assessment of eligibility for continuing healthcare by the NHS.

3.3 The chapter will further consider, where appropriate, a person's right to any particular assessment and the obligations incumbent upon those undertaking the assessment, whether a private individual or public body. It will also set out the process by which such assessments are undertaken.

ASSESSMENT OF MENTAL CAPACITY

The Mental Capacity Act 2005

3.4 The Mental Capacity Act 2005 ('MCA 2005') was implemented on 1 October 2007. The MCA 2005 creates a statutory framework setting out how decisions should be made by and on behalf of people aged 16 and over whose capacity to make their own decisions is in doubt. It identifies what actions others may take in relation to the care or treatment of people lacking capacity to consent to those actions.

3.5 The MCA 2005 was intended to be enabling and supportive of people who lack capacity, not restricting or controlling of their lives. It aims not only to protect people who lack capacity to make particular decisions, but also to maximise their ability to make decisions, or to participate in decision-making, as far as they are able to do so.[1]

1 MCA 2005 Code of Practice, p 19.

3.6 The underlying philosophy of the MCA 2005 is to ensure that any decision made or action taken, on behalf of someone who lacks the capacity to make the decision or act for themselves is made in their best interests.

3.7 Section 42 of the MCA 2005 requires the Lord Chancellor to prepare and issue one or more Codes of Practice. The Government published one such code in 2007, namely the *Mental Capacity Act 2005 Code of Practice* ('MCA Code of Practice').[2]

3.8 The MCA Code of Practice is intended to give practical guidance and examples to illustrate the provisions of the MCA 2005 rather than impose any additional legal or formal requirements.

3.9 The Code of Practice has statutory force, which means that certain categories of people have a legal duty to have regard to it when working with or caring for adults who may lack capacity to make decisions for themselves.[3]

Statutory principles

3.10 Section 1 of the MCA 2005 sets out the five statutory principles or core values that underpin all of the legal requirements in the MCA 2005 and govern its implementation. These five principles are:

(1) A person must be assumed to have capacity unless it is established that they lack capacity.
(2) A person is not to be treated as unable to make a decision unless all practicable steps to help him to do so have been taken without success.
(3) A person is not to be treated as unable to make a decision merely because he makes an unwise decision.
(4) An act done, or decision made, under the MCA 2005 for or on behalf of a person who lacks capacity must be done, or made, in his best interests.
(5) Before the act is done, or the decision is made, regard must be had to whether the purpose for which it is needed can be as effectively achieved in a way that is less restrictive of the person's rights and freedom of action.

3.11 Chapter 2 of the MCA Code of Practice considers these statutory principles in some detail and how they are to be applied.

Defining lack of capacity

3.12 The MCA 2005 preserves in statute the position of the common law that capacity is a functional concept, requiring capacity to be assessed in relation to a particular decision at the time that the decision needs to be made and not a

---

2 https://www.gov.uk/government/publications/mental-capacity-act-code-of-practice.

3 MCA 2005, s 42(4); pp 1–2 of the Code of Practice sets out the categories of people who should 'have regard to' the guidance contained within the Code of Practice.

person's ability to make decisions generally. The consequence of this is that an individual should not be regarded as 'incapable' simply because they have been diagnosed with dementia, or because of any preconceived ideas or assumptions about his or her abilities. Instead, it must be demonstrated that he or she lacks capacity for each specific decision at the time it falls to be made.

3.13 Section 2(1) of the MCA 2005 sets out the definition of a person who lacks capacity as follows:

> 'For the purposes of this Act, a person lacks capacity in relation to a matter if at the material time he is unable to make a decision for himself in relation to the matter because of an impairment of, or a disturbance in the functioning of, the mind or brain.'

3.14 Capacity is therefore not 'all or nothing'. It is both time and issue specific. Furthermore, the inability to make a particular decision must be because of an impairment of, or a disturbance in the functioning of, the mind or brain (ie a mental disability or disorder).

3.15 Section 2(2) of MCA 2005 states that it does not matter whether the impairment or disturbance is permanent or temporary. As such, a person can lack capacity to make a particular decision even if the loss of capacity is only partial or if his or her capacity fluctuates.

3.16 Furthermore, it should be noted that within this definition, a person may lack capacity in relation to one matter (eg handling financial affairs) but not in relation to others (eg where they should live or what care they should receive).

Equal treatment

3.17 Section 2(3) of the MCA 2005 provides that a lack of capacity cannot be established merely by reference to a person's age or appearance, any condition they may have or an aspect of their behaviour, which might lead others to make unjustified assumptions about his or her capacity. This thereby ensures that an individual cannot be labelled incapable simply because he or she has been diagnosed with dementia.

What proof of lack of capacity does the MCA 2005 require?

3.18 Section 2(4) of the MCA 2005 stipulates that any question as to whether a person lacks capacity within the meaning of the MCA 2005 must be decided on the balance of probabilities, ie that it is more likely than not that the individual lacks capacity to make a particular decision at the time it needs to be made.

Qualifying age

3.19 Section 2(5) of the MCA 2005 provides that the powers exercisable under the legislative provisions only apply to adults who lack capacity, defined as those who are aged 16 years or over. There are two exceptions to this rule:

(1) the powers to deal with property and financial affairs may be exercised in relation to a child whose lack of capacity is likely to continue into adulthood;[4] and

(2) no lower age limit is specified for the victim of an offence of ill-treatment or wilful neglect of a person lacking capacity.[5]

Two-stage test of capacity

3.20 The MCA 2005 effectively creates a two-stage process in order to decide whether an individual has the capacity to make a particular decision. The two stages are as follows:

(1) It must be established that there is an 'impairment of, or disturbance in the functioning of, the person's mind or brain'; and

(2) It must be established that the impairment or disturbance is sufficient to render the person unable to make that particular decision at the relevant time.

Stage 1: The diagnostic threshold

3.21 If there is no evidence of an impairment or disturbance, the individual should be presumed to have capacity and his or her ability to make decisions should not be impeded. Paragraph 4.12 of the MCA Code of Practice expressly cites dementia as an example of an impairment or disturbance in the functioning of the mind or brain.

Stage 2: Inability to make a decision

3.22 The second stage of the test of capacity requires that for a person to lack capacity their impairment or disturbance must affect their ability to make the specific decision when they need to. Before this conclusion can be made, the person concerned must be given all practical and appropriate support to help them make the decision for themselves.

3.23 Section 3(1) of MCA 2005 sets out the test for assessing whether a person is unable to make a decision for himself of herself. A person is unable to make a decision if he or she is unable:

(a) to understand the information relevant to the decision,

---

4 MCA 2005, ss 2(6) and 18(3).

5 MCA 2005, s 44.

(b) to retain that information,

(c) to use or weigh that information as part of the process of making the decision, or

(d) to communicate his decision (whether by talking, using sign language or any other means).

3.24 According to the MCA Code of Practice[6] the (a), (b) and (c) of these provisions should be applied together. If a person cannot do any of these three things, they will be treated as unable to make the decision. The fourth, (d), only applies in situations where people cannot communicate their decision in any way. Paragraphs 4.14 to 4.25 of the MCA Code of Practice consider these criteria in much further detail and should be consulted by any person intending to undertake a capacity assessment.

Common law tests of capacity

3.25 There are several common law tests of capacity that were established in case-law prior to the implementation of the MCA 2005. Examples given in the MCA Code of Practice[7] cover:

- capacity to make a will;
- capacity to enter into marriage;
- capacity to make a gift;
- contractual capacity; and
- capacity to litigate.

3.26 The MCA 2005's definition of capacity is in line with the existing common law tests and does not replace them. As such, when cases come before the court on the above issues, judges can adopt the new definition if they think it is appropriate. The MCA 2005 will apply to all other cases relating to financial, healthcare or welfare decisions.

WHEN SHOULD CAPACITY BE ASSESSED?

3.27 The starting point enshrined within the statutory principles of the MCA 2005 should be the presumption of capacity. In the event that doubts arise in relation to a person's capacity to make a particular decision (eg triggered by their own behaviour or through concerns raised by others) the MCA Code of Practice recommends that the following questions should be considered:[8]

- Does the person have all the relevant information they need to make the decision?

---

6 Code of Practice, para 4.15.
7 Code of Practice, para 4.32.
8 Code of Practice, para 4.36.

- If they are making a decision that involves choosing between alternatives, do they have information on all the different options?
- Would the person have a better understanding if information was explained or presented in another way?
- Are there times of day when the person's understanding is better?
- Are there locations where they may feel more at ease?
- Can the decision be put off until the circumstances are different and the person concerned may be able to make the decision?
- Can anyone else help the person to make choices or express a view (for example, a family member or carer, an advocate or someone to help with communication)?

3.28 If all these steps have been taken without enabling that person to make a decision, an assessment of his capacity to make that decision should be made.

WHO SHOULD ASSESS CAPACITY?

3.29 In keeping with the functional approach, the question of who should assess an individual's capacity will depend on the particular decision to be made. Paragraph 4.38 of the MCA Code of Practice notes that usually the person who assesses capacity will be the person who is concerned with the individual at the time the decision has to be made. This can mean that different people may be involved in assessing someone's capacity to make different decisions at different times. For example, a capacity assessment may be made by a partner, carer, other health professional, social worker or solicitor depending on the decision in question.

Reasonable belief of lack of capacity

3.30 For most day-to-day decisions, an assessment is likely to be undertaken by the person caring for them at the time a decision must be made. For example, a care worker might need to assess if the person can agree to being bathed. In such circumstances, it will not be appropriate to carry out a formal assessment of the person's capacity. Instead, it is sufficient that they 'reasonably believe' that the person lacks capacity to make the decision or consent to the action in question.[9] They must be able to point to objective reasons to justify why they hold that belief. Such reasons will depend on individual circumstances and the urgency of the decision.

3.31 The MCA Code of Practice[10] suggests a number of steps that may be helpful in establishing a 'reasonable belief' of lack of capacity:

---

9 MCA 2005, ss 4(8) and 5(1).

10 Code of Practice, para 4.45.

- Start by assuming the person has capacity to make the specific decision. Is there anything to prove otherwise?
- Does the person have a previous diagnosis of disability or mental disorder? Does that condition now affect their capacity to make this decision? If there has been no previous diagnosis, it may be best to get a medical opinion.
- Make every effort to communicate with the person to explain what is happening.
- Make every effort to try to help the person make the decision in question.
- See if there is a way to explain or present information about the decision in a way that makes it easier to understand. If the person has a choice, do they have information about all the options?
- Can the decision be delayed to take time to help the person make the decision, or to give the person time to regain the capacity to make the decision for themselves?
- Does the person understand what decision they need to make and why they need to make it?
- Can they understand information about the decision? Can they retain it, use it and weigh it to make the decision?
- Be aware that the fact that a person agrees with you or assents to what is proposed does not necessarily mean that they have capacity to make the decision.

3.32 Higher expectations are likely to be placed on those appointed to act under formal powers (eg attorneys and deputies) and those acting in a professional capacity (eg doctors, social workers, lawyers) than on family members and friends who are caring for a person lacking capacity without formal authority.

WHEN WILL A FORMAL ASSESSMENT OF CAPACITY BE NECESSARY?

3.33 If a decision is more serious or the outcome more significant, then it is likely that a more formal approach will need to be taken. For example, where consent to medical treatment or examination is required, the doctor or healthcare professional proposing the treatment must decide whether the patient has capacity to consent and should record the assessment process and findings in the person's medical notes. Where a legal transaction is involved (eg creating a Lasting Power of Attorney), the lawyer handling the transaction will need to assess whether the client has capacity to give instructions, perhaps assisted by an opinion from a doctor.

3.34 Where there is a dispute about capacity, assessing capacity is, ultimately, a judicial function as opposed to a medical function. Healthcare professionals are regarded as expert witnesses whose function it is to provide the court with material so that it can reach a decision.[11] However, it should also be noted that medical evidence may not necessarily be determinative. For example, a family member or professional (eg a social worker) with close knowledge of and contact with a person may be in a better position to make a judgment about capacity, than a medical doctor coming to the situation for the first time.

3.35 In the event that a doctor or healthcare professional is requested to undertake an assessment of capacity, he or she should be informed of the specific decision for which the person is being assessed and the relevant legal test (ie the statutory test in the MCA 2005 and any relevant common law tests). In the case of *SC v BS*[12] the opinion of an expert in autism was disregarded as he was unfamiliar with the MCA 2005 test for capacity, referring instead in his report to 'fitness to plead'. This case illustrates that it cannot be assumed that a doctor will necessarily know the correct test to be applied.

3.36 In certain cases it is a requirement of law, or good professional practice, that a formal assessment of capacity is carried out. These include the following situations:

(1) where the Court of Protection is required to determine a person's capacity to make a particular decision;[13]

(2) to establish that a person comes within the jurisdiction of the Court of Protection;[14]

(3) to establish that a person requires the assistance of the Official Solicitor or other litigation friend.[15]

3.37 In other types of cases, obtaining medical evidence is not essential, although highly desirable and recognised as a matter of good practice. One example of this is in relation to testamentary capacity. In *Kenward v Adams*[16] Templeman J established a 'golden rule' where it was held:

> '...When a solicitor is drawing up a will for an aged testator or one who has been seriously ill, it should be witnessed or approved by a medical practitioner, who ought to record his examination of the testator and his findings...'

3.38 Whilst subsequent decisions have established that non-compliance with the golden rule will not automatically demonstrate the invalidity of a will, it will assist the avoidance of disputes or, at least, in the minimisation of their scope.[17]

---

11 *Blackman v Man* [2007] EWHC 3162 (Ch).

12 (Unreported, CoP No.11987961, 7 October 2011).

13 *Masterman-Lister v Brutton& Co and Jewell & Home Counties Dairies* [2002] EWCA Civ 1889, at [54].

14 MCA 2005, ss 15(1) and 16(1).

15 Civil Procedure Rules 1998, SI 1998/3132, r 21.1.

16 (*The Times*, 29 November 1975).

17 *Key v Key* [2010] EWHC 408 (Ch).

REFUSAL OF ASSESSMENT OF CAPACITY

3.39 A person may refuse or object to an assessment of their mental capacity. Paragraph 4.59 of the MCA Code of Practice states that nobody 'can be forced to undergo an assessment of capacity. If someone refuses to open the door to their home, it cannot be forced.'

3.40 If there are serious concerns about a person's mental health, it may be possible to obtain a warrant and force entry under s 135 of the Mental Health Act 1983 ('MHA 1983'). However, the MCA Code of Practice is extremely clear that simply refusing an assessment of capacity is in no way sufficient grounds for an assessment under the MHA 1983.

3.41 If a person lacks capacity to consent or refuse assessment, it will normally be possible for an assessment to proceed so long as the person is compliant and this is to be considered in his or her best interests. In many situations a 'reasonable belief' of lack of capacity will be sufficient.

ASSESSMENT OF SOCIAL CARE NEEDS

3.42 The assessment of a person's community care needs is effectively a 'gateway' to the provision of both residential and non-residential services by social services departments of local authorities.

3.43 Local authority social services in England and Wales have a duty to carry out assessments for people who may be in need of certain services. If an assessment concludes that services are required, these must be provided. These services may include aids and adaptations to the home, meals on wheels, home care, respite schemes, day care, and residential and nursing care.

3.44 The first step for obtaining the correct support is to request a 'community care assessment'. This may also be known as a 'care assessment' or 'needs assessment'. To arrange a community care assessment, the person concerned, a relative or a friend can contact social services directly. Alternatively, a GP, consultant or other professional can make a referral.

The duty to assess

3.45 The NHS and Community Care Act 1990 ('NHSCCA 1990') makes assessment a duty and a service in its own right. Section 47(1) of the NHSCCA 1990 provides:

> '(1) Subject to subsections (5) and (6) below, where it appears to a local authority that any person for whom they may provide or arrange for the provision of community care services may be in need of any such services, the authority—
> (a) shall carry out an assessment of his needs for those services; and
> (b) having regard to the results of that assessment, shall then decide whether his needs call for the provision by them of any such services.'

3.46 The duty to assess a person's need for community care services under s 47(1) arises *where it appears* that the person *may be in need of such services*. This has been described by the Court of Appeal as a 'very low threshold'.[18]

3.47 If an individual's needs are considered to be sufficiently urgent, a local authority may use its powers under NHSCCA 1990, s 47(5) to provide services on a temporary basis until the completion of an assessment.[19]

No need to request an assessment

3.48 Section 47(1) NHSCCA 1990 obliges social services authorities to carry out an assessment of an individual's need for community care services even where the individual has made no request for an assessment. In *R v Gloucestershire CC ex p RADAR*,[20] the court held that a local authority could not discharge its duty to assess under s 47(1) by writing to service users and asking them to reply if they wanted to be considered for assessment.

3.49 All that is required in order to trigger the assessment obligation is that the individual's circumstances have come to the knowledge of the local authority and that he or she may be in need of community care services.

Obligation to assess disabled person

3.50 The effect of s 47(2) of the NHSCCA 1990 means that if at any time during an assessment it appears to the local authority that the person whose needs are being assessed is a disabled person, the authority must proceed to decide whether that person's needs call for the provision of services under the Chronically Sick and Disabled Persons Act 1970 ('CSDPA 1970') without the need for a specific request to do so.[21] The person must be informed of this and of their rights under the CSDPA 1970.

Directions

3.51 Local authorities in England have a duty under Community Care Assessment Directions 2004[22] to:

- consult the person;
- consider whether the person has any carers and, if so, also consult them if the authority 'thinks it appropriate';

---

[18] *R v Bristol CC, ex p Penfold* [1998] 1 CCLR 315.
[19] *R (AA) v Lambeth LBC* [2001] EWCA Admin 741.
[20] (1997–98) 1 CCLR 476.
[21] Disabled Persons (Services, Consultation and Representation) Act 1986, s 4.
[22] There are no equivalent directions that have been issued in Wales. In the absence of such directions, NHSCCA 1990, s 47(4) requires that assessments are to be carried out in such manner and take such form as the local authority consider appropriate.

- take all reasonable steps to reach agreement with the person and, where they think it appropriate, any carers of that person, on the community care services which they are considering providing to meet his or her needs;
- provide information to the person and, where they think it appropriate, any carers of that person, about the amount of the payment (if any) which the person will be liable to make in respect of the community care services which they are considering providing to him.

Policy and Guidance

3.52 All community care assessments should be undertaken in accordance with statutory guidance issued under s 7 of the Local Authority Social Services Act 1970. The Department of Health has issued guidance in England with a view to standardising individual local authority eligibility criteria for community care services. This guidance is entitled, *Prioritising needs in the context of Putting People First* ('Prioritising Needs Guidance'). In Wales, the equivalent guidance published by the Welsh Assembly Government is known as the 'Creating a Unified and Fair System for Assessing and Managing Care' (2002) ('UFSAMC').[23]

The scope of the duty to assess

3.53 The duty to assess and identify community care need is a social services function and cannot be delegated to another body.[24] Furthermore, the identification of need during an assessment is a matter of judgment for the social worker who carries out the assessment. For example, a local authority cannot avoid its obligation to assess a person's needs by exclusively relying on self-assessment by the person concerned. Whilst self-assessment may be used as part of the process, the local authority must still make an appropriate assessment itself.[25]

3.54 Once a local authority has commenced an assessment, there is a duty to inform a relevant Clinical Commissioning Group ('CCG'), health authority or local housing authority to invite them to assist in the assessment if there is a potential need for services by those bodies.[26]

---

23 In Wales this guidance, with relatively minor differences and emphases, is contained in the Assembly guidance 'Created a Unified & Fair System for Assessing & Managing Care' which can be accessed at www.wales.gov.uk/subisocialpolicysocialservices/content/mangingcircular-e.htm.

24 *R v Kirkham MBC, ex p Daykin and Daykin* (1997-8) 1 CCLR 512, at 527B.

25 *R (B) v Cornwall CC & The Brandon Trust* [2009] EWHC 491 (Admin).

26 NHSCCA 1990, s 47(3).

3.55 The duty to assess arises irrespective of the prospect of whether a potential service user may be eligible for services,[27] the financial circumstances of the service user or the service user being ordinarily resident in the local authority's area.[28]

3.56 There are a number of cases stating that local authorities should not necessarily take a person's refusal to be involved in the assessment process as the final word on the matter and that authorities need to be persistent to ensure that vulnerable people are not unwisely leaving themselves at risk.[29]

3.57 A local authority is obliged to provide certain community care services. That duty can be considered discharged if an applicant persistently refuses to co-operate.[30]

3.58 Under s 47(1) of NHSCCA 1990, local authorities have a duty to assess the needs of any person for whom the authority may provide or arrange the provision of community care services and who may be in need of such services. However, because local authorities have a power to provide services to people who live outside of their area, the duty to assess is not restricted to people who are ordinarily resident in the authority's area. This pragmatic approach may be taken in relation to people with firm plans to move to another local authority's area. For example, an elderly grandparent who decides to move to be closer to their family, subject to suitable community care services being available. Such people could be described as 'about to be in need' in the local authority's area, even though they may already be in receipt of services in the area which they are leaving. The person's move must be reasonably certain. Local authorities would not be obliged to assess a person who was merely considering a move to the area.

Future need for services

3.59 Local authorities are required to assess people who are about to be discharged from hospital and may need community care services under the delayed discharges legislation. The courts have recognised that a pragmatic approach needs to be taken in these and similar circumstances. The scope of any assessment is limited to cases of 'reasonably predictable future need'.[31] For example, it was held in the case of *R (on the application of B) v Camden LBC and Camden and Islington Mental Health and Social Care Trust*[32] that the words 'a person...may be in need of such services' refer to a person who may be in need at the time, or who may be about to be in need. That case concerned a detained patient whose conditional discharge had been deferred until suitable

---

27 *R v Bristol CC, ex p Penfold* [1998] 1 CCLR 315.
28 *R v Berkshire CC ex p P* (1997-98) 1 CCLR 141.
29 See for example *R v Kensington & Chelsea RBC, ex p Kujtim* [1999] 4 All ER 161.
30 *R v Kensington and Chelsea LBC, ex p Kujtim* [1999] 4 All ER 161.
31 *R (on the application of NM) v Islington LBC* [2012] EWHC 414 (Admin).
32 [2005] EWHC 1366 (Admin), [2006] LGR 19, 85 BMLR 28.

hostel accommodation could be found. A prisoner who will not be given parole until suitable care arrangements are in place would be in a similar position.

The relevance of financial circumstances

3.60 A local authority's resources are relevant as to whether or not it is necessary to meet the need ie when framing its eligibility criteria.[33] However, once it has been determined that it is necessary to provide services to meet a need, a local authority cannot rely upon its own limited resources as a justification for failing to meet the need.

3.61 By contrast the financial circumstances of an individual are irrelevant to the question of assessment. A person's assets only become relevant at the stage of charging for community care services.[34] In *Penfold*,[35] the court held it is unlawful for a local authority to take the personal resources of an individual into account when deciding whether or not to carry out a community care assessment.

The process of assessment

3.62 Despite the central importance of the assessment in community care law, there is no legislative description of the process. A community care assessment consists of three distinct phases:

(1) information gathering concerning the person's needs and requirements (this will include contacting significant information sources such as family, carers, GP's, housing etc);
(2) a service provision decision; and
(3) formulating a care plan.

The assessment and 'presenting needs'

3.63 The Prioritising Needs Guidance draws a key distinction between the notion of 'presenting needs' which are, in terms of the service user, the problems that they have and those needs for which a local authority will provide help because they fall within the authority's eligibility criteria which are defined as 'eligible needs'.

3.64 Eligibility criteria therefore describe the full range of eligible needs that will be met by local authorities taking their resources into account.

3.65 The Prioritising Needs Guidance grades the eligibility framework into four bands that describe the seriousness of the risk to independence and

---

33 *R v Gloucestershire CC ex p Barry* [1997] AC 584.
34 The issue of charging for community care services is discussed at Chapter 10.
35 *R v Bristol CC, ex p Penfold* [1998] 1 CCLR 315, at [332G].

well-being or other consequences if needs are not addressed. The four bands are 'Critical', 'Substantial' 'Moderate' and 'Low'.[36]

3.66 Once the local authority has set its threshold there is a duty to meet needs insofar as they are assessed to be over the threshold, subject to the qualification that where a range of options would meet the need a local authority is permitted to choose the least expensive. In *R v Gloucestershire County Council, ex parte Barry*,[37] which involved a split decision of 3 to 2, the House of Lords held that the needs of a person and the necessity of making arrangements to meet those needs were relative concepts that had to be judged according to some eligibility criteria, including an acceptable standard of living, which standard was to be set within its area by the local authority balancing the cost of providing a service against the benefit to be obtained from it. In deciding how much weight was to be attached to cost a local authority had to take its resources into account. Accordingly, in assessing the needs of disabled persons and the necessity of meeting those needs, the local authority's resources could be a proper consideration.

How long should someone wait for an assessment?

3.67 There is no prescribed timetable to complete an assessment. A person need only wait a reasonable period of time for an assessment to be provided to them.

3.68 A period of excessive delay can often be easier to detect. For example, the Local Government Ombudsman considered that an adaptation assessment of a home that took three months was 'simply unacceptable'.[38] Furthermore, the failure by a local authority to adhere to its own policy in terms of provision of an assessment is a good indicator that there has been undue delay.

Reassessments and reviews

3.69 Reassessment is not provided for within the legislation but plainly has to take place in line with the Prioritising Needs Guidance requiring regular reviews and an agreement of a date for review at the outset of provision. Reassessment can also be triggered by a scheduled review date, by needs and circumstances changing, and also and certainly where there is a change in the threshold of eligibility, for example where a local authority decides to raise its threshold from substantial to critical.

---

36 These bands and their descriptors are reproduced in full at 6.73 below.

37 [1997] AC 584.

38 Complaint No 05/c/07195 – Northumberland CC, 18 April 2006.

Challenges to community care assessments

3.70 In *Lambeth LBC v Ireneschild*,[39] the Court of Appeal made strong comments regarding challenges to community care assessments under NHSCCA 1990, s 47. Hallett LJ stated at [57]:

> '...one must always bear in mind the context of an assessment of this kind. It is an assessment prepared by a social worker for his or her employers. It is not a final determination of a legal dispute by a lawyer which may be subjected to over zealous textual analysis. Courts must be wary, in my view, of expecting so much of hard pressed social workers that we risk taking them away, unnecessarily, from their front line duties.'

3.71 And furthermore at [71]:

> '...the nature and purpose of a community care assessment...is operational and inevitably judgmental. It must be carried out quickly. I accept the Appellants' argument that a social worker preparing such an assessment cannot be expected to engage in a detailed analysis of the material obtained (often from many sources), decide what particular points have and have not been specifically addressed by the "service user" thus far, and then take steps to ensure that any points which have been missed or not sufficiently addressed are drawn to the attention of the "service user" for his or her response.'

3.72 The court is not the appropriate forum to prescribe the degree of detail to be contained in a care plan drawn up by a local authority following an assessment under NHSCCA 1990, s 47(1) (*R (on the application of Lloyd) v Barking and Dagenham LBC*.[40]

3.73 The recent Supreme Court decision in *R (McDonald) v Kensington and Chelsea RLBC*[41] related to a duty to assess the needs of an older person under NHSCCA 1990, s 47. Lord Dyson JSC gave some useful guidance on the purpose and content of assessments at para 53:

> '...In construing assessments and care plan reviews, it should not be overlooked that these are documents that are usually drafted by social workers. They are not drafted by lawyers, nor should they be. They should be construed in a practical way against the factual background in which they are written and with the aim of seeking to discover the substance of their true meaning.'

3.74 These decisions make it difficult to challenge community care assessments by way of judicial review without having recourse to the complaints procedure first.[42] However, the court is unlikely to criticise proceedings being issued where a failure to meet eligible needs is placing the service user within the realms of physical and/or mental harm.

---

39 [2007] EWCA Civ 234.
40 [2002] 1 FCR 136, CA.
41 [2011] UKSC 33.
42 See Chapter 11.

Care Bill

3.75 The Care Bill is currently proceeding through Parliament and is likely to have a radical impact upon how community care assessments are undertaken in the future. The main effects of the Care Bill in relation to assessments are to codify existing practice and guidance, providing a single statutory base or source, and to bring more detail to particular areas, particularly regarding carers.

3.76 Clauses 9–12 of the Bill set out the relevant provisions in relation to assessments of community care needs (now called 'needs assessments'). Clause 9(1) sets out the trigger for an assessment as being, 'where it appears ... that an adult may have needs'. This is essentially the same as the existing provision in NHSCCA 1990, s 47(1), barring some minor differences in the words used. This reflects the existing position in law that there is no need for a person to have to request an assessment first for the local authority to owe a duty to assess.

3.77 Clause 9(3) stipulates that the duty to assess applies regardless of the authority's view of: (a) the level of the adult's needs for care and support; or (b) the level of the adult's financial resources. This statement effectively puts the current position in the common law and guidance onto a statutory footing, meaning that the threshold to initiate an assessment will continue to be very low.

3.78 Clause 9(4)(a) incorporates by reference to a statutory definition of well-being at clause 1(2) a detailed list of matters that to be covered in a needs assessment. As such, an assessment will need to consider: (a) physical and mental health, emotional well-being and personal dignity; (b) protection from abuse and neglect; (c) control by the individual over day-to-day life (including over care and support); (d) participation in work, education, training or recreation; (e) social and economic well-being; (f) domestic, family and personal relationships; (g) suitability of living accommodation; and (h) the individual's contribution to society. This marks a departure from the present position where the legislation was essentially silent on the content of assessments. In practice this may have little effect as the assessment forms used by many local authorities already seek to identify and assess a similar list of needs.

3.79 The Care Bill also brings specific consideration of the outcomes that the adult wishes to achieve into the assessment process. Clause 9(4)(b)–(d) requires that needs assessments contain the outcomes that the adult wishes to achieve; whether the provision of care and support could contribute to the achievement of those outcomes; and whether the adult's own capabilities and any support available from friends, family or others, and any other matters, could contribute to the achievement of those outcomes. The practical effect of clause 9(4)(d) means that local authorities may decline to provide support where a person is already having a need met by others.

3.80 Clause 11 deals with the position where a person refuses an assessment. The local authority will not be required to assess that person, subject to two exceptions: (1) where the person lacks capacity and an assessment is in their best interests; and (2) where the person is experiencing, or is at risk of, abuse or neglect.

3.81 Finally, and perhaps most significantly, clause 13 stipulates that that there will be national eligibility criteria set by regulations. This will establish national standards for local authority care support and puts the position established by *Barry*[43] on a statutory basis. This will bring about a significant change in the provision of services and achieve a single national standard of social care. This contrasts with the current position whereby a local authority may decide to limit service provision to only those individuals who match the most critical levels of need.

CONTINUING HEALTHCARE ASSESSMENTS

3.82 An individual who has been diagnosed with dementia may often have a variety of associated health needs (whether physical or mental). For a person whose primary continuing need is a 'health need' then they may be eligible for what is called 'NHS continuing healthcare', the name given to a package of care that is arranged and funded solely by the NHS for individuals who are not in hospital and have complex ongoing healthcare needs. It enables them to receive NHS services in a care home, a hospice or in their own home. In certain circumstances a person deemed eligible for continuing health care will have significant financial advantages over a person who is in receipt of social care services only.

3.83 The question of service provision under NHS continuing healthcare is considered in more detail in this book at Chapter 5. The purpose of this section is to consider how a person may be assessed for their eligibility for continuing health care.

The National Framework and Regulations

3.84 In November 2012 the Department of Health published a revised *National Framework for NHS Continuing Healthcare and NHS-funded Nursing Care* ('the Framework Guidance').[44] It sets out the principles and processes of the National Framework for NHS continuing health care and NHS-funded nursing care. The Framework Guidance reflects the new NHS framework and structures created by the Health and Social Care Act 2012 that came into effect on 1 April 2013. It supersedes the previous guidance published in 2009.

---

43 [1997] AC 584.

44 https://www.gov.uk/government/publications/national-framework-for-nhs-continuing-healthcare-and-nhs-funded-nursing-care.

3.85 Standing Rules Regulations[45] have been issued under the National Health Service Act 2006, and directions are issued under the Local Authority Social Services Act 1970 in relation to the National Framework.

3.86 The revised Framework Guidance was accompanied by a revised 'Decision Support Tool' ('DST'),[46] which is a document designed to provide a fair and effective way of establishing individual entitlement to continuing health care and inform consistent decision-making.

3.87 In Wales a similar national framework and DST was published in May 2010 and became effective in August 2010[47] ('the Welsh Framework'). The exact process and wording of the national framework and DST tool may differ between England and Wales. However, the qualifying criteria must remain the same as the same primary legislation and case-law applies. In principle at least, it should be no more difficult or easy to access NHS continuing healthcare in either country.

Definition of continuing healthcare

3.88 The revised Framework Guidance defines continuing healthcare as, '...a package of ongoing care that is arranged and funded solely by the NHS where the individual has been found to have a "primary health need"...Such care is provided to an individual aged 18 or over, to meet needs that have arisen as a result of disability, accident or illness.'[48]

3.89 Paragraph 2.1 of the Welsh Framework defines it as, 'a complete package of ongoing care arranged and solely funded by the NHS, where it has been assessed that the individual's primary need is a health need'.

Determining a 'primary health need'

3.90 The key legal test for continuing health care is whether the person has a 'primary health need'. This flows from the decision of the Court of Appeal, namely *R v North and East Devon Health Authority ex p Coughlan*[49] and followed later in *R (Grogan) v Bexley NHS Care Trust*.[50] These cases are discussed in further detail in Chapter 4.

3.91 Deciding whether there is a 'primary health need' involves looking at the totality of a person's relevant needs. Where an individual has a primary health

---

45 The National Health Service Commissioning Board and Clinical Commissioning Groups (Responsibilities and Standing Rules) Regulations 2012.

46 See Decision Support Tool for NHS Continuing Healthcare (November 2012)(Revised). This can be found at: https://www.gov.uk/government/uploads/system/uploads/attachment_data/file/213139/Decision-Support-Tool-for-NHS-Continuing-Healthcare.pdf.

47 EH/ML/018/10 Welsh Assembly Government Circular: 015/2010. See http://www.wales.nhs.uk/continuingnhshealthcare.

48 Framework Guidance, para 13.

49 [2000] 2 WLR 622.

50 [2006] EWHC 44 (Admin).

need and is therefore eligible for NHS continuing healthcare, the NHS will be responsible for providing all of that individual's assessed health and social care needs, including accommodation, if that is part of the overall need.

3.92 Paragraph 34 of the Framework Guidance states that the primary health need test should be applied so that a person is only ineligible for NHS continuing healthcare if the nursing or other health services are: (a) no more than incidental or ancillary to the provision of residential accommodation which the local authority is under a duty to provide, and (b) are not of a nature beyond which a local authority, whose primary responsibility is to provide social services, could be expected to provide. It is unlawful for a local authority to act beyond the limits of statutory competence and fund a person with nursing needs that are more than merely 'incidental or ancillary' to their social care needs. The distinction between what is a health need and a social care need can often be blurred and may be the subject of dispute between a local authority and a CCG in England or Local Health Board ('LHB') in Wales.

3.93 Paragraph 35 of the Framework Guidance states that certain characteristics of need may help determine whether the 'quality' or 'quantity' of care required is more than the limits of the social care responsibilities of a local authority, as described in *Coughlan*. These are:

- **Nature:** This describes the particular characteristics of an individual's needs (which can include physical, mental health or psychological needs) and the type of those needs. This also describes the overall effect of those needs on the individual, including the type ('quality') of interventions required to manage them.
- **Intensity:** This relates both to the extent ('quantity') and severity ('degree') of the needs and to the support required to meet them, including the need for sustained/ongoing care ('continuity').
- **Complexity:** This is concerned with how the needs present and interact to increase the skill required to monitor the symptoms, treat the condition(s) and/or manage the care. This may arise with a single condition, or it could include the presence of multiple conditions or the interaction between two or more conditions. It may also include situations where an individual's response to their own condition has an impact on their overall needs, such as where a physical health need results in the individual developing a mental health need.
- **Unpredictability:** This describes the degree to which needs fluctuate and thereby create challenges in managing them. It also relates to the level of risk to the person's health if adequate and timely care is not provided. Someone with an unpredictable healthcare need is likely to have either a fluctuating, unstable or rapidly deteriorating condition.

3.94 The Framework Guidance further states that 'each of these characteristics may, in combination or alone, demonstrate a primary health need, because of the quality and/or quantity of care required to meet the individual's needs'. As such, the totality of the overall needs and the effects of the interaction of needs should be carefully considered.[51] In principle, any single characteristic could be sufficient and it would not be necessary for a person's condition to be complex or unpredictable.

Assessment and the National Framework

3.95 The Framework Guidance contains detailed guidance on core values and principles to be applied during any assessment of a person's continuing healthcare needs. In particular:

(i) 'The process of assessment and decision-making should be person-centred. This means placing the individual, their perception of their support needs, and their preferred models of support at the heart of the assessment and care-planning process...the individual's wishes and expectations of how and where the care is delivered, and how their personal information is shared, should be documented and taken into account, along with the risks of different types of provision and fairness of access to resources.'[52]

(ii) 'Access to assessment, decision-making and provision should be fair and consistent. There should be no discrimination on the grounds of race, disability, gender, age, sexual orientation, religion or belief, or type of health need...'[53]

(iii) 'Assessments of eligibility should be organised so that the individual being assessed and their representative understand the process and receive advice and information that will maximise their ability to participate in informed decision-making about their future care.'[54]

Capacity and consent

3.96 A person's informed consent should be obtained before the start of the process of determining whether they may be eligible for continuing healthcare.[55] If there is any concern that they lack capacity to give consent then this will need to be determined in accordance with the MCA 2005 and associated MCA Code of Practice. If the person lacks capacity either to refuse or to consent then a 'best interests' decision will need to be taken as to whether or not to proceed with an eligibility assessment.[56] As with any best interests decision, the assessor must consult with any relevant third party who has a genuine interest in the person's welfare, which will normally include the person's family and/or advocate.

3.97 CCGs or LHBs should ensure that individuals are made aware of local advocacy and other services that may be able to offer advice and support.[57]

---

51 Para 36, Framework Guidance
52 Framework Guidance, para 42; Welsh Framework, para 5.1.
53 Framework Guidance, para 43; Welsh Framework, para 5.3.
54 Framework Guidance, para 44; Welsh Framework, para 5.4.
55 Framework Guidance, paras 45–47; Welsh Framework, para 6.1.
56 Framework Guidance, para 50; Welsh Framework, para 6.5.
57 Framework Guidance, para 53; Welsh Framework, para 6.22.

3.98 In the event that an individual refuses to cooperate with the assessment process, the potential effect that this will have on the ability of the NHS and/or the local authority to provide appropriate services should be carefully explained to them.

Other eligibility issues

3.99 The Framework Guidance provides some further guidance in relation to additional issues that may arise in relation to assessing a person's eligibility for continuing healthcare. In particular:

- 'The decision-making rationale should not marginalise a need just because it is successfully managed: well-managed needs are still needs. Only where the successful management of a healthcare need has permanently reduced or removed an ongoing need, such that the active management of this need is reduced or no longer required, will this have a bearing on NHS continuing healthcare eligibility.'[58]
- 'Financial issues should not be part of the decision on an individual's eligibility for NHS continuing healthcare and it is important that the process of considering and deciding eligibility does not result in any delay to treatment or to appropriate care being put in place.'[59]
- 'The responsibility of the NHS to provide continuing healthcare...is not indefinite, as a person's needs can change...Regular reviews are built into the process to ensure that the care package continues to meet the person's needs.'[60]

3.100 Finally, the Framework Guidance provides a clear and helpful checklist of reasons that are *not* acceptable for declining entitlement to NHS continuing healthcare.[61] It states:

> 'The reasons given for a decision on eligibility should NOT be based on the:
>
> a. person's diagnosis;
> b. setting of care;
> c. ability of the care provider to manage care;
> d. use (or not) of NHS-employed staff to provide care;
> e. need for/presence of 'specialist staff' in care delivery;
> f. the fact that a need is well managed;
> g. the existence of other NHS-funded care; or
> h. any other input-related (rather than needs-related) rationale.'

---

58 Framework Guidance, para 56.
59 Framework Guidance, para 57.
60 Framework Guidance, para 59.
61 Framework Guidance, para 58; Welsh Framework, para 4.4.

The assessment process

Initial screening

3.101 The first step to assess a person's eligibility for NHS continuing healthcare is for a health or social care practitioner to complete the NHS continuing healthcare checklist[62] ('the Checklist'). Originally described as a screening tool, the Department of Health has published the Checklist in order to encourage proportionate assessments. If the Checklist indicates that a person might be eligible for NHS continuing healthcare, then the assessment should proceed to a full assessment using the Decision Support Tool.

3.102 A CCG is also required to take reasonable steps to ensure that individuals are assessed for NHS continuing healthcare in all cases where it appears that there may be a need for such care. Furthermore, if the CCG is to use any screening tool, that tool must be the Checklist.

3.103 The Checklist is usually completed when a nurse, doctor, other qualified healthcare professional or social worker is assessing or reviewing a person's health or social care needs. For example, a nurse could carry out the initial screening before a person leaves hospital or a social worker could do the screening when carrying out a community care assessment.

3.104 The threshold at the Checklist stage has been set deliberately low, to ensure that all those who require a full consideration of their needs do get this opportunity.[63]

3.105 If the Checklist indicates that a person may be eligible for NHS continuing healthcare, the person who completed it will contact the appropriate CCG to arrange a full up-to-date assessment of all their care needs. Furthermore, ADASS guidance suggests that anyone who crosses the checklist threshold, but is subsequently deemed not to qualify for continuing health care is likely to qualify for joint NHS and local authority funding.[64]

Full assessment with Decision Support Tool

3.106 In England, when assessing entitlement to NHS continuing healthcare, CCGs and local authorities are required to use the DST. In Wales, LHBs and local authorities are required to use a similar document that appears in the Welsh Framework.[65]

---

62 NHS Continuing Healthcare Checklist (November 2012).

63 Framework Guidance, para 72.

64 ADASS (2007) *Commentary and Advice for Local Authorities on the National Framework for NHS Continuing Healthcare and NHS-funded Nursing Care*, October 2007 (para 5). See: http://www.adass.org.uk/old/publications/guidance/commentary.pdf.

65 Welsh Framework, Annex 6, pp 68–119.

3.107 The full assessment must be completed by a multidisciplinary team.[66] The assessment will include contributions from all the health and social care professionals involved in the person's care to build an overall picture of their needs.

3.108 To minimise variation in how the principles in the Framework Guidance are interpreted and to inform consistent decision-making, the DST covers 12 'care domains' or generic areas of need. The domains are sub-divided into statements of need, representing low, moderate, high, severe or priority levels of need, depending on the domain. The care domains are: behaviour; cognition; psychological and emotional needs; communication; mobility; nutrition; continence; skin (including tissue viability); breathing; drug therapies and medication (symptom control); altered states of consciousness; and other significant care needs. Further detail about the care domains can be found in Chapter 5.

3.109 The DST is not an assessment in itself, rather, 'it is a way of bringing together and applying evidence in a single practical format, to facilitate consistent, evidence-based decision-making regarding NHS continuing healthcare eligibility'.[67] Completion of the DST should result in an overall picture of the individual's needs that captures their nature, and their complexity, intensity and/or unpredictability – and thus the quality and/or quantity (including continuity) of care required to meet the individual's needs.

3.110 As with the Checklist, use of the DST is not discretionary. However the National Framework emphasises that the guidelines in the DST are indicative only and should not be viewed prescriptively.[68]

3.111 The DST states that a clear recommendation of eligibility for continuing health care would be indicated by any of the following:[69]

- A level of priority needs in any one of the four domains that carry this level.
- A total of two or more incidences of identified severe needs across all care domains.

3.112 A primary health need may also be indicated by the DST where there is:

- one domain recorded as severe, together with needs in a number of other domains; or

---

66 Regulation 21(11) of the Standing Rules Regulations 2012 defines a multi-disciplinary team as consisting of at least two professionals who are from different healthcare professions (ie a profession concerned, wholly or partly, with the physical or mental health of individuals) or one healthcare professional and one person who is responsible for assessing persons for community care services under s 47 of the NHSCCA 1990.

67 Framework Guidance, para 81.

68 Framework Guidance, para 59.

69 *Decision Support Tool for NHS Continuing Healthcare*, para 31.

- a number of domains with high and/or moderate needs.

3.113 The Department of Health recognises that some people's needs may not fit easily into the specified care domains, in which case an additional domain may be inserted. Furthermore, when in doubt about the level at which to place needs in a particular domain, the DST advises the practitioner to choose the higher level of need under consideration and explain the problem.[70]

3.114 The DST is clear that in all cases, the overall need, the interactions between needs in different care domains, and the evidence from risk assessments should be taken into account in deciding whether a recommendation of eligibility for continuing healthcare should be made. It cautions against trying to equate a number of incidences of one level with a number of incidences of another level, as in, for example 'two moderates equals one high'. Instead, the judgement whether someone has a primary health need must be based on what the evidence indicates about the nature and/or complexity and/or intensity and/or unpredictability of the individual's needs.[71]

3.115 The multidisciplinary team will consider the completed DST. Once the team has reached agreement, it should make a recommendation to the CCG or LHB on eligibility. If the CCG or LHB decides a person has a primary health need it must also decide that he or she is eligible for CHC.

3.116 A copy of the completed DST (including the recommendation) should be forwarded to the individual (or, where appropriate, their representative) together with the final decision made by the CCG or LHB, along with the reasons for this decision.

Fast track pathway tool

3.117 In England for a person who is in need an urgent package of care because their condition is deteriorating rapidly and the condition may be entering a terminal phase, the fast track pathway tool may be used instead of the DST. This enables the CCG to arrange for care to be provided as quickly as possible. The fast track pathway tool might be appropriate where the person wishes to return home to die or to allow appropriate end of life support to be arranged.

3.118 Where an 'appropriate clinician'[72] has decided that a person has a primary health need arising from a rapidly deteriorating condition which is entering a terminal phase and has completed the fast track pathway tool with

---

70 *Decision Support* Tool, para 22.

71 *Decision Support* Tool, para 31.

72 The definition of 'appropriate clinician' is set out in reg 21(13) of the Standing Rules Regulations 2012: '(i) "appropriate clinician" means a person who is: (a) responsible for the diagnosis, treatment or care of the person under the 2006 Act in respect of whom a Fast Track Pathway Tool is being completed, and (b) a registered nurse or a registered medical practitioner.'

his or her consent, the CCG must, on receipt of the document, decide that the person is eligible for NHS continuing healthcare.[73] No one who has been identified through the fast-track process as eligible for NHS continuing healthcare should have this funding removed without the eligibility being reviewed.

3.119 In Wales there is no equivalent fast track pathway tool. However, the Welsh Framework does require that a similar fast track system should be developed by LHBs.[74] This requires LHBs to put in place a fast track process that reduces the amount of information required, the time taken to gather information and reduces timescales for making decisions about those individuals.

Timescales

3.120 The time that elapses between the Checklist (or, where no Checklist is used, other notification of potential eligibility) being received by the CCG and the funding decision being made should, in most cases, not exceed 28 days. In acute services, it may be appropriate for the process to take significantly less than 28 days if an individual is otherwise ready for discharge from hospital.[75] Where there are valid and unavoidable reasons for the process taking longer, timescales should be clearly communicated to the person and (where appropriate) their carers and/or representatives.

3.121 Paragraph 5.45 of the Welsh Framework states that the time taken for assessments and agreeing a care package may vary but should be completed in 6 to 8 weeks from initial trigger to agreeing a care package. In some cases much speedier decisions should be taken in the person's best interests (eg in terminal illness) to expedite the process.

Disputing NHS continuing healthcare decisions

3.122 Where a CCG or LHB has decided that a person is not eligible for continuing healthcare it must inform him (or his representative) of the circumstances and manner in which he may apply for a review of the decision if dissatisfied with the procedure followed or with the primary health need decision.[76] For further details on disputing a decision arising out of a continuing healthcare assessment, please refer to Chapter 6.

---

73 Framework Guidance, paras 97–101.

74 Welsh Framework, paras 5.49–5.56.

75 Framework Guidance, para 95.

76 Standing Rules Regulations 2012, reg 21(11).

CHAPTER 4

WELFARE AND BEST INTERESTS

4.1 This chapter considers the key principle of best interests and its importance in decision making for those people who lack the capacity to make decisions for themselves and its application to those with dementia.

4.2 The courts have long recognised the need to act on behalf of and make decisions for a person when that person lacks the mental capacity to make decisions for himself and in those circumstances the court has made those decisions or authorised that acts should be done in that person's best interests.

4.3 Prior to the Mental Capacity Act 2005 ('MCA 2005') the courts had used the inherent jurisdiction to develop the concept of best interests to include medical, social, emotional and ethical best interests. These were taken into account when making decisions on behalf of adults who lacked capacity.

4.4 The landmark legislation of the MCA 2005 has five overarching principles that govern the operation of the Act. Anyone using the MCA 2005 must act with these in mind as a point of reference for their decision making.

4.5 These principles are:

(1) the presumption of capacity: that a person must be presumed to have capacity unless it is established that he lacks capacity;
(2) that a person is not to be treated as being unable to make a decision unless all practical steps have been taken to help him to do so without success;
(3) that a person is not to be treated as unable to make a decision merely because he makes an unwise decision;
(4) that an act done or decision made under the MCA 2005 for or on behalf of a person who lacks capacity must be done, or made, in his best interests;
(5) that, before the act is done or decision made under the MCA 2005, regard must be had to whether the purpose for which the decision or act is needed can be effectively achieved in a way that is less restrictive of the person's rights and freedom of action.

4.6 The aim of the MCA 2005 is to balance the need to protect the vulnerable against the need to preserve and respect individual autonomy, so it is important always to remember that a person's capacity or lack of capacity refers specifically to their capacity to make a particular decision at the time it needs to be made. This is what is meant when the question of capacity is said to be 'issue specific'. If a decision-maker then needs to make the particular decision he must always make it in the best interests of the person concerned.

4.7 This background is particularly important in relation to people who have dementia as there will be instances both where a person will not have capacity to make a decision, which must then be made in their best interests (for example whether to go into a care home), and there will be many occasions where, either with or without help, a person can still make decisions for themselves notwithstanding their diagnosis of dementia (for example whether to refuse to see their sister or to decide what to wear).

WHAT ARE WELFARE DECISIONS?

4.8 Section 17 of the MCA 2005 identifies typical matters that are covered in relation to a person's welfare. They include:

- decisions as to where someone should live;
- who he should see or have contact with;
- who should be prevented from seeing him;
- decisions directing different people to take responsibility for his health or social care;
- giving or refusing consent to treatment by a person providing healthcare.

Personal welfare decisions relate to matters concerning the day-to-day living and care arrangements of a person and consequently are of the utmost concern and delicacy when someone loses capacity to control their own personal arrangements.

4.9 A common example where the court has intervened is where the adult children of an elderly parent with dementia disagree with each other and with the local authority as to where and in what manner their mother or father should be looked after. Both the children and the local authority in such an instance may have opposing views as to what is in the elderly parent's best interests. It is to be hoped, as is often the case, that it would be possible to resolve such an impasse by a meeting with all concerned, or by mediation, but if there is no other way of working out what course of action would be in a person's best interests then an application must be made to the Court of Protection for the Court to decide this specific issue. Chapter 13 details what the Court of Protection can do in this regard.

BEST INTERESTS

4.10 The best interests principle establishes that acting in a person's best interests underpins all actions done for and decisions made on behalf of someone without capacity, but there is no set definition in the MCA 2005; rather the Act sets out in s 4 a checklist of factors that must always be considered in the decision making.

4.11 This template for decision making must be followed for all decisions made that affect someone who lacks capacity. It applies equally to decisions made by the Court of Protection, decisions made by donees under lasting powers of attorney and by court appointed deputies and to decisions made every day in the course of attending to the needs of a person who has lost capacity.

4.12 In determining what is in a person's best interests the decision maker must take into account all the relevant circumstances of which he is aware and which it would be reasonable to regard as relevant such as:

(a) avoiding discrimination on the basis of age and/or appearance;
(b) avoiding making unjustified assumptions on the basis of a person's behaviour or condition;
(c) considering whether it is likely that the person will regain capacity about the matter and if so when that is likely to happen;
(d) so far as is reasonably practicable, he must permit and encourage the person to participate or improve their ability to participate in any act or decision that affects them;
(e) where the decision relates to life-sustaining treatment he must not be motivated in any way by a desire to bring about the person's death, and so must not make assumptions about the person's quality of life;
(f) he must try to find out the person's views: including the past and present wishes and feelings (particularly if there was any written statement made when he had capacity); his beliefs and values which would be likely to influence him if he had capacity and any other factors which he would be likely to consider if he were able to do so;
(g) he must take into account, if it is reasonably practicable to do so, the views of anyone previously named by the person as someone to be consulted in matters of this nature, anyone engaged in caring for the person or interested in his welfare (for example, close relatives or friends, a concerned neighbour); the donee of a lasting power of attorney and any Court of Protection appointed deputy.

4.13 In addition to the s 4 checklist the decision maker must have regard to whether the purpose for which the decision is needed can be effectively achieved in a way that is less restrictive of the person's rights and freedom.

4.14 When the decision maker has taken all the matters in s 4 and the principles of the MCA 2005 into account to make a decision he must reasonably believe that what he does or has decided to do is in the best interests of the person concerned.

How to assess a person's best interests

4.15 Assessments of a person's best interests in relation to particular decisions take place all the time with varying degrees of formality depending on the circumstances.

4.16 An example in practice is the ongoing discussions and assessments that take place in relation to the care of a person with Alzheimers disease. A man had been cared for by his wife at home until she broke her hip and could no longer look after him. A multidisciplinary meeting was held so that all agencies, the wife and any other relations involved who were able to assist could pool their ideas and contribute to the process so that a decision that would be in his best interests could be made for his future care.

Guidance from the Code of Practice in assessing best interests

4.17 In this section we look at the Code of Practice which is an everyday guide to the working of the MCA 2005 and is guidance to which all decision-makers should have regard. Specific decision makers such as donees under lasting powers of attorney and deputies must take the Code of Practice into account.

The Code of Practice and day-to-day decision making

4.18 The MCA 2005 is an empowering piece of legislation, intended to enable individuals to take control of their lives with safeguards for those whose capacity is limited. As stated in the foreword to the Code of Practice, legislation alone is not the whole story. The Code of Practice is practical guidance that supports and explains how the MCA 2005 operates on a day-to-day basis and offers examples of best practice to carers and practitioners.

4.19 The Code of Practice requires that anybody who acts in a professional capacity for, or in relation to, a person who lacks capacity has a legal duty to have regard to its guidance. It also applies generally as guidance and good practice for everyone who looks after or cares for a person who lacks capacity.

4.20 As a clear explanatory tool it is intended to be easily understood by everyone who looks after a vulnerable person, be it a carer or family member or health professional, who is therefore making decisions on a day-to-day basis for people who cannot make decisions for themselves.

4.21 Particularly for those who come into contact with the frail and vulnerable where capacity is fading and failing, the Code of Practice is an invaluable guide to understanding the perspective of the current law and its operation so far as it affects people with dementia.

4.22 It is user-friendly with helpful key terms set out within the various chapters and paragraphs to which they refer.

4.23 As a Code of *good* Practice it is full of examples and explanations of how the MCA 2005 works in everyday life and it uses the device of various scenarios to illustrate particular points in the text.

4.24 Helpfully, at Annex A it provides a list of contact details for organisations that provide information guidance or materials relating to the Mental Capacity Act and the Code of Practice.

Particular guidance in relation to Deprivation of Liberty Safeguards

4.25 The provisions of the MCA 2005 in relation to deprivation of liberty (defined below) were added later and so there is a comprehensive Code of Practice in the same format which supplements the main Code of Practice. It provides guidance and information for those implementing the deprivation of liberty safeguards legislation on a daily basis. More information on the deprivation of a person's liberty is considered later in this section.

4.26 This Code of Practice specifically focuses on providing comprehensive guidance and in some cases step-by-step explanations for people exercising functions relating to the deprivation of liberty safeguards and people acting as a relevant person's representative under those safeguards.

4.27 It is suggested by the writers of this book that it should be mandatory reading for any person concerned in relation to the deprivation and or potential deprivation of liberty or the restriction on the liberty of people they care for and look after, whether they be family members or carers.

Who must have regard to the Code of Practice?

4.28 The following should have regard to the Code of Practice:

- An attorney under a lasting power of attorney.
- A court appointed deputy.
- An Independent Mental Capacity Advocate.
- Anyone acting in a professional capacity in respect of, or in relation to, a person who has lacks capacity, this can include healthcare staff, dentists, chiropodists and people who only occasionally are involved with the care of people who may lack capacity for example ambulance drivers and the police.
- Anyone who is paid to look after a person or the affairs of a person who has lost capacity-that includes for example care assistants in a care home and care workers.
- Anyone carrying out research which has been approved in accordance with the MCA 2005.

4.29 The Code of Practice should be required reading for anybody who comes into contact with people without capacity as it explains and expands the various provisions of the MCA 2005 starting with a definition of mental capacity and lack of capacity.

4.30 The importance of a person's autonomy is so fundamental that the Code of Practice explains at the outset and repeats throughout the code that a person's capacity (or lack of capacity) refers specifically to their capacity to make a particular decision or take a particular action for themselves at the time the decision or action needs to be made.

4.31 This explanation is important as it emphasises that people may lack capacity to do some things but will have capacity to do other things. For example somebody with dementia may be unable to make decisions about whether to stay in a care home, or live on her own but will be able to decide whether to have her hair cut or whether she would like to go on holiday.

4.32 It also reflects the fact that people may lack capacity, for example through illness or the influence of drugs or alcohol or lack of consciousness, but they may also become capacitous and may also learn new ways of communicating so that every decision that might be taken on their behalf has to recalibrate the test of capacity and best interests.

What is covered in the Code of Practice

4.33 The following matters are covered in the Code of Practice:

- The Code explains the MCA 2005 and its key provisions.
- Chapter 1 of the Code introduces the MCA 2005.
- Chapter 2 sets out the five statutory principles behind the MCA 2005 and the way they affect how it is put in practice.
- Chapter 3 explains how the MCA 2005 makes sure that people are given the right help and support to make their own decisions.
- Chapter 4 explains how the MCA 2005 defines 'a person who lacks capacity to make a decision' and sets out a single clear test for assessing whether a person lacks capacity to make a particular decision at a particular time.
- Chapter 5 explains what the MCA 2005 means by acting in the best interests of someone lacking capacity to make a decision for themselves, and describes the checklist set out in the Act for working out what is in someone's best interests.
- Chapter 6 explains how the MCA 2005 protects people providing care or treatment for someone who lacks the capacity to consent to the action being taken.
- Chapter 7 shows how people who wish to plan ahead for the possibility that they might lack the capacity to make particular decisions for themselves in the future are able to grant lasting powers of attorney (LPAs)

to named individuals to make certain decisions on their behalf, and how attorneys appointed under an LPA should act.

- Chapter 8 describes the role of the new Court of Protection, established under the MCA 2005, to make a decision or to appoint a decision maker on someone's behalf in cases where there is no other way of resolving a matter affecting a person who lacks capacity to make the decision in question.
- Chapter 9 explains the procedures that must be followed if someone wishes to make an advance decision to refuse medical treatment to come into effect when they lack capacity to refuse the specified treatment.
- Chapter 10 describes the role of Independent Mental Capacity Advocates appointed under the MCA 2005 to help and represent particularly vulnerable people who lack capacity to make certain significant decisions. It also sets out when they should be instructed.
- Chapter 11 provides guidance on how the MCA 2005 sets out specific safeguards and controls for research involving, or in relation to, people lacking capacity to consent to their participation.
- Chapter 12 explains those parts of the MCA 2005 which can apply to children and young people and how these relate to other laws affecting them.
- Chapter 13 explains how the MCA 2005 relates to the Mental Health Act 1983.
- Chapter 14 sets out the role of the Public Guardian, a new public office established by the MCA 2005 to oversee attorneys and deputies and to act as a single point of contact for referring allegations of abuse in relation to attorneys and deputies to other relevant agencies.
- Chapter 15 examines the various ways that disputes over decisions made under the MCA 2005 or otherwise affecting people lacking capacity to make relevant decisions can be resolved.
- Chapter 16 summarises how the laws about data protection and freedom of information relate to the provisions of the MCA 2005.

Compliance with the Codes

4.34 The Codes have statutory force and failure to comply with either Code could be used as evidence in any court or tribunal in any civil or criminal proceedings, so it is important that anyone working with, or caring for people without capacity make themselves familiar with the provisions of the MCA 2005 and of the Codes. A failure to comply with the codes could be used as evidence of wilful neglect.[1]

1 An offence under MCA 2005, s 44.

DEPRIVATION OF LIBERTY

Restrictions on liberty and deprivation of liberty

4.35 Where someone exercises control over another's person, the degree of control they exert over that person's freedom of action is always subject to scrutiny by the Court of Protection and may amount to a deprivation of liberty that must be authorised by the court.

4.36 Until the MCA 2005 came into force, there was nothing to set out what actions could be lawfully taken by carers and other health professionals in looking after the personal, care and health needs of people who lack the capacity to consent. Everyday actions, unless they could be subsumed under the doctrine of necessity, would, without consent given, otherwise amount to assault, or other civil wrong.[2]

4.37 There is a spectrum of situations that involve decisions that are taken in the best interests of a person who lacks capacity. They range from situations which merely restrict the liberty of a person to those where it can truly be said that a person has been deprived of their liberty.

4.38 In this context hospitals and care homes who look after people with dementia and residents without capacity will need to assess and decide in each particular case whether the restrictions on their liberty in fact amount to a deprivation of liberty which will require the important, prompt and formal process of authorisation.

What constitutes a deprivation of liberty and why is it important?

4.39 The starting point is Article 5 of the European Convention on Human Rights:

> 'Everyone has the right to liberty and security of person. No one shall be deprived of his liberty save in the following cases...and in accordance with a procedure prescribed by law.... (e) the lawful detention of persons ... of unsound mind...'

4.40 There are a number of well-established principles, chief of which are that there needs to be an objective element of confinement in a particular restricted space for a non-negligible length of time; a subjective element, namely no consent to the confinement; and the deprivation is imputable to the state. It is usually the first element that is most problematic because the person lacking capacity cannot give consent and any involvement by the NHS or a local authority will be imputable to the state.

4.41 This is a very complex area of the law which is not fully settled. At the time of publication, the Supreme Court is about to hear an appeal from the

---

2 MCA 2005, ss 5 and 6.

Court of Appeal[3] in a case involving an adult with severe disabilities, both mental and physical. Staff at the care home where he lived employed a number of techniques to manage his care which included some elements of physical restraint. The Court of Appeal held that these were not a deprivation of his liberty, its reasoning being that he would have required such interventions even if cared for at home by his family.

4.42 The present uncertain state of the law can be illustrated by two apparently similar cases where the outcomes were very different.

4.43 In the case of *TG*,[4] TG was a 78-year-old man with dementia and cognitive impairment who was living in a care home. Whilst he was in hospital a dispute arose between his family and the local authority who believed he should receive 24-hour care in a care home rather than go home to his family. The local authority obtained an order that TG be discharged from hospital to an identified care home of the local authority's choosing without notifying the family. When the matter was later heard with all the parties present and or represented in court the court decided that TG should go home to his family. The family claimed that TG had been deprived of his liberty during the time he had spent in the care home. The judge considered there was no deprivation of liberty but that the case was borderline. The matters he considered relevant were that the care home was an ordinary care home with no special restrictions of liberty of the residents; that the family could visit TG and take him out on a generally unrestricted basis, that TG who had lived in a care home in any event for three years before his hospital admission was personally compliant with living in the home and expressed himself as happy and was objectively content there and there had been no occasion where he had objectively been deprived of his liberty.

4.44 On that occasion the judge said:

> 'Whilst I agree that the circumstances of the present case may be near the borderline between mere restrictions of liberty and Article 5 detention, I have come to the conclusion that, looked at as a whole and having regard to all the relevant circumstances, the placement of TG in Towerbridge falls short of engaging Article 5.'

4.45 But in another case:[5] DE was a 76-year-old man who, following a major stroke, had become blind and had significant short-term memory impairment. He also had dementia and lacked capacity to decide where he should live, but was still often able to express his wishes with some clarity and force. DE was married to JE. A time came when JE felt that she could not care for DE, and placed him on a chair on the pavement in front of the house and called the police. The local authority then placed him in two care homes, referred to in the judgment of the court as the X home and the Y home. Within the care homes,

3 *Cheshire West and Chester Council v P* [2011] EWCA Civ 1333.

4 *LLBC v TG* [2007] EWHC 2640 (Fam).

5 *JE v DE and Surrey County Council* [2006] EWHC 3459 (Fam).

DE had a very substantial degree of freedom and lots of contact with the outside world. He was never subject to physical or chemical restraint.

4.46 DE repeatedly expressed the wish to live with JE, and JE also wanted DE to live with her. The local authority would not agree to DE returning to live with, or visit, JE and made it clear that if JE were to persist in an attempt to remove DE, they would contact the police. DE and JE applied to the courts claiming that this was a deprivation of his liberty.

4.47 In his judgment the judge said:

> 'The fundamental issue in this case ... is whether DE has been and is deprived of his liberty to leave the X home and whether DE has been and is deprived of his liberty to leave the Y home. And when I refer to leaving the X home and the Y home, I do not mean leaving for the purpose of some trip or outing approved by SCC or by those managing the institution; I mean leaving in the sense of removing himself permanently in order to live where and with whom he chooses, specifically removing himself to live at home with JE.'

4.48 He then said:

> 'DE was not and is not "free to leave", and was and is, in that sense, completely under the control of [the local authority], because, as [counsel for DE] put it, it was and is [the local authority] who decides the essential matters of where DE can live, whether he can leave and whether he can be with JE.'

4.49 He concluded:

> 'The simple reality is that DE will be permitted to leave the institution in which [the Local Authority] has placed him and be released to the care of JE only as and when, – if ever; probably never, – [the Local Authority] considers it appropriate. [The Local Authority's] motives may be the purest, but in my judgment, [it] has been and is continuing to deprive DE of his liberty.'

4.50 It can be seen that the answer to the question whether a person is being deprived of their liberty or their liberty is being restrained in a particular situation will be different in each case, as each case depends on its own facts.

The Deprivation of Liberty Safeguards

4.51 The MHA 2007, s 50 and Schedules 7 and 8 have amended the MCA 2005 by ss 4A and 4B and Schedules A1 and 1A and introduced a new scheme for the authorisation of a person's deprivation of liberty in particular circumstances, examples of which have been set out above.

4.52 The Deprivation of Liberty Safeguards (DOLS) are a formal set of assessments which are put in place as a legal protection against unlawful detention of a person whenever it appears that a person is, or is likely to be, deprived of their liberty. If the results of all the assessments show that the deprivation of liberty is unavoidable in all the circumstances of the case and is the most appropriate, being the least restrictive, option and in the best interests of the person whose liberty is being deprived then the deprivation will be authorised.

4.53 Decisions made and actions taken under the DOLS must fulfill the requirements of the MCA 2005 and take account of the principles inherent in any decision made or act done for someone without capacity. They cover:

(a) the process of application and assessments needed for authorisation;
(b) the requirements for review, support and representation that must be provided for people subject to an authorisation; and
(c) the mechanism by which people are able to challenge authorisations.

How to authorise a deprivation of liberty

4.54 If a person is eligible to be detained under the MCA 2005 (and not the MHA 1983 where separate powers apply[6]) the deprivation of a person's liberty may be authorised in three ways:

(a) by the Court of Protection making a personal welfare decision under s 15(1)(c) of the Act;
(b) by the managers of a hospital or care home applying to the appropriate officer of the local authority respectively under Sch A1 for a standard or urgent authorisation;
(c) where it is necessary to give life sustaining treatment or do any vital act whilst awaiting a decision from the Court under s 4B of the MCA 2005.

Authorisation by application to the Court of Protection

4.55 In any case where there is an application to the Court of Protection for the Court to consider matters relating to the welfare of an individual, the Court may also need to inquire as to whether that person has been deprived of their liberty. Under s 21A of the Act the Court of Protection may review the lawfulness of any detention of a person in respect of whom a standard or urgent authorisation has been made to provide care or treatment and consider whether the deprivation of liberty can be authorised in the future, or make orders varying or terminating the standard authorisation.

Authorisations by the supervisory body under Schedule A1

4.56 If the manager of a care home is looking after a resident with dementia or is about to accommodate a person with dementia and he is depriving, or is likely to deprive, him of his liberty in the course of his care or treatment, the manager must apply to the supervising authority for an authorisation that the

---

6 See chapter 2.

deprivation of liberty will be lawful unless the circumstances require an urgent authorisation (see below). Similarly the manager must also apply for an authorisation if a resident moves to, or is moved to, a different home notwithstanding there may already be an authorisation in place.

4.57 The authorisation process begins with a request by the manager to the supervisory body for an authorisation of the deprivation of liberty of the particular person. The supervisory body must arrange for six separate assessments to be carried out to determine whether those six prescribed requirements are met so that an authorisation may be granted in relation to the detained resident.

4.58 The six assessments that are required and must be carried out before an authorisation is given:

(a) **Age** – the person in question must be 18 or over.
(b) **Mental Health** – the person must be suffering from a mental disorder within the meaning of the MHA 1983 which includes for this purpose a learning disability.
(c) **Mental Capacity** – the person must lack capacity to make the decision himself as to whether he should be accommodated in the care home or hospital for the purpose of getting the care or treatment concerned.
(d) **Best interests** – that to be looked after in the particular place and in the manner required by the manager is in that person's best interests and the deprivation of liberty that is proposed is necessary to prevent harm to him and is a proportionate response to the likelihood and seriousness of that harm.
(e) **Eligibility** – the person is ineligible for an authorisation under the MCA 2005 if he is already detained under the provisions and framework of detention under the MHA 1983.
(f) **No refusals** – there has been no decision taken, or offer of care or treatment refused by the donee or attorney of a valid LPA (health and welfare) or other advance decision made by the person himself or by his deputy refusing the care or treatment in question.

4.59 When the best interests assessment is carried out, the assessor must use the principles of the Act, the guidance and s 4 checklist that all need to be taken into account when assessing a person's best interests and must also consider these other factors:

- whether there would be any harm to the person if there was no deprivation of liberty;
- what the harm would be;
- how likely is the harm – that is to say is it of a sufficient level of risk to justify the most serious action of depriving the person of their liberty;
- are there any other care options that are less restrictive;

- what can be done to avoid deprivation of liberty in the future.

The starting point of the assessment is in the hospital or care home

4.60 The assessor must first establish whether a deprivation is happening or is likely to occur by consulting with the hospital or care home and examining all the relevant records and care plans prepared for that person.

4.61 If there is a less restrictive option than the original proposal, a deprivation of liberty must not be authorised because it would not be in the person's best interest.

The need for a full best interests assessment

4.62 The consultation process is comprehensive and the assessor must seek out and take account of the range of people connected to the person as set out in s 4(7) of the MCA 2005, for example anyone caring for them or that they have named to be consulted or who is interested in their welfare, their donee under an LPA, or a court appointed deputy and also any Independent Mental Capacity Advocate (IMCA) who has been appointed and assigned specifically to the person being assessed because he does not have anybody to support and speak for him during the assessment process.

4.63 The assessment must document all views taken together with the names and addresses of the people, the reports read and the interviews done. The assessor must look at any assessments and care records and of course, in accordance with the principles of the MCA 2005, involve the person who is being assessed as much as possible in the decision making. If required the assessor should make sure that they can be helped to communicate in the most effective way at a time when they are most alert, for example with somebody close to them present or with the help of a speech therapist.

4.64 In *Hillingdon v Neary*[7] Peter Jackson J reinforced the importance of the process: 'the best interests assessment is anything but a routine piece of paperwork…it should be seen as the cornerstone of the protection that the DOL safeguards offer to people facing deprivation of liberty if they are to be effective as safeguards at all.'

4.65 As part of the assessment the assessor must make recommendations to the supervisory body as to the maximum authorisation period, which must not exceed one year and may recommend conditions to be attached to the authorisation. For example, that the person be assessed by a doctor and a speech therapist on a 2-weekly basis to assess the effect of particular medication.

---

[7] [2011] EWHC 1377 (COP).

If all or any of the criteria in the assessments are not met

4.66 The supervising body must refuse the request for an authorisation if it has not been shown that in all the circumstances detention of the person is in their best interests.

If all criteria in the assessment are met

4.67 The supervisory body must grant the authorisation, set the time period which cannot be longer than that identified in the best interest assessment, attach any conditions identified if appropriate and appoint someone to act as the detained person's representative during the period of the authorisation. The supervisory authority must provide a written record of the authorisation to the managing authority, the person being deprived of their liberty and their representative and any other interested person who was consulted by the best interests assessor.

4.68 Whatever the type of authorisation there are duties on the managing and supervisory authorities to keep records and give copies to the relevant persons, to ensure by taking such steps as are practicable that the relevant person understands the effect of the authorisation and the right to apply to the Court of Protection to review their detention, challenge or determine any question about the authorisation.

Urgent authorisations

4.69 Ideally there should be time for a standard authorisation to be applied for and the assessments to be completed before a person leaves hospital or comes into a care home as it can be requested up to 28 days in advance of the person's arrival.

4.70 Nevertheless it may be the case that an urgent authorisation is necessary which will take effect from the exact time that it is given and can only last for a maximum of 7 days.

4.71 Unlike standard authorisations for which the managing authority has to request from the supervising authority, an urgent authorisation may be given by the managing authority but only if they are required to do as a matter of urgency, this is when:

(1) either the need for the person to be detained is so great that, notwithstanding that they will make an application for a standard authorisation, there should be an immediate authorisation; or
(2) having made a request for a standard authorisation the need for detention is so great that it should start before the outcome of the assessments.

4.72 In cases where the issues are in relation to life-sustaining treatment a person may be deprived of his liberty as long as the purpose is to save his life or to prevent a serious deterioration whilst a decision is sought from the Court of Protection on any question relating to the lawfulness of the deprivation of liberty.

SAFETY MEASURES ESTABLISHED UNDER THE MCA 2005

4.73 In other sections it can be seen how the MCA 2005 protects and safeguards people who lack capacity and how various measures are in place to ensure so far as can be possible that they are not exploited and abused.

4.74 In this section we look at the different safety measures put in place by the MCA 2005 to protect carers from incurring liability for their appropriate actions when caring for vulnerable people without capacity.

4.75 When any action is done or decision is carried out for, or on behalf of a person with dementia, their capacity is issue specific to the act or decision in question; that is it refers specifically to their understanding of and ability to make a particular decision at the time it is needed.

Protection for carers

4.76 In the context of caring for the elderly and particularly for those with dementia whose abilities and frailties in mind and body are increasingly manifest, the MCA 2005 provides in s 5 for carers, whether professional or family members, to be protected from liability if they do an act connected to care or treatment as long as they have first ascertained that the person lacked capacity in relation to the matter in question and that when doing the act the carer reasonably believed that the person lacked capacity in relation to the issue and that it would be in his best interests for the act to be done.

4.77 In the course of everyday care, whether washing or dressing, providing personal care or dental treatment, carers, family members and health care professionals provide a range of services that, but for the exemption from liability, would be criminal or tortious acts. The MCA Code of Practice sets out examples which can be used as guidance where consent would normally be required for certain actions done in connection with care or treatment, but which will not incur liability if they are done with regard to the principles and the various provisions of the MCA 2005.

4.78 Some examples set out in the Code of Practice are about personal matters, for example helping with washing, dressing or personal hygiene; helping with eating and drinking and communication and helping a person to move around.

4.79 The Code sets out some of the hundreds of everyday activities such as helping someone take part in education, social or leisure activities, or going into a person's home to drop off shopping or to see if they are alright. It includes doing the shopping or buying necessary goods with the person's money or arranging household services (for example, arranging repairs or maintenance for gas and electricity supplies), or providing services that help around the home (such as homecare or meals on wheels). Community care services are included as well as helping someone to move home and to clear their former home.

4.80 Other matters are more directed to healthcare and treatment such as carrying out diagnostic examinations and tests (to identify an illness, condition or other problem), providing professional medical, dental and similar treatment or giving medication, taking someone to hospital for assessment or treatment, providing nursing care (whether in hospital or in the community) or carrying out any other necessary medical procedures (for example, taking a blood sample) or therapies (for example, physiotherapy or chiropody) and providing care in an emergency.

When restraint is lawful

4.81 There are times when a carer will have to do something with the intention of restraining a person, for example using a hoist to transfer a person from bed to chair, but the carer will be protected from liability by s 6 of the MCA 2005 if:

(1) having assessed the person's capacity and as long as the carer does the act in the person's best interests;
(2) the carer reasonably believes that it is necessary to prevent harm to the person; and
3) the act is proportionate to the likelihood of the person suffering serious harm.

POWERS OF ATTORNEY REGARDING PERSONAL WELFARE

4.82 People with deteriorating cognitive conditions such as Alzheimer's disease and vascular dementia are encouraged to take as much control over their future care and to order their property and affairs whilst they have capacity to do so. In general there should be wider knowledge of the strategies available to enable people to think ahead and consider how they would like their health and welfare to be delivered by others as their capacity to make those decisions declines. Many people in the early stages of dementia are often so shocked and alarmed by a diagnosis of their deteriorating condition that they become unable to move forward; but others find comfort in having the knowledge and ability to put their affairs in order and their trust in those they have chosen to express their wishes. By making formal arrangements they can give those they trust decision-making abilities when their own capacity to make decisions has gone.

Taking control over future care

4.83 For the first time (by the introduction of the MCA 2005) it has been possible to create a valid power of attorney in relation to health and welfare decisions to endure after the maker or donor has lost capacity to make those decisions himself. This is called a Lasting Power of Attorney for Health and Welfare ('LPAHW'). The LPAHW allows a person (who is 18 or over and has capacity) to set out on a prescribed form his wishes and to nominate a decision maker to make those decisions as far as his personal welfare is concerned in the event that he loses capacity to make those decisions for himself.

4.84 By making a Lasting Power of Attorney for Health and Welfare the donor may direct his attorney or donee (attorney is a technical term as there is no need for the person who is granted the power to be a lawyer) to make decisions about his personal welfare in the event that he loses capacity.

4.85 Those types of decisions may include:

- where he should live, whether he could live for example, at home or in a care home;
- decisions about the sort of care he would like, including contact he would like or not like to have with specified people;
- The LPAHW can provide for a donee to make arrangements so that the donor can have chiropody or dental appointments, and the attorney may consent to or refuse medical examination and treatment on the donor's behalf;
- he may make decisions about assessments for and the provision of community services;
- he may be granted access to personal information about the donor and be able to deal with the donor's personal correspondence and papers and be able to comment on and complain about the donor's care or treatment in his best interests.

4.86 Anecdotally the prompt for people to create Lasting Powers of Attorney very often comes from their adult children when the cognitive difficulties of their parents have become obvious and an LPA may have to be created in a window of capacity. Unfortunately this haste results in occasions where the Office of Public Guardian (OPG)[8] which regulates the registration of LPAs has to refuse the registration of LPA for various reasons of invalidity.

---

8 The OPG is the government agency with responsibility for registration and supervision of EPAs and LPAs. It also has powers to investigate the way in which attorneys carry out their duties.

Creating a valid Lasting Power of Attorney for Health and Welfare

4.87 An Lasting Power of Attorney for Health and Welfare has similarities in its documentary form to a Lasting Power of Attorney for Property and Financial Affairs which is considered in Chapter 8, but it differs in that it may only be used if the donor, the maker, has lost capacity to make decisions about matters concerning his health and welfare. This is not like the LPA for Property and Financial Affairs where, notwithstanding the creation and registration of the LPA, it may also be used before the donor loses capacity and alongside decisions made by the donor in those circumstances.

4.88 An LPA is described by s 9 of the MCA 2005 as a power of attorney under which the donor confers on the donee authority to make decisions about all or any of the following:

(a) a person's personal welfare or specified matters concerning a person's welfare; and
(b) a person's property and affairs or specified matters concerning a person's property and affairs,

and which includes authority to make decisions in circumstances where the person no longer has capacity.

4.89 The LPA is not created unless it is on the prescribed form being either a Lasting Power of Attorney Health and Welfare (LPAHW) or a Lasting Power of Attorney for Property and Financial Affairs (LPAPFA).

4.90 The subject matter of the two different types of decision making make it simpler to have two different instruments as not only does it focus on the particular issue, but it is also possible that there may be different attorneys dealing with the different powers. For example it is quite likely that a donor may want a solicitor to be one of the attorneys dealing with his property and affairs but prefer a relative to act on his behalf and in accordance with his wishes in relation to personal welfare matters.

4.91 Also, and importantly, the Lasting Power of Attorney for Health and Welfare can only be used in circumstances where the donor has lost capacity.

The prescribed form

4.92 The prescribed form for the instrument to create an LPA is a similar form for both an LPA for Property and Financial Affairs and an LPA for Health and Welfare.

4.93 The prescribed form for an LPAHW consists of at least 12 pages, although not every page is appropriate for each case and if there is insufficient space then supplementary pages may be added. The document is seen as consisting of four parts which must all be kept together containing:

(1) the prescribed information which the donor, the attorney and the certificate provider all have to read or have read to them before completing the form;
(2) Part A, the Donor's Declaration;
(3) Part B, the Certificate Provider's Declaration; and
4) Part C, the Attorney's Declaration.

The prescribed information

4.94 The LPAHW sets out clearly at the beginning, in the prescribed information, an explanation and mini guidance concerning the purpose and legal consequences of making an LPA. It directs the person making it, his attorneys and his certificate providers to read it carefully and refers them to the guidance produced by the OPG.

4.95 Crucially it sets out that attorneys cannot do whatever they like. They must follow the principles of the MCA 2005.

4.96 The form and the information are intended to be able to be used by people without legal advice but the number of applications that are referred to the Court of Protection by the OPG for severance suggest that in many cases it would be prudent to seek legal advice before embarking on the creation of an LPA, as the momentous effect of the document once registered is to give a person's autonomy over his decision making to another.

Part A of the LPA

4.97 This sets out the core information about the donor, the attorney(s) and the scope or restriction of their authority. The donor has to specify if he is appointing more than one attorney and whether he is giving them authority to act jointly or jointly and severally (independently) in relation to some but not all matters or in whatever combination.

4.98 Further the donor may appoint replacement attorneys to take effect on the occurrence of a specified event (the disclaimer by an attorney, death or bankruptcy of an attorney, dissolution of the marriage of the attorney, if the spouse of the donor or the donee's incapacity). There is no power for a donee himself to choose another attorney, unlike a trustee who may do so in certain circumstances. See also the potential difficulties involved with replacement attorneys at **8.54** et seq below.

4.99 There is also space for the donor to set out some guidance as to how the attorney should carry out his authority. Whilst not an express restriction on their powers the attorney must take this into account.

4.100 Whilst there is a body of principles that apply to the relationship between attorney and donor regardless of the state of capacity of the donor (see below), it goes without saying that a donor has to consider very carefully who he chooses to act on his behalf as an attorney. However very often it is not the donor but his children or relations that instigate the creation of an LPA and there are therefore some safeguards built into the process.

4.101 One of the safeguards brought in under the MCA 2005 are the notice provisions on registration. In Part A the donor may select up to five named persons (or none) who are to be notified on registration of the power. A named person cannot be an attorney or replacement attorney and if the donor chooses not to notify any named person he must have two certificate providers each providing a certificate of capacity of the donor that he understands the nature of the power he is creating.

Part B of the LPA

4.102 An equally important part and safeguard of the instrument of LPA is the declaration of the certificate provider, a person of a prescribed description, who provides a contemporaneous record at the time the LPA was prepared that:

(1) the donor understands the purpose of the instrument and the scope of the authority conferred under it;
(2) no fraud or undue pressure is being used to induce the donor to create a LPA; and
(3) there is nothing else which would prevent a LPA from being created by the instrument.[9]

4.103 The certificate provider must be chosen by the donor from one of two categories of person: (a) a person who has known the donor for at least 2 years; or (b) a person who, on account of his professional skills and expertise, reasonably considers that he is competent to make the judgments necessary to certify the relevant matters.

4.104 A certificate provider cannot be a family member of the donor, an attorney or family member of the attorney of the LPA or any other LPA or EPA executed by the donor, a director or employee of a trust corporation acting as an attorney under the power of attorney, a business partner or employee of the donor or the attorney appointed under the power of attorney (so another member of a solicitors' firm where the solicitor is the attorney cannot certify that the donor understands what he is doing) and finally but importantly no owner, director, manager or employee of a family member of such a person of any care home in which the donor is living when he executes the LPA.

---

9 MCA 2005, Sch 1, para 2(1)(e).

Part C of the LPA

4.105 The declaration by the attorney in an LPA is an important reminder of the nature of the obligations imposed on the attorney:

(i) that he has read the prescribed information (or has had it read to him), and

(ii) that he understands the duties imposed on a donee of an LPA under ss 1 (the principles) and 4 (best interests).

4.106 This declaration should also be completed by any replacement attorneys, which includes a declaration that if called upon to act by any of the trigger events – the disclaimer by an attorney, death or bankruptcy of an attorney, dissolution of the marriage if the attorney is the donor's spouse or incapacity of the donor – the replacement attorney will notify the OPG returning the original LPA.

4.107 This is important so that the Public Guardian can update his records and endorse the original LPA, which can subsequently be produced by the replacement attorney as his authority to act.

The LPA must be executed in the sequence as set out above: the donor must read or have read to him the prescribed information which is contained on the face of the instrument, as soon as reasonably practicable the donor completes Part A and signs it in the presence of a witness; as soon as reasonably practicable thereafter the certificate provider(s) complete Part B and as soon as is reasonably practicable thereafter the donees must read or have read to them the prescribed information and complete and sign Part C in the presence of a witness.

The LPA is subject to the provisions of the MCA

4.108 The MCA 2005 sets out clearly that unless sections 9, 10 and Schedule 1 of the Act are complied with, no LPA is created nor any authority conferred on a donee. What is particularly important in relation to an LPA for health and welfare (unlike for an LPA for property and affairs) is that it cannot take effect unless the donor can be shown to lack capacity to make his own decisions.

Capacity of donor

4.109 The donor has to have reached the age of 18 and to have capacity to make a Lasting Power of Attorney. As always under the MCA 2005 the test of capacity is time and function specific. That is to say that the donor understands what he is doing by making an LPA. When creating the LPA the donor must understand that he will be giving the attorney either a general power to make all decisions relating to his personal welfare or, if he makes the LPA subject to restrictions or conditions, the donor will be giving the donee a power to make only some particular decisions if called on to do so.

4.110 A donor may want to create and indeed may fill out the prescribed form for an LPA without the assistance of a solicitor. It is implicit that he understands what he is doing. The protection on the donor should come from the certificate provider who is an independent third party (who can be a solicitor or other professional) who confirms that 'the donor understands the purpose of the LPA and the scope of the authority under it' and that no fraud or undue pressure is being used.

4.111 In considering whether a person has the required capacity to make an LPA the following principles of the MCA 2005 apply:

(1) that a person must be assumed to have capacity unless it is established that he lacks capacity; and
(2) that a person is not to be treated as unable to make a decision merely because he makes an unwise decision,

as well as the definition of capacity in section 2: 'if at the material time he is unable to make a decision for himself in relation to the matter because of an impairment of, or a disturbance in the functioning of, the mind or brain'.

The donor's choice of certificate provider

4.112 One of the safeguards against potential abuse of the donor is his choice of certificate provider. Without such a certificate the LPA cannot be registered and used.

4.113 The independence of the certificate provider and his knowledge and experience of the issues involving mental capacity are all helpful safeguards for the donor.

4.114 The professional certificate provider will need to have taken a suitably detailed personal history of the donor and may need to insist on seeing him on his own so as to satisfy the requirements as to undue pressure. The necessity for such professional care becomes obvious if there is a challenge to the Court of Protection about the validity of the LPA.

4.115 An example in practice of a challenge to the validity of an LPA was where the donor had made an LPA appointing her daughter as her sole attorney and excluding her other three children from having anything to do with her. The three children made an application to the Court showing that the certificate provider could not have seen the donor at the relevant time and that the daughter had 'created' the LPA by pressurising her mother to sign a collection of similar pieces of paper.

Registration

4.116 As an LPA cannot take effect until it is registered and the final step to validity is the process of registration. The person making the application to register may be the donor or one of his attorneys.

4.117 Registration of the LPA is also on a formal document (LPA 002) and when submitted must also include the original LPA or a certified copy.

4.118 The notice provisions are the same for personal welfare LPAs as for those for property and affairs. The person applying for registration must give notice in the appropriate form to any persons named by the donor and the OPG will give notice to the donor if the application to register is made by the attorney. Unless the OPG receives a valid notice of objection within 4 weeks from the date of the last notice or there is a defect in the instrument which prevents registration, the OPG must register the LPA.

4.119 Once the instrument that has created the LPA has been registered it will be stamped on each page, notice will be given to the attorney and to the donor that it has been registered and it will be returned to the applicant.

Using an LPA for health and welfare decision making

4.120 If a donor has gone to the trouble and considerable effort of creating a valid LPAHW it is suggested that he makes it very clear to his medical team and particularly to his GP that he has made an LPAHW and he should be encouraged to have a copy lodged with his medical notes. If he has members of his family who have not been given notice of objection to the making of an LPA or its registration it would still be advisable, if possible in the circumstances, to let them know what has been done in the event of decisions needing to be made. In some situations a prominent notice in the donor's home or handbag should alert those who need to know in the event of an emergency that the person has made an LPA.

4.121 Where an LPA has authorised a donee to make decisions about a donor's personal welfare the donee is only authorised to make decisions in circumstances where the donor lacks capacity or the donee reasonably believes the donor to lack capacity.

When can the attorney act

4.122 As has been set out earlier and this section refers, anybody involved in making decisions about providing care for a person without capacity has to have a reasonable belief that the person lacks capacity to do the act or make the decision in question.

4.123 In this case the attorney has to take reasonable steps to establish capacity and he should be able to describe the questions he asked and how he tried to communicate with the person with dementia if he is later challenged about the donor's capacity and how he decided the donor lacked the required capacity. The attorney must have objective reasons for his reasonable belief that the donor lacks capacity.

4.124 As always, the principles and the MCA 2005 apply. In the case of a donee needing to use the LPA and needing to confirm his reasonable belief that the donor lacks capacity the donee may need to be advised by the donor's own doctor or the circumstances may be that a further specialist opinion is required. Some of the circumstances of when more professional advice may be required are set out in the Code of Practice:

- the decision that needs to be made is complicated or has serious consequences;
- an assessor concludes a person lacks capacity, and the person challenges the finding;
- family members, carers and/or professionals disagree about a person's capacity;
- there is a conflict of interest between the assessor and the person being assessed;
- the person being assessed is expressing different views to different people, for example they may be trying to please everyone or telling people what they think they want to hear;
- somebody might challenge the person's capacity to make the decision – either at the time of the decision or later (for example, a family member might challenge a will after a person has died on the basis that the person lacked capacity when they made the will);
- somebody has been accused of abusing a vulnerable adult who may lack capacity to make decisions that protect them;
- a person repeatedly makes decisions that put them at risk or could result in suffering or damage.

The attorney's duties

4.125 In any event the donee or attorney must act within the scope of his powers and must comply with all the provisions of the MCA 2005 and the Code of Practice that apply to donees.

4.126 The standard form for creating an LPA for heath and welfare allows attorneys to make decisions about anything which relates to the donor's personal welfare but the donor may restrict the scope of that power or can add restrictions where they may not wish their attorney to act.

4.127 In the standard form of LPA for health and welfare, decisions about life sustaining treatment are not included within the general power so the donor has to specifically authorise that he wants the attorney to have this authority.

4.128 As with all decisions when someone has lost capacity the attorney must act in the donor's best interests. That process is the one running through all decisions involving people without capacity. It involves applying the best interests checklist and consulting with family members and not being motivated in anyway, for example by pity or guilt by the desire to bring about the donor's death.

4.129 The LPA does not authorise the attorney to restrain the donor except in certain circumstances.

4.130 Where there is any question about the exercise of an attorney's powers under the LPA the attorney may apply to the Court of Protection without seeking prior permission to do so.

Restrictions on acting

4.131 Even if there is a valid LPA for personal welfare the attorney does not have the right to consent to or to refuse treatment if:

- the donor has capacity to do so himself;
- the donor has made an advance decision to refuse the particular treatment after LPA is made;
- the treatment is for life sustaining treatment and there is no specific authority granted by the LPA;
- the patient is detained under the Mental Health Act 1983.

WELFARE DEPUTIES AND THE COURT OF PROTECTION

4.132 Central to the MCA 2005 is the power of the Court of Protection to make decisions and to make orders on behalf of incapable adults and to appoint deputies to make decisions including decisions about a person's health and welfare in that person's best interests if there has been no advance planning by that person when they had capacity to make an LPAHW.

4.133 A decision of the court is to be preferred to the appointment of a deputy and where there is no other way of resolving a dispute, for example where a decision is required as to where someone should live or whether they should have a particular medical treatment, the court will be asked to make an order using its powers under s 16 of the MCA 2005. Chapter 13 explains what the Court of Protection can do.

4.134 Although many applications to the court for welfare orders also ask the court to appoint a welfare deputy, very few welfare deputies are in fact appointed as according to the MCA 2005 the court prefers the decision of a court to the appointment of a deputy.

4.135 However, there are circumstances when decision-making powers will be needed in relation to someone with dementia on a regular or ongoing basis, for example in the course of general treatment and care and where there is no LPA in place. In those circumstances the court may appoint a deputy to make future decisions but their appointment will be as limited in scope and authority as is necessary and for as short a time as possible.

4.136 If a deputy is appointed by the Court, despite not having been chosen by the donor, a deputy will perform a similar function to donees appointed by the donor to be attorneys either in relation to health and welfare matters or in relation to a person's property and affairs.

4.137 The MCA 2005 at s 19(6) confirms that as with a donee of an LPA, a deputy is to be treated as the incapable person's agent in relation to anything done or decided by him within in the scope of his appointment.

When might a deputy be appointed?

4.138 Deputies for personal welfare decisions will only be appointed in the most difficult cases where important or necessary actions cannot be carried out without the court's authority.

4.139 The Code of Practice gives examples where a welfare deputy could be appointed:

- where there are a series of linked welfare decisions to be made over time and it would not be beneficial or appropriate for those decisions to be made by a court all the time;
- the most appropriate way of acting in a person's best interests is to have an appointed deputy who will consult the relevant persons but have the final authority;
- where there is a history of family disputes and a decision maker is needed as it will be detrimental to the person without capacity to have continual wrangling going on over him;
- in the rare cases where it is felt that the person without capacity is at risk of serious harm if decision making is left in the hands of the family and that there should be an independent person making welfare decisions.

4.140 Although the MCA 2005 provides for the appointment of welfare deputies, as set out above the Code of Practice states that deputies for personal welfare decisions will only be required in the most difficult cases. This is illustrated in the case of *MK v JK*[10] in which District Judge Ralton said:

> 'I think it would be very rare for the court to consider it right to delegate its issue-resolving function to a Deputy on any significant issue of principle such as residence, type of care, treatment and such like. The role of resolving such issues

[10] [2013] EWHC 4334 (COP), (2013) MHLO 81.

must remain with the court of justice...I do think that putting in place a State-appointed decision maker – which is what a Deputy is – is a considerable interference with family life and would therefore have to justify the twin requirements of legitimate aim and proportionality. One can never say never, but it is hard at the moment to envisage how in most cases a Personal Welfare Deputy could ever be so justified.'

Who can be a deputy?

4.141 Deputies must be at least 18 years of age. It is important to show that there is no obvious conflict of interest; for example, a paid care worker should not agree to act as a deputy for a resident in their own care home.

4.142 The court may appoint one, two or several deputies and must state whether they can act jointly or jointly and severally (independently) or jointly in some matters and jointly and severally in respect of other matters.

Restrictions on deputies' powers

4.143 In addition to the restrictions placed on a deputy's powers that are imposed under the MCA 2005 (that is, to always follow the principles and act in accordance with the best interests of the person with dementia) the MCA 2005 also restricts the powers that a deputy has. For example:

- a deputy has no power to make a decision for an incapacitated person if he knows or has reasonable grounds for believing that the person has capacity to make the particular decision for himself;
- a deputy cannot stop a named person from having contact to the person without capacity;
- a deputy cannot direct a person responsible for the health of the person without capacity to allow a different person to take over that responsibility;
- a deputy cannot make a decision which is inconsistent with the authority of a donee under an LPA;
- a deputy may not refuse consent to the carrying out or continuation of life-sustaining treatment in relation to the person without capacity;
- a deputy may not do an act that is intended to restrain the person without capacity unless four particular conditions which are set out in s 20 are satisfied:
  - (i) that in doing the MCA 2005 the deputy is acting within the scope of an authority expressly conferred in him by the court;
  - (ii) that the person lacks or the deputy reasonably believes that he lacks capacity in relation to the matter in question;
  - (iii) that the deputy reasonably believes that it is necessary to restrain the person without capacity in order to prevent harm to him; and

(iv) that the restraining act is a proportionate response both to the likelihood of the person suffering harm and the seriousness of that harm.

Duties imposed by the Act on a deputy

4.144 The personal welfare deputy must act in accordance with the MCA 2005's statutory principles and in particular always act in the best interests of the person without capacity. In each situation the deputy must consider whether the person has capacity to make the decision himself and if it is likely that the person may regain capacity, put off the decision until the person is able to make it himself.

4.145 The deputy must act in accordance with the authority granted to him by the court and have regard to the guidance in the Code of Practice.

4.146 A deputy must understand the gravity of the task he has taken on and has a duty of care to carry out his duties with the appropriate skill, care and diligence as if they were managing their own affairs. If the deputy is a paid deputy they are expected to demonstrate a higher degree of skill and care.

4.147 A deputy must act in good faith, respect the confidentiality of the person and neither delegate his duties unless authorised to do so nor take advantage of the situation. Similar to the duties of a donee of an LPA he must indemnify the person against liability to any third party caused by his own negligence.

4.148 If the deputy considers his powers do not cover the matter in question he must apply to the court for the court to either make the decision or to give him greater authority to do so.

4.149 Any breach of a deputy's duties may result in him being removed from the deputyship.

4.150 The OPG both supervises the deputies appointed by the court and also is alert to any suspicion of abuse or exploitation by a deputy that is brought to its attention.

CHAPTER 5

NHS CARE AND TREATMENT

5.1 This chapter sets out several of the more important legal issues concerning the provision of care and treatment by the NHS for those who have dementia, from the purpose and present structure of the service, through the practical problems they and their family and friends may experience as the effects of dementia become more severe, to the very vexed topic of Continuing Healthcare.

NHS RESPONSIBILITIES – OVERVIEW

5.2 The ambition and achievement of the National Health Service Act 1946 in England[1] are now enshrined in the NHS Act 2006 ('NHSA 2006'), as recently amended by the Health and Social Care Act 2012.

5.3 Section 1(1) of the NHSA 2006 conveys the fundamental principle that the Secretary of State for Health is under a duty to continue the promotion in England of a comprehensive health service designed to secure improvement in the physical and mental health of the people of England and in the prevention, diagnosis and treatment of physical and mental illness. By s 1(4) of the same Act these services must be free of charge, unless expressly provided for by statute, and for the most part they are free.

5.4 For the purposes of this Act illness includes any disorder or disability of the mind (it therefore includes dementia) and any injury or disability requiring medical or dental treatment or nursing.[2]

5.5 By s 1H of the NHSA 2006 the NHS Commissioning Board (otherwise known as NHS England) has been created and it too is subject to the s 1(1) duty concurrently with the Secretary of State for Health, except in relation to public health functions.

5.6 By s 1I clinical commissioning groups ('CCG') have been created and their function is to arrange for the provision of services for the purposes of the NHS in England, a role previously given to Primary Care Trusts. These groups are essentially the GPs for a particular geographical area.

---

1 The National Health Service (Wales) Act 2006 applies to Wales.

2 See NHSA 2006, s 275(1).

5.7 By s 3A a CCG must arrange for the provision of the following to such extent as it considers necessary to meet the reasonable requirements of the persons for whom it has responsibility:

- hospital accommodation;
- other accommodation for the purpose of any service provided under the NHSA 2006;
- medical, dental, ophthalmic, nursing and ambulance services;
- such other services or facilities for the care of pregnant women, women who are breastfeeding and young children as the CCG considers are appropriate as part of the health service;
- such other services or facilities for the prevention of illness, the care of persons with illness and the after-care of persons who have had illness as the CCG considers are appropriate as part of the health service;
- such other services or facilities as are required for the diagnosis and treatment of illness.

5.8 Two points in particular arise at this stage. The first is that it is not therefore incumbent upon a CCG to provide all or even any of the treatment, for example, that a person believes would be best for him, because there is, obviously, a limit to resources and the group must balance individual needs and wishes against those of its community as a whole.

5.9 The second is that because the listed services include 'other accommodation for the purpose of any service provided under the NHSA' and 'other services or facilities for the care and after-care of persons who are suffering from or who have suffered from illness', the NHS is able, if it so decides, to provide social care, including in a care or nursing home. There is therefore great potential for tension between CCGs on the one hand and patients (usually in combination with local authorities) on the other when it comes to deciding on eligibility for Continuing Healthcare ('CHC'), by which social care is provided free of charge; whereas a local authority would be under a duty to charge for it if it is residential care (usually in a care or nursing home) and, depending on its policy, may well exercise its power to charge for it if it is non-residential care. Eligibility for CHC is of particular concern to those who have dementia and their families.

5.10 The legislation does not, however, (or at least should not) give rise to any potential for an overlap. This is because s 3A enables a CCG to decide on provision 'to such extent as it considers necessary', which means it is likely that a court would find as between a CCG and a local authority that the former is the primary decision-maker and the latter has to abide by its decisions, if lawfully made (ie if not susceptible to judicial review).[3]

---

3 See *R (St. Helen's BC) v Manchester PCT* [2008] EWCA Civ 931.

5.11 As for the extent of a CCG's community, a group is responsible for all persons who are provided with primary medical services by a member of its group, ie who are registered with a GP who is a member of the CCG. It is also responsible for all persons who usually reside in its area and who are not provided with such services by a member of the group, ie who are not so registered. Exceptions to this general position are set out in regulations[4] and are summarised in guidance issued by NHS England.[5]

DEMENTIA AND THE NHS

5.12 It is beyond the scope of this book to portray and explore in much detail the specific care and treatment that can be provided by the NHS for those with dementia and which is in practice provided by CCGs, whether as a whole or individually, but an indication of this is as follows.

5.13 Unfortunately as matters stand most types of dementia are progressive and cannot be cured. There are exceptions that can be treated with vitamin and hormone supplements and with surgery, but Alzheimer's disease, for example, cannot be cured. At best the effects of it can be delayed, through medication. Otherwise psychological treatment, such as cognitive stimulation (eg problem-solving) and reality orientation therapy (which prompts the patient to focus on such matters as what day it is, where they are and who they are with), can help those with dementia to cope with the symptoms. Another example is behavioural therapy that may involve regular physical exercise designed to make someone less restless, when they would otherwise try to tackle restlessness themselves by wandering, even into the streets.

5.14 A valuable insight into what the NHS (and its local authority colleagues) can and should do for those with dementia (and how it is diagnosed) can be gleaned from specific guidance issued by the National Institute for Health and Care Excellence ('NICE'),[6] which also touches on the more significant legal issues involved. It asserts it is based on the best available evidence for the care and treatment of people with dementia. Its purpose is to make recommendations, in effect as to best practice, rather than make requirements of CCGs.

5.15 An important feature of this guidance is the emphasis it places on forward planning for the person with dementia in discussions with him and those close to him while he still has sufficient capacity to understand what lies

---

4 NHS Commissioning Board and CCGs (Responsibilities and Standing Rules) Regulations 2012, SI 2012/2996 (the '2012 regulations') – see reg 4 and Sch 2.

5 'Who Pays? Determining responsibility for payments to providers', August 2013 – this explains cross-border arrangements as well.

6 NICE clinical guideline 42, 'Dementia – Supporting people with dementia and their carers in health and social care', issued November 2006 and last modified October 2012 – see also the practice guidance 'Living well with dementia: A National Dementia Strategy' issued by the Department of Health in February 2009.

ahead.[7] Such planning should encompass discussions about an advance statement as to treatment (as envisaged by the MCA 2005[8]), an advance decision to refuse treatment (as provided for by the same Act[9]), a Lasting Power of Attorney[10] ('LPA') and a Preferred Place of Care Plan, so that care choices, including as to place of death, can be recorded. Depending on clinical judgment it may also be appropriate to discuss resuscitation in the event of a cardiopulmonary arrest, which is addressed below.

5.16 Another helpful aspect of the guidance is the recommendation that following a diagnosis of dementia, both NHS and local authority professionals should, unless the person with dementia clearly indicates to the contrary, provide him and those close to him with written information about the signs and symptoms of dementia, the course and prognosis of the condition, treatments, local care and support services and groups, sources of financial and legal advice (and advocacy), medico-legal issues (such as driving) and sources of information about dementia.

5.17 As for the person's voluntary carers, whether family or friends, the guidance reminds the NHS and local authority professionals involved to ensure they know of their right to an assessment, so that the local authority can understand the impact on them of caring for the person with dementia and can consider what, if any, support to provide for them.[11]

Refusing treatment

5.18 The common law recognises that a person has the right to refuse anything that would appear to help him, including care and medical treatment, even though refusal may shorten his life considerably, provided he has the mental capacity to make the decision to refuse. If nonetheless someone insists on treating him and this involves physical contact, that constitutes an assault, at the least (subject to the defence of necessity).

5.19 The right to refuse is recognised by the MCA 2005, in particular by s 1(4), which sets out the principle that a person is not to be treated as unable to make a decision merely because he makes an unwise decision, ie a decision that others consider, whether subjectively or objectively, to be unwise.

5.20 The problem for the NHS, as it is for all decision makers but which for obvious reasons is generally more acute than it is for their local authority colleagues, is in determining whether there is the capacity to decide and, if not, what is in the person's best interests, ie whether he should undergo the treatment or not.

---

7 See para 11.4.4.

8 See s 4(6).

9 See ss 24 to 26 and below.

10 See ss 9 to 14 of the MCA 2005.

11 See chapter 7.

5.21 This problem can be alleviated to a significant extent if he has made an advance decision to refuse treatment for the purposes of ss 24 to 26 of the MCA 2005.

5.22 Such a decision is one made by an adult, when he has the capacity to do so, that, in such circumstances as he may specify, specified treatment is not to be carried out or continued by a person providing health care for him. He can express the decision in layman's (as opposed to medical) terms and he can withdraw or alter it at any time as long as he has the capacity to do so.

5.23 The advance decision is not valid if he has: (1) withdrawn it at a time when he had the requisite capacity; or (2) under a later (not earlier) LPA given authority to his attorney to give or refuse consent to the treatment to which the decision relates; or (3) done anything else clearly inconsistent with it remaining his fixed decision. Nor does it apply if at the time of treatment he has the capacity to give or refuse consent to it or if there are reasonable grounds for believing that circumstances exist that he did not anticipate at the time of his decision and that would have affected it had he anticipated them.

5.24 Also, an advance decision does not apply to life-sustaining treatment unless it is verified by a statement by the person concerned ('the patient') to the effect that it is to apply to that treatment even if his life is at risk and it complies with these requirements: it is in writing, signed by him or another person in his presence and by his direction; the signature is made or acknowledged by him in the presence of a witness; and the witness signs it or acknowledges his signature in the patient's presence.

5.25 The Court of Protection can make a declaration as to whether an advance decision exists, is valid and is applicable to a treatment. A person is not prevented from providing life-sustaining treatment or doing any act he reasonably believes to be necessary to prevent a serious deterioration in the patient's condition pending a decision of the court.

5.26 Treatment for these purposes includes a diagnostic or other procedure[12] and life-sustaining treatment is treatment that in the view of the person providing health care for the patient is necessary to sustain life.[13]

5.27 Other than in respect of life-sustaining treatment an advance decision does not have to be in writing and any such decision can be withdrawn without this being committed to writing. Also, an alteration does not have to be in writing in order to apply unless the effect of the alteration is that life-sustaining treatment is to be refused.

5.28 The net effect of these statutory provisions is that if the patient has made an advance decision that is valid and applies to the treatment in question it is as

---

12 See MCA 2005, s 64(1).

13 See MCA 2005, s 4(10).

if he has made the decision himself with the capacity to do so, so that any person who nonetheless gives him that treatment is committing an assault, at the least (subject to the defence of necessity).

Agreeing to treatment

5.29 Section 4(6)(a) of the MCA 2005 provides that in determining the best interests of a person who lacks the requisite capacity the decision maker must consider, amongst other things and so far as is reasonably ascertainable, the person's past and present wishes and, in particular, any relevant written statement made by him when he had capacity.

5.30 By this means a person can, for example, state in advance of losing capacity that he agrees to certain types of treatment or even to any treatment that may prolong his life, but such a statement cannot itself prevent the decision maker from deciding he should not have the treatment, if it is not in his best interests to have it.

5.31 It should be pointed out that, equally, a decision maker in respect of life-sustaining treatment would have to take into account an advance decision in writing to refuse the treatment that was not effective because, for example, there was no witness to it.

Resuscitation

5.32 This issue is at the sharp end of decision making about life-sustaining treatment for a person who lacks capacity and is the subject of a joint statement made by the British Medical Association, the Resuscitation Council (UK) and the Royal College of Nursing, issued in October 2007 (but presently under review).[14]

5.33 The statement concerns cardiopulmonary resuscitation ('CPR'), whose purpose is to try to restore breathing and circulation in a patient in cardiac and/or respiratory arrest. It is a relatively invasive therapy that usually includes chest compressions, attempted defibrillation with electric shocks, injection of drugs and ventilation of the lungs. The survival rate is relatively low, in that if the arrest occurs in hospital the chances of surviving until discharged from hospital are at best about 15–20% and if it occurs elsewhere they are at best 5–10%. There is some risk of brain damage.

5.34 As one would expect the statement conveys a good understanding of the law and is a very helpful guide to how the provisions of the MCA 2005 work in practice. For example, where there are persons who are close to a patient who lacks capacity (ie family or friends) it advises clinicians to ensure that those who do not have any 'legal authority' understand that their role is to help

---

14 'Decisions relating to cardiopulmonary resuscitation.'

inform the decision-making process and that they are not the decision makers. This piece of guidance serves as an excellent vehicle for a demonstration of how the Act is intended to work:[15]

(1) The decision in question is whether CPR should be attempted, this decision to be made either immediately before or shortly before an arrest is expected to occur.

(2) The statement cautions that if the clinicians believe that CPR would not re-start the heart and maintain breathing for a sustained period (ie it is clinically inappropriate[16]) it should not be offered or attempted – but if this is not accepted a second opinion should be offered. This can be a difficult point because it presupposes that the decision to withhold CPR is not a decision to be made by the patient (assuming he has capacity) but by the clinicians, ie the patient cannot insist on CPR being attempted, so that if he lacks capacity there is no best interests decision to be made. Rather than be diverted by that debate, however, what follows assumes there is undoubtedly a best interests decision to be made.

(3) This is a decision the patient would make for himself if he had capacity.

(4) It is life-sustaining treatment and so if he has made a valid and applicable advance decision to refuse such treatment that is the operative decision to the exclusion of all other views.

(5) If not, but if he has executed an LPA that authorises his attorney to make decisions about his personal welfare, the power extends, by statute, to the giving or refusing of consent to the carrying out of or continuation of treatment by a person providing health care for him. However, in order for the power to cover life-sustaining treatment, the instrument creating the power must contain provisions to that effect.[17] If so, the attorney is the decision maker and must therefore make the decision (whether CPR should be attempted) in the best interests of the patient, taking into account the s 4 requirements and therefore the views of the others there mentioned, in particular the clinicians involved and those close to the patient.

(6) Otherwise there may be (but this is very unlikely) a welfare deputy appointed by the Court of Protection, who may have been given the power to give or refuse consent to the carrying out or continuation of treatment by a person providing health care for the patient.[18] Nonetheless he may not refuse consent to life-sustaining treatment.[19]

(7) If there is no valid and applicable advance decision and no welfare attorney with express authority, who then decides on best interests (rather

---

15 See also 'Treatment and care towards the end of life: good practice in decision making', issued by the General Medical Council ('GMC') in 2010, at para 16.

16 Note that the court will not order medical treatment to be carried out if the treating physician or surgeon is unwilling to offer that treatment for clinical reasons conscientiously held by him – see, for example, *AVS v A NHS Foundation Trust* [2011] EWCA Civ 7, at [35].

17 See MCA 2005, s 11(7) and (8).

18 See MCA 2005, s 17(1)(d).

19 See MCA 2005, s 20(5).

than, if different, on whether CPR is clinically appropriate)? The MCA 2005 Code of Practice states that where the decision involves the provision of medical treatment the doctor or other member of healthcare staff responsible for carrying out the particular treatment or procedure is the decision maker.[20] If all involved can agree then all well and good but if not and an application is made to it then only the court itself can break the impasse.[21]

5.35 Another scenario of particular interest is where the patient lacks capacity and there is no-one close to the patient, in which case the MCA 2005 can require the 'NHS body' concerned (now a CCG[22]) to instruct an independent mental capacity advocate ('IMCA')[23] to represent him. Unless the matter is urgent,[24] an IMCA must be instructed if the body is proposing to provide serious medical treatment for a person who lacks capacity to consent to it and it is satisfied there is no-one, other than professionals engaged in providing care or treatment, whom it would be appropriate to consult about best interests.[25] Such treatment means that which involves providing, withholding or withdrawing treatment in circumstances where: (a) in a case where a single treatment is being proposed, there is a fine balance between its benefits to the patient and the burdens and risks it is likely to entail for him; (b) in a case where there is a choice of treatments, a decision as to which one to use is finely balanced, or (c) what is proposed would be likely to involve serious consequences for the patient.[26] The NHS body must then take into account any information given or submissions made by the IMCA.

5.36 The resuscitation statement postulates that it can be argued that a decision not to try CPR because it would not re-start the patient's heart or breathing for a sustained period would not have to involve the instruction of an IMCA on the basis that the withholding of this treatment would not, for the purposes of the regulations, be likely to involve serious consequences for the patient. It recognises, however, that there is uncertainty about this, essentially for the reason set out in paragraph 5.34(2) above.

5.37 The better view probably is that this argument should not prevail, because on any view death is a serious consequence and, in any event, because the structure of the regulation suggests otherwise. Where there is a clear balance in favour of treatment, because the benefits clearly outweigh the burdens/risks, the MCA 2005 does not require an IMCA to be instructed, no doubt because the clinicians will decide to carry out the treatment in any event, in the best

---

20 Paragraph 5.8.

21 See the GMC publication referred to at fn 14 for advice for clinicians on resolving disagreements, at paras 47 to 49.

22 Local Health Board in Wales.

23 See MCA 2005, s 37.

24 Including when an IMCA is not available, at the weekend or in the evening.

25 An IMCA may also need to be instructed by an NHS body or a local authority to represent such a person if accommodation is to be provided for them – see MCA 2005, ss 38 and 39.

26 See reg 4(2) of the Mental Capacity Act 2005 (Independent Mental Capacity Advocates) (General) Regulations 2006, SI 2006/1832; the definition is the same in Wales, see SI 2007/852.

interests of the patient. Where there is a fine balance, however, there is the need for a person who can speak for the patient to be consulted as part of the decision-making process. The serious consequences provision is in the alternative to this and so it must follow that it applies where there is less than a fine balance, ie either nothing in favour of the treatment or, to put it another way, everything against it.

CONTINUING HEALTHCARE

5.38 The current position in England,[27] as from 1 April 2013, is set out in the 'National Framework for NHS Continuing Healthcare and NHS-funded Nursing Care, November 2012 (Revised)'.[28] Its avowed purpose is to focus on the process for establishing eligibility for CHC and the principles of care planning and dispute resolution relevant to this process. As its title indicates it also relates to the provision of NHS-funded care by a registered nurse in nursing homes and it covers packages of care provided jointly by the NHS and a local authority, which topics are addressed below.

5.39 The guidance refers to CHC as a package of ongoing care that is arranged and funded solely by the NHS where an adult has been found to have a 'primary health need' and that is intended to meet needs that have arisen as a result of disability, accident or illness. It can be provided in any setting outside of hospital, whether in a nursing or care home, a hospice or a person's own home.

5.40 The guidance acknowledges that a person who needs ongoing care may require services arranged for by the NHS and/or by local authorities and that they therefore together have a responsibility to ensure that the assessment of eligibility for this and its provision take place in a timely and consistent manner (which is a bold aspiration given the sums of money there can be at stake).

5.41 It explains that even if a person does not qualify for CHC the NHS may nonetheless be responsible for contributing to his health needs, whether by providing services on its own or as part of a joint package with a local authority, whether in a nursing or care home or in a person's own home.

5.42 To a significant extent what then follows in the National Framework is a synopsis of Part 6 of the Standing Rules regulations,[29] which came fully into force on 1 April 2013 and of the accompanying documents.[30] The regulations are particularly important because, for the first time in legislation, they set out

---

27 The equivalent in Wales is 'Continuing NHS Healthcare, The National Framework for Implementation in Wales', May 2010, Welsh Assembly Circular 015/2010.

28 Issued in conjunction with the 'NHS Continuing Healthcare Checklist, November 2012 (Revised)' the Decision Support Tool for NHS Continuing Healthcare, November 2012 (Revised)' and the 'Fast Track Pathway Tool for NHS Continuing Healthcare, November 2012 (Revised) – the 'Checklist', the 'DST' and the 'FTPT'.

29 See fn 4 above – Part 6 comprises regs 20 to 32 inclusive.

30 See fn 28 above.

the test for whether someone has a primary health need, as established by case-law.[31] By reg 21(7), a person has such a need if the nursing or health services he needs are:

- where he is, or is to be accommodated in relevant premises[32] (ie a registered care home), more than incidental or ancillary to the provision of accommodation which a social services authority is, or would be but for a person's means, under a duty to provide, or (in order to cater for non-residential care);
- of a nature beyond which a social services authority whose primary responsibility is to provide social services could be expected to provide.

5.43 If the health body concerned decides that the nursing or health services required, when considered in their totality, fall within either category it must decide that he has a primary health need, in which case it must also decide that he is eligible for CHC.[33]

5.44 It is to be noted that in carrying out its duties under reg 21 the health body must have regard to the National Framework.[34]

5.45 In order to refine this test further the National Framework identifies certain characteristics of need that help to determine whether the nature or the amount of social care needed is outwith the responsibility of a local authority. These characteristics are the nature, intensity, complexity and unpredictability of needs.

Decision Support Tool

5.46 At the heart of the guidance lies the DST, which has been developed by the NHS in an attempt to minimise any variation in the application of the primary health need test. In essence it is a score-sheet for a range of domains, which are:

- behaviour**
- cognition*
- psychological and emotional needs
- communication
- mobility*

---

31 See *Regina v North and East Devon Health Authority ex p Coughlan* [2001] QB 213.

32 These are premises where 'regulated activity' is carried on and for which there is a 'registered person', such activity being the provision of residential accommodation, together with personal or nursing care, as specified in para 2 of Sch 1 to the Health and Social Care Act 2008 (Regulated Activities) Regulations 2010, SI 2010/781 and such a person registered with the Care and Quality Commission under Chapter 2 of Part 1 of the Health and Social Care Act 2008 as a service provider or manager; see reg 20(1) of the Standing Rules regulations.

33 See reg 21(6).

34 See reg 21(12).

- nutrition*
- continence
- skin and tissue viability*
- breathing**
- drug therapies**
- altered states of consciousness**
- other significant health needs*

5.47 For all domains there are these levels of need: no, low, moderate and high. For those with one asterisk there is, in addition, a severe level of need and for those with two asterisks there is also a priority level of need. These levels are expressed as N, L, M, H, S and P in the DST.

5.48 In the DST itself there is an introductory note for each domain followed by an instruction on the content of the assessment followed by a description of need that equates to a particular level of need.

5.49 For example, the introductory note as regards cognition explains that this domain may apply but is not limited to individuals with learning disability and/or acquired and degenerative disorders. It then instructs the user of the tool to describe actual needs (including episodic and fluctuating needs) and to provide the evidence that informs the decision on which level is appropriate, including the frequency and intensity of need, unpredictability, deterioration and any instability. Also, where cognitive impairment has an impact on behaviour this is to be taken into account in the behaviour domain as well.

5.50 These are the descriptions of need in respect of the cognition domain (verbatim) which is the most relevant to a person with dementia:

- Low

  Cognitive impairment which requires some supervision, prompting or assistance with more complex activities of daily living, such as finance and medication, but awareness of basic risks that affect their safety is evident. Or occasional difficulty with memory and decisions/choices requiring support, prompting or assistance. However, the individual has insight into their impairment.
- Moderate

  Cognitive impairment (which may include some memory issues) that requires some supervision, prompting and/or assistance with basic care needs and daily living activities. Some awareness of needs and basic risks is evident. The individual is usually able to make choices appropriate to needs with assistance. However, the individual has limited ability even with supervision, prompting or assistance to make decisions about some aspects of their lives, which consequently puts them at some risk of harm, neglect or health deterioration.
- High

Cognitive impairment that *could* include frequent short-term memory issues and maybe disorientation to time and place. The individual has awareness of only a limited range of needs and basic risks. Although they may be able to make some choices appropriate to need on a limited range of issues they are unable to consistently do so on most issues, even with supervision, prompting or assistance. The individual finds it difficult even with supervision, prompting or assistance to make decisions about key aspects of their lives, which consequently puts them at high risk of harm, neglect or health deterioration.

- Severe
  Cognitive impairment that *may*, for example, include, marked short-term memory issues, problems with long-term memory or severe disorientation to time, place or person.

The individual is unable to assess basic risks even with supervision, prompting or assistance, and is dependent on others to anticipate their basic needs and to protect them from harm, neglect or health deterioration.

5.51 The fundamental point about the DST is that a clear recommendation of eligibility for CHC would be expected if needs reach the priority level in any one of the four domains that include this level or if needs reach the severe level for at least two domains.[35] Where there is one domain at severe level, together with needs in a number of other domains or a number of domains at high and/or moderate levels this may also indicate a primary health need.

Eligibility process

5.52 In general a CCG has the initial responsibility for the eligibility process, ie up until an application for a review is made by a person dissatisfied with a CHC decision, when the NHS Commissioning Board ('the Board') takes over.[36]

5.53 The CCG must take reasonable steps to ensure that an assessment of eligibility is carried out where it appears to it that there may be a need for CHC or a person already in receipt of CHC[37] may no longer be eligible.[38] The use of the word 'may' indicates that in each case there is a low threshold.

5.54 The question of capacity arises at this point. The National Framework cautions that, as with any examination or treatment, informed consent should be obtained for each stage of the eligibility process and for personal information to be shared between those involved in it, for example a local authority in carrying out an assessment of needs and the Board on a review (see below).

---

35 See para 31 of the DST.

36 The Board also has initial responsibility for the eligibility process for some specified groups, for example prisoners and military personnel – see reg 20(2)(b).

37 Including from before 1 April 2013 – see reg 32(1).

38 See reg 21(2).

5.55 It also envisages that some people, with the requisite capacity, may refuse to engage in the eligibility process, in which case there could be tension between the CCG and the local authority concerned. Also, there could be tension between the CCG and the person concerned, if the CCG considers he may no longer be eligible for CHC. The likely result in such cases is that the CCG (and in due course the local authority if there is to be an assessment of needs following screening – see below) should proceed on the basis of information that is otherwise available, including in using the Checklist and in carrying out the assessment of need.

5.56 If, however, the person concerned does not appear to have the requisite capacity, the relevant principles set out in the MCA 2005 must be applied and if it is determined that capacity is lacking a best interests decision must be made, again in accordance with that Act. The National Framework advises that in making such a decision the expectation is that everyone who is potentially eligible for CHC should have the opportunity to be considered for it (and, presumably, the opportunity to retain it if the CCG wants to challenge eligibility). This advice holds good for each decision to be made in respect of the eligibility process, for example a decision to ask the Board for a review of eligibility.

5.57 If the CCG wishes to use an initial screening process to decide whether to undertake an assessment of eligibility it must use the Checklist, inform the person concerned or 'someone lawfully acting on his behalf' in writing of the decision as to whether to carry out a full assessment of eligibility and make a record of the decision.[39]

5.58 The concept of someone lawfully acting on a person's behalf appears elsewhere in the regulations[40] but, in the case of a person who lacks the requisite capacity, it is highly unlikely to refer only to someone who holds a power of attorney (let alone a welfare deputy), because in their absence there should always be someone other than the CCG who can consider the next step in the process of challenging a CHC decision. This may be a family member or a friend or, in their absence, an IMCA. A better term in the circumstances is a person's representative, which in fact is used throughout the National Framework and the accompanying Checklist and DST.

5.59 The stated aim of the Checklist is to allow a variety of people in a variety of settings to refer individuals for a full assessment of eligibility for CHC, so that it can be used in hospital as part of a discharge pathway, by a GP or nurse in a person's home or by a local authority in carrying out a community care assessment.

5.60 The Checklist is based on the DST, so that there are the same 12 domains. For each there are the same descriptions of level of need as there for

---

39 See reg 21(4).

40 See regs 21(10) and 23(3) – and also 21(11), which omits the word 'lawfully'; presumably in error.

the DST but they are grouped into three categories or columns: A, B and C. Column A contains the corresponding description for the high level for each domain, column B the corresponding descriptions for the moderate level and column C the corresponding descriptions for the no and low levels.

5.61 The assessor is instructed to compare the descriptions of need to the person's needs and select the column for each domain that most closely matches his needs. If his needs are the same or greater than anything in column A then A should be selected. For each domain the assessor should give a brief reference to where the evidence for his conclusion is to be found.

5.62 Where it can reasonably be anticipated that the individual's needs are likely to increase in the next 3 months (eg because of an expected deterioration in his condition), this should be reflected in the columns selected. Where the extent of a need may appear to be less because good care and treatment is reducing the effect of a condition, the need should be recorded in the Checklist as if that care and treatment was not being provided.

5.63 Crucially, the guidance states that a full assessment for CHC is required if there are (at least):

- two or more domains selected in column A;
- five or more domains selected in column B or one selected in column A and four in B;
- one domain selected in column A if it is one of the four that has a priority level of need (see **5.46**), whatever the other selections are.

5.64 Also crucially (and enigmatically), the guidance states that there may also be circumstances where a full assessment is considered necessary even though the individual does not apparently meet the indicated threshold.

5.65 The Checklist commentary states that the person assessed and/or his representative should be advised that if they disagree with the decision they may ask the CCG to reconsider it, who should then review the result taking into account any new information available. This might result in a further Checklist being completed. The CCG must then give a clear and written response as soon as reasonably practicable, to include details of the right to make a complaint under the NHS complaints procedure.[41] Under the regulations there is no right to a review of a screening decision.

5.66 If a person is not screened out there must be an assessment of needs, which must be carried out by a multi-disciplinary team.[42] This must be an accurate reflection of the person's need as at the date of the assessment of

---

41 See Chapter 11 for information about making a complaint.

42 A team consisting of at least two professionals who are from different healthcare professions (ie a profession concerned, wholly or partly, with the physical or mental health of individuals)

eligibility and the team must use this assessment of needs to complete the DST. Also, the CCG must ensure that it uses the completed DST to inform its decision on eligibility.

5.67 The National Framework guidance requires this assessment of needs to be a comprehensive assessment of an individual's health and social care needs and their desired outcomes and he must be given every opportunity to participate in it and given the option of being supported or represented by another in order to achieve this.

5.68 As set out above, if the CCG decides he has a primary health need it must also decide that he is eligible for CHC.

5.69 This process does not, however, have to be followed where an appropriate clinician[43] decides that a person has a primary health need arising from a rapidly deteriorating condition and that the condition may be entering a terminal phase and he has completed a Fast Track Pathway Tool ('FTPT') stating reasons for the decision.

5.70 A CCG must, on receipt of a FTPT so completed, decide that that person is eligible for CHC.

5.71 Where an assessment of eligibility has been carried out or a CCG has received a completed FTPT it must notify the person assessed (or his representative) in writing of the eligibility decision, the reasons for it and, where applicable the matters referred to in reg 21(11) (see below) and it must make a record of the decision. The DST commentary states that the decision should normally be made within 28 days.

5.72 By reg 21(11), where a CCG has decided that a person is not eligible for CHC it must inform him (or his representative) of the circumstances and manner in which he may apply for a review of the decision if dissatisfied with the procedure followed or with the primary health need decision.

5.73 Each CCG should have its own resolution procedure, ordinarily to be used before the matter is referred to the Board. The National Framework requires it to include timescales and to be publicly available. A copy should be sent to a person who seeks a review.

5.74 Where a person (or his representative) is dissatisfied with the procedure or the decision and he has used the resolution procedure but it has not resolved

---

or one healthcare professional and one person who is responsible for assessing persons for community care services under s 47 of the National Health Service and Community Care Act 1990 – see reg 21(11).

43 A person who is responsible for the diagnosis, treatment or care of the person concerned under the NHSA 2006 and who is a registered nurse or a registered medical practitioner – see reg 21(11).

the matter or he has not used the procedure and the Board is satisfied that requiring him to do so would cause undue delay, he may apply in writing to the Board for a review of the decision.

5.75 Following receipt of an application the Board may refer the matter for a decision to a review panel consisting of a chair, one CCG member (from a CCG whose procedure or decision is not the subject of the review) and one social services authority member (from an authority whose area is not situated in all or part of the area of the CCG whose procedure or decision is the subject of the review). The procedure and operation of the review panel are to be a matter for the chair, having regard to the National Framework.[44]

5.76 The National Framework states that a panel's recommendation should be accepted by the Board in all but exceptional circumstances and if the Board does not accept it, it must explain its reasons in writing to the person concerned, the CCG and the panel's chair.

5.77 The Board must, as soon as reasonably practicable, give notice in writing of the review decision and the reasons for it to the applicant and, where a CCG has made the decision, to it as well.

5.78 The CCG whose decision has been reviewed must, unless it determines there are exceptional reasons not to do so (for which purpose it must have regard to the National Framework), implement the decision of the review panel as soon as reasonably practicable.

5.79 Joint working between CCGs and local authorities in respect of the initial process is governed, so far as CCGs are concerned, by the Standing Rules regulations and, so far as local authorities are concerned, by corresponding directions made under s 7A of the Local Authority Social Services Act 1970.[45]

5.80 A CCG must consult with an authority before making a decision about eligibility (or ineligibility) and must co-operate with it in arranging for persons to participate in a multi-disciplinary team. Likewise, when consulted the authority must, so far as it is reasonably practicable, provide advice and assistance to the CCG and must, when asked to do so, co-operate as regards participation in the team. This does not affect an authority's duty to carry out an assessment under s 47 of the National Health Service and Community Care Act ('NHSCCA').

5.81 Where there is a dispute between a CCG and an authority about an eligibility decision or, where the person concerned is ineligible for CHC, about the contribution each is to make to a joint package of care for him, both bodies

---

44 If, as at 1 April 2013, a screening process was not complete or a review was outstanding the regulations still apply – see reg 32.

45 The NHS Continuing Healthcare (Responsibilities of Social Services Authorities) Directions 2013.

must, having regard to the National Framework, agree a dispute resolution procedure and resolve their disagreement in accordance with it.

5.82 Both CCGs and local authorities must throughout have due regard to the need to promote and secure the continuity of appropriate services for persons who are receiving community care services under s 47 of the NHSCCA on the date on which they are found to be eligible for CHC or who have been in receipt of CHC but are found to be no longer eligible for it or who are otherwise determined to be ineligible for it.

JOINT PACKAGES OF CARE

5.83 A person may not be eligible for CHC and yet receive NHS medical care as part of a joint package agreed between a CCG and a local authority. This will be so where his needs as a whole are not beyond the powers of an authority to meet but some of them, as identified by the DST, are not of a nature that the authority should meet on its own.

NHS-FUNDED NURSING CARE

5.84 By reason of s 49 of the Health and Social Care Act 2001 a local authority cannot provide 'nursing care by a registered nurse', which care comprises any services provided by a registered nurse that involves the provision of care or the planning, supervision or delegation of the provision of care, other than services that, having regard to their nature and the circumstances of their provision, do not need to be provided by a registered nurse.

5.85 It is important to note that this section concerns the provision of care rather than treatment. In *Minister of Health v General Committee of the Royal Midland Counties Home for Incurables Leamington Spa*[46] the Court of Appeal considered the former to be 'the homely art of making people comfortable and providing for their well-being so far as their condition allows' and the latter to be 'the exercise of professional skill to remedy the disease or disability, or to lessen its ill-effects or the pain and suffering which it occasions'.

5.86 Where it appears to a CCG in respect of a person for whom it has responsibility that he is resident in 'relevant premises'[47] or may need to become resident in such premises and may be in need of nursing care,[48] it must carry out an assessment of the need for nursing care ('nursing assessment') – unless he is in receipt of CHC. Before it does so, however, the CCG must consider

---

46 [1950] Ch 530.

47 See fn 7 above.

48 This means 'nursing care by a registered nurse', which has the same meaning as in s 49 of the Health and Social Care Act 2001.

whether it owes him a duty under reg 21(2) as regards eligibility for CHC and, if so, it must comply with reg 21 before it carries out a nursing assessment.

5.87 Where the CCG has carried out an assessment of eligibility for CHC but decided he is ineligible it must nevertheless use that assessment, wherever reasonably practicable, in making a nursing assessment.

5.88 Where the CCG determines that a person has a need for nursing care and he has agreed with it that he does want to be provided with such care then the CCG must pay the 'registered person',[49] in effect the home, the flat rate in respect of his nursing care unless or until it is later determined he does not need such care or he leaves the home or he becomes eligible for CHC or (of course) he dies. These same regulations provide that the flat rate (at the time of publication) is £108.70 per week.[50]

5.89 Although the use of the words 'has agreed' suggests that the resident must have the capacity to decide to agree or not there can be little doubt that his representative could agree on his behalf, alternatively that a best interests decision could be made in favour of the payment being made.

5.90 Where before 1 April 2013 a PCT was making a flat rate payment to a home under directions made in 2007[51] the CCG must continue to make them, unless or until one of the trigger events described above occurs.

5.91 Before 1 October 2007 there were three rates or bands of payment (high, medium and low) for nursing care but these were abolished in favour of a flat rate, save that payments at the high rate continued for those entitled to them before then. The Standing Rules regulations continue this protection for them, unless or until one of the trigger events described above occurs or unless the following paragraph applies.

5.92 Where a person in respect of whom a high band payment is being made has a nursing assessment on or after 1 April 2013 and following this it is determined that his need has diminished to the extent that if former guidance on nursing care[52] were applied he would be eligible only for a medium or low band payment, the CCG must give him (and where appropriate his representative) and the home written notice of the outcome of the assessment and must, no sooner than 14 days from when the notice is given, make the flat rate payment, unless or until as above.

---

49 See fn 7 above.

50 See reg 20(1).

51 NHS (Nursing Care in Residential Accommodation) (England) Directions 2007.

52 'Guidance on Free Nursing Care in Nursing Homes' dated 25 September 2001 and 'NHS Funded Nursing Care Practice Guidance and Workbook (August 2001) dated 5 September 2001, as supplemented by 'NHS Continuing Health Care: Action following the Grogan Judgment' dated 3 March 2006.

5.93 The high band rate is (at the time of publication) £149.60 per week.[53]

5.94 A CCG is not, however, prevented from providing nursing care for a person on a temporary basis without carrying out a nursing assessment if, in its opinion, his condition is such that it is needed urgently.

5.95 The Standing Rules regulations do not provide for a procedure for a review of a nursing care decision but the associated practice guidance[54] states that if the individual (or, presumably, his representative) is dissatisfied with the outcome of such a decision he is entitled to ask for a review before he makes, if then necessary, a complaint. This certainly gives rise to a legitimate expectation of a review, so that a CCG (or, arguably, the Board) would have to carry one out, perhaps in keeping with the wording of the regulations as regards a CHC review. Helpfully this guidance also mentions that the CCG should provide information about advocacy services from Healthwatch,[55] local Independent Complaints Advocacy Services (ICAS) and/or other local advocacy providers who can support the aggrieved through the process.

---

[53] See reg 20(1).

[54] See 'NHS-funded Nursing Care Practice Guide July 2013 (Revised)', para 57.

[55] This is a committee of the CQC whose aim is to be 'the new consumer champion for health and adult social care in England'.

CHAPTER 6

LOCAL AUTHORITY CARE

6.1 The purpose of this chapter is to map out in summary form the core underpinning for the current provision of care by local authorities. Such provision is presently governed by a bewildering (even to lawyers) and sometimes overlapping hotch-potch of statutes, regulations, directions, orders and guidance (both policy and practice guidance[1]) that for many years has needed to be transformed and modernised by the introduction of one all-embracing statute, albeit with attendant regulations and guidance. This is soon to be achieved, in England, when the Care Bill has passed through Parliament.[2]

6.2 One of the reforms intended by this Bill is to give local authorities much greater freedom to decide on the nature of the care services a person may need rather than, as the current legislation does, to prescribe more or less exactly what these could be. The vehicle for this particular reform is at the date of publication clause 8, which gives general examples of what may be provided to meet needs:

(1) accommodation in a care home or in premises of some other type;

(2) care and support at home or in the community;

(3) counselling and other types of social work;

(4) goods and facilities;

(5) information, advice and advocacy.

6.3 That said there is generally little difficulty in local authorities acknowledging that they can provide the type of care and support that someone with dementia typically needs, without having to delve too far (if at all) into the legislation and its accompanying guidance. Aside from residential care, in a nursing or care home, such care and support is likely to be personal care at home, home help, meals at home, day centres and equipment. Where there tends to be difficulty is with regard to the extent of care an authority is able and

---

1 For this purpose 'policy guidance' is statutory guidance issued under s 7(1) of the Local Authority Social Services Act 1970 ('LASSA 1970'), by which local authorities must, in the exercise of their social services functions, act under the general guidance of the SSH – 'practice guidance' is non-statutory and local authorities need only have regard to it.

2 Its equivalent in Wales is the Social Services and Well-being (Wales) Bill.

willing to provide, which difficulty is likely to intensify as life expectancy increases – and, subject to any breakthroughs in treatment, more and more people with dementia.

SERVICE PROVISION DECISION

6.4 Once a local authority has carried out an assessment of a person's needs for community care services, under s 47 of the National Health Service and Community Care Act 1990 ('NHSCCA 1990'), it must decide whether his needs call for the provision by it of any such services.[3]

6.5 These services are defined by s 46(3) of the same Act as being those a local authority may provide or arrange to be provided under Part III of the National Assistance Act 1948 ('NAA 1948'), s 45 of the Health and Services and Public Health Act 1968 ('HSPHA 1968'), Schedule 20 to the National Health Service Act 2006 ('NHSA 2006') (and Schedule 15 to the National Health Service (Wales) Act 2006) and s 117 of the Mental Health Act 1983 ('MHA 1983').

6.6 Part III of the NAA 1948 provides for two types of service, namely residential care under s 21 and non-residential care under s 29. For the most part the other community care enactments provide for non-residential care, save that s 117 of the MHA 1983 can also be (and often is) the foundation for the provision of residential care as well.

Section 21 of the NAA 1948

6.7 By s 21(1)(a), a local authority can come under a duty to make arrangements for providing residential accommodation for persons aged 18 or over who by reason of age, illness, disability or any other circumstance are in need of care and attention that is not otherwise available to them. Whether there is a duty to accommodate such a person or only a power to do so depends on whether the Secretary of State for Health has made a direction (ie imposed a duty) or given his approval (ie created a power), a mechanism that s 21 has in common with s 29 of the same Act and some of the other community care enactments.[4] The precise terms of these directions and approvals can give rise to intricate legal arguments but do not need to be explored at all for the purposes of this book.

6.8 By reason of s 21(5), accommodation includes 'board and other services, amenities and requisites' provided in connection with it unless their provision is considered to be unnecessary. Although this does not specify the provision of care it is generally recognised that it is covered by this phrase, not least because it is difficult to see how else it could be provided for in legislation.

---

3 See the closing words of sub-s (1).

4 See the three appendices to Local Authority Circular ('LAC') (93)10 concerning, respectively, ss 21 and 29 of the NAA 1948 and Sch 20 to the NHSA 2006.

6.9 For the purposes of s 21(1)(a), a need for care and attention is a need to be looked after and looking after someone means doing something for him that he cannot, or cannot be expected to do for himself, for example household tasks or personal care such as feeding, washing and toileting.[5] It does not include medical treatment, nor the provision of anything that the NHS has decided to or must provide,[6] so that if a person has been found to be eligible for Continuing Healthcare ('CHC') in the form of accommodation (and care with it) in a care or nursing home a local authority is prohibited from providing this service instead.

6.10 As for whether the care and attention needed is otherwise available, there are two facets to this. The first is that it must not be available otherwise than by the provision of accommodation under s 21, ie the need must be accommodation-related.[7] If a person with dementia, for example, can no longer manage in his own home, even with a substantial package of care, then he has reached the point when the care and attention he needs is only available in a care or nursing home. The position is very different where the person concerned is homeless (for example, a destitute asylum-seeker), in which case in order to obtain accommodation under s 21 he need only show that he needs some care and attention, which if he had a home he could have in the form of a care package there. If this is so he will be provided with ordinary accommodation, rather than accommodation in a care or nursing home. It is beyond the scope of this book to explore any further the complexities of community care for persons who have no recourse to public funds.

6.11 The second facet is that the care and attention may be otherwise available if the person concerned can afford to pay for residential care himself in the sense that his resources are above the limit set by regulations made under s 22 of the NAA 1948.[8] Local authorities generally refer to such a person as a 'self-funder'.

6.12 The fact that a person may appear to an authority on first presentation to be a self-funder does not, however, mean that on this basis it can avoid a duty to assess his needs for services under s 47 of the NHSCCA 1990, for which there is a very low threshold. Nor, if it is established following a financial assessment that he is indeed a self-funder, does it necessarily mean that the authority is not under a duty to make arrangements for providing accommodation for him. Indeed, the basis of charging for residential care is that those who, according to the charging regulations, can afford to repay the authority in full for its cost must do so, the premise, arguably, being that the authority must accommodate self-funders who want it to do so, perhaps in

---

5 See *R (M) v Slough BC* [2008] UKHL 52, at [33].

6 See s 21(8), which provides that nothing in the section authorises or requires a local authority to make any provision authorised or required under the NHSA 2006.

7 See *R (SL) v Westminster CC* [2013] UKSC 27.

8 National Assistance Act (Assessment of Resources) Regulations 1992, SI 1992/2977 – also see the 'Charging for Residential Accommodation Guidance' ('CRAG') which explains and expands on them. See also Chapter 10.

order to have the advantage of the cheaper rates available to local authorities as bulk-purchasers. The better view, however, is likely to be that an authority can find there is no duty if the self-funder can make his own arrangements or has a family member or friend (or attorney or Court of Protection deputy) who can make them on his behalf – and that it is only under a duty to make the arrangements for him if he has no such assistance available.

Which local authority is responsible for providing accommodation?

6.13 The local authority that is responsible for providing residential accommodation under section 21(1)(a) is the one in whose area the person concerned is 'ordinarily resident'. This phrase is not defined by the NAA 1948 but case-law has established that for its purposes a person's ordinary residence is where he has chosen to live for settled purposes as part of the regular order of his life for the time being, whether of short or long duration.[9] Where a person lacks the capacity to decide where to live there is a variation to this test, to the effect that if his parents remain close to him he is resident where they are and if he is not close to them (or, obviously, if they are dead) only the remainder of the test applies, i e where he lives as part of the regular order of his life.[10]

6.14 Although both tests appear to be relatively straightforward their application can be very complicated indeed and can give rise to protracted disputes between local authorities. As far as the service-user is concerned, however, the existence of such a dispute should not impact on the provision of services for him, because one of the authorities involved (sometimes there are more than two) should take provisional responsibility pending the outcome of the dispute.

6.15 The intricacies of the law on ordinary residence are beyond the scope of this book but some knowledge of the procedure by which they are resolved will be of assistance.

6.16 By s 32(1) of the NAA 1948 any expenditure incurred by one local authority in providing accommodation under s 21 for a person ordinarily resident in the area of another authority (or in providing non-residential care under s 29 of the same Act – see below[11]) is recoverable from the other authority. By s 32(3), if the authorities involved cannot agree on where he is ordinarily resident the dispute must be referred to the Secretary of State for Health (or the Welsh Ministers[12]) who will then determine the issue in

---

9 See *R v Barnet LBC ex p Shah* [1983] 2 AC 309, referred to below as '*Shah*'.

10 See *R v Waltham Forest LBC ex p Vale* (unreported) – but note that at the time of publication the first limb is the subject of an appeal, from the decision in *R (Cornwall CC) v SSH* [2012] EWHC 3739.

11 Or services under s 2 of the Chronically Sick and Disabled Persons Act 1970 ('CSDPA 1970) – see s 2(1A) of that Act.

12 Arrangements have been made between the SSH and the Welsh Ministers about cross-border disputes.

accordance with the 'Ordinary Residence Guidance' issued by his department (originally in April 2011 and since updated in March 2013). If an authority is aggrieved by a determination it can challenge it by means of judicial review.

6.17 Paragraph 5 of this guidance refers to how the assessment process and the provision of services should never be held up because of uncertainty about which authority is responsible. This is founded on directions issued[13] under the NAA 1948 and under s 7A of the Local Authority Social Services Act 1970 ('LASSA 1970') (which means that local authorities must follow them) that set out the steps to be taken by authorities when they are in dispute. Direction 2 states that they must not allow the existence of the dispute to prevent, delay or otherwise adversely affect the provision of services and one of them must take provisional responsibility for their provision. If the authorities cannot agree on which is to do so, the one in whose area the person concerned is living must take provisional responsibility, and if he is homeless the one in whose area he is physically present should do so.

6.18 It should be noted that although the outcome of such a dispute could affect the nature and extent of services to be provided for the person concerned (particularly in a s 29 case) neither these directions nor the guidance contemplate his participation in the determination and as far as the authors know no-one in this position has ever sought to intervene. He would, however, be named as a matter of course as an interested party if, following a determination under s 32(3), a local authority decided to bring a claim for a judicial review against the Secretary of State and so he could therefore at this later stage become actively involved in the dispute, if he wished.

6.19 If the person concerned is not ordinarily resident in any local authority's area, typically because he is homeless, the responsible authority is the one for the area in which he is present at the time he is in need of residential accommodation.

6.20 Another aspect of s 24 that is of considerable importance in ordinary residence disputes is that it contains two deeming provisions.[14] The first is that if a person is provided with accommodation under s 21 he is deemed for the purposes of the NAA 1948 to continue to be ordinarily resident in the area in which he had this status immediately before the accommodation was provided for him. It follows that if the authority in which he is ordinarily resident as a matter of fact accommodates him outside its area it nonetheless remains responsible for him, as a matter of law, for as long it continues to accommodate him, even though otherwise, as a matter of fact, he may become ordinarily resident (in accordance with the test in *Shah*[15]) in the new area. This provision can be of particular significance where a person has settled in the care or nursing home in the new area and the original authority then stops paying for

---

13 Ordinary Residence Disputes (National Assistance Act 1948) Directions 2010.

14 A deeming provision is a statutory device by which a state of affairs is deemed to exist even though it may not exist as a matter of fact.

15 See fn 9.

him for a while, either because he is temporarily a self-funder or temporarily eligible for CHC. When his care is again paid for by a local authority he may well find it is the new authority that does so.

6.21 The second deeming provision concerns the provision of accommodation by the NHS, whether in a hospital or elsewhere. Where a person is provided with this he is deemed to be ordinarily resident in the area in which he had this status beforehand, whether or not in fact he continues to be ordinarily resident there.

Arrangements for accommodation

6.22 Although the NAA 1948 envisages that local authorities can themselves manage accommodation to be used for s 21 purposes, in practice they rely instead on the voluntary and private sectors. This is catered for by s 26 of the same Act, some parts of which are of particular interest and significance. Firstly, it enables the arrangements to be made with a voluntary organisation (which includes a housing association) or with any other person who is not a local authority where the organisation or person manages premises that provide for reward accommodation that falls within s 21.

6.23 Secondly, such arrangements may not be made if they are for accommodation together with nursing or personal care for persons such as are mentioned in s 3(2) of the Care Standards Act 2000 ('CSA 2000') unless the accommodation is in a care home (as defined by that Act) managed by the organisation or person and it or he is registered under Chapter 2 of Part 1 of the Health and Social Care Act 2008 ('HSCA 2008') in respect of a regulated activity carried on in the home (or in the case of a home in Wales, registered under Part 2 of the CSA 2000 in respect of it).

6.24 The key concepts here are as follows:

- Those who come within s 3(2) of the CSA 2000 are persons who are or have been ill, who have or have had a mental disorder, who are disabled or infirm and who are or have been dependent on alcohol or drugs.
- In general an establishment is a care home if it provides accommodation, together with nursing or personal care, for any of these persons.[16]
- The HSCA 2008 established, for England, the Care Quality Commission ('CQC'), whose functions under the same Act include the registration of service providers and managers in respect of regulated activities[17] involving or in connection with the provision of health or social care.

---

16 See s 3(1) of the CSA 2000 – and note the exceptions in s 3(3) as regards Wales and in s 3(4) as regards England.

17 As prescribed by the Health and Social Care Act 2008 (Regulated Activities) Regulations 2010, SI 2010/781 (as amended) (the 'Regulated Activities Regulations').

- Such activities include the provision of residential accommodation, together with nursing or personal care.[18]
- Nursing care means any services provided by a nurse and involving the provision of care or the planning, supervision or delegation of the provision of care, other than any services which, having regard to their nature and the circumstances in which they are provided, do not need to be provided by a nurse.[19]
- Personal care means physical assistance given to a person in connection with eating or drinking, toileting, washing or bathing, dressing, oral care, or the care of skin, hair and nails – or the prompting, together with supervision, of a person, in relation to the performance of any of these activities where that person is unable to make a decision for themselves in relation to performing such an activity without such prompting and supervision.[20]
- The registration of care homes in Wales, by the Care and Social Services Inspectorate in Wales ('CSSIW'), is still governed by Part 2 of the CSA 2000.

6.25 The net effect is that if, for example, a person with dementia needs accommodation together with nursing or personal care a local authority can only place him in a nursing or care home that is registered with the CQC or the CSSIW.

6.26 Thirdly, no arrangements may be made for the provision of accommodation with nursing unless the clinical commissioning group ('CCG') (or, in Wales, the Local Health Board ('LHB')) has consented or unless they need to be made urgently pending the receipt of such consent.[21]

Choice of accommodation

6.27 Another important aspect of the provision of residential care is that to some extent a person (or his representative) can choose a different home to the one the authority would ordinarily place them in, even if it is more expensive.

6.28 This is catered for by directions made under s 7A of the LASSA 1970 and by accompanying guidance.[22] The directions provide that where an authority has decided that accommodation should be provided under s 21 of the NAA 1948 for a person, it shall make arrangements for him to be accommodated at the place of his choice within England and Wales if he has indicated this to be

---

18 But this does not apply to the provision of accommodation to an individual by an adult placement carer under the terms of a carer agreement or in a school or in a further education institution or 16 to 19 Academy.

19 See reg 2 of the Regulated Activities Regulations.

20 Ibid.

21 See NAA 1948, s 26(1C).

22 National Assistance Act 1948 (Choice of Accommodation) Directions 1992 and LAC(2004)20.

his wish. Such accommodation is known as 'preferred accommodation'. Its provision is, however, subject to four conditions:

(1) the accommodation must appear to the authority to be suitable in relation to his needs as assessed by it;
(2) its cost would not require the authority to pay more than it would usually expect to pay having regard to his assessed needs;
(3) the accommodation is available;
(4) the persons in charge of it provide it subject to the authority's usual terms and conditions.

6.29 For the most part the guidance explains how these directions are intended to work in practice but it also explains the concept of 'topping-up', whereby a resident (actual or prospective) chooses accommodation that is more expensive than the authority is prepared to pay for but where (usually) a third party, such as a family member, is willing and able to pay the difference.[23]

6.30 In respect of both preferred accommodation and topping-up, the guidance acknowledges that there will be cases where the resident lacks the capacity to decide about these concepts and advises that in these circumstances it would be reasonable to expect an authority to act on the preference expressed by his 'advocate, carer or legal guardian' unless in its opinion this would be against the resident's best interests. Clearly nowadays decision-making in this regard would be guided by and would need to comply fully with the requirements of the MCA 2005.

6.31 As regards topping-up, a resident can do this himself during the 12-week property disregard period[24] or where he has entered into a deferred payments agreement[25] with the authority (in which case the top-up is added to the deferred contribution). Further information about both of these concepts is set out in Chapter 10.

Section 29 of the NAA 1948

6.32 By this section a local authority can come under a duty to make arrangements for promoting the welfare of persons aged 18 or over who are blind, deaf or dumb or who suffer from mental disorder of any description or who are substantially and permanently handicapped by illness, injury or congenital deformity.

---

23 See s 54 of the Health and Social Care Act 2001 and, made under it, the National Assistance (Residential Accommodation) (Additional Payments and Assessment of Resources) (Amendment) (England) Regulations 2001, SI 2001/3441.

24 In the case of a resident who becomes a permanent resident in respect of his first period of permanent residence the value of any dwelling which he would otherwise normally occupy as his only or main residence is, subject to certain conditions, disregarded for 12 weeks – see paragraph 1A of Schedule 4 to the charging regulations, paragraph 7.004 of CRAG paragraph 12 of the annex to LAC(2001)10.

25 See chapter 10.

6.33 The section goes on to give specific examples of such arrangements, including the giving of instruction in their own homes or elsewhere in methods of overcoming the effects of their disabilities and for providing recreational facilities in their homes or elsewhere. The scope of the section has been widened considerably since its inception by directions made by the Secretary of State for Health[26] and by s 2 of the Chronically Sick and Disabled Persons Act 1970 ('CSDPA 1970').

Section 2 of the CSDPA 1970

6.34 This is an adjunct to s 29. It does not use the approval/direction mechanism but instead directly imposes specific duties on local authorities in relation to those who come within that other section.

6.35 Section 2 provides that where an authority has functions under s 29 in respect of a person who is ordinarily resident in its area and it is satisfied it is necessary to make certain arrangements in order to meet his needs then it comes under a duty to do so. These arrangements include such fundamental matters as the provision of practical assistance in the home and the provision of facilities designed to secure greater safety, comfort and convenience but also arguably less fundamental ones (at least nowadays), such as the provision of wireless, television and library facilities.

Section 45 of the HSPHA 1968

6.36 The purpose of this section is to require or empower local authorities to make arrangements for promoting the welfare of 'old people' (which term is not defined) by means of non-residential care, on the basis there will be some who do not come within the terms of s 29 of the NAA 1948 (and s 2 of the CSDPA 1970). In common with that section it uses the mechanism of enabling the Secretary of State for Health to approve/direct the arrangements to be made.

6.37 As it happens only approvals have been made[27] and these empower local authorities to provide a range of services for the elderly that are similar to those that can, or must be provided under s 29 of the NAA 1948.

Schedule 20 to the NHSA 2006

6.38 The purpose of this Schedule is to enable local authorities to provide non-residential care for expectant and nursing mothers and for those who may become ill or who are or have been ill. Again, it employs the approval/direction mechanism and again, like s 29, there are in the section itself and in the approvals and directions made under it[28] specific examples of such services, most notably, for our purposes, centres or other facilities for keeping such

---

[26] See appendix 2 to LAC(93)10.
[27] See DHSS Circular 19/71.
[28] See Appendix 3 to LAC(93)10.

persons suitably occupied. It also enables local authorities to provide home help and laundry facilities for households where there is such a person or someone who is aged or handicapped as a result of having suffered from illness or by congenital deformity.

Section 117 of the MHA 1983

6.39 This requires certain persons who leave hospital[29] to be provided, if they need them, with 'after-care services', by both the NHS and local authorities. These services can include general social work, help with problems concerning accommodation and family relationships and the provision of domiciliary services, day centre use and residential care, as well as psychiatric treatment. The MHA 1983's English Code of Practice[30] describes after-care as being a vital component in patients' overall treatment and care – 'As well as meeting their immediate needs for health and social care, after-care should aim to support them in regaining their skills, or learning new skills, in order to cope with life outside hospital.'

6.40 Those who can be provided with after-care services under s 117 are those who have been detained in hospital under the MHA 1983, the ethos behind the need for special treatment for them being that they are likely to be those who most need intensive support once they are back in the community, otherwise they may have to return to hospital.

6.41 They include, in particular, those who have been admitted to hospital (and detained there) under s 3 of the MHA 1983. Others who benefit are those who have been admitted to hospital pursuant to a hospital order made under s 37 of the Act (made on conviction in a magistrates' or Crown Court) or transferred there under s 45A (by the Crown Court) or ss 47 or 48 (from prison).

6.42 The responsibility for providing these services is shared, jointly, in each person's case by, in England, a CCG or, in Wales, a LHB and, in both countries, by a social services authority, ie a local authority that has social services functions. In general the duty continues until the NHS body and the local authority concerned are satisfied that the 'patient' is no longer in need of such services. They cannot, however, be so satisfied in the case of a community patient, ie a patient in respect of whom a community treatment order made under s 17A of the same Act is in force.[31]

---

29 Including on s 17 leave.

30 See para 27.5 – by s 118 of the MHA the SSH (and the Welsh Ministers) must maintain a code of practice that mental health professionals must follow unless, in accordance with *R (Munjaz) v Mersey Care NHS Trust* [2005] UKHL 58, there is good reason not to.

31 A patient who has been detained for treatment under s 3 and who is discharged from hospital for treatment in the community but who remains subject to recall to hospital.

6.43 The responsible NHS body is determined by reference to s 3(1A) of the National Health Service Act 2006 and regulations made under it.[32] In England the position is that if a person is registered with a GP then the responsible body is the CCG of which the GP is a member. In Wales the responsible body is the LHB for the area in which the person concerned considers he is usually resident.

6.44 The responsible social services authority is the one in whose area the patient is resident or to which he is sent on discharge by the hospital in which he was detained. 'Resident' for these purposes means where he was living at the time he was detained, no matter whether on discharge he has a home he can return to there.[33] If he was not resident anywhere at that time, which in practice is highly unlikely, the responsible authority is the one for the area to which the hospital sends him. There can be disputes between local authorities about responsibility but a person's discharge should not be delayed because of this and it is generally accepted, and would be ordered by the High Court if there had to be a claim for judicial review, that one authority must accept provisional responsibility pending the outcome of any dispute and that the other should reimburse it if it loses.

6.45 There is also some scope for disputes between NHS bodies and local authorities, as regards cost-sharing, including as to whether the patient is instead eligible for CHC – and would therefore have no need for after-care services. The National Framework for NHS Continuing Healthcare and NHS-funded Nursing Care[34] expresses the view that it is not necessary to assess eligibility for CHC if all the services needed by the patient are to be provided as after-care services under s 117, because both CHC and s 117 after-care are provided for free – see below.

6.46 This is a naive view, because although it does not matter to the patient which category of care he receives it does matter to the local authority concerned, in that if he is eligible for CHC it does not have to pay towards it.

6.47 The National Framework is on firmer ground, however, when it advises that such a patient may also have or may develop care needs that are not related to their mental disorder, in which case a decision on eligibility for CHC may be needed.[35]

6.48 The generally acknowledged test for deciding whether to provide a service as an after-care service is whether it is to be provided in order to meet an assessed need that arises from the person's mental disorder aimed at reducing his chances of being re-admitted to hospital for treatment for that disorder.[36]

---

[32] See regs 4 and 14 of the NHS Commissioning Board and CCGs (Responsibilities and Standing Rules) Regulations 2012, SI 2012/2996.

[33] See *R v Mental Health Review Tribunal ex p Hall* [1993] 3 All ER 1323.

[34] See para 121.

[35] See para 122.

[36] See *R (Mwanza) v Greenwich LBC* [2010] EWHC 1462, at [63] and [67], and para 31.2 of the Welsh Code of Practice.

6.49 As mentioned above, a crucial point about the provision of after-care in the form of social care is that its recipient cannot be charged for it, so that any residential or non-residential care provided is for free. There was a time when local authorities sought to charge those who had been placed in residential care, on the basis that s 117 was simply a gateway to other community care services and the substantive provision made in such a case was under s 21 of the NAA 1948, but in the case of *Stennett*[37] the House of Lords decided this was not so.

Accommodation

6.50 Although the issue of charging is therefore now well-settled another issue of some importance has emerged in the wake of the decision in *Stennett*, namely the nature of the accommodation that can be provided under s 117 – in particular, does it have to be specialist accommodation, such as a care or nursing home, or can it be ordinary (or bare) accommodation?

6.51 In *Stennett* it was agreed between the parties that a placement in a care home was within the scope of s 117(2) and the House concurred. Lord Steyn looked upon such accommodation as a caring environment that took the place of the hospital where treatment, for example medication, could continue if it was needed. In a 2011 case, *DM*,[38] Langstaff J explained the position more fully. He considered that a person receiving after-care is receiving care that is intrinsically linked to the medical treatment he has been receiving, in hospital, for his mental disorder, and that the background to this was the shift in policy away from, for most individuals, long-term detention for the purpose of treatment to a regime that bridged the gap between hospital and, if possible, an unsupported return to the community.

6.52 In *Mwanza*,[39] Hickinbottom J was faced with an attempt to use s 117 to obtain ordinary accommodation for a person who was unlawfully present in the UK and for his family as well. The judge therefore had to focus on the purpose of an after-care service, which he accepted is to meet a need arising from the disorder with the aim of preventing re-admission to hospital. He went on to contemplate that in theory ordinary accommodation (a 'mere roof over the head', as he put it) can meet such a need but accepted that in practice it was difficult to envisage this.

6.53 More recently, in the case of *Afework*,[40] Mostyn J has looked at this issue. He too could not think of an example of how ordinary accommodation could meet such a need and considered that the reason for this was that both in practice and in law it cannot do so. His judgment goes beyond this point, however, in that he found that for a placement in accommodation to qualify under s 117(2) it must be involuntary.

---

37 *R v Manchester CC ex p Stennett* [2002] UKHL 34.

38 *R (DM) v Doncaster MBC* [2011] EWHC 3652.

39 See fn 35 above.

40 *R (Afework) v Camden LBC* [2013] EWHC 1637.

6.54 His conclusions were as follows:

(1) The need for accommodation must be a direct result of the reason that the ex-patient was detained in the first place ('the original condition').
(2) The requirement must be for enhanced specialist accommodation to meet needs directly arising from the original condition.
(3) The ex-patient is being placed in the accommodation on an involuntary (in the sense of being incapacitated) basis arising as result of the original condition.

6.55 The first two findings are relatively uncontroversial but the last most certainly is. For example, if a patient has the capacity to decide where to live and chooses a particular care home he will, presumably, be placed there under s 21 of the NAA 1948 instead and must therefore be charged by the local authority for this.

6.56 This third finding appears to be derived from comments made by Lord Steyn in *Stennett* concerning how a tribunal can direct a patient to live at a particular placement on discharge and how it can therefore hardly be said that he freely chooses this accommodation. This, however, overlooks both the fact that he may have chosen it, albeit from a restricted range of similar placements, and that there are very many patients who have been detained, under s 3 in particular, and who are discharged without having to apply to a tribunal, for example if they again comply with their medication programme once back in hospital and appear committed to do so once back in the community. This decision is likely to give rise to further litigation on the point.

Planning for after-care

6.57 Although the duty to provide after-care services only begins when the person concerned leaves hospital, the planning for their provision should start as soon as he is admitted to hospital and the responsible NHS body and local authority must be involved in this.[41]

6.58 Those eligible for after-care on leaving hospital will have this planned for them through the Care Programme Approach ('CPA'), which is the framework that supports and co-ordinates mental health care for people with severe mental health problems in secondary mental health services.[42]

6.59 In addition to the patient himself, those involved in planning should include:

- His responsible clinician

---

41 See para 27.8 of the English Code of Practice and para 31. 7 of the Welsh Code.

42 See 'Refocusing the Care Programme Approach, Policy and Positive Practice Guidance' issued by the DH in March 2008 – since June 2012 it has been superseded in Wales by Part 2 of the Mental Health (Wales) Measure 2010.

- Nurses and other professionals involved in caring for the patient in hospital
- A clinical psychologist, community mental health nurse and other members of the community team
- The patient's GP and primary care team
- Subject to the patient's views, any carer who will be involved in looking after him outside hospital, the patient's nearest relative[43] or other family members
- A representative of any relevant voluntary organisations
- In the case of a restricted patient,[44] the probation service
- A representative of housing authorities, if accommodation is an issue
- An employment expert, if employment is an issue
- An independent mental health advocate,[45] if the patient has one
- An independent mental capacity advocate,[46] if the patient has one
- The patient's attorney or deputy, if the patient has one
- Any other representative nominated by the patient.

6.60 The English Code of Practice[47] advises that a thorough assessment of needs is likely to involve consideration of the following:

- Continuing mental healthcare in the community or as an out-patient
- The psychological needs of the patient and, where appropriate, of their family and carers
- Physical healthcare
- Daytime activities or employment
- Appropriate accommodation
- Identified risk and safety issues
- Any specific needs arising from, for example, co-existing physical disability, sensory impairment, learning disability or autistic spectrum disorder
- Any specific needs arising from drug, alcohol or substance misuse (if relevant)
- Any parenting or caring needs
- Social, cultural or spiritual needs
- Counselling and personal support
- Assistance in welfare rights and managing finances

---

43 He has a key formal role under the MHA 1983 in assisting the patient – his identity is determined by reference to s 26.

44 Generally a patient who is subject to a restriction order made under s 41 of the MHA 1983 – see s 79(1) for the full definition.

45 See MHA 1983, s 130A.

46 See Chapter 4.

47 See para 27.13.

- The involvement of authorities and agencies in a different area, if the patient is not going to live locally
- The involvement of other agencies, for example the probation service or voluntary organisations
- For a restricted patient, the conditions which the Secretary of State for Justice or the Tribunal has imposed or is likely to impose on their conditional discharge
- Contingency plans (should the patient's mental health deteriorate) and crisis contact details.

6.61 The professionals involved should, in discussion with the patient, agree an outline of his needs and a timescale for the implementation of the various aspects of the after-care plan. All key people with specific responsibilities should be identified and if approval for any aspect of the plan needs to be obtained from anyone senior to them it is important this does not result in any delay to the implementation of the plan.

6.62 The plan should, of course, be fully recorded in writing and once agreed it is essential that any proposed changes to it are discussed with the patient and others involved with him before they are implemented. There should be regular reviews, which are for the designated care co-ordinator to arrange.

Ending after-care

6.63 In general the duty to provide after-care services only ceases when the NHS body and the local authority concerned are agreed, following consultation with the person concerned and any representative of his, that such services are no longer needed because his mental health has improved. The English Code of Practice[48] warns against them being withdrawn or refused solely because he has been discharged from the care of specialist mental health services to the care of his GP, because an arbitrary period has passed, because he is deprived of his liberty under the MCA 2005, because he returns to hospital informally or is admitted to hospital for treatment under s 2 of the MHA 1983,[49] because is no longer on supervised community treatment or s 17 leave or because he has previously been unwilling to have them.

6.64 The English Code of Practice[50] also cautions that even if a former patient becomes well-settled in the community he may still continue to need after-care, for example in order to prevent a relapse or further deterioration.

---

48 See para 27.19 – and see para 31.13 of the Welsh Code.

49 There is some controversy about whether the duty to provide after-care services ceases automatically on the patient being detained again under other provisions of the Act, in particular s 3, on the basis that a fresh detention triggers a fresh duty when he again leaves hospital.

50 See para 27.21.

PRIORITISING NEED

6.65 Neither the NHSCCA 1990 nor any of the community care enactments, or any other legislation, explains how a local authority is to decide how to apply the service provision test, namely whether a person's needs call for the provision of community care services. Instead there is policy guidance that does so, namely 'Prioritising need in the context of Putting People First: A whole system approach to eligibility for social care', issued by the Department of Health in 2010. It relates to all of the community care enactments.

6.66 Its predecessor was the Fair Access to Care ('FACS') guidance issued in 2003. Although this has been superseded, some authorities and, indeed the Department of Health itself, still refer to it, in particular to 'FACS criteria'.[51]

6.67 The Prioritising Need guidance is described as guidance on eligibility criteria for adult social care and has been issued under s 7(1) of the LASSA 1970, which means it must be followed unless there is good reason not to do so.

6.68 It stems from the decision of the House of Lords in 1997, in a case known as *Barry*,[52] that a local authority can take its resources into account in deciding whether a person has a need for a service under s 2 of the CSDPA 1970 and/or whether it is necessary to meet the need. This decision is highly controversial, because it is capable of reducing a duty imposed by Parliament on local authorities to the status of a power, but even so the concept at its core, that need is relative, lives on in the guidance, which specifically requires local authorities to take account of their own resources.

6.69 Another perspective is that the guidance can also elevate a power to provide a community care service to the status of a duty, i e if a local authority is required to provide a service in order to meet an eligible need it must provide it, even though by statute it only has a discretion to do so.

6.70 The stated aim of Prioritising Need is to assist local authorities in determining eligibility for social care in a way that is fair, transparent and consistent and that accounts for the needs of their communities as well as the needs of the individuals within them for support.

6.71 The essential feature of the guidance is that it distinguishes between 'presenting needs' and 'eligible needs'. The former are those matters that the individual would like to be met and the latter are those of them that come within the authority's eligibility criteria and that it will therefore meet.

6.72 In order to assist local authorities in deciding what their criteria should be the guidance contains an eligibility framework, which is graded into four bands, namely critical, substantial, moderate and low. These bands describe the

---

51 See 6.71.

52 *R v Gloucestershire CC ex p Barry* [1997] AC 584.

seriousness of the risk to independence and well-being or other consequences if needs are not addressed. A local authority can decide for itself, on taking into account its resources, which bands or even which levels within bands, to cover but it is difficult to contemplate how an authority could ever fail to cover the critical band at the least. Not many now cover the low band and so the usual issue in practice is whether the authority in question covers critical, substantial and moderate or just critical and substantial. This variation in provision between authorities has given rise to concerns about there being a 'postcode lottery'.

6.73 These bands and their descriptors are as follows:

- Critical – when:
  - life is, or will be, threatened; and/or
  - significant health problems have developed or will develop; and/or
  - there is, or will be, little or no choice and control over vital aspects of the immediate environment; and/or
  - serious abuse or neglect has occurred or will occur; and/or
  - there is, or will be, an inability to carry out vital personal care or domestic routines; and/or
  - vital involvement in work, education or learning cannot or will not be sustained; and/or
  - vital social support systems and relationships cannot or will not be sustained; and/or
  - vital family and other social roles and responsibilities cannot or will not be undertaken.
- Substantial – when:
  - there is, or will be, only partial choice and control over the immediate environment; and/or
  - abuse or neglect has occurred or will occur; and/or
  - there is, or will be, an inability to carry out the majority of personal care or domestic routines; and/or
  - involvement in many aspects of work, education or learning cannot or will not be sustained; and/or
  - the majority of social support systems and relationships cannot or will not be sustained; and/or
  - the majority of family and other social roles and responsibilities cannot or will not be undertaken.
- Moderate – when:
  - there is, or will be, an inability to carry out several personal care or domestic routines; and/or
  - involvement in several aspects of work, education or learning cannot or will not be sustained; and/or
  - several social support systems and relationships cannot or will not be sustained; and/or
  - several family and other social roles and responsibilities cannot or will not be undertaken.

- Low – when:
  - there is, or will be, an inability to carry out one or two personal care or domestic routines; and/or
  - involvement in one or two aspects of work, education or learning cannot or will not be sustained; and/or
  - one or two social support systems and relationships cannot or will not be sustained; and/or
  - one or two family and other social roles and responsibilities cannot or will not be undertaken.

6.74 Local authorities should seek to agree with the individual concerned and/or his representative what his eligible needs, if any, are and they should be recorded, so as to avoid disputes in the future. Once they are identified an authority should, if possible, take steps to meet them in a way that coincides with the individual's aspirations.

6.75 In determining an individual's need for assistance an authority should take into account the support that existing carers (in particular family members, friends, and neighbours) are willing and able to offer but should nonetheless identify all needs that can be met by community care services, whether or not they are being currently being met. If the carer is willing and able to continue to meet a particular need then this can be recorded as a need on the care plan but that it is being fully met, so that it does not become an eligible need.

6.76 If an individual has eligible needs the authority must work with him and/or his representative to develop a plan for his care and support. In advance of the Care Act coming into force it does not matter if this plan is referred to as a care plan, support plan or a care and support plan but the first of these terms is most commonly used. The essence of such a plan is that it sets out what the eligible needs are and how they will be met.

6.77 The Prioritising Need guidance, at para 121, specifies those matters that should be included in the plan, namely:

- A note of the eligible needs identified during assessment
- Agreed outcomes and how support will be organised to meet those outcomes
- A risk assessment including any actions to be taken to manage identified risks
- Contingency plans to manage emergency changes
- Any financial contributions the individual is assessed to pay
- Support which carers and others are willing and able to provide
- Support to be provided to address needs identified through the carer's assessment, where appropriate
- A review date.

6.78 Once an authority has decided that an individual has an eligible need it must meet the need and cannot refuse to do so because of a lack of resources. In deciding how to meet the need, however, it can take its resources into account, ie it can choose the cheapest option, but must ensure it fully meets the need.

CARE BILL

6.79 A significant reform is that the Bill introduces the concept of eligibility criteria to the service provision decision stage, thereby making the application of such criteria a statutory function rather than one governed only by guidance.

6.80 By means of the current clause 13, where an authority is satisfied on the basis of a needs assessment that an individual has needs for care and support it must determine whether any of them meet the eligibility criteria and, if any of them do, consider what could be done to meet those that do. The exercise of this duty is to be prescribed by regulations and a person's needs will meet the criteria if they rank at or above the level of need set out in the regulations by reference to specified levels of need or, if the regulations so require, set by an authority for its area by reference to such levels. This will enable the Government, if it wishes, to tackle concerns about variations in service provision by imposing nationwide levels of need that must be met by all local authorities.

6.81 The following are other examples of how the Care Act is likely to refine the assessment, service provision decision and care-planning procedures already in place.

6.82 By means of the current clause 18, where an authority has carried out a needs assessment and, where applicable, a financial assessment, it must meet those needs that meet its eligibility criteria if the individual is ordinarily resident in its area or is present in its area but of no settled residence, if his accrued costs do not exceed the cap on care costs, and if there is no charge for meeting those needs or if one of the following applies: his resources are at or below the financial limit; his resources are above this limit but he has asked the authority to meet his needs; he lacks the capacity to arrange for the provision of care and support and there is no person authorised to do so under the MCA 2005 or otherwise in a position to do so on his behalf.

6.83 Where an authority is required to meet needs under clause 18 it must prepare a care and support plan, tell the individual which (if any) of these needs can be met by direct payments and help him to decide how to have them met. Where it has carried out a needs assessment but is not required to meet any needs (and chooses not to do so) it must give the individual a written record of the assessment, a written record of any financial assessment it has carried out and advice and information about what can be done to meet the needs or to prevent or delay the development of needs in the future.

6.84 Clause 25 then explains what must be included in a care and support plan, namely it must:

- Specify the needs identified by the needs assessment
- Specify whether, or to what extent, the needs meet the eligibility criteria
- Specify the needs the authority is going to meet and how it is going to meet them
- Specify which outcomes the individual wishes to achieve in day-to-day life the provision of care and support could be relevant to
- Include his personal budget.

6.85 Where some or all of the needs are to be met by direct payments the plan must also specify the needs that are to be so met, how it is they will be met by such payments and their amount and frequency.

6.86 Clause 25 also provides that in preparing a care and support plan the authority must, so far as it is feasible, consult the individual, any carer he has and any other person he asks it to consult. Once completed the authority must give a copy of the plan to the individual, any carer he has if he asks the authority to do so and any other person he asks to be given a copy. Where an individual has a carer the authority can combine the care and support plan (for the individual) with the support plan (for the carer) if both agree.

6.87 By clause 27 an authority must keep under review the care and support plans it has prepared. It may revise such a plan and in deciding whether or how to do so it must have regard to the outcomes that the individual wishes to achieve in day-to-day living and, insofar as it is feasible to do so, must consult the individual, any carer he has and any other person he asks it to consult. If the authority is then satisfied that the individual's circumstances have changed in a way that affects the plan it must, to the extent it considers appropriate, carry out a needs assessment and (where applicable) a financial assessment, following which it again exercises the function under clause 13 and revises the plan accordingly.

CHAPTER 7

CARERS

7.1 A carer for the purposes of this chapter is someone who provides 'care' (see below) for another and who does not do so under a contract or for a voluntary organisation, ie a family member, friend, neighbour, etc.[1] Therefore, if, for example, a family member provides care but is paid for doing so by the person cared for, through direct payments, he is not a carer.

7.2 Many carers do not expect anything from the State to assist them in their role and expect others to have the same attitude but the reality is that there are carers who are not so fortunate that they can otherwise manage and who do need some support. The process by which Parliament has sought to achieve a balance between these two positions is an interesting one, featuring as it has a gradual progression from simply taking into account the informal care available in deciding what additional care the State should provide, to active involvement by the carer in local authorities making such decisions, to separate assessment of a carer's needs, to the provision of services for the carer himself, if an authority so chooses.

7.3 This is a very welcome progression, the next stage in which is, by means of the Care Act, the imposition on local authorities of a duty to provide services for a carer if they need them.

THE STATUTES

7.4 The current statutory bases for the assessment of and the provision of services for carers are the Carers (Recognition and Services) Act 1995 ('CRSA 1995'), the Carers and Disabled Children Act 2000 ('CDCA 2000') and the Carers (Equal Opportunities) Act 2004 ('CEOA 2004'). In practice they have superseded an earlier recognition by statute of the importance of a carer's role in providing care, in the Disabled Persons (Services, Consultation and Representation Act) 1986 ('DPSCRA 1986'), s 8 of which requires a local authority on making a service provision decision in respect of a disabled person living at home to have regard to the ability of a carer to continue to provide care.

---

1 See DPSCRA 1986, s 8(1)(a), NHSCCA 1990, s 46(3), CRSA 1995, s 1(3) and CDCA 2000, s 1(3) – and clause 10 of the Care and Support Bill.

7.5 Carers also have a statutory role to play in supporting those they care for when their needs for community care services are assessed under s 47 of the NHS and Community Care Act 1990 ('NHSCCA 1990')[2]. The Community Care Assessment Directions 2004, made under that section, requires a local authority to consider whether the person being assessed has carers and, where it thinks it appropriate, it must consult with them. It must also take all reasonable steps to reach agreement about the services it is considering providing, both with the person being assessed and, where it thinks it appropriate, with any carer.

7.6 Each of these statutes refers to 'care' but none of them define it. The best approach probably is to apply the opening words of Baroness Hale's explanation in *R (M) v Slough BC*[3] of what is meant by care and attention for the purposes of s 21 of the National Assistance Act 1948 ('NAA 1948'), namely looking after someone by *doing something for him which he cannot or should not be expected to do for himself*. A carer could therefore be an advocate or someone who simply provides emotional support. A person who gives another a lift to the shops in his car would not ordinarily be looked upon as a carer but he may be if he also helps with the shopping and/or with taking it into the other's home.

7.7 The principal purpose of the first statute in time, the CRSA 1995, was to introduce the concept of an assessment of a carer's ability to provide care, that of the CDCA 2000 was to build on this and, for the first time, to enable services to be provided to a carer and that of the CEOA 2004 was, chiefly, to amend the other two so as to impose duties on local authorities to inform carers of their right to such an assessment and to consider the impact of caring on other aspects of their life, such as work.

Assessments for carers

7.8 Where a local authority carries out an assessment of an adult's needs for community care services,[4] ie a 'community care assessment', and an individual, 'the carer', provides or intends to provide a substantial amount of care on a regular basis for him, the carer can ask the authority, before it makes its service provision decision, to carry out an assessment of his ability to provide and to continue to provide care,[5] ie a carer's assessment. If he asks, the authority must carry out the assessment and take its results into account in making the service provision decision in respect of the person cared for. The assessment must include consideration of whether the carer works or wishes to work and whether he is undertaking or wishes to undertake education, training or any leisure activity.

---

2 See Chapter 3 for detailed information about community care assessments.

3 [2008] UKHL 52, at [33].

4 Under NHSCCA 1990, s 47.

5 CRSA 1995, s 1(1).

7.9 In support of this assessment duty, where a local authority is carrying out a community care assessment and it appears that an individual may be entitled to ask for a carer's assessment it must tell him of his entitlement before it makes its service provision decision in respect of the person cared for.[6]

7.10 The concept of a 'substantial amount of care on a regular basis' is common to the four statutes referred to in **7.3** but none of them define this phrase. Nor is there any case-law on the point but it is likely the courts would find there to be a low threshold for a carer's assessment, if only because the amount of care provided could not be properly evaluated in advance of one. If a failure to assess were alleged they would no doubt look at the decision through the prism of rationality, ie whether the local authority had made a decision verging on the absurd. If, however, there were to be a challenge it is far more likely that it would be in the form of a complaint to the authority and then, if necessary, a complaint to the Local Government Ombudsman.[7]

7.11 Where an individual aged 16 or over, 'the carer' for its purposes, provides or intends to provide a substantial amount of care on a regular basis for another individual aged 18 or over, 'the person cared for', and asks a local authority for an assessment of his ability to provide and to continue to provide care, ie a carer's assessment,[8] it must carry one out if satisfied that the person cared for is someone for whom it may provide or arrange for the provision of community care services.[9] Again, the assessment (and one carried out under s 6 of the same Act – see immediately below) must include consideration of whether the carer works or wishes to work and/or is undertaking or wishes to undertake education, training or any leisure activity.[10]

7.12 Incidentally, the National Framework guidance in respect of Continuing Healthcare ('CHC'),[11] advises[12] clinical commissioning groups ('CCG') that if it becomes apparent during the CHC assessment process that a carer may have a right to a carer's assessment, they should refer him to the appropriate local authority. This begs the question whether a carer for someone who is eligible for CHC has such a right (and could be provided with services), to which the answer is probably not because, depending on the precise circumstances, the authority would not be satisfied that the person cared for is someone for who it may provide community care services. In any event a person who receives CHC is unlikely to need a substantial amount of care from a voluntary carer as well.

---

6 CRSA 1995, s 1(2B).

7 See Chapter 11.

8 CDCA 2000, s 1.

9 Therefore, as regards territorial jurisdiction, the duty to carry out the carer's assessment (and the corresponding power to provide services for the carer) lies with the local authority that is responsible for the provision of community care services for the person cared for; generally the one for the area in which he is ordinarily resident.

10 See CDCA 2000, s 1(3A).

11 See Chapters 3 and 5 for more information about continuing health care.

12 At para 54.

7.13 If it appears to a local authority that it would be required to carry out a carer's assessment on being asked to do so by a carer it must inform him that he may be entitled to such an assessment in relation to the person cared for unless it has previously carried one out or informed him he may be entitled to one.[13]

7.14 The CDCA 2000 therefore introduced the concept of a carer's right to an assessment independent of a corresponding community care assessment and in practice its provisions prevail over those of the CRSA 1995.

7.15 The Prioritising Need guidance[14] emphasises that local authorities should grade the extent of risk to the sustainability of the caring role into one of the four categories it promotes in respect of community care services, namely critical, substantial, moderate and low, for which the descriptors are approximately the same.[15] For example, there is a critical risk to the sustainability of the caring role if:

- the carer's life may be threatened;
- major health problems have developed or will develop;
- there is, or will be, an extensive loss of autonomy for the carer in decisions about the nature of tasks he will perform and how much time he will give to his caring role;
- there is, or will be, an inability to look after his own domestic needs and other daily routines while sustaining his caring role;
- involvement in employment or other responsibilities is, or will be, at risk;
- many significant social support systems and relationships are, or will be, at risk.

7.16 As the guidance explains, this grading system is a formal determination of the degree to which a carer's ability to sustain that role is compromised or threatened either in the present or in the foreseeable future by the absence of appropriate support.

Services for carers

7.17 The local authority must consider the carer's assessment and decide whether the carer has needs in relation to the care which he provides or intends to provide and, if so, whether these needs could be satisfied, in whole or in part, by services it may provide and, if so, whether or not to provide such services.[16]

7.18 These services are any that the authority sees fit to provide and that will, in its view, help the carer care for the person cared for. The authority therefore

---

13 CDCA 2000, s 6A.
14 See Chapter 6 for more information about this guidance.
15 See paras 99 to 102 of this guidance and para 70 of the practice guidance on the CDCA 2000.
16 CDCA 2000, s 2.

has a power or discretion to provide a service and is not under a duty to do so. Such services may take the form of physical help or other forms of support.

7.19 A service, although provided to the carer, may take the form of a service delivered to the person cared for if it is one that could fall within community care services and both the carer and the person cared for agree it is to be so delivered. Such a service may not, however, include anything of an intimate nature except in prescribed circumstances, as set out in regulations made under the CDCA 2000.[17]

7.20 By these regulations a service is of an intimate nature if it involves:

- lifting, washing, grooming, feeding, dressing, bathing, toileting, administering medicines or otherwise having physical contact with the person cared for; or
- assistance in connection with these actions; or
- supervising him whilst he is dressing, bathing or using the toilet.

7.21 A service of an intimate nature may be provided if:

- during the delivery of a non-intimate service the person cared for asks the carer to provide one; or
- the person cared for lacks capacity within the meaning of the MCA 2005 to consent to the provision of an intimate nature and it is provided in accordance with the principles of that Act (essentially, in his best interests); or
- the person cared for is in a situation in which he is likely to suffer serious personal harm unless a service of an intimate nature is provided to him and the person providing a non-intimate service reasonably believes it is necessary to provide a service of an intimate nature because the likelihood of such harm is imminent.

7.22 The net effect of this aspect of the CDCA 2000 is that a service can be delivered as a service to the carer (subject to the intimate nature point) even though it could instead be delivered as a community care service to the person cared for. It appears that the reason for this is that some people who are cared for do not want care or support from a local authority as a community care service (and who, necessarily, have the capacity to make this decision) but will accept it as a service to their carer.

7.23 Examples of other services for carers include holidays, driving lessons, travel assistance (including help with taxi fares and with running a car), training (eg moving and handling classes), laundry, gardening, help with

---

17 Carers (Services) and Direct Payments (Amendment) (England) Regulations 2001, SI 2001/441.

housework – even a mobile phone, a computer or an entry phone. There is no limit on the type of service, provided it serves the statutory purpose of helping the carer care for the person cared for.

7.24 By s 3 of the CDCA 2000 and regulations made under it[18] a local authority can issue vouchers to be used by the person cared for to pay for community care services on a temporary basis while the carer has a break. It appears that with the increase in use of direct payments that the voucher system is not much used any more.

7.25 One continuing point of interest, however, is that s 3 shows that respite or short break care (whether residential or non-residential) is in law a community care service rather than a service for a carer, so that a local authority may have to provide it, to meet an eligible need in accordance with the Prioritising Need guidance, rather than have a discretion to do so under s 2 of the CDCA 2000.

Short breaks

7.26 As regards those with dementia, the Department of Health has recognised the importance of short breaks for those who care for them and has in recent years issued a fact-sheet that explains what they can comprise and, by reference to research studies, how their provision can be improved.[19] Of interest, it describes the variety of care involved, namely:

- day care outside the home, at a centre;
- support in the home, eg a sitting service;
- overnight care away from home, in a care home or hospital, commonly for one or two weeks at a time;
- 'host family care', where the person cared for and the carer both stay with another family;
- adult placement, ie the person cared for stays with another family;
- emergency breaks, usually at home.

Therapy

7.27 The guidance on dementia produced by the National Institute for Health and Care Excellence ('NICE')[20] recommends that those carrying out carers' assessments should seek to identify any psychological distress and the psychological impact of caring for someone with dementia and monitor this

---

18 Carers and Disabled Children (Vouchers) (England) Regulations 2003, SI 2003/1216.

19 *Creative Models of Short Breaks (Respite Care) for People with Dementia*, produced by the Care Services Improvement Partnership, February 2008 – helpfully, it also gives details of providers of short breaks for those with dementia and their carers.

20 NICE clinical guideline 42, 'Dementia, Supporting people with dementia and their carers in health and social care', issued November 2006 and last modified October 2012 – see Chapter 5.

even after they cease to provide care.[21] If needed, they should be offered psychological therapy, including cognitive behavioural therapy, conducted by a specialist practitioner.

7.28 This guidance also recommends that care plans for such carers should involve a range of 'tailored interventions', that consist of or include the following:

- individual or group psycho-education;
- peer-support groups with other carers, tailored to the needs of individuals depending on the stage of dementia of the person being cared for and other characteristics;
- support and information by telephone and through the internet;
- training courses about dementia, services and benefits;
- communication and problem solving in the care of people with dementia; and
- involvement of other family members as well as the primary carer in family meetings.

7.29 It too recognises the value to carers of respite and short-break services.

Failure to provide services

7.30 The Prioritising Need guidance cautions that a local authority cannot adopt a policy that it will never exercise its power to provide services for carers, because that would amount to an unlawful fettering of its discretion and that if a carer is found to have a critical need it is likely the authority will have to meet it.[22] This would have to be on the basis that no reasonable authority would do anything other than meet such a need, i e it would be irrational to do otherwise.

7.31 The guidance also suggests that a failure to meet a carer's critical need could amount to a breach of Article 8 of the ECHR but in practice it could be very difficult to establish this.

Direct payments and charging

7.32 By s 57 of the Health and Social Care Act 2001[23] a local authority can make direct payments to carers in lieu of providing them with 'direct services' under s 2 of the CDCA 2000. The procedures are the same as for direct payments in lieu of other services (see Chapter 10).

---

21 See para 1.11.2.
22 See para 100 of this guidance.
23 See sub-s (2)(b).

7.33 By s 17 of the Health and Social Services and Social Security Adjudications Act 1983[24] a local authority can charge a carer for services provided under s 2 of the CDCA 2000. The procedures are the same as for charging for other non-residential services under that Act (see Chapter 10).

Co-operation between local authorities

7.34 If a local authority forms the view that a carer's ability to provide and to continue to provide care might be enhanced by the provision of services (whether for him or for the person cared for) by another local authority or a local housing authority or an NHS body that other authority or body must give due consideration to the request.[25] For example, a local authority may ask a CCG for lifting and handling equipment or training, in which case it would be expected to assist or explain why it could not.

CARE BILL

7.35 The CRSA 1995, the CDCA 2000 and the CEOA 2004 do not currently appear in the list of those to be repealed by the Care Act but they will be repealed 'or where appropriate amended in due course'.[26] This is not surprising in the light of the changes intended to be wrought by the Act in respect of carers, the more important of which are summarised below (based on the current state of the Bill[27]).

7.36 Clause 8 sets out examples of what can be provided to meet a carer's needs for support, such as support at home or in the community, counselling, advocacy, other social work, goods and facilities, information and advice. The same clause also gives examples of how an authority can meet these needs, whether by itself providing a service or by arranging for another to do so or by making direct payments.

7.37 By clause 10 where it appears to an authority that a carer may have needs for support, whether currently or in the future, it must carry out a 'carer's assessment', i e it must assess whether he does have such needs or is likely to do so in the future and, if he does, what they are or are likely to be.

7.38 A carer is defined as an adult who provides or intends to provide care for another adult (note that there is no quantity or regularity requirement – nor at present is there any definition of care, for this or any other purpose) but is not to be regarded as one if he provides or intends to provide it under or by virtue of a contract or as voluntary work – unless the authority considers that the relationship is such that it would be appropriate for him to be regarded as a carer, which is an interesting change to the current state of the law.

---

24 See sub-s (2)(f).

25 CEOA 2004, s 3.

26 See para 82 of the Detailed Notes on the Bill.

27 As at 1 October 2013.

7.39 A carer's assessment must include an assessment of whether he is able, and will continue to be able, to provide care and whether he is willing, and will continue to be willing, to do so. In carrying out the assessment the authority must have regard to whether the carer works or wishes to do so and whether he is participating in or wishes to participate in education, training or recreation. It must also, so far as it is feasible to do so, consult the carer and any person he asks it to consult.

7.40 By clause 11 where a carer refuses an assessment the authority is not required to carry one out.

7.41 By clause 12 provision is intended to be made for regulations that govern the procedure for carrying out a carer's assessment.

7.42 By clause 13 where an authority is satisfied on the basis of a carer's assessment that a carer has needs for support it must determine, in accordance with regulations to be made under this section, whether any of the needs meet the eligibility criteria and, if any of them do, consider what could be done to meet those that do.

7.43 By clause 14 an authority may impose a charge for meeting a carer's needs for support.

7.44 By clause 17 where an authority thinks that, were it to meet a carer's needs for support, it would impose a charge on the carer, it must assess the level of his financial resources and the amount (if any) which he would be likely to be able to pay towards the cost of support.

7.45 By clause 20 where an authority has carried out a carer's assessment and, where applicable, a financial assessment, it must meet those needs that meet the eligibility criteria if the adult needing care is ordinarily resident in its area or is present in its area but of no settled residence and if there is no charge for meeting those needs or if one of the following applies: the authority is satisfied that the carer's financial resources are at or below the financial limit; the authority is satisfied his financial resources are above the financial limit but he nonetheless asks the authority to meet the needs. The imposition of a duty on a local authority to meet a carer's eligible needs is a very significant change indeed.

7.46 Where the authority is satisfied there is no duty to meet a carer's needs for support, it may nonetheless meet any of them but insofar as they involve the provision of care and support to the adult needing care it may do so only if the adult agrees.

7.47 By clause 24 where an authority is required to meet a carer's needs for support or decides to exercise its power to do so it must prepare a support plan for him.

7.48 By clause 25 a support plan is a document prepared by an authority that:

- specifies the needs identified by the carer's assessment;
- specifies whether, or to what extent, the needs meet the eligibility criteria;
- specifies the needs that the authority is going to meet and how it is going to meet them;
- includes the carer's personal budget.

7.49 Where some or all of the needs are to be met by direct payments the support plan must also specify the needs to be so met, how they will be met by them and their amount and frequency.

7.50 In preparing a support plan the authority must, so far as it is feasible, consult the carer, the adult needing care, if the carer asks it to do so, and any other person the carer asks it to consult.

7.51 In seeking to ensure that the support plan is proportionate to the needs to be met, the authority must have regard in particular to whether the carer is able, and will continue to be able, to provide care, whether he is willing, and will continue to be willing, to do so, whether he works or wishes to do so and whether he is participating in or wishes to participate in education, training or recreation.

7.52 The authority must give a copy of the support plan to the carer, the adult needing care and any other person the carer asks it to give a copy to. The authority may combine a care and support plan for an individual with a support plan for a carer if both agree.

7.53 By clause 26 a personal budget for a carer is a statement that specifies the amount that the authority assesses as the cost of meeting those of his needs it must or chooses to meet, the amount he must pay towards the cost and the amount the authority must pay. It may also specify other amounts of public money that are available for spending on matters relating to his housing, health care or welfare.

7.54 By clause 27 an authority must keep under review support plans for carers that it has prepared. It may revise such a plan and deciding whether or how to do so it must have regard in particular to whether the carer is able, and will continue to be able, to provide care, whether he is willing, and will continue to be willing, to do so, whether he works or wishes to do so and whether he is participating in or wishes to participate in education, training or recreation. It must also, insofar as it is feasible, consult the carer, the adult needing care if the carer asks the authority to do so and any other person the carer asks it to consult. If the authority is satisfied that the carer's circumstances have changed in a way that affects his support plan, it must, to the extent it thinks appropriate, carry out a carer's assessment and (where applicable) a financial assessment. It must then again exercise its function under clause 13 and revise the support plan accordingly.

7.55 Clause 31 applies where a personal budget for a carer specifies an amount that the authority must pay towards the cost of meeting his needs and he asks it to meet some or all of those needs by making payments to him or to a person nominated by him. If four conditions are then met the authority must make direct payments. The first condition is that the carer has, or the authority believes he has, capacity to make the request and, where there is a nominated person, that person agrees to receive them. The second is that the carer or his nominee is not prohibited by regulations from receiving such payments. The third is that the authority is satisfied that he or his nominee is capable of managing them by himself or with whatever help the authority thinks he will be able to access. The fourth is that the authority is satisfied that making direct payments is an appropriate way to meet the needs in question.

CHAPTER 8

LASTING AND ENDURING POWERS OF ATTORNEY

8.1 It is a feature of English law that an individual has always enjoyed the freedom to manage his own affairs with as little interference from the State as possible. This chapter considers the legal tools available to enable a person to plan ahead and to choose how they would like their affairs managed and by whom in the event that they become incapacitated by dementia or some other mental disability.

8.2 For many years creating an Enduring Power of Attorney ('EPA') was the means by which a person could control who would carry on his business and manage his financial affairs in the event he became unable to do so because of mental incapacity. When the Mental Capacity Act 2005 ('MCA 2005') came into force on 1 October 2007, it provided a new statutory framework for powers of attorney designed to survive the incapacity of the donor now called Lasting Power of Attorney ('LPA'). This chapter considers both EPAs and LPAs.

WHAT IS A POWER OF ATTORNEY?

8.3 A standard power of attorney, sometimes called a bare power, is a formal document whereby one person (the donor) gives another person (the attorney or donee) the power to act on his behalf and in his name.

8.4 When properly granted by a person who is over 18 who has the mental capacity to do so, powers of attorney are widely used as a form of agency to enable the financial affairs of the donor to be conducted by his attorney in his absence or when he does not wish to act for himself for some other reason. The attorney is said to stand in the shoes of the donor so that any act carried out by him is treated as an act carried out by the donor. Consequently, the attorney and any third party can assume that the donor knows and approves of what is being done on his behalf.

8.5 A power of attorney can be revoked by the donor at any time. Crucially, a standard power of attorney is automatically revoked and becomes legally invalid if the donor becomes mentally incapable of managing his own property and affairs. The rationale behind this is that the attorney can only do what he has been given authority by the donor to do and if the donor lacks capacity then he is unable to continue to give that authority. Provided that the statutory requirements have been complied with, an EPA or an LPA will not cease to have effect once the donor has lost capacity.

OBLIGATIONS ON AN ATTORNEY

8.6 Any power of attorney, whether a standard power of attorney, an EPA or an LPA, imposes at its heart the same basic obligations upon the attorney. Therefore, it is sensible for the donor to be aware of the skills required and expected when considering whether to appoint a particular person as his attorney or one of his attorneys. It is also important for the attorney to know that the donor does not confer on his attorney the opportunity to do whatever he likes with the donor's property and affairs.

8.7 The attorney owes a fiduciary duty to the donor. That is, a strict duty:

- not act to benefit himself or any other person from the donor's estate;
- not to let his personal interests conflict with those of the donor;
- to act in good faith; and
- to keep proper accounts.

The attorney must also keep all monies held in his position as attorney separate from his own funds and in accounts in the donor's name.

8.8 An attorney owes a duty of care and skill commensurate to the service that he is providing to the donor. If he is a solicitor, the standard expected is no less than the care and skill expected from a reasonably competent solicitor; if he is a layman and is not being paid for his services, the standard is no less than the care and skill a person would expect to exercise when acting for himself.

8.9 The attorney may not delegate his authority nor disclose confidential information and, as he is personally chosen, he cannot appoint a new attorney or successor.

8.10 The attorney may only act within his power and he may not do something as an attorney that only the donor can do, for example vote or swear an affidavit.

8.11 As the standard power of attorney is revoked by the incapacity of the donor, the attorney must not continue to act once the dementia has advanced to a stage where the donor is no longer able to make informed decisions as to whether the power should continue. An EPA or an LPA will, subject to various conditions, continue as described below.

ENDURING POWERS OF ATTORNEY

What is an enduring power of attorney?

8.12 An EPA is a special form of power of attorney, created in accordance with the Enduring Powers of Attorney Act 1985 ('EPAA 1985'). The power must be granted using the prescribed form and can be used by an attorney to deal with the property and financial affairs of the donor in the same way as a standard power of attorney whilst he still has sufficient mental capacity to understand the nature and effect of the power granted. However, provided that the attorney follows the prescribed registration process, the EPA (unlike a standard power of attorney) can also be used notwithstanding that the donor has lost that capacity.

8.13 The donor may grant the attorney general powers to deal with all of his property and affairs or may grant more limited specific powers. The EPA may not grant the attorney the power to make welfare decisions. There are also statutory restrictions that will bind the attorney and to which the attorney has to have regard.

8.14 Until the MCA 2005 came into force on 1 October 2007, an EPA was the only type of power of attorney that could still be used once the donor's dementia had reached the stage where he no longer understood the issues relevant to whether he could grant a power of attorney. EPAs that were validly granted before that date remain in effect and can still be registered once the dementia reaches the point where registration is required. No new EPAs could be granted once the MCA 2005 came into force.

8.15 There can be a substantial period between an EPA being granted and registration being required. Until registration, an EPA is a private arrangement between the donor and the attorney so there is no way of knowing how many valid (and also invalid) EPAs have been created but not yet registered. For that reason, the MCA 2005 brings the operation of existing EPAs into its framework by regulating their operation even though it does not allow for any more to be created.

Why there was a need to replace enduring powers of attorney

8.16 Creating a standard power of attorney is a relatively straightforward process and, by extension, the creation of an EPA, although it required a more complicated document, was just as easy albeit that it required the attorney to register the EPA with the Office of the Public Guardian[1] ('OPG') for it to be effective once the donor lost capacity.

8.17 The success of the EPA is shown by its widespread take-up. However, the system provided little protection and there was great opportunity for the trust

---

1 The OPG is the government agency with responsibility for registration and supervision of EPAs and LPAs. It also has powers to investigate the way in which attorneys carry out their duties.

of the donor to be abused. Consequently, after consultation Parliament attempted to reconcile the competing principles: that individuals should be able to be as autonomous as possible and to entrust the management of their affairs to whomsoever they wanted with as little interference from the courts or anyone else on the one hand; and, that there should be greater safeguards to protect the vulnerable from the unscrupulous attorney on the other.

8.18 In order to address these concerns without undermining the arrangements already put in place by many people (possibly hundreds of thousands) the MCA 2005 repealed the EPAA 1985 so that no new EPAs could be created. However, whilst providing for EPAs created before 1 October 2007 to remain effective, it added some safeguards for donors by requiring them to operate within the MCA 2005 framework, thereby imposing additional obligations upon an attorney acting under an EPA to act in the donor's best interests. Attorneys acting under EPAs are also are bound by the principles of the MCA 2005 and must have regard to the Code of Practice.[2]

Enduring powers of attorney – the legal process

8.19 Although no new EPAs can be created, as we have seen there are still very many in use and there are likely to be many more stored away in a safe place, ready to be used when an attorney believes that the donor is or is becoming mentally incapable of managing his or her property and affairs. The provisions applying to existing EPAs are set out in Schedule 4, MCA 2005.

The creation of a valid EPA

8.20 To be valid, an EPA must have been made when the donor had capacity to grant it. An EPA has to be in the prescribed form which contains important explanatory information which the donor by signing the document acknowledges that he has understood. The test of a person's capacity to manage and administer his property and affairs is a question of functional capacity and involves weighing up all the circumstances as explained in Chapter 3. The donor will be presumed to have had the capacity to make the EPA by his witnessed signature on the document but this presumption may be rebutted. The burden of proving that the donor did not have capacity or that his signature was procured under pressure or duress is on the person making that assertion.

8.21 An EPA can only deal with a donor's property and affairs and cannot grant powers in respect of welfare decisions. Where the EPA contains invalid provisions, the court will sever them rather than declare the EPA invalid; for example, the court will sever a provision in an EPA that purports to authorise the attorney to 'make a choice on my behalf for any residential care needed for me in the future' as that would be ineffective as part of the EPA because it sought to authorise personal welfare decision making. Notwithstanding that the

---

2 See Chapter 4 for more general information about the Code of Practice.

MCA 2005 now provides for personal welfare decisions to be made by an attorney acting under an LPA, it does not import any such powers into an EPA which remains specifically for dealing with a donor's property and financial affairs.

8.22 To be valid, an EPA must be in the prescribed form and have been executed by the donor and attorney or attorneys before 1 October 2007.[3] In the case of *Re Freeman*[4] the donor signed Part B of the EPA instrument on 14 April 2006 but the attorney did not sign Part C until 3 October 2008. The OPG refused to register the EPA on the ground that an instrument could not be a valid EPA unless the attorney had signed before 1 October 2007. On the attorney's application, the court declared that the instrument was not a valid EPA.

8.23 The OPG will, however, register an EPA that appoints joint and several attorneys if at least one attorney has signed before 1 October 2007, even though other(s) did not; in that case registration will be limited to the attorney(s) who signed before that date.

Loss of capacity

8.24 It is difficult to watch a person's mental health deteriorate to the point where it appears that they are losing or have lost the capacity to make decisions about their financial affairs. Very often a person with dementia becomes adept at compensating for the loss of faculties and it is equally hard for many relatives, for understandable emotional reasons, to accept the fact that the person is losing or has lost capacity. However, it is important that an attorney remains alert for signs that the time has come when the EPA must be registered.

8.25 The key points in recognising that the donor is no longer able to deal with his property and affairs such that the EPA must be registered are the facts that:[5]

a) the inability to manage must arise by reason of a mental disorder which is more than a temporary impairment of intellectual function shown by a failure of memory, orientation, comprehension and learning capacity; and
(b) he no longer understands the information relevant to the decision that he has to make.

8.26 When acting for people with dementia the point at which capacity is lost or the time when capacity is fluctuating is the most difficult time for both donor and attorney because the attorney must register the power for him to be able to

3 MCA 2005, s 66(2) provides that an EPA cannot be 'created' after commencement.
4 (2010) COP (an order of District Judge Ralton made on 7 September 2010).
5 This definition is a combined result of Sch 1, para 23(1) to, and s 1(2) of the Mental Health Act 1983 and the definition set out by the Department of Health and Social Security in its review of the Mental Health Act 1959.

act or to continue to act. An attorney may expose himself to personal liability if he acts or continues to act at a time when the EPA needs to be registered but is not.

8.27 Both donor and attorney may find it difficult to come to terms with the realisation that the donor can no longer make decisions for himself and may wish to put off the moment of registration. On a practical level, waiting until the last moment to register is not advisable because the registration process can take time, even if there are no issues as to its validity. Further, once the EPA has been registered, it is generally not enough merely to produce a registered EPA or registered LPA to a bank or other organisation; their bureaucracy works in a ponderous way and most organisations will need at least 6 weeks to adjust their own systems to recognise the EPA. This can be problematic if urgent business needs to be conducted.

Steps to be taken once capacity becomes an issue

8.28 The attorney is under a duty when he believes the donor is or is becoming mentally incapable to give notice to the donor and prescribed relatives that he intends to apply to register the EPA. He must apply to the OPG for the registration of the EPA.

Notice

8.29 Before the EPA can be used on behalf of the donor the attorney will have to notify the donor of his intention to register it and also notify at least three relatives who are in a prescribed order of 'classes' to be notified.[6] Importantly, the notice will give the donor an opportunity to say if he believes that he still has capacity and to object to the registration. It also provides an opportunity for the donor and any person notified of the application to assert that the donor was forced in some way to execute the EPA and it was done against his will. Any person notified can object to the registration and can apply to the Court of Protection asking it to refuse to register the EPA or to revoke it.

Registration

8.30 The court has powers to refuse the registration of an EPA if it is satisfied that the donor has revoked the power, remains capable, has died or has become bankrupt. Registration may also be refused if the court finds that fraud or undue influence have been used to procure the EPA or, having regard to all the circumstances and, in particular, the donor's relationship or connection with the attorney, the attorney is unsuitable.

8.31 Examples are legion where unscrupulous 'friends' or 'helpful neighbours' of donors have made themselves indispensable to the donor and who have produced EPAs to assist them to look after someone with dementia. If alerted to the problem, the court will look into the circumstances and could refuse the

---

6 These are defined in MCA 2005, Sch 4, para 6.

registration of an EPA where there is evidence of wrongdoing. An example of such a case would be the scenario where a porter of a block of flats befriends a very rich old lady in his block who has moderate dementia and applies to register an EPA which she purported to make appointing him as her attorney. It transpires on objection by her family that the porter has made himself indispensable to the lady and has isolated her from her family and persuaded her to create an EPA. Registration in these circumstances would be refused.

8.32 If no objections are received within 5 weeks of the last notice being served the OPG must register the power. The website http://www.justice.gov.uk/forms/opg/enduring-power-of-attorney provides a pack that can be downloaded which contains the forms and guidance material needed in order to apply to register an EPA.

What can the attorney do whilst he is waiting for the EPA to be registered?

8.33 Once an application for registration is made the attorney may take action under the power to maintain the donor or prevent loss to his estate or to maintain himself or others insofar as the scope of his authority allows.

LASTING POWERS OF ATTORNEY – THE LEGAL PROCESS

Definition

8.34 The MCA 2005 introduced an entirely new type of power of attorney[7] known as a Lasting Power of Attorney (LPA). From 1 October 2007, it became possible to appoint an attorney to make health and welfare decisions in the event that the donor lost the capacity to make those decisions for himself.[8] Alongside the health and welfare LPA, the LPA (property and affairs) replaced the EPA as the method by which one person can appoint another to make financial decisions should he lose the capacity to do so in the future. Anyone granting a power of attorney after 1 October 2007, intending that it will continue if he should become incapacitated, must ensure that it is a valid LPA. LPAs are authorised by the Court of Protection and must comply with the provisions set out in the MCA 2005 and the Code of Practice.

What is included as property and affairs?

8.35 The Code of Practice sets out guidance as to the matters that come within the scope of property and affairs. Once a person with dementia loses capacity

---

7 At s 9 of the MCA 2005.

8 This is a Lasting Power of Attorney LPA (health and welfare) but unlike the LPA (property and affairs) it can only be used once a donor has lost capacity. See Chapter 4 for more information about health and welfare LPAs.

to make everyday decisions about these matters, the attorney will need to make those decisions in accordance with the provisions and principles of the MCA 2005.

8.36 Property and affairs is defined in the Code of Practice to include:

- buying or selling property;
- opening, closing or operating any bank, building society or other account;
- giving access to the donor's financial information;
- claiming, receiving and using (on the donor's behalf) all benefits, pensions, allowances and rebates (unless the Department for Work and Pensions has already appointed someone and everyone is happy for this to continue);
- receiving any income, inheritance or other entitlement on behalf of the donor;
- dealing with the donor's tax affairs;
- paying the donor's mortgage, rent and household expenses;
- insuring, maintaining and repairing the donor's property;
- investing the donor's savings;
- making limited gifts on the donor's behalf;
- paying for private medical care and residential care or nursing home fees;
- applying for any entitlement to funding for NHS care, social care or adaptations;
- using the donor's money to buy a vehicle or any equipment or other help they need;
- repaying interest and capital on any loan taken out by the donor.

Capacity of the donor

8.37 On making an LPA the donor has to understand what it is and the effect on him of conferring authority on his attorney to make decisions on his behalf when he has lost the capacity to do so himself. The test of capacity under the MCA 2005 is time and function specific so that it is possible that the capacity of the donor will vary according to the specific decision to be taken. There is a distinction between the capacity to create an LPA and the capacity to manage one's property and affairs. For example, a donor may be unable to manage his property and affairs himself because they are too complex but he can perfectly understand the necessity of arranging matters so that, when his dementia is more advanced, the person or people whom he has chosen for their expertise or other qualities will be able to manage his affairs on his behalf and that any attorney will take account of any guidance or particular instruction or restriction that he has specified.

Who can be an attorney?

8.38 The only statutory requirement is that an attorney may be either a trust corporation or an individual who is over 18 and who is not a bankrupt at the time the LPA is made. If the attorney subsequently becomes bankrupt he will no longer be able to act.

8.39 More than one person may be appointed to act as an attorney and the donor must specify how the attorney is to act as is set out below. It is to be hoped that a donor when acting on his own or assisted by a solicitor to create an LPA will think very carefully about the qualities he would like in the person he is entrusting to make decisions on his behalf. It is suggested it is not enough that the person is kind or a member of the family or a 'dependable neighbour'. An attorney must be trustworthy, competent and reliable with the skills, ability and willingness to carry out the tasks of an attorney which are serious and may be perceived by someone not committed to the task as burdensome.

Requirements for the creation of an LPA

8.40 Creating an LPA is a two stage process. The instrument has to be completed in the prescribed form by a donor with capacity and then the instrument has to be registered with the OPG in accordance with Schedule 1 to the MCA 2005. Notwithstanding that the instrument itself may be completed, an LPA is not effective unless and until it is registered. This contrasts with the EPA as we have seen, where an attorney who has applied to register the EPA may continue to perform some decision-making tasks before the instrument is registered.

8.41 The guidance in the Code of Practice suggests that an LPA should be registered soon after it has been completed by the donor so as to avoid delay when it needs to be used.

The instrument

8.42 The website of the OPG[9] provides information packs and links to download all of the forms and materials necessary to create and to register an LPA.

8.43 There are different prescribed forms for an LPA for property and financial affairs ('LPAPFA') and for an LPA for health and welfare ('LPAHW'),[10] the reasons for this are that the two different types of LPAs are likely to involve completely different considerations and often are granted to different attorneys. Further, the LPAPFA once registered may be used whether or not the donor has lost capacity whereas the LPAHW may only be used if the donor lacks capacity.

---

9 http://www.justice.gov.uk/about/opg.
10 See Chapter 4 which deals with LPAHWs.

The requirements of the form

8.44 It cannot be emphasised too strongly that the instrument of an LPA (ie the document creating it) has to be filled in correctly and with care as the OPG will not register it and will apply to the court to sever any invalid provisions. This will add further delay to the process time for registration which at the time of publication stands at a minimum of 9 weeks in cases where there is no impediment to registration.

8.45 The prescribed form for an LPAPFA consists of a minimum of 11 pages, although not all sections will apply to everyone. If there is insufficient space then supplementary pages may be added.

8.46 The document is made up of four parts which must all be kept together containing:

(I) the prescribed information which the donor, the attorney and the certificate provider all have to read or have read to them before completing the form;

(II) Part A, the Donor's Declaration;

(III) Part B, the Certificate Provider's Declaration; and

(IV) Part C, the Attorney's Declaration.

The prescribed information

8.47 The form for an LPA for property and affairs has a section at the beginning setting out clearly the prescribed information giving an explanation and brief guidance on the purpose and legal consequences of making an LPA. It directs the person making it, his attorneys and his certificate providers to read it carefully and refers them to the guidance produced by the OPG.

8.48 Crucially it sets out that attorneys cannot do whatever they like. They must follow the principles of the MCA 2005. In the case of *Re Buckley*[11] the senior judge of the Court of Protection was clear: 'Attorneys should be aware of the law regarding their role and responsibilities. Ignorance is no excuse. I am not suggesting that attorneys should be able to pass an examination on the provisions of the Mental Capacity Act 2005, but they should at least be familiar with the "information you must read" on the LPA itself and the provisions of the Mental Capacity Act 2005 Code of Practice.' Section 42(4)(a) of the MCA 2005 expressly stipulates that it is the duty of an attorney acting under an LPA to have regard to the Code of Practice.

8.49 The form and the information are intended to be capable of being used by people without legal advice but the number of applications that are referred to the Court of Protection for severance because one or other of the clauses or restrictions could invalidate the document suggest that in many cases it would

---

11 A judgment of the senior judge given on 22 January 2013.

be prudent to seek legal advice before embarking on the creation of an LPA. Further, given that the momentous effect of the document once registered is to give a person's autonomy over his decision making to another, serious consideration should be given to obtaining professional legal advice.

8.50 The OPG publishes extensive guidance to assist anybody contemplating making an LPA. This includes: LPA 103 *Lasting powers of attorney: a guide for people who want to make a Property and Affairs Lasting Power of Attorney*, guidance for registering an LPA: LPA 108 *Lasting powers of attorney: a guide to registering a Lasting Power of Attorney* and also guidance for people offering themselves as attorneys: LPA 105 *Lasting powers of attorney: a guide for people taking on the role of a Property and Affairs attorney under a Lasting Power of Attorney.*

Part A of the LPA

8.51 This section of the form is about the donor and his attorney(s) and defines the scope of, or any restrictions upon, of their authority. The donor has to specify whether he is appointing more than one attorney and, if so, whether he is giving them authority to act together or independently that is 'jointly or severally' in relation to all matters or in relation to some but not all matters or in whatever combination of the two.

What does acting jointly and severally mean

8.52 A donor may choose one or more attorneys. If choosing more than one attorney, the donor has to decide whether they act together or independently of each other. In the MCA 2005 the concept of whether they act *together* and *independently* is drafted using the more legalistic terms of *jointly and severally. Jointly* means all must act *together* and *severally* means each attorney can act *independently* of the others.

8.53 For example, the donor may appoint three attorneys who are authorised to act on their own for low value transactions but must act together for higher value transactions. However, care must be taken to ensure that contradictory provisions are not made as they will be invalid. An example of such a contradictory provision is where the attorneys were appointed to act at any time either on their own or together that was then contradicted by a provision that they must act together in transactions over £2,000. Similarly, appointing three attorneys and ticking the 'independently and together' box on the form but then specifying that two out of the three attorneys had to act together and that no attorney could act alone was invalid.

Replacement attorneys

8.54 The donor (and not a donee) may appoint other attorneys as a replacement for an original attorney but only if one of the trigger events specified in s 13 of the MCA 2005 ends the appointment of the original attorney. The events are: the disclaimer by an attorney of his appointment, the death or bankruptcy of an attorney, the dissolution of the marriage or civil partnership if the donor appoints his spouse or civil partner or an attorney loses mental capacity.

8.55 Any LPA which purports to allow an attorney to find replacement attorneys to take over his responsibilities in the event of his death or mental incapacity will be severed on the ground that s 10(8)(a) of the MCA 2005 invalidates any provision in an LPA giving an attorney power to appoint a substitute or successor.

8.56 The validity of provisions which are intended to replace original attorneys with new attorneys are frequently scrutinised by the Court of Protection and may be severed if found to be invalid. A simple example that shows how careful a donor must be was a case[12] where the donor said that a replacement attorney should act if any attorney was 'not available through travel or living abroad'. As that was not a trigger event it was invalid.

8.57 In another case,[13] the donor and the proposed replacement attorneys challenged the application of the OPG to sever the clear provisions that the donor had set out in her property and affairs LPA stipulating that successive replacement attorneys should act in the event that her sole attorney became incapable and the replacement attorney subsequently became unable to act. The donor had appointed her husband as sole attorney and then her sons and finally her niece as replacement attorneys. It appears she had created the LPA in this way in order to attempt to avoid the difficulties she had experienced when acting herself, individually, as an attorney under an EPA.

8.58 Notwithstanding her expressed wishes, the court granted the application for severance of the provision on the construction of s 10(8) saying that the way to achieve what the donor wanted was to have made two LPAs: the first one appointing her husband to be the sole attorney and one son to be the sole replacement attorney; and the other appointing her other son to be the sole attorney and her niece to the sole replacement attorney, with a condition that the second instrument will not come into effect until the first instrument has ceased to be operable for any reason.

8.59 The court reiterated that caution must be exercised in drafting the LPA otherwise could it have the effect of negating the donor's intention. For example, if the donor appointed A and B to act jointly, and C to act as a replacement attorney, A's bankruptcy, death or disclaimer would terminate A and B's joint appointment, and C would become the sole attorney, rather than act jointly with B.

---

12 *Re Jenkins* (an order of the senior judge made on 2 September 2008).

13 *Re Boff* (a judgment of the senior judge given on 16 August 2013).

Placing restrictions or conditions on attorneys

8.60 In section 6 of the form the donor may place restrictions on the attorney's powers or specify conditions under which he can act.

8.61 First the donor has to decide whether he wants his attorney or attorneys to act on his behalf at any time or only when he lacks capacity. A donor may specifically direct that he does not want the attorney to register the LPA until he lacks, or the attorney has reason to believe that he lacks, capacity to make a particular decision. If, for example, he decides that the LPA can only be used when he lacks capacity, the donor may specify anything he wants the attorney to do to confirm that he does indeed lack capacity to make the decision in question. For example, a donor could specify that the LPA will only apply if his GP confirms in writing that he lacks capacity to make specific decisions about his property or financial matters. If the donor does not so specify, the OPG will not ask for medical evidence to confirm the loss of capacity. However, the OPG does notify the donor on receipt of the application to register and that will give him an opportunity to object to the registration.

8.62 The donor has made a proactive decision to create an LPA for the smooth running of his financial affairs in the event he loses capacity. It is also prudent to set out the particular way he would like his affairs ordered by way of conditions imposed upon the attorney(s). For example, to specify that he would like the attorney to keep a record of all the decisions he makes on the donor's behalf and submit them on a monthly basis to the donor's accountant.

8.63 A common clause in an LPA is to authorise the donor's solicitor to disclose the donor's will to his attorney. Common restrictions that are often seen are ones which prevent the attorney from investing or dealing with the donor's funds where he has already appointed a fund manager to carry out those duties or a condition putting a limit on the amount of money the attorney may spend or gift in a particular year. A donor may make stricter conditions than the parameters set out in the MCA 2005 but cannot make provision for the attorney to make more extensive gifts than allowed by the Act (as detailed below).

8.64 Unless there are valid written restrictions in the LPA an attorney may make all and any decisions about the donor's property and affairs so long as it is in line with the principles and provisions of the MCA 2005 and does not conflict with his fiduciary duties as attorney.

The powers and obligations of an attorney acting under an LPA when investing the donor's funds

8.65 The apparent misconception that an attorney acting under an LPA can do whatever he likes with a donor's funds and that he can do whatever the donor could or would have done personally if he had the capacity to manage their own affairs is illustrated frequently in the types of case that have come before the Court of Protection following an investigation by the OPG.

8.66 In the case of *Re Buckley* above[14] where an elderly lady appointed her niece to be her sole attorney under an LPA, the OPG applied to revoke and cancel the LPA following concerns raised by the donor's close friend and only person named to be notified on the registration of the LPA. On investigation into the sale of the donor's property by the attorney, it became clear that the attorney had invested over £87,000 into setting up a reptile breeding business as her aunt 'loved animals and she was sure that would be what her aunt wanted' and the attorney had misappropriated over £43,000 into her own account.

8.67 In that case, the senior judge repeated the fiduciary obligations on an attorney and the requirement of an attorney to act in the donor's best interests. The obligations on an attorney are likened to those of trustees to exercise such care and skill as is reasonable in the circumstances when investing the donor's assets. The court suggested that until such time as the OPG offered its own guidance to attorneys and deputies on the investment of funds that, as they have fiduciary duties which are similar to trustees, they should comply with the provisions of the Trustee Act 2000 as regards investment criteria and the requirement to obtain and consider proper advice.

8.68 Like trustees, attorneys should have regard to the standard investment criteria when exercising any power of investment. There are two standard criteria: the suitability of the investments and the need to diversify the investments so far as it is appropriate in the circumstances.

8.69 Under the Trustee Act 2000, trustees are required to obtain and consider proper advice about the way in which their powers of investment should be exercised. In the context of an LPA, the average age of a donor is about 80 years old. Age and life expectancy are two of the most important factors in considering investments and the court has given guidance as to short term investments. Consideration should be given to depositing moneys in interest bearing accounts with reputable banks or building societies offering relatively instant access or National Savings and Investments where there is a 100% guarantee from HM Treasury on all deposits.

8.70 The court reiterated the importance of the fiduciary relationship between donor and attorney which is underlined in Chapter 7 of the Code of Practice (see 8.99): to keep the donor's moneys and property separate from their own or that of any other person, and further to make any investments in the donor's name or if that is not possible to execute a declaration of trust or other formal record that acknowledges the donor's beneficial interest in the asset.

8.71 The court recommended that an attorney intending to invest or deal with donor's funds should have regard to guidance set out by the OPG *Investing for Patients* alongside the amended short term investment code which is reproduced below:

---

14 *Re Buckley* a judgment of the senior judge given on 22 January 2013.

Table 8.1 OPG Investing for Patients Guidance

Investment code	Approximate value	Investment requirement	Usual investment strategy
ST1	*£0–£85,000*	Available quickly – safe	Cash deposit that provides a competitive rate when compared with base rates and NS&I returns
ST2	*Over £85,000*	All or part available quickly – very little risk acceptable	Cash deposits with different financial institutions, including NS&I, which stay below the FSCS limits and/or a gilt portfolio to provide returns that compare favourably with base rates
ST3	*Cash with an existing portfolio*	Aim to make all, or part, available quickly – reducing risk commensurate with P's requirements	Depending on the nature of the portfolio, a liquidation process should be adopted using the annual CGT allowance. The cash funds should be retained in cash deposits with different financial institutions, including NS&I, which stay within the FSCS limits; and/or a gilt portfolio to provide returns that compare favourably with base rates

Gifts

8.72 The MCA 2005 prohibits an attorney disposing of the donor's property by making gifts unless the gifts are on customary occasions to related or connected persons of the donor or to any charity to whom the donor already made donations or might have been expected to donate *and* the value of each gift is not unreasonable looking at all the circumstances particularly the size of the donor's estate.

8.73 Customary occasions when gifts are permitted include birthdays, Christmas and other religious festivals, weddings and civil partnerships, christening presents, graduation presents and housewarming gifts but the donor must heed the provisions of the MCA 2005 and the gift must be proportional having regard to the size of the donor's estate. Even if a donor tries to authorise a different type of gift by specifying it in the LPA, it will still be invalid if it is outside the categories of acceptable gifts set out in s 12.

8.74 The following have been held by the courts to be invalid gifts: gifts to pay school fees of grandchildren; repayment of a student loan; and a provision to continue to make the regular gifts (not on birthdays etc) that a donor was making at the time the LPA was made. In these cases, where an attorney wants to make a different or more complicated gift he can apply to the Court of Protection under s 23(4) of the MCA 2005 for permission to make a gift outside the permitted categories.[15]

8.75 In the case of *Buckley* (see **8.66**) the court reiterated that the attorney *must* make an application to the court in any of the following cases:

(a) gifts that exceed the limited scope of the authority conferred on attorneys by s 12 of the MCA 2005;
(b) loans to the attorney or to members of the attorney's family;
(c) any investment in the attorney's own business;
(d) sales or purchases at an undervalue; and
(e) any other transactions in which there is a conflict between the interest of the donor and the interest of the attorney.

8.76 In that case, the attorney used £43,317 of the donor's money by gifting it to herself claiming that she had the donor's permission to do so, whilst at the same time admitting that the donor was increasingly confused and unable to understand or retain the information relevant to understanding how to handle her finances.

The donor's guidance to his attorneys

8.77 The restrictions to be placed on an attorney's powers have to be clear and unambiguous and not incompatible with the provisions of the MCA 2005

[15] See Chapter 9 for more information about the court's approach to approving gifts.

otherwise the OPG will use his powers of severance or could refuse to register the LPA. An alternative method by which the donor can ensure that his wishes are taken into account is to give his attorneys guidance as to how he would like things done. This guidance is not binding on the attorneys but it will be a clear indication of what the donor would like and the attorney should consider it in his decision making.

8.78 For those reasons it is suggested that using the guidance section of the LPA form as a means of setting out a donor's wishes is the preferable option where a donor is not using a solicitor to create his LPA. Guidance which an attorney must consider before making a decision is persuasive and instructive rather than of itself being legally binding. However, even so, the courts are vigilant in overseeing the guidance provisions and considering their compatibility with the terms of the LPA notwithstanding they are usually made with the best of intentions.

8.79 As in the case of *Re Norris*,[16] the donor made LPAs for property and financial affairs and for health and welfare and included the following guidance in both LPAs: 'At all times to make decisions in the best interests of [my wife] during her lifetime.' On the application of the OPG, the provision was severed as being potentially inconsistent with the requirement in s 1(5) of the MCA 2005 that any act done or decision made must be done or made in the donor's best interests.

8.80 Where a donor has the capacity to make an LPA but needs matters to be explained to him in a very clear and simple way and he also communicates in simple terms, it will be sensible to record his wishes in the manner in which he has expressed them in the guidance section.

Safeguards for LPAs

8.81 Whilst there are clear duties incumbent on an attorney acting under an LPA which affect the relationship between the attorney and donor regardless of the state of capacity of the donor, it goes without saying that a donor has to consider very carefully who he chooses to act as his attorney. However, very often it is not the donor but his children or other relatives that instigate the creation of an LPA and there are, therefore, some safeguards built into the process.

8.82 One of the safeguards brought in under the MCA 2005 are the notice provisions on registration. In part A the donor may select up to five named persons (or none) who are to be notified upon the registration of the power. A named person cannot be an attorney or replacement attorney. If the donor chooses not to notify any named person, he must have two certificate providers each providing a certificate of capacity confirming that the donor is able to understand the nature of the power he is creating.

---

16 *Re Norris* (an order of the senior judge made on 25 July 2012).

8.83 In the case of *Buckley* which is set out at 8.66, it was the concern of Miss Buckley's friend Shirley, the sole named person who was to be notified on registration of the LPA, that uncovered the misappropriation. Shirley alerted the OPG because: 'she was so worried that Miss Buckley's money will get stolen and that she won't be able to stay in the nursing home...it's nearly £1000 per week. She cannot afford for her money to be taken. She needs every penny.'

Part B of the LPA

8.84 An equally important part and safeguard to the instrument of an LPA is the declaration of the certificate provider, a person of a prescribed description, who provides a contemporaneous record that at the time the LPA was prepared:

(a) the donor understands the purpose of the instrument and the scope of the authority conferred under it;
(b) no fraud or undue pressure is being used to induce the donor to create a lasting power of attorney; and
(c) there is nothing else that would prevent a lasting power of attorney from being created by the instrument.

8.85 The certificate provider must be chosen by the donor from one of two categories of person:

(a) a person who has known the donor for at least 2 years; or
(b) a person who on account of his relevant professional skills and expertise considers that he is competent to make the judgments necessary to certify the relevant matters.

Who can be a certificate provider?

8.86 A certificate provider cannot be a family member of the donor; an attorney (or family member of the attorney) appointed under the LPA or any other LPA or EPA executed by the same donor; a director or employee of a trust corporation acting as an attorney under the power; a business partner or employee of the donor or the attorney appointed under the power (so where a solicitor is the attorney, another member of his firm cannot certify that the donor understands what he is doing); and, finally but importantly, an owner, director, manager or employee (or the family member of such a person) of any care home in which the donor is living when he executes the LPA.

8.87 The certificate provider has a responsibility to talk to the donor in private away from his attorney and to certify that he has done so otherwise the certificate is not valid.

8.88 An example of how even an ostensibly simple instruction can be ambiguous and likely to be scrutinised by the court is in the case of *Re Gibbs*:[17] the certificate provider ticked the box to confirm that he had discussed the LPA with the donor and that the attorneys were not present, he also ticked the box to say that the LPA had been discussed with the donor in the presence of other persons, identified by name as the attorneys. The court directed that the LPA was valid (the certificate provider having confirmed by letter that he had interviewed the donor on her own as well as with the attorneys present).

Part C of the LPA

8.89 As with an EPA, the declaration by the attorney in an LPA is an important reminder of the nature of the obligations imposed on the attorney to the effect that he:

(a) has read the prescribed information or a prescribed part of it (or has had it read to him); and

(b) understands the duties imposed on a donee of a lasting power of attorney under sections 1 (the principles) and 4 (best interests).

8.90 The attorney's declaration should also be completed by any replacement attorneys who must in addition make a declaration that if called upon to act by any of the trigger events (ie the disclaimer by an attorney, death or bankruptcy of an attorney, dissolution of the marriage or incapacity) the replacement attorney will notify the OPG and return the original LPA to the OPG. This is important so that the OPG has notice of the event and can update the records and also so that the OPG can endorse the original LPA which can subsequently be produced by the replacement attorney as his authority to act.

8.91 The LPA must be executed in sequence as set out above: the donor must read or have read to him the prescribed information which is contained on the face of the instrument, as soon as reasonably practicable the donor completes part A and signs it in the presence of a witness; as soon as reasonably practicable thereafter the certificate provider(s) complete part B and as soon as is reasonably practicable thereafter the attorneys must read or have read to them the prescribed information and complete and sign Part C in the presence of a witness.

Registration

8.92 As an LPA is not valid until it is registered, the final step is registration with the OPG. The OPG has issued Guidance on registration as well as the forms required to do so (see above). Registration of the LPA is also on a formal document (LPA 002) that, when submitted, must also include the original LPA or a certified copy.

---

[17] An order of the senior judge made on 9 September 2008.

8.93 The procedure is summarised as follows: notification to specified persons by the donor or putative attorneys of incipient registration; application to register made to the OPG in prescribed form accompanied by attached LPA instrument and fee for registration which is £130 (at the time of publication). It is a criminal offence to make false statements in connection with obtaining an LPA.

8.94 If there are no valid notices of objections within 6 weeks and no problems raised on the form, the OPG will register the LPA. This will be at least 6 weeks after the last notice was given.

Reasons for non-registration

8.95 If the OPG finds a provision on the LPA form which he considers would make the LPA unworkable or ineffective, the application must be referred to the Court of Protection before registration can take place. If an objection to registration is made to the OPG by any of the specified persons, the LPA cannot be registered unless and until the Court of Protection so directs. An objection has to be made formally on form COP7.

Where the Office of the Public Guardian must refuse to register

8.96 The OPG must refuse to register an LPA if is not made in accordance with the MCA 2005 or where the application is not accompanied by the original or a certified copy. Where the Court of Protection has already appointed a deputy and it appears to the OPG that the powers conferred on the deputy would conflict with the attorney's powers, the OPG must refer the application to the Court of Protection. See Chapter 10 for information about court appointed deputies.

8.97 If there is a provision in the LPA which would prevent the power from operating as an LPA then it must be referred to the Court of Protection. The Court of Protection can sever any such clause or restriction and the LPA will then be registered with a note on the register to that effect.

Revocation

8.98 After the LPA has been registered, if the donor wishes to revoke it he may do so by making a deed of revocation. He may do this at any time whilst he has the mental capacity to do so and the court will direct that the power be revoked if it is satisfied as to capacity. The LPA may be revoked by the court upon an application by another person where it is satisfied that it is proper to do so. The OPG will make an application for the LPA to be revoked where it has found evidence that the attorney has acted improperly.

The Code of Practice

8.99 As seen in Chapter 4, the Code of Practice provides practical guidance and best practice on how the MCA 2005 should be applied to everyday situations. It particularly applies to attorneys acting under LPAs. The Code is set out in a way that makes it accessible to layman and lawyer alike; it includes various scenarios which illustrate the point being made, for example:

> **'Scenario: Making decisions in a donor's best interests**
>
> Mr Young has been a member of the Green Party for a long time. He has appointed his solicitor as his attorney under a property and affairs LPA. But Mr Young did not state in the LPA that investments made on his behalf must be ethical investments. When the attorney assesses his client's best interests, however, the attorney considers the donor's past wishes, values and beliefs. He makes sure that he only invests in companies that are socially and environmentally responsible.'

8.100 As well as being required reading for attorneys acting under LPAs, it is suggested that Chapter 7 of the Code of Practice entitled *What does the Act say about Lasting Powers of Attorney?* is of great help to any person proposing to make an LPA. This chapter specifically deals with LPAs and describes how attorneys appointed under an LPA should act.

8.101 Attorneys acting under LPAs have to have regard to the relevant guidance in the Code of Practice when acting or making decisions on behalf of someone who lacks capacity to make the relevant decision for himself. They are well advised to familiarise themselves with the workings of the whole Code but particularly the following chapters: Chapter 2 which sets out how the principles in the MCA 2005 should be applied; Chapter 3 as to the steps to be taken to try to assist the person to make decisions himself; guidance on assessing capacity and the definition of lack of capacity in Chapter 4; and Chapter 5 which gives guidance on working out where a donor's best interest lies.

CHAPTER 9

PROPERTY AND AFFAIRS IN THE COURT OF PROTECTION

9.1 This chapter considers and explains the role of the Court of Protection in making decisions about the financial affairs of those affected by dementia.

9.2 The Court of Protection has for many years been concerned with the property and financial affairs of those who were considered mentally incapable of managing such matters. In the past, the approach taken by the court was somewhat patriarchal with the wishes and feelings of the patient (as those subject to the court's jurisdiction were known) being a long way down the list of factors to be taken into account. As a rule, the court made orders on the basis of what was objectively thought to be prudent regardless of what the patient would have wanted. The expansion of the court as a result of the enactment of the Mental Capacity Act 2005 (MCA 2005) brought about a concerted change of attitude and a much greater willingness to make decisions that might be viewed as carrying more risk where that accords with the expressed wishes of the person affected.

9.3 Another significant change brought about by the MCA 2005 was to the way in which capacity was determined. Previously, the court had simply considered that a person either did or did not have the general capacity to manage his financial affairs. Now, the court must consider the question of capacity in relation to each decision to be made and to ask whether the person has the capacity (with help if necessary) to make this particular decision. For many people with dementia, it will be clear that the ability to retain and weigh up information is so impaired that even relatively simple financial decisions will not be possible. However, for others, particularly in the early stages of the illness, some decisions could be made with help and the court is not permitted to interfere or overrule such decisions, even if they might appear unwise.

JURISDICTION

9.4 The Court of Protection is empowered to make decisions on behalf of a person who lacks the capacity to make that decision for himself. A firm distinction is drawn between decisions about a person's *welfare* and those concerning his *property and affairs*. As seen in chapter 4, welfare decisions typically concern matters such as where the person should live, who he should have contact with and whether or not a particular medical treatment should be administered. The most common property and affairs decisions concern the person's former home and whether it should be sold or the tenancy surrendered.

9.5 This distinction is, in part, the result of the court's long history in determining what should happen to the property and affairs of those who lack capacity, whereas its power to make welfare decisions is quite recent. Before the MCA 2005, there were no statutory provisions for such decisions to be made on behalf of another person and those decisions had to be decided by the High Court under its inherent jurisdiction (see chapter 15 for more information about the inherent jurisdiction). There is also another reason for the distinction between the two types of decision and that is that, generally, welfare decisions by the court are only needed when there is a dispute. If all concerned agree that a particular residential home is best, there is no need for the court to become involved. The types of dispute and the remedies available from the court are discussed in chapter 13. In contrast, unless there is a lasting power of attorney or an enduring power of attorney, the sanction of the court will always be required in property and affairs decisions even if all concerned agree. This is because no bank or solicitor (for example) will act on the instructions of a third party without proper authorisation. Consequently, the necessary financial transactions require an order from the court.

9.6 There are of course some cases which require the court to consider decisions that encompass both welfare and property and affairs. One common example is where an elderly person with Alzheimer's disease is living in a property that is in a state of disrepair and he does not want to move but is not sure whether or not he has the money to pay for the repairs. The court has to consider whether the person has capacity to manage his day to day finances and perhaps to appoint someone to investigate and manage the financial position in the interim. If there is no money for repairs, the court will then consider whether the person has the capacity to decide to continue to live in the unrepaired property and, if not, whether it would be in his best interest to move elsewhere. Whilst the welfare and financial issues are clearly intertwined, the court does tend to treat them separately and it is usual for two separate orders to be made at hearings; one dealing with the welfare issues and the other with the financial matters.

9.7 The Court of Protection may only make a decision on behalf of a person who is unable to make the decision for himself. The court is required to presume that a person has capacity unless there is evidence that he lacks capacity and so any application to the court must be supported by this evidence. See chapter 3 for information about capacity assessments. Where the person has mild to moderate dementia, his capacity is likely to fluctuate and this has a significant influence on the way the court approaches the question of whether or not it has the power to make the orders sought.

9.8 The court is required when making decisions for a person who lacks capacity to consider whether the desired purpose can be achieved in a way that is less restrictive of the person's rights and freedom of action. This should lead the court to ask questions such as whether the person would be able to manage if he had help or whether he could manage his day to day expenses if the more complex transactions were managed by someone else. It is therefore sensible to carefully consider these points before contemplating an application to the court and, where possible, to try out any less restrictive options.

9.9 The MCA 2005 permits the court to either make a decision on behalf of the person who lacks capacity or to appoint another person to make decisions on his behalf. Where another person is appointed to make the decisions, that person is referred to as the deputy. The court may appoint a deputy to make welfare decisions but rarely does so (see chapter 4).

9.10 In practice, the court will usually appoint a deputy where there is a need for ongoing management of the person's financial affairs. This is because it is not reasonably practicable for the court to take the day to day decisions necessary. Where that ongoing decision making is not required, the court should make the necessary decision rather than appoint a deputy for property and affairs. An example of when that would be appropriate is a person who needs to surrender a secure tenancy whose only income comes from a state pension and welfare benefits that are already being received by an appointee.[1] Once the court has authorised the surrender of the tenancy, there is no need for any further input and the appointee can continue to receive the pension and benefits without the court's involvement.

9.11 The types of decision that can be made by the court are set out in s 16 of the MCA 2005 and include:

- the control and management of P's property;
- the sale, exchange, charging, gift or other disposition of P's property;
- the acquisition of property in P's name or on P's behalf;
- the carrying on, on P's behalf, of any profession, trade or business;
- the taking of a decision which will have the effect of dissolving a partnership of which P is a member;
- the carrying out of any contract entered into by P;
- the discharge of P's debts and of any of P's obligations, whether legally enforceable or not;
- the settlement of any of P's property, whether for P's benefit or for the benefit of others;
- the execution for P of a will;
- the exercise of any power (including a power to consent) vested in P whether beneficially or as trustee or otherwise;
- the conduct of legal proceedings in P's name or on P's behalf.

---

1 An appointee is a person who receives another person's state benefits as a result of an application to the Department of Work and Pensions.

9.12 Not all of these decisions can be delegated by the court to a deputy for property and affairs. For example, the decision to execute a will can only be made by the court.

APPLICATIONS TO THE COURT OF PROTECTION

9.13 The provisions of the MCA 2005 set out the nature and extent of the court's powers. The administrative and legal framework within which the court operates is contained in the Court of Protection Rules 2007 ('the COP Rules'). There are also a number of Practice Directions which set out in detail what the court requires in particular circumstances; for example there are Practice Directions on service of documents and urgent applications.[2]

Permission

9.14 Before starting the application, it is important to consider whether permission is required. Section 50 of the MCA 2005 stipulates that unless it or the COP Rules provide otherwise, the permission of the court is required before an application can be made. Most applications relating to property and affairs do not require permission[3] and can be made by anybody. The exceptions are certain applications under the Trustee Act 1925 and applications relating to gifts, settlements or wills where the application is not made by a person in one of the specified classes (see Rule 52 for the full details).

9.15 Some applications to the court will involve mixed issues, some of which do not require permission and others that do. If a single application is made, the issues that do not require permission will not be considered until permission has been given to make the application. Alternatively, two separate applications could be made (and two separate fees paid) so that the issues that do not require permission can be considered without waiting for permission for the other application. Whether it is sensible to make one application or two will depend on the circumstances. For example, it is common for the court to be asked to decide whether it would be in a person's best interest to move into a care home. That application requires permission because it is a welfare issue. It is usual for the court also to be asked for an order that the former home be sold to meet the cost and to appoint a deputy for property and affairs to manage the person's finances on an ongoing basis. That application does not need permission. If the person will need a deputy whether or not he moves to a care home then it would be sensible to make two separate applications. If the deputy is only needed if the former home is sold then a single application would be appropriate.

9.16 If permission is required, the court will consider carefully whether or not the application should be heard and in doing so will have particular regard to

---

[2] These can be obtained from http://www.judiciary.gov.uk/publications-and-reports/practice-directions/cop-practice-directions.

[3] Rule 51(2)(a) of the COP Rules.

the reasons for the application, the benefit to the person about whom the application would be made and whether that benefit could be achieved in some other way.

9.17 The request for permission is made by submitting a COP2 permission form accompanied by a draft of the application for which permission is sought using form COP1 and an assessment of capacity using form COP3. The application fee also will need to be paid. It is important to explain carefully in the draft application what the benefit of the application is and why it cannot readily be achieved without court proceedings.

The application

9.18 The application must be made on form COP1. The application fee at the time of writing is £400. There are two classes of persons who may have an interest in the application that must be listed. These are respondents and persons notified and, in practice, it can be difficult to distinguish between the two. The notes to the form define the respondents as *any person who you reasonably believe has an interest which means they ought to be heard by the court* whereas the persons to be notified are *other people who are likely to have an interest in being notified of your application*. Respondents must be served with a copy of the application form and all documents filed with the application whereas persons to be notified are simply informed that an application has been issued and of the orders sought.

9.19 It is good practice to list as a respondent any person closely connected to the matter who is likely to object to the order being sought. It might also be appropriate to list as a respondent a person who will support the application if that person might otherwise have been thought likely to make an application himself.

9.20 There is a Practice Direction (PD9B) giving details of who is to be notified of an application. There is a presumption that close family members (spouse or civil partner, any other partner, parents and children) will have an interest in being notified of the application. If the applicant is aware of circumstances which mean that a close family member should not be notified of the application, evidence in support of the decision not to notify that person will be required. The obligation to notify is not limited to family members and may include close friends, particularly those who have been providing informal care. The Practice Direction states '[i]n some cases, P may be closer to persons who are not relatives and if so, it will be appropriate to notify them instead of family members'. Attempts must be made to identify at least three people who are likely to have an interest in being notified of the application.

9.21 The COP1 application must be accompanied by an assessment of capacity using form COP3 or a witness statement explaining:

- why the applicant has not been able to obtain an assessment of capacity;

- what attempts have been made to obtain an assessment of capacity; and
- why he believes that the person lacks the capacity to make the decision that is the subject of the application.

9.22 At this stage, the evidence of capacity need not be in its final form, particularly if capacity is disputed. However, there does need to be sufficient evidence for the court to have reasonable grounds for believing that the person *may* lack capacity. This is because the MCA 2005 contains a presumption of capacity and the court has no powers to make orders or give directions unless there are reasonable grounds for thinking that presumption might be rebutted.

9.23 Depending on the type of application, it may be necessary to file other forms or evidence with the application. It will often be helpful to supplement the information on the COP1 with a witness statement containing the relevant facts and any material of which the court ought to be made aware but this is not strictly necessary if the application form contains all the important information.

9.24 Practice Direction 9A sets out the requirements for other documents that must be filed with the application form as follows:

Table 9.1 Practice Direction 9A: required documents

Type of document or instrument	When document is to be filed
Any order granting permission.	If permission is required.
Assessment of capacity form (COP3).	Unless already filed with the permission form.
Annex A: Supporting information for property and affairs applications (COP1A).	Where an order relating to P's property and affairs is sought.
Annex B: Supporting information for personal welfare applications (COP1B).	Where an order relating to P's personal welfare is sought.
Lasting power of attorney or enduring power of attorney.	Where the application concerns the court's power under section 22 or 23 of, or Schedule 4 to, the Act (where available).
Deputy's declaration (COP4).	Where the application is for the appointment of a deputy.
Order appointing a deputy.	Where the application relates to or is made by a deputy.
Order appointing a litigation friend.	Where the application is made by, or where the application relates to the appointment of, a litigation friend.

Type of document or instrument	When document is to be filed
Order of the Court of Protection.	Where the application relates to the order.
Order of another court (and where the judgment is not in English, a translation of it into English: (i) certified by a notary public or other qualified person; or (ii) accompanied by written evidence confirming that the translation is accurate).	Where the application relates to an order made by another court.

Urgent applications

9.25 There is a procedure for urgent applications to be put before a judge very quickly. However, this is intended to be used only when there is an immediate danger or risk to the person concerned. Urgent applications about property and affairs are rare but do arise on occasion such as when an imminent financial transaction needs to be stopped because the funds will otherwise be irrecoverable. The procedure for urgent applications is set out in Practice Direction 10B.

The order sought

9.26 Some care needs to be taken in formulating the details of the order(s) sought from the court. It has already been noted above that MCA 2005 requires the court to favour making a decision on behalf of the person who lacks capacity rather than appointing a deputy. The timing of the application and the extent of the person's dementia will both have an important bearing on the court's attitude as to what order it should make. The question of whether there is another method of achieving the desired purpose which involves a lesser degree of interference with the person's right to autonomy should always be considered diligently and objectively.

9.27 The starting point should be to ask whether there is going to be a need for ongoing decision making on a regular basis in respect of the person's property and affairs. If so, then the court is likely to appoint a deputy to make those decisions rather than the matter having to come back before the court each time. In answering that question, the court will take account of the person's current financial position and (if applicable) his ability to make some decisions for himself.

9.28 This approach is illustrated in the case of *G v E*[4] where the court declined to appoint a deputy for property and affairs because, at the time of the hearing, E's income consisted of benefits alone and his saving were less than £1,000. The

4 [2010] EWHC 2512 (COP).

court was aware that he expected to be awarded a significant sum of damages in forthcoming proceedings but held that the appointment of a financial deputy should be considered then.

9.29 If the appointment of a deputy is not appropriate or is not appropriate at this time, the court should be asked to make the necessary decision(s) on behalf of the person. The court will need to be satisfied that the person lacks the capacity to make this particular decision and that it is the least intrusive means of achieving a necessary or desirable purpose. This can lead to difficulties where the dementia is at an early stage or where the extent of impairment fluctuates. The court will not impose a decision on a person who may well be able to make the decision for himself on another day. It is, therefore, important to explore alternative options and to provide the court with good evidence as to why they will not achieve the desired purpose.

9.30 Some of the most common types of order sought are considered in more detail later in this chapter.

The court's approach

9.31 In many cases where the application relates to property and affairs, there is no dispute as to whether the order sought should be granted and the court will be satisfied that it can grant the application without holding a hearing or requiring the person with dementia to be made a party to the proceedings. However, where there is a dispute, the court will usually order that the person be made a party to the application and, if the person does not have capacity to litigate, a litigation friend will be required to conduct the litigation on his behalf. The identity of an appropriate litigation friend will depend upon the nature and facts of the dispute. Where the dispute is between members of the family, it will not normally be appropriate for any of them to act as the litigation friend. Where there is no other suitable litigation friend,[5] the court will invite the Official Solicitor to act instead. The Official Solicitor is a litigation friend of last resort. He will normally instruct solicitors to act for the person and those costs will need to be met from his funds (unless he is entitled to public funding). The Official Solicitor will not accept the court's invitation to act until he has satisfied himself that (i) there is no one else who could be litigation friend; and, (ii) the legal costs will be paid. This can result in a delay before the court can properly consider the merits of the application.[6]

9.32 The evidence needed to support the application will depend on the nature of the application and whether it is likely to be disputed. In cases where capacity is not disputed, the COP3 assessment is usually sufficient. However, where capacity is disputed, expert evidence is likely to be required.

---

5 See r 140 of the Court of Protection Rules 2007 and Practice Direction 17A.

6 Further information about the official solicitor's criteria for acceptance of appointment as litigation friend can be found at www.justice.gov.uk/about/ospt.

9.33 In all property and affairs applications form COP1A must be filed. This form is headed 'Annex A: Supporting information for property and affairs application'. It is a long form requiring details of the person's income, assets and expenditure. Much of this information may not be known to the person making the application and it can be difficult to obtain information from banks and solicitors where there is no formal power of attorney and there has been no order from the court. These difficulties are recognised by the court and the COP1A should be completed to the best of the applicant's knowledge, clearly indicating where figures are provisional or are estimated. If the court needs further or more accurate information, it can make an interim order authorising the applicant to undertake further investigations. That order should provide sufficient authority for the required information to be obtained.

9.34 The other evidence in support of the application should be given in one or more witness statements which must be included in or attached to form COP24. The witness statement must be verified by a statement of truth.[7] Any documents referred to in the witness statement should be exhibited to it. Practice Direction 14A gives further requirements as to the format and content of witness statements.

Costs

9.35 The way in which the court deals with the costs of the proceedings is different for welfare applications and property and affairs matters. The usual rule in welfare applications is that each party bears its own costs and the court will only depart from that where there is good reason, usually because a party has acted unreasonably in some way that has caused costs to be incurred that would not otherwise have been necessary.

9.36 In contrast, the usual rule for property and affairs is that all the costs should come from assets of the person to whom the application relates. Again, this rule is only departed from where there is a good reason why another party should pay some or all of the costs. In practice, such orders are only made where the court views the conduct of a party as being wholly unreasonable and having caused unnecessary cost. Where an application has been brought in good faith for an order concerning the property and affairs of a person with dementia, the applicant should not normally be ordered to pay the costs even if the application is refused.

9.37 Where a single application has been made seeking orders that concern both welfare issues and property and affairs, the court will usually make two separate orders and will deal with the costs separately in each order: the welfare order containing a provision that there be no order for costs in respect of the welfare issues; and, the property and affairs order providing that the costs of the property and affairs issues be met from the patient's estate.

---

7 That means it must end with the words 'I believe that the facts stated in this witness statement are true' and the signature of the person making the statement.

9.38 Where the court awards costs, these can be paid on a fixed cost basis[8] or subject to summary assessment by the judge or a detailed assessment by a costs officer.[9]

Common types of decision

9.39 Under the MCA 2005, the court is empowered to make a decision on behalf of a person who lacks capacity. Alternatively, it may appoint a deputy to make decisions on that person's behalf. In deciding which of these options to adopt in any particular case, the court is required to have regard to the principle that a decision of the court is to be preferred to the appointment of a deputy.[10] Although the court is more likely to appoint a deputy for property and affairs than a welfare deputy, it will still consider carefully whether a particular decision can, or should, be delegated to a deputy. A number of the decisions most commonly required are considered below.

Sale of property

9.40 Where a person has permanently moved into residential care leaving the former home empty, there is usually an expectation that it will be sold. Although property is an asset that is likely to appreciate in value, the court recognises that empty properties are vulnerable to vandalism and burglary and that maintenance can be a heavy burden.

9.41 Issues arise when the move to residential care has been on a trial basis or where the person believes that he will be able to return home in the future. The court will want to be satisfied that there is no real prospect of the person being able to return home with support before it will authorise the irreversible step of selling the property. In practice, this can present difficulties as most people with dementia could live at home if live-in carers were employed. However, for most people, the cost would be prohibitive and the quality of life that could be achieved questionable. Where such issues arise, it might be sensible to also ask the court to make a welfare decision about where it would be in the best interest of the person to reside.

9.42 In some cases, it may be preferable to rent the property to tenants rather than to sell it. This is particularly so where the property is left to a named person in the will. Whether or not rental is a practical option will largely depend upon whether there is someone who is willing and able to manage the property on an ongoing basis. If the property is to be let rather than sold, that need for ongoing management would necessitate the appointment of a deputy.

9.43 Where the former home is occupied, the question of whether or not it should be sold is much more difficult and each case will turn on its own facts.

---

8 As provided for by Practice Direction 19B.

9 Rule 164 of the Court of Protection Rules 2007.

10 See s 16(2) and (4) of MCA 2005.

At one end of the spectrum, where the property is occupied by a fit and healthy adult child who has not provided significant care and the proceeds of sale are required to meet the costs of the residential care home, the court is highly likely to order a sale. At the other end, where the property is occupied by a person who has provided a substantial amount of care for many years and there are sufficient other assets from which the care fees can be paid, it is unlikely that the sale would be authorised.

9.44 The question of what should happen to the proceeds of sale once the property has been sold also needs to be considered. In most cases, the proceeds will need to be invested and the care home bills settled on an ongoing basis. This will usually necessitate the appointment of a deputy for property and affairs. Where property that has been sold is bequeathed in a will or would have passed under an intestacy, the beneficiary is entitled to what remains of the proceeds of sale at death.[11] There is, therefore, a duty to preserve the proceeds to the extent compatible with the best interest of the person with dementia.

Surrender of tenancy

9.45 Many of the same issues arise in respect of surrendering a tenancy as when authorisation is sought to sell the former home. However, a rented home is not an appreciating asset and so, unless there are issues as to whether the person will be able to return home in the future or it is occupied by a person able to pay the rent, the court will almost always find it in the person with dementia's best interest to surrender the tenancy and put an end to their financial obligations.

9.46 Secure tenants, assured tenants and Rent Act tenants all lose their security of tenure if the property is no longer occupied as the principal or only home. This may result in the landlord seeking possession once it has become clear that an admission to residential care is likely to be permanent. If there is no real prospect of a return home, the court is unlikely to find it in the person's best interest to resist such a claim.

Gifts

9.47 The court's authority will be needed to make a substantial gift using funds belonging to the person with dementia. The exceptions are those gifts that the person would customarily make such as on birthdays and at Christmas and small charitable gifts. The key features are that the gifts must be of a similar nature and value to those that the person made before the onset of their illness. Gifts over a particular threshold will always need to be authorised by the court. The level of the threshold will depend upon the resources of the person concerned. In one case,[12] the court held that that gifts up to the

---

11 Paragraph 8 of Schedule 2 to MCA 2005.

12 *Re GM* [2013] COPLR 290.

Inheritance Tax exempt amount of £3,000 per year plus small gifts of up to £250 to 10 people was the appropriate threshold; whereas in another case where the person had more modest means[13] a threshold of £1,000 per year was appropriate.

9.48 Where the authorisation of a gift is sought, the court will need evidence to explain why this gift should be made and to demonstrate that it can be made without causing hardship. If the local authority is providing a financial contribution towards the costs of a residential care home, or is likely to in the future, the effect of the gift upon that funding will need to be considered (see chapter 10).

9.49 The court's approach to whether or not a gift should be authorised is very much dependent upon the facts of the case at hand. However, some general guidance can be obtained from the following three cases:

(1) The court was asked to give retrospective authority for very large sums gifted by the deputies to charities and to themselves and their immediate families. The gifts to the charities were authorised as was one gift of £2,500 to a family member, which an investigation by the Public Guardian had suggested P would have wanted to make. The other gifts over and above the appropriate annual threshold were not authorised and the deputies were personally liable to reimburse P's estate for those unauthorised gifts.[14]

(2) The court was asked to order a deputy for property and affairs to make payments to P's adult daughter by way of maintenance. The judge could only make that order if it was in P's best interest to do so. In considering whether it was in P's best interest to maintain her daughter, the judge found that best interest was not the same as self-interest and that it could be in a person's best interest to behave altruistically. He took the view that P would have wanted to support her daughter and that was an important consideration. There were no countervailing factors which suggested that it would not be in P's best interest to make the maintenance payments and the court ordered that they be made.[15]

(3) P had been injured at birth and had received substantial compensation. The deputy sought the court's authority to transfer £325,000 into a trust with the intention of reducing the inheritance tax liability for P's estate to the benefit of his parents after his death. The court declined to authorise the transfer. It held that the purpose for which P had been awarded compensation and the assumptions upon which it was based were factors which militated against the proposed trust. In principle all of the funds paid to P as compensation for his injury would be needed. If the calculations were correct, the last pound of compensation would be spent in the minute of his death and so it was not in his best interest to divest

---

13 *Re Joan Treadwell (Deceased)* [2013] EWHC 2409 (Cop).

14 *Re GM* [2013] COPLR 290.

15 *Re G(TJ)* [2010] EWHC 3005 (COP).

himself of such a large amount of capital. The court also commented that it was not its function *to anticipate, ring-fence or maximise any potential inheritance for the benefit of family members.*[16]

Statutory wills

9.50 The court is provided with a power under s 18 of MCA 2005 to execute a will on behalf of an adult who does not have the mental capacity to do so. This power cannot be delegated to a deputy for property and affairs. In the past, the court has been reticent about making such wills and would do so only where necessary in order to prevent the intention of an existing will being defeated. Further, in setting the terms of the will to be made, the court would attempt to ascertain what the person lacking capacity would have done with the benefit of competent professional advice. The modern approach, since the MCA 2005 came into force is to approve the making of a will where that is in the best interest of the person concerned. As previously stated, best interest is not limited to self interest and this is particularly pertinent in respect of applications for a statutory will. The court has recognised that '*having done the right thing by his will*' and being remembered for that after death are relevant concerns.[17]

9.51 The court must be satisfied that the person with dementia lacks the capacity to make the will himself. Where the dementia is advanced, this is unlikely to present any issues. However, where capacity fluctuates, the court may not be satisfied that the test is met. In the case of *A, B & C v X, Y & Z*[18] the court declined to make a general declaration that X, who had dementia, did not have the capacity to make a will. However, the court strongly qualified that finding by saying that there were many times when he did lack testamentary capacity and that such periods were likely to become more frequent, such that any will now made would be seriously open to challenge unless accompanied by contemporary medical evidence asserting capacity.

9.52 In practice, where a person has made a will before the onset of dementia which now needs to be amended (for example, because it refers to a specific property but the person with dementia has moved to a new property) the court is likely to order the execution of an amended will. Approval for a statutory will is also likely where the person's estate has dwindled to a level where any distribution now made would be substantially different from that envisaged at the time that the will was made.

9.53 Further, the court is likely to approve a statutory will where there has been a significant change in circumstances such that a person who did not have dementia would have been likely to revisit the terms of an existing will or to make a will where he had previously not seen any need to do so. Where there

---

16 *Re JDS; KGS v JDS* [2012] EWHC 302 (COP).

17 *Re M* COPLR Con Vol 828 at paragraph 38.

18 [2012] COP EWHC 2400 at paragraph 37.

have been changes to the system of taxation, the court is likely to authorise a statutory will that achieved the same result as the existing will but in a more tax-efficient manner.

9.54 The position is much less obvious where there are likely to be significant disputes about the existing will after death. The Court of Protection does not have the power to declare a will to be invalid; that is a matter for the Chancery Division of the High Court. However, it does have the power to execute a new will thereby revoking the contentious one. The circumstances in which the court will use that power to prevent a future dispute are generally those where the beneficiaries are able to agree the terms thereby resolving the underlying conflict and removing the likelihood of future litigation.

FINANCIAL DEPUTIES

9.55 The court will only appoint a deputy for property and affairs where it is satisfied that it is necessary to do so because there is a need for ongoing day to day decision making that would not be practical or appropriate to be brought before the court. The court is unlikely to be satisfied that a deputy is necessary if the person's only income is welfare benefits and/or the state pension because the Secretary of State for Work and Pensions has a simple procedure whereby an appointee may apply for and receive these payments on behalf of the person who lacks capacity.[19] Where a person has income from other sources and substantial capital assets, the need for a deputy will be obvious.

9.56 It may be necessary to appoint an interim deputy for property and affairs where the court needs to be fully appraised of the person's financial position in order to make other decisions about what is in his best interest. For example, in proceedings in the family court for financial remedies in a divorce where one of the parties has dementia, there are likely to be concurrent proceedings in the Court of Protection for a decision as to where it would be in his best interest to live. To answer that question, the court will need to know whether it is financially viable for the person to remain in the former matrimonial home before making a decision. A deputy may well be appointed for the duration of the proceedings to investigate the position and manage the financial affairs until the court has made a decision.

9.57 Careful consideration should be given to the identity of the proposed deputy. The duties as set out below can be quite onerous and it is important that the person is willing and able to take on the task. In many cases, it would be natural to propose that the spouse be appointed deputy. However, where the spouse is also taking a substantial role in caring for the person with dementia, it may be advisable for an adult child to take the role of deputy. Alternatively, the court may appoint more than one person to act as deputy, either jointly and severally or successively. Although the court has the power to appoint joint

19 Regulation 33 of the Social Security (Claims and Payments) Regulations 1987. For details of how to apply, see https://www.gov.uk/become-appointee-for-someone-claiming-benefits.

deputies where there is a dispute, it is unlikely to do so if that would mean every decision became contentious and increased the level of conflict. In such circumstances, it is likely to attempt to identify an alternative deputy.

9.58 Where there is no suitable deputy from amongst the family or close friends, a panel deputy may be considered. That is a solicitor from the list maintained by the Office of the Public Guardian (OPG) who is suitably experienced and willing to act as a deputy. A panel deputy is paid at professional rates for the work that is carried out in the role of deputy and this cost will come from the assets of the person who lacks capacity. Many local authorities will also agree to act a deputy for property and affairs, although some will only do so where the person lacking capacity is in residential care arranged through the local authority. The local authority is also entitled to be paid for the work done but this is at a lower rate than a panel deputy.

9.59 The application process is as described above. Permission is not needed and, where the need is clear cut and the application is uncontentious, the order appointing the deputy for property and affairs is usually made without a hearing. Where there is a dispute as to who should be appointed deputy, the court may decide to hold a hearing. Although the court will consider all of the circumstances of the case, 'generally speaking the order of preference is:

- "P's spouse or partner;
- any other relative who takes a close personal interest in P's affairs;
- a close friend;
- a professional advisor, such as the family solicitor, or accountant;
- a *local authority's Social Services Department; and finally*
- a panel deputy, as deputy of last resort."'[20]

9.60 When the court makes an order appointing the deputy for property and affairs, it will draw up that order setting out the extent of the deputy's authority. The deputy must notify the person who lacks capacity that an order has been made. The order will authorise the deputy to make decisions within the scope of its terms but only where the person is unable to make the decision for himself. It is important to bear in mind that a person who lacks the capacity to make the complex decisions required to manage his financial affairs on an ongoing basis may still be capable of making one-off decisions about specific issues.

Where the person's capacity fluctuates, this may mean that he has capacity to make the particular decision at times but not at others. In those circumstances, the deputy would be required to consider not only whether the person can make this decision for himself (with help if necessary) but also whether he

---

[20] *Re AS* (unreported decision of Senior Judge Lush 7 December 2012).

would be able to do so during a more lucid interlude. Only if the deputy was satisfied on both counts would he be authorised by the order to make the decision on that person's behalf.

9.61 The court will usually require the deputy (unless it is a local authority) to provide the Office of the Public Guardian with security of an amount commensurate with the value of the estate of the person lacking capacity.[21] The purpose of the security is to protect the person lacking capacity from any loss incurred as a result of negligence or some other default by the deputy. The starting point for the level of that security is the amount of the funds that are in the deputy's control and might be lost in the event of total default. The premium payable to acquire that level of security is then considered in the context of the person lacking capacity's resources to assess whether it would be an unjustifiable or wasteful use of resources when balanced against the benefit of the protection offered. The court will then set the level of security taking account of these matters.[22]

9.62 The Office of the Public Guardian also has an ongoing responsibility to supervise deputies appointed by the court. The nature of that supervision will vary depending on the size and complexity of the estate of the person. There are four levels of supervision with varying degrees of scrutiny with an annual charge which (at the time of publication) is £320 for levels 1, 2 and 2A and £35 per annum for level 3 (minimal supervision).

9.63 The deputy is entitled to be reimbursed out of the person lacking capacity's estate for reasonable expenses incurred in managing his property and affairs. This will include the premium payable for the security bond referred to above. The deputy is not entitled to any remuneration for the work done as deputy unless the court has ordered otherwise. The court will not order that the deputy receive any remuneration unless it has appointed a solicitor or other professional deputy or the local authority has been appointed.

9.64 Where the court is satisfied that the deputy has or intends to act in way that is (i) contrary to his authority; or (ii) not in the person lacking capacity's best interests, the court may revoke the appointment.[23] Where the deputy is no longer able or willing to act or where he dies, the court may discharge the order or may vary it to appoint another person in his place.[24]

DEPUTIES' OBLIGATIONS

9.65 When an order is made by the court appointing a deputy for property and affairs, it will set out the extent of the deputy's powers. The deputy may

---

21 As provided for by MCA 2005, s 19(9).

22 See *Re H (A Minor and Incapacitated Person); Baker v H and the Official Solicitor* [2009] COPLR Con Vol 606.

23 See s 16(8).

24 See s 16(7).

only make decisions and take actions that are (i) authorised within that order; and (ii) in the best interest of the person lacking capacity. If the deputy believes that it is in the person's best interest for a decision or action to be taken which is outside the scope of the powers in the order, he must ask the court to either make that particular decision or, if appropriate, to extend his powers to authorise the deputy to make that decision.

9.66 It is also important that a deputy considers whether any decision contemplated is one that the person could make themselves or could make with assistance. This is not always straight forward when there is a moderate degree of dementia. Where capacity is fluctuating with lucid spells experienced from time to time and the decision does not need to be made urgently, the deputy would be expected to try to discuss the matter with the person, perhaps on several occasions, before concluding that he cannot make this particular decision. Where the dementia is advanced, it will be more obvious that the person cannot make a considered decision about matters of financial importance.

9.67 Complications can also arise for a deputy where there is a lasting power of attorney ('LPA') in effect. The court is not permitted to give a deputy the authority to make any decision which is inconsistent with a lawful decision made a person holding a lasting power of attorney.[25] In this context a lawful decision is one that is within the authority given by the LPA and has been made in the person lacking capacity's best interest. This usually arises where there is a welfare LPA and a financial deputy. The deputy will need to consider whether any decision he proposes to make would be inconsistent with the attorney's decisions. For example, if the attorney has made a decision under the LPA that the person should go in to residential care, the deputy for property and affairs would have no power to purchase a new home for him to live in.

9.68 The deputy is required to apply the principles set out in s 1 of the MCA 2005 and to have regard to the guidance in the Code of Practice[26] issued under s 42 of the MCA 2005.[27] It is therefore important that a deputy is familiar with the Code of Practice in general and s 8 in particular. A deputy who has not complied with the Code of Practice could potentially face criminal prosecution[28] or could incur civil liability for any losses that resulted from that failure.

9.69 Clearly, the deputy must make decisions that are in the person's best interest and must take reasonable care to ensure that he does not cause financial loss. The deputy acts as agent for the person with dementia and so there is a fiduciary duty. This means that the deputy must not take advantage of the

---

25 See s 20(4).

26 Available from http://www.justice.gov.uk/protecting-the-vulnerable/mental-capacity-act.

27 Section 42(4)(b).

28 The MCA 2005 creates specific offences of ill-treating or wilfully neglecting a person who lacks capacity s 44. A deputy for property and affairs could well face allegations of neglect which carries a maximum sentence of five years imprisonment.

position for his own benefit. The deputy must act in good faith and may not delegate his duties to another person. The deputy must also keep money belonging to the person with dementia separate from his own money and must keep adequate and accurate records to be able to account for his actions undertaken on the person's behalf.

9.70 There are occasions when the potential arises for a conflict of interest between the deputy and the person with dementia. For example, the deputy may be the joint owner of a property. However, the court takes a pragmatic view of such situations. Most deputies have some degree of interest in the person's estate and it would be impractical to exclude them all from appointment as deputies because of such theoretical possibilities. However, where the deputy proposes to take some action which does give rise to a more tangible conflict, such as where he proposes to buy out the person's interest in a jointly-owned property, the matter should be referred to the court for directions. The court may well ask the Official Solicitor to represent the person with dementia in respect of that particular issue to ensure that his interest is seen to be adequately protected.

9.71 In a recent unreported case,[29] the court held that there was no real conflict of interest where the local authority that had been appointed as deputy for property and affairs sought to realise assets in order to pay its charges for residential care provided to the person concerned. The court reasoned that the person would have to pay the fees whether or not he lacked capacity. If it was in P's best interest to live in a care home then there was no real choice, the fees had to be paid.

FINANCIAL ABUSE

9.72 Where there are concerns that an attorney or deputy may be using the funds of the person with dementia improperly, these should be reported to the Office of the Public Guardian as it is responsible for supervising the use of such powers. Where the Office of the Public Guardian is satisfied that an attorney or a deputy has acted contrary to the person's interest, it may apply to the court to revoke the appointment.[30] An application can also be brought by any person who has sufficient connection to the person with dementia.

9.73 Where financial abuse is suspected, it may also be appropriate to approach the local authority for the area in which the person with dementia is living. The local authority has a statutory duty to safeguard vulnerable adults[31] and should investigate such allegations. However, the local authority does not

---

[29] *Re RGS No 2* COP Case No 11831647.

[30] In respect of attorneys see MCA 2005, s 13, in respect of deputies see s 16(8).

[31] This duty arises from the guidance issued by the Department of Health under Section 7 of the Local Authority Social Services Act 1970 *'No Secrets' guidance on developing and implementing multi-agency policies and procedures to protect vulnerable adults from abuse.*

have powers to compel the disclosure of bank accounts records or other documents and so there are practical limits to the extent of those investigations.

CHAPTER 10

FUNDING FOR CARE SERVICES

10.1 Many people with dementia receive a substantial amount of care from their family and friends. However, there usually comes a point where the extent of the care needed exceeds that which can be sustained. Even the most loving and dedicated carer will need a break from time to time for the sake of their own well-being. This chapter explores the legal issues that arise when engaging care services or arranging residential care on a self-funding basis and explains the regime for charging when such services are provided with the assistance of the local social services authority.

10.2 In recent years, there has been a huge growth in the number of private care agencies that provide services to people in their own homes. This probably comes as a result of the trend within local authorities to outsource such services to the private sector rather than running such services 'in-house'. However, that growth has also been driven by a change in attitude towards the elderly and a much greater willingness to accommodate the desire to remain at home. This is particularly important for a person with dementia where the need for familiar surroundings is acute. It is, arguably, easier than at any time before to secure the services needed to enable the person to stay in his own home; whether that is entirely through arrangements made without any involvement of the local authority, with financial assistance only from the local authority or through services provided by the local authority. Issues can arise with contractual arrangements and employment relationships where the care is arranged privately and the costs met from the person's own resources. Many people will be entitled to assistance from the local authority, which might take the form of a financial contribution towards the cost of those care needs that have been assessed as eligible needs or it might be in the form of services. The allocation of an individual or personal budget and the financial assessment are complex processes that are not always well explained or understood.

10.3 When residential care does become the appropriate option, the selection of the care home and arrangements for admission may be made without local authority involvement or the arrangements may be made by the local authority in consultation with the family. Even where the arrangements are entirely private, some regard should be given to the criteria and assessment regime, whereby the local authority arranges or funds the accommodation, if there is any prospect that the person's resources will be depleted to the extent that local authority assistance may be needed at some point in the future. Whilst a person who is funding their own care has a free choice of care home at whatever price he is willing to pay, the same is not true of those who will need assistance, where there is a maximum weekly rate and complex rules as to the circumstances in which a more expensive care home can be used and how the difference in cost may be funded. The position in respect of the person's own home is often an emotive issue because it may have to be sold to fund the residential care placement. The treatment of such properties in the financial assessment process is explained below, along with the option for deferring the sale until after death. The financial assessment regime incorporates a number of anti-avoidance measures that enable the local authority to look past financial transactions intended to reduce the amount that a person will contribute towards the cost of residential care. There are also powers to force the sale of property where debts are accruing for residential care.

10.4 The cost of the sort of care services needed by those with dementia is of considerable concern and it is an understandable complaint that it is unfair for those who have been financially prudent and acquired assets to have to sell those assets to pay the full cost of their care whilst those who have been profligate and saved nothing are funded by the public purse. These issues have been the subject of several reports by bodies such as the Dilnot Commission, the Kings Fund and the Law Commission and the Government has resolved to address these concerns. Although not yet finalised, the draft Care Bill attempts to simplify the myriad of legislation that currently applies to social care and is likely to bring about some significant changes in the course of 2015. The Government has also announced more profound changes, with the introduction of a lifetime cap in the amount a person must pay towards the cost of social care and this is expected to be implemented in 2016. The final part of this chapter considers these changes.

CARE AT HOME

Self-funded care

10.5 Many people prefer to make their own arrangements and engage a care agency or employ a carer directly without any involvement from the local authority. Where the person is unlikely to qualify for any financial assistance from the local authority this approach is understandable. However, every person who appears to be in need of community care services is entitled to an assessment by the local authority.[1] Even if it is proposed to purchase care separately, the assessment of needs by an experienced social worker is likely to be extremely useful in defining what services should be purchased.

10.6 There are many agencies providing social care services and these are regulated and inspected by the Care Quality Commission (although at the time of writing many care providers had not yet been inspected for the first time). It is important to be clear about the services being engaged and, in particular, who

[1] Section 47 of the National Health Service and Community Care Act 1990. See Chapter 3 for more information about assessments.

will visit, when and what tasks will be carried out on each visit. These details should be set out in a written care plan that will form the basis of the contract with the care agency. The contract itself must include a commitment that the care services will be provided and set out the fee to be paid for those services. The care agency should be responsible for arranging cover in the event that the usual carer is unable to attend for whatever reason.

10.7 Issues arise where the person receiving the care has dementia and there is no person with formal authority to act on his behalf (ie there is no one with a power or attorney and no deputy). This is because the care agency will want to be sure that the contract is legally enforceable. A contract signed by a person with dementia is a valid contract, even if he did not have capacity.[2] However, such a contract is liable to be set aside by a court if the fees are not paid and the care agency tried to enforce it on the grounds that was no true meeting of minds because the person with dementia cannot have understood what was being agreed. The care agency is likely to insist that the contract is signed by someone else. In doing so, it is important that the person signing understands that he is personally liable to pay the fees to the agency and must then look to the person with dementia for reimbursement.

10.8 Difficulties can also arise in making the payment. It is not uncommon for care services to commence when the dementia is at a relatively early stage when there are periods of sound capacity during which payments are made. As the condition deteriorates these become fewer and further apart and substantial arrears accrue. By the time it is clear that the person will not be able to make the payment himself, there is a large debt and the agency are threatening to withdraw from the contract. It is important to recognise that this may occur and to put in place measures to minimise the likelihood of a breakdown in the relationship with the care agency. This could be a very simple measure, such as the person concerned putting in place a standing order to pay the fees, or a more comprehensive one, such as him executing a lasting power of attorney, both of which must be done before capacity is permanently lost. Once there has been a permanent loss of capacity, an application to the Court of Protection may be needed.[3]

10.9 The alternative to engaging a care agency to provide the care services is to employ carers directly. Although there are a great many obligations placed upon an employer for such matters as tax and national insurance there are organisations that can help with this.[4] As an employer, there are also responsibilities to ensure the health and safety of the employee(s) and to ensure that appropriate equipment and training are provided. It is also important to

---

2 Capacity is discussed in detail in Chapter 3.

3 See Chapter 9.

4 There are a large number of organisations that offer employment administration services for people receiving direct payments from the local authority. A number of these also offer services to those funding their own care. See as an example, The Rowan Organisation www.therowan.org.

ensure that there is an appropriate insurance policy in place to cover employer's liability before the employee starts work.

10.10 As with engaging an agency, it is important to set down clearly in writing when the carer(s) are expected to attend and what tasks will be carried out. It is very common for a person with dementia to forget that the carer has already carried out a particular task and to complain that it has not been done. Some mechanism (such as a daily log book or spot checks) will be needed so that the carer's work can be monitored and problems dealt with. It is also important to plan not only for the times when the carer is on holiday but also for unexpected absences with little or no notice such as an illness or sudden bereavement.

10.11 Careful thought needs to be given to the selection and interview process. It will be necessary to advertise the position and to provide contact details for interested candidates. It may be unwise for the person with dementia to give their own details in the advert even when the dementia is at an early stage and he is capable of arranging the interviews. This is because of the risk that this information will be used by an unscrupulous person wanting to take advantage of his vulnerability rather than to apply for the position. Interviews should be conducted by at least two people and it is good practice to keep a note of why the successful candidate was selected. It is beyond the scope of this book to cover employment law in any detail.

Local authority funded care at home

10.12 Where the person with dementia is or may be eligible for assistance from the local authority towards the cost of his care, it should be approached as soon as possible. The starting point for obtaining services is an assessment of need and the local authority must carry out that assessment if it appears that the person *may have* a need for community care services.[5] In doing so, it must assess the person's needs against its eligibility criteria and decide whether the assessed needs call for the provision by the local authority of any services.

10.13 The modern practice is for the local authority to carry out the assessment of need and to allocate a personal budget for non-residential care for that person based on the amount that the local authority would have to spend if it were to provide those services itself. This is sometimes less than might be expected. Most local authorities use a resource allocation system to produce an indicative budget which, based on an analysis of others with similar care needs, should be sufficient to meet the assessed needs. There has been considerable controversy about the use of resource allocation systems but the

---

[5] Section 47 of the National Health Service and Community Care Act 1990. See Chapter 3 for more information about assessments.

courts have upheld their use as being a lawful starting point provided that there is proper consideration of whether the indicative budget is actually appropriate in each case.[6]

10.14 Once the individual budget has been agreed, the person needing care has a choice as to whether to take services directly from the local authority's Social Services department or whether to take the money as a direct payment[7] (subject to any contribution) and arrange the services himself. A mixture of the two is also possible with some services provided by the local authority and some arranged privately.

Care from social services

10.15 The nature and extent of the service provided by social services to meet the eligible assessed needs will be agreed in consultation with the person with dementia and his family. This may give only limited choice as to what services are provided and how often but the local authority should not refuse to provide those services that are needed to meet assessed eligible needs solely because the person with dementia has sufficient funds to purchase those services himself.[8]

10.16 The carers will be arranged by the local authority and may be local authority employees or, more commonly, will be from an agency which the local authority has contracted to provide services on its behalf. The local authority will contract with the care provider on the basis of the agreed care plan and will be responsible for paying the fees. The local authority will collect any contribution assessed as being payable and may take steps, including court proceedings, to recover any sums that are outstanding. It may not, however, refuse to provide or withdraw services because of issues regarding payment.[9] It may, therefore be advisable, where there is likely to be some difficulty or delay in getting formal arrangements in place to pay for care, to ask the local authority to provide such services as it deems necessary until those arrangements are fully in place.

10.17 There is another good reason to consider the direct provision of service by the local authority, even where it is likely that the full cost will be met by the person receiving the care. The local authority purchases care services in bulk from local providers and is required to adopt a formal process for inviting and evaluating tenders. This competition is designed, amongst other things, to ensure that the local authority obtains value for money and it usually results in

---

6 See *R (on the application of Savva) v Royal Borough of Kensington and Chelsea* [2010] EWCA Civ 1209 at [16] to [18].

7 Direct payments are only available for non-residential care services, although they may be used to pay for short periods of respite care.

8 This was made clear by the Department of Health in the Fair Access to Care Services Practice Guidance: Implementation Questions and Answer published in 2003. See question 8.5.

9 Paragraph 99 of *Fairer Charging Policies for Home Care and Other Non-residential Social Service* June 2013 in England and para 116 of Welsh Assembly Government *Introducing More Consistency in Local Authorities' Charging for Non-Residential Social Services* April 2011 for Wales.

the local authority paying rates that are significantly below that which an individual would pay to the same agency. Consequently, care services provided through the local authority are often more cost effective. Further, there is no reason why a person with sufficient resources cannot purchase additional care services to top-up what has been provided by the local authority.

Direct Payments

10.18 Where the person does not wish to take a service directly, he may be able to receive a payment with which to arrange his own care instead.[10] These are known as direct payments[11] and are subject to the same system for assessing contributions as services provided by the local authority. The amount of the direct payment will be the amount of the personal budget (as described above) but the person receiving the care may have to pay a contribution (as described below) towards the cost. Confusingly, some local authorities pay the full amount needed to meet the assessed care needs[12] and then require the person receiving the care to make a regular payment back to the local authority of the assessed contribution. However, it has become quite rare for such gross payment arrangements to be made and it is now usual for the net amount[13] to be paid by the local authority with the person expected to use that money together with his contribution to pay for the care.

10.19 As originally enacted, direct payments were not available to those who lacked the capacity to consent to them being made and this often excluded people with dementia. However, the legislation was amended in 2009[14] to enable direct payments to be made to a 'suitable person' on behalf of the person who lacks capacity. A suitable person includes an attorney acting under a lasting power of attorney or a deputy appointed by the Court of Protection or, if the local authority agrees, a family member or a close friend who is willing to manage the direct payment.[15]

10.20 In addition to there being a suitable person to receive the direct payments on behalf of the person with dementia, the local authority must be satisfied that the eligible care needs as assessed can be met by the provision of a direct payment and that the person to whom payment will be made is capable of managing the direct payment,[16] with such assistance as may be available to

---

10 The local authority cannot refuse a direct payment if the criteria are met unless there is some very good reason. See *Guidance on Direct Payments England 2009*, para 15 (Department of Health) for England and *Direct Payments Guidance 2011*, para 1.17 (Welsh Assembly Government) for Wales.

11 These are made pursuant to s 57 of the Health and Social Care Act 2001.

12 This is a gross payment as defined in s 57(4).

13 See s 57(5).

14 By the Health and Social Care Act 2008.

15 Where there is a person with a power of attorney or a deputy whose powers include the power to make decisions about securing care services, that person must also agree to a person other than another attorney or deputy receiving the direct payments. See s 57(1C) for the detail.

16 Regulation 8(5) of the Community Care, Services for Carers and Children's Services (Direct Payments) (England) Regulations 2009, SI 2009/1887 (the '2009 Regulations') and reg 9(5) of

him. The local authority must also be satisfied that the person receiving the payment will act in the best interests of the person needing care.[17] Where the person who will receive the payment is not a close relative (as defined by the regulations) or a friend who has previously been involved in his care, the local authority may need to carry out a criminal records check.[18] If these criteria are met, the local authority must agree to make a direct payment.[19]

10.21 The direct payment may only be used to purchase residential care for up to four weeks in any year.[20] It cannot be used to pay the partner or close relative of the person receiving the care who lives in the same household unless the local authority consider it necessary for the care service to be provided by that person regardless of where he lives.[21] The local authority is entitled to impose conditions[22] when agreeing a direct payment and will usually require a separate bank account to be set up to receive the direct payments and to use to pay for the care services. This also makes the task of monitoring the use of the direct payments more straightforward. It is important to note that whilst additional or different care services may be purchased by topping up from other resources, the direct payment and the assessed contribution must be used to meet the eligible care needs as assessed by the local authority. It would be permissible to engage an assistant to spend on a particular activity than had been assessed as necessary by making a greater contribution to cover the additional cost but it would not be permissible to use the direct payment to employ that assistant to carry out completely unrelated duties.

10.22 The local authority is required to monitor the use of the direct payment and will require the person receiving it on behalf of the individual needing care to keep records of how it has been spent.[23] Where the direct payment has not been spent or has been spent other than on meeting the assessed care needs, the local authority may demand that all or part is repaid.[24] The local authority may also ask for repayment where any condition imposed in respect of the direct payment has not been adhered to.[25] Although the power to require repayment is wide ranging, the local authority would still be susceptible to challenge on ordinary public law principles if it used those powers in an unreasonable manner.

---

the Community Care, Services for Carers and Children's Services (Direct Payments) (Wales) Regulations 2011, SI 2011/1667 (W191) (the '2011 Regulations').

17 As above.

18 2009 Regulations, reg 8(2)(c); 2011 Regulations, reg 9(2)(c).

19 See fn 9.

20 2009 Regulations, reg 13; 2011 Regulations, reg 14.

21 2009 Regulations, reg 12; 2011 Regulations, reg 13.

22 2009 Regulations, reg 12(4); 2011 Regulations, reg 13(4).

23 For more information about monitoring the use of direct payments see paras 220–233 in the Guidance on Direct Payments England 2009 and paras 7.1–7.15 in the Welsh Assembly Government Direct Payments Guidance 2011.

24 Regulation 15 of the 2009 Regulations and reg 16 of the 2011 Regulations.

25 Ibid.

10.23 Subject to the requirement to use the direct payment to meet the assessed care needs, the recipient is in the same position as a person who funds his own care. He may choose to engage an agency or may employ carers directly and will need to consider the issues set out above in respect of self-funded care. Each local authority is required to provide support, training and guidance for those receiving direct payments and will be able to provide details of organisations that can assist with the administration of paying wages and similar issues.

Financial contributions

10.24 Where the local authority provides care services to a person in their own home, it may make a reasonable charge for providing that service.[26] Where direct payments are made, the local authority must determine the amount that it is reasonable for the person to contribute towards the cost of the services.[27] Charges may not be made for: community equipment, such as raised toilet seats and shower stools, or minor adaptations[28] below £1,000; where the person has dementia as a result of Creutzfeldt–Jakob disease;[29] or where the person has been assessed by the NHS as requiring continuing health care[30] (see Chapter 6). Where the person with dementia has been detained under s 3 of the Mental Health Act 1983 and is being provided with after care services, he cannot be asked to make any contribution.[31]

The position in England

10.25 Otherwise, each local authority is able to set its own policy as to what services it will charge for and the amount of the charge. However, in defining its policy, it must comply[32] with the standards set down by the Department of

---

26 Section 17 of the Health and Social Services and Social Security Adjudications Act 1983 ('HASSASSA 1983').

27 2009 Regulations, regs 9(2) and 10(2); 2011 Regulations, regs 10(2) and 11(2) .

28 Community Care (Delayed Discharges, etc) Act (Qualifying Services (England) Regulations 2003, SI 2003/1196 and LAC (2003) 14. These exclusions apply in England, please see below for the position in Wales.

29 See para 79 of *Fairer Charging Policies for Home Care and Other Non-residential Social Services* June 2013 in England and para 32 of Welsh Assembly Government *Introducing More Consistency in Local Authorities' Charging for Non-Residential Social Services* April 2011 for Wales.

30 It was established in the case of *R v North and East Devon Health Authority, ex p Coughlan (Secretary of State for Health and another intervening)* [2000] 3 All ER 850 that where a person's primary need was for health care, all of the care must be provided free of charge by the NHS.

31 See para 7 of the June 2011 guidance for England and para 32 of the April 2011 Guidance for Wales. This is the result of the decision of the House of Lords in *R v Manchester City Council, ex p Stennett* [2002] 4 All ER 124.

32 It is guidance issued under s 7(1) of the Local Authority Social Services Act 1970, which means that it must be followed unless there is good reason not to.

Health in *Fairer Charging Policies for Home Care and Other Non-residential Services.*[33] This document sets out a number of ground rules, the most important being:

- The local authority must set the charge at a level that leaves the person paying with sufficient income to live. This is defined as being the amount that is or would be received in the applicable welfare benefits plus a buffer of 25%.
- Disability Related Expenditure must be taken into account where incurred by a person with a disability who has little or no choice but to incur that expenditure because of the disability.
- The charge for a service cannot be more than the cost to the local authority of providing that service.

10.26 The applicable welfare benefit for a person aged below the equivalent state retirement age for women[34] will be Income Support (IS) including the premiums for age, disability and family but not any supplements for severe disability. Where the person is over that age, he will qualify for pension credit and the standard rate of guarantee credit of pension credit (ie excluding the additional amount for severe disability) will be the applicable basic rate. The 25% buffer will be added to these rates. The transition to universal credit began in October 2013 but is not scheduled to be complete until April 2017 and the current guidance[35] is that local authorities should continue to use income support and pension credit rates pending further guidance.

10.27 The local authority will require detailed information about the person with dementia's financial circumstances. Where this is not known and further investigation is required, the local authority should make a provisional assessment based on the available information, which can be revised when the remaining information has been obtained. This may be preferable to a long period in which no assessment is made resulting in a large debt being payable immediately once the person's position has been established. If no information is provided to the local authority, it is likely to make a full-cost assessment on the grounds that the onus is upon the person being assessed to show that he cannot reasonably afford to pay the full cost.[36]

---

33 This guidance was originally issued in 2001 (see LAC (2001) 32) and applied to England and Wales. It was most recently revised in England in June 2013. The Welsh Guidance is now substantially different as discussed below.

34 This was 60 but is being increased to 66 over a number of years. There is a helpful tool for calculating the date upon which a person is entitled to Pension Credit at https://www.gov.uk/calculate-state-pension.

35 As at 30 September 2013.

36 HASSASSA1983, s 17(3). Although less clear, it seems likely that the same principle will apply to the question of how much it is reasonable for a person to contribute towards the cost of his care services under regs 9 and 10 of the 2009 Regulations.

Income and capital

10.28 The local authority will assess the person's income taking into account welfare benefits, pensions and any private income. From this, any earnings, working tax credits, child tax credits, working families' tax credit and disabled persons tax credit must be disregarded as to do otherwise would create barriers to work for disabled people.[37] At the time of writing, there is no guidance on the treatment of universal credit for working people with disabilities.

10.29 Capital assets and savings may be taken into account and treated in accordance with the Charging for Residential Accommodation Guide (CRAG) as set out in detail below. Almost all local authorities do so and will assess a person as liable to pay the full cost of his care if he has capital assets in excess of the upper threshold (£23,250 as at 1 October 2013). Importantly, unlike for residential care, the capital value of a property will not be included in that assessment where home care services are concerned if it is occupied as his main or only home. The value of any second home or other property held will be taken into account. Capital and savings will be disregarded if the total value is below the lower capital threshold (£14,250 as at 1 October 2013). Where the total capital and savings are between these amounts, £1 of income is added per week for every £250 (or part of £250) above the lower capital threshold. This is referred to as tariff income.

10.30 As with residential care, issues arise when property appears to have been given away at a time when it was foreseeable that home care would be needed. This is covered in detail in the section below on residential care. There are, however, a number of important differences. Where a person is found to have deprived himself of income with the intention of reducing the amount that he would have to pay for his care services, the *Fairer Charging Guidance* does not provide any express power for the local authority to treat a person as having notional income to the value of the income given away. The position with capital is different; the *Fairer Charging Guidance* permits a local authority to treat capital on the same basis as in CRAG.[38] The provisions relating to deprivation of capital could, arguably, be applied so that the amount given away will be treated as notional capital. That proposition is controversial. However, as the local authority is permitted to make such charge as it considers reasonable, it can take income and capital deprivation into account by this route. Unlike residential care, there is no power to transfer liability for unpaid home care charges to the recipient of the assets given away.

Disability-related benefits and expenditure

10.31 Many people are surprised to find that they are assessed as liable to make a contribution towards the costs of home care services when their income is entirely from state benefits. This will be the case where the local authority

---

37 See *Fairer Charging Policies for Home Care and Other non-residential Social Services* June 2013, paras 31 and 76–77.

38 See paras 62–63 of the June 2013 guidance.

takes into account income from disability-related benefits. Almost all authorities do and the reason is because these benefits are paid in order to help people obtain the extra care needed or meet the extra costs incurred as a result of disability. If the local authority is providing some of that extra care, then it does not seem unreasonable that such benefits are included in the assessment of income.

10.32 Special rules apply where the benefit is paid to cover both day and night time care. This will apply to attendance allowance ('AA') paid at the higher rate; the care component of disability living allowance ('DLA') paid at the highest rate; constant attendance allowance ('CAA') paid at the intermediate or exceptional rates; and exceptionally severe disability allowance ('ESDA'). If, as is often the case, the care package put in place by the local authority does not include the provision of care at night (because this care is provided by a spouse or relative living in the same house) then the difference between the rate without night care and the rate paid must be disregarded.[39] The effect of this is that AA can be included at the lower rate only; DLA at the lower or middle rate; and CAA at the part or full day rate. ESDA cannot be included.

10.33 The position with the daily living component of personal independence payments ('PIP') is more complex because there is no distinction made between day and night care. The *Fairer Charging Guidance* requires local authorities to consider the totality of the person's needs and the extent to which those needs are met other than by the services that it has assessed as being necessary to meet eligible needs. It would appear reasonable for the local authority to take account of the entire PIP where it was providing 24-hour care. At the time of writing, PIP has only just been introduced for new claimants and few local authorities have updated their policies to set out how they will be treated. It seems likely that there will be a period of uncertainty about this benefit.

10.34 The mobility component of DLA or PIP cannot be taken into account as income. In calculating the amount that a person can reasonably afford to contribute towards the cost of the care services, the local authority must take account of disability-related expenditure. The manner in which local authorities treat disability-related expenditure varies considerably. Most have some form of default amount which will be allowed without proof of expenditure and in many cases this will adequately cover the extra expenditure. However, where the person's needs require a greater level of expenditure, the local authority must carry out a proper assessment and make allowance for items *where the user has little or no choice other than to incur the expenditure, in order to maintain independence or quality of life*.[40]

10.35 Two issues commonly arise in respect of the detailed assessment of disability-related expenditure: these are whether the particular item was reasonably necessary; and what evidence is required in support of the claimed

---

39 *R (on the application of Carton) v Coventry City Council* (2001) 4 CCL Rep 41.

40 *Fairer Charging Policies for Home Care and other non-residential Social Services* June 2013, para 49.

expenditure. The local authority should be flexible as to how this part of the assessment is carried out and will often undertake a home visit to do so. There is no prescribed list of what does or does not constitute reasonable disability-related expenditure.

10.36 In deciding what expenditure is reasonably necessary, the care plan or support plan will be the starting point but that will not necessarily show the full extent of the disability-related expenditure. For example, a person who is no longer able to go out is likely to incur higher heating and energy costs as a result but it is unlikely that this would be specifically mentioned in the care plan. Where special equipment is purchased, the cost of maintaining it should be allowed and the replacement cost spread over the lifetime of that particular item. The local authority does not have to allow the actual costs, if the need could be addressed in a more cost effective manner. For example, the cost of purchasing incontinence supplies is not usually allowed as these can be obtained from the NHS.

10.37 The local authority is only entitled to ask for reasonable evidence and should not insist on unduly onerous requirements for evidence before agreeing to allow a particular item of expenditure. It will usually ask for some evidence that the expenditure has been incurred and it is advisable to provide receipts or copies of bills whenever possible. Where the cost of assistance with tasks such as gardening and cleaning is claimed, evidence of actual payment is likely to be needed, especially if these services are being performed by a relative or close friend.

The amount charged

10.38 For some services, there will simply be a fixed flat-rate fee regardless of the financial assessment. This is typically for services that are a replacement for everyday expenditure such as Meals on Wheels. For most services though, the local authority will calculate the contribution to be paid by reference to the person's capital and income. The most that a person can be asked to contribute is the actual costs to the local authority of providing the service. This maximum can be fairly readily ascertained where the care services are being provided by social services. However, it is less straightforward where direct payments are being made.

10.39 Where the local authority makes a direct payment instead of providing care services, it must assess the contribution in exactly the same way[41] and must ensure that it does not charge the person receiving direct payments for a service that would be provided without charge if he were receiving services from the local authority. For example, some local authorities do not charge for attendances at a day centre; if the person with dementia has an individual budget that includes a sum to attend a day centre paid as a direct payment, that part of the budget should not be excluded when calculating the maximum

---

41 See the Introduction to Fairer Contributions Guidance 2010: *Calculating an Individual's Contribution to their Personal Budget* (Department of Health).

contribution. Wherever the service would have been provided free of charge by the local authority or at a subsidy then that will affect the maximum contribution from a person receiving direct payments.[42]

10.40 Many local authorities have set a maximum weekly charge. Where this is applicable, the person receiving home care services should not be asked to contribute more than this sum regardless of his means.

10.41 Once the local authority has assessed the contribution to be made towards the cost of the care services, it must provide an explanation in writing and must inform the person of his right to ask for a review of the assessment if he thinks it is wrong. If he is still not satisfied once the review has been carried out, he can complain through the statutory complaints process. See Chapter 11 for details.

10.42 Where social services are providing services and the person does not pay the assessed contribution, the local authority must continue to meet the assessed needs and may not withhold services until payment is made.[43] If a person does not pay, its only options are to try to persuade him or the person assisting with his finances to do so or to bring court proceedings. Unlike where charges are owed in respect of residential care, there is no power to declare a charge against property owned by the person in order to secure the debt.

10.43 Where the person has dementia and lacks the capacity to litigate, a claim for arrears of contributions is likely to be disproportionately costly. The local authority may instead start proceedings in the Court of Protection for a declaration that it is in the person's best interest for his bills to be paid.

The Welsh position

10.44 Since 11 April 2011,[44] local authorities in Wales must follow the Welsh Assembly Government's (WAG) guidance '*Introducing More Consistency in Local Authorities' Charging for Non-Residential Social Services*'. Prior to that, those authorities were following the WAG Fairer Charging guidance that was similar to the English version described above and both systems continue to have much in common. There are some important differences and these are discussed in this section.

10.45 Welsh local authorities may not charge for transport to attend a day centre where attendance at the day centre and transport to it are included in the assessment of need. Where this requirement is met and the person receives direct payments, the transport cost must not be included in calculation of direct

---

42 See Fairer Contributions Guidance 2010: *Calculating an Individual's Contribution to their Personal Budget* (Department of Health) at paras 2.10–2.18.

43 *Fairer Charging Policies for Home Care and other non-residential Social Services* June 2013, para 99.

44 This was the date that the regulations made under the Social Care Charges (Wales) Measure 2010 came into effect replacing the power to charge under s 17 of HASSASSA 1983 in respect of Welsh local authorities.

payment contribution. Unlike in England, the Welsh Assembly Government has not used its power to exempt community equipment or minor adaptions from charges.[45] As in England, intermediate care is free of charge for up to 6 weeks.

10.46 Regulations set out the detailed process for the conduct of the financial assessment (referred to throughout the guidance as a means assessment). Unless it is only providing services which are a substitute for ordinary every day expenditure for which it is reasonable to impose a flat-rate charge (such as Meals on Wheels, for example), the local authority must send a written invitation to the person who is to receive home care services containing the prescribed information and offering to carry out a financial assessment. Once the financial assessment is complete, the local authority must send a statement of the charge to be imposed. Until this is done, the local authority may not impose any charge or ask the person to make any contribution. This means that direct payments must be paid as gross payments until the statement of charge has been sent. Although it does not expressly say so, the guidance appears to prohibit local authorities from recovering any charges for services provided prior to that date.

10.47 Capital and savings may be assessed in the same way as for residential care[46] but local authorities are permitted to adopt a more generous treatment. The treatment of income is the same as for England except that the buffer to be added to the basic welfare rate is 35% instead of 25% and everyone is entitled to a further 10% for disability-related expenditure making the buffer effectively 45%. Those with higher disability-related expenditure are entitled to a detailed assessment.

10.48 The applicable welfare benefit for the basic rate may be Income Support or Pension Credit Guarantee Credit and these are calculated in the same way as for English authorities as described above. In Wales, the applicable welfare benefit may also be Employment and Support Allowance ('ESA') in which case it is calculated as the personal allowance and any additional amount to which the person is entitled but need not include additional amounts for severe disability or, where the person is also a carer any additional amount received in that regard.

10.49 The very big difference in Wales is the statutory imposition of a £50 per week maximum charge (at the time of publication) or contribution (excluding any flat rate charges). Whatever his financial position or the costs of the care being provided, no person can be asked to pay or contribute more than this amount.

---

45 Section 16 of the Community Care (Delayed Discharges, etc) Act 2003 empowers the Welsh Assembly to make equivalent provisions to those in England but this power has not been deployed.

46 As set out in the Welsh Assembly Government Charging for Residential Accommodation Guide (WAG CRAG).

10.50 In Wales, there is also a statutory right to request a review of any decision relating to charging. Local authorities must have a suitably trained person to carry out such reviews and that person must not have been involved in the original financial assessment. Importantly, the person receiving the care services can elect not to pay whilst the review is carried out. Where that person is receiving direct payments, this means that the local authority must make gross payments until the review has been completed.

RESIDENTIAL CARE

10.51 When the time comes that the person with dementia can no longer manage at home, it will be necessary to select a residential care home that has the facilities to care for people with dementia. There are many to choose from with some charging as little as £325 per week whilst others charge £1,400 or more per week. All must be registered with the Care Quality Commission and are inspected regularly. The inspection reports are a good source of information about the standard of care provided. The website www.carehome.co.uk is also a useful source of information.

Self-funded care

10.52 Anybody with savings above the upper capital threshold (currently £23,250) will have to meet the full cost of the care home and some local authorities are reluctant to provide any assistance whatsoever. However, the person is entitled to an assessment from social services[47] regardless of his financial means. The assessment may provide useful information that will help him and his family select an appropriate home. It is important to consider the likely progress of the dementia and the facilities available at the care home to reduce the risk that the person may have to move to a different care home in the future.

10.53 Where the person would not have capital above the threshold if his home were disregarded, he will be entitled to financial assistance from the local authority for the first 12 weeks of any permanent admission to residential care and may then, subject to the local authority's agreement, be able to defer payment of part of the fees until his home is sold or until after his death through a deferred payment agreement. These are explained in more detail below.

10.54 The local authority should not refuse to make the arrangements with the care home unless it is satisfied that the person is able to make those arrangements for himself or that there is a relative or friend who is willing and able to make the arrangements for him.[48] If the dementia has advanced to a stage where the person does not have the capacity to make the decision as to which home to go to or to enter into the contract and there is no attorney or

---

47 Pursuant to s 47 of the NHS and Community Care Act 2001.

48 See LAC (98) 19, paras 9 and 10 and in Wales Welsh Office Circular 27/98.

deputy authorised to make those decisions on his behalf, the local authority ought to make the arrangements. If it does so, it will then recover the full cost. The position where the local authority does so is explained in more detail below.

10.55 Where the person is not entitled to any assistance and is able (with the help of a relative or friend) to make the arrangements with the care home, he will be able to choose whichever home he wants. It is important to know what is included in the weekly fee and what he will be charged extra for. This information should be provided in writing along with the other important terms that will apply such as whether there is a trial period and what notice must be given to terminate the contract. It is also important to know what must be paid for if the person dies and how quickly his room must be cleared. In theory, it should be possible to negotiate the terms of the contract but the reality is that most care homes will insist on their standard terms and conditions.

10.56 As with home care services, the care home will want to be sure that the contract is legally enforceable. A contract signed by a person with dementia is a valid contract, even if he did not have capacity.[49] However, such a contract is liable to be set aside by a court if the fees were not paid and the care home is likely to insist that the contract is signed by someone else. Unless there is a formal power of attorney or a deputy, the person signing is personally liable to pay the fees to the care home and must then look to the person with dementia for reimbursement.

10.57 As with non-residential care services, difficulties can also arise in making the payment where there is no attorney or deputy. Whilst there are periods of sound capacity, payments are made. As the condition deteriorates these become fewer and further apart and substantial arrears accrue. By the time it is clear that the person will not be able to make the payment himself, there is a large debt. It is important to recognise that this may occur and to put in place measures to minimise the likelihood of a problems. This could be very simple measures such as putting in place a standing order to pay the fees at the outset or more comprehensive such as the execution of a lasting power of attorney, both of which must be done before capacity is permanently lost. Once there has been a permanent loss of capacity, an application to the Court of Protection may be needed.[50]

10.58 Where the person's financial resources are depleted and are approaching the upper capital threshold, the local authority should be approached. Because the local authority places so many people in care homes, it is able to negotiate rates that can be considerably lower than those paid by a person funding his own care. This can create problems where the care home is unwilling to lower the rate for an existing resident to that which would be paid by the local

---

49 See Chapter 3 for a detailed discussion of capacity.

50 See Chapter 9.

authority if this were a new placement. If the local authority is unable to persuade the care home to agree the reduction, it may be possible to terminate the self-funding contract and put a local authority placement agreement in its place.

10.59 A person who needs to be in a care home and is not receiving any assistance with the cost from the local authority or the NHS is entitled to claim AA (if he meets the eligibility criteria for it).

Assistance from the local authority with residential care

10.60 If the person with dementia is likely to be entitled to assistance from the local authority, he must approach the local authority where he is or was last ordinarily resident. It can be quite complex to identify the correct local authority where the person has spent time in an institution. Any time spent in hospital or other NHS accommodation does not count towards ordinary residence nor does any time in a care home where the arrangements were made by a local authority. In those cases, the person remains ordinarily resident in the place where he lived before admission. However, time spent in a care home where the arrangements were made privately without the involvement of the local authority is likely to count to establish ordinary residence in the area of that care home.[51]

Choice of accommodation

10.61 Each local authority has a maximum amount that it will usually pay for a care home placement. However, the person being admitted is entitled to choose a more expensive home[52] if the difference (referred to as the Top-Up) can be paid from one of the permitted resources, this usually means that a third-party must agree to pay the Top-Up. It is important to note that the person can only be asked to pay the Top-Up where he has chosen a more expensive care home. If the only care home being offered that can meet his needs is more expensive than the local authority's usual maximum, it must pay the difference.

10.62 The rules on what resources may be used to pay the Top-Up are designed to prevent the person who is receiving care from depleting his own resources more quickly than would otherwise be the case because he has chosen an expensive home. This is because once his resources are depleted, the burden of paying for his care from the public purse will be greater. A person is permitted to pay the Top-Up from his own funds where (i) he has resources that

---

51 *R (on the application of Greenwich London BC) v Secretary of State for Health* [2006] EWHC 2576 (Admin).

52 National Assistance Act 1948 (Choice of Accommodation) Directions 1992 in England and National Assistance Act 1948 (Choice of Accommodation) Directions 1993 in Wales.

are otherwise disregarded in the financial assessment (such as a personal injury trust, for example); or (ii) he is receiving the 12-week property disregard or has a deferred payment agreement.[53]

Financial assessment

10.63 Where a local authority makes the arrangements for a person to receive care, either in one of its own care homes or in a private care home, it is required to recover the full cost of that care unless it is satisfied that the person cannot reasonably afford to pay the full cost.[54] The local authority may charge a reasonable amount for up to 8 weeks but after that must carry out a financial assessment in accordance with the applicable regulations[55] as explained in detail in the Charging for Residential Accommodation Guide (CRAG). As the local authority is required to recover the full cost of the placement unless it is satisfied that the person cannot reasonably afford to pay that amount, it is entitled to make a full cost assessment where the person is unwilling to disclose sufficient details of his financial circumstances.

10.64 Where the person with dementia has been detained under s 3 of the Mental Health Act 1983 and is being provided with residential accommodation as an after care service, he cannot be asked to make any contribution.[56]

Income

10.65 With very limited exceptions,[57] all income is taken into account including income which would be available if an application was made. This means that any benefits to which a person is entitled will be taken into account regardless of whether those benefits have been claimed or are being paid. The person receiving care must be left with a prescribed amount for his personal expenses. This is currently £23.90 per week, although the local authority has a discretion to allow a higher rate in appropriate circumstances.[58] Consequently, even those with no savings or capital assets, will be assessed as liable to contribute towards the cost of the placement. A person above the qualifying age for pension credit is likely to be assessed as liable to pay £121.50 per week at current rates.

---

53 National Assistance (Residential Accommodation) (Additional Payments and Assessment of Resources) (Amendment) (England) Regulations 2001, SI 2001/3441 and National Assistance (Residential Accommodation) (Additional Payments, Relevant Contributions and Assessment of Resources) (Wales) Regulations 2003, SI 2003/931 (W121). See also *R v East Sussex ex p Ward* CCLR June 2000.

54 National Assistance Act 1948, ss 22 and 26.

55 National Assistance (Assessment of Resources) Regulations 1992, SI 1992/2977.

56 See para 7 of the June 2011 guidance for England and para 32 of the April 2011 Guidance for Wales. This is the result of the decision of the House of Lords in *R v Manchester City Council, ex p Stennett* [2002] 4 All ER 124. See Chapter 6 for more information about services under s 117 of the Mental Health Act 1983.

57 These are set out in section 8 of CRAG.

58 An example of when a higher rate might be allowed is when benefits are being paid as a couple and the partner at home needs to be provided for.

Savings and capital assets

10.66 Savings and capital assets are disregarded where the total value is below the lower capital threshold (currently £14,250) and have no impact on the financial assessment. Where the person has savings and capital assets above the upper capital threshold (currently £23,250), he will be liable to contribute the full cost of his care. Where the person has savings in between those two amount, he will be treated as having an additional £1 per week of income for every £250 above the lower capital threshold and his contribution will be calculated according to his income including this sum. This is sometimes called tariff income in local authority assessments.[59]

10.67 Sections 6 and 7 of CRAG set out how capital and property are to be assessed. The guidance is long and detailed but the general approach is that the value of the asset less the costs of disposal will be taken into account. Where money is held in joint accounts it is deemed to be held in equal shares. Some assets are disregarded for a period and others are disregarded entirely. The rules about the treatment of funds which have originated from a settlement in respect of a personal injury are extremely complex and are set out in section 10 of CRAG. In many cases such funds will be disregarded. The most common disputes arise out of the valuation of jointly owned property and as to whether the value of the former home should be disregarded. These are now considered.

Jointly owned property

10.68 Where property is jointly owned, the local authority must assess the value of the person's interest and not just assign a proportion of the value of the property to that person.[60] This creates difficulties for local authorities where the other owners have a vested interest in the property having a low value (perhaps because the joint owner will inherit the other half on the resident's death). There is a comment in CRAG[61] that where the joint owners do not wish to sell and there is no willing purchaser from amongst the family, the value of the interest could effectively be nil. It is doubtful that this comment is right in the majority of cases because it ignores the likelihood of a court making an order that the property be sold against the joint owner's wishes where the funds are needed to pay for his care. However, where there is a dispute as to the value of an interest in property, the local authority must obtain a professional valuation.

Disregarded property

10.69 The value of the former home of the person being admitted to residential care must be disregarded if the admission is temporary and he

---

59 See paras 6.009–9.010 of CRAG.

60 The report of the Local Government Ombudsman Investigation into complaint no 10 014 187 against West Sussex County Council made it clear that the local authority is required to obtain a valuation of the resident's share of the property and may not simply value the property as a whole.

61 CRAG, paragraph 7.019.

intends to return home. There has to be some realistic chance that he will be able to do so. The former home must also be disregarded where it is occupied by the spouse, civil partner or a person with whom he lived as if married. It must also be disregarded if it is occupied by a relative who is over 60 or is incapacitated.[62] The local authority has a discretion to disregard the property in other circumstances and will generally do so where the property is occupied by a person who has given up his own home to care for the person now going into residential care. The guidance requires the local authority to balance the use of this discretion with the need to ensure that residents with assets are not maintained at public expense.[63]

The 12-week disregard and deferred payment agreements

10.70 There are two important provisions that will make a difference to a person who would not have capital in excess of the upper capital threshold if the value of his former home were disregarded. Everyone being admitted to residential care is entitled to have the value of his former home disregarded for the first 12 weeks.[64] For many people, this means that they will be entitled to financial assistance from the local authority for this 12-week period. At the end of that time, the person will be liable to pay the full cost of the placement unless he has entered into a deferred payment agreement with the local authority.[65] A person who has previously been funding his own care is entitled to the 12-week disregard from the time that he approaches the local authority for assistance.

10.71 Under a deferred payment agreement, the person is still required to meet the full cost of his placement but is able to defer part of his contribution until the property is sold or until 56 days after his death. There is a duty on local authorities to consider a request for a deferred payments agreement but it is not obliged to agree to the request and the degree of willingness to enter into these agreements varies significantly. The amount deferred is secured by a charge against the property. However, the local authority is not permitted to terminate the agreement once in place and so it must be confident at the outset that the property offers sufficient security for the debt that is likely to accrue.

10.72 If a direct payment agreement is put in place, the person will be assessed with the value of the former home disregarded. He will be required to pay the assessed contribution each week in the normal way. The balance of the care home fees accrues as a debt which is payable when the property is sold or 56 days after death. As a person with a deferred payment agreement will eventually be paying the full cost of the care home, he is entitled to claim AA (if he meets the eligibility criteria).

---

[62] CRAG paragraph 7.003.

[63] CRAG paragraph 7.011.

[64] CRAG paragraphs 7.004–7.006.

[65] As provided for by s 55 of the Health and Social Care Act 2001. See also LAC (2001) 25 for England and NAFWC 21/2003 for Wales.

Anti-avoidance provisions

10.73 The local authority is entitled to treat a person as still possessing capital of which he has deprived himself for the purpose of decreasing the amount that he may be liable to pay for his accommodation.[66] The local authority has to prove that avoiding part or all of the charges was a significant part of this person's reasoning process[67] but the courts have taken a realistic approach to what must be proved. In the case of *Yule v South Lanarkshire Council*[68] the court made the point that 'the local authority cannot look into the mind of the person making the disposition of capital or of others who may be concerned in the transaction. It can only look at the nature of the disposal within the context of the time at which and the circumstances in which that disposal took place'. Consequently, the local authority may satisfy the burden of proving the necessary purpose or intention by establishing primary facts from which that intention can be inferred in the absence of some other reasonable explanation.

10.74 The purpose of giving away assets may be mixed and avoiding charges or reducing the amount payable need not be the main reason. The finding in *Yule* was that 'it is open to a local authority to reach a view as to the purpose of a transaction such as the present, without any specific finding as to the exact state of knowledge or intention of the applicant, so long as the primary facts are such as reasonably to lead to the inference that the purpose was at least in part that specified in [the regulations].'

10.75 Further, there is often more than one operative reason for the transfer of assets and it will often be the case that the motive to defeat the local authority and the motive to secure family protection will co-exist in such a way that even the transferor himself may be unable to say which was uppermost in his mind. What has to be shown is that avoiding the charges was *one of* the reasons for the transfer and not simply a by-product.[69]

10.76 Each case will turn on its own facts but the following factors are likely to be significant in most cases:

- Any recorded discussions about possible admission to residential care.
- Receipt of non-residential services, particularly where the package of care has been increasing.
- The provision of information about the way in which charges are assessed.
- Gifts made when there was no need to make an outright gift at that time.
- Whether the claimed purpose could have been achieved without making an outright gift.

---

66 Regulation 25 of the National Assistance Act (Assessment of Resources) Regulations 1992.

67 *R (on the application of Beeson) v Dorset County Council* [2002] EWCA Civ 1812.

68 [2001] SC 203.

69 See *Inland Revenue Commissioners v Hashmi* [2002] EWCA Civ 981.

10.77 Where the gift or disposition has been concealed from the local authority or inconsistent explanations have been given, this will tend to suggest that there has been a deliberate deprivation. However, whilst important, such matters are not determinative.

10.78 It is also important for the local authority to satisfy itself that the gift or disposition has been made willingly by the resident and to rule out the possibility of financial exploitation. This is important for two reasons: (i) the local authority has a statutory duty to safeguard vulnerable persons from such abuse; and (ii) a person who has been abused or exploited does not have the necessary intention so cannot have deprived *himself* of assets.

Transfer of liability

10.79 Establishing the required intention, allows the local authority to treat the person as still possessing the assets given away when conducting the financial assessment. Usually, this will result in a full cost assessment. However, difficulties inevitably arise when the assessed charges are not paid. The local authority could bring proceedings against the resident and obtain judgment for the sum outstanding but this is likely to be fruitless because he no longer possesses assets against which that judgment can be enforced.

10.80 To have any real prospect of recovery, the claim must be brought against those who have received the gift. There are two potential routes for such a claim. First, where the assets were given away at a time when the person was already in residential care, or they were given away in the 6 months before his admission to residential care, liability for the unpaid fees (up to the value of the gift received) is transferred to the recipient.[70]

10.81 Where the assets have been transferred outside that timeframe, a claim may be brought under s 423 of the Insolvency Act 1986. Although that section is headed 'Transactions to defraud creditors', it applies to any transaction intended to put assets out of the reach of future creditors. The test is whether the transaction was entered into for the purpose of (a) putting assets beyond the reach of a person who is making, or may at some time make, a claim against him, or (b) otherwise prejudicing the interests of such a person in relation to the claim which he is making or may make. Although the wording is somewhat different the intention to be proved is the same.

Arrears of contributions

10.82 Where a person does not pay the assessed contribution to the care home, the local authority must do so. It may not terminate the placement because of unpaid contributions. Where a person has been admitted to residential accommodation and does not pay the assessed contribution, the

---

70 By s 21 of HASSASSA 1983. The test in HASSASSA 1983 is worded slightly differently from that in reg 25 of the 1992 Regulations in that a person must transfer assets *knowingly and with the intention of avoiding charges*. There is unlikely to be any material difference resulting from this wording.

local authority may by declaration create a charge over any interest in land owned by the person.[71] The charge takes effect as a legal mortgage over the property and secures such sums as owed from time to time. The local authority may bring possession proceedings in the county court to obtain vacant possession and may then sell the property as mortgagee in possession.

10.83 The local authority may also bring an ordinary claim for the arrears but this is likely to encounter difficulties where the person has dementia and does not have the capacity to participate in the litigation. It is also open to the local authority to petition for bankruptcy where the arrears are unpaid but this is rarely likely to be reasonable where the person owing the debt has dementia.

Nursing contribution

10.84 Where the person with dementia has been assessed as needing care from a registered nurse whilst in the care home, he should receive a contribution towards the care home fees from the NHS. This is known as Registered Nursing Care Contribution and is currently £109.79 per week in England and £120.55 per week in Wales. This is not means tested but a person funding his own care home who has not been assessed by the local authority will need to ask for an assessment.

The position in Wales

10.85 The system for funding residential care in Wales is broadly the same as that described above. However, there is no lower capital threshold[72] and so no tariff income. Where the person's total capital assets are below the upper capital threshold (which is currently slightly higher than in England at £23,750[73]), those assets are disregarded entirely. The personal expenses allowance is also slightly higher in Wales at £24.00 per week.[74]

PROPOSED REFORMS

10.86 At the time of publication, there have been a number of significant changes announced to the system for funding care in England and draft legislation in the form of the Care Bill 2013 has been proposed. Much of the bill is focused on consolidating the labyrinth of provisions that currently apply (as anyone looking at the footnotes in this book can see) into one comprehensive and coherent act. There will be a single regime for financial assessment for both residential and non-residential care services. There are also

---

[71] HASSASSA 1983, s 22.

[72] See para 6.004of the WAG CRAG. At the time of writing there had not been a 2013 update and the version in force is that dated April 2012.

[73] Regulation 20A of the National Assistance (Assessment of Resources) Regulations 1992 was amended as of 8 April 2013 such that the threshold is £23,750. However, at the time of writing, WAG CRAG had not been amended since then and still refers to a threshold of £23,250.

[74] Paragraph 5.005 WAG CRAG.

changes proposed that will require the local authority to provide care or make the arrangements for care where the person wishes regardless of his financial means and to ensure that deferred payment agreements are available for all. The work on this part of the Bill is well advanced and is likely to be brought into effect first; although the timetable for that is not yet clear, it appears likely that it will be in 2015.

10.87 The more momentous changes that have been announced are in response to the recommendation made in the Dilnot Commission[75] that there be a cap on the amount that a person is required to contribute towards the cost of his care. It has been announced that this will be set at £72,000 for 2016 and will increase each year in line with inflation. Once the person has reached that cap, the local authority will have to meet the full cost of his care. Where the person is in residential care, part of the fees paid will not count towards the cap as these are considered to be the costs of board and lodgings rather than care costs. The proposal is that £10,000 per year (adjusted for inflation from 2010–11) will be disregarded in this way. The upper capital threshold is also being raised substantially (the proposal is to £100,000 adjusted for inflation) so many more people will be entitled to financial assistance from the local authority. There will be a duty on local authorities to keep records of how much has been spent towards the cap.

10.88 The current proposal is that this part of the Care Bill will come into force in 2016.

---

75 The Commission on Funding of Care and Support headed by Andrew Dilnot was established in 2010; its report *Fairer Care Funding* was published on 4 July 2011. It recommended a lower cap.

CHAPTER 11

CHALLENGING DECISIONS AND MAKING COMPLAINTS

11.1 A variety of problems and issues may arise in respect of someone with dementia. It will be important for everyone involved for any such difficulties to be resolved promptly and appropriately.

11.2 The potential benefits of resolving disputes without recourse to the courts should not be underestimated. Methods other than litigation may be cheaper, quicker and less stressful. The potential benefits of alternative dispute resolution will be considered in the next chapter. This chapter will provide information about how to make complaints and attempt to resolve certain problems without going to court including by approaching the relevant ombudsman.

11.3 At the conclusion of this chapter contact details are set out of some organisations that may be able to help.

COMPLAINTS

Complaints in general

11.4 Generally it is important, both so that the problem is resolved swiftly and that any investigation that needs to take place has the best information possible available to it, that complaints are made quickly. There are time limits that apply in respect of complaining in certain situations that are set out below.

11.5 If the complaint is about a particular professional, it is wise to keep a note of their name, their job title and the address of their place of work. It is a good idea to write down the date and exact time that any relevant event took place. If an incident took place in a hospital, the ward on which it happened should be noted. If the concern is about a series of events, a note of when and where each incident took place should be kept. If there has been a particular incident and there are witnesses, they should be asked for their name and contact details.

11.6 It is important to retain copies of all documents relating to the complaint. This would include, for example, any assessments that give rise to the complaint, any response to the complaint, and any changes to the assessment made as a result of the complaint. If informal processes (as set out below) are unsuccessful, it is generally sensible for complaints to be put in writing and copies of them retained. A record of how and when the complaint was submitted should also be kept (together with, for example, a receipt of postage if the complaint was sent by registered post). Original documents should be kept in a safe place and not given to, for example, the agency the complaint is about.

11.7 It may well prove important to have all of this information if further steps need to be taken such as going to court. Also if, for example, a local authority suggests that it never received a copy of a complaint, it will be necessary to produce a copy of it together with a record of how and when it was submitted.

11.8 It should be remembered that despite the merits of making complaints and attempting to resolve matters informally, if the problem is not satisfactorily resolved, there is no substitution for obtaining full and proper legal advice on the issue.

11.9 It should also be borne in mind that strict time limits apply should a challenge to a decision in court (a 'judicial review') need to be brought. Chapter 14 should be carefully considered on this point.

Informal processes

11.10 It is a good idea to attempt to solve disputes directly with the individual or agency concerned first. Making a formal complaint may be time consuming and stressful. If there has just been a mistake or confusion it may be that matters can be sorted out without the need to make a formal complaint.

11.11 This could be done by an informal face to face discussion with, for example, the social worker concerned if it is thought that there is a mistake in their assessment of the needs of the person with dementia. A request could also be made to speak with their manager if the discussion with the individual concerned is not fruitful. If the problem is about the health care in a hospital that the person with dementia has received, the ward manager, senior nurse on duty or the hospital receptionist could be spoken to. If the difficulty relates to a GP, they should be approached first. If the problem relates to the NHS in England, the Patient Advice and Liaison Service (PALS) may be able to assist. If the concern is in respect of the NHS in Wales, a Community Health Council (CHC) may be able to help.

11.12 Even if the matter is resolved informally it is wise to retain a note of what the problem was and how it was resolved in case of future problems. If, for example, it is accepted that there was a mistake in an assessment by a social worker, a copy of an amended assessment should be requested within a reasonable time and retained.

FORMAL COMPLAINTS

11.13 If an informal discussion has not solved the issue, the next stage is to make a formal complaint to the individual or agency. How to do this in relation to those with dementia is set out below. The following sections aim to provide a guide as to who can make a complaint (including whether representatives of the person with dementia can make the complaint), what will happen to the complaint, and what the body in question must do in respect of matters such as making individuals aware of its complaints procedure.

11.14 It is important to note that often different processes apply in respect of services in England and Wales. The processes are set out below to the extent it appears they are likely to be particularly relevant to complaints in respect of or on behalf of persons with dementia[1] and certain matters are outside the scope of this work.[2]

Complaints about care homes and care providers in England

11.15 Those carrying out certain 'regulated activities' must be registered with the Care Quality Commission ('CQC').[3] 'Regulated activities' include (with some exceptions): (i) the provision of personal care for persons who, by reason of old age, illness or disability are unable to provide it for themselves and which is provided in a place where they are living at the time the care is provided; and (ii) the provision of residential accommodation together with nursing or personal care.[4]

11.16 For the purposes of assessing, and preventing or reducing the impact of, unsafe or inappropriate care or treatment, the 'registered person' (a person who is the service provider or registered manager in respect of a regulated activity ie individuals registered with the CQC) must have an effective system in place ('the complaints system') for identifying, receiving, handling and responding appropriately to complaints and comments made by service users, or persons acting on their behalf, in relation to the carrying on of the regulated activity.[5] A 'service user' is a person who receives services provided in the course of a regulated activity (ie the person with dementia).

11.17 The registered person must bring the complaints system to the attention of service users and persons acting on their behalf in a suitable manner and

---

1 References to statutory material should not therefore be taken to include the entirety of the statute or statutory instrument.

2 For example approaching the Housing Ombudsman. Complaints about bodies such as the Care Quality Commission ('CQC'), Care and Social Services Inspectorate Wales ('CSSIW') and the Healthcare Inspectorate Wales ('HIW)' together with approaching professional regulators are also outside the scope of this chapter.

3 Health and Social Care Act 2008, s 10.

4 Schedule 1 to the Health and Social Care Act 2008 (Regulated Activities) Regulations 2010 (as amended) ('HSCARAR 2010'). The contents of this part of the Chapter are based upon HSCARAR 2010 and each individual reference is not as such included.

5 HSCARAR 2010, reg 19.

format. This may mean, for example, that the complaints system for a care home should be brought to the attention of an adult child acting on behalf of an elderly parent with dementia.

11.18 Support to bring a complaint or make a complaint (where such assistance is necessary) must be provided to service users and those acting on their behalf. The registered person must ensure that any complaint made is fully investigated and, so far as reasonably practicable, resolved to the satisfaction of the service user or the person acting on the service user's behalf. They must also take appropriate steps to coordinate a response to a complaint where that complaint relates to care or treatment provided to a service user in circumstances where the provision of such care or treatment has been shared with, or transferred to, others.

11.19 The registered person has to send to the CQC (when requested to do so) a summary of the complaints and responses made.

Complaints about social services and the NHS in England

11.20 The Local Authority Social Services and National Health Service Complaints (England) Regulations 2009 provide that each responsible body (which includes local authorities and NHS bodies) must make arrangements for the handling and consideration of complaints.[6] The arrangements must be such as to ensure that:

(a) complaints are dealt with efficiently;
(b) complaints are property investigated;
(c) complainants are treated with respect and courtesy;
(d) complainants receive, so far as is reasonably practical:
  (i) assistance to enable them to understand the procedure in relation to complaints, or
  (ii) advice on where they may obtain such assistance;
(e) complainants receive a timely and appropriate response;
(f) complainants are told the outcome of the investigation of their complaint; and
(g) action is taken if necessary in the light of the outcome of a complaint.

11.21 A complaint may be made by a person who receives or has received services from a responsible body (for example the person with dementia) or a person who is affected or likely to be affected by the action, omission or decision of the responsible body which is the subject of the complaint. A complaint may also be made by a representative of such a person in certain circumstances, including if they are unable to make the complaint themselves

6 'LASSNHSCER 2009', SI 2009/309. The contents of this part of the chapter are based upon LASSNHSCER 2009 and as such each individual reference is not included.

because of lack of capacity within the meaning of the Mental Capacity Act 2005 ('MCA 2005'). Chapter 3 explains what this means.

11.22 There is provision in the regulations[7] for complaints not to be considered if the complaint is made by a representative on behalf of a person who lacks capacity and the responsible body is satisfied that the representative is not conducting the complaint in the best interests of that person. If this happens, the responsible body must notify the representative in writing and state the reason for its decision.

11.23 There is a duty upon responsible bodies in certain circumstances to handle the complaint in accordance with the regulations. These include a complaint made to a local authority about the exercise of its social services functions and a complaint to an NHS body about the exercise of its functions. Certain complaints are not required to be dealt with in accordance with the regulations. These include complaints the subject matter of which have been previously investigated under the regulations, and complaints that are being (or have been) investigated by a Local Commissioner or Health Service Commissioner (see further below for what this means).

11.24 There is a time limit for making a complaint of no later than 12 months after the date on which the matter that is the subject of the complaint occurred or (if later) the date on which that matter came to the notice of the complainant. The time limit does not apply if the complainant had good reasons for not making the complaint within that time limit and notwithstanding the delay it is still possible to investigate the complaint effectively and fairly.

11.25 A complaint may be made orally, in writing or electronically. If it is made orally, the responsible body must make a written record of the complaint and provide a copy of the written record to the complainant.

11.26 In most cases, the responsible body must acknowledge the complaint not later than 3 working days after the day on which it receives the complaint. When it does so, it must offer to discuss with the complainant (at a time to be agreed with him) the manner and timing of the way the complaint will be dealt with. If the complainant does not accept the offer of a discussion, the responsible body must determine the response period and notify the complainant of that period in writing.

11.27 The responsible body must investigate the complaint in a manner appropriate to resolve it speedily and efficiently and during the investigation keep the complainant informed, as far as reasonably practicable, as to the

---

7 See LASSNHSCER 2009, reg 5(4) and 5(5).

progress of the investigation.[8] Should it appear that such a complaint is not being dealt with promptly, it may assist to cite this provision to the responsible body.

11.28 As soon as reasonably practicable after completing the investigation, the responsible body must send the complainant a written response including:

(a) a report which includes:
  (i) an explanation of how the complaint has been considered; and
  (ii) the conclusions reached in relation to the complaint, including any matters for which the complaint specifies, or the responsible body considers, that remedial action is needed;
(b) confirmation as to whether the responsible body is satisfied that any action needed in consequence of the complaint has been taken or is proposed to be taken;
(c) where the complaint relates wholly or in part to the functions of a local authority, details of the complainant's right to take their complaint to a Local Commissioner under the Local Government Act 1974 (see below for what this means);
(d) except where the complaint relates only to the functions of a local authority, details of the complainant's right to take their complaint to the Health Service Commissioner under the 1993 Act (see below for what this means).

11.29 If the responsible body does not send the complainant such a response within 6 months (commencing on the day the complaint was received) or any longer period agreed before the expiry of 6 months, the responsible body must notify the complainant in writing accordingly and explain the reason why, and send such a response as soon as reasonably practicable after the relevant period.

11.30 Each responsible body must make information available to the public as to its arrangements for dealing with complaints and how further information about those arrangements may be obtained. Such information should therefore be made available to those caring for someone with dementia.

11.31 Each responsible body must maintain records of each complaint received, the subject matter and outcome of each complaint, and where they informed the complainant of the response period or any amendments to that period whether a report was then sent within that period.

11.32 Annual reports must be prepared by each responsible body which include the number of complaints received; the number they decided were well-founded; the number which they were informed had been referred to the Health Service Commissioner or Local Commissioner; and a summary of the subject matter of complaints they received, any matters of general importance arising out of those complaints or the way in which the complaints were

---

8 LASSNHSCER 2009, reg 14(b).

handled and any matters where action had been or was to be taken to improve services as a consequence of those complaints. They must ensure that the annual report is available to any person on request.

NHS Constitution for England

11.33 The NHS Constitution for England sets out the following rights:

(a) to have any complaint made about NHS services acknowledged within three working days and to have it properly investigated;
(b) to discuss the manner in which the complaint is to be handled, and to know the period within which the investigation is likely to be completed and the response sent;
(c) to be kept informed of progress and to know the outcome of any investigation into the complaint, including an explanation of the conclusions and confirmation that any action needed in consequence of the complaint has been taken or is proposed to be taken;
(d) to take the complaint to the independent Parliamentary and Health Service Ombudsman or Local Government Ombudsman if not satisfied with the way the complaint was dealt with by the NHS (see below for what this means);
(e) to make a claim for judicial review if the individual concerned thinks they have been directly affected by an unlawful act or decision of an NHS body or local authority (see Chapter 14 for an explanation of judicial review);
(f) to compensation where the individual has been harmed by negligent treatment (see Chapter 15 for further information about this).

11.34 The NHS Constitution also sets out that it promises to ensure that the individual concerned is treated with courtesy and receives appropriate support throughout the handling of a complaint, and that the fact they have complained will not adversely affect their future treatment. It promises to ensure that when mistakes happen or the individual concerned is harmed while receiving health care they receive an appropriate explanation and apology, delivered with sensitivity and recognition of the trauma they have experienced, and know that lessons will be learned to help avoid a similar incident occurring again. It also commits to ensure that the organisation learns lessons from complaints and claims and uses those to improve NHS services.

Complaints about care homes in Wales

11.35 The relevant regulations are the Care Homes (Wales) Regulations 2002 (as amended) ('CHWR 2002').[9] They apply in relation to care homes in Wales.

---

[9] SI 2002/324 (W37). The contents of this part of the Chapter are based upon CHWR 2002 and as such each individual reference is not included.

11.36 The registered person (the person registered under the Care Standards Act 2000 ('CSA 2000') as the manager of the care home or a person carrying on the care home) has to compile a written statement ('the statement of purpose') which includes a statement of the arrangements for dealing with complaints. They are required to make this available upon request for inspection at any reasonable time by any 'service user' and any representative of a service user. The service user means any person accommodated in the care home who is in need of nursing or personal care by reason of disability, infirmity, past or present illness, past or present mental disorder or past or present dependence on alcohol or drugs. In the context of this book, the service user is therefore the person with dementia who is accommodated in the care home in Wales and in need of nursing or personal care by reason of their dementia.

11.37 In addition to the statement of purpose, the registered person is required to produce a written guide to the care home ('the service user's guide') which is to include a summary of the complaints procedure established. He is required to provide a copy of the current version of the service user's guide to each service user when first accommodated in the home, and to provide further copies at the request of the service user. Moreover should, for example, a family member of the person with dementia request a copy of the service user's guide, the registered person is required to make a copy of the current version of it available for inspection by them at the care home or provide a copy to them.[10]

11.38 The registered person is required to prepare and follow a written procedure ('the complaints procedure') for considering complaints made to them by a service user or person acting on the service user's behalf. The complaints procedure must be appropriate to the needs of service users and must include provision for the consideration of complaints made about the registered person. He is obliged to ensure that the following persons are aware of the existence of the complaints procedure, and must take all reasonable steps to give a copy of the complaints procedure in an appropriate format (or such format as may be requested) to the following:

(a) service users;

(b) representatives of service users; and

(c) any authority which has arranged for the accommodation of a service user at the care home.[11]

11.39 There should be no difficulties in obtaining a copy of the complaints procedure as the representative of a service user with dementia. If difficulties are experienced, it may be of assistance to quote the above paragraph to the care home.

---

[10] CHWR 2002, reg 5(2)(d).

[11] CHWR 2002, reg 23(4).

11.40 What is more, the registered person must ensure that the staff employed at the care home are informed about, given a copy of and appropriately trained in the operation of the complaints procedure.

11.41 The complaints procedure itself must include:

(a) the name, address and telephone number of the appropriate office of the National Assembly; and
(b) the procedure, if any, that has been notified to the registered person by the National Assembly for the making of complaints to it.

11.42 The complaints procedure must include provision for the 'local' resolution of complaints at an early stage where appropriate. Where the complaints procedure includes provision for a formal consideration, this provision must be approved by the National Assembly (and approval of the National Assembly will only be given where the complaints procedure includes provision for the formal consideration to be undertaken by a person who is independent of the management of the home).

11.43 The complaints procedure must be operated in accordance with the principle that the welfare of the service user is safeguarded and promoted and account must be taken of the ascertainable wishes and feelings of the service user.

11.44 When a complaint is made, the registered person must advise the complainant of their right to complain at any time to the National Assembly or, where relevant, to the authority which has arranged for the accommodation of the service user at the care home.

11.45 It is important to note that the registered person must inform the complainant of the availability of any advocacy services which the registered person believes may be of assistance to the complainant.

11.46 The registered person can in any case where it is appropriate to do so, and with the agreement of the complainant, make arrangements for conciliation, mediation or other assistance for the purposes of resolving the complaint (see Chapter 12 for the potential benefits of alternative methods of dispute resolution).

11.47 The registered person is obliged to keep a written record of any complaint, the outcome of the investigation and any action taken in response.

11.48 The registered person is also obliged to supply to the appropriate office of the National Assembly at its request a statement containing a summary of the complaints made during the preceding 12 months and the action taken in response to each complaint.

11.49 Complaints that are dealt with locally must be resolved by the registered person as soon as reasonably practicable and in any event within 14 days. This time limit may be extended for up to a further 14 days with the agreement of the complainant.

11.50 Where the complaint is resolved under this procedure the registered person must confirm in writing to the complainant the agreed resolution. The registered person must also, at the request of the National Assembly or any authority who has arranged for the accommodation of a service user at the care home, confirm the local resolution of a complaint.

11.51 Complaints that are dealt with by way of formal consideration must be resolved 'as soon as reasonably practicable' and in any event within 35 days of the request for formal consideration. If the complaint has not been resolved within 35 days of the request for formal consideration, the registered person must notify the appropriate office of the National Assembly of the complaint and the reasons for the delay in resolution. The time limit of 35 days may be extended with the agreement of the complainant.

11.52 The outcome of a formal consideration must be confirmed in writing by the registered person to the complainant and must summarise the nature and substance of the complaint, the conclusions and the action to be taken as a result. The registered person must send a copy of the written response to a complaint to the appropriate office of the National Assembly and any authority which has arranged for the accommodation of the service user at the care home.

Complaints about social services in Wales

11.53 The regulations that apply in respect of complaints about social services in Wales are the Social Services Complaints Procedure (Wales) Regulations 2005.[12]

11.54 Any complaints procedure set up under the regulations must be operated in accordance with the principle that the welfare of the service user should be safeguarded and promoted. It is set out that account should be taken of the ascertainable wishes and feelings of the service user.

11.55 Each local authority has a duty to make arrangements in accordance with the regulations for the handling and consideration of complaints. The arrangements must be in writing (a 'complaints procedure').

11.56 Each local authority must ensure that their staff are informed about and appropriately trained in the operation of the complaints procedure.

---

12 'SSCPWR 2005', SI 2005/3366 (W263). The contents of this part of the chapter are based upon SSCPWR 2005 and as such references are not given to each individual regulation.

11.57 So far as is generally relevant for the purposes of this book, those that may make complaints are set out as follows:

(a) Any person to whom the local authority has a power or duty to provide, or secure the provision of, a service which (if provided) would be provided as a social service function and whose need or possible need for such a service has (by whatever means) come to the attention of the local authority (ie the 'service user').

(b) A representative acting on behalf of a service user where the service user has requested the representative to act on his or her behalf or is not capable of making the complaint personally.

11.58 A complaint may also be made by a representative in respect of a person who has died.

11.59 Any representative making a complaint on behalf of a person who is not capable of making the complaint personally or who has died must, in the opinion of the local authority, have or have had an interest in the person's welfare and be suitable to act as representative. If the local authority is of the opinion that the person does not have sufficient interest in the person's welfare or is not a suitable person to act as a representative the authority must notify the person in writing immediately stating the reasons for that opinion. If such a notification is given and the service user is alive the local authority must, if it considers it appropriate to do so having regard to the understanding of the service user, provide them with a copy of the notification.

11.60 Complaints may be about the exercise of the local authority's social services functions. The regulations do not require arrangements to be made for the investigation of any complaint which has been previously investigated under the regulations, under any former complaints procedure or by a Commissioner for Local Administration (see below for what this means).

11.61 If a complaint relates wholly or partly to services provided in respect of which a person is registered under the Care Standards Act 2000, the local authority must within 2 working days of receipt do the following: (a) send details of the complaint to the person registered to provide that service; (b) request the person to whom details are sent to notify the authority within 10 working days of the outcome of their consideration of the complaint; and (c) inform the complainant of the action that has been taken under (a) and (b).

11.62 This does not apply if the complaint has already been considered by the registered person or if the local authority is of the opinion that for the complaint to be so considered would be likely to compromise or prejudice the investigation of the complaint under these regulations or might compromise or prejudice an investigation by the National Assembly.

11.63 Complaints may be made orally or in writing (including electronically) to any member of the staff of the local authority employed or engaged in relation to the social services function of it.

11.64 The local authority must inform the complainant of the availability of any advocacy services which the complaints officer believes may be of assistance to the complainant.[13] Those with dementia or those involved in complaining on behalf of a person with dementia should not hesitate to request this information and it may assist to quote this regulation to the local authority.

Local resolution

11.65 The first stage of resolving the complaint is known as 'local resolution'. The local authority must take all reasonable steps to resolve the complaint as soon as is reasonably practicable and within 10 working days from the date the complaint was made (this may be extended by up to a further 10 working days on request of the complainant or with the complainant's agreement). The local authority may (in any case where it would be appropriate to do so and if the complainant agrees) make arrangements for conciliation, mediation or other assistance in order to try to resolve the complaint. Chapter 12 details the potential benefits of alternative methods of dispute resolution such as mediation. If the complaint is resolved by 'local resolution', the local authority must confirm to the complainant the agreed resolution in writing.

11.66 If the complaint has not been resolved by local resolution within 20 working days, the local authority must (as soon as practicable) notify the complainant in writing of their right to request that the complaint be formally considered, the procedure for requesting this and the date by which such a request must be made. The complainant may request 'formal consideration' at any time within 30 working days of the date on which the complaint was first made.

Formal consideration

11.67 'Formal consideration' means that the local authority must investigate the complaint to the extent necessary and in the manner which appears to the authority most appropriate to resolve it speedily and efficiently. They must compile a formal written record of the complaint as soon as is reasonably practicable and send it to the person making the complaint with an invitation to comment on its accuracy. The local authority must then consider any comments made and in the light of those make any amendments to the record which are necessary to ensure it is (in the opinion of the authority) an accurate record of the complaint. Save where arrangements have been made within local consideration for conciliation, mediation or other assistance, the local authority may in formal consideration (again where it would be appropriate to do so and

---

[13] SSCPWR 2005, reg 16.

with the agreement of the person making the complaint) make arrangements for the same for the purposes of resolving the complaint.

11.68 The local authority must explain to the complainant how the complaint will be investigated and send a copy of the complaint to any person who is the subject of the complaint unless this has already been done or notification at that time would prejudice the consideration of the complaint.

11.69 The local authority has to take all reasonable steps to keep the person making the complaint informed about the progress of its formal consideration of the complaint.

11.70 The local authority must then prepare a written response to the complaint which (i) summarises its nature and substance; (ii) describes the investigation under formal consideration and summarises the conclusions; (iii) explains what action will be taken to resolve it; (iv) where appropriate contains an apology to the complainant; and (v) identifies what other action (if any) will be taken in the light of the complaint. This response must be sent to the complainant within 25 days from when the local authority received the request for formal consideration unless the local authority has notified the complainant otherwise. The local authority is able to take longer in certain circumstances where there has been difficulty in the determination of its nature or substance; the complaint involves more than one body; the complaint has been treated as subject to concurrent consideration or where the complainant has agreed to a later response if it is not possible for the response to be sent within 25 working days. The local authority does have to notify the complainant of the reason for the delay, the date by which it expects to send the response and must send its response as soon as reasonably practicable.

11.71 The response must include information about the complainant's right to request an independent panel hearing, the procedure for requesting such a hearing and the time within such a request must be made.

Independent panel hearing

11.72 The next stage is therefore an 'independent panel hearing'. A complainant may request that a complaint is further considered by an independent panel in circumstances including the following:

(a) where a local authority has decided it will not consider a complaint in a case where it is of the opinion that the person making a complaint on behalf of the service user (where the service user is not capable of making the complaint personally or has died) does not have sufficient interest in the person's welfare or is not a suitable person to act as a representative;
(b) where for any reason formal consideration has not been completed within 3 months of the date on which the complaint was made; and
(c) Where the complainant is dissatisfied with the result of formal consideration by the local authority.

11.73 The request for further consideration by an independent panel must be made to the Assembly within 20 working days of the day on which the written response from the formal consideration was sent to the complainant, or within 20 working days of the notification of the decision set out in subparagraph (a) above. If the request is made as a result of subparagraph (b) above, it must be made within 20 working days of the complainant becoming aware that the local authority has not been sent a written response to the complaint within 3 months of when it was made.

11.74 The local authority shall then, as soon as practicable, inform the Assembly of the request. The Assembly must acknowledge receipt of the request in writing within 2 working days. It must ask the complainant to provide within 20 working days (if one has not already been provided) a written statement setting out the basis of the complaint and why the complainant is dissatisfied with the local authority's response. It must inform the local authority complained about in writing and send it a copy of the complainant's letter requesting a panel hearing and (when available) a copy of their written statement. It must also request from the local authority the complaints file and any information and documents relevant to the complaint.

11.75 The Assembly has to convene a panel of 3 members (one from a list of persons with social services experience, two from a list of lay persons one of whom must be appointed to chair the panel) to further consider the complaint within 20 working days of receipt of the complainant's written statement.

11.76 The panel must ensure that the person making the complaint and any person who is the subject of the complaint are given the opportunity to present their case orally or (if they want to) in writing.

11.77 The chair of the panel must prepare a written report which summarises the findings of fact made by the panel relevant to the complaint; summarises the conclusions of the panel; recommends what action (if any) should be taken to resolve the complaint; recommends what other action (if any) should be taken as a result of the complaint; and sets out the reasons for their findings, conclusions and recommendations. The report may include suggestions which the panel consider would improve the services of the local authority or which would otherwise be effective for the purpose of resolving the complaint. The report has to be delivered to the Assembly within 5 working days of the conclusion of the panel hearing.

11.78 The Assembly has to send copies of the report to the complainant, any person on whose behalf a complaint has been made by a representative, the panel members and the Chief Executive and Director of Social Services for the authority which was complained against. If the time frame above cannot be adhered to, the Assembly must write to those that are entitled to a copy of the report explaining the reason for the delay and when it will be available.

11.79 When the local authority has received a copy of the panel's report, it must within 15 working days of receipt decide what action it will take in the light of the recommendations of the panel and notify the complainant and any person on whose behalf a complaint has been made by a representative of its decision. That notification must explain the complainant's right to complain to the Public Services Ombudsman for Wales (see further below).

11.80 There are provisions within the regulations for each local authority to monitor the arrangements they have made with a view to ensuring they comply with the regulations and to prepare annual reports.

Complaints about the NHS in Wales

11.81 If the dispute is about the NHS in Wales and it has not been possible to resolve it by speaking with the organisation concerned the next stage would be to get in touch with the Health Board's Concerns Team or the relevant NHS Trust.

11.82 The relevant regulations are the National Health Service (Concerns, Complaints and Redress Arrangements) (Wales) Regulations 2011 (as amended).[14] They use the word 'concern' to include complaints, notifications of incidents concerning patient safety and (except for certain circumstances) claims for compensation.

11.83 There are certain general principles that apply to any arrangements set up under the regulations for the handling and investigation of concerns. They must be such as to ensure that:

(a) there is a single point of entry for the submission of concerns;
(b) concerns are dealt with efficiently and openly;
(c) concerns are properly investigated;
(d) provision should be made to establish the expectations of the person notifying the concern and to seek to secure their involvement in the process;
(e) persons who notify concerns are treated with respect and courtesy;
(f) persons who notify concerns are advised of:
    (i) the availability of assistance to enable them to pursue their concern;
    (ii) advice as to where they may obtain such assistance if it is required; and
    (iii) the name of the person in the relevant responsible body who will act as their contact throughout the handling of their concern;
(g) a Welsh NHS body must give consideration to the making of an offer of redress where its investigation into the matters raised in a concern reveal that there is a qualifying liability (see further below);

---

14 SI 2011/704 (W108). The contents of this part of the chapter are based upon these regulations: as such individual references are not given to each regulation.

(h) persons who notify concerns receive a timely and appropriate response;
(i) persons who notify concerns are advised of the outcome of the investigation;
(j) appropriate action is taken in the light of the outcome of the investigation; and
(k) account is taken of any guidance that may be issued from time to time by the Welsh Ministers.

11.84 There is a duty on a responsible body (which includes a Welsh NHS body) to make arrangements in accordance with the regulations for the handling and investigation of concerns. The arrangements must be published in a variety of media, formats and languages. A copy of the arrangements must be given free of charge to any person who requests it, in the format that has been requested. Each responsible body must ensure that its staff are informed about and receive appropriate training in respect of the operation of the arrangements for the reporting, handling and investigation of concerns.

11.85 There is an obligation upon responsible bodies to handle concerns in accordance with the arrangements set out in the regulations if provisions are followed in respect of notification, those that may notify concerns, the matters that may be notified and the period within which concerns must be notified.

11.86 Concerns may be notified in writing, electronically or verbally (either by telephone or in person to any member of the staff of the responsible body, the exercise of whose functions is the subject of the concern).

11.87 Concerns may be notified by certain individuals including:

(a) a person who is receiving or has received services from a responsible body in relation to the services being received or having been received;
(b) a person who is affected, or likely to be affected by the action, omission or decision of a responsible body (the exercise of whose functions is the subject of the concern); and
(c) a representative acting on behalf of (a) or (b) who has died, is unable to notify the concern themselves because they lack capacity within the meaning of the MCA 2005 or has requested the representative to act on their behalf.

11.88 If a representative notifies a concern on behalf of a person who lacks capacity within the meaning of the MCA 2005 and the responsible body is satisfied that there are reasonable grounds to conclude that the representative is not a suitable person to act as representative or is not pursuing the concern in the best interests of the person on whose behalf the concern has been notified, the concern may not be considered or further considered pursuant to the regulations and the responsible body must notify the representative in writing and state the reason for the decision unless it is satisfied that it is necessary to continue to investigate any issue raised by the concern (though is then under no obligation to provide a response unless it considers that it is reasonable to do so).

11.89 Concerns may be notified to, for example but not limited to, Welsh NHS bodies about any matter connected with the exercise of its functions.

11.90 Certain matters are excluded from consideration including concerns which are being or have been investigated by the Public Services Ombudsman for Wales (see further below), concerns the subject matter of which have previously been considered in accordance with these regulations or previous relevant complaints procedures, and concerns the subject matter of which is or becomes the subject of civil proceedings.

11.91 Save for verbal concerns resolved satisfactorily no later than the next working day, should the responsible body make a decision that the concern is excluded from consideration, it must as soon as reasonably practicable notify in writing the person who made the notification of its decision and the reason for it.

11.92 Concerns must be notified no later than 12 months after the date on which the matter which is the subject of the concern occurred or (if later) the date on which the matter came to the notice of the person making the notification. This time limit does not apply if the responsible body is satisfied that the person making the notification had good reasons for not doing so within that time limit and notwithstanding the delay it is still possible to investigate the concern effectively and fairly. Concerns may not be notified 3 or more years after the date on which the matter occurred or (if later) 3 or more years from the date on which the matter came to the notice of the patient. It should be borne in mind that dates of knowledge referred to are to the patient's date of knowledge and not any representative's date of knowledge.

11.93 The procedure for handling and investigating concerns is as follows (save for those in respect of which there are specific provisions or verbal concerns resolved satisfactorily no later than the next working day).

11.94 The responsible body must acknowledge receipt of the notification of the concern not later than 2 working days after the day on which it is received (this may be made in writing or electronically depending on how the concern was notified) and at the same time offer to discuss with the person who notified the concern (at a time to be agreed with that person) the following:

(a) the manner in which the investigation of the concern will be handled (including consent to the use of medical records);
(b) the availability of advocacy and support services which may be of assistance to that person;[15] and

---

[15] NHSCCRAWR 2011, reg 22(4)(b).

(c) the period within which the investigation is likely to be completed and the response likely to be sent.

11.95 If the offer of a discussion is not accepted, the responsible body must consider and make a decision upon these matters and write to the person as such.

11.96 A copy of the notification of the concern must be sent to any person who is the subject of it unless already done or it would, in the reasonable opinion of the responsible body, prejudice its consideration of the matters raised.

11.97 The responsible body must investigate the matters raised in the manner which appears to that body to be most appropriate to reach a conclusion in respect of those matters 'thoroughly, speedily and efficiently' having particular regard (save in certain circumstances) to matters which include the following:

(a) the carrying out of an initial assessment of the concern to assist in its determination of the depth and parameters of the investigation required (and keeping this determination under review);
(b) the method and timing of communication with the person who notified or who is affected by the concern;
(c) the most appropriate method of involving the person who notified the concern (including discussion about how the investigation is conducted);
(d) the level and type of support required by any staff of the responsible body who are involved in the matters raised by the concern;
(e) whether the person investigating the matters raised by the concern requires independent medical or other advice;
(f) whether the concern may be capable of resolution by making use of alternative dispute resolution (as to which see Chapter 12); and
(g) (save in certain circumstances) where the responsible body is a Welsh NHS body and the concern includes an allegation that harm has or may have been caused, the likelihood of any qualifying liability, the duty to consider redress (see further below) and where appropriate consideration of the additional redress requirements.

11.98 Save for where a Welsh NHS body decided that there is or may be a qualifying liability and a Welsh NHS body produces an interim report (as to which see further below), a responsible body must prepare a written response to the concern which has been investigated which:

(a) summarises the nature and substance of the matter raised in the concern;
(b) describes the investigation undertaken;
(c) contains copies of any expert opinions that the person investigating the concern has received;
(d) contains a copy of any relevant medical records (where appropriate);

(e) contains an apology (where appropriate);

(f) identifies what action (if any) will be taken in light of the outcome of the investigation;

(g) contains details of the right to notify the concern to the Public Services Ombudsman for Wales (see further below);

(h) offers the opportunity to discuss the contents of the response; and

(i) is signed.

11.99 If there is an allegation that harm has or may have been caused, a responsible body that is a Welsh NHS body must, if it is of the view that there is no qualifying liability, give reasons in the response for this decision.

11.100 The responsible body must take all reasonable steps to send a response within 30 working days from when notification of the concern was received. If they are unable to do so, they must notify the person who raised the concern, explain the reason why and send the response as soon as reasonably practicable and within 6 months from when notification of the concern was received. If exceptional circumstances mean this 6-month period cannot be kept to, the responsible body must advise the person who notified the concern of the reasons for the delay and when a response may be expected.

11.101 There are provisions within the regulations for consideration of 'redress' which means offers of compensation (in satisfaction of any right to bring civil proceedings) in a sum not exceeding £25,000, explanations, written apologies and giving reports on the action that has been (or would be) taken to prevent similar cases where an investigation of a concern is being undertaken by a Welsh NHS body and it determines that a qualifying liability[16] exists or may exist. The detail of these provisions lies outside the scope of this book.

11.102 Each responsible body must ensure that it has in place arrangements to review the outcome of any concern that has been subject to an investigation under the regulations in order to ensure that any deficiencies identified in its action or provision of services are acted upon and monitored so that any lessons learned are identified and promulgated throughout that body to improve the services it provides and to avoid such deficiencies recurring. Provisions also apply in respect of monitoring the operation of the arrangements for dealing with concerns under the regulations and the preparation of annual reports.

---

[16] A liability in tort owed in respect of or consequent upon personal injury or loss arising out of or in connection with breach of a duty of care; please see Chapter 15 for further discussion of these issues.

COMPLAINTS TO OMBUDSMEN

11.103 This part of the chapter considers three different ombudsmen: the Local Government Ombudsman and Parliamentary and Health Service Ombudsman in relation to England and the Public Services Ombudsman for Wales.

11.104 Depending on the nature of the complaint, if the complainant is not satisfied by the outcome of a formal complaint as above, the next stage may be to approach an ombudsman. The sections below explain how to approach these ombudsmen, what matters they may investigate, how they do so and what happens to the outcome of their investigations. Should the conclusion of a complaint to one of these ombudsmen not be satisfactory, there may be a remedy by way of judicial review and Chapter 14 should be considered in this regard.

Local Government Ombudsman

11.105 The Local Government Ombudsmen (LGO) are also referred to as the Commissioners for Local Administration. The statutory framework is set out in the Local Government Act 1974 (as amended)[17] ('LGA 1974'). For the purposes of this chapter, the current Local Government Ombudsman is referred to using 'LGO'.[18]

11.106 In the context of adult social care, for example, the LGO is able to consider complaints about care in a residential home and personal care at home whether arranged direct with a care provider (either funded by a local authority or by a service user himself) or provided by a local authority. Separate procedures are set out for local government administration, and for investigation of complaints about privately arranged or funded adult social care, and each is detailed below.

11.107 The LGO has produced a very helpful leaflet entitled 'How to complain about a care home or care in your home' which is available on their website (see end of the chapter for useful contact details).

---

[17] The contents of this part of the chapter are based upon the LGA 1974: particular references are not given to every section.

[18] As to remedies and the LGO see *R (Bradley) v SS Work and Pensions* [2008] EWCA Civ 36, at [139] which states: 'In cases involving the local government ombudsman ("LGO"), the citizen who has invoked his assistance has – in law – no substantive remedy against the local authority concerned if that authority rejects the LGO's conclusion. It is true that the citizen could apply for judicial review of the local authority's decision not to implement the LGO's findings, but the system, as I understand it, depends upon the convention that if a local authority wishes to avoid findings of maladministration made by a LGO, it must apply for judicial review to quash the decision.' See Chapter 14 for consideration of judicial review.

Complaints about local government administration

11.108 Matters that may be investigated include:

(a) alleged or apparent maladministration in connection with the exercise of an authority's administrative functions;
(b) an alleged or apparent failure in a service which it was an authority's function to provide; and
(c) an alleged or apparent failure to provide such a service.

11.109 When determining whether to initiate, continue or discontinue an investigation the LGO shall (subject to statutory provisions) act in accordance with his own discretion. He can decide not to investigate a matter or to discontinue an investigation of a matter if he is satisfied with action which the authority concerned has taken or proposes to take.

11.110 Amongst several other authorities, any local authority is subject to investigation.

11.111 Before proceeding to investigate a matter, the LGO shall satisfy himself that the matter has been brought (by or on behalf of the person affected) to the notice of the authority to which it relates and that that authority has been afforded a reasonable opportunity to investigate the matter and respond, or in the particular circumstances it is not reasonable to expect the matter to be brought to the notice of that authority or for that authority to be afforded a reasonable opportunity to investigate and respond.

11.112 There are certain matters in respect of which the LGO is not permitted to conduct an investigation. These include any action in respect of which the person affected has or had a remedy by way of proceedings in any court of law provided that he may do so if satisfied that in the particular circumstances it is not reasonable to expect the person affected to resort or have resorted to it.

11.113 Complaints may only be made by the following:

(a) a member of the public who claims to have sustained injustice in consequence of the matter;
(b) a person authorised in writing by such a member of the public to act on his behalf; or
(c) where a member of the public by whom a complaint about a matter might have been made has died or is otherwise unable to authorise a person to act on his behalf, his personal representative (if any) or a person who appears to a Local Commissioner to be suitable to represent him.

11.114 Complaints must be made in writing and before the end of the period of 12 months beginning with the day on which the person affected first had notice of the matter or if they died without having notice of the matter, the day on which their personal representatives first had notice of the matter or (if earlier) the day on which the complainant first had notice of the matter. The LGO is able to disapply the requirements for writing and the time limit in relation to a particular complaint. Complaints may be referred to the LGO by an authority.

11.115 Where the LGO proposes to investigate a matter under this heading he has to give the authority and any person who is alleged in the complaint (or who otherwise appears to the LGO to have taken or authorised the relevant action) an opportunity to comment. Investigations are conducted in private. His powers include requiring any member or officer of the authority (or any other person who in his opinion is able to) to furnish information or produce documents relevant to the investigation (and as such he has the same powers as the High Court in respect of the attendance and examination of witnesses, and the production of documents).

11.116 After completing an investigation, the LGO has to prepare a report of its results and send it to the persons concerned (unless he is satisfied with action the authority has taken or proposes to take and it is not appropriate to prepare and send a report, in which case he may instead prepare a statement of his reasons for the decision and send a copy of this). He can include recommendations in this report (as to which, see further below). Generally, the persons concerned are any complainant, anyone referring the matter, the authority and any other authority or person who is alleged in the complaint or who appears to the LGO to have taken or authorised the action.

11.117 If he decides not to investigate a matter or to discontinue an investigation of a matter he has to prepare a statement of his reasons and send a copy to each of the persons concerned.

11.118 Generally, apart from identifying the authority (or authorities) the report is not to mention any person's name or contain particulars likely (in the opinion of the LGO) to identify any person unless after taking into account the public interest and the interests of any complainant (and other persons) he considers it necessary.

11.119 There are provisions for the authority to make reports available for inspection by the public for a period of 3 weeks at his discretion.

11.120 If the LGO reports that there has been maladministration in connection with the exercise of the authority's administrative functions, a failure in a service which it was the function of an authority to provide or a failure to provide such a service, it is the duty of the authority concerned to consider the report and (within 3 months from when they received it or any longer agreed period) notify the LGO of the action which they have taken or propose to take. If he is not satisfied with the action (or if a notification is not received, or if he does not receive confirmation that proposed action has been taken, within the time limits), he has to make a further report setting out facts and making recommendations. The recommendations are with respect to action which in the opinion of the LGO the authority should take to remedy any injustice sustained by the person affected as a result and to prevent injustice being caused in the future as a result of similar maladministration or failures in services (or to provide a service).

11.121 The LGO may also require the authority to arrange for a statement to be published including matters such as any recommended action which the authority has not taken. Provisions are in place for any further report to be referred to the authority when it has been considered by a person other than the authority and it is proposed that no action should be taken on the report or the recommended action should not be taken. The authority is able to make payments or provide benefits to the person who has suffered injustice in consequence of the maladministration or failure.

11.122 The LGO is able to publish all or part of reports or statements (or summaries) if after taking into account the public interest and the interests of any complainant and other persons, he considers it appropriate to do so.

Complaints about privately arranged or funded adult social care

11.123 A LGO may also investigate the matters (subject to certain exceptions) that relate to action taken by an adult social care provider in connection with the provision of adult social care and either:

(a) a complaint which satisfies the requirements about who can complain and the procedure for making complaints (see below) has been made to the LGO; or

(b) the matter has come to the LGO's attention during the course of an investigation (before the person affected or their personal representatives had notice of the matter, or in any other case before the end of 12 months from the day the person affected (or their personal representatives if they died without having notice) first had notice unless this requirement is disapplied by the LGO) and it appears to the LGO that a member of the public has, or may have, suffered injustice in consequence of the matter.

11.124 Before investigating, the LGO must be satisfied that the matter has been brought to the notice of the adult social care provider and that the provider has been given a reasonable opportunity to investigate and respond, or in the particular circumstances it is not reasonable to expect that to happen.

11.125 When deciding whether to initiate, continue or discontinue an investigation the LGO must (subject to relevant parts of the Act) act in accordance with his own discretion. If the LGO is satisfied with action the adult social care provider has taken or proposes to take he may decide not to investigate, or to discontinue an investigation.

11.126 The following can complain under these provisions: a member of the public who claims to have sustained injustice in consequence of the matter; a person authorised in writing by them to act on their behalf; or where they have died or are otherwise unable to authorise a person to act on their behalf, their personal representatives or a person who appears to the LGO to be suitable to represent them.

11.127 Complaints must be made in writing and before the end of 12 months beginning with the day on which the person affected first had notice of the matter (or if they died without having notice of it, the day on which their personal representatives first had notice or (if earlier) the day the complainant first had notice). These requirements may be disapplied in relation to particular complaints. Provisions also apply in respect of matters coming to the attention of the LGO during investigations.

11.128 The adult social care provider, any person who is alleged in the complaint to have taken or authorised the action and any person who otherwise appears to have taken or authorised the action must be given an opportunity to comment on the matter. Investigations are conducted in private. The LGO has powers to require information to be furnished or documents to be produced.

11.129 The LGO must prepare a written statement if he decides not to investigate the matter or decides to discontinue an investigation setting out his reasons for his decision. He must also prepare a written statement if he completes an investigation setting out his conclusions and any recommendations which in his opinion the adult social care provider should take to remedy any injustice sustained by the person affected and prevent injustice being caused in the future in consequence of similar action. Copies of the statements must be sent to any complainant, the adult social care provider, any person alleged to have taken or authorised the action and any other person who appears to the LGO to have taken or authorised such action. He may send copies of the statement to the Care Quality Commission and any local authority which appears to him to have an interest in the subject matter. The statement must identify the adult social care provider unless it is an individual (or a particular individual would in his opinion be likely to be identified as a result) and he considers it is not appropriate for the individual to be identified. It must not mention any person's name (other than the provider) or contain particulars which are in the LGO's opinion likely to identify any other person (and can be taken out without impairing the effectiveness of the statement) unless after taking into account the public interest as well as the interests of that person, the complainant and other persons, he considers it necessary to do so.

11.130 The adult social care provider must consider any statement containing recommendations and notify the LGO within one month starting from the date when the provider received the statement (or longer agreed period) of the action it has taken or proposes to take. The LGO may require the provider to arrange for an adverse findings notice to be published if he does not receive the notification within the time limit, is satisfied before the expiry of that time limit that the provider has decided to take no action, is not satisfied with the action the provider has taken or proposes to take or does not within a month of the end of that period (or longer agreed period) receive confirmation that the provider has taken proposed action to his satisfaction.

11.131 Provisions apply in respect of the publication of such a notice. The LGO can publish all or part of his statements, or a summary of the matter if (after taking into account the competing interests) he considers it appropriate to do so.

Parliamentary and Health Service Ombudsman

11.132 The Parliamentary and Health Service Ombudsman combines two separate statutory roles. The statutory basis for the Parliamentary Ombudsman (also known as the Parliamentary Commissioner for Administration) is the Parliamentary Commissioner Act 1967 (as amended). The statutory basis for the Health Service Ombudsman (also known as the Health Service Commissioner) is the Health Service Commissioners Act 1993 (as amended). Each will be discussed in turn.[19]

Parliamentary Commissioner for Administration

11.133 Various government departments, corporations and unincorporated bodies are subject to investigation by the Parliamentary Commissioner for Administration, for example the CQC, the Department for Communities and Local Government and the Department of Health.

11.134 The Commissioner may investigate any action taken by or on behalf of any such department or authority in the exercise of their administrative functions where a written complaint is made to a member of the House of Commons by a member of the public who claims to have sustained injustice in consequence of maladministration in connection with the action and the complaint is referred to the Commissioner with the consent of the person that made it by a member of the House of Commons with a request to conduct an investigation. The Commissioner is not permitted to investigate actions in respect of which the person aggrieved has or had rights or remedies before a tribunal or court, though may do so if satisfied that in the particular circumstances it is not reasonable to expect him to resort (or have resorted) to them. Certain other matters may not be investigated.

11.135 It is important to recognise therefore that if an investigation by an Ombudsman is sought in respect of these types of matters, the next stage is to contact the local MP and ask that they refer to the complaint to the Parliamentary Ombudsman. There is a blank document available on the

---

[19] Again, the contents of this part of the chapter are based upon these statutory provisions so individual references to each section are not included.

website of the Parliamentary and Health Service Ombudsman which may assist with this – one section of it needs to be completed by an MP.[20]

11.136 In deciding whether to initiate, continue or discontinue an investigation, the Commissioner shall (subject to other provisions) act in accordance with her own discretion.

11.137 Complaints may be made by individuals or by bodies of persons (but not various bodies eg local authorities). Should the person who might have made a complaint have died or for any reason be unable to act for himself, the complaint may be made by his personal representative or a member of his family or other individual suitable to represent him. The complaint must be made to a member of the House of Commons not later than 12 months from the day on which the person aggrieved first had notice of the alleged matters, but the Commissioner can investigate complaints made outside that time period if she considers there are 'special circumstances' which make it proper to do so.

11.138 The principal officer of the department or authority, and any person who is alleged in the complaint to have taken or authorised the action complained of, will be given an opportunity to comment. Investigations shall be conducted in private. The procedure for conducting the investigation will be as the Commissioner considers appropriate in the circumstances of the case. The Commissioner is able to require relevant information to be furnished and documents produced.

11.139 Where the Commissioner decides not to conduct an investigation, she has to send a statement of her reasons to the member of the House of Commons who made the request. Where an investigation is conducted, a report of the results of the investigation shall be sent to the member of the House of Commons, together with the principal officer of the department or authority (and any other person who is alleged in the complaint to have taken or authorised the action). If it appears to the Commissioner that injustice has been caused to the aggrieved person in consequence of maladministration and that the injustice has not been (or will not be) remedied she may if she thinks fit lay before each House of Parliament a special report upon the case.

Health Service Commissioner

11.140 The Health Service Commissioner for England may investigate complaints about the NHS in England (with some exceptions). Complaints about the NHS in Wales should be directed towards the Public Services Ombudsman for Wales (as to which see below). The office of the Health Service Commissioner for Wales has been abolished.

11.141 The Commissioner may investigate various alleged failures in service provided, failures to provide services or maladministration when complaints are

---

20 http://www.ombudsman.org.uk/make-a-complaint/how-to-complain/what-can-we-help-with.

duly made to her by or on behalf of a person that they have sustained injustice or hardship as a result of the same. In deciding whether to initiate, continue or discontinue investigations, she acts in accordance with her own discretion. She is not permitted to conduct investigations if the aggrieved person has or had in relation to the action, rights before a tribunal or remedies by way of court proceedings unless she is satisfied that in the particular circumstances it is not reasonable to expect them to resort (or to have resorted) to them. She is not permitted to conduct investigations unless she is satisfied that various complaints procedures have been invoked and exhausted, or in the particular circumstances it is not reasonable to expect it to be invoked or (as the case may be) exhausted.[21]

11.142 Complaints may be made by individuals or bodies of persons (other than public authorities, eg local authorities). Complaints must be made in writing. Complaint forms are available on the website of the Parliamentary and Health Service Ombudsman. The complaint will not be entertained unless it is made by the person aggrieved or where he has died or is for any reason unable to act for himself, by his personal representative, a member of his family or some body or individual suitable to represent him. Complaints will not be entertained if they are made more than a year after the day on which the person aggrieved first had notice of the matters alleged unless the Commissioner considers it reasonable to do so (with certain exceptions). Provisions exist for complaints to be referred to the Commissioner by health service bodies.

11.143 The body (or other provider) and other relevant individuals must be given an opportunity to comment on any allegations in the complaint. Investigations are conducted in private. The procedure for conducting an investigation is as the Commissioner considers appropriate in the circumstances. The Commissioner has powers to require information and documents relevant to the investigation to be supplied.

11.144 Where the Commissioner conducts investigations, she has to send a report of the results of it to various individuals including (i) the person who made the complaint; (ii) to any member of the House of Commons who to her knowledge assisted in the making of the complaint (or if they are no longer a member to such other member as she thinks appropriate); (iii) the body (or other provider or person); and (iv) any person who is alleged in the complaint to have taken or authorised the action (if applicable to the type of complaint made) and may send it to such other persons as she thinks appropriate.

11.145 If the Commissioner decides not to conduct an investigation she has to send a statement of her reasons to the person who made the complaint and to

---

21 It was held by the Court of Appeal that the health service's commissioner's functions were limited to the investigation of complaints, having no power of investigation at large in *R (on the application of Cavanagh v Health Service Commissioner; R (on the application of Bhatt) v Health Service Commissioner; R (on the application of Redmond) v Health Service Commissioner* [2005] EWCA Civ 1578.

any member of the House of Commons as defined above and is again able to send it to such other persons as she thinks appropriate.

11.146 If it appears to the Commissioner after having conducted an investigation that the aggrieved person has sustained injustice or hardship as set out in the Act and it has not been and will not be remedied, she may (if she thinks fit) lay before each House of Parliament a special report on the case.

Public Services Ombudsman for Wales

11.147 For public services in Wales, the relevant body is the Public Services Ombudsman for Wales (PSOW). The statutory basis for the body is the Public Services Ombudsman (Wales) Act 2005 ('PSOWA 2005').[22]

11.148 The PSOW may investigate a complaint in respect of a matter if it has been duly made or referred to him, and the matter is one which he is entitled to investigate. A complaint is 'duly made' if it is made by a person who is entitled to make it, being:

(a) a member of the public who claims or claimed to have sustained injustice or hardship in consequence of a matter which the Ombudsman is entitled to investigate (see below);
(b) a person authorised by the person aggrieved to act on his behalf;
(c) if the person aggrieved is not capable of authorising a person to act on his behalf (for example because he has died) a person who appears to the ombudsman to be appropriate to act on behalf of the person aggrieved.

11.149 To be 'duly made', the following requirements must also be satisfied in respect of it:

(a) the complaint must be made in writing; and
(b) the complaint must be made to the PSOW before the end of the period of one year starting on the day on which the person aggrieved first has notice of the matters alleged in the complaint.

11.150 There is an online form available on the website.[23]

11.151 A complaint is 'duly referred' to the PSOW if it is referred to him by a listed authority, the complaint was made to the listed authority by a person who would have been entitled to make the complaint to the PSOW, the complaint was made to the listed authority before the end of the period of one year starting on the day on which the person aggrieved first had notice of the matters alleged in the complaint, the complaint was referred to the Ombudsman in writing; and the complaint was referred to the Ombudsman

---

22 The contents of this part of the chapter are based upon PSOWA 2005: individual references to each section are not included.

23 http://www.ombudsman-wales.org.uk/en/Making%20a%20complaint.aspx.

before the end of the period of one year starting on the day on which the complaint was made to the listed authority.

11.152 The PSOW may investigate a complaint even if the requirements of it being made in writing and within one year (and referred within one year if applicable) are not met.

11.153 'Listed authorities' include (among others) the Welsh Assembly Government, the National Assembly for Wales Commission, a local authority in Wales, the Care Council for Wales, a Local Health Board, an NHS trust managing a hospital in Wales, and a Community Health Council.

11.154 The PSOW is entitled to investigate the following matters:

(a) alleged maladministration by a listed authority in connection with relevant action;
(b) an alleged failure in a relevant service provided by a listed authority; and
(c) an alleged failure by a listed authority to provide a relevant service.

11.155 With the exception of the Welsh Assembly Government, the PSOW may not investigate matters arising in connection with the discharge of functions not in relation to Wales.

11.156 Moreover, the PSOW may not investigate if the person aggrieved has or had various rights or remedies including appeal to a tribunal or by way of court proceedings unless the Ombudsman is satisfied that in the particular circumstances it is not reasonable to expect the person to resort, or to have resorted, to the right or remedy.

11.157 The PSOW may only investigate a matter if he is satisfied that it has been brought to the attention of the listed authority to which it relates by or on behalf of the person aggrieved, and the authority has been given a reasonable opportunity to investigate and respond to it. However, this does not prevent him investigating a matter if he is satisfied that it is reasonable in the particular circumstances for him to investigate the matter despite the fact that these requirements have not been met.

11.158 There are certain matters that the PSOW may not investigate. He may not question the merits of a decision made without maladministration by a listed authority in the exercise of a discretion (though this does not apply to the merits of a decision to the extent that it was taken in consequence of the exercise of professional judgment which appears to him to be exercisable in connection with the provision of health and social care).

11.159 It is for the ombudsman to decide whether to begin, continue or discontinue an investigation and he may take any action which he thinks may assist in making this decision. If he decides not to begin an investigation into a complaint in respect of a listed authority or to discontinue such an investigation he must prepare a statement of the reasons for his decision and must send a copy of this to the person who made the complaint and the listed authority (and may send it to any other persons he thinks appropriate). He can also publish this statement if, after taking account of the interests of the person aggrieved and any other persons he thinks appropriate, he considers it to be in the public interest to do so. Provisions apply in respect of whether information such as mentioning the name of any person in respect of which the complaint was made should be included in the statements.

11.160 As to alternative resolution of complaints, the ombudsman may take any action he thinks appropriate with a view to resolving a complaint. Any such action must be taken in private.

11.161 If he conducts an investigation, the PSOW must give the listed authority an opportunity to comment on any allegations contained in the complaint and give any other person who is alleged in the complaint to have taken (or authorised) the action complained of an opportunity to comment on any allegations relating to them. Investigations must be conducted in private. He may require individuals to supply information or produce documents relevant to the investigation. For the purposes of his investigation he has the same powers as the High Court in respect of the attendance and examination of witnesses and the production of documents.

11.162 After conducting an investigation into a complaint, he must prepare a report on his findings and send a copy of the report to all the appropriate persons which include the person who made the complaint, the listed authority and any other person who is alleged in the complaint to have taken or authorised the action complained and the First Minister for Wales (unless the listed authority is itself the Welsh Assembly Government or is a local authority in Wales) among others. He can publish the report if he considers it to be in the public interest to do so (having taken account of the interests of the aggrieved person and any other persons he thinks appropriate). Provisions apply in respect of not including matters such as the name of any person other than the listed authority in the report sent or published unless (after taking account of the interests of the person aggrieved and any other persons he thinks appropriate) he considers it to be in the public interest to include that information in that version of the report. Generally, a listed authority in respect of whom an investigation has been conducted, and who received a copy of a report, must make copies of the report available for a period of at least three weeks, both at one or more of their offices and on their website (if they have one) and give notice of that (though the Ombudsman does have the power to direct that this is not to apply in relation to a particular report).

11.163 If the PSOW has concluded that the aggrieved person sustained injustice or hardship in consequence of the matter investigated, the listed authority must consider the report and notify the PSOW before the end of the permitted period (one month beginning on the date on which the authority receives the report or any longer period specified by the PSOW in writing) the action it has taken or proposes to take in response to it, and the period before the end of which it proposes to have taken that action (if it has not already done so). If the PSOW is satisfied that the listed authority has wilfully disregarded his report without lawful excuse, he may issue a certificate to that effect to the High Court.

11.164 There is an alternative procedure if, after having conducted his investigation into a complaint about a listed authority, the PSOW concludes that the aggrieved person has not sustained injustice or hardship as a consequence of the matter investigated and he is satisfied that the public interest does not require the procedure which includes that set out above to apply. The alternative procedure also applies if, after he has conducted an investigation into a complaint about a listed authority, he concludes that the aggrieved person has sustained injustice or hardship in consequence of the matter investigated, the listed authority agrees to implement any recommendations he makes before the end of the permitted period (a period agreed between the PSOW, the listed authority and the person who made the complaint or if the PSOW thinks no such agreement can be reached, the period specified by him in writing), and he is satisfied that the public interest does not require the procedure which includes that set out above to apply. The PSOW can instead decide to prepare a different report on his findings, and provisions apply in respect of sending and publishing the report (and whether matters such as the name of any person other than the listed authority should be included).

11.165 In certain circumstances the PSOW may prepare a special report (eg if he concluded that the person aggrieved had sustained injustice or hardship in consequence of the matter investigated and he has not received the notification required from the listed authority before the end of the period allowed; or if he received the notification but is not satisfied with the action the listed authority has taken or proposes to take together with other circumstances). A special report sets out the facts on the basis of which these provisions apply and makes such recommendations as the Ombudsman thinks fit with respect to the action which in his opinion should be taken to remedy the injustice or hardship to the person aggrieved and to prevent similar injustice or hardship being caused in the future. Provisions apply in respect of sending and supplying copies of the special report, and he may also publish it. Provisions apply as to the inclusion of names (other than the listed authority) and potentially identifying particulars. Specific provisions apply should the special report be made in a case where the complaint was made about the Welsh Assembly Government or the National Assembly for Wales Commission.

11.166 The Ombudsman must send a copy of this special report to various persons as set out in the provisions. He may also publish it.

11.167 A listed authority must take reasonable steps to provide information to the public about the right to make a complaint to the PSOW in respect of the authority, the right of the authority to refer a complaint to the PSOW, the time limits for making and referring complaints to the PSOW and how to contact the

PSOW. Such information must be included in or provided with documents published by the listed authority which contain information about relevant services provided by them to members of the public or their procedures for dealing with complaints, and also in any documents issued by the authority responding to a complaint made to it by a person who might be entitled to make the complaint to the PSOW.

11.168 The listed authority may make a payment to, or provide any other benefit for, the person aggrieved in respect of the matter which is the subject of the complaint.[24]

WEBSITES THAT MAY BE HELPFUL

11.169 The following websites may be helpful:

- NHS in Wales: www.wales.nhs.uk/ourservices/directory and www.puttingthingsright.wales.nhs.uk
- NHS in England: www.nhs.uk/Service-Search and www.nhs.uk/choiceintheNHS/Rightsandpledges/complaints/Pages/NHScomplaints.aspx
- PALS services: www.nhs.uk/Service-Search/patient-advice-and-liaison-services-(pals)/LocationSearch/363
- Community Health Councils: www.communityhealthcouncils.org.uk
- Local councils in England and Wales: www.gov.uk/complain-about-your-council
- Local Government Ombudsman: www.lgo.org.uk
- Parliamentary and Health Service Ombudsman: www.ombudsman.org.uk
- Public Services Ombudsman for Wales: www.ombudsman-wales.org.uk
- Healthwatch England: www.healthwatch.co.uk
- Care Quality Commission: www.cqc.org.uk
- Care and Social Services Inspectorate Wales: http://wales.gov.uk/cssiwsubsite/newcssiw/?lang=e
- Healthcare Inspectorate Wales: http://www.hiw.org.uk/
- Members of Parliament: http://findyourmp.parliament.uk/

24 PSOWA 2005, s 34(2).

CHAPTER 12

RESOLVING DISPUTES: MEDIATION AND ALTERNATIVE DISPUTE RESOLUTION

12.1 It is inevitable that despite the best ordered arrangements put in place for those with dementia, disagreements can often get started and almost imperceptibly positions can become intractable between families and carers, local authority and hospital staff and care home management.

12.2 A diagnosis of dementia in a relation can have, and is likely to have, a profound effect on the whole family. Family members may find it difficult to adjust to the fact that someone, usually a parent, who until the decline of their mental capacity was robust and decisive, now needs support and will need increasing help not only to do the things they previously took for granted but also to maintain their individuality and self-worth.

12.3 A consequence is that family members will often become the champion of the person with dementia, rightly battling for their rights and freedoms but not infrequently running into conflict with the very organisations and personnel they depend on to assist the person with dementia.

12.4 What starts out as a disagreement can rapidly escalate to become a dispute that could lead to litigation. In this section we look at mediation and a number of other forms of dispute resolution that are alternatives to going to court. Mediation is the most common and best known type of alternative dispute resolution as it is generally the most appropriate method and is most effective. In a great many cases, mediation can be used as a beneficial alternative to conventional litigation whether in the Court of Protection or elsewhere.

12.5 It is suggested that litigation should be seen as the last resort for the resolution of any dispute, particularly in the Court of Protection, and should only be used there where the subject matter of a decision is so serious that only a court can make it, or where the decision of the court is required under the Mental Capacity Act 2005 ('MCA 2005').

ALTERNATIVE DISPUTE RESOLUTION

12.6 Alternative dispute resolution ('ADR') is a means of resolving disputes by using an independent third party who may help and facilitate the parties to reach their own solution but who cannot impose a solution on them.

12.7 The concept of using less confrontational methods of dispute resolution that are quicker, more cost effective and are in the interests of justice has been the acknowledged preferred choice of the judiciary and parties alike where the situation and subject matter take a dispute beyond the win or lose criterion.

12.8 Disputes involving people with dementia, their care and welfare, and their property and affairs are rarely matters where there is one decision to be made and where the dispute is over when the decision is made. Generally in these types of dispute the parties to the dispute will need to continue their relationship with each other and will have to work together to provide care and help for the person with dementia long after a case has been concluded. The polarised positions of the parties which are often entrenched by the adversarial and accusatory nature of court proceedings can permanently destroy trust and make an ongoing relationship impossible. That could, in turn result in the person with dementia having to go into residential care at an earlier stage than might otherwise have been necessary or even being given notice to leave a residential placement where the staff were unable to cope with the continuing unresolved issues between the family.

12.9 ADR is voluntary, as the parties chose to use this type of dispute resolution and can withdraw at any time from the process before a solution is agreed. It is collaborative in that it is the parties' intention to choose to mediate and therefore to attempt to reach a solution through mediation. It is different from litigation in that litigation is not voluntary and parties have to accept the judgment of the court which can be imposed upon them and which may well carry costs implications.

Recognising disputes at their start

12.10 It is always to be hoped that disputes and disagreements can be resolved informally without having to go to court and there are several routes within organisations such as social services and the health service that are designed to settle disagreements. For example, in every hospital setting the Patients Advice and Liaison Service ('PALS')[1] is available, and there are complaints procedures as well as processes for dispute resolution in social services[2] and the health service and in care homes which are discussed in chapter 11.

---

1 The Patient Advice and Liaison Service ('PALS') offers confidential advice, support and information on health-related matters. They provide a point of contact for patients, their families and their carers. PALS officers found in local hospitals.

2 See Chapter 11.

12.11 As it is very often a lack of communication that has led to the break down between parties, early resolution of conflicts will depend on the parties being facilitated to be able to properly communicate with each other as well as understanding the need to so.

The person at the centre of the dispute

12.12 In mediation, as in any situation concerning the capacity of a person in respect of whom decisions are to be taken, the principles of the MCA 2005 and the requirement that any decision has to be taken in a person's best interest applies.

12.13 It is always helpful and best practice if there is an independent person or advocate present to represent and if necessary, speak for the person without capacity. The presence of someone acting on the incapacitated person's behalf serves not only to convey their wishes and feelings but also to remind the parties to the dispute that they are dealing with the best interest of a person with their own unique identity and values, not merely a collection of different issues.

The availability of professional advocates

12.14 Advocacy services are used otherwise than in the litigation context, that is, in any dispute resolution or other situation whether formal or otherwise to help someone with dementia communicate their wishes and to say what they want, to make sure their rights are respected and upheld, to represent their interests and get to the services they need. They are on the side of the person with dementia and are usually provided by the voluntary sector and not linked with any agency that would be involved with the person. Having an advocate who is able to say what the person who lacks capacity wants, may be sufficient to settle a disagreement, as this maybe the first time relatives are able to hear what the person would like rather than any person or agency imposing their own perspectives on that person's choice.

12.15 A suitable advocate in this context is someone who is independent of the person with dementia; a family member is not always suitable as it depends on the issue that is involved. In some situations a family member may find it difficult to be objective.

12.16 Generally local authorities and various voluntary organisations all have advocacy services that can and will be provided free of charge to people without capacity or to those who need the services of an advocate. Enquiries can be made to each authority who will have details of local independent advocacy services.

12.17 In some situations the responsible authority[3] must make arrangements for persons to be available to represent and support people who lack capacity. For example, where the local authority or NHS body propose to make arrangements for the accommodation of a person who lacks the capacity to agree to the accommodation or the local authority wants to move a person to a different residential home and there is no person who it would be appropriate for them to consult in determining what would be in the person's best interests, the local authority or NHS body must instruct an Independent Mental Capacity Advocate ('IMCA') to represent that person.[4] Similarly an IMCA must be appointed and account taken of any submissions made by the IMCA in a situation where an NHS body intends to provide serious medical treatment to a person and there is no appropriate adult available to speak up for them,[5] or where issues arise as to a person's deprivation of liberty.[6]

12.18 It should be noted that if court proceedings have begun and a litigation friend has been appointed by the court that person would be a suitable advocate to represent a person with dementia in a mediation setting.

What can be done when the family and the professionals disagree

12.19 In situations where a breakdown of communication occurs, for example, about the type of care that a local authority proposes for a person with dementia, it is always advisable to try and arrange a meeting in a neutral setting so that the family can have the time to explain their concerns. The clinicians and care professionals can also explain in a clear and unhurried way and in layman's terms what appears to them to be happening in relation to the care of the person with dementia, why a course of action is suggested and what the options are.

12.20 It is not unusual for clinicians and professional carers to come across as impatient and indeed omnipotent and for family members to misunderstand or be unable to take in information as they may be scared or shocked or just not used to dealing with people for whom terms like 'capacity' and 'best interests decision making' are second nature. It is important that each party is able to listen to the other and to acknowledge their different perspectives and concerns.

12.21 It may be helpful for the relevant professional to have a colleague to explain things and who could give a second opinion. In appropriate circumstances, offering to get independent expert advice is another way of showing a family that the professional social worker, for example, is alert to the families' concerns and prepared to look at other options. It is always open to the family to obtain a second opinion and families may be helped by being reminded of that.

---

3 MCA 2005, s 35.
4 MCA 2005, s 39.
5 MCA 2005, s 37.
6 MCA 2005, s 39A.

12.22 Equally it may be helpful for a family member to bring another person to the meeting who is also able to contribute to the discussion as a supporter of the family but who, by not being involved, may be able to explain the various concerns in a different way.

12.23 It is important to make sure the meetings are person centred so that the person with dementia, the one for whom the decisions are to be taken, is at the centre of the discussions. One of the ways that this may be achieved is by having an advocate to speak for him and if necessary remind the meeting of its focus.

12.24 Very often arranging a multidisciplinary conference to which the family is invited can be helpful to show the wide range of expertise that goes into decision making and that can itself allay concerns, for example that a person is being bundled out of his home for no reason.

12.25 On many occasions taking the time to listen to the family's concerns and worries and allowing them time to consider and ask questions is sufficient to deflect any potential dispute.

12.26 It has to be remembered that the chronic lack of time and resources may have the effect of making professionals less available to the people they look after. This may mean they are less attentive to the signals of families bewildered by the system who, in turn, may feel that their concerns for their family member are not being listened to or taken seriously and very soon this lack of real communication will lead to breakdown.

Going to court

12.27 Despite the Court of Protection Rules (see **12.56**) and the court-led case management, preparing a case for trial is a time consuming and emotionally debilitating process for all parties. It is also expensive both in respect of the litigation as well as the enormous amount of time taken up by the parties to the litigation, who may have to take time off work to prepare documents or obtain evidence. Sides have to be taken and positions become immovable.

12.28 Among the indirect costs of conflict are the damage to reputations and team morale, the damage to participants' self-esteem and the huge emotional costs involved for all. One of the most difficult aspects of the aftermath of a court hearing is that parties have to continue their relationship once the evidence is given and the hearing is over. In such circumstances, it is often difficult to build up trust which is crucial to the caring process and, once that trust is lost, it will not inure to the best interests of the person with dementia who has been and will continue to be at the centre of the dispute.

MEDIATION

What is mediation?

12.29 Mediation as a form of ADR is a process in which an independent third party, known as a mediator, helps both sides come to an agreement.

12.30 Mediation has the potential to be one of the fastest, most cost effective and least stressful ways to resolve disputes without the need to go to court. Unlike the court process, which is by its nature adversarial, a mediation can be therapeutic and empowering for the participants and beneficial for the continuance of long term working relationships.

12.31 A mediator facilitates communication between all the parties to the mediation and is there to promote understanding of each other's interests and position and to focus the parties on the issues and their interests.

12.32 A mediation is not a court hearing, it is a structured process facilitated by the mediator that enables the parties to be more creative in their way of problem solving. Consequently, the parties have more flexibility and control over the outcome.

12.33 A mediation is informal in that it is a voluntary process and disputes can be mediated at any stage. A mediation is a private process and mediators keep information that is told to them by one party confidential unless and until they are given permission to disclose it to the other party.

12.34 If the mediation does not resolve the dispute, anything said or done in the process remains confidential and cannot be used in any court proceedings. This enables the parties to explore possible solutions to resolve the dispute without fear of undermining their positions if they do have to go to court. That safe environment in which the parties can communicate freely is fundamental to the success of mediation as a method of resolving disputes.

Types of dispute that can be mediated

12.35 In relation to the personal welfare of a person with dementia he, his family, or his advocate may disagree with the assessment of his capacity; the family may disagree with the standard of care and nature or extent of the welfare services provided by healthcare and social services; they may take issue with the decisions made by local authorities as to whether they are in the person's best interests or whether care could be provided at home.

12.36 There is wide scope for disagreements when a lasting power of attorney ('LPA') is created or exercised, there are disagreements about where someone should live and how that place should be paid for. Family members once notified about the creation or registration of an LPA are often disappointed and horrified at the purported decision of a donor to make a particular person their attorney and that may in turn be the continuation of a larger family dispute.

This sort of family falling out which often involves the wider family is frequently mediated. It is interesting to note that conflict more frequently arises between family members over the creation of an LPA for property and financial affairs than for health and welfare! Entrenched family dynamics are usually at the heart of the very many intractable arguments within families which centre around the care of a family member who has lost capacity. Such disputes are often a continuation of the dynamics that previously existed but were perhaps controlled by the very person who is now dependent on those same relatives.

The process

12.37 The parties involved in the dispute agree to appoint a trained and accredited mediator. Many barristers and solicitors are trained mediators and specialise in mediations of a particular type which usually reflects their specialist practices. Although all trained and accredited mediators should be able to mediate any dispute it is advisable to choose a mediator that specialises in Court of Protection work as those mediators are used to mediating disputes that involve many differently interested people, are skilled at rapidly assimilating information and understand about evaluating and acting in the best interests of person. The Council of the Bar and the Law Society websites together with Barristers and Solicitors websites are a good starting point to select an appropriate mediator.

12.38 Where the dispute involves healthcare services or social services, the professional workers involved will often be familiar with the process of mediation and should welcome it. They will usually take the lead in contacting a mediator and arranging a venue. The mediator is independent so taking charge of the arrangements is a practical necessity and has no tactical benefit.

12.39 The mediator will circulate an agreement to be signed which contractually binds all the parties to the process of mediation, deals with the fees of the mediator and requires the parties to keep all information disclosed during the course of mediation confidential.

12.40 Where the mediation takes place and how it is conducted is dependent on the parties and the mediator. A mediation is a very adaptable process and it can be arranged to suit the nature of the dispute and the needs of the parties. Flexibility is important as the mediation can take place at a venue convenient to the parties and, unlike a court hearing, may be able to be arranged on a few days' or weeks' notice.

12.41 What is important is that the parties who come to the mediation must have the authority to settle the dispute at the mediation. For example, there is no point in having extensive discussions about funding a course of treatment if it transpires during the course of the mediation that the person present who is willing to agree to that funding has in fact insufficient seniority or managerial status in the Clinical Commissioning Group ('CCG') to authorise it.

The structure

12.42 The nature of a mediation varies with the subject matter; the parties; the complexity of the issue, and the stage it has reached but the structure of a mediation is generally similar.

12.43 A mediation often begins with pre-mediation meetings and goes on to joint meetings between the parties and the mediator, and then individual meetings in which the mediator will go between the parties in separate rooms.

Pre-mediation meeting

12.44 As the mediation process depends on the building of communication between the parties, the mediator will, from the outset of her instruction, begin to build a communication base between the parties.

12.45 It is usual for the mediator to contact all parties before the mediation is due to begin to acquaint them with the process and to answer any queries or worries they may have.

12.46 Each party to the mediation will be told that they come to the mediation on an equal footing with the purpose of trying to find a workable solution and are told that it makes no difference to the mediator or to the mediation whether a party comes on their own or with legal representation and/or supporters.

The mediation

12.47 The mediator will usually have asked for all sides individually to have put their position in writing before the mediation begins so that the issues are flagged up at the outset.

12.48 The process of mediation is all about constructive listening for all the parties present at the mediation. It is an integral part of the process for the mediator and, importantly, for the other parties to hear from each person present at the mediation as to what their position or understanding of the dispute is and what they would like as an outcome. It is to be noted that often what a person actually says is very different and more instructive of what they want than the position that they set out in writing.

12.49 The progress and direction the mediation takes is governed by the mediator and will usually consist of several sessions where the mediator listens to each party separately and where the mediator 'shuttles' between them all to facilitate a solution.

12.50 The mediation only becomes binding when everyone present has come to an agreement and it has been put in writing and signed by the all the parties and the mediator.

THE COURT OF PROTECTION AND ITS APPROACH TO MEDIATION

12.51 Traditionally the court is seen as the arbiter of claims and applications are made to the court with the intention that the dispute will be resolved by an adjudication by a judge. There are some matters that can only be heard by the court and cannot be mediated, for example, fact-finding hearings where there are allegations of physical or financial abuse that need to be adjudicated by a judge; allegations of neglect or decisions relating to deputies or attorneys. Equally, there are other matters which have occupied the court for a disproportionate amount of time in the way of Dickensian litigation and where the court has emphasised time and again that such a case would have benefited from mediation.

12.52 This is illustrated well in a recent case involving (among other matters) the capacity of a man who had had a stroke to bring chancery proceedings because he wanted to make pecuniary gifts to a friend of his. The judge found that he did not have capacity in relation to the litigation but had very clear and fervent wishes which could not be met by the case being heard in court. During the course of a 73-page judgment the judge opined: 'It is the kind of case which cries out for mediation and a realistic settlement.' And later: 'A trial of the action is likely to be a painful and damaging experience for all concerned and I repeat my hope that the parties will even now be able to come to a settlement.'[7]

Mediation in the framework of the MCA 2005

12.53 The comprehensive statutory framework of the MCA 2005 is founded on the concepts of capacity and best interests. Any litigation or mediation which necessarily involves a person who lacks capacity must come to decisions that are in that person's best interests.

12.54 Also before the act is done or decision made, regard must be had as to whether the purpose for which it is needed can be achieved in a way that is less restrictive of the person's rights and freedom of action.

12.55 The Code of Practice provides guidance on the best ways to settle disputes and promotes the use of mediation. It acknowledges that mediation is generally less stressful, more cost effective and a quicker route to settling disputes than going to court.

Court of Protection Rules

12.56 The MCA 2005 created the Court of Protection as a superior court of record with the same powers, rights, privileges and authority as the High Court. The Court of Protection Rules 2007[8] are, as in any other court, designed

---

7 See *Re S, D v R and S* [2010] EWHC 2405 (COP).

8 SI 2007/1744.

to assist courts to deal justly and fairly with cases. The court will endeavour to give effect to that overriding objective. Further, the parties to any application also have a duty to help the court in furthering the overriding objective.

Mediation as part of the overriding objective

12.57 The overriding objective (set out in the Court of Protection Rules, r 3), is to enable the court to deal with cases justly having regard to the principles contained in the MCA 2005. The court will actively manage cases so that they are dealt with expeditiously, as reasonably practicable and fairly and so that the person without capacity whose interests are at the centre of the litigation are properly considered.

12.58 Active case management includes encouraging the parties to co-operate with each other in the conduct of the proceedings, to identify the issues and to identify any person who should be a party to the proceedings.

12.59 Under r 5(e) of the Court of Protection Rules the parties are encouraged to use an ADR procedure if the court considers that appropriate.

12.60 Similarly, any ADR process adopted must have those tenets at the forefront of any settlement.

When is the right time to go to mediation?

12.61 As suggested earlier in this section (see **12.11**), the sooner parties recognise that their disagreement is becoming intractable and that they are just not communicating with each other, the better. That is the time to consider mediation as a way of clearing the blockage of non-communication, which can serve to enhance the future relationships with all sides for the benefit of the person with dementia, who is very often caught in the middle.

12.62 However, the parties to a dispute are often not adept at recognising how quickly they can become stuck and may be unable to see any view other than their own in their dealings with each other. Often they do not appreciate that the financial outlay in the short term of a mediation can result in tremendous cost saving in the long term.

12.63 It is also a feature of mediation that where the parties have been ordered by the court to attend mediation, the mediation is more likely to succeed.

When litigation begins

12.64 Parties should, in accordance with the Court of Protection Rules, be alert to the beneficial outcomes of mediation and consider the alternative of a properly funded independent mediation before starting proceedings.

12.65 The mediation is likely to be in the form already described above. Otherwise it is counterproductive to a successful outcome if any of the parties are put in the position of thinking that the mediator was not independent or that their concerns were not heard or that the other party or parties were simply paying lip-service to the process of facilitated communication.

12.66 It is suggested that on any application to the court concerning a person who lacks capacity where the application relates to matters concerning that person's personal welfare or property and affairs, the application should include a request for an order that the parties attend mediation. The court will consider whether the circumstances are such that the hearing should be stayed or adjourned to give the parties an opportunity to attend mediation and whether the order should state: 'that the parties attend mediation with a view to reaching an agreement'. Generally a judge will give such a direction as it underlines the importance the court places on an agreement or solution agreed between the parties rather than an order imposed by the court, which brings with it the hazards and costs of litigation together with the likely breakdown of trust between the parties and the difficulties of rebuilding that trust that has already been discussed earlier at **12.28**.

12.67 It is appropriate, if any of the parties are publicly funded, that the order which adjourns a case for the parties to attend mediation includes an appropriate clause stating that the court considers that the costs of the mediation are an appropriate disbursement on the funded party's public funding certificate.

12.68 During the proceedings, a number of professionals (such as independent social workers, or speech and language therapists for example) may make assessments and provide reports to the court. The independence and expertise of these professionals can be very useful at the mediation if that can be achieved in a cost effective manner.

The cost of not mediating

12.69 Whilst the court actively encourages the parties to mediate rather than litigate the court has no power to force them to do so. Indeed it is the voluntary nature of an agreement to mediate that is part of its success. However, a refusal to mediate may have consequences in costs at the end of a trial. The court may exercise its discretion at the end of a trial when it is deciding whether to award costs against a party if it considers that a party's refusal to mediate the dispute was unreasonable. Any reason for refusing to mediate should be flagged up as soon as mediation is suggested so that it might be overcome and any request from a party to mediate should be answered immediately so as not to be seen to be an unreasonable refusal to mediate.[9]

---

9 *Halsey v Milton Keynes General NHS Trust; Steel v Joy* [2004] EWCA Civ 576, [2004] 1 WLR 3002.

WHAT CHARACTERISTICS OF THE PROCESS MAKES A MEDIATION SUCCEED?

12.70 If the parties decide to go to mediation rather than to start or continue litigation, they know that they are embarking on a process that is in effect tailor made for them. It is in a place of their choice rather than a court with a trained and accredited mediator who will usually be experienced in this area of the law.

12.71 The whole day (or whatever arranged time to suit the circumstances) is set aside and there are no interruptions to the process which is informal and user friendly. An experienced mediator has constructive listening and communication skills and is adept at reassuring the parties to the mediation that they are being listened to and that their arguments are being facilitated. Where disputes revolve around family relationships and family functioning a mediation will also focus on the emotional dynamic between the parties and, by allowing the parties to each have their say and 'open up', the mediator can incrementally build trust between the parties so as to enable a more creative solution to be put together.

12.72 The fact that parties are able to speak in controlled situations where all the participants in the mediation have an equal status is unusual and unlikely in a court arena and is empowering. Overall the parties want to be able to find a solution to their problem whilst being able to save face and dignity as it is likely that the (possibly enforced) relationship between them will have to continue long after the litigation or mediation has finished.

12.73 Even if the mediation is not successful in that the parties do not come to an agreed solution, the process of mediation, or other form of ADR, is almost always a useful process in itself, promoting communication between the parties and enabling them to narrow the issues that need to be determined by the court.

OTHER TYPES OF ADR

12.74 Where any dispute concerns the incapacity of a person, not only do decisions have to be made in that person's best interests but it is also important that the solution is person-centred and founded on the principles and concepts of the MCA 2005 as well as taking into account the competing interests of several other parties. The types of ADR described below which are mentioned for completeness are generally used in commercial matters and may be less suitable for Court of Protection cases.

Conciliation

12.75 Although mediation and conciliation are often used interchangeably and in both a neutral third party is nominated to assist the parties to resolve their issues, conciliation is distinguished from mediation as the conciliator's role is often interventionist and will be more likely to recommend solutions and narrow the issues.

12.76 It may be a semantic difference, but the success of resolving disagreements that have been mediated rather than conciliated is often due to the fact that the parties in a mediation are conscious of having the responsibility of creating a workable solution rather than living with a solution being imposed on them.

Arbitration

12.77 Arbitration is the private, judicial determination of a dispute by an independent third party. The disputing parties hand over their power to decide the dispute to an arbitrator, or a panel of arbitrators, who they have selected as being qualified to decide who is right and who is wrong. Arbitration is an alternative to court action, and generally, just as final and binding, unlike mediation, negotiation and conciliation in which it is always possible for the parties to walk away.

Early neutral evaluation

12.78 This usually occurs once proceedings have begun where the parties choose to submit their case to a neutral third party to evaluate their respective prospects of success if the matter were to continue to trial. The opinion of the evaluator is to help the parties agree a settlement. For example, this could involve the agreed instruction of an independent social worker to give his view of the likely outcome of any proceedings as regards best interests.

Negotiation

12.79 Negotiation is usually seen as the first step in dispute resolution. It is valuable in the context of meeting competing needs where each party is able to bargain with the outcome of a particular situation. Although frequently successful in the short term, negotiations can often be a precursor to the parties requiring a formal mediation as negotiations often break down if the parties perceive that one of them has an unequal bargaining position and stalemate results. Negotiation is driven by representatives claiming the rights and liability of their clients, whereas mediation rather turns the process to each party's respective needs and interests.

CHAPTER 13

REMEDIES IN THE COURT OF PROTECTION

13.1 If other methods of attempting to resolve a dispute involving a person with dementia have been unsuccessful or are unsuitable, an application to the Court of Protection may need to be considered.

13.2 The Court of Protection is a 'superior court of record' which has in connection with its jurisdiction the same powers, rights, privileges and authority as the High Court.[1]

13.3 As explained in Chapters 4 and 9 of this book, the Court of Protection may be able to make decisions on behalf of persons with dementia if they do not have the capacity (bearing in mind that the test for capacity is decision specific under the Mental Capacity Act 2005 ('MCA 2005') to make those decisions themselves. The issue of assessment of capacity is considered in detail in Chapter 3.

13.4 The key difference between decisions made about a person's welfare and those concerning his property and affairs, and the rationale for this distinction, is explained in Chapter 9. For example, a decision about the welfare of an elderly parent with dementia may need to be made should the adult children disagree with each other and with the local authority about where their parent should live. A decision about the property and affairs of a person with dementia may be, for example, whether the home of a person with dementia should be sold. As explained in Chapter 9 some disputes may concern both welfare and property and affairs, for example where a person with dementia is living in a property in a state of disrepair and does not want to move but is not sure whether he has the funds to pay for the repairs.

13.5 This chapter will explain what the Court of Protection has the power to do when one of these disputes arises (in other words the 'remedies' that the Court of Protection is able to grant). It will also consider the circumstances in which these remedies may be granted when disputes concerning people with dementia arise.

13.6 Before any application to the Court of Protection is made, informal methods of resolving the dispute should be thought about. The dispute may, for

---

1 MCA 2005, ss 45 and 47.

example, be capable of resolution by approaching the relevant Ombudsman (see Chapter 11) or by mediation (see Chapter 12).

13.7 The benefits of methods of resolving disputes, if possible, without going to the Court of Protection should not be minimised. Applications to the Court of Protection can be costly and time consuming. At the end of this Chapter consideration is given to 'costs' (the legal fees associated with the litigation) and how the court exercises its discretion on this. Careful consideration should be given to the costs consequences of making an application to the Court of Protection before doing so.

13.8 What is more, litigation can be risky. There is no substitute for obtaining proper legal advice on the merits of your case from a qualified lawyer.

13.9 Some disputes that may arise in respect of a person with dementia must be decided by the High Court by way of a process called judicial review. This is a very different process to an application to the Court of Protection and Chapter 14 explains these types of disputes.

13.10 Other remedies that may be available depending on the nature of your dispute and what has happened are considered in Chapter 15. These include negligence claims in respect of the care given to a person with dementia.

WHAT CAN THE COURT OF PROTECTION DO?

13.11 The powers that the Court of Protection has are statutory powers derived from the Mental Capacity Act 2005 ('MCA 2005').

Declarations

13.12 The Court of Protection has the power to make declarations.[2] A declaration is a formal legal pronouncement. The court may make declarations as to:

(a) whether a person has or lacks capacity to make a decision specified in the declaration;

(b) whether a person has or lacks capacity to make decisions on such matters as are described in the declaration;

(c). the lawfulness or otherwise of any act done, or yet to be done, in relation to that person ('act' includes an omission and a course of conduct).

Declarations on capacity

13.13 The Court of Protection can use its powers to make declarations as to whether a person who has dementia has, or does not have, the capacity to make

---

2 MCA 2005, s 15.

a particular decision (for example whether they have capacity to make a decision about whether they want to have contact with their adult children). More broadly, it can use this power to decide whether a person who has dementia has, or does not have, the capacity to make decisions on matters set out in the declaration.

13.14 As detailed in Chapters 4 and 9, it is important to remember that the Court of Protection can only exercise its powers if the person with dementia lacks capacity to make the decision for himself. In every case, the Court of Protection will need to make a declaration that the person with dementia lacks the necessary capacity before it makes any other orders.

13.15 Chapter 4 sets out the principles in the MCA 2005.[3] As a reminder, the person with dementia must be assumed to have capacity unless it is established that he lacks capacity. He is not to be treated as unable to make a decision unless all practicable steps to help him to do so have been taken without success. He is not to be treated as unable to make a decision merely because he makes an unwise decision. For example, an elderly parent with dementia is not to be treated as unable to make a decision about whether he should remain living at home just because the decision he has made is considered by his children to be unwise.

13.16 The principles continue that an act done, or decision made, under the MCA 2005 for or on behalf of a person who lacks capacity must be done, or made, in his best interests. The law surrounding 'best interests' is fully set out in Chapter 4 and is not repeated here. Before the act is done, or the decision is made, regard must be had to whether the purpose for which it is needed can be as effectively achieved in a way that is less restrictive of the rights and freedom of action of the person.

13.17 A person lacks capacity in relation to a matter if at the material time he is unable to make a decision for himself in relation to the matter because of an impairment of, or a disturbance in the functioning of, the mind or brain[4] (sometimes called the 'diagnostic test'). It does not matter whether the impairment or disturbance is permanent or temporary. A lack of capacity cannot be established merely by reference to (a) a person's age or appearance, or (b) a condition of his, or an aspect of his behaviour, which might lead others to make unjustified assumptions about his capacity. Any question about whether a person with dementia lacks capacity is decided on the balance of probabilities (whether it is more likely than not).

13.18 A person is considered to be unable to make a decision for himself if he is unable:

(a) to understand the information relevant to the decision;

---

3 MCA 2005, s 1.
4 MCA 2005, s 2.

(b) to retain that information;

(c) to use or weigh that information as part of the process of making the decision; or

(d) to communicate his decision (whether by talking, using sign language or any other means).[5]

13.19 This is sometimes called the 'functional test'. The Code of Practice provides guidance as to what these four factors mean. In respect of (b), an example is given at para 4.20 and reproduced below:

> **'Scenario: Assessing a person's ability to retain information**
>
> Walter, an elderly man, is diagnosed with dementia and has problems remembering things in the short term. He can't always remember his great-grandchildren's names, but he recognises them when they come to visit. He can also pick them out on photographs. Walter would like to buy premium bonds (a type of financial investment) for each of his great-grandchildren. He asks his solicitor to make the arrangements. After assessing his capacity to make financial decisions, the solicitor is satisfied that Walter has capacity to make this decision, despite his short-term memory problems.'

13.20 It is envisaged that it may be necessary to use a variety of means to communicate relevant information, that it is not always necessary for a person to comprehend all peripheral details and that it is recognised that different individuals may give different weight to different factors.[6]

13.21 The observation that 'we must be careful not to set the test of capacity to marry too high, lest it operate as an unfair, unnecessary and indeed discriminatory bar against the mentally disabled'[7] has been held to apply to other questions of capacity.[8] Mr Justice Baker was of the view that courts must guard against imposing too high a test of capacity to decide issues such as residence because to do so would run the risk of discriminating against persons with a mental disability. He stated that there was no reason for adopting an approach that a finding of a lack of capacity should only be made where the quality of the evidence in support of such a finding is 'compelling'. The question of incapacity must be construed in accordance with the statutory test 'no more and no less'. He also held that in assessing the question of capacity the court must consider all the relevant evidence. Clearly, the opinion of an independently-instructed expert will be likely to be of very considerable importance, but in many cases the evidence of other clinicians and professionals who have experience of treating and working with the person concerned will be just as important and, in some cases, more important. In assessing that evidence

---

[5] MCA 2005, s 3(1).

[6] *LBL v RYJ and VJ* [2010] COPLR Con Vol 809, per Macur J at [24].

[7] *Re E (An Alleged Patient); Sheffield City Council v E and S* [2004] EWHC 2808 (Fam); [2005] 1 FLR 965 (a case about capacity to marry before the implementation of the MCA 2005, per Munby J (as he then was) at [144]).

[8] *PH v A Local Authority* [2012] COPLR 128.

the court must be aware of the difficulties which may arise as a result of the close professional relationship between the clinicians treating, and the key professionals working with, the person concerned.

13.22 A person is not to be regarded as unable to understand the information relevant to a decision if he is able to understand an explanation of it given to him in a way that is appropriate to his circumstances (using simple language, visual aids or any other means)[9] and the fact that he is able to retain the information relevant to a decision for a short period only does not prevent him from being regarded as able to make the decision.[10] The information relevant to a decision includes information about the reasonably foreseeable consequences of deciding one way or another or failing to make the decision.[11]

13.23 The Court of Protection is able to seek a medical opinion on the issue of capacity from, for example, a Special Visitor (see **13.61** for information as to what a Special Visitor is).

13.24 Capacity can be particularly difficult to assess in respect of those with dementia whose illness is progressing gradually. It is important to remember that the capacity of persons with dementia is assessed in respect of whether they are able to make a particular decision or take a particular action for themselves at the time the decision or action needs to be taken (see the MCA Code of Practice for further explanation of this). It may be that there is disagreement as to whether the individual with dementia has capacity and it may be difficult to determine at what point an individual with dementia lacks capacity on a particular issue. The case of *A,B & C v X, Y and Z*[12] discussed in Chapter 9 considered this in the context of whether a person with dementia lacked the capacity to make a will. In that case, the court declined to make a general declaration that X (who has dementia) did not have the capacity to make a will. However, the court strongly qualified that finding by saying that there were many times when he did lack testamentary capacity and such periods were likely to become more frequent, such that any will now made would be seriously open to challenge unless accompanied by contemporary medical evidence asserting capacity.

13.25 As expressed in *RT v LT and A Local Authority*[13] (in the context of a decision on capacity), the essential judicial task is to apply the plain words of the MCA 2005 to the facts of the case before the court. There will be cases in which it may be necessary to look at authority (case-law) on the question of capacity but Sir Nicholas Wall, when he was President of the Family Division, said in that case that his strong hope was that the overwhelming majority of cases will be sensibly resolved by the application of the plain words of the MCA 2005 to the facts of the case.

---

9 MCA 2005, s 3(2).
10 MCA 2005, s 3(3).
11 MCA 2005, s 3(4).
12 [2012] COP EWHC 2400, at [37].
13 [2010] COPLR Con Vol 1061.

13.26 The Court of Protection is able to make 'interim declarations' as to the capacity of a person with dementia before the dispute is finally resolved. This means that the Court of Protection can make orders or give directions in certain circumstances even if the issue of the capacity of the person with dementia is not finally resolved. The Court of Protection may do so if:[14]

(a) there is reason to believe that the person lacks capacity in relation to the matter;
(b) the matter is one to which the Court of Protection's powers under the MCA 2005 extend; and
(c) it is in the person's best interests to make the order, or give the directions, without delay.

13.27 In the case of *Re F (Interim Declarations)*[15] HHJ Marshall held that what is required in order to satisfy this section of the MCA 2005:

> 'is simply sufficient evidence to justify a reasonable belief that P may lack capacity in the relevant regard. There are various phrases which might be used to describe this, such as "good" or "serious cause for concern" or "a real possibility" that P lacks capacity, but the concept behind each of them is the same, and is really quite easily recognised...the "gateway" test for the engagement of the court's powers under s 48 must be lower than that of evidence sufficient, in itself, to rebut the presumption of capacity.'

13.28 The rest of this chapter presumes that the person with dementia lacks the requisite capacity.

Declarations on medical treatment

13.29 A type of declaration that the Court of Protection has the power to make is a declaration that certain medical treatment can be carried out. Chapter 5 considers this issue further.

13.30 The words of warning spoken by the Court of Appeal in *AVS (By His Litigation Friend, CS) v NHS Foundation Trust and B PCT*[16] should be heeded. The court will not order medical treatment to be carried out if the treating physician or surgeon is unwilling to offer that treatment for clinical reasons conscientiously held by that medical practitioner. Sometimes the court's intervention is sought and is necessary to overcome a reluctance or reticence to undertake the treatment for fear of doing so would be unlawful. In this case the court was being invited to do no more nor less than to declare that if a medical practitioner is willing, ready and able to perform the treatment, it would be in the best interests of the patient to do so. It was a purely hypothetical matter which would not force the hospital concerned to provide treatment against their clinicians' clinical judgment. It was held by the court that to use a

---

14 MCA 2005, s 48.
15 [2009] COPLR Con Vol 390.
16 [2011] COPLR Con Vol 219.

declaration of the court to twist the arm of some other clinician, as yet unidentified, to carry out the procedures or to put pressure upon the Secretary of State to provide a hospital where the procedures may be undertaken was an abuse of process of the court and should not be tolerated.

Other declarations

13.31 The Court of Protection can use its power to make declarations to state, for example, where the person with dementia should live. It may be that one adult child of an elderly parent with dementia thinks that they should remain at home, another adult child thinks that they should move into care home X and the local authority thinks that they should live in care home Y. The Court of Protection could make a declaration as to what is in the elderly parent's best interests.

13.32 A declaration could state, for example, that a proposal by a local authority to place a person with dementia into a residential care home is lawful. Declarations may state who the person with dementia should, or should not, have contact with and in what way. The case example at the end of this section (see **13.35**) illustrates this point.

13.33 The Court of Protection is able to make declarations that certain acts do or do not amount to a deprivation of the liberty of a person with dementia, for example being in a care home with particular rules in place as to whether they are able to leave. Chapter 4 considers this issue in detail and provides helpful examples of cases which did, and did not, amount to deprivations of liberty.

13.34 The Court of Protection also has the power to make a declaration as to whether an advance decision exists, is valid, and is applicable to treatment.[17] Advance decisions are discussed fully in Chapter 5. The Court of Protection held in *A Local Authority v E*[18] that for an advance decision relating to life-sustaining treatment to be valid and applicable, there should be clear evidence establishing on the balance of probability that the maker had capacity at the relevant time which was when the advance decision was made. Where the evidence of capacity is doubtful or equivocal it is not appropriate to uphold the decision. In that case, the case should have been brought before the court long before it was, her condition having been seen by those treating her as raising an ethical predicament since at least 2009 (if not before) and the application having been made in May 2012. Jackson J also made clear that in a case with legal, moral and ethical dimensions it is important for the court to ensure that it is informed of the actual practical possibilities and not be drawn into theorising.

---

17 MCA 2005, s 26(4).

18 [2012] COPLR 441.

Case example – dementia, capacity and best interests

13.35 An example of a case (albeit fact specific) concerning the determination of the capacity of a woman with vascular dementia, delay and the local authority's duties in the context of a personal welfare dispute is *Re MM*.[19]

13.36 The 80-year-old woman concerned had been cohabiting with a man (also 80 years old) for about 4 years. She then went into a care home. The woman's daughters contended that the relationship between the man and the woman was one of friendship only and not an intimate personal relationship as he alleged. The judge accepted that it was an intimate personal relationship and the local authority accepted that as a public authority it had a duty to respect the Article 8 rights of the man and the woman.

13.37 The woman's daughters became concerned that negative behaviour and verbal comments made by the man during his visits to the woman were having a detrimental effect on her well-being. The manager of the care home also expressed the view that he had spoken to the woman and other residents in a harsh tone. He accepted he had behaved inappropriately in some ways and agreed to reduce his visits from daily to every other day.

13.38 The local authority tried to ascertain the woman's wishes with regard to contact. Her response to the social worker was that she was happy for him to visit. The care home manager was concerned that the man's behaviour appeared to unsettle the woman and make her anxious and frustrated. The Court of Protection took the view that there were legitimate concerns which needed careful investigation and it was appropriate for the local authority to consider his behaviour and its impact upon her. It was also appropriate that the local authority should attempt to resolve matters by discussion with the man.

13.39 A meeting took place. The conclusions included that there was a need to establish whether the woman had the capacity to make decisions as to who visited her, and that if she were assessed as not having capacity to make her own decisions about who she was to see, her family as next of kin would make decisions in her best interests. At the end of the meeting the man was informed that he would no longer be permitted to visit the woman pursuant to the decision of her daughters. It was clear that the local authority had based their views about forbidding the man to visit the woman upon their understanding that as next of kin her daughters were entitled to make a decision about who was able to visit her. There was no evidence that the social workers made their own professional assessment of her best interests or that they gave any guidance to the care home or her daughters about how her best interests would be determined. Neither of the social workers considered whether an outright ban on the woman having any direct contact with the man was a proportionate response to the risks to the woman that might arise from the man's alleged conduct (the identified risk was distress and upset, not physical harm).

---

[19] [2009] COPLR Con Vol 881.

13.40 The local authority sought to obtain a medical assessment but this was not obtained until 10 months later. They were alerted to the very real possibility that the woman lacked capacity. As set out above, if there is a doubt about an individual's capacity the presumption of capacity will prevail and it is her declared wish that should be respected. The judge was clear that where the capacity is in issue and if it has been determined that a medical opinion is necessary before taking any action or steps in respect of determining either the Article 8 rights or the best interests of that person, then it is incumbent on the local authority to act with all expediency in securing determination of that capacity. Either the woman's declared wish should be respected (to see the man) or if the local authority sought to take action to impose their view of her best interests then it was unacceptable to allow a period of 10 months to pass without determination of the issue of whether or not she did lack capacity (the lack of capacity would then entitle the local authority to pursue a course of action to secure what was in their view in the woman's best interests). The view had been taken erroneously by the social workers and the care home that, as next of kin, the woman's daughters were entitled to make a decision about who visited her. The local authority maintained that the decision to exclude the man from the care home was one taken by the home and as such the local authority had no control over the decision. The care home made it clear that they would say it was not their decision. The local authority subsequently started proceedings in the Court of Protection. Once this was done, the court ordered observed contact and an independent social work expert recommended that contact between the man and the woman should continue in the future. A declaration was made that there should be weekly contact between the man and the woman in the presence of the man's daughter, such contact being in the woman's best interests.

13.41 The judgment of the Court of Protection sets out that no one at the relevant time was asserting that the woman had capacity, and thus it was the view generally held by those involved with her that the local authority had a duty to act upon what they considered to be the last capable wish that she had expressed and consider how her best interests and welfare could be served and protected. It was not sufficient to merely promote the wishes of the next of kin without any consideration of the woman's wishes or exploration of her best interests. The local authority had assumed some responsibility for the woman and should have sought to guide the care home as to the correct approach for the care home to take (which they did not do). They did not undertake the exercise of seeing if a total ban was proportionate, or whether supervised contact may be feasible. The man's application for a declaration that his Article 8 rights had been breached by denial of contact with the woman was granted. Her Honour Judge Moir was clear that the application to the Court of Protection could and should have been made sooner.

Making decisions and appointing deputies

13.42 If the person with dementia lacks capacity in relation to matters concerning their personal welfare or property and affairs the court may make the decision(s) on their behalf or appoint a person (a 'deputy') to make decisions on their behalf.[20]

13.43 These powers of the Court of Protection are subject to the provisions of the MCA 2005 and in particular MCA 2005, s 1 (the Principles, see **13.15–13.16**) and MCA 2005, s 4 (best interests).

13.44 When the court is deciding whether it is in the best interests of a person to appoint a deputy, it must have regard to the following principles (as well as MCA 2005, s 4 concerning best interests):

(a) that a decision by the court is to be preferred to the appointment of a deputy to make a decision; and
(b) that the powers conferred on a deputy should be as limited in scope and duration as is reasonably practicable in the circumstances.

13.45 The Court of Protection has the power to make further orders or directions, and confer on a deputy powers or impose on him duties, as it thinks necessary or expedient for giving effect to, or otherwise in connection with, an order making a decision or appointment of a deputy. Without prejudice to the principles in the previous paragraph, the Court of Protection may make the order making a decision, give directions or make an appointment of a deputy on the terms that it considers are in the person's best interests even though there is no application before the court for those terms.

13.46 The Court of Protection can vary or discharge an order it makes by way of a subsequent order.

13.47 The Court of Protection is able to revoke the appointment of a deputy, and to vary the powers conferred on a deputy.[21] In order to do either of those things the court is required to be satisfied that:

(a) the deputy has behaved, or is behaving, in a way that contravenes the authority conferred on him by the court or is not in the best interests of the person; or
(b) the deputy proposes to behave in a way that would contravene that authority or would not be in the best interests of the person.

13.48 The court can require a deputy to give to the Public Guardian (see **13.62** for an explanation of what the Office of the Public Guardian ('OPG') is) security for the due discharge of his functions and submit reports. As explained

---

20 MCA 2005, s 16.
21 MCA 2005, s 16(8).

in Chapter 9, the purpose of the security is to protect the person with dementia from any loss incurred as a result of negligence or some other default by the deputy.

Decisions and deputies – personal welfare

13.49 In the context of personal welfare, the power to make decisions or appoint a deputy extends in particular to:[22]

(a) deciding where the person is to live;
(b) deciding what contact, if any, the person is to have with any specified persons;
(c) making an order prohibiting a named person from having contact with the person;
(d) giving or refusing consent to the carrying out or continuation of a treatment by a person providing health care for the person;
(e) giving a direction that a person responsible for the health care of a person allow a different person to take over that responsibility.

13.50 As detailed above, a decision of the Court of Protection is to be preferred to the appointment of a deputy. Chapter 4 gives a full explanation of welfare deputies and their obligations. Many applications to the Court of Protection for welfare orders also ask for the appointment of a welfare deputy but very few welfare deputies are in fact appointed. In the recent case of *MK v JK*[23] the judge said 'one can never say never, but it is hard at the moment to envisage how in most cases a Personal Welfare Deputy could ever be so justified'. Sometimes it may be that the circumstances justify the appointment of a welfare deputy (for example if decision making powers will be needed in respect of the person with dementia on a regular or ongoing basis and there is no lasting power of attorney in place) but their appointment will be as limited in scope and authority as is necessary, and for as short a time as possible. The court may appoint more than one deputy.

13.51 It is important to remember that a deputy has no power to make a decision for an incapacitated person if he has reasonable grounds for believing that the person has capacity to make the particular decision for himself.

13.52 There are certain things that a deputy is not permitted to do. For example, a deputy is not permitted to be given power to prohibit a particular person from having contact with the individual concerned.[24] A deputy may not refuse consent to the carrying out or continuation of life-sustaining treatment in relation to the person.[25] There are restrictions on a deputy doing an act that is intended to restrain the person who lacks capacity (see Chapter 4).

---

22 MCA 2005, s 17.
23 [2013] EWHC 4334 (COP); [2013] MHLO 81.
24 MCA 2005, s 20(2).
25 MCA 2005, s 20(5).

Decisions and deputies – property and affairs

13.53 As to property and affairs, the power to make decisions or appoint deputies extends in particular to:[26]

(a) the control and management of the property of the person;

(b) the sale, exchange, charging, gift or other disposition of the property of the person;

(c) the acquisition of property in the name of the person or on their behalf;

(d) the carrying on, on the behalf of the person, of any profession, trade or business;

(e) the taking of a decision which will have the effect of dissolving a partnership of which the person is a member;

(f) the carrying out of any contract entered into by the person;

(g) the discharge of the debts of the person and of any of their obligations (whether legally enforceable or not);

(h) the settlement of any of the property of the person, whether for his benefit or for the benefit of others;

(i) the execution for the person of a will;

(j) the exercise of any power (including a power to consent) vested in the person whether beneficially or as trustee or otherwise;

(k) the conduct of legal proceedings in the name of the person or on their behalf.

13.54 The court can give a deputy the power to take possession or control of property of the person and exercise powers in respect of it (including powers of investment).

13.55 As explained in Chapter 9, the court will only appoint a deputy for property and affairs where it is satisfied that it is necessary to do so because of a need for ongoing day-to-day decision making that would not be practical or appropriate to be brought before the court. An order of the court should be made rather than appointing a deputy if, for example, the only income of a person with dementia comes from a state pension and welfare benefits that are already being received by an appointee and who now needs to surrender a secure tenancy. This would be a particular decision that needed to be made, rather than there being the need for ongoing decision making.

13.56 The Court of Protection has the power to appoint joint deputies. If there is no suitable deputy from amongst the family or close friends of a person with dementia, the Court of Protection may consider appointing a 'panel deputy'. It may be that a local authority would agree to act as the deputy of a person with dementia. Full discussion on the relevant issues concerning deputies and persons with dementia is contained in Chapter 9. It is important to remember

---

[26] MCA 2005, s 18.

that the order appointing the deputy will authorise them to make decisions on behalf of the person within the scope of its terms but only where he is unable to make the decision for himself. It may be, for example, that a person with dementia is capable of making one-off decisions about specific issues even though he is unable to make the complex decisions required to manage his financial affairs on an ongoing basis.

13.57 Should the capacity of a person with dementia be fluctuating, he may have capacity to make the particular decision at times but not at others. That would mean that any deputy would need to consider not only whether the person with dementia could make the decision for himself (with help if necessary) but also whether he would be able to do so during a more lucid interlude. Only if the deputy was satisfied on both matters would he be authorised to make the decision on the person's behalf.

13.58 In the context of property and affairs, a deputy is not permitted to do certain things such as the execution for a person who lacks capacity of a will.

Other powers

13.59 The Court of Protection has in connection with its jurisdiction the same powers, rights, privileges and authority as the High Court.[27]

13.60 When considering a question relating to the person who lacks capacity, the Court of Protection may wish for professionals to report to it with further information. The Court of Protection has the power to 'call for reports'.[28] It may require a local authority or an NHS body to arrange for a report to be made dealing with matters it sets out. The Court of Protection may also require a report to be made to it by the OPG or a Court of Protection Visitor. The court may direct that the report be made in writing or orally.

13.61 A Court of Protection Visitor is either a 'Special Visitor' or a 'General Visitor'. In order to be a Special Visitor, the person must be a medical practitioner (or have other suitable qualifications or training) and have special knowledge of and experience in cases of impairment of or disturbance in the functioning of the mind or brain. A General Visitor does not need to have a medical qualification.[29] In order to carry out their functions, the Court of Protection Visitors may, for example, examine and take copies of health records and local authority records relating to the person lacking capacity and may interview them in private. Reports by Special Visitors may, for example, be of assistance to the Court of Protection when it is considering an issue about capacity.

---

27 MCA 2005, s 47(1).
28 MCA 2005, s 49.
29 MCA 2005, s 61.

13.62 The OPG has specified functions,[30] some of which have been discussed in earlier chapters.[31] They include directing a Court of Protection Visitor to visit individuals such as a person for whom a deputy is appointed, and make a report on certain matters, receiving security which the court requires a person to give for the discharge of his functions, and reporting to the court on such matters relating to proceedings under the MCA 2005 as the court requires. In order to carry out his functions the OPG may also examine and take copies of documents including health and local authority records so far as they relate to the person who lacks capacity, and may interview that person in private.

13.63 The Court of Protection has the power to determine any question relating to whether one or more of the requirements for the creating of a lasting power of attorney ('LPA') have been met, and whether the power has been revoked or has otherwise come to an end. In certain circumstances, the Court of Protection can also direct that an instrument purporting to create the LPA is not to be registered, or if the person concerned lacks the capacity to do so revoke the instrument or the LPA. The Court of Protection is able to determine any question as to the meaning or effect of a LPA, or an instrument purporting to create one. It can give directions with respect to decisions that the donee of a LPA has authority to make and which the person concerned lacks capacity to make. It can also give any consent or authorisation to act which the donee would have to obtain from the person concerned if he had capacity to give it.

13.64 Other powers of the Court of Protection in respect of donees include requiring him to supply information or produce documents or things in his possession as done, or relieve him (wholly or partly) from any liability he has or may have incurred on account of a breach of his duties as donee. As explained in Chapters 8 and 9, the Court of Protection can authorise the making of gifts which are not permitted gifts.

13.65 As to enduring powers of attorney ('EPAs'), where an instrument has been registered the Court of Protection also has powers including determining any question as to the meaning or effect of the instrument, requiring the attorney to supply information or produce documents or things in his possession as attorney and relieving him wholly or partly from any liability he has or may have incurred on account of a breach of his duties as attorney.[32]

13.66 Chapter 4 gives further detail about LPAs in the context of personal welfare, and Chapter 8 about LPAs in a financial context.

---

30 MCA 2005, s 58(1).

31 Including Chapters 8 and 9.

32 MCA 2005, Sch 4.

WILL THE DECISIONS OF THE COURT OF PROTECTION BE MADE PUBLIC?

13.67 Whether members of the public (or indeed other individuals that know the person with dementia) will be able to sit in court during a hearing in the Court of Protection and will be able to obtain information about the proceedings may be a concern.

13.68 The general rule is that hearings in the Court of Protection are held in private.[33] That means that the only people allowed to attend are the parties: 'P' (the individual with dementia in these circumstances); any person acting in the proceedings as a litigation friend (for an explanation of what a litigation friend is see Chapter 9 in the context of property and financial affairs, and Chapter 4 in the context of welfare matters); any legal representative of the parties, the person with dementia, and the litigation friend; and any court officer.[34]

13.69 The Court of Protection does have the power to order that a hearing (or part of it) be held in public.

13.70 The Court of Protection can make orders allowing people to attend a private hearing or excluding them from attending. It can also make orders excluding people from attending a public hearing.

13.71 Whether the proceedings are held in public or private, the Court of Protection can make orders allowing information relating to the proceedings to be published, or allowing its judgment or order (the text or a summary of the whole of it or a part of it) to be published. If the Court of Protection takes this course of action, it can do so 'on such terms as it thinks fit'.[35] These can include restrictions on the publication of the identity of individuals and a prohibition on the publication of any information that may lead to a person being identified. This could mean that the judgment of a case is published (it may, for example, contain an interesting legal issue) but the identity of the person with dementia it concerned is not revealed.[36]

13.72 The test for making any of the orders referred to above is that 'it appears to the court that there is good reason for making the order'.[37] Such an order can be made at any time, and either on the court's own initiative or by a person making an application.

13.73 The President of the Court of Protection, Sir James Munby P, has recently distributed a draft of proposed Guidance on the Publication of Judgments which would apply in the Court of Protection for comment and

---

33 Court of Protection Rules 2007, SI 2007/1744 (COPR 2007), r 90(1).

34 COPR 2007, r 90(2).

35 COPR 2007, r 91(3).

36 The practice of the court is to assign initials by which the parties will be identified eg A, *B and C v X, Y and Z*.

37 COPR 2007, r 93(1).

discussion. He is of the view that there is a need for 'greater transparency in order to improve public understanding of the court process and confidence in the court system'. The effect of the Guidance would be an increase in the number of judgments available for publication, even if they would often need to be published in appropriately anonymised form.

13.74 It is important to note that at the time of publication this is a draft document. In that draft Munby P suggests that in cases involving the personal welfare jurisdiction of the Court of Protection, where the judgment relates to the making or refusal of any order authorising a change of the placement of an adult from one with a family member to a home, any order arguably involving a deprivation of liberty, any order involving the giving or withholding of significant medical treatment or any order involving a restraint on publication of information relating to the proceedings, the starting point be that the judgment should be published unless there are compelling reasons why it should not. As to all other cases the starting point would be that a judgment (where available) may be published whenever a party or an accredited member of the media applies for an order permitting publication, and the judge concludes that the judgment may be published taking account of the rights arising under any relevant provisions of the European Convention on Human Rights, including Articles 6 (right to a fair hearing), 8 (respect for private and family life) and 10 (freedom of expression).

13.75 The draft Guidance provides that in any event, a judgment should be published where the court considers that publication is in the public interest, whether or not a request is made by a party or the media. When considering whether a judgment should be published, the judge should address certain questions (whether or not anyone has raised them) which include the extent of any anonymisation and before making a decision on such matters the judge should invite representations from the parties and (if present) any accredited members of the media. Generally where a judge authorises publication of a judgment, public authorities and expert witnesses should be named in the published judgment unless there are compelling reasons not to and anonymity in the published judgment should not extend beyond protecting the privacy of the families involved unless there are good reasons to do so.

13.76 Munby P sets out that he proposes to adopt an incremental approach to this by way of initial Guidance followed by further Guidance and in due course more formal Practice Directions and changes to the Court of Protection Rules 2007 (changes to primary legislation being unlikely in the near future). It remains to be seen what, if any, changes are made to the draft Guidance as a result of comment and discussion.

COSTS

13.77 As set out above, it is suggested that careful consideration is given to costs before making any application to the Court of Protection. This section considers the court's powers to direct that one party to the litigation has to pay the legal costs (which can be eye-wateringly high) of the other party. In addition, that party is likely to have to pay its own legal costs.

13.78 Subject to the COPR 2007, the costs of and incidental to all proceedings in the Court of Protection are 'in its discretion'.[38] The Court of Protection has full power to determine by whom, and to what extent, the costs are to be paid. It may disallow or order the legal (or other representatives concerned) to meet the whole or part of any wasted costs. The threshold for a wasted costs order is high. Wasted costs are defined as meaning any costs incurred by a party (a) as a result of any improper, unreasonable or negligent act or omission on the part of any legal or other representative or any employee of such a representative; or (b) which, in the light of any such act or omission occurring after they were incurred, the court considers it is unreasonable to expect that party to pay.[39]

13.79 The general rules are:

(a) Where the proceedings concern a person's property and affairs, the costs of the proceedings (or of that part of the proceedings that concerns his property and affairs) shall be paid by him or charged to his estate.[40]
(b) Where the proceedings concern a person's personal welfare there will be no order as to the costs of the proceedings (or of that part of the proceedings that concerns his personal welfare).[41]

13.80 Given the difference in the general rules set out above, if the proceedings concern both property and affairs, and personal welfare, the court (insofar as practicable) will apportion the costs as between the respective issues.[42]

13.81 The Court of Protection is able to depart from the general rule 'if the circumstances so justify'.[43] In deciding whether departure is justified, the Court of Protection will have regard to all the circumstances, including:

(a) the conduct of the parties;
(d) whether a party has succeeded on part of his case even if he has not been wholly successful; and
(e) the role of any public body involved in the proceedings.

13.82 The 'conduct of the parties' includes:

(a) conduct before, as well as during, the proceedings;

---

38 MCA 2005, s 55.
39 MCA 2005, s 55(6).
40 COPR 2007, r 156.
41 COPR 2007, r 157.
42 COPR 2007, r 158.
43 COPR 2007, r 159.

(b) whether it was reasonable for a party to raise, pursue or contest a particular issue;
(c) the manner in which a party has made or responded to an application or a particular issue; and
(d) whether a party who has succeeded in his application or response to an application, in whole or in part, exaggerated any matter contained in his application or response.

13.83 In certain circumstances (for example where solicitors are appointed to act as deputy for preparing an income tax return on behalf of P) fixed costs apply though in some cases may seek a detailed assessment of costs.[44]

13.84 The Court of Protection has the power to award costs on both the 'standard' and 'indemnity' basis.[45]

13.85 In the case of *G v E (Costs)*,[46] Baker J ordered a local authority to pay costs on a combination of the standard and indemnity basis. He was 'entirely satisfied' that the local authority's blatant disregard of the processes of the MCA 2005 and their obligation to respect the individual's rights under the ECHR amounted to misconduct which justified departing from the general rule and considered the local authority's conduct (up to the point at which it conceded the deprivation of liberty issue) amounted to a 'significant degree of unreasonableness' so as to give rise to a liability for costs on an indemnity basis.

13.86 Litigants should be alive to their conduct in the Court of Protection and the possible impact on orders for costs. Exaggerating matters in the application may result in the Court departing from the 'general rule' even if the application succeeds.

13.87 In the case of *Re S; D v R (The Deputy of S) and S (Costs)*[47] an order was made for a litigant in a property and affairs case to pay their own costs together with a proportion of the deputy's costs after a certain date. Henderson J reached this decision because the litigant's conduct resulted in a hearing being substantially longer and more complicated than it should have been.

13.88 If the case 'settles' (the parties agree a compromise without needing a trial) the Court of Protection still has the power to make a costs order.

13.89 In the case of *Re AH (Costs): AH and Others v Hertfordshire Partnership NHS Foundation Trust*[48] nine individuals who were resident at a unit earmarked for closure sought declarations as to their best interests as regards their continued residence and care arrangements. The case of one

---

[44] Court of Protection Practice Direction 19B.
[45] Disputes are resolved in favour of the paying party on the standard basis, and in favour of the receiving party on the indemnity basis.
[46] [2010] COPLR Con Vol 454.
[47] [2012] COPLR 154.
[48] [2012] COPLR 327.

individual, AH, was determined by way of a contested hearing (Jackson J deciding it was not in his best interests to move to the placement proposed for him). Thereafter, the other cases were compromised. Each of the individuals brought an application that the respondents pay half of their costs of the proceedings and the earlier investigations. The costs involved were substantial (AH's were £78,000). There was no suggestion in this case of any bad faith on the part of any of the respondents, nor of 'flagrant misconduct'. It was undoubtedly a major piece of litigation, potentially concerning the future of about 30 residents.

13.90 Jackson J decided that on the facts of AH's case some departure from the general rule was justified to the extent that the two public bodies involved were directed to each pay one quarter of his costs from the date upon which proceedings were issued until their conclusion. This decision was fact-specific. Factors that the judge relied on in reaching it included the reluctance of the public bodies to share information in the pre-action phase, the lack of a best interests' assessment worth the name, and that the application made on AH's behalf was wholly successful in circumstances where the evidence as a whole pointed strongly to the eventual result.

13.91 As to the other applications, those that had been compromised, Jackson J was unable to identify and significant difference between the circumstances of those cases and the case of AH. The position of these cases was different in that they had not been tried in the same manner but the judge was not impressed by the submission that as no findings had been made and the cases were compromised from pragmatic cost-saving motives that it could not be said the residents succeeded. The judge made the same orders (distinctions being drawn depending on timings of offers to settle).

13.92 As to medical treatment cases, Jackson J held in the case of *Re D (Costs)*[49] that an order for half costs represented a reasonable starting point, from which the court could depart if there is reason to do so. That case involved an application brought by an NHS Trust for a declaration that it was lawful and in the best interests of D (who was in a permanent vegetative state) to withdraw active medical treatment. The application was granted. The Official Solicitor who acted as D's litigation friend applied for an order that the NHS Trust should pay half of his costs, and they were ordered to do so.

---

[49] [2012] COPLR 499.

CHAPTER 14

JUDICIAL REVIEW

14.1 This chapter explains the nature of judicial review and when a claim for judicial review may be appropriate. A summary of the current procedure both before and after proceedings are issued is then provided; recent and proposed changes to the procedure are also considered. The final part of this chapter considers the relationship between judicial review claims and proceedings in the Court of Protection.

14.2 Examples of when a person may consider bringing a claim for judicial review on behalf of a person with dementia are when a local authority has decided to provide services which members of the family believe are inadequate, or the NHS has completed a continuing healthcare assessment which has failed to take account of important material.

14.3 It is important to be aware at the outset of this chapter that a claim for judicial review should not be brought without careful consideration of the relevant law and facts and the costs consequences for the losing party, taking into account, as regards those costs consequences, the risks of an appeal by the losing party.

14.4 Because the law and procedure are both complex, judicial review claims are usually brought by parties represented by solicitors and barristers who specialise in this area of the law. It also follows that judicial review claims are often pursued and defended when the case has wide significance and by those who, one way or another, have the resources to make or defend the claim.

WHAT IS JUDICIAL REVIEW?

14.5 A claim for judicial review is a claim in which the court is asked to review the lawfulness of an enactment or of a decision, action or failure to act in relation to a public function.[1] In practice, a claim for judicial review is usually based on a challenge to a decision of a public body.

14.6 Examples of public bodies are central government departments (where the claim is often made against the relevant Secretary of State as the political

---

1 See CPR, r 54.1(2)(a).

head of the department) and local authorities. Other examples include certain regulatory bodies such as the Nursing and Midwifery Council.

14.7 The court has the power to give the following types of relief: a mandatory order (that is an order requiring a public body to do something), a prohibiting order (that is an order stopping a public body from doing something), a quashing order (that is an order striking down a decision), and a declaration (a formal pronouncement of the court on a matter in issue).[2] Damages and restitution may also be claimed but cannot be claimed on their own.[3]

14.8 The remedies are therefore sought in public law or, to use another similar description of the relevant area of law, administrative law. Claims for judicial review should be distinguished from claims for private law remedies which, for example, may be brought as contractual or tortious claims for damages.[4] This is important because private law claims are heard by different courts that have different rules and procedures.

14.9 Judicial review claims are brought in the Administrative Court and, for historical reasons, are brought in the name of the Crown on behalf of a claimant. Claims are therefore given the title 'The Queen on behalf of (the name of the claimant) v (the name of the defendant)' or 'Regina (name of claimant….) v name of defendant/s)', often shortened in turn to 'R (name of claimant….) v (name of defendant/s)'.

14.10 It follows from the above brief description of the nature of judicial review that, in principle, there is scope for bringing judicial review claims to challenge the provision of services for people with dementia by public bodies such as local authorities. However, in practice, there are strict legal and procedural criteria which limit the circumstances in which such claims can be brought and which are discussed below.

MATTERS THAT MAY LIMIT THE AVAILABILITY OF JUDICIAL REVIEW

14.11 First, judicial review is a discretionary remedy. Even if the public body concerned is found to have acted unlawfully, the court may refuse to grant the relief sought. For example, the court may find that a local authority failed to have regard to a matter that it ought to have considered when carrying out an assessment of community care needs but refuse to quash the decision because consideration of that matter would not have made a material difference to the services that the local authority would provide.

---

2 CPR, r 54.2.

3 CPR, r 54.3.

4 See *R (Broadway Care Centre Limited) v Caerphilly County Borough Council* [2012] EWHC 37 (Admin) and *R (Davis and another) v West Sussex County Council* [2012] EWHC 2152 (QB).

14.12 Secondly, public bodies are given a wide discretion as regards their decisions. It is not enough to show that a different person would have reached a different decision. To be unreasonable in law, the decision must be one that no reasonable person could have come to having properly appraised himself of the relevant material; this test of 'irrationality'[5] is a high hurdle to overcome.

14.13 Thirdly, if the court decides that the decision was unlawful only because it was procedurally unfair, it may grant only a very limited remedy, often simply ordering the public body to make a fresh decision in a lawfully correct way. It is, therefore, possible that all that will happen after the proceedings is that the public body will go through a further decision-making process and will come to the same conclusion but this time do so in a lawful way that cannot then properly be challenged again.

14.14 However, notwithstanding the above qualifications, a claim for judicial review can, in the right circumstances, provide a powerful means of ensuring that a public body provides a person or group of people with dementia the services that they are entitled to.

14.15 Careful consideration will need to be given as to how the proceedings can be funded. See Chapter 15 for detailed discussion of this issue.

JUDICIAL REVIEW: HOW DOES THE COURT MAKE ITS DECISIONS?

14.16 Claims for judicial review are decided in the Administrative Court on the following basis:

(1) by applying the relevant principles of administrative law;
(2) by applying the relevant procedure which is set out in the Civil Procedure Rules ('CPR');[6]
(3) by a judge deciding what in the circumstances of a particular case, is the just result.

14.17 The main legal principles of administrative law which may provide grounds for a claim for judicial review are set out in **14.29** to **14.41**.

14.18 It is important to bear in mind that administrative law is complex and evolving and what follows is a summary of the basic principles. For more detailed analysis of the relevant law, reference should be made to one or more of the specialist books on the subject.[7] Moreover, administrative law is

---

5 Irrationality is sometimes referred to as *Wednesbury* unreasonableness after the famous case of *Associated Provincial Picture Houses v Wednesbury Corporation* [1948] 1 KB 223.

6 Part 54. See 'Judicial and Statutory Review' on the justice.gov.uk website: http://www.justice.gov.uk/courts/procedure-rules/civil/rules/.

7 See, for example, Michael Fordham QC, *Judicial Review Handbook*, 6th edn, Hart Publishing.

constantly developing and the law may be significantly changed by new cases or by legislation.[8] Any person considering judicial review proceedings or their legal representative should therefore always ensure that they have undertaken a search for recent relevant cases on one of the online facilities such as the free service provided by the British and Irish Legal Information Institute ('BAILII').[9]

14.19 Also, *Civil Procedure, The White Book Service 2013* (often called 'The White Book'), as well as containing the relevant provisions of the CPR, provides helpful detailed notes on the relevant law and procedure which include references to some of the important cases.

14.20 It is also essential to note that, on a superficial reading of all the grounds for judicial review referred to below, it may be thought that it would be relatively easy to persuade a judge to grant the relief sought by the claimant on one or more of those grounds. In practice, judges in the Administrative Court can be cautious in interfering with the functions of public bodies. This is especially important to remember as, in claims for judicial review, the losing party usually has to bear all of the costs.

TIME LIMITS AND STANDING

14.21 Claims must be brought promptly and in any event within 3 months of the disputed decision having been made. Shorter time limits apply to some claims as discussed later in this chapter. The time limit cannot be extended by agreement between the parties to the dispute but can be extended by the court where there is a good reason for the delay. It should be noted that the courts are often reluctant to extend the time limit unless the claim appears strong.

14.22 A claim for judicial review must be brought by a person who has a sufficient interest in the subject matter, sometimes referred to as standing. In this context 'interest' means more than simply a person who would like a different decision to be made; the person must be directly affected by the outcome in some way.

14.23 In addition, if proceedings are being issued or defended by a person who has, or may have dementia and therefore lacks capacity, or may lack capacity to conduct litigation, further issues may arise including whether a litigation friend should be appointed to act on that person's behalf. It is likely that medical evidence will need to be obtained in order to ascertain whether the person has capacity to conduct litigation. The Official Solicitor may need to be appointed as the person's litigation friend. For further details about this see Chapter 15.

---

8 The Government maintains a database of legislation at www.legislation.gov.uk. Please note however that it is not completely up to date.

9 See www.bailii.org.

LIMITED SCOPE OF JUDICIAL REVIEW

14.24 All public bodies take their authority from a statute or other legal enactment. This means that a public body is not entitled to carry out an action or activity unless it has been granted a legal power to carry out that action or activity. Public bodies must not exceed their legal powers or breach their legal duties (often grouped together as their legal obligations). They must not act beyond their legal powers and when they do so it is said to be 'ultra vires'.

14.25 However, judicial review is limited in its scope; that scope is essentially to supervise public bodies' powers and duties. Just because a judge may agree with a claimant that a different decision might have been preferable that is not in itself sufficient to justify the court granting the claimant any remedy as the public body has to be shown to have acted contrary to its duties or outside the ambit of its powers.

14.26 Apart from anything else, this principle of discretion is based on the pragmatic need to ensure that the numerous decisions made every day by public bodies are not challenged in court proceedings just because a party may, albeit with some justification, be unhappy with the decision made.

14.27 Importantly, the court can make orders prior to a full hearing and, where appropriate will do so very quickly. For example, where a local authority has decided to withdraw a particular care service being provided to a person with dementia, the court could make an interim order requiring the local authority to continue the service until the claim for judicial review has been determined. This can be a powerful means of quickly achieving the desired outcome, for example, by encouraging a defendant public authority to settle the matter and ensure that the right services are delivered to a person or group of persons who have dementia in order to avoid a contested hearing followed by a public judgment where they may be found to be at fault.

14.28 Also, there are certain circumstances in which the Court will grant a monetary remedy. These are rare and usually occur when there has been a prolonged failure by the public body comply with its duties that has caused unnecessary suffering to the person concerned.

CHALLENGING DECISIONS OF PUBLIC BODIES: GROUNDS FOR JUDICIAL REVIEW

14.29 In order properly to bring or to defend a claim for judicial review, it is necessary to have a thorough understanding of the principles below. There may be one or more grounds for a claim which will only become apparent by applying the principles. For example, a local authority may have acted in such a way so as to justify a claim based upon an assertion that there has been an unjustified breach of a legitimate expectation. Equally, a thorough knowledge of the relevant principles of administrative law may enable the public body successfully to defeat a claim made on this basis.

14.30 The main grounds for judicial review can be categorised as illegality, irrationality and procedural impropriety.

Illegality

14.31 Public bodies must not make decisions which are based on a material error of law. This principle is of considerable significance and can result in a claim for judicial review being based upon a detailed analysis of domestic statutory provisions or EU law in order to establish that the decision made is unlawful.

14.32 Statutory equality duties must be complied with, including the public sector equality duty[10] to have regard to the need to: eliminate discrimination, victimisation and harassment; advance equality of opportunity; and foster good relations between those who share a relevant protected characteristic and those who do not. The protected characteristics most relevant to those with dementia are disability and age. Breaches of these requirements could provide a basis for challenging the lawfulness of the decision of the public body.[11]

14.33 It is also important to be aware that public bodies have to act in accordance with the European Convention on Human Rights ('ECHR'). Judicial review claims are therefore often brought on the basis that rights contained in the ECHR ('Convention rights') have been breached. Convention rights may be especially significant when considering the rights of people with dementia; for example, Article 3, which prohibits torture, inhuman or degrading treatment; Article 5 which protects the right to liberty, where a breach may lead to an unlawful deprivation of liberty; Article 8 which protects the right to respect for private life and family life; Article 14 which prohibits discrimination.

14.34 It is important to be aware that any allegation of a breach of Convention rights must be made in accordance with the relevant law that has developed since the ECHR was incorporated into the law of the United Kingdom by the Human Rights Act 1998 which came into force in October 2000. Vague allegations that there has been a breach of human rights are insufficient. However, properly formulated, an allegation of a breach of Convention rights can be a powerful means of ensuring that a public body, such as a local authority, treats people with dementia lawfully.[12]

---

10 This is contained in s 149 of the Equality Act 2010.

11 See for example, *R (South Western Care Homes and others) v Devon County Council* [2012] EWHC 2967 (Admin).

12 A claim for damages may also arise out of a breach of human rights. For further details on this see Chapter 15.

14.35 The recent decision of Lang J in *R(A) v Chief Constable of Kent Constabulary*[13] contains an important analysis of Convention rights and of the different role of the court in human rights cases compared with ordinary judicial review cases. Moreover, in some cases, a breach of Convention rights can give rise to a claim for damages; see further Chapter 15.

Irrationality

14.36 A public body must not act unreasonably or irrationally. This is an important principle of administrative law which is often relied upon by claimants in claims for judicial review. However, in practice, it can be very difficult to establish that a decision was irrational; indeed, in one case *Nottinghamshire CC v Secretary of State for the Environment*,[14] Lord Scarman stated that he regarded irrationality as meaning that the decision maker 'has taken leave of his senses'.

Procedural impropriety

14.37 Unfairness or breach of natural justice is also a ground for a judicial review claim. Again it is important to be aware that a claim cannot be brought on the basis of some vague allegation that the decision was unfair. However, certain important rights are contained within this principle which can provide a basis for a claim. For example, the principle of fairness includes the right to be heard which, in practice, often means a person is entitled to make representations or to make comments which have to be taken into account (and to be shown to have been taken into account) by the decision maker. The requirement for consultation can also be important in this context; see the examples provided below.

14.38 A public body must not operate a policy which is inflexible and applied without exceptions. This is because such a policy is said to fetter its discretion; that is that the policy actually prohibits the exercise discretion. Where the public body has been given a discretion, it must consider exercising that discretion in every case. Also, it must not breach a legitimate expectation, act with bad faith or an improper motive and must ensure equal treatment, consistency and relevancy in its decision-making.

14.39 A public body must not be biased or appear to be biased in its decision-making. The test for apparent bias is whether a fair minded and informed observer would think there is a risk of bias.

14.40 A failure to give a reason for a decision can also render a decision procedurally unfair and therefore unlawful and susceptible to a claim for judicial review.

---

13 [2013] EWHC 424 (Admin).

14 [1986] AC 240, at pp 247–248.

14.41 Public bodies must not make decisions which are based on a material error of fact. However, as the determination of factual questions is primarily for the public body to decide it will not be easy to persuade a judge to conclude that a decision is unlawful because of an error of fact.

THE PROCEDURE FOR JUDICIAL REVIEW

14.42 Part 54 of the Civil Procedure Rules contains detailed rules for the filing of the claim form and the acknowledgement of service and for the other procedural requirements which have to be complied with before the final hearing of the claim. The Practice Directions that accompany the rules also set out a number of important relevant provisions. What follows is a brief summary of the procedure and reference should be made to the actual CPR 54 and the Practice Directions for the full details of the requirements that have to be complied with.

14.43 The courts have made clear that judicial review proceedings should only be issued as a last resort. This is also important bearing in mind the costs and uncertain outcome of any claim for judicial review; see further below.

14.44 There is therefore a pre-action protocol for judicial review, or 'PAP' which should be used in order to try and avoid proceedings. Failure to follow the protocol may be a relevant factor when the court decides whether or not to award costs so any party considering making a claim for judicial review or defending a claim should be aware of its requirements.

14.45 The essential requirements contained in the protocol are as follows. First the parties should consider whether some form of alternative dispute resolution would be more suitable than litigation and, if so, endeavour to agree which form to adopt. Secondly, whilst the protocol makes clear that it will not be appropriate in an urgent case, in non-urgent cases, before making a claim, the claimant should send the defendant a letter before claim (sometimes called a 'PAP' letter), identifying the issues in dispute in order to establish if litigation can be avoided, giving usually at least 14 days to respond before proceedings are issued. Thirdly, defendants should normally respond within 14 days setting out their position in response. The protocol has annexed to it a standard format for the letter before claim and the letter in response which should be followed.

14.46 It is also important to emphasise that a detailed understanding of the relevant principles of administrative law is essential when preparing the letter before claim and the letter in reply which are required by the relevant pre-action protocol; see further below. A properly formulated letter before claim can often result in the public body agreeing to make a fresh decision or to make some other important concession, bearing in mind the risk of a significant liability for costs if proceedings are issued and the public body then agrees to grant the relief sought in the letter before claim.

14.47 Assuming that proceedings have not been avoided, the claim for judicial review is issued in the Administrative Court in London or one of the authorised regional centres.[15] The claim must be made using the prescribed form. Any applicable fee has to be paid by the claimant and the claim form is 'sealed' or stamped by the court office upon issue.

14.48 The claim form must be filed promptly and, subject to the amendments to the rules referred to below, must be filed not later than 3 months after the grounds to make the claim first arose unless an enactment specifies a shorter time limit.[16]

14.49 It should be noted in passing that CPR, r 54.5(A1) shortens the time limits in certain cases (challenges to planning decisions and to decisions governed by the Public Contracts Regulations 2006) where the grounds for the claim arose on or after 1 July 2013. The pre-action protocol referred to below has also been changed to reflect these changes in the CPR.

14.50 Although the time limits in CPR, r 54.5 cannot be extended by agreement between the parties they can be extended by the court. Moreover, at the other end of the scale, even if the claim was issued within the relevant time limit, the court can refuse to grant the relief sought if it decides that the claim form was not filed promptly.

14.51 The issue of whether the relevant time periods have been complied with and whether the claimant is guilty of delay which is fatal to his claim is often contested by the parties and there are a number of decided cases which consider this issue.[17]

14.52 The claim form must be sent to the public body whose decision is being challenged within 7 days of being sealed by the court.[18] There may also be other persons that could be affected by the outcome of the claim for judicial review and the process provides a mechanism for naming these other persons as interested parties. For example, if a CCG decision to refuse continuing healthcare is being challenged, it may be appropriate to name the local authority as an interested party because if the NHS does not provide care, the local authority may have to. Where an interested party is named, it should also be sent a copy of the claim within 7 days.

14.53 The defendant must file a form known as an acknowledgement of service within 21 days of receiving the claim form. It must also send a copy to the claimant not later than 7 days after it is filed.[19]

---

15 These are Birmingham, Cardiff, Leeds and Manchester.

16 See CPR, r 54.5.

17 For example, the court rejected a claim because it was out of time in the case of *R (Nash) v Barnet LBC* [2013] EWCA Civ 1004.

18 See CPR, r 54.7.

19 See CPR, r 54.8.

14.54 CPR, r 54.8 also sets out a number of other requirements. The acknowledgement of service should state whether the claim is contested and, if so, must set out a summary of the grounds for contesting the claim often called 'the defendant's summary grounds'.

14.55 Although there is a section in the acknowledgement of service for setting out the defendant's summary grounds, in practice, if the defendant is legally represented, the defendant's summary grounds consist of a separate document prepared by the defendant's legal representatives which is filed with the acknowledgement of service together with any witness statements and other documents that the defendant may rely upon.

14.56 Preparing the defendant's summary grounds and any evidence in support is a crucial part of preparing the defence to the claim as the defendant will be very likely be asking the court to refuse to grant permission to proceed with the claim.

14.57 Although the time for filing the acknowledgement of service cannot be extended by agreement between the parties, judges sometimes, when granting interim relief, shorten or abridge the time for filing and serving the acknowledgement of service. Where this is done, the parties must comply with the shortened timetable.

14.58 The court's permission is required to proceed with a claim for judicial review.[20] The requirement for permission is an important part of the judicial review procedure. The test is whether the claim is properly arguable. It is effectively a screening procedure whereby the court decides whether or not the claim is strong enough to justify granting permission to proceed to a final hearing with all the preparation, costs and court time that will usually result from a final hearing.

14.59 Once the acknowledgement of service has been filed and served the court therefore decides whether or not to grant permission to proceed with the claim. This decision can be made by a judge 'on the papers', that is, solely on consideration of the documents lodged at court by all parties i e without a hearing. The claimant has the right to request that the decision is reconsidered at a hearing if permission is refused on the papers.[21] Alternatively, sometimes the court, of its own motion, orders a hearing to decide whether permission should be granted.

14.60 If permission to proceed with the claim is refused, then the claimant can ask for permission to appeal to the Court of Appeal. In practice permission to appeal is not granted very often. In addition CPR, r 52.15 which deals with

---

20 CPR, r 54.4.

21 This is subject to the new r 54.12(7); see CPR, r 54.12. The new r 54.12(7) applies where the claim form is filed on or after 1 July 2013. It provides that where the court refuses permission to proceed and records that the application is 'totally without merit' in accordance with r 23.12, the claimant may not request that decision to be reconsidered at a hearing.

judicial review appeals has been amended so that where the court refuses permission to proceed and records that the application is totally without merit an appeal to the Court of Appeal will only be available on paper and not by way of oral submission.

14.61 If permission to proceed with the claim is granted then the case has to be prepared by both parties for the final hearing which will usually be listed for a hearing before a judge in the Administrative Court although, exceptionally, the court may determine the claim without a hearing where all parties agree.[22]

14.62 The CPR sets out various procedural requirements that have to be complied with before the final hearing. In particular, the defendant has the right to file and serve further detailed grounds setting out any additional grounds they may rely upon and any further written evidence; see CPR, r 54.14. In contrast, the claimant requires the court's permission if he seeks to rely upon any grounds other than those for which he has been given permission to proceed.[23]

14.63 Certain variations on the usual procedure set out above should be noted, especially the powers of the court to order a 'rolled up' hearing and/or an expedited hearing. A 'rolled up' hearing is a hearing where the court considers at the same time (in practice in the judgment handed down after the hearing) whether to grant permission to proceed with the claim and, if so, whether to grant the relief sought by the claimant. An expedited hearing is a hearing which is given listing priority and should therefore be heard a lot quicker than a case in the general list.

APPLICATIONS FOR INTERIM RELIEF

14.64 An application for interim relief is often made when a claim for judicial review is issued. Whether or not such an application succeeds can be of crucial importance.

14.65 An application for interim relief which is often combined with an application for urgent consideration is usually considered by a judge 'on the papers'; that is, just on consideration of the documents provided by the claimant and without a court hearing although a court hearing may follow, especially if there is an application to discharge the order granting interim relief which contains a request for an oral hearing.

14.66 The judge is, therefore, when determining an application for interim relief on the papers, restricted to seeing what the claimant decides that he should see. In other words it is a form of without notice hearing[24] and it is absolutely essential that the claimant provides the judge with full and frank

---

22 See CPR, r 54.18.

23 See CPR, r 54.15.

24 That is a hearing that only one party is formally aware of.

disclosure of any relevant information even if it is information that may assist the defendant as opposed to the claimant.

WHAT JUDGES TAKE INTO ACCOUNT IN MAKING THEIR DECISION

14.67 When considering all of the complex principles of administrative law and the numerous procedural requirements that apply when a claim for judicial review is made, it is important not to lose sight of the fact that, when applying the law and the procedure, what a judge is trying to do is to make a just and fair decision.

14.68 However, no two judges will view a case in exactly the same way. Inevitably, individual judges, will apply their own notions of 'justice' and 'fairness' to the circumstances of the case. Moreover the possibility of an appeal is also important to take into account when deciding whether to issue or to defend a claim for judicial review. Thus, a party may win in the Administrative Court and then lose the appeal; a party could even win in the Administrative Court, lose in the Court of Appeal by a majority and win in the Supreme Court by a majority.

14.69 Also, after proceedings have been issued, further information can come to light or there can be further developments which affect the outcome of a claim, possibly to the point where the outcome of the claim has become irrelevant or where events have overtaken the decision originally complained of. These are also known as academic claims and are rarely entertained by the court. Judicial review litigation is therefore particularly uncertain in its outcome. An apparently strong claim can be lost and an apparently weak claim can be won when, perhaps after several years, the case is finally determined at an appeal hearing. Whilst only a very small number of cases end up in the Supreme Court, appeals to the Court of Appeal are more frequent.

14.70 It is therefore important to consider at as early a stage as possible whether a claim should be brought or defended, taking into account the potential costs, the ability to pay them, the possible wider importance of the issues involved, the uncertain outcome of litigation and the possibility of winning in the Administrative Court and then losing on appeal.

COSTS

14.71 The Court has a discretion whether to award costs and the general rule is that the losing party has to pay the costs of the winning party. Those costs can be substantial, although legally aided parties are usually personally protected from costs orders.[25] It is therefore no coincidence that the majority of

[25] There are some circumstances in which a legally aided party may have to pay costs but that is beyond the scope of this text.

claims for judicial review involve parties that are either legally aided or are companies, private individuals or large public organisations that have sufficient funds available to fund the costs of the litigation.

RELATIONSHIP BETWEEN PROCEEDINGS IN THE COURT OF PROTECTION AND JUDICIAL REVIEW

14.72 There is some debate about whether the Court of Protection can require a public body, typically a local authority, to provide a welfare service which the court considers to be in P's best interests but which the body is not willing to provide. The likely answer to this lies in an understanding of the court's fundamental role, which is to make decisions for P that he could and would make if he had the capacity to do so himself, and in identifying what the decision in issue is.

14.73 A person with the capacity to do so may decide that it is in his best interests to be provided with a particular community care service or level of service but on any view he cannot then simply require a local authority to provide it, without the authority considering whether he needs it, in balance with the needs of other members of its community. The material decision is not his decision to have the service no matter what the authority may think but his decision (assuming he has the requisite capacity) to accept or refuse what, if anything, the authority offers him. If he is dissatisfied his remedy is to complain and/or bring a claim for judicial review.

14.74 Likewise, if a person lacks the capacity to decide what he needs, the material decision to be taken on his behalf by the Court of Protection is not, in the abstract, that it is in his best interests to have a particular service but to decide if it is in his best interests to have what is on offer from the local authority.[26] If his litigation friend considers there to be scope for a challenge to the offer then he can complain or bring a claim for judicial review, whether after the Court of Protection proceedings have concluded or whilst they are still on foot. Indeed, the same judge may be able to hear both cases on the same occasion, if he is a High Court family judge who is also approved to sit in the Administrative Court.

14.75 Otherwise, for example, there would be no logical reason why the court could not require the DWP to pay P more in benefits than he is entitled to, simply because it found it was in his best interests to have more money.

14.76 The competing view is based on the concept that the local authority is required by the Mental Capacity Act 2005 ('MCA 2005') to act in a person's best interests in deciding on service provision but this is misconceived because it misses the point about what the material decision is.

---

[26] See *A Local Authority v PB and P* [2011] EWHC 502 and *Re SK* [2012] EWHC 1990.

14.77 By s 1(5) of the MCA 2005, a decision made under the Act *for or on behalf of* a person who lacks capacity must be made in his best interests. The focus therefore is on a decision he would otherwise make. It is not for P to decide what community care services a local authority should offer him and so there can be no question of a local authority having to make this decision for or on behalf of him for the purposes of the Act.[27]

14.78 This does not mean that, depending on the circumstances, the Court of Protection cannot persuade, or even cajole, a local authority to provide a form or level of service that it was not otherwise minded to provide.

[27] See *R (Chatting) v Viridian Housing* [2012] EWHC 3595, at [100], which is the clearest exposition yet of this point in a judgment.

CHAPTER 15

OTHER COURT PROCEEDINGS

15.1 The previous chapters in this section of the book focus on the remedies that are considered most important in relation to people with dementia. This chapter considers other remedies that may be relevant in certain circumstances: the protections afforded to vulnerable adults under the inherent jurisdiction, damages claims for personal injuries, professional negligence and breach of human rights together with discrimination claims and remedies arising out of contractual disputes. The important related issues of litigation capacity and funding claims are also considered. A case example is provided in the undue influence section whereby a daughter successfully applied to set aside a number of transactions her father had made before he died.

USING THE INHERENT JURISDICTION OF THE HIGH COURT

15.2 The High Court can exercise its inherent jurisdiction to protect vulnerable adults who are not considered to lack capacity within the meaning of the Mental Capacity Act 2005 ('MCA 2005') but who may nevertheless need protecting. The jurisdiction could, therefore, be of importance in relation to someone who has early or relatively mild dementia, perhaps because they are in the early stages of Alzheimer's disease, and who retains capacity in relation to some matters but may nevertheless need protecting when making decisions in relation to those matters. The jurisdiction may also be of importance to someone who has fluctuating capacity in relation to decision making in some situations and therefore needs protecting during the periods when he has capacity.

15.3 In an appropriate case this may mean that an application under the inherent jurisdiction is made in the High Court, to a High Court judge sitting in the Family Division. In some circumstances where there are concerns that a person has fluctuating capacity an application under the inherent jurisdiction may be made at the same time as an application under the MCA 2005, the application being issued in the Court of Protection with a request that it is transferred to the High Court to be heard by a judge in the Family Division of the High Court who also has Court of Protection jurisdiction so that the judge can exercise the inherent jurisdiction insofar as is necessary.

15.4 In the case of *A Local Authority and others v DL*,[1] the Court of Appeal confirmed that the High Court's inherent jurisdiction had survived the passing of the MCA 2005. The Court of Appeal made it clear that the High Court's inherent jurisdiction is available to make declarations and, if necessary, put protective measures in place in relation to vulnerable adults who do not fall within the 2005 Act but who are, or are reasonably believed to be, for some reason deprived of the capacity to make the relevant decision, or disabled from making a free choice, or incapacitated or disabled from giving or expressing a real and genuine consent by reason of such things as constraint, coercion, undue influence or other vitiating factor.

15.5 In *DL*, the facts themselves provide a good example of how the inherent jurisdiction may be used in this context. The appellant, DL, was a man in his fifties who lived with his elderly parents. The local authority had become concerned about DL's aggressive and controlling behaviour towards his parents, one of whom, the mother, still retained capacity to make decisions about her residence and welfare. The behaviour included seeking to coerce his father into transferring the ownership of the house into DL's name, placing considerable pressure on both parents to have the mother moved into a care home against her wishes, physical assaults, verbal threats, controlling the parents' movements in and out of the house and controlling who might visit them including health care and other professionals.

15.6 The judge who initially heard the case had made a wide-ranging interim injunction restraining DL's behaviour, making the injunction under the court's inherent jurisdiction in respect of his mother and under the MCA 2005 in respect of his father. This two-jurisdiction approach was approved by the Court of Appeal, which confirmed that this was the approach to be taken in the future in these types of cases.

15.7 In another case relating to the use of the inherent jurisdiction *A NHS Trust v Dr A*,[2] Baker J made clear that when using the inherent jurisdiction, the court must act in best interests of the person who is the subject matter of the case even if strictly the principles of the MCA 2005 do not apply to those cases under the inherent jurisdiction. Baker J stated that:

> 'When deciding what order to make on behalf of a person who lacks capacity, whether under the MCA or under its inherent jurisdiction, the Court must act in his best interests…'

15.8 Having referred to s 4 of the MCA 2005, Baker J went on to state in para 49 of the judgment that:

> 'Although as a matter of strict law these principles do not apply when the court is exercising its inherent jurisdiction, they are manifestly applicable in those circumstances because best interests lies at the heart of the inherent jurisdiction. As

1 [2012] EWCA Civ 253.
2 [2013] EWHC 2442 (COP).

Munby J (as he then was) observed in *Re SA (Vulnerable Adult with Capacity)* [2005] EWHC 2942 (Fam) at paragraph 96, when exercising the inherent jurisdiction, it is "elementary that the court exercises its powers by reference to the incompetent adult's best interests".'

15.9 So it can be seen that there may well be circumstances where the inherent jurisdiction may need to be invoked in relation to a person with dementia who nevertheless retains capacity in relation to at least some matters.

LITIGATION CAPACITY IN CIVIL PROCEEDINGS

15.10 Persons with dementia who lack the requisite capacity may be involved, as claimants or defendants, in a wide range of litigation relating both to events that occurred before they lost this capacity (or even developed dementia) and to those that have occurred since. In order to ensure that their interests are properly represented the courts have developed the concept of a litigation friend (formerly a next friend) who is appointed to conduct the litigation on their behalf, including by instructing solicitors.

15.11 If an adult party to civil proceedings,[3] whether as a claimant or defendant or otherwise, lacks the capacity to conduct those proceedings[4] he is known as a 'protected party' and he needs a litigation friend to conduct them on his behalf.[5] This requirement is set out in the Civil Procedure Rules ('CPR') Pt 21, together with other associated rules.

15.12 A person may not, without the permission of the court, make an application against a protected party before proceedings have started or take any steps in proceedings except issuing and serving a claim form or applying for the appointment of a litigation friend unless he already has a litigation friend.[6] If during proceedings a party loses the capacity to conduct them no party may take any further step without the permission of the court until he has one. Further, any step taken before a protected party has a litigation friend has no effect unless the court orders otherwise.

15.13 A deputy appointed by the Court of Protection with power to conduct proceedings on behalf of a protected party[7] is entitled to be his litigation friend in any proceedings to which his power extends.[8] Otherwise a person may act as one if:

- he can fairly and competently conduct proceedings on behalf of the protected party;

---

3 For this purpose, proceedings in the County Court, the High Court and the Court of Appeal Civil Division.

4 As determined in accordance with the principles set out in the MCA 2005.

5 This is also the case in the Court of Protection – see Court of Protection Rules, rr 140 to 149.

6 CPR, r 21.3.

7 See MCA 2005, s 18(1)(k).

8 CPR, r 21.4.

- he has no adverse interest;
- where the protected party is a claimant, he undertakes to pay any costs which the protected party may be ordered to pay, subject to any right he may have to be repaid from his assets.

15.14 In order to become a litigation friend without a court order a Court of Protection deputy needs to file an official copy of the order that confers his power and any other person must file a certificate of suitability stating that he satisfies the conditions set out above either, if he acts for a claimant, when the claim is made or, if he acts for a defendant, when he first takes a step in the proceedings on behalf of the protected party.[9]

15.15 The certificate of suitability[10] must contain the following:

- the litigation friend's consent to act as one;
- a statement that he knows or believes that the party lacks capacity to conduct the proceedings;
- the grounds for this belief – if it is based on medical or other expert opinion he must attach any relevant document to this effect;
- a statement that he can fairly and competently conduct the proceedings and has no adverse interest;
- an undertaking as to costs.

15.16 The court may appoint a litigation friend on the application of a person who wants to have this role or on the application of another party.[11] It can also direct that a person may not act as a litigation friend, terminate the appointment of one and appoint a substitute.[12]

15.17 Where a claim is made by or on behalf of a protected party or against one, no settlement, compromise or payment and no acceptance of payment into court is valid without the approval of the court.[13]

15.18 Where money is recovered or money paid into court accepted by or on behalf of or for the benefit of a protected party, it is to be dealt with in accordance with directions made by the court.[14] If so, a litigation friend who has incurred expenses on behalf of the protected party in the proceedings is entitled to be reimbursed out of this money to the extent it has been reasonably incurred and is reasonable in amount.[15]

---

9 CPR, r 21.5.
10 Practice Form N235.
11 CPR, r 21.6.
12 CPR, r 21.7.
13 CPR, r 21.10.
14 CPR, r 21.11.
15 CPR, r 21.12.

PROFESSIONAL NEGLIGENCE CLAIMS

15.19 A professional negligence claim is a claim against a member of a profession who is alleged to have breached their duty of care by failing to adhere to a reasonable standard, or failing to provide their services with reasonable care and skill. Claims can therefore be brought against any professional who it is alleged is responsible for a negligent act or omission; for example, doctors, solicitors, financial advisers and accountants.

15.20 A professional negligence claim should only be brought or defended after careful consideration of all of the relevant legal and factual issues. Advice from a solicitor who specialises in the relevant area of the law is essential. An expert report from a suitably qualified expert is usually also necessary especially in medical negligence claims.

15.21 Moreover, a claim against a professional person will usually be defended by specialist solicitors acting on behalf of that professional person who are in turn instructed by his insurers. So the legal costs of a defendant who is a professional person will usually be funded by his insurers.

15.22 So whilst this is important for the professional who, understandably may be very anxious about the criticism of his professional skills and will need properly funded representation, it also means that, given the risks that the losing party will have to pay the successful party's substantial legal costs, it is important that any professional negligence claim is only brought when the issues of how the claim will be funded and how any costs order will be paid in the event that the claim is unsuccessful have been fully and carefully explored preferably with the advice of reputable solicitors who specialise in the relevant area.

15.23 Professional negligence claims can arise where a person has or may have dementia. A common issue for a professional person, such as a solicitor, who is advising a client, is whether a person who has or may have dementia, has capacity to make the relevant decisions.

15.24 In the case of *Lorraine Studholm Feltham v Freer Bouskell*,[16] a professional negligence claim was brought against a firm of solicitors. The judge stated that where a solicitor is instructed to prepare and execute a new will, he has an obligation to carry out those instructions within a reasonable period of time and, moreover, he has to carry them out expeditiously where the testator is very elderly as it is foreseeable that the testator may not live very long. The solicitor had been unsure whether the client genuinely intended to change her will and had delayed obtaining a medical report on capacity to see if she raised the matter again. This judgment is important for clients who have or may have dementia; if a solicitor has concerns as to his client's mental capacity, he must either refuse to accept instructions whilst, at the same time, making the position clear to the client or promptly take steps to satisfy himself as to the

---

16 [2013] EWHC 1952 (Ch).

client's mental capacity. The judge went on to find that the solicitor had failed to obtain a medical report promptly enough.

15.25 This case is therefore an important reminder of the professional obligations of solicitors when taking instructions from a client who they consider may lack capacity due to dementia or, for some other reason. The same principles may apply to accountants and financial advisers etc. A claim for professional negligence may arise in respect of medical professionals and this will be considered below.

DAMAGES FOR BREACH OF HUMAN RIGHTS

15.26 The power to award damages for breach of a Convention right is derived from section 8 of the Human Rights Act 1998. No award of damages should be made unless, taking into account all of the circumstances of the case, including any other relief or remedy granted, the court is satisfied that the award is necessary to afford just satisfaction to the person in whose favour it is made.[17]

15.27 The courts are reluctant to find that there has been a breach of a positive obligation to provide welfare support or community care under Article 8 of the Convention. In *R (McDonald) v Kensington and Chelsea Royal London Borough Council*,[18] the claim was made that the local authority's decision to stop the provision of a night-time carer with incontinence pads being used instead amounted to a breach of Article 8. The claim failed, the court finding that the appellant's human dignity and autonomy had been respected.[19]

15.28 A relatively rare example of a case where, due to a failure to provide community care in accordance with the local authority's statutory obligations under s 21 of the National Assistance Act 1948, the court did find that there was a breach of Article 8 obligations was the decision of the Administrative Court in *R (Bernard) v The London Borough of Enfield*.[20] However, as Lord Brown said in *R (McDonald) v Kensington and Chelsea* when approving the decision in *Bernard*[21] the consequences of the local authority's breach of its statutory obligations in *Bernard* to provide the family for 20 months with accommodation to suit the claimant's disability were appalling; the wife was doubly incontinent and, because there was no wheelchair access to the lavatory, she was forced to defecate and urinate on the living-room floor and she was unable to play any part in looking after her six children.

---

17 See the decision of the Supreme Court in *Rathbone v Penine Care NHS Foundation Trust* [2012] 2 All ER 381, at [82] and *R (Anufrijeva) v Southwark London Borough Council* [2004] 2 WLR 603.

18 [2012] LGR 107.

19 See the judgment, at [19].

20 [2003] LGR 423.

21 See para [17] of the judgment.

15.29 Moreover, although an award of damages for a breach of the human rights of a person with dementia may appear logically to follow from a judicial finding that there has been a breach of that person's human rights, the court can choose not to award damages if it decides that a finding that there has been a breach of human rights is of itself sufficient justice.

15.30 Thus there is usually a reluctance by the courts in the United Kingdom to award damages following a finding that there has been a breach of a person's human rights. In the case of *Re C (A Child)*,[22] an appeal to the Court of Appeal by a mother against a refusal to award compensation even though the judge had found that her Article 8 rights had been breached concerning the rehabilitation of her child was dismissed by the Court of Appeal, Thorpe LJ stating (at [58]) that 'in the circumstances of this case it is not necessary to afford to the mother any just satisfaction other than that resulting from the declaration finding a violation of her rights'.[23]

15.31 Moreover, not only are awards of damages relatively rare, in addition, even where it is decided to award damages, awards for breaches of human rights are usually quite modest; see, for example, the decision of the Supreme Court in *R (Faulkner) v Secretary of State for Justice*.[24] However the courts are occasionally willing to award significant sums. In *R (Bernard) v London Borough of Enfield* (see **15.28**), the judge awarded £10,000 damages.

15.32 It should also be noted that claims brought under the Human Rights Act 1998 should be started within one year or such longer period as the court considers equitable having regard to all the circumstances.[25]

DISCRIMINATION

15.33 The Equality Act 2010 (hereafter 'the Act') brings all anti-discrimination legislation under one act, replacing previous legislation such as the Disability Discrimination Act 1995. The Act makes it illegal for people to be treated less favourably because of a disability.

15.34 The Act recognises that 'equality' for disabled people does not mean equality of treatment but, in order to address the absence of a level playing field, must mean striving at least towards equality of outcome. In order to achieve that aim it is insufficient that disabled people are treated the same as those who are not disabled. As Lord Brown put it in *Lewisham LBC v Malcolm*:[26]

---

22 [2007] EWCA Civ 2.

23 See also *R (Greenfield) v Secretary of State for the Home Department* [2005] 1WLR 673.

24 [2013] UKSC 23.

25 Human Rights Act 1998, s 7(5)(b).

26 [2008] UKHL 43, [2008] 1 AC 1399, [2008] 4 All ER 525, at [114].

'...where Parliament is clearly intent not merely on levelling the playing field for the disabled but in securing positive discrimination in their favour it does so by requiring reasonable adjustments to be made to cater for their special difficulties.'

15.35 The Act provides protection from discrimination, harassment and victimisation in a number of different spheres including housing, the workplace, the provision of goods and services, public services, the provision of education and clubs and other associations.

15.36 The circumstances where a person with dementia may rely upon the Act are many and varied. For example:

(a) An employee dismissed because of his forgetfulness.
(b) A person expelled from the social club she/he has enjoyed for years because of her/his confused episodes.
(c) A person unable to remember to turn off the cooker in his/her rented property and facing danger of eviction.
(d) A person denied access to a hotel or respite home.

15.37 The provisions of the Act dealing with disability are complex and often counter intuitive. The Act provides that the Equality and Human Rights Commission should provide a code of guidance. Further where a court or tribunal is dealing with any claim under the Act it must have regard to that guidance. The code of guidance that has been produced by the Equality and Human Rights Commission is written in very accessible terms and is illustrated with examples. In any case an advisor may find reference to the code very helpful, It can be accessed from the Equality and Human Rights Commission ('EHRC') website.

15.38 A detailed explanation of the Act is outside the scope of this work and what follows is a very short synopsis. That said it is considered advisable that anyone in the position of giving advice should consider the possible remedies and protections identified below.

Disability

15.39 In order for a person to qualify for protection (with some exceptions) it is necessary to establish that the person suffers from a 'disability'. The very nature of dementia means that any person suffering from the disease is likely to satisfy this requirement from the onset of any symptoms. The definition of disability of the purposes of the Act is found in subs 6(1) of the Act which states:

'A person (P) has a disability if —

(a) P has a physical or mental impairment, and
(b) the impairment has a substantial and long-term adverse effect on P's ability to carry out normal day-to-day activities.'

15.40 The expression 'substantial' has been held to mean 'more than trivial' and is accordingly a very low threshold. Other provisions make it likely that those with dementia will fall within the statutory definition. First, Sch 1, para 2(1) provides:

> '(1) The effect of an impairment is long-term if —
>
> (i) it has lasted for at least 12 months,
> (ii) it is likely to last for at least 12 months, or
> (iii) it is likely to last for the rest of the life of the person affected.'

15.41 In addition Sch 1, para 8 provides for 'Progressive Conditions'. Whilst there is no specific definition of progressive conditions it is likely that dementia would fall within such a description. Paragraph 8 provides:

> '(1) This paragraph applies to a person (P) if —
>
> (a) P has a progressive condition,
> (b) as a result of that condition P has an impairment which has (or had) an effect on P's ability to carry out normal day-to-day activities, but
> (c) the effect is not (or was not) a substantial adverse effect.
>
> (2) P is to be taken to have an impairment which has a substantial adverse effect if the condition is likely to result in P having such an impairment.
>
> (3) Regulations may make provision for a condition of a prescribed description to be treated as being, or as not being, progressive.'

Definition of discrimination

15.42 'Discrimination' within the Act includes direct discrimination, indirect discrimination and discrimination 'arising from a disability'. The three forms of discrimination are very different. Each has its own statutory definition.

15.43 Direct discrimination is essentially less favourable treatment motivated consciously or subconsciously by disability. A clear example would be where a work colleague made unpleasant jokes at the expense of a person with dementia. In the field of services a further example would be a hotel which, simply on the grounds that a potential guest revealed that they had dementia, rather than any effects it might potentially have, declined a booking. Direct discrimination is not capable of justification and in the protected spheres is always unlawful. A person who is themselves not disabled at all can complain of direct discrimination on the grounds of disability. This is referred to as 'discrimination by association'. This would cover discrimination where the victim was perceived to have a disability even if they did not. It would also cover less favourable treatment of a person associated with a disabled person. These principles were established in *EBR Attridge Law LLP v Coleman*

(No 2)[27] under the pre-existing legislation but put beyond doubt by the drafting of the Act. It is important to remember that this applies only to direct discrimination and not to duties to make adjustments.

15.44 Indirect discrimination is more complex. Essentially it is necessary to show that the potential discriminator has some policy, criterion or practice that places people with the disability at a disadvantage and in particular places that the disabled person at a disadvantage relative to a non-disabled comparator. It will not be unlawful discrimination if the potential discriminator can show that the policy criterion or practice is 'a proportionate means of achieving a legitimate aim'. An example of indirect discrimination might be a call centre operator who insisted that its staff memorise a script rather than refer to notes and who could not show why this was necessary for the proper running of the business.

15.45 Discrimination 'arising from' disability restricts less favourable treatment on the grounds of the consequences of disability. Take, for example, a supermarket which asks a carer and a person with dementia not to return to the shop after the person with dementia had wandered off and got distressed. Here the action is not taken simply because the person had dementia but because of the effects of the illness. This will be unlawful unless the shop can show that its treatment, the exclusion, was a proportionate means of achieving a legitimate aim. Unlikely in this example, but clearly a possibility in other cases.

15.46 Other prohibited conduct includes victimisation and harassment; these are treated separately from 'discrimination' within the Act. A person will victimise another where he subjects the other to a detriment because that person has done a 'protected act'. The acts that are protected are: bringing a claim under the Act, giving evidence or doing anything else in connection with the Act or making an allegation that there has been a breach of any provision of the Act. There is a requirement of good faith before an act is 'protected'. The definition of harassment is that a person harasses another if he or she engages in unwanted conduct related to a relevant protected characteristic, and the conduct has the purpose or effect of violating another person's dignity, or creating an intimidating, hostile, degrading, humiliating or offensive environment for that other person. It can be seen that there can be some overlap between direct discrimination and harassment. The advantage of the latter is that no comparative exercise is required. As a consequence it would not be open to a person who makes jokes about those with dementia to say that he would make similar jokes about people without dementia.

Reasonable adjustments and the provision of auxiliary aids

15.47 The most significant provisions in relation to achieving equality of outcome are those which require positive steps to be taken to alleviate disadvantage. The scope of the duty depends upon the field in which the

[27] [2010] IRLR 10.

disadvantage arises. Section 20 of the Act sets out the duty to make reasonable adjustments or to provide auxiliary aids and then various schedules set out how that duty is to apply in the fields of work, premises and education. It is important to note that the duty is a qualified duty; that is to say, it is a duty to take steps that are reasonable. Section 22 allows Parliament to make regulations setting out circumstances where it may or may not be reasonable to make adjustments and indeed to disapply the duties.

15.48 The code of practice produced by the EHRC in relation to employment suggests that some of the factors that ought to be taken into account in deciding whether or not a step is reasonable would include:

- whether taking any particular steps would be effective in preventing the substantial disadvantage;
- the practicability of the step;
- the financial and other costs of making the adjustment and the extent of any disruption caused;
- the extent of the employer's financial or other resources;
- the availability to the employer of financial or other assistance to help make an adjustment (such as advice through Access to Work); and
- the type and size of the employer.

15.49 An important question is the cost. Clearly the Act requires employers, hotel owners, shopkeepers etc to incur some cost in alleviating the disadvantages to the disabled. The question is what the limits might be. In *Cordell v Foreign and Commonwealth Office*,[28] Ms Cordell, who was profoundly deaf, suggested that it was reasonable to expect the Foreign and Commonwealth Office to spend about £230,000 per annum providing English-speaking lip speaker support so as to enable her to take up a post in Kazakhstan. The Employment Tribunal and the Employment Appeal Tribunal (permission to appeal was refused by the Court of Appeal) disagreed. However the Employment Appeal Tribunal clearly considered that Ms Cordell's contentions were arguable.

15.50 The decision of the Court of Appeal in *ZH v Metropolitan Police Commissioner*[29] was an example of the willingness of the courts to find that there had been discrimination in relation to a severely autistic and epileptic boy who during a visit to a local swimming pool in 2008 (ie before the Equality Act 2010 came into force), jumped into the pool and was then lifted out by lifeguards and police officers and forcibly restrained by police officers. The Court of Appeal upheld the decision of the judge in the court below. Lord Dyson MR, considering the then relevant provisions of the Disability Discrimination Act 1995 considered the scope of the duty to make reasonable adjustments stating as follows:

---

28 UKEAT/0016/11/SM.

29 [2013] EWCA Civ 69.

> '67. What is reasonable will depend on the facts of the particular case. Section 21E(2) states in terms that it is the duty of the authority to take such steps as it is reasonable in all the circumstances of the case to have to make to change the practice, policy or procedure so that (relevantly for the present case) it no longer has detrimental effect. I accept that police officers are not required to make medical diagnoses. They are not doctors. But the important feature of the present case is that, even before they restrained ZH, they knew that he was autistic and epileptic. They knew (or ought to have known) that autistic persons are vulnerable and have limited understanding. Further, I see no basis for holding that the duty to make reasonable adjustments is not a continuing duty. In my view, the judge was entitled to reach the conclusion that he did on this issue. It was a decision on the particular facts of this case. I reject the submission that his decision makes practical policing unduly difficult or impossible.'

15.51 Given the similar obligations in the Equality Act 2010 to make reasonable adjustments this case remains an important example of the need to make reasonable adjustments.

Time limits and jurisdiction

15.52 The forum for bringing a claim under the Act depends upon the sphere in which the discrimination is said to have occurred. For claims relating to work (a far wider concept than ordinary employment) then claims must be brought in the Employment Tribunal generally within 3 months of the act or end of the act complained of. An extension may be sought on 'just and equitable grounds' but that discretion is used sparingly.

15.53 The forum for claims in the sphere of education is the First-tier Tribunal (formerly the SENDIST). All other claims must be brought in the civil courts. For these claims a time limit of 6 months from the date of the act complained of applies. Once again the time limits can be extended upon just and equitable grounds.

Remedies

15.54 Where discrimination or other prohibited conduct is established then damages can be recovered. The basis of assessment is the tortious basis. Damages are available (even in the absence of a personal injury) for 'injury to feelings', ie for hurt, distress, anger etc. Aggravated damages may also be available.

15.55 In addition to pecuniary claims additional remedies include declaratory relief and a 'recommendation'. Clearly if the purpose of any claim is to improve circumstances for others then these are valuable remedies.

Public sector equality duty

15.56 Section 149 of the Act sets out important provisions in relation to the equality duty of public authorities in the exercise of their functions. Section 149 of the Act requires a public body, in the exercise of its functions, to have due regard to the need to eliminate discrimination, harassment and victimisation, to advance equality of opportunity and foster good relations between persons who share a relevant protected characteristic and persons who do not share it.[30] The relevant protected characteristics are age, disability, gender reassignment, pregnancy and maternity, race, religion or belief, sex and sexual orientation.[31]

15.57 The Act has already resulted in a number of reported cases where the courts have been asked to consider the ambit of the public sector equality duty contained in s 149 of the Act; see also the section on judicial review remedies in Chapter 14.

15.58 The level of difficulty involved in challenging the exercise of a public body's public sector equality duty under s 149 of the Act is well illustrated in the case of *R (on the application of D) v Worcester County Council*.[32] The claimant was 17 years old and had a number of needs, deriving from medical conditions, which included learning disability, attention deficit hyperactivity disorder, auditory processing difficulties and epilepsy. He challenged the local authority policy to limit funding to the cost of a care home placement. He alleged that, in adopting the policy, the local authority had (amongst other things) failed to comply with its public sector equality duty under s 149 of the Equality Act 2010.

15.59 The judge reviewed the relevant law and dismissed the claim, holding that the local authority had not failed to have a proper understanding of the potential detriment to disabled people and how the true detriment might be mitigated.

Sources of help

15.60 The EHRC has a statutory duty to promote equality and will, in appropriate cases, give advice and assistance and on occasions provide representation. Where issues of discrimination arise an advisor will find a large body of useful information on the EHRC website.

15.61 Public funding remains available for some discrimination cases.

CONTRACTUAL DISPUTES

15.62 There are a number of issues that may be of particular relevance to a person who has or may have dementia and is involved in a dispute over a contract and the main ones are set out in the following paragraphs.[33]

---

30 Section 149(1).

31 See s 149(7).

32 [2013] EWHC 2490 (Admin).

33 For detailed discussion on contract law reference should be made to specialist texts, see for example *Chitty on Contracts* 31st edn.

Contractual incapacity

15.63 A contract that would otherwise be valid may be invalidated due to the incapacity of one of the contracting parties.

15.64 Subject to the exception referred to below, the general rule is that a person who lacks capacity is bound by the contract unless he can establish, first, that his lack of capacity resulted in him not knowing what he was doing and, secondly, that the other contracting party was aware of his incapacity; see *Imperial Loan Co Ltd v Stone*.[34]

15.65 If the two matters referred to in the preceding paragraph can be established, then the contract is voidable[35] at the option of the person who lacks capacity. Moreover, in *Sutton v Sutton*,[36] it was held that a gift as well as a contract is rendered voidable rather than void[37] by mental incapacity.

15.66 Evidential issues may arise when a lack of capacity is asserted. However, the Court of Protection may, under the MCA 2005, make appropriate decisions as regards whether a person has the requisite capacity and grant other related relief in appropriate circumstances.

15.67 There is an exception to the above position. Section 7 of the MCA 2005 states as follows:

> '(1) If necessary goods or services are supplied to a person who lacks capacity to contract for the supply, he must pay a reasonable price for them.
>
> (2) "Necessary" means suitable to a person's condition in life and to his actual requirements at the time when the goods or services are supplied.'

Duress and undue influence

15.68 A contract may be avoided for a number of reasons, such as misrepresentation or fraud. However, it is of particular importance to someone who is or may be vulnerable due to dementia that a contract may be avoided where there has been duress or undue influence.

Duress

15.69 A person may be able to avoid a contract for duress if the other party has applied some form of illegitimate pressure which effects their decision to enter into the contract. There are a number of types of illegitimate pressure, including violence to the person or threats of violence, threats to destroy or

---

34 [1892] 1 QB 599.

35 Voidable means it can be declared to have no effect but remains effective until such a declaration is made.

36 [2009] EWHC 2576 (Ch).

37 If a contract is void, it is of no effect regardless of whether there has been a declaration.

damage property and economic duress, that is, threats of an economic nature. The agreement to the contract has to have been caused by the duress. If duress is established the contract is voidable.

Undue influence

15.70 A contract may be voidable for undue influence. A distinction is sometimes made between *actual undue influence*, where one party was subjected to actual pressure from the other party and *presumed undue influence*, which is where one party takes advantage of a position of trust and confidence to the clear disadvantage of the other party.

15.71 In some cases, such as where there is a parent/child, solicitor/client or trustee/beneficiary relationship, there is an irrebuttable relationship of trust and confidence and the burden of proof then shifts to the party in whom trust and confidence was reposed to establish that the contract was entered into on a full, free and informed basis; evidence of independent legal advice should be sufficient to establish this.

15.72 It is important to stress that the question of whether there has been undue influence will depend upon the circumstances of the individual case. However, subject to that qualification, an illustrative example of a case where undue influence was established is the case of *Pearce v Beverley*.[38]

A case example: Pearce v Beverley

15.73 The claim was brought by Colette Pearce, following the death of her father John Pearce. The claimant sought to challenge a number of transactions made by her father, which were said by the claimant to have been subject to the undue influence of the defendant, Elisabeth Beverley, with whom John Pearce had had a relationship. Those transactions were as follows:[39]

'1. The transfer on 19 June 2006 of 1 Rose Grove, Luddenfoot, Halifax ('1 Rose Grove') into the joint names of John Pearce and Elizabeth Beverley.

2. The sale of 1 Rose Grove on 14 September 2007 with the net sale proceeds of £117,080.33

3. The Purchase of 23 Turn Lea, Midgley, Halifax ('23 Turn Lea') on 14 September 2007 into the joint names of John Pearce and Elizabeth Beverley for £124,500. Although the net proceeds of sale of 1 Rose Grove were used to pay in part for the purchase there was in addition a loan of £47,000 from the Leeds Building Society. There was an overall surplus of £48,907.05 arising out of the transaction. This sum was paid into a joint account in the name of Elizabeth Beverley and John Pearce.

4. The sale on 31 August 2007 of 38 Mitchell Street, Sowerby Bridge ('38 Mitchell Street') for £62,000. The net proceeds of sale amounting to £61,415.17 were paid into the joint bank account.

---

38 [2013] EWHC 2627 (Ch).

39 See the judgment at [2].

5. The execution, on 20 June 2007, by John Pearce of will under which he left his whole estate to Elizabeth Beverley.
6. The payment on 29 September 2008 to Elizabeth Beverley of £24,511 being the net proceeds of sale of the Liverpool Victoria ('LV') life policy.
7. The purchase on 16 May 2008 by Elizabeth Beverley of 48 Burnley Road, Mytholmroyd ('48 Burnley Road') to Elizabeth Beverley.
8. The purchase on 24 August 2010 by Elizabeth Beverley and her husband, Gary Michael Beverley of 1 Hebble Vale Drive, Halifax for £170,000.'

15.74 The claim was contested and the judge heard from a number of witnesses. The issues the judge considered included the issue of whether John Pearce had early dementia. Although the judge was unable to make a finding of dementia he did decide that John Pearce had been infirm and vulnerable and had placed trust and confidence in Elisabeth Beverley in relation to his financial affairs.[40] The judge held that a number of transactions had been subject to the undue influence of the defendant who the judge did not consider to be a reliable witness, finding that there were inconsistencies in her evidence.[41] In finding that there had been undue influence the judge decided that each of the transactions in question called for an explanation from Elisabeth Beverley.[42] The burden of proof had shifted to her to establish that the transactions were not procured by an abuse of her position of influence but rather resulted from the free exercise of John Pearce's will as a result of full, free and informed thought and she had failed to discharge that burden of proof.[43] The judge accordingly concluded as follows:[44]

> '1. I hold that the will dated 20th June 2007 was not validly executed by John Pearce. In the absence of any other will I hold that he died intestate. It follows that his estate passes to his daughter.
>
> 2. I hold that the transfer of 1 Rose Grove into the joint names of John Pearce and Elizabeth Beverley was procured by undue influence and was liable to be set aside subject to crediting Elizabeth Beverley with the £16,116.86 in respect of her contribution in March 2006.
>
> 3. I hold that 23 Turn Lea was purchased with the net proceeds of sale of 1 Rose Grove and that the estate of John Pearce have a tracing remedy with the result that 23 Turn Lea is held on trust for the estate. As there was a mortgage of £47,000 questions of equitable accounting may arise in respect of the period since death.
>
> 4. I hold that the payments of £48,907.05, £61,415.17 and £24,511 paid into the joint account were procured by undue influence and the payments were liable to be set aside. It is common ground that the purchase price for 48 Burnley Road of £76,000 was paid out of the first two of these sums. I accordingly hold that 48

40 See the judgment at [98] and [99].
41 See the judgment at [89].
42 See the judgment at [100].
43 See the judgment at [106].
44 See the judgment at [107].

Burnley Road is held on trust for the estate. There may need to be equitable accounting in relation to any outgoings, occupational rent, moneys spent on repairs and rents received.'

15.75 It can be seen from the above extract from the judgment that the judge's conclusions demonstrate the willingness of the courts, in an appropriate case, to make wide ranging orders setting aside transactions procured by undue influence.

PERSONAL INJURY CLAIMS

15.76 A claim for damages for personal injuries is a claim for monetary compensation for the injuries sustained as a result of the negligent act or omission of another person. That person could be a car driver, another work employee, a doctor, health professional or a carer in a care home.

15.77 There is an established body of law both in relation to how liability is determined in personal injury claims and how damages are quantified and relevant specialist texts should be referred to where necessary.

15.78 There is a wide range of circumstances in which damages claims for personal injuries may arise in relation to someone with dementia. For example, dementia can result from a head injury that causes haemorrhaging in the brain. In general people who have had severe head or whiplash injuries also appear to be at increased risk of developing dementia.

15.79 Dementia can result from a reaction to medication or from a brain tumour, from vitamin deficiencies or from multiple sclerosis. People with Down's Syndrome who live into their 50s and 60s are at particular risk of developing Alzheimer's disease because of the difference in their chromosomal makeup. Whilst there is no established test for any cause of dementia including Alzheimer's disease, a medical diagnosis can usually be made by excluding other causes which may present similar symptoms. Moreover, whilst there is currently no cure for Alzheimer's disease, there are some drug treatments that may temporarily reduce the effect of some symptoms or possibly slow down their progression.

15.80 It follows from the above very brief summary of some of the causes of dementia that not only may dementia be caused by head injuries sustained as a result of an accident. There may, in addition, be a number of ways in which it could be asserted that dementia had been caused or exacerbated by the negligence of a doctor or other health professional; for example, a claim could possibly be made on the basis of allegations of wrong diagnosis, wrong prescription of drugs or allegations of medical negligence which results in Down's Syndrome.[45]

---

[45] See *Margaret Anne McLelland v Greater Glasgow Health Board* 1998 SCLR 1081 considered further at 15.89.

15.81 In all cases where the issue of whether the accident has caused dementia or may do so in the future, expert medical evidence will be necessary and each case will depend upon its own medical evidence. Medical negligence claims are considered further at **15.88–15.90**.

15.82 However, by way of general example, a claim for damages for personal injuries caused by an accident, such as road traffic accident or an accident at work, where there have been serious head injuries or serious whiplash, may include a claim for substantial damages for dementia that has been caused by the accident.

15.83 If a person has dementia and has been involved in an accident, complex issues may still arise in relation to causation.

15.84 Thus, in the Scottish case of *Taylor v Sands and Co-Operative Insurance Ltd*,[46] the claimant (called the pursuer in Scotland) was seriously injured in a road traffic accident. She sustained a severe brain injury. As a result there was said to be major impairment to her cognitive functioning. Her communication was severely impaired and she had global and profound acquired dementia and profound retro-amnesia. It was unlikely there would be any significant improvement. She was unable to return to any form of gainful employment.

15.85 Liability was admitted. But the calculation of damages was made more complicated by the fact that she had been involved in a previous accident and by other issues. The position was explained in the judgment as follows:

> '[4] The situation in this case is complicated by the fact that Clare was previously involved in a road traffic accident on 26 July 2000 in which she sustained what the pursuer avers was a moderate brain injury, causing her to suffer minor cognitive difficulties. She avers that at the time of the present action, Clare was still in the recuperative phase of her earlier injury. At the time of the earlier accident, she was setting up a recruitment consultancy business.
>
> [5] A further complicating factor is that in response to averments from the defender, the pursuer admits that in 1999 and 2000 Clare suffered from work related stress, which prevented her from working, having suffered panic attacks and agoraphobia in 1997.
>
> [6] The pursuer's position is that but for the present accident, it is likely that she would have recovered from her earlier head injury, would have been independent for all activities of daily living and enjoying a relatively normal social life. All her current disabilities are attributed to the injuries sustained.
>
> [7] The defenders aver that the earlier head injury was a severe one and that as a result of her previous physical and psychological history, her employment prospects were limited.'

---

46 [2006] CSOH 186.

15.86 As the hearing was only a hearing to determine what interim damages should be awarded, although the judge reviewed the medical and other evidence when deciding what sum to award, she did not carry out a full investigation of causation. However, it can be seen from the parts of the judgment cited above that the judgment provides a helpful example of some of the complex issues of causation that can arise when damages are claimed in a case where the claimant asserts that the accident has caused dementia.

15.87 Of course, personal injury claims may also arise when a person is injured in a care home where some or all of the residents have dementia.

Medical negligence claims

15.88 It will be apparent, even from a brief analysis of some of the other causes of dementia, that there may be circumstances in which a person with dementia may have a claim against a doctor or other health professional; such claims are called medical negligence claims or clinical negligence claims.

15.89 In the Scottish case of *Margaret Anne McLelland v Greater Glasgow Health Board*[47] liability for medical negligence was established as a result of a failure to diagnose Down's Syndrome in a foetus and damages were recoverable as a result of the consequential loss of opportunity to terminate the pregnancy. The medical evidence established that the child subsequently born, by the age of 40, would have a higher chance of pre-senile dementia than is present in the general population and damages were awarded to reflect the likely increased costs of care after the age of 40.

15.90 The case of *Spargo v North Essex District Health Authority*[48] also provides an example of medical negligence where there was misdiagnosis of organic brain damage syndrome.

FUNDING A CLAIM

15.91 If a formal legal remedy is being considered with the possibility of court proceedings being issued or defended, then the issue of costs has to be considered very carefully, especially with reference to what the costs could be, who will be likely to pay them and how they can be funded. A range of funding options may be available. Large commercial organisations and public bodies such as central government departments or local authorities and wealthy individuals should have sufficient resources to fund the costs of making or defending their position in court proceedings. Private individuals with limited financial resources will have to carefully consider the funding options before getting involved in legal proceedings.

---

47 1998 SCLR 1081.

48 37 BMLR 99.

15.92 Sometimes legal insurance to cover the obtaining of legal advice and proceedings is available to private individuals, perhaps as part of a household or other general insurance policy although such cover is likely to be subject to merits criteria and to a financial limit which, if exceeded, can result in a major personal liability for costs for the insured party which would not be covered by the insurance policy. So the terms of a policy always need to be checked carefully.

15.93 A number of other funding options may be available in certain circumstances, such as legal aid (public funding) conditional fee agreements (sometimes called 'no win no fee agreements': although a payment may be required to insure the costs to be paid if the claimant loses), or contingency fee agreements where the lawyers receive a percentage of any damages recovered.

15.94 The exceptions to the above positions are in cases where there is a small money claim which can be made or defended in the small claims court where only very limited costs should usually be incurred.

15.95 If the dispute is a complex one or one where the emotions run high, the party wishing to bring the claim may only be able to put their case effectively with the assistance of legal or other representation. Consideration may have to be given as to who will represent the person with dementia (the person who is central to the dispute).

15.96 Legal representation involves instructing a solicitor, who in turn may instruct a barrister. Some barristers can also be instructed directly. If there is an informal method of dispute resolution being used, some form of informal advocate may be appropriate and most local authorities carry lists of independent advocates who can be approached.

15.97 Increasingly because of the strictures on public funding there is a rise of litigants in person, that is claimants or defendants who feel so strongly about their case that they are prepared to go to court to present it themselves.

15.98 Litigants should always bear in mind that however strongly they may feel that they are in the right and however optimistic the advice may be that they have been given by a solicitor or barrister, the outcome of court proceedings is never certain. Quite simply, the judge may not agree with you, preferring the position of another party.

15.99 Court proceedings can result in a major liability for costs and so before deciding to issue or defend proceedings all of the above issues will need to be considered very carefully. It is always essential to be clear what the worst case scenario could be as regards liability for costs, also taking into account the risks of an appeal by the losing party.

APPENDIX 1

STATUTORY MATERIALS

MENTAL CAPACITY ACT 2005

PART 1
PERSONS WHO LACK CAPACITY

The principles

1 The principles

(1) The following principles apply for the purposes of this Act.

(2) A person must be assumed to have capacity unless it is established that he lacks capacity.

(3) A person is not to be treated as unable to make a decision unless all practicable steps to help him to do so have been taken without success.

(4) A person is not to be treated as unable to make a decision merely because he makes an unwise decision.

(5) An act done, or decision made, under this Act for or on behalf of a person who lacks capacity must be done, or made, in his best interests.

(6) Before the act is done, or the decision is made, regard must be had to whether the purpose for which it is needed can be as effectively achieved in a way that is less restrictive of the person's rights and freedom of action.

Preliminary

2 People who lack capacity

(1) For the purposes of this Act, a person lacks capacity in relation to a matter if at the material time he is unable to make a decision for himself in relation to the matter because of an impairment of, or a disturbance in the functioning of, the mind or brain.

(2) It does not matter whether the impairment or disturbance is permanent or temporary.

(3) A lack of capacity cannot be established merely by reference to –

- (a) a person's age or appearance, or
- (b) a condition of his, or an aspect of his behaviour, which might lead others to make unjustified assumptions about his capacity.

(4) In proceedings under this Act or any other enactment, any question whether a person lacks capacity within the meaning of this Act must be decided on the balance of probabilities.

(5) No power which a person ('D') may exercise under this Act –

- (a) in relation to a person who lacks capacity, or
- (b) where D reasonably thinks that a person lacks capacity,

is exercisable in relation to a person under 16.

(6) Subsection (5) is subject to section 18(3).

3 Inability to make decisions

(1) For the purposes of section 2, a person is unable to make a decision for himself if he is unable –

- (a) to understand the information relevant to the decision,
- (b) to retain that information,
- (c) to use or weigh that information as part of the process of making the decision, or
- (d) to communicate his decision (whether by talking, using sign language or any other means).

(2) A person is not to be regarded as unable to understand the information relevant to a decision if he is able to understand an explanation of it given to him in a way that is appropriate to his circumstances (using simple language, visual aids or any other means).

(3) The fact that a person is able to retain the information relevant to a decision for a short period only does not prevent him from being regarded as able to make the decision.

(4) The information relevant to a decision includes information about the reasonably foreseeable consequences of –

- (a) deciding one way or another, or
- (b) failing to make the decision.

4 Best interests

(1) In determining for the purposes of this Act what is in a person's best interests, the person making the determination must not make it merely on the basis of –

- (a) the person's age or appearance, or
- (b) a condition of his, or an aspect of his behaviour, which might lead others to make unjustified assumptions about what might be in his best interests.

(2) The person making the determination must consider all the relevant circumstances and, in particular, take the following steps.

(3) He must consider –

- (a) whether it is likely that the person will at some time have capacity in relation to the matter in question, and
- (b) if it appears likely that he will, when that is likely to be.

(4) He must, so far as reasonably practicable, permit and encourage the person to participate, or to improve his ability to participate, as fully as possible in any act done for him and any decision affecting him.

(5) Where the determination relates to life-sustaining treatment he must not, in considering whether the treatment is in the best interests of the person concerned, be motivated by a desire to bring about his death.

(6) He must consider, so far as is reasonably ascertainable –

- (a) the person's past and present wishes and feelings (and, in particular, any relevant written statement made by him when he had capacity),
- (b) the beliefs and values that would be likely to influence his decision if he had capacity, and
- (c) the other factors that he would be likely to consider if he were able to do so.

(7) He must take into account, if it is practicable and appropriate to consult them, the views of –

- (a) anyone named by the person as someone to be consulted on the matter in question or on matters of that kind,
- (b) anyone engaged in caring for the person or interested in his welfare,
- (c) any donee of a lasting power of attorney granted by the person, and
- (d) any deputy appointed for the person by the court,

as to what would be in the person's best interests and, in particular, as to the matters mentioned in subsection (6).

(8) The duties imposed by subsections (1) to (7) also apply in relation to the exercise of any powers which –

- (a) are exercisable under a lasting power of attorney, or
- (b) are exercisable by a person under this Act where he reasonably believes that another person lacks capacity.

(9) In the case of an act done, or a decision made, by a person other than the court, there is sufficient compliance with this section if (having complied with the requirements of subsections (1) to (7)) he reasonably believes that what he does or decides is in the best interests of the person concerned.

(10) 'Life-sustaining treatment' means treatment which in the view of a person providing health care for the person concerned is necessary to sustain life.

(11) 'Relevant circumstances' are those –

- (a) of which the person making the determination is aware, and
- (b) which it would be reasonable to regard as relevant.

4A Restriction on deprivation of liberty

(1) This Act does not authorise any person ('D') to deprive any other person ('P') of his liberty.

(2) But that is subject to –

- (a) the following provisions of this section, and
- (b) section 4B.

(3) D may deprive P of his liberty if, by doing so, D is giving effect to a relevant decision of the court.

(4) A relevant decision of the court is a decision made by an order under section 16(2)(a) in relation to a matter concerning P's personal welfare.

(5) D may deprive P of his liberty if the deprivation is authorised by Schedule A1 (hospital and care home residents: deprivation of liberty).

Amendment: Mental Health Act 2007.

4B Deprivation of liberty necessary for life-sustaining treatment etc

(1) If the following conditions are met, D is authorised to deprive P of his liberty while a decision as respects any relevant issue is sought from the court.

(2) The first condition is that there is a question about whether D is authorised to deprive P of his liberty under section 4A.

(3) The second condition is that the deprivation of liberty –

- (a) is wholly or partly for the purpose of –
  - (i) giving P life-sustaining treatment, or
  - (ii) doing any vital act, or
- (b) consists wholly or partly of –
  - (i) giving P life-sustaining treatment, or
  - (ii) doing any vital act.

(4) The third condition is that the deprivation of liberty is necessary in order to –

- (a) give the life-sustaining treatment, or
- (b) do the vital act.

(5) A vital act is any act which the person doing it reasonably believes to be necessary to prevent a serious deterioration in P's condition.

Amendment: Mental Health Act 2007.

5 Acts in connection with care or treatment

(1) If a person ('D') does an act in connection with the care or treatment of another person ('P'), the act is one to which this section applies if –

- (a) before doing the act, D takes reasonable steps to establish whether P lacks capacity in relation to the matter in question, and
- (b) when doing the act, D reasonably believes –
  - (i) that P lacks capacity in relation to the matter, and
  - (ii) that it will be in P's best interests for the act to be done.

(2) D does not incur any liability in relation to the act that he would not have incurred if P –

- (a) had had capacity to consent in relation to the matter, and
- (b) had consented to D's doing the act.

(3) Nothing in this section excludes a person's civil liability for loss or damage, or his criminal liability, resulting from his negligence in doing the act.

(4) Nothing in this section affects the operation of sections 24 to 26 (advance decisions to refuse treatment).

6 Section 5 acts: limitations

(1) If D does an act that is intended to restrain P, it is not an act to which section 5 applies unless two further conditions are satisfied.

(2) The first condition is that D reasonably believes that it is necessary to do the act in order to prevent harm to P.

(3) The second is that the act is a proportionate response to –

- (a) the likelihood of P's suffering harm, and

(b) the seriousness of that harm.

(4) For the purposes of this section D restrains P if he –

(a) uses, or threatens to use, force to secure the doing of an act which P resists, or
(b) restricts P's liberty of movement, whether or not P resists.

(5) (*repealed*)

(6) Section 5 does not authorise a person to do an act which conflicts with a decision made, within the scope of his authority and in accordance with this Part, by –

(a) a donee of a lasting power of attorney granted by P, or
(b) a deputy appointed for P by the court.

(7) But nothing in subsection (6) stops a person –

(a) providing life-sustaining treatment, or
(b) doing any act which he reasonably believes to be necessary to prevent a serious deterioration in P's condition,

while a decision as respects any relevant issue is sought from the court.

Amendment: Mental Health Act 2007.

7 Payment for necessary goods and services

(1) If necessary goods or services are supplied to a person who lacks capacity to contract for the supply, he must pay a reasonable price for them.

(2) 'Necessary' means suitable to a person's condition in life and to his actual requirements at the time when the goods or services are supplied.

8 Expenditure

(1) If an act to which section 5 applies involves expenditure, it is lawful for D –

(a) to pledge P's credit for the purpose of the expenditure, and
(b) to apply money in P's possession for meeting the expenditure.

(2) If the expenditure is borne for P by D, it is lawful for D –

(a) to reimburse himself out of money in P's possession, or
(b) to be otherwise indemnified by P.

(3) Subsections (1) and (2) do not affect any power under which (apart from those subsections) a person –

(a) has lawful control of P's money or other property, and
(b) has power to spend money for P's benefit.

Lasting powers of attorney

9 Lasting powers of attorney

(1) A lasting power of attorney is a power of attorney under which the donor ('P') confers on the donee (or donees) authority to make decisions about all or any of the following –

(a) P's personal welfare or specified matters concerning P's personal welfare, and
(b) P's property and affairs or specified matters concerning P's property and affairs,

and which includes authority to make such decisions in circumstances where P no longer has capacity.

(2) A lasting power of attorney is not created unless –

- (a) section 10 is complied with,
- (b) an instrument conferring authority of the kind mentioned in subsection (1) is made and registered in accordance with Schedule 1, and
- (c) at the time when P executes the instrument, P has reached 18 and has capacity to execute it.

(3) An instrument which –

- (a) purports to create a lasting power of attorney, but
- (b) does not comply with this section, section 10 or Schedule 1,

confers no authority.

(4) The authority conferred by a lasting power of attorney is subject to –

- (a) the provisions of this Act and, in particular, sections 1 (the principles) and 4 (best interests), and
- (b) any conditions or restrictions specified in the instrument.

10 Appointment of donees

(1) A donee of a lasting power of attorney must be –

- (a) an individual who has reached 18, or
- (b) if the power relates only to P's property and affairs, either such an individual or a trust corporation.

(2) An individual who is bankrupt or is a person in relation to whom a debt relief order is made may not be appointed as donee of a lasting power of attorney in relation to P's property and affairs.

(3) Subsections (4) to (7) apply in relation to an instrument under which two or more persons are to act as donees of a lasting power of attorney.

(4) The instrument may appoint them to act –

- (a) jointly,
- (b) jointly and severally, or
- (c) jointly in respect of some matters and jointly and severally in respect of others.

(5) To the extent to which it does not specify whether they are to act jointly or jointly and severally, the instrument is to be assumed to appoint them to act jointly.

(6) If they are to act jointly, a failure, as respects one of them, to comply with the requirements of subsection (1) or (2) or Part 1 or 2 of Schedule 1 prevents a lasting power of attorney from being created.

(7) If they are to act jointly and severally, a failure, as respects one of them, to comply with the requirements of subsection (1) or (2) or Part 1 or 2 of Schedule 1 –

- (a) prevents the appointment taking effect in his case, but
- (b) does not prevent a lasting power of attorney from being created in the case of the other or others.

(8) An instrument used to create a lasting power of attorney –

(a) cannot give the donee (or, if more than one, any of them) power to appoint a substitute or successor, but
(b) may itself appoint a person to replace the donee (or, if more than one, any of them) on the occurrence of an event mentioned in section 13(6)(a) to (d) which has the effect of terminating the donee's appointment.

Amendment: SI 2012/2404.

11 Lasting powers of attorney: restrictions

(1) A lasting power of attorney does not authorise the donee (or, if more than one, any of them) to do an act that is intended to restrain P, unless three conditions are satisfied.

(2) The first condition is that P lacks, or the donee reasonably believes that P lacks, capacity in relation to the matter in question.

(3) The second is that the donee reasonably believes that it is necessary to do the act in order to prevent harm to P.

(4) The third is that the act is a proportionate response to –

(a) the likelihood of P's suffering harm, and
(b) the seriousness of that harm.

(5) For the purposes of this section, the donee restrains P if he –

(a) uses, or threatens to use, force to secure the doing of an act which P resists, or
(b) restricts P's liberty of movement, whether or not P resists,

or if he authorises another person to do any of those things.

(6) (*repealed*)

(7) Where a lasting power of attorney authorises the donee (or, if more than one, any of them) to make decisions about P's personal welfare, the authority –

(a) does not extend to making such decisions in circumstances other than those where P lacks, or the donee reasonably believes that P lacks, capacity,
(b) is subject to sections 24 to 26 (advance decisions to refuse treatment), and
(c) extends to giving or refusing consent to the carrying out or continuation of a treatment by a person providing health care for P.

(8) But subsection (7)(c) –

(a) does not authorise the giving or refusing of consent to the carrying out or continuation of life-sustaining treatment, unless the instrument contains express provision to that effect, and
(b) is subject to any conditions or restrictions in the instrument.

Amendment: Mental Health Act 2007.

12 Scope of lasting powers of attorney: gifts

(1) Where a lasting power of attorney confers authority to make decisions about P's property and affairs, it does not authorise a donee (or, if more than one, any of them) to dispose of the donor's property by making gifts except to the extent permitted by subsection (2).

(2) The donee may make gifts –

(a) on customary occasions to persons (including himself) who are related to or connected with the donor, or
(b) to any charity to whom the donor made or might have been expected to make gifts,

if the value of each such gift is not unreasonable having regard to all the circumstances and, in particular, the size of the donor's estate.

(3) 'Customary occasion' means –

(a) the occasion or anniversary of a birth, a marriage or the formation of a civil partnership, or
(b) any other occasion on which presents are customarily given within families or among friends or associates.

(4) Subsection (2) is subject to any conditions or restrictions in the instrument.

13 Revocation of lasting powers of attorney etc

(1) This section applies if –

(a) P has executed an instrument with a view to creating a lasting power of attorney, or
(b) a lasting power of attorney is registered as having been conferred by P,

and in this section references to revoking the power include revoking the instrument.

(2) P may, at any time when he has capacity to do so, revoke the power.

(3) P's bankruptcy, or the making of a debt relief order (under Part 7A of the Insolvency Act 1986) in respect of P, revokes the power so far as it relates to P's property and affairs.

(4) But where P is bankrupt merely because an interim bankruptcy restrictions order has effect in respect of him or where P is subject to an interim debt relief restrictions order (under Schedule 4ZB of the Insolvency Act 1986), the power is suspended, so far as it relates to P's property and affairs, for so long as the order has effect.

(5) The occurrence in relation to a donee of an event mentioned in subsection (6) –

(a) terminates his appointment, and
(b) except in the cases given in subsection (7), revokes the power.

(6) The events are –

(a) the disclaimer of the appointment by the donee in accordance with such requirements as may be prescribed for the purposes of this section in regulations made by the Lord Chancellor,
(b) subject to subsections (8) and (9), the death or bankruptcy of the donee or the making of a debt relief order (under Part 7A of the Insolvency Act 1986) in respect of the donee or, if the donee is a trust corporation, its winding-up or dissolution,
(c) subject to subsection (11), the dissolution or annulment of a marriage or civil partnership between the donor and the donee,
(d) the lack of capacity of the donee.

(7) The cases are –

(a) the donee is replaced under the terms of the instrument,

(b) he is one of two or more persons appointed to act as donees jointly and severally in respect of any matter and, after the event, there is at least one remaining donee.

(8) The bankruptcy of a donee or the making of a debt relief order (under Part 7A of the Insolvency Act 1986) in respect of a donee does not terminate his appointment, or revoke the power, in so far as his authority relates to P's personal welfare.

(9) Where the donee is bankrupt merely because an interim bankruptcy restrictions order has effect in respect of him or where the donee is subject to an interim debt relief restrictions order (under Schedule 4ZB of the Insolvency Act 1986),, his appointment and the power are suspended, so far as they relate to P's property and affairs, for so long as the order has effect.

(10) Where the donee is one of two or more appointed to act jointly and severally under the power in respect of any matter, the reference in subsection (9) to the suspension of the power is to its suspension in so far as it relates to that donee.

(11) The dissolution or annulment of a marriage or civil partnership does not terminate the appointment of a donee, or revoke the power, if the instrument provided that it was not to do so.

Amendment: SI 2012/2404.

14 Protection of donee and others if no power created or power revoked

(1) Subsections (2) and (3) apply if –

(a) an instrument has been registered under Schedule 1 as a lasting power of attorney, but
(b) a lasting power of attorney was not created,

whether or not the registration has been cancelled at the time of the act or transaction in question.

(2) A donee who acts in purported exercise of the power does not incur any liability (to P or any other person) because of the non-existence of the power unless at the time of acting he –

(a) knows that a lasting power of attorney was not created, or
(b) is aware of circumstances which, if a lasting power of attorney had been created, would have terminated his authority to act as a donee.

(3) Any transaction between the donee and another person is, in favour of that person, as valid as if the power had been in existence, unless at the time of the transaction that person has knowledge of a matter referred to in subsection (2).

(4) If the interest of a purchaser depends on whether a transaction between the donee and the other person was valid by virtue of subsection (3), it is conclusively presumed in favour of the purchaser that the transaction was valid if –

(a) the transaction was completed within 12 months of the date on which the instrument was registered, or
(b) the other person makes a statutory declaration, before or within 3 months after the completion of the purchase, that he had no reason at the time of the transaction to doubt that the donee had authority to dispose of the property which was the subject of the transaction.

(5) In its application to a lasting power of attorney which relates to matters in addition to P's property and affairs, section 5 of the Powers of Attorney Act 1971 (protection where power is revoked) has effect as if references to revocation included the cessation of the power in relation to P's property and affairs.

(6) Where two or more donees are appointed under a lasting power of attorney, this section applies as if references to the donee were to all or any of them.

General powers of the court and appointment of deputies

15 Power to make declarations

(1) The court may make declarations as to –

- (a) whether a person has or lacks capacity to make a decision specified in the declaration;
- (b) whether a person has or lacks capacity to make decisions on such matters as are described in the declaration;
- (c) the lawfulness or otherwise of any act done, or yet to be done, in relation to that person.

(2) 'Act' includes an omission and a course of conduct.

16 Powers to make decisions and appoint deputies: general

(1) This section applies if a person ('P') lacks capacity in relation to a matter or matters concerning –

- (a) P's personal welfare, or
- (b) P's property and affairs.

(2) The court may –

- (a) by making an order, make the decision or decisions on P's behalf in relation to the matter or matters, or
- (b) appoint a person (a 'deputy') to make decisions on P's behalf in relation to the matter or matters.

(3) The powers of the court under this section are subject to the provisions of this Act and, in particular, to sections 1 (the principles) and 4 (best interests).

(4) When deciding whether it is in P's best interests to appoint a deputy, the court must have regard (in addition to the matters mentioned in section 4) to the principles that –

- (a) a decision by the court is to be preferred to the appointment of a deputy to make a decision, and
- (b) the powers conferred on a deputy should be as limited in scope and duration as is reasonably practicable in the circumstances.

(5) The court may make such further orders or give such directions, and confer on a deputy such powers or impose on him such duties, as it thinks necessary or expedient for giving effect to, or otherwise in connection with, an order or appointment made by it under subsection (2).

(6) Without prejudice to section 4, the court may make the order, give the directions or make the appointment on such terms as it considers are in P's best interests, even though no application is before the court for an order, directions or an appointment on those terms.

(7) An order of the court may be varied or discharged by a subsequent order.

(8) The court may, in particular, revoke the appointment of a deputy or vary the powers conferred on him if it is satisfied that the deputy –

(a) has behaved, or is behaving, in a way that contravenes the authority conferred on him by the court or is not in P's best interests, or

(b) proposes to behave in a way that would contravene that authority or would not be in P's best interests.

16A Section 16 powers: Mental Health Act patients etc

(1) If a person is ineligible to be deprived of liberty by this Act, the court may not include in a welfare order provision which authorises the person to be deprived of his liberty.

(2) If –

(a) a welfare order includes provision which authorises a person to be deprived of his liberty, and

(b) that person becomes ineligible to be deprived of liberty by this Act,

the provision ceases to have effect for as long as the person remains ineligible.

(3) Nothing in subsection (2) affects the power of the court under section 16(7) to vary or discharge the welfare order.

(4) For the purposes of this section –

(a) Schedule 1A applies for determining whether or not P is ineligible to be deprived of liberty by this Act;

(b) 'welfare order' means an order under section 16(2)(a).

Amendment: Mental Health Act 2007.

17 Section 16 powers: personal welfare

(1) The powers under section 16 as respects P's personal welfare extend in particular to –

(a) deciding where P is to live;

(b) deciding what contact, if any, P is to have with any specified persons;

(c) making an order prohibiting a named person from having contact with P;

(d) giving or refusing consent to the carrying out or continuation of a treatment by a person providing health care for P;

(e) giving a direction that a person responsible for P's health care allow a different person to take over that responsibility.

(2) Subsection (1) is subject to section 20 (restrictions on deputies).

18 Section 16 powers: property and affairs

(1) The powers under section 16 as respects P's property and affairs extend in particular to –

(a) the control and management of P's property;

(b) the sale, exchange, charging, gift or other disposition of P's property;

(c) the acquisition of property in P's name or on P's behalf;

(d) the carrying on, on P's behalf, of any profession, trade or business;

(e) the taking of a decision which will have the effect of dissolving a partnership of which P is a member;
(f) the carrying out of any contract entered into by P;
(g) the discharge of P's debts and of any of P's obligations, whether legally enforceable or not;
(h) the settlement of any of P's property, whether for P's benefit or for the benefit of others;
(i) the execution for P of a will;
(j) the exercise of any power (including a power to consent) vested in P whether beneficially or as trustee or otherwise;
(k) the conduct of legal proceedings in P's name or on P's behalf.

(2) No will may be made under subsection (1)(i) at a time when P has not reached 18.

(3) The powers under section 16 as respects any other matter relating to P's property and affairs may be exercised even though P has not reached 16, if the court considers it likely that P will still lack capacity to make decisions in respect of that matter when he reaches 18.

(4) Schedule 2 supplements the provisions of this section.

(5) Section 16(7) (variation and discharge of court orders) is subject to paragraph 6 of Schedule 2.

(6) Subsection (1) is subject to section 20 (restrictions on deputies).

19 Appointment of deputies

(1) A deputy appointed by the court must be –

(a) an individual who has reached 18, or
(b) as respects powers in relation to property and affairs, an individual who has reached 18 or a trust corporation.

(2) The court may appoint an individual by appointing the holder for the time being of a specified office or position.

(3) A person may not be appointed as a deputy without his consent.

(4) The court may appoint two or more deputies to act –

(a) jointly,
(b) jointly and severally, or
(c) jointly in respect of some matters and jointly and severally in respect of others.

(5) When appointing a deputy or deputies, the court may at the same time appoint one or more other persons to succeed the existing deputy or those deputies –

(a) in such circumstances, or on the happening of such events, as may be specified by the court;
(b) for such period as may be so specified.

(6) A deputy is to be treated as P's agent in relation to anything done or decided by him within the scope of his appointment and in accordance with this Part.

(7) The deputy is entitled –

(a) to be reimbursed out of P's property for his reasonable expenses in discharging his functions, and

(b) if the court so directs when appointing him, to remuneration out of P's property for discharging them.

(8) The court may confer on a deputy powers to –

(a) take possession or control of all or any specified part of P's property;
(b) exercise all or any specified powers in respect of it, including such powers of investment as the court may determine.

(9) The court may require a deputy –

(a) to give to the Public Guardian such security as the court thinks fit for the due discharge of his functions, and
(b) to submit to the Public Guardian such reports at such times or at such intervals as the court may direct.

20 Restrictions on deputies

(1) A deputy does not have power to make a decision on behalf of P in relation to a matter if he knows or has reasonable grounds for believing that P has capacity in relation to the matter.

(2) Nothing in section 16(5) or 17 permits a deputy to be given power –

(a) to prohibit a named person from having contact with P;
(b) to direct a person responsible for P's health care to allow a different person to take over that responsibility.

(3) A deputy may not be given powers with respect to –

(a) the settlement of any of P's property, whether for P's benefit or for the benefit of others,
(b) the execution for P of a will, or
(c) the exercise of any power (including a power to consent) vested in P whether beneficially or as trustee or otherwise.

(4) A deputy may not be given power to make a decision on behalf of P which is inconsistent with a decision made, within the scope of his authority and in accordance with this Act, by the donee of a lasting power of attorney granted by P (or, if there is more than one donee, by any of them).

(5) A deputy may not refuse consent to the carrying out or continuation of life-sustaining treatment in relation to P.

(6) The authority conferred on a deputy is subject to the provisions of this Act and, in particular, sections 1 (the principles) and 4 (best interests).

(7) A deputy may not do an act that is intended to restrain P unless four conditions are satisfied.

(8) The first condition is that, in doing the act, the deputy is acting within the scope of an authority expressly conferred on him by the court.

(9) The second is that P lacks, or the deputy reasonably believes that P lacks, capacity in relation to the matter in question.

(10) The third is that the deputy reasonably believes that it is necessary to do the act in order to prevent harm to P.

(11) The fourth is that the act is a proportionate response to –

(a) the likelihood of P's suffering harm, and
(b) the seriousness of that harm.

(12) For the purposes of this section, a deputy restrains P if he –

(a) uses, or threatens to use, force to secure the doing of an act which P resists, or
(b) restricts P's liberty of movement, whether or not P resists,

or if he authorises another person to do any of those things.

(13) (*repealed*)

Amendment: Mental Health Act 2007.

21 Transfer of proceedings relating to people under 18

(1) The Lord Chief Justice, with the concurrence of the Lord Chancellor, may by order make provision as to the transfer of proceedings relating to a person under 18, in such circumstances as are specified in the order –

(a) from the Court of Protection to a court having jurisdiction under the Children Act 1989, or
(b) from a court having jurisdiction under that Act to the Court of Protection.

(2) The Lord Chief Justice may nominate any of the following to exercise his functions under this section –

(a) the President of the Court of Protection;
(b) a judicial office holder (as defined in section 109(4) of the Constitutional Reform Act 2005).

Amendment: SI 2006/1016.

Powers of the court in relation to Schedule A1

Amendment: Mental Health Act 2007.

21A Powers of court in relation to Schedule A1

(1) This section applies if either of the following has been given under Schedule A1 –

(a) a standard authorisation;
(b) an urgent authorisation.

(2) Where a standard authorisation has been given, the court may determine any question relating to any of the following matters –

(a) whether the relevant person meets one or more of the qualifying requirements;
(b) the period during which the standard authorisation is to be in force;
(c) the purpose for which the standard authorisation is given;
(d) the conditions subject to which the standard authorisation is given.

(3) If the court determines any question under subsection (2), the court may make an order –

(a) varying or terminating the standard authorisation, or
(b) directing the supervisory body to vary or terminate the standard authorisation.

(4) Where an urgent authorisation has been given, the court may determine any question relating to any of the following matters –

(a) whether the urgent authorisation should have been given;
(b) the period during which the urgent authorisation is to be in force;
(c) the purpose for which the urgent authorisation is given.

(5) Where the court determines any question under subsection (4), the court may make an order –

(a) varying or terminating the urgent authorisation, or
(b) directing the managing authority of the relevant hospital or care home to vary or terminate the urgent authorisation.

(6) Where the court makes an order under subsection (3) or (5), the court may make an order about a person's liability for any act done in connection with the standard or urgent authorisation before its variation or termination.

(7) An order under subsection (6) may, in particular, exclude a person from liability.

Amendment: Mental Health Act 2007.

Powers of the court in relation to lasting powers of attorney

22 Powers of court in relation to validity of lasting powers of attorney

(1) This section and section 23 apply if –

(a) a person ('P') has executed or purported to execute an instrument with a view to creating a lasting power of attorney, or
(b) an instrument has been registered as a lasting power of attorney conferred by P.

(2) The court may determine any question relating to –

(a) whether one or more of the requirements for the creation of a lasting power of attorney have been met;
(b) whether the power has been revoked or has otherwise come to an end.

(3) Subsection (4) applies if the court is satisfied –

(a) that fraud or undue pressure was used to induce P –
  (i) to execute an instrument for the purpose of creating a lasting power of attorney, or
  (ii) to create a lasting power of attorney, or
(b) that the donee (or, if more than one, any of them) of a lasting power of attorney –
  (i) has behaved, or is behaving, in a way that contravenes his authority or is not in P's best interests, or
  (ii) proposes to behave in a way that would contravene his authority or would not be in P's best interests.

(4) The court may –

(a) direct that an instrument purporting to create the lasting power of attorney is not to be registered, or
(b) if P lacks capacity to do so, revoke the instrument or the lasting power of attorney.

(5) If there is more than one donee, the court may under subsection (4)(b) revoke the instrument or the lasting power of attorney so far as it relates to any of them.

(6) 'Donee' includes an intended donee.

23 Powers of court in relation to operation of lasting powers of attorney

(1) The court may determine any question as to the meaning or effect of a lasting power of attorney or an instrument purporting to create one.

(2) The court may –

- (a) give directions with respect to decisions –
  - (i) which the donee of a lasting power of attorney has authority to make, and
  - (ii) which P lacks capacity to make;
- (b) give any consent or authorisation to act which the donee would have to obtain from P if P had capacity to give it.

(3) The court may, if P lacks capacity to do so –

- (a) give directions to the donee with respect to the rendering by him of reports or accounts and the production of records kept by him for that purpose;
- (b) require the donee to supply information or produce documents or things in his possession as donee;
- (c) give directions with respect to the remuneration or expenses of the donee;
- (d) relieve the donee wholly or partly from any liability which he has or may have incurred on account of a breach of his duties as donee.

(4) The court may authorise the making of gifts which are not within section 12(2) (permitted gifts).

(5) Where two or more donees are appointed under a lasting power of attorney, this section applies as if references to the donee were to all or any of them.

Advance decisions to refuse treatment

24 Advance decisions to refuse treatment: general

(1) 'Advance decision' means a decision made by a person ('P'), after he has reached 18 and when he has capacity to do so, that if –

- (a) at a later time and in such circumstances as he may specify, a specified treatment is proposed to be carried out or continued by a person providing health care for him, and
- (b) at that time he lacks capacity to consent to the carrying out or continuation of the treatment,

the specified treatment is not to be carried out or continued.

(2) For the purposes of subsection (1)(a), a decision may be regarded as specifying a treatment or circumstances even though expressed in layman's terms.

(3) P may withdraw or alter an advance decision at any time when he has capacity to do so.

(4) A withdrawal (including a partial withdrawal) need not be in writing.

(5) An alteration of an advance decision need not be in writing (unless section 25(5) applies in relation to the decision resulting from the alteration).

25 Validity and applicability of advance decisions

(1) An advance decision does not affect the liability which a person may incur for carrying out or continuing a treatment in relation to P unless the decision is at the material time –

(a) valid, and
(b) applicable to the treatment.

(2) An advance decision is not valid if P –

(a) has withdrawn the decision at a time when he had capacity to do so,
(b) has, under a lasting power of attorney created after the advance decision was made, conferred authority on the donee (or, if more than one, any of them) to give or refuse consent to the treatment to which the advance decision relates, or
(c) has done anything else clearly inconsistent with the advance decision remaining his fixed decision.

(3) An advance decision is not applicable to the treatment in question if at the material time P has capacity to give or refuse consent to it.

(4) An advance decision is not applicable to the treatment in question if –

(a) that treatment is not the treatment specified in the advance decision,
(b) any circumstances specified in the advance decision are absent, or
(c) there are reasonable grounds for believing that circumstances exist which P did not anticipate at the time of the advance decision and which would have affected his decision had he anticipated them.

(5) An advance decision is not applicable to life-sustaining treatment unless –

(a) the decision is verified by a statement by P to the effect that it is to apply to that treatment even if life is at risk, and
(b) the decision and statement comply with subsection (6).

(6) A decision or statement complies with this subsection only if –

(a) it is in writing,
(b) it is signed by P or by another person in P's presence and by P's direction,
(c) the signature is made or acknowledged by P in the presence of a witness, and
(d) the witness signs it, or acknowledges his signature, in P's presence.

(7) The existence of any lasting power of attorney other than one of a description mentioned in subsection (2)(b) does not prevent the advance decision from being regarded as valid and applicable.

26 Effect of advance decisions

(1) If P has made an advance decision which is –

(a) valid, and
(b) applicable to a treatment,

the decision has effect as if he had made it, and had had capacity to make it, at the time when the question arises whether the treatment should be carried out or continued.

(2) A person does not incur liability for carrying out or continuing the treatment unless, at the time, he is satisfied that an advance decision exists which is valid and applicable to the treatment.

(3) A person does not incur liability for the consequences of withholding or withdrawing a treatment from P if, at the time, he reasonably believes that an advance decision exists which is valid and applicable to the treatment.

(4) The court may make a declaration as to whether an advance decision –

(a) exists;
(b) is valid;
(c) is applicable to a treatment.

(5) Nothing in an apparent advance decision stops a person –

(a) providing life-sustaining treatment, or
(b) doing any act he reasonably believes to be necessary to prevent a serious deterioration in P's condition,

while a decision as respects any relevant issue is sought from the court.

Excluded decisions

27 Family relationships etc

(1) Nothing in this Act permits a decision on any of the following matters to be made on behalf of a person –

(a) consenting to marriage or a civil partnership,
(b) consenting to have sexual relations,
(c) consenting to a decree of divorce being granted on the basis of two years' separation,
(d) consenting to a dissolution order being made in relation to a civil partnership on the basis of two years' separation,
(e) consenting to a child's being placed for adoption by an adoption agency,
(f) consenting to the making of an adoption order,
(g) discharging parental responsibilities in matters not relating to a child's property,
(h) giving a consent under the Human Fertilisation and Embryology Act 1990,
(i) giving a consent under the Human Fertilisation and Embryology Act 2008.

(2) 'Adoption order' means –

(a) an adoption order within the meaning of the Adoption and Children Act 2002 (including a future adoption order), and
(b) an order under section 84 of that Act (parental responsibility prior to adoption abroad).

Amendment: Human Fertilisation and Embryology Act 2008.

28 Mental Health Act matters

(1) Nothing in this Act authorises anyone –

(a) to give a patient medical treatment for mental disorder, or
(b) to consent to a patient's being given medical treatment for mental disorder,

if, at the time when it is proposed to treat the patient, his treatment is regulated by Part 4 of the Mental Health Act.

(1A) Subsection (1) does not apply in relation to any form of treatment to which section 58A of that Act (electro-convulsive therapy, etc) applies if the patient comes within subsection (7) of that section (informal patient under 18 who cannot give consent).

(1B) Section 5 does not apply to an act to which section 64B of the Mental Health Act applies (treatment of community patients not recalled to hospital).

(2) 'Medical treatment', 'mental disorder' and 'patient' have the same meaning as in that Act.

Amendments: Mental Health Act 2007; SI 2008/1900.

29 Voting rights

(1) Nothing in this Act permits a decision on voting at an election for any public office, or at a referendum, to be made on behalf of a person.

(2) 'Referendum' has the same meaning as in section 101 of the Political Parties, Elections and Referendums Act 2000.

Research

30 Research

(1) Intrusive research carried out on, or in relation to, a person who lacks capacity to consent to it is unlawful unless it is carried out –

- (a) as part of a research project which is for the time being approved by the appropriate body for the purposes of this Act in accordance with section 31, and
- (b) in accordance with sections 32 and 33.

(2) Research is intrusive if it is of a kind that would be unlawful if it was carried out –

- (a) on or in relation to a person who had capacity to consent to it, but
- (b) without his consent.

(3) A clinical trial which is subject to the provisions of clinical trials regulations is not to be treated as research for the purposes of this section.

(3A) Research is not intrusive to the extent that it consists of the use of a person's human cells to bring about the creation in vitro of an embryo or human admixed embryo, or the subsequent storage or use of an embryo or human admixed embryo so created.

(3B) Expressions used in subsection (3A) and in Schedule 3 to the Human Fertilisation and Embryology Act 1990 (consents to use or storage of gametes, embryos or human admixed embryos etc.) have the same meaning in that subsection as in that Schedule.

(4) 'Appropriate body', in relation to a research project, means the person, committee or other body specified in regulations made by the appropriate authority as the appropriate body in relation to a project of the kind in question.

(5) 'Clinical trials regulations' means –

- (a) the Medicines for Human Use (Clinical Trials) Regulations 2004 and any other regulations replacing those regulations or amending them, and
- (b) any other regulations relating to clinical trials and designated by the Secretary of State as clinical trials regulations for the purposes of this section.

(6) In this section, section 32 and section 34, 'appropriate authority' means –

(a) in relation to the carrying out of research in England, the Secretary of State, and
(b) in relation to the carrying out of research in Wales, the National Assembly for Wales.

Amendment: Human Fertilisation and Embryology Act 2008; SI 2009/2232.

31 Requirements for approval

(1) The appropriate body may not approve a research project for the purposes of this Act unless satisfied that the following requirements will be met in relation to research carried out as part of the project on, or in relation to, a person who lacks capacity to consent to taking part in the project ('P').

(2) The research must be connected with –

(a) an impairing condition affecting P, or
(b) its treatment.

(3) 'Impairing condition' means a condition which is (or may be) attributable to, or which causes or contributes to (or may cause or contribute to), the impairment of, or disturbance in the functioning of, the mind or brain.

(4) There must be reasonable grounds for believing that research of comparable effectiveness cannot be carried out if the project has to be confined to, or relate only to, persons who have capacity to consent to taking part in it.

(5) The research must –

(a) have the potential to benefit P without imposing on P a burden that is disproportionate to the potential benefit to P, or
(b) be intended to provide knowledge of the causes or treatment of, or of the care of persons affected by, the same or a similar condition.

(6) If the research falls within paragraph (b) of subsection (5) but not within paragraph (a), there must be reasonable grounds for believing –

(a) that the risk to P from taking part in the project is likely to be negligible, and
(b) that anything done to, or in relation to, P will not –
   (i) interfere with P's freedom of action or privacy in a significant way, or
   (ii) be unduly invasive or restrictive.

(7) There must be reasonable arrangements in place for ensuring that the requirements of sections 32 and 33 will be met.

32 Consulting carers etc

(1) This section applies if a person ('R') –

(a) is conducting an approved research project, and
(b) wishes to carry out research, as part of the project, on or in relation to a person ('P') who lacks capacity to consent to taking part in the project.

(2) R must take reasonable steps to identify a person who –

(a) otherwise than in a professional capacity or for remuneration, is engaged in caring for P or is interested in P's welfare, and
(b) is prepared to be consulted by R under this section.

(3) If R is unable to identify such a person he must, in accordance with guidance issued by the appropriate authority, nominate a person who –

(a) is prepared to be consulted by R under this section, but
(b) has no connection with the project.

(4) R must provide the person identified under subsection (2), or nominated under subsection (3), with information about the project and ask him –

(a) for advice as to whether P should take part in the project, and
(b) what, in his opinion, P's wishes and feelings about taking part in the project would be likely to be if P had capacity in relation to the matter.

(5) If, at any time, the person consulted advises R that in his opinion P's wishes and feelings would be likely to lead him to decline to take part in the project (or to wish to withdraw from it) if he had capacity in relation to the matter, R must ensure –

(a) if P is not already taking part in the project, that he does not take part in it;
(b) if P is taking part in the project, that he is withdrawn from it.

(6) But subsection (5)(b) does not require treatment that P has been receiving as part of the project to be discontinued if R has reasonable grounds for believing that there would be a significant risk to P's health if it were discontinued.

(7) The fact that a person is the donee of a lasting power of attorney given by P, or is P's deputy, does not prevent him from being the person consulted under this section.

(8) Subsection (9) applies if treatment is being, or is about to be, provided for P as a matter of urgency and R considers that, having regard to the nature of the research and of the particular circumstances of the case –

(a) it is also necessary to take action for the purposes of the research as a matter of urgency, but
(b) it is not reasonably practicable to consult under the previous provisions of this section.

(9) R may take the action if –

(a) he has the agreement of a registered medical practitioner who is not involved in the organisation or conduct of the research project, or
(b) where it is not reasonably practicable in the time available to obtain that agreement, he acts in accordance with a procedure approved by the appropriate body at the time when the research project was approved under section 31.

(10) But R may not continue to act in reliance on subsection (9) if he has reasonable grounds for believing that it is no longer necessary to take the action as a matter of urgency.

33 Additional safeguards

(1) This section applies in relation to a person who is taking part in an approved research project even though he lacks capacity to consent to taking part.

(2) Nothing may be done to, or in relation to, him in the course of the research –

(a) to which he appears to object (whether by showing signs of resistance or otherwise) except where what is being done is intended to protect him from harm or to reduce or prevent pain or discomfort, or

(b) which would be contrary to –
  (i) an advance decision of his which has effect, or
  (ii) any other form of statement made by him and not subsequently withdrawn,

of which R is aware.

(3) The interests of the person must be assumed to outweigh those of science and society.

(4) If he indicates (in any way) that he wishes to be withdrawn from the project he must be withdrawn without delay.

(5) P must be withdrawn from the project, without delay, if at any time the person conducting the research has reasonable grounds for believing that one or more of the requirements set out in section 31(2) to (7) is no longer met in relation to research being carried out on, or in relation to, P.

(6) But neither subsection (4) nor subsection (5) requires treatment that P has been receiving as part of the project to be discontinued if R has reasonable grounds for believing that there would be a significant risk to P's health if it were discontinued.

34 Loss of capacity during research project

(1) This section applies where a person ('P') –

(a) has consented to take part in a research project begun before the commencement of section 30, but
(b) before the conclusion of the project, loses capacity to consent to continue to take part in it.

(2) The appropriate authority may by regulations provide that, despite P's loss of capacity, research of a prescribed kind may be carried out on, or in relation to, P if –

(a) the project satisfies prescribed requirements,
(b) any information or material relating to P which is used in the research is of a prescribed description and was obtained before P's loss of capacity, and
(c) the person conducting the project takes in relation to P such steps as may be prescribed for the purpose of protecting him.

(3) The regulations may, in particular, –

(a) make provision about when, for the purposes of the regulations, a project is to be treated as having begun;
(b) include provision similar to any made by section 31, 32 or 33.

Independent mental capacity advocate service

35 Appointment of independent mental capacity advocates

(1) The responsible authority must make such arrangements as it considers reasonable to enable persons ('independent mental capacity advocates') to be available to represent and support persons to whom acts or decisions proposed under sections 37, 38 and 39 relate or persons who fall within section 39A, 39C or 39D.

(2) The appropriate authority may make regulations as to the appointment of independent mental capacity advocates.

(3) The regulations may, in particular, provide –

(a) that a person may act as an independent mental capacity advocate only in such circumstances, or only subject to such conditions, as may be prescribed;
(b) for the appointment of a person as an independent mental capacity advocate to be subject to approval in accordance with the regulations.

(4) In making arrangements under subsection (1), the responsible authority must have regard to the principle that a person to whom a proposed act or decision relates should, so far as practicable, be represented and supported by a person who is independent of any person who will be responsible for the act or decision.

(5) The arrangements may include provision for payments to be made to, or in relation to, persons carrying out functions in accordance with the arrangements.

(6) For the purpose of enabling him to carry out his functions, an independent mental capacity advocate –

(a) may interview in private the person whom he has been instructed to represent, and
(b) may, at all reasonable times, examine and take copies of –
  (i) any health record,
  (ii) any record of, or held by, a local authority and compiled in connection with a social services function, and
  (iii) any record held by a person registered under Part 2 of the Care Standards Act 2000 or Chapter 2 of Part I of the Health and Social Care Act 2008,

which the person holding the record considers may be relevant to the independent mental capacity advocate's investigation.

(6A) In subsections (1) and (4), 'the responsible authority' means –

(a) in relation to the provision of the services of independent mental capacity advocates in the area of a local authority in England, that local authority, and
(b) in relation to the provision of the services of independent mental capacity advocates in Wales, the Welsh Ministers.

(6B) In subsection (6A)(a), 'local authority' has the meaning given in section 64(1) except that it does not include the council of a county or county borough in Wales.

(7) In this section, section 36 and section 37, 'the appropriate authority' means –

(a) in relation to the provision of the services of independent mental capacity advocates in England, the Secretary of State, and
(b) in relation to the provision of the services of independent mental capacity advocates in Wales, the National Assembly for Wales.

Amendment: Mental Health Act 2007; Health and Social Care Act 2012; SI 2010/813.

36 Functions of independent mental capacity advocates

(1) The appropriate authority may make regulations as to the functions of independent mental capacity advocates.

(2) The regulations may, in particular, make provision requiring an advocate to take such steps as may be prescribed for the purpose of –

(a) providing support to the person whom he has been instructed to represent ('P') so that P may participate as fully as possible in any relevant decision;
(b) obtaining and evaluating relevant information;

(c) ascertaining what P's wishes and feelings would be likely to be, and the beliefs and values that would be likely to influence P, if he had capacity;
(d) ascertaining what alternative courses of action are available in relation to P;
(e) obtaining a further medical opinion where treatment is proposed and the advocate thinks that one should be obtained.

(3) The regulations may also make provision as to circumstances in which the advocate may challenge, or provide assistance for the purpose of challenging, any relevant decision.

37 Provision of serious medical treatment by NHS body

(1) This section applies if an NHS body –

(a) is proposing to provide, or secure the provision of, serious medical treatment for a person ('P') who lacks capacity to consent to the treatment, and
(b) is satisfied that there is no person, other than one engaged in providing care or treatment for P in a professional capacity or for remuneration, whom it would be appropriate to consult in determining what would be in P's best interests.

(2) But this section does not apply if P's treatment is regulated by Part 4 or 4A of the Mental Health Act.

(3) Before the treatment is provided, the NHS body must instruct an independent mental capacity advocate to represent P.

(4) If the treatment needs to be provided as a matter of urgency, it may be provided even though the NHS body has not been able to comply with subsection (3).

(5) The NHS body must, in providing or securing the provision of treatment for P, take into account any information given, or submissions made, by the independent mental capacity advocate.

(6) 'Serious medical treatment' means treatment which involves providing, withholding or withdrawing treatment of a kind prescribed by regulations made by the appropriate authority.

(7) 'NHS body' has such meaning as may be prescribed by regulations made for the purposes of this section by –

(a) the Secretary of State, in relation to bodies in England, or
(b) the National Assembly for Wales, in relation to bodies in Wales.

Amendment: Mental Health Act 2007.

38 Provision of accommodation by NHS body

(1) This section applies if an NHS body proposes to make arrangements –

(a) for the provision of accommodation in a hospital or care home for a person ('P') who lacks capacity to agree to the arrangements, or
(b) for a change in P's accommodation to another hospital or care home,

and is satisfied that there is no person, other than one engaged in providing care or treatment for P in a professional capacity or for remuneration, whom it would be appropriate for it to consult in determining what would be in P's best interests.

(2) But this section does not apply if P is accommodated as a result of an obligation imposed on him under the Mental Health Act.

(2A) And this section does not apply if –

(a) an independent mental capacity advocate must be appointed under section 39A or 39C (whether or not by the NHS body) to represent P, and
(b) the hospital or care home in which P is to be accommodated under the arrangements referred to in this section is the relevant hospital or care home under the authorisation referred to in that section.

(3) Before making the arrangements, the NHS body must instruct an independent mental capacity advocate to represent P unless it is satisfied that –

(a) the accommodation is likely to be provided for a continuous period which is less than the applicable period, or
(b) the arrangements need to be made as a matter of urgency.

(4) If the NHS body –

(a) did not instruct an independent mental capacity advocate to represent P before making the arrangements because it was satisfied that subsection (3)(a) or (b) applied, but
(b) subsequently has reason to believe that the accommodation is likely to be provided for a continuous period –
    (i) beginning with the day on which accommodation was first provided in accordance with the arrangements, and
    (ii) ending on or after the expiry of the applicable period,

it must instruct an independent mental capacity advocate to represent P.

(5) The NHS body must, in deciding what arrangements to make for P, take into account any information given, or submissions made, by the independent mental capacity advocate.

(6) 'Care home' has the meaning given in section 3 of the Care Standards Act 2000.

(7) 'Hospital' means –

(a) in relation to England, a hospital as defined by section 275 of the National Health Service Act 2006; and
(b) in relation to Wales, a health service hospital as defined by section 206 of the National Health Service (Wales) Act 2006 or an independent hospital as defined by section 2 of the Care Standards Act 2000.

(8) 'NHS body' has such meaning as may be prescribed by regulations made for the purposes of this section by –

(a) the Secretary of State, in relation to bodies in England, or
(b) the National Assembly for Wales, in relation to bodies in Wales.

(9) 'Applicable period' means –

(a) in relation to accommodation in a hospital, 28 days, and
(b) in relation to accommodation in a care home, 8 weeks.

(10) For the purposes of subsection (1), a person appointed under Part 10 of Schedule A1 to be P's representative is not, by virtue of that appointment, engaged in providing care or treatment for P in a professional capacity or for remuneration.

Amendments: Mental Health Act 2007; SI 2010/813.

39 Provision of accommodation by local authority

(1) This section applies if a local authority propose to make arrangements –

(a) for the provision of residential accommodation for a person ('P') who lacks capacity to agree to the arrangements, or
(b) for a change in P's residential accommodation,

and are satisfied that there is no person, other than one engaged in providing care or treatment for P in a professional capacity or for remuneration, whom it would be appropriate for them to consult in determining what would be in P's best interests.

(2) But this section applies only if the accommodation is to be provided in accordance with –

(a) section 21 or 29 of the National Assistance Act 1948, or
(b) section 117 of the Mental Health Act,

as the result of a decision taken by the local authority under section 47 of the National Health Service and Community Care Act 1990.

(3) This section does not apply if P is accommodated as a result of an obligation imposed on him under the Mental Health Act.

(3A) And this section does not apply if –

(a) an independent mental capacity advocate must be appointed under section 39A or 39C (whether or not by the local authority) to represent P, and
(b) the place in which P is to be accommodated under the arrangements referred to in this section is the relevant hospital or care home under the authorisation referred to in that section.

(4) Before making the arrangements, the local authority must instruct an independent mental capacity advocate to represent P unless they are satisfied that –

(a) the accommodation is likely to be provided for a continuous period of less than 8 weeks, or
(b) the arrangements need to be made as a matter of urgency.

(5) If the local authority –

(a) did not instruct an independent mental capacity advocate to represent P before making the arrangements because they were satisfied that subsection (4)(a) or (b) applied, but
(b) subsequently have reason to believe that the accommodation is likely to be provided for a continuous period that will end 8 weeks or more after the day on which accommodation was first provided in accordance with the arrangements,

they must instruct an independent mental capacity advocate to represent P.

(6) The local authority must, in deciding what arrangements to make for P, take into account any information given, or submissions made, by the independent mental capacity advocate.

(7) For the purposes of subsection (1), a person appointed under Part 10 of Schedule A1 to be P's representative is not, by virtue of that appointment, engaged in providing care or treatment for P in a professional capacity or for remuneration.

Amendments: Mental Health Act 2007.

39A Person becomes subject to Schedule A1

(1) This section applies if –

(a) a person ('P') becomes subject to Schedule A1, and
(b) the managing authority of the relevant hospital or care home are satisfied that there is no person, other than one engaged in providing care or treatment for P in a professional capacity or for remuneration, whom it would be appropriate to consult in determining what would be in P's best interests.

(2) The managing authority must notify the supervisory body that this section applies.

(3) The supervisory body must instruct an independent mental capacity advocate to represent P.

(4) Schedule A1 makes provision about the role of an independent mental capacity advocate appointed under this section.

(5) This section is subject to paragraph 161 of Schedule A1.

(6) For the purposes of subsection (1), a person appointed under Part 10 of Schedule A1 to be P's representative is not, by virtue of that appointment, engaged in providing care or treatment for P in a professional capacity or for remuneration.

Amendment: Mental Health Act 2007.

39B Section 39A: supplementary provision

(1) This section applies for the purposes of section 39A.

(2) P becomes subject to Schedule A1 in any of the following cases.

(3) The first case is where an urgent authorisation is given in relation to P under paragraph 76(2) of Schedule A1 (urgent authorisation given before request made for standard authorisation).

(4) The second case is where the following conditions are met.

(5) The first condition is that a request is made under Schedule A1 for a standard authorisation to be given in relation to P ('the requested authorisation').

(6) The second condition is that no urgent authorisation was given under paragraph 76(2) of Schedule A1 before that request was made.

(7) The third condition is that the requested authorisation will not be in force on or before, or immediately after, the expiry of an existing standard authorisation.

(8) The expiry of a standard authorisation is the date when the authorisation is expected to cease to be in force.

(9) The third case is where, under paragraph 69 of Schedule A1, the supervisory body select a person to carry out an assessment of whether or not the relevant person is a detained resident.

Amendment: Mental Health Act 2007.

39C Person unrepresented whilst subject to Schedule A1

(1) This section applies if –

(a) an authorisation under Schedule A1 is in force in relation to a person ('P'),

- (b) the appointment of a person as P's representative ends in accordance with regulations made under Part 10 of Schedule A1, and
- (c) the managing authority of the relevant hospital or care home are satisfied that there is no person, other than one engaged in providing care or treatment for P in a professional capacity or for remuneration, whom it would be appropriate to consult in determining what would be in P's best interests.

(2) The managing authority must notify the supervisory body that this section applies.

(3) The supervisory body must instruct an independent mental capacity advocate to represent P.

(4) Paragraph 159 of Schedule A1 makes provision about the role of an independent mental capacity advocate appointed under this section.

(5) The appointment of an independent mental capacity advocate under this section ends when a new appointment of a person as P's representative is made in accordance with Part 10 of Schedule A1.

(6) For the purposes of subsection (1), a person appointed under Part 10 of Schedule A1 to be P's representative is not, by virtue of that appointment, engaged in providing care or treatment for P in a professional capacity or for remuneration.

Amendment: Mental Health Act 2007.

39D Person subject to Schedule A1 without paid representative

(1) This section applies if –

- (a) an authorisation under Schedule A1 is in force in relation to a person ('P'),
- (b) P has a representative ('R') appointed under Part 10 of Schedule A1, and
- (c) R is not being paid under regulations under Part 10 of Schedule A1 for acting as P's representative.

(2) The supervisory body must instruct an independent mental capacity advocate to represent P in any of the following cases.

(3) The first case is where P makes a request to the supervisory body to instruct an advocate.

(4) The second case is where R makes a request to the supervisory body to instruct an advocate.

(5) The third case is where the supervisory body have reason to believe one or more of the following –

- (a) that, without the help of an advocate, P and R would be unable to exercise one or both of the relevant rights;
- (b) that P and R have each failed to exercise a relevant right when it would have been reasonable to exercise it;
- (c) that P and R are each unlikely to exercise a relevant right when it would be reasonable to exercise it.

(6) The duty in subsection (2) is subject to section 39E.

(7) If an advocate is appointed under this section, the advocate is, in particular, to take such steps as are practicable to help P and R to understand the following matters –

- (a) the effect of the authorisation;
- (b) the purpose of the authorisation;

(c) the duration of the authorisation;
(d) any conditions to which the authorisation is subject;
(e) the reasons why each assessor who carried out an assessment in connection with the request for the authorisation, or in connection with a review of the authorisation, decided that P met the qualifying requirement in question;
(f) the relevant rights;
(g) how to exercise the relevant rights.

(8) The advocate is, in particular, to take such steps as are practicable to help P or R –

(a) to exercise the right to apply to court, if it appears to the advocate that P or R wishes to exercise that right, or
(b) to exercise the right of review, if it appears to the advocate that P or R wishes to exercise that right.

(9) If the advocate helps P or R to exercise the right of review –

(a) the advocate may make submissions to the supervisory body on the question of whether a qualifying requirement is reviewable;
(b) the advocate may give information, or make submissions, to any assessor carrying out a review assessment.

(10) In this section –

'relevant rights' means –
(a) the right to apply to court, and
(b) the right of review;

'right to apply to court' means the right to make an application to the court to exercise its jurisdiction under section 21A;
'right of review' means the right under Part 8 of Schedule A1 to request a review.

Amendment: Mental Health Act 2007.

39E Limitation on duty to instruct advocate under section 39D

(1) This section applies if an advocate is already representing P in accordance with an instruction under section 39D.

(2) Section 39D(2) does not require another advocate to be instructed, unless the following conditions are met.

(3) The first condition is that the existing advocate was instructed –

(a) because of a request by R, or
(b) because the supervisory body had reason to believe one or more of the things in section 39D(5).

(4) The second condition is that the other advocate would be instructed because of a request by P.

Amendment: Mental Health Act 2007.

40 Exceptions

(1) The duty imposed by section 37(3), 38(3) or (4), 39(4) or (5), 39A(3), 39C(3) or 39D(2) does not apply where there is –

(a) a person nominated by P (in whatever manner) as a person to be consulted on matters to which that duty relates,

(b) a donee of a lasting power of attorney created by P who is authorised to make decisions in relation to those matters, or
(c) a deputy appointed by the court for P with power to make decisions in relation to those matters.

(2) A person appointed under Part 10 of Schedule A1 to be P's representative is not, by virtue of that appointment, a person nominated by P as a person to be consulted in matters to which a duty mentioned in subsection (1) relates.

Amendment: Mental Health Act 2007.

41 Power to adjust role of independent mental capacity advocate

(1) The appropriate authority may make regulations –

(a) expanding the role of independent mental capacity advocates in relation to persons who lack capacity, and
(b) adjusting the obligation to make arrangements imposed by section 35.

(2) The regulations may, in particular –

(a) prescribe circumstances (different to those set out in sections 37, 38 and 39) in which an independent mental capacity advocate must, or circumstances in which one may, be instructed by a person of a prescribed description to represent a person who lacks capacity, and
(b) include provision similar to any made by section 37, 38, 39 or 40.

(3) 'Appropriate authority' has the same meaning as in section 35.

Miscellaneous and supplementary

42 Codes of practice

(1) The Lord Chancellor must prepare and issue one or more codes of practice –

(a) for the guidance of persons assessing whether a person has capacity in relation to any matter,
(b) for the guidance of persons acting in connection with the care or treatment of another person (see section 5),
(c) for the guidance of donees of lasting powers of attorney,
(d) for the guidance of deputies appointed by the court,
(e) for the guidance of persons carrying out research in reliance on any provision made by or under this Act (and otherwise with respect to sections 30 to 34),
(f) for the guidance of independent mental capacity advocates,
(fa) for the guidance of persons exercising functions under Schedule A1,
(fb) for the guidance of representatives appointed under Part 10 of Schedule A1,
(g) with respect to the provisions of sections 24 to 26 (advance decisions and apparent advance decisions), and
(h) with respect to such other matters concerned with this Act as he thinks fit.

(2) The Lord Chancellor may from time to time revise a code.

(3) The Lord Chancellor may delegate the preparation or revision of the whole or any part of a code so far as he considers expedient.

(4) It is the duty of a person to have regard to any relevant code if he is acting in relation to a person who lacks capacity and is doing so in one or more of the following ways –

(a) as the donee of a lasting power of attorney,
(b) as a deputy appointed by the court,
(c) as a person carrying out research in reliance on any provision made by or under this Act (see sections 30 to 34),
(d) as an independent mental capacity advocate,
(da) in the exercise of functions under Schedule A1,
(db) as a representative appointed under Part 10 of Schedule A1,
(e) in a professional capacity,
(f) for remuneration.

(5) If it appears to a court or tribunal conducting any criminal or civil proceedings that –

(a) a provision of a code, or
(b) a failure to comply with a code,

is relevant to a question arising in the proceedings, the provision or failure must be taken into account in deciding the question.

(6) A code under subsection (1)(d) may contain separate guidance for deputies appointed by virtue of paragraph 1(2) of Schedule 5 (functions of deputy conferred on receiver appointed under the Mental Health Act).

(7) In this section and in section 43, 'code' means a code prepared or revised under this section.

Amendments: Mental Health Act 2007.

43 Codes of practice: procedure

(1) Before preparing or revising a code, the Lord Chancellor must consult –

(a) the National Assembly for Wales, and
(b) such other persons as he considers appropriate.

(2) The Lord Chancellor may not issue a code unless –

(a) a draft of the code has been laid by him before both Houses of Parliament, and
(b) the 40 day period has elapsed without either House resolving not to approve the draft.

(3) The Lord Chancellor must arrange for any code that he has issued to be published in such a way as he considers appropriate for bringing it to the attention of persons likely to be concerned with its provisions.

(4) '40 day period', in relation to the draft of a proposed code, means –

(a) if the draft is laid before one House on a day later than the day on which it is laid before the other House, the period of 40 days beginning with the later of the two days;
(b) in any other case, the period of 40 days beginning with the day on which it is laid before each House.

(5) In calculating the period of 40 days, no account is to be taken of any period during which Parliament is dissolved or prorogued or during which both Houses are adjourned for more than 4 days.

44 Ill-treatment or neglect

(1) Subsection (2) applies if a person ('D') –

(a) has the care of a person ('P') who lacks, or whom D reasonably believes to lack, capacity,
(b) is the donee of a lasting power of attorney, or an enduring power of attorney (within the meaning of Schedule 4), created by P, or
(c) is a deputy appointed by the court for P.

(2) D is guilty of an offence if he ill-treats or wilfully neglects P.

(3) A person guilty of an offence under this section is liable –

(a) on summary conviction, to imprisonment for a term not exceeding 12 months or a fine not exceeding the statutory maximum or both;
(b) on conviction on indictment, to imprisonment for a term not exceeding 5 years or a fine or both.

SCHEDULES

Schedule A1
Hospital and Care Home Residents: Deprivation of Liberty

Amendment: Mental Health Act 2007.

PART 1
AUTHORISATION TO DEPRIVE RESIDENTS OF LIBERTY ETC

1 Application of Part

(1) This Part applies if the following conditions are met.

(2) The first condition is that a person ('P') is detained in a hospital or care home –for the purpose of being given care or treatment –in circumstances which amount to deprivation of the person's liberty.

(3) The second condition is that a standard or urgent authorisation is in force.

(4) The third condition is that the standard or urgent authorisation relates –

(a) to P, and
(b) to the hospital or care home in which P is detained.

The managing authority of the hospital or care home may deprive P of his liberty by detaining him as mentioned in paragraph 1(2).

3 No liability for acts done for purpose of depriving P of liberty

(1) This paragraph applies to any act which a person ('D') does for the purpose of detaining P as mentioned in paragraph 1(2).

(2) D does not incur any liability in relation to the act that he would not have incurred if P –

(a) had had capacity to consent in relation to D's doing the act, and
(b) had consented to D's doing the act.

4 No protection for negligent acts etc

(1) Paragraphs 2 and 3 do not exclude a person's civil liability for loss or damage, or his criminal liability, resulting from his negligence in doing any thing.

(2) Paragraphs 2 and 3 do not authorise a person to do anything otherwise than for the purpose of the standard or urgent authorisation that is in force.

(3) In a case where a standard authorisation is in force, paragraphs 2 and 3 do not authorise a person to do anything which does not comply with the conditions (if any) included in the authorisation.

Amendment: Mental Health Act 2007.

PART 2
INTERPRETATION: MAIN TERMS

5 Introduction

This Part applies for the purposes of this Schedule.

6 Detained resident

'Detained resident' means a person detained in a hospital or care home –for the purpose of being given care or treatment –in circumstances which amount to deprivation of the person's liberty.

7 Relevant person etc

In relation to a person who is, or is to be, a detained resident –

'relevant person' means the person in question;
'relevant hospital or care home' means the hospital or care home in question;
'relevant care or treatment' means the care or treatment in question.

8 Authorisations

'Standard authorisation' means an authorisation given under Part 4.

9 'Urgent authorisation' means an authorisation given under Part 5.

10 'Authorisation under this Schedule' means either of the following –

(a) a standard authorisation;
(b) an urgent authorisation.

11 (1) The purpose of a standard authorisation is the purpose which is stated in the authorisation in accordance with paragraph 55(1)(d).

(2) The purpose of an urgent authorisation is the purpose which is stated in the authorisation in accordance with paragraph 80(d).

Amendment: Mental Health Act 2007.

PART 3
THE QUALIFYING REQUIREMENTS

12 The qualifying requirements

(1) These are the qualifying requirements referred to in this Schedule –

(a) the age requirement;
(b) the mental health requirement;
(c) the mental capacity requirement;
(d) the best interests requirement;
(e) the eligibility requirement;
(f) the no refusals requirement.

(2) Any question of whether a person who is, or is to be, a detained resident meets the qualifying requirements is to be determined in accordance with this Part.

(3) In a case where –

(a) the question of whether a person meets a particular qualifying requirement arises in relation to the giving of a standard authorisation, and
(b) any circumstances relevant to determining that question are expected to change between the time when the determination is made and the time when the authorisation is expected to come into force,

those circumstances are to be taken into account as they are expected to be at the later time.

13 The age requirement

The relevant person meets the age requirement if he has reached 18.

14 The mental health requirement

(1) The relevant person meets the mental health requirement if he is suffering from mental disorder (within the meaning of the Mental Health Act, but disregarding any exclusion for persons with learning disability).

(2) An exclusion for persons with learning disability is any provision of the Mental Health Act which provides for a person with learning disability not to be regarded as suffering from mental disorder for one or more purposes of that Act.

15 The mental capacity requirement

The relevant person meets the mental capacity requirement if he lacks capacity in relation to the question whether or not he should be accommodated in the relevant hospital or care home for the purpose of being given the relevant care or treatment.

16 The best interests requirement

(1) The relevant person meets the best interests requirement if all of the following conditions are met.

(2) The first condition is that the relevant person is, or is to be, a detained resident.

(3) The second condition is that it is in the best interests of the relevant person for him to be a detained resident.

(4) The third condition is that, in order to prevent harm to the relevant person, it is necessary for him to be a detained resident.

(5) The fourth condition is that it is a proportionate response to –

(a) the likelihood of the relevant person suffering harm, and
(b) the seriousness of that harm,

for him to be a detained resident.

17 The eligibility requirement

(1) The relevant person meets the eligibility requirement unless he is ineligible to be deprived of liberty by this Act.

(2) Schedule 1A applies for the purpose of determining whether or not P is ineligible to be deprived of liberty by this Act.

18 The no refusals requirement

The relevant person meets the no refusals requirement unless there is a refusal within the meaning of paragraph 19 or 20.

19 (1) There is a refusal if these conditions are met –

(a) the relevant person has made an advance decision;
(b) the advance decision is valid;
(c) the advance decision is applicable to some or all of the relevant treatment.

(2) Expressions used in this paragraph and any of sections 24, 25 or 26 have the same meaning in this paragraph as in that section.

20 (1) There is a refusal if it would be in conflict with a valid decision of a donee or deputy for the relevant person to be accommodated in the relevant hospital or care home for the purpose of receiving some or all of the relevant care or treatment –

(a) in circumstances which amount to deprivation of the person's liberty, or
(b) at all.

(2) A donee is a donee of a lasting power of attorney granted by the relevant person.

(3) A decision of a donee or deputy is valid if it is made –

(a) within the scope of his authority as donee or deputy, and
(b) in accordance with Part 1 of this Act.

Amendment: Mental Health Act 2007.

PART 4
STANDARD AUTHORISATIONS

21 Supervisory body to give authorisation

Only the supervisory body may give a standard authorisation.

22 The supervisory body may not give a standard authorisation unless –

(a) the managing authority of the relevant hospital or care home have requested it, or

(b) paragraph 71 applies (right of third party to require consideration of whether authorisation needed).

23 The managing authority may not make a request for a standard authorisation unless –

(a) they are required to do so by paragraph 24 (as read with paragraphs 27 to 29),
(b) they are required to do so by paragraph 25 (as read with paragraph 28), or
(c) they are permitted to do so by paragraph 30.

24 Duty to request authorisation: basic cases

(1) The managing authority must request a standard authorisation in any of the following cases.

(2) The first case is where it appears to the managing authority that the relevant person –

(a) is not yet accommodated in the relevant hospital or care home,
(b) is likely –at some time within the next 28 days –to be a detained resident in the relevant hospital or care home, and
(c) is likely –
  (i) at that time, or
  (ii) at some later time within the next 28 days,
  to meet all of the qualifying requirements.

(3) The second case is where it appears to the managing authority that the relevant person –

(a) is already accommodated in the relevant hospital or care home,
(b) is likely –at some time within the next 28 days –to be a detained resident in the relevant hospital or care home, and
(c) is likely –
  (i) at that time, or
  (ii) at some later time within the next 28 days,
  to meet all of the qualifying requirements.

(4) The third case is where it appears to the managing authority that the relevant person –

(a) is a detained resident in the relevant hospital or care home, and
(b) meets all of the qualifying requirements, or is likely to do so at some time within the next 28 days.

(5) This paragraph is subject to paragraphs 27 to 29.

25 Duty to request authorisation: change in place of detention

(1) The relevant managing authority must request a standard authorisation if it appears to them that these conditions are met.

(2) The first condition is that a standard authorisation –

(a) has been given, and
(b) has not ceased to be in force.

(3) The second condition is that there is, or is to be, a change in the place of detention.

(4) This paragraph is subject to paragraph 28.

26 (1) This paragraph applies for the purposes of paragraph 25.

(2) There is a change in the place of detention if the relevant person –

(a) ceases to be a detained resident in the stated hospital or care home, and
(b) becomes a detained resident in a different hospital or care home ('the new hospital or care home').

(3) The stated hospital or care home is the hospital or care home to which the standard authorisation relates.

(4) The relevant managing authority are the managing authority of the new hospital or care home.

27 Other authority for detention: request for authorisation

(1) This paragraph applies if, by virtue of section 4A(3), a decision of the court authorises the relevant person to be a detained resident.

(2) Paragraph 24 does not require a request for a standard authorisation to be made in relation to that detention unless these conditions are met.

(3) The first condition is that the standard authorisation would be in force at a time immediately after the expiry of the other authority.

(4) The second condition is that the standard authorisation would not be in force at any time on or before the expiry of the other authority.

(5) The third condition is that it would, in the managing authority's view, be unreasonable to delay making the request until a time nearer the expiry of the other authority.

(6) In this paragraph –

(a) the other authority is –
    (i) the decision mentioned in sub-paragraph (1), or
    (ii) any further decision of the court which, by virtue of section 4A(3), authorises, or is expected to authorise, the relevant person to be a detained resident;
(b) the expiry of the other authority is the time when the other authority is expected to cease to authorise the relevant person to be a detained resident.

28 Request refused: no further request unless change of circumstances

(1) This paragraph applies if –

(a) a managing authority request a standard authorisation under paragraph 24 or 25, and
(b) the supervisory body are prohibited by paragraph 50(2) from giving the authorisation.

(2) Paragraph 24 or 25 does not require that managing authority to make a new request for a standard authorisation unless it appears to the managing authority that –

(a) there has been a change in the relevant person's case, and
(b) because of that change, the supervisory body are likely to give a standard authorisation if requested.

29 Authorisation given: request for further authorisation

(1) This paragraph applies if a standard authorisation –

(a) has been given in relation to the detention of the relevant person, and
(b) that authorisation ('the existing authorisation') has not ceased to be in force.

(2) Paragraph 24 does not require a new request for a standard authorisation ('the new authorisation') to be made unless these conditions are met.

(3) The first condition is that the new authorisation would be in force at a time immediately after the expiry of the existing authorisation.

(4) The second condition is that the new authorisation would not be in force at any time on or before the expiry of the existing authorisation.

(5) The third condition is that it would, in the managing authority's view, be unreasonable to delay making the request until a time nearer the expiry of the existing authorisation.

(6) The expiry of the existing authorisation is the time when it is expected to cease to be in force.

30 Power to request authorisation

(1) This paragraph applies if –

(a) a standard authorisation has been given in relation to the detention of the relevant person,
(b) that authorisation ('the existing authorisation') has not ceased to be in force,
(c) the requirement under paragraph 24 to make a request for a new standard authorisation does not apply, because of paragraph 29, and
(d) a review of the existing authorisation has been requested, or is being carried out, in accordance with Part 8.

(2) The managing authority may request a new standard authorisation which would be in force on or before the expiry of the existing authorisation; but only if it would also be in force immediately after that expiry.

(3) The expiry of the existing authorisation is the time when it is expected to cease to be in force.

(4) Further provision relating to cases where a request is made under this paragraph can be found in –

(a) paragraph 62 (effect of decision about request), and
(b) paragraph 124 (effect of request on Part 8 review).

31 Information included in request

A request for a standard authorisation must include the information (if any) required by regulations.

32 Records of requests

(1) The managing authority of a hospital or care home must keep a written record of –

(a) each request that they make for a standard authorisation, and
(b) the reasons for making each request.

(2) A supervisory body must keep a written record of each request for a standard authorisation that is made to them.

33 Relevant person must be assessed

(1) This paragraph applies if the supervisory body are requested to give a standard authorisation.

(2) The supervisory body must secure that all of these assessments are carried out in relation to the relevant person –

(a) an age assessment;
(b) a mental health assessment;
(c) a mental capacity assessment;
(d) a best interests assessment;
(e) an eligibility assessment;
(f) a no refusals assessment.

(3) The person who carries out any such assessment is referred to as the assessor.

(4) Regulations may be made about the period (or periods) within which assessors must carry out assessments.

(5) This paragraph is subject to paragraphs 49 and 133.

34 Age assessment

An age assessment is an assessment of whether the relevant person meets the age requirement.

35 Mental health assessment

A mental health assessment is an assessment of whether the relevant person meets the mental health requirement.

36 When carrying out a mental health assessment, the assessor must also –

(a) consider how (if at all) the relevant person's mental health is likely to be affected by his being a detained resident, and
(b) notify the best interests assessor of his conclusions.

37 Mental capacity assessment

A mental capacity assessment is an assessment of whether the relevant person meets the mental capacity requirement.

38 Best interests assessment

A best interests assessment is an assessment of whether the relevant person meets the best interests requirement.

39 (1) In carrying out a best interests assessment, the assessor must comply with the duties in sub-paragraphs (2) and (3).

(2) The assessor must consult the managing authority of the relevant hospital or care home.

(3) The assessor must have regard to all of the following –

(a) the conclusions which the mental health assessor has notified to the best interests assessor in accordance with paragraph 36(b);
(b) any relevant needs assessment;
(c) any relevant care plan.

(4) A relevant needs assessment is an assessment of the relevant person's needs which –

(a) was carried out in connection with the relevant person being accommodated in the relevant hospital or care home, and
(b) was carried out by or on behalf of –
 (i) the managing authority of the relevant hospital or care home, or
 (ii) the supervisory body.

(5) A relevant care plan is a care plan which –

(a) sets out how the relevant person's needs are to be met whilst he is accommodated in the relevant hospital or care home, and
(b) was drawn up by or on behalf of –
 (i) the managing authority of the relevant hospital or care home, or
 (ii) the supervisory body.

(6) The managing authority must give the assessor a copy of –

(a) any relevant needs assessment carried out by them or on their behalf, or
(b) any relevant care plan drawn up by them or on their behalf.

(7) The supervisory body must give the assessor a copy of –

(a) any relevant needs assessment carried out by them or on their behalf, or
(b) any relevant care plan drawn up by them or on their behalf.

(8) The duties in sub-paragraphs (2) and (3) do not affect any other duty to consult or to take the views of others into account.

40 (1) This paragraph applies whatever conclusion the best interests assessment comes to.

(2) The assessor must state in the best interests assessment the name and address of every interested person whom he has consulted in carrying out the assessment.

41 Paragraphs 42 and 43 apply if the best interests assessment comes to the conclusion that the relevant person meets the best interests requirement.

42 (1) The assessor must state in the assessment the maximum authorisation period.

(2) The maximum authorisation period is the shorter of these periods –

(a) the period which, in the assessor's opinion, would be the appropriate maximum period for the relevant person to be a detained resident under the standard authorisation that has been requested;
(b) 1 year, or such shorter period as may be prescribed in regulations.

(3) Regulations under sub-paragraph (2)(b) –

(a) need not provide for a shorter period to apply in relation to all standard authorisations;
(b) may provide for different periods to apply in relation to different kinds of standard authorisations.

(4) Before making regulations under sub-paragraph (2)(b) the Secretary of State must consult all of the following –

(a) each body required by regulations under paragraph 162 to monitor and report on the operation of this Schedule in relation to England;
(b) such other persons as the Secretary of State considers it appropriate to consult.

(5) Before making regulations under sub-paragraph (2)(b) the National Assembly for Wales must consult all of the following –

(a) each person or body directed under paragraph 163(2) to carry out any function of the Assembly of monitoring and reporting on the operation of this Schedule in relation to Wales;
(b) such other persons as the Assembly considers it appropriate to consult.

43 The assessor may include in the assessment recommendations about conditions to which the standard authorisation is, or is not, to be subject in accordance with paragraph 53.

44 (1) This paragraph applies if the best interests assessment comes to the conclusion that the relevant person does not meet the best interests requirement.

(2) If, on the basis of the information taken into account in carrying out the assessment, it appears to the assessor that there is an unauthorised deprivation of liberty, he must include a statement to that effect in the assessment.

(3) There is an unauthorised deprivation of liberty if the managing authority of the relevant hospital or care home are already depriving the relevant person of his liberty without authority of the kind mentioned in section 4A.

45 The duties with which the best interests assessor must comply are subject to the provision included in appointment regulations under Part 10 (in particular, provision made under paragraph 146).

46 Eligibility assessment

An eligibility assessment is an assessment of whether the relevant person meets the eligibility requirement.

47 (1) Regulations may –

(a) require an eligibility assessor to request a best interests assessor to provide relevant eligibility information, and
(b) require the best interests assessor, if such a request is made, to provide such relevant eligibility information as he may have.

(2) In this paragraph –

'best interests assessor' means any person who is carrying out, or has carried out, a best interests assessment in relation to the relevant person;
'eligibility assessor' means a person carrying out an eligibility assessment in relation to the relevant person;
'relevant eligibility information' is information relevant to assessing whether or not the relevant person is ineligible by virtue of paragraph 5 of Schedule 1A.

48 No refusals assessment

A no refusals assessment is an assessment of whether the relevant person meets the no refusals requirement.

49 Equivalent assessment already carried out

(1) The supervisory body are not required by paragraph 33 to secure that a particular kind of assessment ('the required assessment') is carried out in relation to the relevant person if the following conditions are met.

(2) The first condition is that the supervisory body have a written copy of an assessment of the relevant person ('the existing assessment') that has already been carried out.

(3) The second condition is that the existing assessment complies with all requirements under this Schedule with which the required assessment would have to comply (if it were carried out).

(4) The third condition is that the existing assessment was carried out within the previous 12 months; but this condition need not be met if the required assessment is an age assessment.

(5) The fourth condition is that the supervisory body are satisfied that there is no reason why the existing assessment may no longer be accurate.

(6) If the required assessment is a best interests assessment, in satisfying themselves as mentioned in sub-paragraph (5), the supervisory body must take into account any information given, or submissions made, by –

- (a) the relevant person's representative,
- (b) any section 39C IMCA, or
- (c) any section 39D IMCA.

(7) It does not matter whether the existing assessment was carried out in connection with a request for a standard authorisation or for some other purpose.

(8) If, because of this paragraph, the supervisory body are not required by paragraph 33 to secure that the required assessment is carried out, the existing assessment is to be treated for the purposes of this Schedule –

- (a) as an assessment of the same kind as the required assessment, and
- (b) as having been carried out under paragraph 33 in connection with the request for the standard authorisation.

50 Duty to give authorisation

(1) The supervisory body must give a standard authorisation if –

- (a) all assessments are positive, and
- (b) the supervisory body have written copies of all those assessments.

(2) The supervisory body must not give a standard authorisation except in accordance with sub-paragraph (1).

(3) All assessments are positive if each assessment carried out under paragraph 33 has come to the conclusion that the relevant person meets the qualifying requirement to which the assessment relates.

51 Terms of authorisation

(1) If the supervisory body are required to give a standard authorisation, they must decide the period during which the authorisation is to be in force.

(2) That period must not exceed the maximum authorisation period stated in the best interests assessment.

52 A standard authorisation may provide for the authorisation to come into force at a time after it is given.

53 (1) A standard authorisation may be given subject to conditions.

(2) Before deciding whether to give the authorisation subject to conditions, the supervisory body must have regard to any recommendations in the best interests assessment about such conditions.

(3) The managing authority of the relevant hospital or care home must ensure that any conditions are complied with.

54 Form of authorisation

A standard authorisation must be in writing.

55 (1) A standard authorisation must state the following things –

- (a) the name of the relevant person;
- (b) the name of the relevant hospital or care home;
- (c) the period during which the authorisation is to be in force;
- (d) the purpose for which the authorisation is given;
- (e) any conditions subject to which the authorisation is given;
- (f) the reason why each qualifying requirement is met.

(2) The statement of the reason why the eligibility requirement is met must be framed by reference to the cases in the table in paragraph 2 of Schedule 1A.

56 (1) If the name of the relevant hospital or care home changes, the standard authorisation is to be read as if it stated the current name of the hospital or care home.

(2) But sub-paragraph (1) is subject to any provision relating to the change of name which is made in any enactment or in any instrument made under an enactment.

57 Duty to give information about decision

(1) This paragraph applies if –

- (a) a request is made for a standard authorisation, and
- (b) the supervisory body are required by paragraph 50(1) to give the standard authorisation.

(2) The supervisory body must give a copy of the authorisation to each of the following –

- (a) the relevant person's representative;
- (b) the managing authority of the relevant hospital or care home;
- (c) the relevant person;
- (d) any section 39A IMCA;

(e) every interested person consulted by the best interests assessor.

(3) The supervisory body must comply with this paragraph as soon as practicable after they give the standard authorisation.

58 (1) This paragraph applies if –

(a) a request is made for a standard authorisation, and
(b) the supervisory body are prohibited by paragraph 50(2) from giving the standard authorisation.

(2) The supervisory body must give notice, stating that they are prohibited from giving the authorisation, to each of the following –

(a) the managing authority of the relevant hospital or care home;
(b) the relevant person;
(c) any section 39A IMCA;
(d) every interested person consulted by the best interests assessor.

(3) The supervisory body must comply with this paragraph as soon as practicable after it becomes apparent to them that they are prohibited from giving the authorisation.

59 Duty to give information about effect of authorisation

(1) This paragraph applies if a standard authorisation is given.

(2) The managing authority of the relevant hospital or care home must take such steps as are practicable to ensure that the relevant person understands all of the following –

(a) the effect of the authorisation;
(b) the right to make an application to the court to exercise its jurisdiction under section 21A;
(c) the right under Part 8 to request a review;
(d) the right to have a section 39D IMCA appointed;
(e) how to have a section 39D IMCA appointed.

(3) Those steps must be taken as soon as is practicable after the authorisation is given.

(4) Those steps must include the giving of appropriate information both orally and in writing.

(5) Any written information given to the relevant person must also be given by the managing authority to the relevant person's representative.

(6) They must give the information to the representative as soon as is practicable after it is given to the relevant person.

(7) Sub-paragraph (8) applies if the managing authority is notified that a section 39D IMCA has been appointed.

(8) As soon as is practicable after being notified, the managing authority must give the section 39D IMCA a copy of the written information given in accordance with sub-paragraph (4).

60 Records of authorisations

A supervisory body must keep a written record of all of the following information –

(a) the standard authorisations that they have given;

(b) the requests for standard authorisations in response to which they have not given an authorisation;
(c) in relation to each standard authorisation given: the matters stated in the authorisation in accordance with paragraph 55.

61 Variation of an authorisation

(1) A standard authorisation may not be varied except in accordance with Part 7 or 8.

(2) This paragraph does not affect the powers of the Court of Protection or of any other court.

62 Effect of decision about request made under paragraph 25 or 30

(1) This paragraph applies where the managing authority request a new standard authorisation under either of the following –

(a) paragraph 25 (change in place of detention);
(b) paragraph 30 (existing authorisation subject to review).

(2) If the supervisory body are required by paragraph 50(1) to give the new authorisation, the existing authorisation terminates at the time when the new authorisation comes into force.

(3) If the supervisory body are prohibited by paragraph 50(2) from giving the new authorisation, there is no effect on the existing authorisation's continuation in force.

63 When an authorisation is in force

(1) A standard authorisation comes into force when it is given.

(2) But if the authorisation provides for it to come into force at a later time, it comes into force at that time.

64 (1) A standard authorisation ceases to be in force at the end of the period stated in the authorisation in accordance with paragraph 55(1)(c).

(2) But if the authorisation terminates before then in accordance with paragraph 62(2) or any other provision of this Schedule, it ceases to be in force when the termination takes effect.

(3) This paragraph does not affect the powers of the Court of Protection or of any other court.

65 (1) This paragraph applies if a standard authorisation ceases to be in force.

(2) The supervisory body must give notice that the authorisation has ceased to be in force.

(3) The supervisory body must give that notice to all of the following –

(a) the managing authority of the relevant hospital or care home;
(b) the relevant person;
(c) the relevant person's representative;
(d) every interested person consulted by the best interests assessor.

(4) The supervisory body must give that notice as soon as practicable after the authorisation ceases to be in force.

66 When a request for a standard authorisation is 'disposed of'

A request for a standard authorisation is to be regarded for the purposes of this Schedule as disposed of if the supervisory body have given –

(a) a copy of the authorisation in accordance with paragraph 57, or
(b) notice in accordance with paragraph 58.

67 Right of third party to require consideration of whether authorisation needed

For the purposes of paragraphs 68 to 73 there is an unauthorised deprivation of liberty if –

(a) a person is already a detained resident in a hospital or care home, and
(b) the detention of the person is not authorised as mentioned in section 4A.

68 (1) If the following conditions are met, an eligible person may request the supervisory body to decide whether or not there is an unauthorised deprivation of liberty.

(2) The first condition is that the eligible person has notified the managing authority of the relevant hospital or care home that it appears to the eligible person that there is an unauthorised deprivation of liberty.

(3) The second condition is that the eligible person has asked the managing authority to request a standard authorisation in relation to the detention of the relevant person.

(4) The third condition is that the managing authority has not requested a standard authorisation within a reasonable period after the eligible person asks it to do so.

(5) In this paragraph 'eligible person' means any person other than the managing authority of the relevant hospital or care home.

69 (1) This paragraph applies if an eligible person requests the supervisory body to decide whether or not there is an unauthorised deprivation of liberty.

(2) The supervisory body must select and appoint a person to carry out an assessment of whether or not the relevant person is a detained resident.

(3) But the supervisory body need not select and appoint a person to carry out such an assessment in either of these cases.

(4) The first case is where it appears to the supervisory body that the request by the eligible person is frivolous or vexatious.

(5) The second case is where it appears to the supervisory body that –

(a) the question of whether or not there is an unauthorised deprivation of liberty has already been decided, and
(b) since that decision, there has been no change of circumstances which would merit the question being decided again.

(6) The supervisory body must not select and appoint a person to carry out an assessment under this paragraph unless it appears to the supervisory body that the person would be –

(a) suitable to carry out a best interests assessment (if one were obtained in connection with a request for a standard authorisation relating to the relevant person), and

(b) eligible to carry out such a best interests assessment.

(7) The supervisory body must notify the persons specified in sub-paragraph (8) –

(a) that the supervisory body have been requested to decide whether or not there is an unauthorised deprivation of liberty;
(b) of their decision whether or not to select and appoint a person to carry out an assessment under this paragraph;
(c) if their decision is to select and appoint a person, of the person appointed.

(8) The persons referred to in sub-paragraph (7) are –

(a) the eligible person who made the request under paragraph 68;
(b) the person to whom the request relates;
(c) the managing authority of the relevant hospital or care home;
(d) any section 39A IMCA.

70 (1) Regulations may be made about the period within which an assessment under paragraph 69 must be carried out.

(2) Regulations made under paragraph 129(3) apply in relation to the selection and appointment of a person under paragraph 69 as they apply to the selection of a person under paragraph 129 to carry out a best interests assessment.

(3) The following provisions apply to an assessment under paragraph 69 as they apply to an assessment carried out in connection with a request for a standard authorisation –

(a) paragraph 131 (examination and copying of records);
(b) paragraph 132 (representations);
(c) paragraphs 134 and 135(1) and (2) (duty to keep records and give copies).

(4) The copies of the assessment which the supervisory body are required to give under paragraph 135(2) must be given as soon as practicable after the supervisory body are themselves given a copy of the assessment.

71 (1) This paragraph applies if –

(a) the supervisory body obtain an assessment under paragraph 69,
(b) the assessment comes to the conclusion that the relevant person is a detained resident, and
(c) it appears to the supervisory body that the detention of the person is not authorised as mentioned in section 4A.

(2) This Schedule (including Part 5) applies as if the managing authority of the relevant hospital or care home had, in accordance with Part 4, requested the supervisory body to give a standard authorisation in relation to the relevant person.

(3) The managing authority of the relevant hospital or care home must supply the supervisory body with the information (if any) which the managing authority would, by virtue of paragraph 31, have had to include in a request for a standard authorisation.

(4) The supervisory body must notify the persons specified in paragraph 69(8) –

(a) of the outcome of the assessment obtained under paragraph 69, and
(b) that this Schedule applies as mentioned in sub-paragraph (2).

72 (1) This paragraph applies if –

(a) the supervisory body obtain an assessment under paragraph 69, and

(b) the assessment comes to the conclusion that the relevant person is not a detained resident.

(2) The supervisory body must notify the persons specified in paragraph 69(8) of the outcome of the assessment.

73 (1) This paragraph applies if –

(a) the supervisory body obtain an assessment under paragraph 69,
(b) the assessment comes to the conclusion that the relevant person is a detained resident, and
(c) it appears to the supervisory body that the detention of the person is authorised as mentioned in section 4A.

(2) The supervisory body must notify the persons specified in paragraph 69(8) –

(a) of the outcome of the assessment, and
(b) that it appears to the supervisory body that the detention is authorised.

Amendment: Mental Health Act 2007.

PART 5
URGENT AUTHORISATIONS

74 Managing authority to give authorisation

Only the managing authority of the relevant hospital or care home may give an urgent authorisation.

75 The managing authority may give an urgent authorisation only if they are required to do so by paragraph 76 (as read with paragraph 77).

76 Duty to give authorisation

(1) The managing authority must give an urgent authorisation in either of the following cases.

(2) The first case is where –

(a) the managing authority are required to make a request under paragraph 24 or 25 for a standard authorisation, and
(b) they believe that the need for the relevant person to be a detained resident is so urgent that it is appropriate for the detention to begin before they make the request.

(3) The second case is where –

(a) the managing authority have made a request under paragraph 24 or 25 for a standard authorisation, and
(b) they believe that the need for the relevant person to be a detained resident is so urgent that it is appropriate for the detention to begin before the request is disposed of.

(4) References in this paragraph to the detention of the relevant person are references to the detention to which paragraph 24 or 25 relates.

(5) This paragraph is subject to paragraph 77.

77 (1) This paragraph applies where the managing authority have given an urgent authorisation ('the original authorisation') in connection with a case where a person is, or is to be, a detained resident ('the existing detention').

(2) No new urgent authorisation is to be given under paragraph 76 in connection with the existing detention.

(3) But the managing authority may request the supervisory body to extend the duration of the original authorisation.

(4) Only one request under sub-paragraph (3) may be made in relation to the original authorisation.

(5) Paragraphs 84 to 86 apply to any request made under sub-paragraph (3).

78 Terms of authorisation

(1) If the managing authority decide to give an urgent authorisation, they must decide the period during which the authorisation is to be in force.

(2) That period must not exceed 7 days.

79 Form of authorisation

An urgent authorisation must be in writing.

80 An urgent authorisation must state the following things –

(a) the name of the relevant person;
(b) the name of the relevant hospital or care home;
(c) the period during which the authorisation is to be in force;
(d) the purpose for which the authorisation is given.

81 (1) If the name of the relevant hospital or care home changes, the urgent authorisation is to be read as if it stated the current name of the hospital or care home.

(2) But sub-paragraph (1) is subject to any provision relating to the change of name which is made in any enactment or in any instrument made under an enactment.

82 Duty to keep records and give copies

(1) This paragraph applies if an urgent authorisation is given.

(2) The managing authority must keep a written record of why they have given the urgent authorisation.

(3) As soon as practicable after giving the authorisation, the managing authority must give a copy of the authorisation to all of the following –

(a) the relevant person;
(b) any section 39A IMCA.

83 Duty to give information about authorisation

(1) This paragraph applies if an urgent authorisation is given.

(2) The managing authority of the relevant hospital or care home must take such steps as are practicable to ensure that the relevant person understands all of the following –

(a) the effect of the authorisation;
(b) the right to make an application to the court to exercise its jurisdiction under section 21A.

(3) Those steps must be taken as soon as is practicable after the authorisation is given.

(4) Those steps must include the giving of appropriate information both orally and in writing.

84 Request for extension of duration

(1) This paragraph applies if the managing authority make a request under paragraph 77 for the supervisory body to extend the duration of the original authorisation.

(2) The managing authority must keep a written record of why they have made the request.

(3) The managing authority must give the relevant person notice that they have made the request.

(4) The supervisory body may extend the duration of the original authorisation if it appears to them that –

(a) the managing authority have made the required request for a standard authorisation,
(b) there are exceptional reasons why it has not yet been possible for that request to be disposed of, and
(c) it is essential for the existing detention to continue until the request is disposed of.

(5) The supervisory body must keep a written record that the request has been made to them.

(6) In this paragraph and paragraphs 85 and 86 –

(a) 'original authorisation' and 'existing detention' have the same meaning as in paragraph 77;
(b) the required request for a standard authorisation is the request that is referred to in paragraph 76(2) or (3).

85 (1) This paragraph applies if, under paragraph 84, the supervisory body decide to extend the duration of the original authorisation.

(2) The supervisory body must decide the period of the extension.

(3) That period must not exceed 7 days.

(4) The supervisory body must give the managing authority notice stating the period of the extension.

(5) The managing authority must then vary the original authorisation so that it states the extended duration.

(6) Paragraphs 82(3) and 83 apply (with the necessary modifications) to the variation of the original authorisation as they apply to the giving of an urgent authorisation.

(7) The supervisory body must keep a written record of –

(a) the outcome of the request, and

(b) the period of the extension.

86 (1) This paragraph applies if, under paragraph 84, the supervisory body decide not to extend the duration of the original authorisation.

(2) The supervisory body must give the managing authority notice stating –

(a) the decision, and
(b) their reasons for making it.

(3) The managing authority must give a copy of that notice to all of the following –

(a) the relevant person;
(b) any section 39A IMCA.

(4) The supervisory body must keep a written record of the outcome of the request.

87 No variation

(1) An urgent authorisation may not be varied except in accordance with paragraph 85.

(2) This paragraph does not affect the powers of the Court of Protection or of any other court.

88 When an authorisation is in force

An urgent authorisation comes into force when it is given.

89

(1) An urgent authorisation ceases to be in force at the end of the period stated in the authorisation in accordance with paragraph 80(c) (subject to any variation in accordance with paragraph 85).

(2) But if the required request is disposed of before the end of that period, the urgent authorisation ceases to be in force as follows.

(3) If the supervisory body are required by paragraph 50(1) to give the requested authorisation, the urgent authorisation ceases to be in force when the requested authorisation comes into force.

(4) If the supervisory body are prohibited by paragraph 50(2) from giving the requested authorisation, the urgent authorisation ceases to be in force when the managing authority receive notice under paragraph 58.

(5) In this paragraph –

'required request' means the request referred to in paragraph 76(2) or (3);
'requested authorisation' means the standard authorisation to which the required request relates.

(6) This paragraph does not affect the powers of the Court of Protection or of any other court.

90 (1) This paragraph applies if an urgent authorisation ceases to be in force.

(2) The supervisory body must give notice that the authorisation has ceased to be in force.

(3) The supervisory body must give that notice to all of the following –

(a) the relevant person;
(b) any section 39A IMCA.

(4) The supervisory body must give that notice as soon as practicable after the authorisation ceases to be in force.

Amendment: Mental Health Act 2007.

PART 6
ELIGIBILITY REQUIREMENT NOT MET: SUSPENSION OF STANDARD AUTHORISATION

91 (1) This Part applies if the following conditions are met.

(2) The first condition is that a standard authorisation –

(a) has been given, and
(b) has not ceased to be in force.

(3) The second condition is that the managing authority of the relevant hospital or care home are satisfied that the relevant person has ceased to meet the eligibility requirement.

(4) But this Part does not apply if the relevant person is ineligible by virtue of paragraph 5 of Schedule 1A (in which case see Part 8).

92 The managing authority of the relevant hospital or care home must give the supervisory body notice that the relevant person has ceased to meet the eligibility requirement.

93 (1) This paragraph applies if the managing authority give the supervisory body notice under paragraph 92.

(2) The standard authorisation is suspended from the time when the notice is given.

(3) The supervisory body must give notice that the standard authorisation has been suspended to the following persons –

(a) the relevant person;
(b) the relevant person's representative;
(c) the managing authority of the relevant hospital or care home.

94 (1) This paragraph applies if, whilst the standard authorisation is suspended, the managing authority are satisfied that the relevant person meets the eligibility requirement again.

(2) The managing authority must give the supervisory body notice that the relevant person meets the eligibility requirement again.

95 (1) This paragraph applies if the managing authority give the supervisory body notice under paragraph 94.

(2) The standard authorisation ceases to be suspended from the time when the notice is given.

(3) The supervisory body must give notice that the standard authorisation has ceased to be suspended to the following persons –

(a) the relevant person;

(b) the relevant person's representative;
(c) any section 39D IMCA;
(d) the managing authority of the relevant hospital or care home.

(4) The supervisory body must give notice under this paragraph as soon as practicable after they are given notice under paragraph 94.

96 (1) This paragraph applies if no notice is given under paragraph 94 before the end of the relevant 28 day period.

(2) The standard authorisation ceases to have effect at the end of the relevant 28 day period.

(3) The relevant 28 day period is the period of 28 days beginning with the day on which the standard authorisation is suspended under paragraph 93.

97 The effect of suspending the standard authorisation is that Part 1 ceases to apply for as long as the authorisation is suspended.

Amendment: Mental Health Act 2007.

PART 7
STANDARD AUTHORISATIONS: CHANGE IN SUPERVISORY RESPONSIBILITY

98 Application of this Part

(1) This Part applies if these conditions are met.

(2) The first condition is that a standard authorisation –

(a) has been given, and
(b) has not ceased to be in force.

(3) The second condition is that there is a change in supervisory responsibility.

(4) The third condition is that there is not a change in the place of detention (within the meaning of paragraph 25).

99 For the purposes of this Part there is a change in supervisory responsibility if –

(a) one body ('the old supervisory body') have ceased to be supervisory body in relation to the standard authorisation, and
(b) a different body ('the new supervisory body') have become supervisory body in relation to the standard authorisation.

100 Effect of change in supervisory responsibility

(1) The new supervisory body becomes the supervisory body in relation to the authorisation.

(2) Anything done by or in relation to the old supervisory body in connection with the authorisation has effect, so far as is necessary for continuing its effect after the change, as if done by or in relation to the new supervisory body.

(3) Anything which relates to the authorisation and which is in the process of being done by or in relation to the old supervisory body at the time of the change may be continued by or in relation to the new supervisory body.

(4) But –

(a) the old supervisory body do not, by virtue of this paragraph, cease to be liable for anything done by them in connection with the authorisation before the change; and
(b) the new supervisory body do not, by virtue of this paragraph, become liable for any such thing.

Amendment: Mental Health Act 2007.

PART 8
STANDARD AUTHORISATIONS: REVIEW

101 Application of this Part

(1) This Part applies if a standard authorisation –

(a) has been given, and
(b) has not ceased to be in force.

(2) Paragraphs 102 to 122 are subject to paragraphs 123 to 125.

102 Review by supervisory body

(1) The supervisory body may at any time carry out a review of the standard authorisation in accordance with this Part.

(2) The supervisory body must carry out such a review if they are requested to do so by an eligible person.

(3) Each of the following is an eligible person –

(a) the relevant person;
(b) the relevant person's representative;
(c) the managing authority of the relevant hospital or care home.

103 Request for review

(1) An eligible person may, at any time, request the supervisory body to carry out a review of the standard authorisation in accordance with this Part.

(2) The managing authority of the relevant hospital or care home must make such a request if one or more of the qualifying requirements appear to them to be reviewable.

104 Grounds for review

(1) Paragraphs 105 to 107 set out the grounds on which the qualifying requirements are reviewable.

(2) A qualifying requirement is not reviewable on any other ground.

105 Non-qualification ground

(1) Any of the following qualifying requirements is reviewable on the ground that the relevant person does not meet the requirement –

(a) the age requirement;
(b) the mental health requirement;
(c) the mental capacity requirement;

(d) the best interests requirement;
(e) the no refusals requirement.

(2) The eligibility requirement is reviewable on the ground that the relevant person is ineligible by virtue of paragraph 5 of Schedule 1A.

(3) The ground in sub-paragraph (1) and the ground in sub-paragraph (2) are referred to as the non-qualification ground.

106 Change of reason ground

(1) Any of the following qualifying requirements is reviewable on the ground set out in sub-paragraph (2) –

(a) the mental health requirement;
(b) the mental capacity requirement;
(c) the best interests requirement;
(d) the eligibility requirement;
(e) the no refusals requirement.

(2) The ground is that the reason why the relevant person meets the requirement is not the reason stated in the standard authorisation.

(3) This ground is referred to as the change of reason ground.

107 Variation of conditions ground

(1) The best interests requirement is reviewable on the ground that –

(a) there has been a change in the relevant person's case, and
(b) because of that change, it would be appropriate to vary the conditions to which the standard authorisation is subject.

(2) This ground is referred to as the variation of conditions ground.

(3) A reference to varying the conditions to which the standard authorisation is subject is a reference to –

(a) amendment of an existing condition,
(b) omission of an existing condition, or
(c) inclusion of a new condition (whether or not there are already any existing conditions).

108 Notice that review to be carried out

(1) If the supervisory body are to carry out a review of the standard authorisation, they must give notice of the review to the following persons –

(a) the relevant person;
(b) the relevant person's representative;
(c) the managing authority of the relevant hospital or care home.

(2) The supervisory body must give the notice –

(a) before they begin the review, or
(b) if that is not practicable, as soon as practicable after they have begun it.

(3) This paragraph does not require the supervisory body to give notice to any person who has requested the review.

109 Starting a review

To start a review of the standard authorisation, the supervisory body must decide which, if any, of the qualifying requirements appear to be reviewable.

110 No reviewable qualifying requirements

(1) This paragraph applies if no qualifying requirements appear to be reviewable.

(2) This Part does not require the supervisory body to take any action in respect of the standard authorisation.

111 One or more reviewable qualifying requirements

(1) This paragraph applies if one or more qualifying requirements appear to be reviewable.

(2) The supervisory body must secure that a separate review assessment is carried out in relation to each qualifying requirement which appears to be reviewable.

(3) But sub-paragraph (2) does not require the supervisory body to secure that a best interests review assessment is carried out in a case where the best interests requirement appears to the supervisory body to be non-assessable.

(4) The best interests requirement is non-assessable if –

(a) the requirement is reviewable only on the variation of conditions ground, and
(b) the change in the relevant person's case is not significant.

(5) In making any decision whether the change in the relevant person's case is significant, regard must be had to –

(a) the nature of the change, and
(b) the period that the change is likely to last for.

112 Review assessments

(1) A review assessment is an assessment of whether the relevant person meets a qualifying requirement.

(2) In relation to a review assessment –

(a) a negative conclusion is a conclusion that the relevant person does not meet the qualifying requirement to which the assessment relates;
(b) a positive conclusion is a conclusion that the relevant person meets the qualifying requirement to which the assessment relates.

(3) An age review assessment is a review assessment carried out in relation to the age requirement.

(4) A mental health review assessment is a review assessment carried out in relation to the mental health requirement.

(5) A mental capacity review assessment is a review assessment carried out in relation to the mental capacity requirement.

(6) A best interests review assessment is a review assessment carried out in relation to the best interests requirement.

(7) An eligibility review assessment is a review assessment carried out in relation to the eligibility requirement.

(8) A no refusals review assessment is a review assessment carried out in relation to the no refusals requirement.

113 (1) In carrying out a review assessment, the assessor must comply with any duties which would be imposed upon him under Part 4 if the assessment were being carried out in connection with a request for a standard authorisation.

(2) But in the case of a best interests review assessment, paragraphs 43 and 44 do not apply.

(3) Instead of what is required by paragraph 43, the best interests review assessment must include recommendations about whether –and, if so, how –it would be appropriate to vary the conditions to which the standard authorisation is subject.

114 Best interests requirement reviewable but non-assessable

(1) This paragraph applies in a case where –

- (a) the best interests requirement appears to be reviewable, but
- (b) in accordance with paragraph 111(3), the supervisory body are not required to secure that a best interests review assessment is carried out.

(2) The supervisory body may vary the conditions to which the standard authorisation is subject in such ways (if any) as the supervisory body think are appropriate in the circumstances.

115 Best interests review assessment positive

(1) This paragraph applies in a case where –

- (a) a best interests review assessment is carried out, and
- (b) the assessment comes to a positive conclusion.

(2) The supervisory body must decide the following questions –

- (a) whether or not the best interests requirement is reviewable on the change of reason ground;
- (b) whether or not the best interests requirement is reviewable on the variation of conditions ground;
- (c) if so, whether or not the change in the person's case is significant.

(3) If the supervisory body decide that the best interests requirement is reviewable on the change of reason ground, they must vary the standard authorisation so that it states the reason why the relevant person now meets that requirement.

(4) If the supervisory body decide that –

- (a) the best interests requirement is reviewable on the variation of conditions ground, and
- (b) the change in the relevant person's case is not significant,

they may vary the conditions to which the standard authorisation is subject in such ways (if any) as they think are appropriate in the circumstances.

(5) If the supervisory body decide that –

(a) the best interests requirement is reviewable on the variation of conditions ground, and
(b) the change in the relevant person's case is significant,

they must vary the conditions to which the standard authorisation is subject in such ways as they think are appropriate in the circumstances.

(6) If the supervisory body decide that the best interests requirement is not reviewable on –

(a) the change of reason ground, or
(b) the variation of conditions ground,

this Part does not require the supervisory body to take any action in respect of the standard authorisation so far as the best interests requirement relates to it.

116 Mental health, mental capacity, eligibility or no refusals review assessment positive

(1) This paragraph applies if the following conditions are met.

(2) The first condition is that one or more of the following are carried out –

(a) a mental health review assessment;
(b) a mental capacity review assessment;
(c) an eligibility review assessment;
(d) a no refusals review assessment.

(3) The second condition is that each assessment carried out comes to a positive conclusion.

(4) The supervisory body must decide whether or not each of the assessed qualifying requirements is reviewable on the change of reason ground.

(5) If the supervisory body decide that any of the assessed qualifying requirements is reviewable on the change of reason ground, they must vary the standard authorisation so that it states the reason why the relevant person now meets the requirement or requirements in question.

(6) If the supervisory body decide that none of the assessed qualifying requirements are reviewable on the change of reason ground, this Part does not require the supervisory body to take any action in respect of the standard authorisation so far as those requirements relate to it.

(7) An assessed qualifying requirement is a qualifying requirement in relation to which a review assessment is carried out.

117 One or more review assessments negative

(1) This paragraph applies if one or more of the review assessments carried out comes to a negative conclusion.

(2) The supervisory body must terminate the standard authorisation with immediate effect.

118 Completion of a review

(1) The review of the standard authorisation is complete in any of the following cases.

(2) The first case is where paragraph 110 applies.

(3) The second case is where –

(a) paragraph 111 applies, and
(b) paragraph 117 requires the supervisory body to terminate the standard authorisation.

(4) In such a case, the supervisory body need not comply with any of the other provisions of paragraphs 114 to 116 which would be applicable to the review (were it not for this sub-paragraph).

(5) The third case is where –

(a) paragraph 111 applies,
(b) paragraph 117 does not require the supervisory body to terminate the standard authorisation, and
(c) the supervisory body comply with all of the provisions of paragraphs 114 to 116 (so far as they are applicable to the review).

119 Variations under this Part

Any variation of the standard authorisation made under this Part must be in writing.

120 Notice of outcome of review

(1) When the review of the standard authorisation is complete, the supervisory body must give notice to all of the following –

(a) the managing authority of the relevant hospital or care home;
(b) the relevant person;
(c) the relevant person's representative;
(d) any section 39D IMCA.

(2) That notice must state –

(a) the outcome of the review, and
(b) what variation (if any) has been made to the authorisation under this Part.

121 Records

A supervisory body must keep a written record of the following information –

(a) each request for a review that is made to them;
(b) the outcome of each request;
(c) each review which they carry out;
(d) the outcome of each review which they carry out;
(e) any variation of an authorisation made in consequence of a review.

122 Relationship between review and suspension under Part 6

(1) This paragraph applies if a standard authorisation is suspended in accordance with Part 6.

(2) No review may be requested under this Part whilst the standard authorisation is suspended.

(3) If a review has already been requested, or is being carried out, when the standard authorisation is suspended, no steps are to be taken in connection with that review whilst the authorisation is suspended.

123 Relationship between review and request for new authorisation

(1) This paragraph applies if, in accordance with paragraph 24 (as read with paragraph 29), the managing authority of the relevant hospital or care home make a request for a new standard authorisation which would be in force after the expiry of the existing authorisation.

(2) No review may be requested under this Part until the request for the new standard authorisation has been disposed of.

(3) If a review has already been requested, or is being carried out, when the new standard authorisation is requested, no steps are to be taken in connection with that review until the request for the new standard authorisation has been disposed of.

124 (1) This paragraph applies if –

(a) a review under this Part has been requested, or is being carried out, and
(b) the managing authority of the relevant hospital or care home make a request under paragraph 30 for a new standard authorisation which would be in force on or before, and after, the expiry of the existing authorisation.

(2) No steps are to be taken in connection with the review under this Part until the request for the new standard authorisation has been disposed of.

125 In paragraphs 123 and 124 –

(a) the existing authorisation is the authorisation referred to in paragraph 101;
(b) the expiry of the existing authorisation is the time when it is expected to cease to be in force.

Amendment: Mental Health Act 2007.

PART 9
ASSESSMENTS UNDER THIS SCHEDULE

126 Introduction

This Part contains provision about assessments under this Schedule.

127 An assessment under this Schedule is either of the following –

(a) an assessment carried out in connection with a request for a standard authorisation under Part 4;
(b) a review assessment carried out in connection with a review of a standard authorisation under Part 8.

128 In this Part, in relation to an assessment under this Schedule –

'assessor' means the person carrying out the assessment;
'relevant procedure' means –
(a) the request for the standard authorisation, or
(b) the review of the standard authorisation;
'supervisory body' means the supervisory body responsible for securing that the assessment is carried out.

129 Supervisory body to select assessor

(1) It is for the supervisory body to select a person to carry out an assessment under this Schedule.

(2) The supervisory body must not select a person to carry out an assessment unless the person –

(a) appears to the supervisory body to be suitable to carry out the assessment (having regard, in particular, to the type of assessment and the person to be assessed), and
(b) is eligible to carry out the assessment.

(3) Regulations may make provision about the selection, and eligibility, of persons to carry out assessments under this Schedule.

(4) Sub-paragraphs (5) and (6) apply if two or more assessments are to be obtained for the purposes of the relevant procedure.

(5) In a case where the assessments to be obtained include a mental health assessment and a best interests assessment, the supervisory body must not select the same person to carry out both assessments.

(6) Except as prohibited by sub-paragraph (5), the supervisory body may select the same person to carry out any number of the assessments which the person appears to be suitable, and is eligible, to carry out.

130 (1) This paragraph applies to regulations under paragraph 129(3).

(2) The regulations may make provision relating to a person's –

(a) qualifications,
(b) skills,
(c) training,
(d) experience,
(e) relationship to, or connection with, the relevant person or any other person,
(f) involvement in the care or treatment of the relevant person,
(g) connection with the supervisory body, or
(h) connection with the relevant hospital or care home, or with any other establishment or undertaking.

(3) The provision that the regulations may make in relation to a person's training may provide for particular training to be specified by the appropriate authority otherwise than in the regulations.

(4) In sub-paragraph (3) the 'appropriate authority' means –

(a) in relation to England: the Secretary of State;
(b) in relation to Wales: the National Assembly for Wales.

(5) The regulations may make provision requiring a person to be insured in respect of liabilities that may arise in connection with the carrying out of an assessment.

(6) In relation to cases where two or more assessments are to be obtained for the purposes of the relevant procedure, the regulations may limit the number, kind or combination of assessments which a particular person is eligible to carry out.

(7) Sub-paragraphs (2) to (6) do not limit the generality of the provision that may be made in the regulations.

131 Examination and copying of records

An assessor may, at all reasonable times, examine and take copies of –

(a) any health record,
(b) any record of, or held by, a local authority and compiled in accordance with a social services function, and
(c) any record held by a person registered under Part 2 of the Care Standards Act 2000 or Chapter 2 of Part 1 of the Health and Social Care Act 2008,

which the assessor considers may be relevant to the assessment which is being carried out.

132 Representations

In carrying out an assessment under this Schedule, the assessor must take into account any information given, or submissions made, by any of the following –

(a) the relevant person's representative;
(b) any section 39A IMCA;
(c) any section 39C IMCA;
(d) any section 39D IMCA.

133 Assessments to stop if any comes to negative conclusion

(1) This paragraph applies if an assessment under this Schedule comes to the conclusion that the relevant person does not meet one of the qualifying requirements.

(2) This Schedule does not require the supervisory body to secure that any other assessments under this Schedule are carried out in relation to the relevant procedure.

(3) The supervisory body must give notice to any assessor who is carrying out another assessment in connection with the relevant procedure that they are to cease carrying out that assessment.

(4) If an assessor receives such notice, this Schedule does not require the assessor to continue carrying out that assessment.

134 Duty to keep records and give copies

(1) This paragraph applies if an assessor has carried out an assessment under this Schedule (whatever conclusions the assessment has come to).

(2) The assessor must keep a written record of the assessment.

(3) As soon as practicable after carrying out the assessment, the assessor must give copies of the assessment to the supervisory body.

135 (1) This paragraph applies to the supervisory body if they are given a copy of an assessment under this Schedule.

(2) The supervisory body must give copies of the assessment to all of the following –

(a) the managing authority of the relevant hospital or care home;
(b) the relevant person;
(c) any section 39A IMCA;
(d) the relevant person's representative.

(3) If –

(a) the assessment is obtained in relation to a request for a standard authorisation, and
(b) the supervisory body are required by paragraph 50(1) to give the standard authorisation,

the supervisory body must give the copies of the assessment when they give copies of the authorisation in accordance with paragraph 57.

(4) If –

(a) the assessment is obtained in relation to a request for a standard authorisation, and
(b) the supervisory body are prohibited by paragraph 50(2) from giving the standard authorisation,

the supervisory body must give the copies of the assessment when they give notice in accordance with paragraph 58.

(5) If the assessment is obtained in connection with the review of a standard authorisation, the supervisory body must give the copies of the assessment when they give notice in accordance with paragraph 120.

136 (1) This paragraph applies to the supervisory body if –

(a) they are given a copy of a best interests assessment, and
(b) the assessment includes, in accordance with paragraph 44(2), a statement that it appears to the assessor that there is an unauthorised deprivation of liberty.

(2) The supervisory body must notify all of the persons listed in sub-paragraph (3) that the assessment includes such a statement.

(3) Those persons are –

(a) the managing authority of the relevant hospital or care home;
(b) the relevant person;
(c) any section 39A IMCA;
(d) any interested person consulted by the best interests assessor.

(4) The supervisory body must comply with this paragraph when (or at some time before) they comply with paragraph 135.

Amendment: Mental Health Act 2007; SI 2010/813.

PART 10
RELEVANT PERSON'S REPRESENTATIVE

137 The representative

In this Schedule the relevant person's representative is the person appointed as such in accordance with this Part.

138 (1) Regulations may make provision about the selection and appointment of representatives.

(2) In this Part such regulations are referred to as 'appointment regulations'.

139 Supervisory body to appoint representative

(1) The supervisory body must appoint a person to be the relevant person's representative as soon as practicable after a standard authorisation is given.

(2) The supervisory body must appoint a person to be the relevant person's representative if a vacancy arises whilst a standard authorisation is in force.

(3) Where a vacancy arises, the appointment under sub-paragraph (2) is to be made as soon as practicable after the supervisory body becomes aware of the vacancy.

140 (1) The selection of a person for appointment under paragraph 139 must not be made unless it appears to the person making the selection that the prospective representative would, if appointed –

(a) maintain contact with the relevant person,
(b) represent the relevant person in matters relating to or connected with this Schedule, and
(c) support the relevant person in matters relating to or connected with this Schedule.

141 (1) Any appointment of a representative for a relevant person is in addition to, and does not affect, any appointment of a donee or deputy.

(2) The functions of any representative are in addition to, and do not affect –

(a) the authority of any donee,
(b) the powers of any deputy, or
(c) any powers of the court.

142 Appointment regulations

Appointment regulations may provide that the procedure for appointing a representative may begin at any time after a request for a standard authorisation is made (including a time before the request has been disposed of).

143 (1) Appointment regulations may make provision about who is to select a person for appointment as a representative.

(2) But regulations under this paragraph may only provide for the following to make a selection –

(a) the relevant person, if he has capacity in relation to the question of which person should be his representative;
(b) a donee of a lasting power of attorney granted by the relevant person, if it is within the scope of his authority to select a person;
(c) a deputy, if it is within the scope of his authority to select a person;
(d) a best interests assessor;
(e) the supervisory body.

(3) Regulations under this paragraph may provide that a selection by the relevant person, a donee or a deputy is subject to approval by a best interests assessor or the supervisory body.

(4) Regulations under this paragraph may provide that, if more than one selection is necessary in connection with the appointment of a particular representative –

(a) the same person may make more than one selection;

(b) different persons may make different selections.

(5) For the purposes of this paragraph a best interests assessor is a person carrying out a best interests assessment in connection with the standard authorisation in question (including the giving of that authorisation).

144 (1) Appointment regulations may make provision about who may, or may not, be –

(a) selected for appointment as a representative, or
(b) appointed as a representative.

(2) Regulations under this paragraph may relate to any of the following matters –

(a) a person's age;
(b) a person's suitability;
(c) a person's independence;
(d) a person's willingness;
(e) a person's qualifications.

145 Appointment regulations may make provision about the formalities of appointing a person as a representative.

146 In a case where a best interests assessor is to select a person to be appointed as a representative, appointment regulations may provide for the variation of the assessor's duties in relation to the assessment which he is carrying out.

147 Monitoring of representatives

Regulations may make provision requiring the managing authority of the relevant hospital or care home to –

(a) monitor, and
(b) report to the supervisory body on,

the extent to which a representative is maintaining contact with the relevant person.

148 Termination

Regulations may make provision about the circumstances in which the appointment of a person as the relevant person's representative ends or may be ended.

149 Regulations may make provision about the formalities of ending the appointment of a person as a representative.

150 Suspension of representative's functions

(1) Regulations may make provision about the circumstances in which functions exercisable by, or in relation to, the relevant person's representative (whether under this Schedule or not) may be –

(a) suspended, and
(b) if suspended, revived.

(2) The regulations may make provision about the formalities for giving effect to the suspension or revival of a function.

(3) The regulations may make provision about the effect of the suspension or revival of a function.

151 Payment of representative

Regulations may make provision for payments to be made to, or in relation to, persons exercising functions as the relevant person's representative.

152 Regulations under this Part

The provisions of this Part which specify provision that may be made in regulations under this Part do not affect the generality of the power to make such regulations.

153 Effect of appointment of section 39C IMCA

Paragraphs 159 and 160 make provision about the exercise of functions by, or towards, the relevant person's representative during periods when –

(a) no person is appointed as the relevant person's representative, but
(b) a person is appointed as a section 39C IMCA.

Amendment: Mental Health Act 2007.

PART 11
IMCAS

154 Application of Part

This Part applies for the purposes of this Schedule.

155 The IMCAs

A section 39A IMCA is an independent mental capacity advocate appointed under section 39A.

156 A section 39C IMCA is an independent mental capacity advocate appointed under section 39C

157 A section 39D IMCA is an independent mental capacity advocate appointed under section 39D.

158 An IMCA is a section 39A IMCA or a section 39C IMCA or a section 39D IMCA.

159 Section 39C IMCA: functions

(1) This paragraph applies if, and for as long as, there is a section 39C IMCA.

(2) In the application of the relevant provisions, references to the relevant person's representative are to be read as references to the section 39C IMCA.

(3) But sub-paragraph (2) does not apply to any function under the relevant provisions for as long as the function is suspended in accordance with provision made under Part 10.

(4) In this paragraph and paragraph 160 the relevant provisions are –

(a) paragraph 102(3)(b) (request for review under Part 8);

(b) paragraph 108(1)(b) (notice of review under Part 8);
(c) paragraph 120(1)(c) (notice of outcome of review under Part 8).

160 (1) This paragraph applies if –

(a) a person is appointed as the relevant person's representative, and
(b) a person accordingly ceases to hold an appointment as a section 39C IMCA.

(2) Where a function under a relevant provision has been exercised by, or towards, the section 39C IMCA, there is no requirement for that function to be exercised again by, or towards, the relevant person's representative.

161 Section 39A IMCA: restriction of functions

(1) This paragraph applies if –

(a) there is a section 39A IMCA, and
(b) a person is appointed under Part 10 to be the relevant person's representative (whether or not that person, or any person subsequently appointed, is currently the relevant person's representative).

(2) The duties imposed on, and the powers exercisable by, the section 39A IMCA do not apply.

(3) The duties imposed on, and the powers exercisable by, any other person do not apply, so far as they fall to be performed or exercised towards the section 39A IMCA.

(4) But sub-paragraph (2) does not apply to any power of challenge exercisable by the section 39A IMCA.

(5) And sub-paragraph (3) does not apply to any duty or power of any other person so far as it relates to any power of challenge exercisable by the section 39A IMCA.

(6) Before exercising any power of challenge, the section 39A IMCA must take the views of the relevant person's representative into account.

(7) A power of challenge is a power to make an application to the court to exercise its jurisdiction under section 21A in connection with the giving of the standard authorisation.

Amendment: Mental Health Act 2007.

PART 12
MISCELLANEOUS

162 Monitoring of operation of Schedule

(1) Regulations may make provision for, and in connection with, requiring one or more prescribed bodies to monitor, and report on, the operation of this Schedule in relation to England.

(2) The regulations may, in particular, give a prescribed body authority to do one or more of the following things –

(a) to visit hospitals and care homes;
(b) to visit and interview persons accommodated in hospitals and care homes;
(c) to require the production of, and to inspect, records relating to the care or treatment of persons.

(3) 'Prescribed' means prescribed in regulations under this paragraph.

163 (1) Regulations may make provision for, and in connection with, enabling the National Assembly for Wales to monitor, and report on, the operation of this Schedule in relation to Wales.

(2) The National Assembly may direct one or more persons or bodies to carry out the Assembly's functions under regulations under this paragraph.

164 Disclosure of information

(1) Regulations may require either or both of the following to disclose prescribed information to prescribed bodies –

(a) supervisory bodies;
(b) managing authorities of hospitals or care homes.

(2) 'Prescribed' means prescribed in regulations under this paragraph.

(3) Regulations under this paragraph may only prescribe information relating to matters with which this Schedule is concerned.

165 Directions by National Assembly in relation to supervisory functions

(1) The National Assembly for Wales may direct a Local Health Board to exercise in relation to its area any supervisory functions which are specified in the direction.

(2) Directions under this paragraph must not preclude the National Assembly from exercising the functions specified in the directions.

(3) In this paragraph 'supervisory functions' means functions which the National Assembly have as supervisory body, so far as they are exercisable in relation to hospitals (whether NHS or independent hospitals, and whether in Wales or England).

166 (1) This paragraph applies where, under paragraph 165, a Local Health Board ('the specified LHB') is directed to exercise supervisory functions ('delegated functions').

(2) The National Assembly for Wales may give directions to the specified LHB about the Board's exercise of delegated functions.

(3) The National Assembly may give directions for any delegated functions to be exercised, on behalf of the specified LHB, by a committee, sub-committee or officer of that Board.

(4) The National Assembly may give directions providing for any delegated functions to be exercised by the specified LHB jointly with one or more other Local Health Boards.

(5) Where, under sub-paragraph (4), delegated functions are exercisable jointly, the National Assembly may give directions providing for the functions to be exercised, on behalf of the Local Health Boards in question, by a joint committee or joint sub-committee.

167 (1) Directions under paragraph 165 must be given in regulations.

(2) Directions under paragraph 166 may be given –

(a) in regulations, or
(b) by instrument in writing.

168 The power under paragraph 165 or paragraph 166 to give directions includes power to vary or revoke directions given under that paragraph.

169 Notices

Any notice under this Schedule must be in writing.

170 Regulations

(1) This paragraph applies to all regulations under this Schedule, except regulations under paragraph 162, 163, 167 or 183.

(2) It is for the Secretary of State to make such regulations in relation to authorisations under this Schedule which relate to hospitals and care homes situated in England.

(3) It is for the National Assembly for Wales to make such regulations in relation to authorisations under this Schedule which relate to hospitals and care homes situated in Wales.

171 It is for the Secretary of State to make regulations under paragraph 162.

172 It is for the National Assembly for Wales to make regulations under paragraph 163 or 167.

173 (1) This paragraph applies to regulations under paragraph 183.

(2) It is for the Secretary of State to make such regulations in relation to cases where a question as to the ordinary residence of a person is to be determined by the Secretary of State.

(3) It is for the National Assembly for Wales to make such regulations in relation to cases where a question as to the ordinary residence of a person is to be determined by the National Assembly.

Amendment: Mental Health Act 2007.

PART 13
INTERPRETATION

174 Introduction

This Part applies for the purposes of this Schedule.

175 Hospitals and their managing authorities

(1) 'Hospital' means –

(a) an NHS hospital, or
(b) an independent hospital.

(2) 'NHS hospital' means –

(a) a health service hospital as defined by section 275 of the National Health Service Act 2006 or section 206 of the National Health Service (Wales) Act 2006, or
(b) a hospital as defined by section 206 of the National Health Service (Wales) Act 2006 vested in a Local Health Board.

(3) 'Independent hospital' –

(a) in relation to England, means a hospital as defined by section 275 of the National Health Service Act 2006 that is not an NHS hospital; and
(b) in relation to Wales, means a hospital as defined by section 2 of the Care Standards Act 2000 that is not an NHS hospital.

176 (1) 'Managing authority', in relation to an NHS hospital, means –

(a) if the hospital –
 (i) is vested in the appropriate national authority for the purposes of its functions under the National Health Service Act 2006 or of the National Health Service (Wales) Act 2006, or
 (ii) consists of any accommodation provided by a local authority and used as a hospital by or on behalf of the appropriate national authority under either of those Acts,

 the Local Health Board or Special Health Authority responsible for the administration of the hospital;
(aa) in relation to England, if the hospital falls within paragraph (a)(i) or (ii) and no Special Health Authority has responsibility for its administration, the Secretary of State;
(b) if the hospital is vested in a National Health Service trust or NHS foundation trust, that trust;
(c) if the hospital is vested in a Local Health Board, that Board.

(2) For this purpose the appropriate national authority is –

(a) in relation to England: the Secretary of State;
(b) in relation to Wales: the National Assembly for Wales;
(c) in relation to England and Wales: the Secretary of State and the National Assembly acting jointly.

177

'Managing authority', in relation to an independent hospital, means –
 (a) in relation to England, the person registered, or required to be registered, under Chapter 2 of Part 1 of the Health and Social Care Act 2008 in respect of regulated activities (within the meaning of that Part) carried on in the hospital, and
 (b) in relation to Wales, the person registered, or required to be registered, under Part 2 of the Care Standards Act 2000 in respect of the hospital.

178 Care homes and their managing authorities

'Care home' has the meaning given by section 3 of the Care Standards Act 2000.

179

'Managing authority', in relation to a care home, means –
 (a) in relation to England, the person registered, or required to be registered, under Chapter 2 of Part 1 of the Health and Social Care Act 2008 in respect of the provision of residential accommodation, together with nursing or personal care, in the care home, and
 (b) in relation to Wales, the person registered, or required to be registered, under Part 2 of the Care Standards Act 2000 in respect of the care home.

180 Supervisory bodies: hospitals

(1) The identity of the supervisory body is determined under this paragraph in cases where the relevant hospital is situated in England.

(2) If the relevant person is ordinarily resident in the area of a local authority in England, the supervisory body are that local authority.

(3) If the relevant person is not ordinarily resident in England and the National Assembly for Wales or a Local Health Board commission the relevant care or treatment, the National Assembly are the supervisory body.

(4) In any other case, the supervisory body are the local authority for the area in which the relevant hospital is situated.

(4A) 'Local authority' means –

(a) the council of a county;
(b) the council of a district for which there is no county council;
(c) the council of a London borough;
(d) the Common Council of the City of London;
(e) the Council of the Isles of Scilly.

(5) If a hospital is situated in the areas of two (or more) local authorities, it is to be regarded for the purposes of sub-paragraph (4) as situated in whichever of the areas the greater (or greatest) part of the hospital is situated.

181 (1) The identity of the supervisory body is determined under this paragraph in cases where the relevant hospital is situated in Wales.

(2) The National Assembly for Wales are the supervisory body.

(3) But if the relevant person is ordinarily resident in the area of a local authority in England, the supervisory body are that local authority.

(4) 'Local authority' means –

(a) the council of a county;
(b) the council of a district for which there is no county council;
(c) the council of a London borough;
(d) the Common Council of the City of London;
(e) the Council of the Isles of Scilly.

182 Supervisory bodies: care homes

(1) The identity of the supervisory body is determined under this paragraph in cases where the relevant care home is situated in England or in Wales.

(2) The supervisory body are the local authority for the area in which the relevant person is ordinarily resident.

(3) But if the relevant person is not ordinarily resident in the area of a local authority, the supervisory body are the local authority for the area in which the care home is situated.

(4) In relation to England 'local authority' means –

(a) the council of a county;
(b) the council of a district for which there is no county council;
(c) the council of a London borough;

(d) the Common Council of the City of London;
(e) the Council of the Isles of Scilly.

(5) In relation to Wales 'local authority' means the council of a county or county borough.

(6) If a care home is situated in the areas of two (or more) local authorities, it is to be regarded for the purposes of sub-paragraph (3) as situated in whichever of the areas the greater (or greatest) part of the care home is situated.

183 Supervisory bodies: determination of place of ordinary residence

(1) Subsections (5) and (6) of section 24 of the National Assistance Act 1948 (deemed place of ordinary residence) apply to any determination of where a person is ordinarily resident for the purposes of paragraphs 180, 181 and 182 as those subsections apply to such a determination for the purposes specified in those subsections.

(2) In the application of section 24(6) of the 1948 Act by virtue of subsection (1) to any determination of where a person is ordinarily resident for the purposes of paragraph 182,section 24(6) is to be read as if it referred to a hospital vested in a Local Health Board as well as to hospitals vested in the Secretary of State and the other bodies mentioned in section 24(6).

(3) Any question arising as to the ordinary residence of a person is to be determined by the Secretary of State or by the National Assembly for Wales.

(4) The Secretary of State and the National Assembly must make and publish arrangements for determining which cases are to be dealt with by the Secretary of State and which are to be dealt with by the National Assembly.

(5) Those arrangements may include provision for the Secretary of State and the National Assembly to agree, in relation to any question that has arisen, which of them is to deal with the case.

(6) Regulations may make provision about arrangements that are to have effect before, upon, or after the determination of any question as to the ordinary residence of a person.

(7) The regulations may, in particular, authorise or require a local authority to do any or all of the following things –

(a) to act as supervisory body even though it may wish to dispute that it is the supervisory body;
(b) to become the supervisory body in place of another local authority;
(c) to recover from another local authority expenditure incurred in exercising functions as the supervisory body.

184 Same body managing authority and supervisory body

(1) This paragraph applies if, in connection with a particular person's detention as a resident in a hospital or care home, the same body are both –

(a) the managing authority of the relevant hospital or care home, and
(b) the supervisory body.

(2) The fact that a single body are acting in both capacities does not prevent the body from carrying out functions under this Schedule in each capacity.

(3) But, in such a case, this Schedule has effect subject to any modifications contained in regulations that may be made for this purpose.

185 Interested persons

Each of the following is an interested person –

(a) the relevant person's spouse or civil partner;
(b) where the relevant person and another person of the opposite sex are not married to each other but are living together as husband and wife: the other person;
(c) where the relevant person and another person of the same sex are not civil partners of each other but are living together as if they were civil partners: the other person;
(d) the relevant person's children and step-children;
(e) the relevant person's parents and step-parents;
(f) the relevant person's brothers and sisters, half-brothers and half-sisters, and stepbrothers and stepsisters;
(g) the relevant person's grandparents;
(h) a deputy appointed for the relevant person by the court;
(i) a donee of a lasting power of attorney granted by the relevant person.

186 (1) An interested person consulted by the best interests assessor is any person whose name is stated in the relevant best interests assessment in accordance with paragraph 40 (interested persons whom the assessor consulted in carrying out the assessment).

(2) The relevant best interests assessment is the most recent best interests assessment carried out in connection with the standard authorisation in question (whether the assessment was carried out under Part 4 or Part 8).

187 Where this Schedule imposes on a person a duty towards an interested person, the duty does not apply if the person on whom the duty is imposed –

(a) is not aware of the interested person's identity or of a way of contacting him, and
(b) cannot reasonably ascertain it.

188 The following table contains an index of provisions defining or otherwise explaining expressions used in this Schedule –

age assessment	paragraph 34
age requirement	paragraph 13
age review assessment	paragraph 112(3)
appointment regulations	paragraph 138
assessment under this Schedule	paragraph 127
assessor (except in Part 8)	paragraph 33
assessor (in Part 8)	paragraphs 33 and 128
authorisation under this Schedule	paragraph 10
best interests (determination of)	section 4

best interests assessment	paragraph 38
best interests requirement	paragraph 16
best interests review assessment	paragraph 112(6)
care home	paragraph 178
change of reason ground	paragraph 106
complete (in relation to a review of a standard authorisation)	paragraph 118
deprivation of a person's liberty	section 64(5) and (6)
deputy	section 16(2)(b)
detained resident	paragraph 6
disposed of (in relation to a request for a standard authorisation)	paragraph 66
eligibility assessment	paragraph 46
eligibility requirement	paragraph 17
eligibility review assessment	paragraph 112(7)
eligible person (in relation to paragraphs 68 to 73)	paragraph 68
eligible person (in relation to Part 8)	paragraph 102(3)
expiry (in relation to an existing authorisation)	paragraph 125(b)
existing authorisation (in Part 8)	paragraph 125(a)
hospital	paragraph 175
IMCA	paragraph 158
in force (in relation to a standard authorisation)	paragraphs 63 and 64
in force (in relation to an urgent authorisation)	paragraphs 88 and 89
ineligible (in relation to the eligibility requirement)	Schedule 1A
interested person	paragraph 185
interested person consulted by the best interests assessor	paragraph 186
lack of capacity	section 2
lasting power of attorney	section 9
managing authority (in relation to a care home)	paragraph 179
managing authority (in relation to a hospital)	paragraph 176 or 177
maximum authorisation period	paragraph 42
mental capacity assessment	paragraph 37
mental capacity requirement	paragraph 15

mental capacity review assessment	paragraph 112(5)
mental health assessment	paragraph 35
mental health requirement	paragraph 14
mental health review assessment	paragraph 112(4)
negative conclusion	paragraph 112(2)(a)
new supervisory body	paragraph 99(b)
no refusals assessment	paragraph 48
no refusals requirement	paragraph 18
no refusals review assessment	paragraph 112(8)
non-qualification ground	paragraph 105
old supervisory body	paragraph 99(a)
positive conclusion	paragraph 112(2)(b)
purpose of a standard authorisation	paragraph 11(1)
purpose of an urgent authorisation	paragraph 11(2)
qualifying requirements	paragraph 12
refusal (for the purposes of the no refusals requirement)	paragraphs 19 and 20
relevant care or treatment	paragraph 7
relevant hospital or care home	paragraph 7
relevant managing authority	paragraph 26(4)
relevant person	paragraph 7
relevant person's representative	paragraph 137
relevant procedure	paragraph 128
review assessment	paragraph 112(1)
reviewable	paragraph 104
section 39A IMCA	paragraph 155
section 39C IMCA	paragraph 156
section 39D IMCA	paragraph 157
standard authorisation	paragraph 8
supervisory body (except in Part 8)	paragraph 180, 181 or 182
supervisory body (in Part 8)	paragraph 128 and paragraph 180, 181 or 182
unauthorised deprivation of liberty (in relation to paragraphs 68 to 73)	paragraph 67
urgent authorisation	paragraph 9
variation of conditions ground	paragraph 107

Amendment: Mental Health Act 2007, s 50(5), Sch 7, Health and Social Care Act 2012, s 55(2), Sch 5, paras 133, 136(1)–(6), SI 2010/813.

Schedule 1
Lasting Powers of Attorney: Formalities

Section 9

PART 1
MAKING INSTRUMENTS

1 General requirements as to making instruments

(1) An instrument is not made in accordance with this Schedule unless –

(a) it is in the prescribed form,
(b) it complies with paragraph 2, and
(c) any prescribed requirements in connection with its execution are satisfied.

(2) Regulations may make different provision according to whether –

(a) the instrument relates to personal welfare or to property and affairs (or to both);
(b) only one or more than one donee is to be appointed (and if more than one, whether jointly or jointly and severally).

(3) In this Schedule –

(a) 'prescribed' means prescribed by regulations, and
(b) 'regulations' means regulations made for the purposes of this Schedule by the Lord Chancellor.

2 Requirements as to content of instruments

(1) The instrument must include –

(a) the prescribed information about the purpose of the instrument and the effect of a lasting power of attorney,
(b) a statement by the donor to the effect that he –
  (i) has read the prescribed information or a prescribed part of it (or has had it read to him), and
  (ii) intends the authority conferred under the instrument to include authority to make decisions on his behalf in circumstances where he no longer has capacity,
(c) a statement by the donor –
  (i) naming a person or persons whom the donor wishes to be notified of any application for the registration of the instrument, or
  (ii) stating that there are no persons whom he wishes to be notified of any such application,
(d) a statement by the donee (or, if more than one, each of them) to the effect that he –
  (i) has read the prescribed information or a prescribed part of it (or has had it read to him), and
  (ii) understands the duties imposed on a donee of a lasting power of attorney under sections 1 (the principles) and 4 (best interests), and
(e) a certificate by a person of a prescribed description that, in his opinion, at the time when the donor executes the instrument –
  (i) the donor understands the purpose of the instrument and the scope of the authority conferred under it,

(ii) no fraud or undue pressure is being used to induce the donor to create a lasting power of attorney, and
(iii) there is nothing else which would prevent a lasting power of attorney from being created by the instrument.

(2) Regulations may –

(a) prescribe a maximum number of named persons;
(b) provide that, where the instrument includes a statement under sub-paragraph (1)(c)(ii), two persons of a prescribed description must each give a certificate under sub-paragraph (1)(e).

(3) The persons who may be named persons do not include a person who is appointed as donee under the instrument.

(4) In this Schedule, 'named person' means a person named under sub-paragraph (1)(c).

(5) A certificate under sub-paragraph (1)(e) –

(a) must be made in the prescribed form, and
(b) must include any prescribed information.

(6) The certificate may not be given by a person appointed as donee under the instrument.

3 Failure to comply with prescribed form

(1) If an instrument differs in an immaterial respect in form or mode of expression from the prescribed form, it is to be treated by the Public Guardian as sufficient in point of form and expression.

(2) The court may declare that an instrument which is not in the prescribed form is to be treated as if it were, if it is satisfied that the persons executing the instrument intended it to create a lasting power of attorney.

PART 2
REGISTRATION

4 Applications and procedure for registration

(1) An application to the Public Guardian for the registration of an instrument intended to create a lasting power of attorney –

(a) must be made in the prescribed form, and
(b) must include any prescribed information.

(2) The application may be made –

(a) by the donor,
(b) by the donee or donees, or
(c) if the instrument appoints two or more donees to act jointly and severally in respect of any matter, by any of the donees.

(3) The application must be accompanied by –

(a) the instrument, and
(b) any fee provided for under section 58(4)(b).

(4) A person who, in an application for registration, makes a statement which he knows to be false in a material particular is guilty of an offence and is liable –

(a) on summary conviction, to imprisonment for a term not exceeding 12 months or a fine not exceeding the statutory maximum or both;
(b) on conviction on indictment, to imprisonment for a term not exceeding 2 years or a fine or both.

5 Subject to paragraphs 11 to 14, the Public Guardian must register the instrument as a lasting power of attorney at the end of the prescribed period.

6 Notification requirements

(1) A donor about to make an application under paragraph 4(2)(a) must notify any named persons that he is about to do so.

(2) The donee (or donees) about to make an application under paragraph 4(2)(b) or (c) must notify any named persons that he is (or they are) about to do so.

7 As soon as is practicable after receiving an application by the donor under paragraph 4(2)(a), the Public Guardian must notify the donee (or donees) that the application has been received.

8 (1) As soon as is practicable after receiving an application by a donee (or donees) under paragraph 4(2)(b), the Public Guardian must notify the donor that the application has been received.

(2) As soon as is practicable after receiving an application by a donee under paragraph 4(2)(c), the Public Guardian must notify –

(a) the donor, and
(b) the donee or donees who did not join in making the application,

that the application has been received.

9 (1) A notice under paragraph 6 must be made in the prescribed form.

(2) A notice under paragraph 6, 7 or 8 must include such information, if any, as may be prescribed.

10 Power to dispense with notification requirements

The court may –

(a) on the application of the donor, dispense with the requirement to notify under paragraph 6(1), or
(b) on the application of the donee or donees concerned, dispense with the requirement to notify under paragraph 6(2),

if satisfied that no useful purpose would be served by giving the notice.

11 Instrument not made properly or containing ineffective provision

(1) If it appears to the Public Guardian that an instrument accompanying an application under paragraph 4 is not made in accordance with this Schedule, he must not register the instrument unless the court directs him to do so.

(2) Sub-paragraph (3) applies if it appears to the Public Guardian that the instrument contains a provision which –

(a) would be ineffective as part of a lasting power of attorney, or
(b) would prevent the instrument from operating as a valid lasting power of attorney.

(3) The Public Guardian –

(a) must apply to the court for it to determine the matter under section 23(1), and
(b) pending the determination by the court, must not register the instrument.

(4) Sub-paragraph (5) applies if the court determines under section 23(1) (whether or not on an application by the Public Guardian) that the instrument contains a provision which –

(a) would be ineffective as part of a lasting power of attorney, or
(b) would prevent the instrument from operating as a valid lasting power of attorney.

(5) The court must –

(a) notify the Public Guardian that it has severed the provision, or
(b) direct him not to register the instrument.

(6) Where the court notifies the Public Guardian that it has severed a provision, he must register the instrument with a note to that effect attached to it.

12 Deputy already appointed

(1) Sub-paragraph (2) applies if it appears to the Public Guardian that –

(a) there is a deputy appointed by the court for the donor, and
(b) the powers conferred on the deputy would, if the instrument were registered, to any extent conflict with the powers conferred on the attorney.

(2) The Public Guardian must not register the instrument unless the court directs him to do so.

13 Objection by donee or named person

(1) Sub-paragraph (2) applies if a donee or a named person –

(a) receives a notice under paragraph 6, 7 or 8 of an application for the registration of an instrument, and
(b) before the end of the prescribed period, gives notice to the Public Guardian of an objection to the registration on the ground that an event mentioned in section 13(3) or (6)(a) to (d) has occurred which has revoked the instrument.

(2) If the Public Guardian is satisfied that the ground for making the objection is established, he must not register the instrument unless the court, on the application of the person applying for the registration –

(a) is satisfied that the ground is not established, and
(b) directs the Public Guardian to register the instrument.

(3) Sub-paragraph (4) applies if a donee or a named person –

(a) receives a notice under paragraph 6, 7 or 8 of an application for the registration of an instrument, and
(b) before the end of the prescribed period –
    (i) makes an application to the court objecting to the registration on a prescribed ground, and

(ii) notifies the Public Guardian of the application.

(4) The Public Guardian must not register the instrument unless the court directs him to do so.

14 Objection by donor

(1) This paragraph applies if the donor –

(a) receives a notice under paragraph 8 of an application for the registration of an instrument, and
(b) before the end of the prescribed period, gives notice to the Public Guardian of an objection to the registration.

(2) The Public Guardian must not register the instrument unless the court, on the application of the donee or, if more than one, any of them –

(a) is satisfied that the donor lacks capacity to object to the registration, and
(b) directs the Public Guardian to register the instrument.

15 Notification of registration

Where an instrument is registered under this Schedule, the Public Guardian must give notice of the fact in the prescribed form to –

(a) the donor, and
(b) the donee or, if more than one, each of them.

16 Evidence of registration

(1) A document purporting to be an office copy of an instrument registered under this Schedule is, in any part of the United Kingdom, evidence of –

(a) the contents of the instrument, and
(b) the fact that it has been registered.

(2) Sub-paragraph (1) is without prejudice to –

(a) section 3 of the Powers of Attorney Act 1971 (proof by certified copy), and
(b) any other method of proof authorised by law.

PART 3
CANCELLATION OF REGISTRATION AND NOTIFICATION OF SEVERANCE

17 (1) The Public Guardian must cancel the registration of an instrument as a lasting power of attorney on being satisfied that the power has been revoked –

(a) as a result of the donor's bankruptcy or a debt relief order (under Part 7A of the Insolvency Act 1986) having been made in respect of the donor, or
(b) on the occurrence of an event mentioned in section 13(6)(a) to (d).

(2) If the Public Guardian cancels the registration of an instrument he must notify –

(a) the donor, and
(b) the donee or, if more than one, each of them.

18 The court must direct the Public Guardian to cancel the registration of an instrument as a lasting power of attorney if it –

(a) determines under section 22(2)(a) that a requirement for creating the power was not met,
(b) determines under section 22(2)(b) that the power has been revoked or has otherwise come to an end, or
(c) revokes the power under section 22(4)(b) (fraud etc).

19 (1) Sub-paragraph (2) applies if the court determines under section 23(1) that a lasting power of attorney contains a provision which –

(a) is ineffective as part of a lasting power of attorney, or
(b) prevents the instrument from operating as a valid lasting power of attorney.

(2) The court must –

(a) notify the Public Guardian that it has severed the provision, or
(b) direct him to cancel the registration of the instrument as a lasting power of attorney.

20 On the cancellation of the registration of an instrument, the instrument and any office copies of it must be delivered up to the Public Guardian to be cancelled.

PART 4
RECORDS OF ALTERATIONS IN REGISTERED POWERS

21 Partial revocation or suspension of power as a result of bankruptcy

If in the case of a registered instrument it appears to the Public Guardian that under section 13 a lasting power of attorney is revoked, or suspended, in relation to the donor's property and affairs (but not in relation to other matters), the Public Guardian must attach to the instrument a note to that effect.

22 Termination of appointment of donee which does not revoke power

If in the case of a registered instrument it appears to the Public Guardian that an event has occurred –

(a) which has terminated the appointment of the donee, but
(b) which has not revoked the instrument,

the Public Guardian must attach to the instrument a note to that effect.

23 Replacement of donee

If in the case of a registered instrument it appears to the Public Guardian that the donee has been replaced under the terms of the instrument the Public Guardian must attach to the instrument a note to that effect.

24 Severance of ineffective provisions

If in the case of a registered instrument the court notifies the Public Guardian under paragraph 19(2)(a) that it has severed a provision of the instrument, the Public Guardian must attach to it a note to that effect.

25 Notification of alterations

If the Public Guardian attaches a note to an instrument under paragraph 21, 22, 23 or 24 he must give notice of the note to the donee or donees of the power (or, as the case may be, to the other donee or donees of the power).

Amendments: SI 2012/2404.

Schedule 1A
Persons Ineligible to be Deprived of Liberty by this Act

PART 1
INELIGIBLE PERSONS

1 Application

This Schedule applies for the purposes of –

(a) section 16A, and
(b) paragraph 17 of Schedule A1.

2 Determining ineligibility

A person ('P') is ineligible to be deprived of liberty by this Act ('ineligible') if –

(a) P falls within one of the cases set out in the second column of the following table, and
(b) the corresponding entry in the third column of the table – or the provision, or one of the provisions, referred to in that entry – provides that he is ineligible.

	Status of P	*Determination of ineligibility*
Case A	P is – (a) subject to the hospital treatment regime, and (b) detained in a hospital under that regime.	P is ineligible.
Case B	P is – (a) subject to the hospital treatment regime, but (b) not detained in a hospital under that regime.	See paragraphs 3 and 4.
Case C	P is subject to the community treatment regime.	See paragraphs 3 and 4.
Case D	P is subject to the guardianship regime.	See paragraphs 3 and 5.
Case E	P is – (a) within the scope of the Mental Health Act, but	See paragraph 5.

	(b) not subject to any of the mental health regimes.	

3 Authorised course of action not in accordance with regime

(1) This paragraph applies in cases B, C and D in the table in paragraph 2.

(2) P is ineligible if the authorised course of action is not in accordance with a requirement which the relevant regime imposes.

(3) That includes any requirement as to where P is, or is not, to reside.

(4) The relevant regime is the mental health regime to which P is subject.

4 Treatment for mental disorder in a hospital

(1) This paragraph applies in cases B and C in the table in paragraph 2.

(2) P is ineligible if the relevant care or treatment consists in whole or in part of medical treatment for mental disorder in a hospital.

5 P objects to being a mental health patient etc

(1) This paragraph applies in cases D and E in the table in paragraph 2.

(2) P is ineligible if the following conditions are met.

(3) The first condition is that the relevant instrument authorises P to be a mental health patient.

(4) The second condition is that P objects –

(a) to being a mental health patient, or
(b) to being given some or all of the mental health treatment.

(5) The third condition is that a donee or deputy has not made a valid decision to consent to each matter to which P objects.

(6) In determining whether or not P objects to something, regard must be had to all the circumstances (so far as they are reasonably ascertainable), including the following –

(a) P's behaviour;
(b) P's wishes and feelings;
(c) P's views, beliefs and values.

(7) But regard is to be had to circumstances from the past only so far as it is still appropriate to have regard to them.

PART 2
INTERPRETATION

6 Application

This Part applies for the purposes of this Schedule.

7 Mental health regimes

The mental health regimes are –

(a) the hospital treatment regime,
(b) the community treatment regime, and
(c) the guardianship regime.

8 Hospital treatment regime

(1) P is subject to the hospital treatment regime if he is subject to –

(a) a hospital treatment obligation under the relevant enactment, or
(b) an obligation under another England and Wales enactment which has the same effect as a hospital treatment obligation.

(2) But where P is subject to any such obligation, he is to be regarded as not subject to the hospital treatment regime during any period when he is subject to the community treatment regime.

(3) A hospital treatment obligation is an application, order or direction of a kind listed in the first column of the following table.

(4) In relation to a hospital treatment obligation, the relevant enactment is the enactment in the Mental Health Act which is referred to in the corresponding entry in the second column of the following table.

Hospital treatment obligation	*Relevant enactment*
Application for admission for assessment	Section 2
Application for admission for assessment	Section 4
Application for admission for treatment	Section 3
Order for remand to hospital	Section 35
Order for remand to hospital	Section 36
Hospital order	Section 37
Interim hospital order	Section 38
Order for detention in hospital	Section 44
Hospital direction	Section 45A
Transfer direction	Section 47
Transfer direction	Section 48
Hospital order	Section 51

9 Community treatment regime

P is subject to the community treatment regime if he is subject to –

(a) a community treatment order under section 17A of the Mental Health Act, or
(b) an obligation under another England and Wales enactment which has the same effect as a community treatment order.

10 Guardianship regime

P is subject to the guardianship regime if he is subject to –

(a) a guardianship application under section 7 of the Mental Health Act,
(b) a guardianship order under section 37 of the Mental Health Act, or

(c) an obligation under another England and Wales enactment which has the same effect as a guardianship application or guardianship order.

11 England and Wales enactments

(1) An England and Wales enactment is an enactment which extends to England and Wales (whether or not it also extends elsewhere).

(2) It does not matter if the enactment is in the Mental Health Act or not.

12 P within scope of Mental Health Act

(1) P is within the scope of the Mental Health Act if –

(a) an application in respect of P could be made under section 2 or 3 of the Mental Health Act, and
(b) P could be detained in a hospital in pursuance of such an application, were one made.

(2) The following provisions of this paragraph apply when determining whether an application in respect of P could be made under section 2 or 3 of the Mental Health Act.

(3) If the grounds in section 2(2) of the Mental Health Act are met in P's case, it is to be assumed that the recommendations referred to in section 2(3) of that Act have been given.

(4) If the grounds in section 3(2) of the Mental Health Act are met in P's case, it is to be assumed that the recommendations referred to in section 3(3) of that Act have been given.

(5) In determining whether the ground in section 3(2)(c) of the Mental Health Act is met in P's case, it is to be assumed that the treatment referred to in section 3(2)(c) cannot be provided under this Act.

13 Authorised course of action, relevant care or treatment & relevant instrument

In a case where this Schedule applies for the purposes of section 16A –

'authorised course of action' means any course of action amounting to deprivation of liberty which the order under section 16(2)(a) authorises;
'relevant care or treatment' means any care or treatment which –
(a) comprises, or forms part of, the authorised course of action, or
(b) is to be given in connection with the authorised course of action;

'relevant instrument' means the order under section 16(2)(a).

14 In a case where this Schedule applies for the purposes of paragraph 17 of Schedule A1 –

'authorised course of action' means the accommodation of the relevant person in the relevant hospital or care home for the purpose of being given the relevant care or treatment;
'relevant care or treatment' has the same meaning as in Schedule A1;
'relevant instrument' means the standard authorisation under Schedule A1.

15 (1) This paragraph applies where the question whether a person is ineligible to be deprived of liberty by this Act is relevant to either of these decisions –

(a) whether or not to include particular provision ('the proposed provision') in an order under section 16(2)(a);
(b) whether or not to give a standard authorisation under Schedule A1.

(2) A reference in this Schedule to the authorised course of action or the relevant care or treatment is to be read as a reference to that thing as it would be if –

(a) the proposed provision were included in the order, or
(b) the standard authorisation were given.

(3) A reference in this Schedule to the relevant instrument is to be read as follows –

(a) where the relevant instrument is an order under section 16(2)(a): as a reference to the order as it would be if the proposed provision were included in it;
(b) where the relevant instrument is a standard authorisation: as a reference to the standard authorisation as it would be if it were given.

16 Expressions used in paragraph 5

(1) These expressions have the meanings given –

'donee' means a donee of a lasting power of attorney granted by P;
'mental health patient' means a person accommodated in a hospital for the purpose of being given medical treatment for mental disorder;
'mental health treatment' means the medical treatment for mental disorder referred to in the definition of 'mental health patient'.

(2) A decision of a donee or deputy is valid if it is made –

(a) within the scope of his authority as donee or deputy, and
(b) in accordance with Part 1 of this Act.

17 Expressions with same meaning as in Mental Health Act

(1) 'Hospital' has the same meaning as in Part 2 of the Mental Health Act.

(2) 'Medical treatment' has the same meaning as in the Mental Health Act.

(3) 'Mental disorder' has the same meaning as in Schedule A1 (see paragraph 14).

Amendment: Mental Health Act 2007.

Schedule 2
Property and Affairs: Supplementary Provisions

Section 18(4)

1 Wills: general

Paragraphs 2 to 4 apply in relation to the execution of a will, by virtue of section 18, on behalf of P.

2 Provision that may be made in will

The will may make any provision (whether by disposing of property or exercising a power or otherwise) which could be made by a will executed by P if he had capacity to make it.

3 Wills: requirements relating to execution

(1) Sub-paragraph (2) applies if under section 16 the court makes an order or gives directions requiring or authorising a person ('the authorised person') to execute a will on behalf of P.

(2) Any will executed in pursuance of the order or direction –

- (a) must state that it is signed by P acting by the authorised person,
- (b) must be signed by the authorised person with the name of P and his own name, in the presence of two or more witnesses present at the same time,
- (c) must be attested and subscribed by those witnesses in the presence of the authorised person, and
- (d) must be sealed with the official seal of the court.

4 Wills: effect of execution

(1) This paragraph applies where a will is executed in accordance with paragraph 3.

(2) The Wills Act 1837 has effect in relation to the will as if it were signed by P by his own hand, except that –

- (a) section 9 of the 1837 Act (requirements as to signing and attestation) does not apply, and
- (b) in the subsequent provisions of the 1837 Act any reference to execution in the manner required by the previous provisions is to be read as a reference to execution in accordance with paragraph 3.

(3) The will has the same effect for all purposes as if –

- (a) P had had the capacity to make a valid will, and
- (b) the will had been executed by him in the manner required by the 1837 Act.

(4) But sub-paragraph (3) does not have effect in relation to the will –

- (a) in so far as it disposes of immovable property outside England and Wales, or
- (b) in so far as it relates to any other property or matter if, when the will is executed –
  - (i) P is domiciled outside England and Wales, and
  - (ii) the condition in sub-paragraph (5) is met.

(5) The condition is that, under the law of P's domicile, any question of his testamentary capacity would fall to be determined in accordance with the law of a place outside England and Wales.

5 Vesting orders ancillary to settlement etc

(1) If provision is made by virtue of section 18 for –

- (a) the settlement of any property of P, or
- (b) the exercise of a power vested in him of appointing trustees or retiring from a trust,

the court may also make as respects the property settled or the trust property such consequential vesting or other orders as the case may require.

(2) The power under sub-paragraph (1) includes, in the case of the exercise of such a power, any order which could have been made in such a case under Part 4 of the Trustee Act 1925.

6 Variation of settlements

(1) If a settlement has been made by virtue of section 18, the court may by order vary or revoke the settlement if –

(a) the settlement makes provision for its variation or revocation,
(b) the court is satisfied that a material fact was not disclosed when the settlement was made, or
(c) the court is satisfied that there has been a substantial change of circumstances.

(2) Any such order may give such consequential directions as the court thinks fit.

7 Vesting of stock in curator appointed outside England and Wales

(1) Sub-paragraph (2) applies if the court is satisfied –

(a) that under the law prevailing in a place outside England and Wales a person ('M') has been appointed to exercise powers in respect of the property or affairs of P on the ground (however formulated) that P lacks capacity to make decisions with respect to the management and administration of his property and affairs, and
(b) that, having regard to the nature of the appointment and to the circumstances of the case, it is expedient that the court should exercise its powers under this paragraph.

(2) The court may direct –

(a) any stocks standing in the name of P, or
(b) the right to receive dividends from the stocks,

to be transferred into M's name or otherwise dealt with as required by M, and may give such directions as the court thinks fit for dealing with accrued dividends from the stocks.

(3) 'Stocks' includes –

(a) shares, and
(b) any funds, annuity or security transferable in the books kept by any body corporate or unincorporated company or society or by an instrument of transfer either alone or accompanied by other formalities,

and 'dividends' is to be construed accordingly.

8 Preservation of interests in property disposed of on behalf of person lacking capacity

(1) Sub-paragraphs (2) and (3) apply if –

(a) P's property has been disposed of by virtue of section 18,
(b) under P's will or intestacy, or by a gift perfected or nomination taking effect on his death, any other person would have taken an interest in the property but for the disposal, and
(c) on P's death, any property belonging to P's estate represents the property disposed of.

(2) The person takes the same interest, if and so far as circumstances allow, in the property representing the property disposed of.

(3) If the property disposed of was real property, any property representing it is to be treated, so long as it remains part of P's estate, as if it were real property.

(4) The court may direct that, on a disposal of P's property –

(a) which is made by virtue of section 18, and
(b) which would apart from this paragraph result in the conversion of personal property into real property,

property representing the property disposed of is to be treated, so long as it remains P's property or forms part of P's estate, as if it were personal property.

(5) References in sub-paragraphs (1) to (4) to the disposal of property are to –

(a) the sale, exchange, charging of or other dealing (otherwise than by will) with property other than money;
(b) the removal of property from one place to another;
(c) the application of money in acquiring property;
(d) the transfer of money from one account to another;

and references to property representing property disposed of are to be construed accordingly and as including the result of successive disposals.

(6) The court may give such directions as appear to it necessary or expedient for the purpose of facilitating the operation of sub-paragraphs (1) to (3), including the carrying of money to a separate account and the transfer of property other than money.

9 (1) Sub-paragraph (2) applies if the court has ordered or directed the expenditure of money –

(a) for carrying out permanent improvements on any of P's property, or
(b) otherwise for the permanent benefit of any of P's property.

(2) The court may order that –

(a) the whole of the money expended or to be expended, or
(b) any part of it,

is to be a charge on the property either without interest or with interest at a specified rate.

(3) An order under sub-paragraph (2) may provide for excluding or restricting the operation of paragraph 8(1) to (3).

(4) A charge under sub-paragraph (2) may be made in favour of such person as may be just and, in particular, where the money charged is paid out of P's general estate, may be made in favour of a person as trustee for P.

(5) No charge under sub-paragraph (2) may confer any right of sale or foreclosure during P's lifetime.

10 Powers as patron of benefice

(1) Any functions which P has as patron of a benefice may be discharged only by a person ('R') appointed by the court.

(2) R must be an individual capable of appointment under section 8(1)(b) of the 1986 Measure (which provides for an individual able to make a declaration of communicant status, a clerk in Holy Orders, etc to be appointed to discharge a registered patron's functions).

(3) The 1986 Measure applies to R as it applies to an individual appointed by the registered patron of the benefice under section 8(1)(b) or (3) of that Measure to discharge his functions as patron.

(4) 'The 1986 Measure' means the Patronage (Benefices) Measure 1986 (No 3).

Schedule 4
Provisions Applying to Existing Enduring Powers of Attorney

Section 66(3)

PART 1
ENDURING POWERS OF ATTORNEY

1 Enduring power of attorney to survive mental incapacity of donor

(1) Where an individual has created a power of attorney which is an enduring power within the meaning of this Schedule –

- (a) the power is not revoked by any subsequent mental incapacity of his,
- (b) upon such incapacity supervening, the donee of the power may not do anything under the authority of the power except as provided by sub-paragraph (2) unless or until the instrument creating the power is registered under paragraph 13, and
- (c) if and so long as paragraph (b) operates to suspend the donee's authority to act under the power, section 5 of the Powers of Attorney Act 1971 (protection of donee and third persons), so far as applicable, applies as if the power had been revoked by the donor's mental incapacity,

and, accordingly, section 1 of this Act does not apply.

(2) Despite sub-paragraph (1)(b), where the attorney has made an application for registration of the instrument then, until it is registered, the attorney may take action under the power –

- (a) to maintain the donor or prevent loss to his estate, or
- (b) to maintain himself or other persons in so far as paragraph 3(2) permits him to do so.

(3) Where the attorney purports to act as provided by sub-paragraph (2) then, in favour of a person who deals with him without knowledge that the attorney is acting otherwise than in accordance with sub-paragraph (2)(a) or (b), the transaction between them is as valid as if the attorney were acting in accordance with sub-paragraph (2)(a) or (b).

2 Characteristics of an enduring power of attorney

(1) Subject to sub-paragraphs (5) and (6) and paragraph 20, a power of attorney is an enduring power within the meaning of this Schedule if the instrument which creates the power –

- (a) is in the prescribed form,
- (b) was executed in the prescribed manner by the donor and the attorney, and
- (c) incorporated at the time of execution by the donor the prescribed explanatory information.

(2) In this paragraph, 'prescribed' means prescribed by such of the following regulations as applied when the instrument was executed –

(a) the Enduring Powers of Attorney (Prescribed Form) Regulations 1986,
(b) the Enduring Powers of Attorney (Prescribed Form) Regulations 1987,
(c) the Enduring Powers of Attorney (Prescribed Form) Regulations 1990,
(d) the Enduring Powers of Attorney (Welsh Language Prescribed Form) Regulations 2000.

(3) An instrument in the prescribed form purporting to have been executed in the prescribed manner is to be taken, in the absence of evidence to the contrary, to be a document which incorporated at the time of execution by the donor the prescribed explanatory information.

(4) If an instrument differs in an immaterial respect in form or mode of expression from the prescribed form it is to be treated as sufficient in point of form and expression.

(5) A power of attorney cannot be an enduring power unless, when he executes the instrument creating it, the attorney is –

(a) an individual who has reached 18 and is not bankrupt or is not subject to a debt relief order (under Part 7A of the Insolvency Act 1986), or
(b) a trust corporation.

(6) A power of attorney which gives the attorney a right to appoint a substitute or successor cannot be an enduring power.

(7) An enduring power is revoked by the bankruptcy of the donor or attorney or the making of a debt relief order (under Part 7A of the Insolvency Act 1986) in respect of the donor or attorney.

(8) But where the donor or attorney is bankrupt merely because an interim bankruptcy restrictions order has effect in respect of him or where the donor or attorney is subject to an interim debt relief restrictions order, the power is suspended for so long as the order has effect.

(9) An enduring power is revoked if the court –

(a) exercises a power under sections 16 to 20 in relation to the donor, and
(b) directs that the enduring power is to be revoked.

(10) No disclaimer of an enduring power, whether by deed or otherwise, is valid unless and until the attorney gives notice of it to the donor or, where paragraph 4(6) or 15(1) applies, to the Public Guardian.

3 Scope of authority etc of attorney under enduring power

(1) If the instrument which creates an enduring power of attorney is expressed to confer general authority on the attorney, the instrument operates to confer, subject to –

(a) the restriction imposed by sub-paragraph (3), and
(b) any conditions or restrictions contained in the instrument,

authority to do on behalf of the donor anything which the donor could lawfully do by an attorney at the time when the donor executed the instrument.

(2) Subject to any conditions or restrictions contained in the instrument, an attorney under an enduring power, whether general or limited, may (without obtaining any consent) act under the power so as to benefit himself or other persons than the donor to the following extent but no further –

(a) he may so act in relation to himself or in relation to any other person if the donor might be expected to provide for his or that person's needs respectively, and
(b) he may do whatever the donor might be expected to do to meet those needs.

(3) Without prejudice to sub-paragraph (2) but subject to any conditions or restrictions contained in the instrument, an attorney under an enduring power, whether general or limited, may (without obtaining any consent) dispose of the property of the donor by way of gift to the following extent but no further –

(a) he may make gifts of a seasonal nature or at a time, or on an anniversary, of a birth, a marriage or the formation of a civil partnership, to persons (including himself) who are related to or connected with the donor, and
(b) he may make gifts to any charity to whom the donor made or might be expected to make gifts,

provided that the value of each such gift is not unreasonable having regard to all the circumstances and in particular the size of the donor's estate.

Amendment: SI 2012/2404.

PART 2
ACTION ON ACTUAL OR IMPENDING INCAPACITY OF DONOR

4 Duties of attorney in event of actual or impending incapacity of donor

(1) Sub-paragraphs (2) to (6) apply if the attorney under an enduring power has reason to believe that the donor is or is becoming mentally incapable.

(2) The attorney must, as soon as practicable, make an application to the Public Guardian for the registration of the instrument creating the power.

(3) Before making an application for registration the attorney must comply with the provisions as to notice set out in Part 3 of this Schedule.

(4) An application for registration –

(a) must be made in the prescribed form, and
(b) must contain such statements as may be prescribed.

(5) The attorney –

(a) may, before making an application for the registration of the instrument, refer to the court for its determination any question as to the validity of the power, and
(b) must comply with any direction given to him by the court on that determination.

(6) No disclaimer of the power is valid unless and until the attorney gives notice of it to the Public Guardian; and the Public Guardian must notify the donor if he receives a notice under this sub-paragraph.

(7) A person who, in an application for registration, makes a statement which he knows to be false in a material particular is guilty of an offence and is liable –

(a) on summary conviction, to imprisonment for a term not exceeding 12 months or a fine not exceeding the statutory maximum or both;
(b) on conviction on indictment, to imprisonment for a term not exceeding 2 years or a fine or both.

(8) In this paragraph, 'prescribed' means prescribed by regulations made for the purposes of this Schedule by the Lord Chancellor.

PART 3
NOTIFICATION PRIOR TO REGISTRATION

5 Duty to give notice to relatives

Subject to paragraph 7, before making an application for registration the attorney must give notice of his intention to do so to all those persons (if any) who are entitled to receive notice by virtue of paragraph 6.

6 (1) Subject to sub-paragraphs (2) to (4), persons of the following classes ('relatives') are entitled to receive notice under paragraph 5 –

(a) the donor's spouse or civil partner,
(b) the donor's children,
(c) the donor's parents,
(d) the donor's brothers and sisters, whether of the whole or half blood,
(e) the widow, widower or surviving civil partner of a child of the donor,
(f) the donor's grandchildren,
(g) the children of the donor's brothers and sisters of the whole blood,
(h) the children of the donor's brothers and sisters of the half blood,
(i) the donor's uncles and aunts of the whole blood,
(j) the children of the donor's uncles and aunts of the whole blood.

(2) A person is not entitled to receive notice under paragraph 5 if –

(a) his name or address is not known to the attorney and cannot be reasonably ascertained by him, or
(b) the attorney has reason to believe that he has not reached 18 or is mentally incapable.

(3) Except where sub-paragraph (4) applies –

(a) no more than 3 persons are entitled to receive notice under paragraph 5, and
(b) in determining the persons who are so entitled, persons falling within the class in sub-paragraph (1)(a) are to be preferred to persons falling within the class in sub-paragraph (1)(b), those falling within the class in sub-paragraph (1)(b) are to be preferred to those falling within the class in sub-paragraph (1)(c), and so on.

(4) Despite the limit of 3 specified in sub-paragraph (3), where –

(a) there is more than one person falling within any of classes (a) to (j) of sub-paragraph (1), and
(b) at least one of those persons would be entitled to receive notice under paragraph 5,

then, subject to sub-paragraph (2), all the persons falling within that class are entitled to receive notice under paragraph 5.

7 (1) An attorney is not required to give notice under paragraph 5 –

(a) to himself, or
(b) to any other attorney under the power who is joining in making the application,

even though he or, as the case may be, the other attorney is entitled to receive notice by virtue of paragraph 6.

(2) In the case of any person who is entitled to receive notice by virtue of paragraph 6, the attorney, before applying for registration, may make an application to the court to be dispensed from the requirement to give him notice; and the court must grant the application if it is satisfied –

(a) that it would be undesirable or impracticable for the attorney to give him notice, or
(b) that no useful purpose is likely to be served by giving him notice.

8 Duty to give notice to donor

(1) Subject to sub-paragraph (2), before making an application for registration the attorney must give notice of his intention to do so to the donor.

(2) Paragraph 7(2) applies in relation to the donor as it applies in relation to a person who is entitled to receive notice under paragraph 5.

9 Contents of notices

A notice to relatives under this Part of this Schedule must –

(a) be in the prescribed form,
(b) state that the attorney proposes to make an application to the Public Guardian for the registration of the instrument creating the enduring power in question,
(c) inform the person to whom it is given of his right to object to the registration under paragraph 13(4), and
(d) specify, as the grounds on which an objection to registration may be made, the grounds set out in paragraph 13(9).

10 A notice to the donor under this Part of this Schedule –

(a) must be in the prescribed form,
(b) must contain the statement mentioned in paragraph 9(b), and
(c) must inform the donor that, while the instrument remains registered, any revocation of the power by him will be ineffective unless and until the revocation is confirmed by the court.

11 Duty to give notice to other attorneys

(1) Subject to sub-paragraph (2), before making an application for registration an attorney under a joint and several power must give notice of his intention to do so to any other attorney under the power who is not joining in making the application; and paragraphs 7(2) and 9 apply in relation to attorneys entitled to receive notice by virtue of this paragraph as they apply in relation to persons entitled to receive notice by virtue of paragraph 6.

(2) An attorney is not entitled to receive notice by virtue of this paragraph if –

(a) his address is not known to the applying attorney and cannot reasonably be ascertained by him, or
(b) the applying attorney has reason to believe that he has not reached 18 or is mentally incapable.

12 Supplementary

Despite section 7 of the Interpretation Act 1978 (construction of references to service by post), for the purposes of this Part of this Schedule a notice given by post is to be regarded as given on the date on which it was posted.

PART 4
REGISTRATION

13 Registration of instrument creating power

(1) If an application is made in accordance with paragraph 4(3) and (4) the Public Guardian must, subject to the provisions of this paragraph, register the instrument to which the application relates.

(2) If it appears to the Public Guardian that –

(a) there is a deputy appointed for the donor of the power created by the instrument, and

(b) the powers conferred on the deputy would, if the instrument were registered, to any extent conflict with the powers conferred on the attorney,

the Public Guardian must not register the instrument except in accordance with the court's directions.

(3) The court may, on the application of the attorney, direct the Public Guardian to register an instrument even though notice has not been given as required by paragraph 4(3) and Part 3 of this Schedule to a person entitled to receive it, if the court is satisfied –

(a) that it was undesirable or impracticable for the attorney to give notice to that person, or

(b) that no useful purpose is likely to be served by giving him notice.

(4) Sub-paragraph (5) applies if, before the end of the period of 5 weeks beginning with the date (or the latest date) on which the attorney gave notice under paragraph 5 of an application for registration, the Public Guardian receives a valid notice of objection to the registration from a person entitled to notice of the application.

(5) The Public Guardian must not register the instrument except in accordance with the court's directions.

(6) Sub-paragraph (7) applies if, in the case of an application for registration –

(a) it appears from the application that there is no one to whom notice has been given under paragraph 5, or

(b) the Public Guardian has reason to believe that appropriate inquiries might bring to light evidence on which he could be satisfied that one of the grounds of objection set out in sub-paragraph (9) was established.

(7) The Public Guardian –

(a) must not register the instrument, and

(b) must undertake such inquiries as he thinks appropriate in all the circumstances.

(8) If, having complied with sub-paragraph (7)(b), the Public Guardian is satisfied that one of the grounds of objection set out in sub-paragraph (9) is established –

(a) the attorney may apply to the court for directions, and

(b) the Public Guardian must not register the instrument except in accordance with the court's directions.

(9) A notice of objection under this paragraph is valid if made on one or more of the following grounds –

(a) that the power purported to have been created by the instrument was not valid as an enduring power of attorney,
(b) that the power created by the instrument no longer subsists,
(c) that the application is premature because the donor is not yet becoming mentally incapable,
(d) that fraud or undue pressure was used to induce the donor to create the power,
(e) that, having regard to all the circumstances and in particular the attorney's relationship to or connection with the donor, the attorney is unsuitable to be the donor's attorney.

(10) If any of those grounds is established to the satisfaction of the court it must direct the Public Guardian not to register the instrument, but if not so satisfied it must direct its registration.

(11) If the court directs the Public Guardian not to register an instrument because it is satisfied that the ground in sub-paragraph (9)(d) or (e) is established, it must by order revoke the power created by the instrument.

(12) If the court directs the Public Guardian not to register an instrument because it is satisfied that any ground in sub-paragraph (9) except that in paragraph (c) is established, the instrument must be delivered up to be cancelled unless the court otherwise directs.

14 Register of enduring powers

The Public Guardian has the function of establishing and maintaining a register of enduring powers for the purposes of this Schedule.

PART 5
LEGAL POSITION AFTER REGISTRATION

15 Effect and proof of registration

(1) The effect of the registration of an instrument under paragraph 13 is that –

(a) no revocation of the power by the donor is valid unless and until the court confirms the revocation under paragraph 16(3);
(b) no disclaimer of the power is valid unless and until the attorney gives notice of it to the Public Guardian;
(c) the donor may not extend or restrict the scope of the authority conferred by the instrument and no instruction or consent given by him after registration, in the case of a consent, confers any right and, in the case of an instruction, imposes or confers any obligation or right on or creates any liability of the attorney or other persons having notice of the instruction or consent.

(2) Sub-paragraph (1) applies for so long as the instrument is registered under paragraph 13 whether or not the donor is for the time being mentally incapable.

(3) A document purporting to be an office copy of an instrument registered under this Schedule is, in any part of the United Kingdom, evidence of –

(a) the contents of the instrument, and
(b) the fact that it has been so registered.

(4) Sub-paragraph (3) is without prejudice to section 3 of the Powers of Attorney Act 1971 (proof by certified copies) and to any other method of proof authorised by law.

16 Functions of court with regard to registered power

(1) Where an instrument has been registered under paragraph 13, the court has the following functions with respect to the power and the donor of and the attorney appointed to act under the power.

(2) The court may –

(a) determine any question as to the meaning or effect of the instrument;
(b) give directions with respect to –
  (i) the management or disposal by the attorney of the property and affairs of the donor;
  (ii) the rendering of accounts by the attorney and the production of the records kept by him for the purpose;
  (iii) the remuneration or expenses of the attorney whether or not in default of or in accordance with any provision made by the instrument, including directions for the repayment of excessive or the payment of additional remuneration;
(c) require the attorney to supply information or produce documents or things in his possession as attorney;
(d) give any consent or authorisation to act which the attorney would have to obtain from a mentally capable donor;
(e) authorise the attorney to act so as to benefit himself or other persons than the donor otherwise than in accordance with paragraph 3(2) and (3) (but subject to any conditions or restrictions contained in the instrument);
(f) relieve the attorney wholly or partly from any liability which he has or may have incurred on account of a breach of his duties as attorney.

(3) On application made for the purpose by or on behalf of the donor, the court must confirm the revocation of the power if satisfied that the donor –

(a) has done whatever is necessary in law to effect an express revocation of the power, and
(b) was mentally capable of revoking a power of attorney when he did so (whether or not he is so when the court considers the application).

(4) The court must direct the Public Guardian to cancel the registration of an instrument registered under paragraph 13 in any of the following circumstances –

(a) on confirming the revocation of the power under sub-paragraph (3),
(b) on directing under paragraph 2(9)(b) that the power is to be revoked,
(c) on being satisfied that the donor is and is likely to remain mentally capable,
(d) on being satisfied that the power has expired or has been revoked by the mental incapacity of the attorney,
(e) on being satisfied that the power was not a valid and subsisting enduring power when registration was effected,
(f) on being satisfied that fraud or undue pressure was used to induce the donor to create the power,

(g) on being satisfied that, having regard to all the circumstances and in particular the attorney's relationship to or connection with the donor, the attorney is unsuitable to be the donor's attorney.

(5) If the court directs the Public Guardian to cancel the registration of an instrument on being satisfied of the matters specified in sub-paragraph (4)(f) or (g) it must by order revoke the power created by the instrument.

(6) If the court directs the cancellation of the registration of an instrument under sub-paragraph (4) except paragraph (c) the instrument must be delivered up to the Public Guardian to be cancelled, unless the court otherwise directs.

17 Cancellation of registration by Public Guardian

The Public Guardian must cancel the registration of an instrument creating an enduring power of attorney –

(a) on receipt of a disclaimer signed by the attorney;
(b) if satisfied that the power has been revoked by the death or bankruptcy of the donor or attorney or the making of a debt relief order (under Part 7A of the Insolvency Act 1986) in respect of the donor or attorney or, if the attorney is a body corporate, by its winding up or dissolution;
(c) on receipt of notification from the court that the court has revoked the power;
(d) on confirmation from the court that the donor has revoked the power.

Amendments: SI 2012/2404.

PART 6
PROTECTION OF ATTORNEY AND THIRD PARTIES

18 Protection of attorney and third persons where power is invalid or revoked

(1) Sub-paragraphs (2) and (3) apply where an instrument which did not create a valid power of attorney has been registered under paragraph 13 (whether or not the registration has been cancelled at the time of the act or transaction in question).

(2) An attorney who acts in pursuance of the power does not incur any liability (either to the donor or to any other person) because of the non-existence of the power unless at the time of acting he knows –

(a) that the instrument did not create a valid enduring power,
(b) that an event has occurred which, if the instrument had created a valid enduring power, would have had the effect of revoking the power, or
(c) that, if the instrument had created a valid enduring power, the power would have expired before that time.

(3) Any transaction between the attorney and another person is, in favour of that person, as valid as if the power had then been in existence, unless at the time of the transaction that person has knowledge of any of the matters mentioned in sub-paragraph (2).

(4) If the interest of a purchaser depends on whether a transaction between the attorney and another person was valid by virtue of sub-paragraph (3), it is conclusively presumed in favour of the purchaser that the transaction was valid if –

(a) the transaction between that person and the attorney was completed within 12 months of the date on which the instrument was registered, or

(b) that person makes a statutory declaration, before or within 3 months after the completion of the purchase, that he had no reason at the time of the transaction to doubt that the attorney had authority to dispose of the property which was the subject of the transaction.

(5) For the purposes of section 5 of the Powers of Attorney Act 1971 (protection where power is revoked) in its application to an enduring power the revocation of which by the donor is by virtue of paragraph 15 invalid unless and until confirmed by the court under paragraph 16 –

(a) knowledge of the confirmation of the revocation is knowledge of the revocation of the power, but
(b) knowledge of the unconfirmed revocation is not.

19 Further protection of attorney and third persons

(1) If –

(a) an instrument framed in a form prescribed as mentioned in paragraph 2(2) creates a power which is not a valid enduring power, and
(b) the power is revoked by the mental incapacity of the donor,

sub-paragraphs (2) and (3) apply, whether or not the instrument has been registered.

(2) An attorney who acts in pursuance of the power does not, by reason of the revocation, incur any liability (either to the donor or to any other person) unless at the time of acting he knows –

(a) that the instrument did not create a valid enduring power, and
(b) that the donor has become mentally incapable.

(3) Any transaction between the attorney and another person is, in favour of that person, as valid as if the power had then been in existence, unless at the time of the transaction that person knows –

(a) that the instrument did not create a valid enduring power, and
(b) that the donor has become mentally incapable.

(4) Paragraph 18(4) applies for the purpose of determining whether a transaction was valid by virtue of sub-paragraph (3) as it applies for the purpose or determining whether a transaction was valid by virtue of paragraph 18(3).

PART 7
JOINT AND JOINT AND SEVERAL ATTORNEYS

20 Application to joint and joint and several attorneys

(1) An instrument which appoints more than one person to be an attorney cannot create an enduring power unless the attorneys are appointed to act –

(a) jointly, or
(b) jointly and severally.

(2) This Schedule, in its application to joint attorneys, applies to them collectively as it applies to a single attorney but subject to the modifications specified in paragraph 21.

(3) This Schedule, in its application to joint and several attorneys, applies with the modifications specified in sub-paragraphs (4) to (7) and in paragraph 22.

(4) A failure, as respects any one attorney, to comply with the requirements for the creation of enduring powers –

- (a) prevents the instrument from creating such a power in his case, but
- (b) does not affect its efficacy for that purpose as respects the other or others or its efficacy in his case for the purpose of creating a power of attorney which is not an enduring power.

(5) If one or more but not both or all the attorneys makes or joins in making an application for registration of the instrument –

- (a) an attorney who is not an applicant as well as one who is may act pending the registration of the instrument as provided in paragraph 1(2),
- (b) notice of the application must also be given under Part 3 of this Schedule to the other attorney or attorneys, and
- (c) objection may validly be taken to the registration on a ground relating to an attorney or to the power of an attorney who is not an applicant as well as to one or the power of one who is an applicant.

(6) The Public Guardian is not precluded by paragraph 13(5) or (8) from registering an instrument and the court must not direct him not to do so under paragraph 13(10) if an enduring power subsists as respects some attorney who is not affected by the ground or grounds of the objection in question; and where the Public Guardian registers an instrument in that case, he must make against the registration an entry in the prescribed form.

(7) Sub-paragraph (6) does not preclude the court from revoking a power in so far as it confers a power on any other attorney in respect of whom the ground in paragraph 13(9)(d) or (e) is established; and where any ground in paragraph 13(9) affecting any other attorney is established the court must direct the Public Guardian to make against the registration an entry in the prescribed form.

(8) In sub-paragraph (4), 'the requirements for the creation of enduring powers' means the provisions of –

- (a) paragraph 2 other than sub-paragraphs (8) and (9), and
- (b) the regulations mentioned in paragraph 2.

21 Joint attorneys

(1) In paragraph 2(5), the reference to the time when the attorney executes the instrument is to be read as a reference to the time when the second or last attorney executes the instrument.

(2) In paragraph 2(6) to (8), the reference to the attorney is to be read as a reference to any attorney under the power.

(3) Paragraph 13 has effect as if the ground of objection to the registration of the instrument specified in sub-paragraph (9)(e) applied to any attorney under the power.

(4) In paragraph 16(2), references to the attorney are to be read as including references to any attorney under the power.

(5) In paragraph 16(4), references to the attorney are to be read as including references to any attorney under the power.

(6) In paragraph 17, references to the attorney are to be read as including references to any attorney under the power.

22 Joint and several attorneys

(1) In paragraph 2(7), the reference to the bankruptcy of the attorney is to be read as a reference to the bankruptcy of the last remaining attorney under the power; and the bankruptcy of any other attorney under the power causes that person to cease to be an attorney under the power.

(1A) In paragraph 2(7), the reference to the making of a debt relief order (under Part 7A of the Insolvency Act 1986) in respect of the attorney is to be read as a reference to the making of a debt relief order in respect of the last remaining attorney under the power; and the making of a debt relief order in respect of any other attorney under the power causes that person to cease to be an attorney under the power.

(2) In paragraph 2(8), the reference to the suspension of the power is to be read as a reference to its suspension in so far as it relates to the attorney in respect of whom the interim bankruptcy restrictions order has effect.

(2A) In paragraph 2(8), the reference to the suspension of the power is to be read as a reference to its suspension in so far as it relates to the attorney in respect of whom the interim debt relief restrictions order has effect.

(3) The restriction upon disclaimer imposed by paragraph 4(6) applies only to those attorneys who have reason to believe that the donor is or is becoming mentally incapable.

Amendments: SI 2012/2404.

PART 8
INTERPRETATION

23 (1) In this Schedule –

'enduring power' is to be construed in accordance with paragraph 2,

'mentally incapable' or 'mental incapacity', except where it refers to revocation at commonlaw, means in relation to any person, that he is incapable by reason of mental disorder of managing and administering his property and affairs and 'mentally capable' and 'mental capacity' are to be construed accordingly,

'notice' means notice in writing, and

'prescribed', except for the purposes of paragraph 2, means prescribed by regulations made for the purposes of this Schedule by the Lord Chancellor.

(1A) In sub-paragraph (1), 'mental disorder' has the same meaning as in the Mental Health Act but disregarding the amendments made to that Act by the Mental Health Act 2007.

(2) Any question arising under or for the purposes of this Schedule as to what the donor of the power might at any time be expected to do is to be determined by assuming that he had full mental capacity at the time but otherwise by reference to the circumstances existing at that time.

Amendments: Mental Health Act 2007, ss 1(4), 55, Sch 1, Pt 2, para 23(1)-(3), Sch 11, Pt 1.

MENTAL HEALTH ACT 1983

PART I
APPLICATION OF ACT

1 Application of Act: 'mental disorder'

(1) The provisions of this Act shall have effect with respect to the reception, care and treatment of mentally disordered patients, the management of their property and other related matters.

(2) In this Act–

'mental disorder' means any disorder or disability of the mind; and
'mentally disordered' shall be construed accordingly;

and other expressions shall have the meanings assigned to them in section 145 below.

(2A) But a person with learning disability shall not be considered by reason of that disability to be –

(a) suffering from mental disorder for the purposes of the provisions mentioned in subsection (2B) below; or
(b) requiring treatment in hospital for mental disorder for the purposes of sections 17E and 50 to 53 below,

unless that disability is associated with abnormally aggressive or seriously irresponsible conduct on his part.

(2B) The provisions are –

(a) sections 3, 7, 17A, 20 and 20A below;
(b) sections 35 to 38, 45A, 47, 48 and 51 below; and
(c) section 72(1)(b) and (c) and (4) below.

(3) Dependence on alcohol or drugs is not considered to be a disorder or disability of the mind for the purposes of subsection (2) above.

(4) In subsection (2A) above, 'learning disability' means a state of arrested or incomplete development of the mind which includes significant impairment of intelligence and social functioning.

Amendments: Mental Health Act 2007.

PART II
COMPULSORY ADMISSION TO HOSPITAL AND GUARDIANSHIP

Procedure for hospital admission

2 Admission for assessment

(1) A patient may be admitted to a hospital and detained there for the period allowed by subsection (4) below in pursuance of an application (in this Act referred to as 'an application for admission for assessment') made in accordance with subsections (2) and (3) below.

(2) An application for admission for assessment may be made in respect of a patient on the grounds that–

(a) he is suffering from mental disorder of a nature or degree which warrants the detention of the patient in a hospital for assessment (or for assessment followed by medical treatment) for at least a limited period; and
(b) he ought to be so detained in the interests of his own health or safety or with a view to the protection of other persons.

(3) An application for admission for assessment shall be founded on the written recommendations in the prescribed form of two registered medical practitioners, including in each case a statement that in the opinion of the practitioner the conditions set out in subsection (2) above are complied with.

(4) Subject to the provisions of section 29(4) below, a patient admitted to hospital in pursuance of an application for admission for assessment may be detained for a period not exceeding 28 days beginning with the day on which he is admitted, but shall not be detained after the expiration of that period unless before it has expired he has become liable to be detained by virtue of a subsequent application, order or direction under the following provisions of this Act.

3 Admission for treatment

(1) A patient may be admitted to a hospital and detained there for the period allowed by the following provisions of this Act in pursuance of an application (in this Act referred to as 'an application for admission for treatment') made in accordance with this section.

(2) An application for admission for treatment may be made in respect of a patient on the grounds that–

(a) he is suffering from mental disorder of a nature or degree which makes it appropriate for him to receive medical treatment in a hospital; and
(b) . . .
(c) it is necessary for the health or safety of the patient or for the protection of other persons that he should receive such treatment and it cannot be provided unless he is detained under this section; and
(d) appropriate medical treatment is available for him.

(3) An application for admission for treatment shall be founded on the written recommendations in the prescribed form of two registered medical practitioners, including in each case a statement that in the opinion of the practitioner the conditions set out in subsection (2) above are complied with; and each such recommendation shall include–

(a) such particulars as may be prescribed of the grounds for that opinion so far as it relates to the conditions set out in paragraphs (a) and (d) of that subsection; and
(b) a statement of the reasons for that opinion so far as it relates to the conditions set out in paragraph (c) of that subsection, specifying whether other methods of dealing with the patient are available and, if so, why they are not appropriate.

(4) In this Act, references to appropriate medical treatment, in relation to a person suffering from mental disorder, are references to medical treatment which is appropriate in his case, taking into account the nature and degree of the mental disorder and all other circumstances of his case.

Amendments: Mental Health Act 2007.

4 Admission for assessment in cases of emergency

(1) In any case of urgent necessity, an application for admission for assessment may be made in respect of a patient in accordance with the following provisions of this section, and any application so made is in this Act referred to as 'an emergency application'.

(2) An emergency application may be made either by an approved mental health professional or by the nearest relative of the patient; and every such application shall include a statement that it is of urgent necessity for the patient to be admitted and detained under section 2 above, and that compliance with the provisions of this Part of this Act relating to applications under that section would involve undesirable delay.

(3) An emergency application shall be sufficient in the first instance if founded on one of the medical recommendations required by section 2 above, given, if practicable, by a practitioner who has previous acquaintance with the patient and otherwise complying with the requirements of section 12 below so far as applicable to a single recommendation, and verifying the statement referred to in subsection (2) above.

(4) An emergency application shall cease to have effect on the expiration of a period of 72 hours from the time when the patient is admitted to the hospital unless–

- (a) the second medical recommendation required by section 2 above is given and received by the managers within that period; and
- (b) that recommendation and the recommendation referred to in subsection (3) above together comply with all the requirements of section 12 below (other than the requirement as to the time of signature of the second recommendation).

(5) In relation to an emergency application, section 11 below shall have effect as if in subsection (5) of that section for the words 'the period of 14 days ending with the date of the application' there were substituted the words 'the previous 24 hours'.

Amendments: Mental Health Act 2007.

5 Application in respect of patient already in hospital

(1) An application for the admission of a patient to a hospital may be made under this Part of this Act notwithstanding that the patient is already an in-patient in that hospital or, in the case of an application for admission for treatment, that the patient is for the time being liable to be detained in the hospital in pursuance of an application for admission for assessment; and where an application is so made the patient shall be treated for the purposes of this Part of this Act as if he had been admitted to the hospital at the time when that application was received by the managers.

(2) If, in the case of a patient who is an in-patient in a hospital, it appears to the registered medical practitioner or approved clinician in charge of the treatment of the patient that an application ought to be made under this Part of this Act for the admission of the patient to hospital, he may furnish to the managers a report in writing to that effect; and in any such case the patient may be detained in the hospital for a period of 72 hours from the time when the report is so furnished.

(3) The registered medical practitioner or approved clinician in charge of the treatment of a patient in a hospital may nominate one (but not more than one) person to act for him under subsection (2) above in his absence.

(3A) For the purposes of subsection (3) above –

(a) the registered medical practitioner may nominate another registered medical practitioner, or an approved clinician, on the staff of the hospital; and
(b) the approved clinician may nominate another approved clinician, or a registered medical practitioner, on the staff of the hospital.

(4) If, in the case of a patient who is receiving treatment for mental disorder as an in-patient in a hospital, it appears to a nurse of the prescribed class–

(a) that the patient is suffering from mental disorder to such a degree that it is necessary for his health or safety or for the protection of others for him to be immediately restrained from leaving the hospital; and
(b) that it is not practicable to secure the immediate attendance of a practitioner or clinician for the purpose of furnishing a report under subsection (2) above,

the nurse may record that fact in writing; and in that event the patient may be detained in the hospital for a period of six hours from the time when that fact is so recorded or until the earlier arrival at the place where the patient is detained of a practitioner having power to furnish a report under that subsection.

(5) A record made under subsection (4) above shall be delivered by the nurse (or by a person authorised by the nurse in that behalf) to the managers of the hospital as soon as possible after it is made; and where a record is made under that subsection the period mentioned in subsection (2) above shall begin at the time when it is made.

(6) The reference in subsection (1) above to an in-patient does not include an in-patient who is liable to be detained in pursuance of an application under this Part of this Act or a community patient and the references in subsections (2) and (4) above do not include an in-patient who is liable to be detained in a hospital under this Part of this Act or a community patient.

(7) In subsection (4) above 'prescribed' means prescribed by an order made by the Secretary of State.

Amendments: Mental Health Act 2007.

6 Effect of application for admission

(1) An application for the admission of a patient to a hospital under this Part of this Act, duly completed in accordance with the provisions of this Part of this Act, shall be sufficient authority for the applicant, or any person authorised by the applicant, to take the patient and convey him to the hospital at any time within the following period, that is to say–

(a) in the case of an application other than an emergency application, the period of 14 days beginning with the date on which the patient was last examined by a registered medical practitioner before giving a medical recommendation for the purposes of the application;
(b) in the case of an emergency application, the period of 24 hours beginning at the time when the patient was examined by the practitioner giving the medical recommendation which is referred to in section 4(3) above, or at the time when the application is made, whichever is the earlier.

(2) Where a patient is admitted within the said period to the hospital specified in such an application as is mentioned in subsection (1) above, or, being within that hospital, is treated by virtue of section 5 above as if he had been so admitted, the application shall be sufficient authority for the managers to detain the patient in the hospital in accordance with the provisions of this Act.

(3) Any application for the admission of a patient under this Part of this Act which appears to be duly made and to be founded on the necessary medical recommendations may be acted upon without further proof of the signature or qualification of the person by whom the application or any such medical recommendation is made or given or of any matter of fact or opinion stated in it.

(4) Where a patient is admitted to a hospital in pursuance of an application for admission for treatment, any previous application under this Part of this Act by virtue of which he was liable to be detained in a hospital or subject to guardianship shall cease to have effect.

Guardianship

7 Application for guardianship

(1) A patient who has attained the age of 16 years may be received into guardianship, for the period allowed by the following provisions of this Act, in pursuance of an application (in this Act referred to as 'a guardianship application') made in accordance with this section.

(2) A guardianship application may be made in respect of a patient on the grounds that–

(a) he is suffering from mental disorder of a nature or degree which warrants his reception into guardianship under this section; and
(b) it is necessary in the interests of the welfare of the patient or for the protection of other persons that the patient should be so received.

(3) A guardianship application shall be founded on the written recommendations in the prescribed form of two registered medical practitioners, including in each case a statement that in the opinion of the practitioner the conditions set out in subsection (2) above are complied with; and each such recommendation shall include–

(a) such particulars as may be prescribed of the grounds for that opinion so far as it relates to the conditions set out in paragraph (a) of that subsection; and
(b) a statement of the reasons for that opinion so far as it relates to the conditions set out in paragraph (b) of that subsection.

(4) A guardianship application shall state the age of the patient or, if his exact age is not known to the applicant, shall state (if it be the fact) that the patient is believed to have attained the age of 16 years.

(5) The person named as guardian in a guardianship application may be either a local social services authority or any other person (including the applicant himself); but a guardianship application in which a person other than a local social services authority is named as guardian shall be of no effect unless it is accepted on behalf of that person by the local social services authority for the area in which he resides, and shall be accompanied by a statement in writing by that person that he is willing to act as guardian.

Amendments: Mental Health Act 2007

8 Effect of guardianship application, etc

(1) Where a guardianship application, duly made under the provisions of this Part of this Act and forwarded to the local social services authority within the period allowed by subsection (2) below is accepted by that authority, the application shall, subject to

regulations made by the Secretary of State, confer on the authority or person named in the application as guardian, to the exclusion of any other person–

(a) the power to require the patient to reside at a place specified by the authority or person named as guardian;

(b) the power to require the patient to attend at places and times so specified for the purpose of medical treatment, occupation, education or training;

(c) the power to require access to the patient to be given, at any place where the patient is residing, to any registered medical practitioner, approved mental health professional or other person so specified.

(2) The period within which a guardianship application is required for the purposes of this section to be forwarded to the local social services authority is the period of 14 days beginning with the date on which the patient was last examined by a registered medical practitioner before giving a medical recommendation for the purposes of the application.

(3) A guardianship application which appears to be duly made and to be founded on the necessary medical recommendations may be acted upon without further proof of the signature or qualification of the person by whom the application or any such medical recommendation is made or given, or of any matter of fact or opinion stated in the application.

(4) If within the period of 14 days beginning with the day on which a guardianship application has been accepted by the local social services authority the application, or any medical recommendation given for the purposes of the application, is found to be in any respect incorrect or defective, the application or recommendation may, within that period and with the consent of that authority, be amended by the person by whom it was signed; and upon such amendment being made the application or recommendation shall have effect and shall be deemed to have had effect as if it had been originally made as so amended.

(5) Where a patient is received into guardianship in pursuance of a guardianship application, any previous application under this Part of this Act by virtue of which he was subject to guardianship or liable to be detained in a hospital shall cease to have effect.

Amendments: Mental Health Act 2007.

9 Regulations as to guardianship

(1) Subject to the provisions of this Part of this Act, the Secretary of State may make regulation–

(a) for regulating the exercise by the guardians of patients received into guardianship under this Part of this Act of their powers as such; and

(b) for imposing on such guardians, and upon local social services authorities in the case of patients under the guardianship of persons other than local social services authorities, such duties as he considers necessary or expedient in the interests of the patients.

(2) Regulations under this section may in particular make provision for requiring the patients to be visited, on such occasions or at such intervals as may be prescribed by the regulations, on behalf of such local social services authorities as may be so prescribed, and shall provide for the appointment, in the case of every patient subject to the guardianship of a person other than a local social services authority, of a registered medical practitioner to act as the nominated medical attendant of the patient.

10 Transfer of guardianship in case of death, incapacity, etc of guardian

(1) If any person (other than a local social services authority) who is the guardian of a patient received into guardianship under this Part of this Act–

(a) dies; or
(b) gives notice in writing to the local social services authority that he desires to relinquish the functions of guardian,

the guardianship of the patient shall thereupon vest in the local social services authority, but without prejudice to any power to transfer the patient into the guardianship of another person in pursuance of regulations under section 19 below.

(2) If any such person, not having given notice under subsection (1)(b) above, is incapacitated by illness or any other cause from performing the functions of guardian of the patient, those functions may, during his incapacity, be performed on his behalf by the local social services authority or by any other person approved for the purposes by that authority.

(3) If it appears to the county court, upon application made by an approved mental health professional acting on behalf of the local social services authority, that any person other than a local social services authority having the guardianship of a patient received into guardianship under this Part of this Act has performed his functions negligently or in a manner contrary to the interests of the welfare of the patient, the court may order that the guardianship of the patient be transferred to the local social services authority or to any other person approved for the purpose by that authority.

(4) Where the guardianship of a patient is transferred to a local social services authority or other person by or under this section, subsection (2)(c) of section 19 below shall apply as if the patient had been transferred into the guardianship of that authority or person in pursuance of regulations under that section.

(5) In this section 'the local social services authority', in relation to a person (other than a local social services authority) who is the guardian of a patient, means the local social services authority for the area in which that person resides (or resided immediately before his death).

Amendment: Mental Health Act 2007.

General provisions as to applications and recommendations

11 General provisions as to applications

(1) Subject to the provisions of this section, an application for admission for assessment, an application for admission for treatment and a guardianship application may be made either by the nearest relative of the patient or by an approved mental health professional ; and every such application shall specify the qualification of the applicant to make the application.

(1A) No application mentioned in subsection (1) above shall be made by an approved mental health professional if the circumstances are such that there would be a potential conflict of interest for the purposes of regulations under section 12A below.

(2) Every application for admission shall be addressed to the managers of the hospital to which admission is sought and every guardianship application shall be forwarded to the local social services authority named in the application as guardian, or, as the case may be, to the local social services authority for the area in which the person so named resides.

(3) Before or within a reasonable time after an application for the admission of a patient for assessment is made by an approved mental health professional, that professional shall take such steps as are practicable to inform the person (if any) appearing to be the nearest relative of the patient that the application is to be or has been made and of the power of the nearest relative under section 23(2)(a) below.

(4) An approved mental health professional may not make an application for admission for treatment or a guardianship application in respect of a patient in either of the following cases –

- (a) the nearest relative of the patient has notified that professional, or the local social services authority on whose behalf the professional is acting, that he objects to the application being made; or
- (b) that professional has not consulted the person (if any) appearing to be the nearest relative of the patient, but the requirement to consult that person does not apply if it appears to the professional that in the circumstances such consultation is not reasonably practicable or would involve unreasonable delay.(5) None of the applications mentioned in subsection (1) above shall be made by any person in respect of a patient unless that person has personally seen the patient within the period of 14 days ending with the date of the application.

(6) (*repealed*)

(7) Each of the applications mentioned in subsection (1) above shall be sufficient if the recommendations on which it is founded are given either as separate recommendations, each signed by a registered medical practitioner, or as a joint recommendation signed by two such practitioners.

Amendments: Mental Health Act 2007.

12 General provisions as to medical recommendations

(1) The recommendations required for the purposes of an application for the admission of a patient under this Part of this Act or a guardianship application (in this Act referred to as 'medical recommendations') shall be signed on or before the date of the application, and shall be given by practitioners who have personally examined the patient either together or separately, but where they have examined the patient separately not more than five days must have elapsed between the days on which the separate examinations took place.

(2) Of the medical recommendations given for the purposes of any such application, one shall be given by a practitioner approved for the purposes of this section by the Secretary of State as having special experience in the diagnosis or treatment of mental disorder; and unless that practitioner has previous acquaintance with the patient, the other such recommendation shall, if practicable, be given by a registered medical practitioner who has such previous acquaintance.

(2A) A registered medical practitioner who is an approved clinician shall be treated as also approved for the purposes of this section under subsection (2) above as having special experience as mentioned there.

(3) No medical recommendation shall be given for the purposes of an application mentioned in subsection (1) above if the circumstances are such that there would be a potential conflict of interest for the purposes of regulations under section 12A below.

Amendments: Care Standards Act 2000; Health and Social Care (Community Health and Standards) Act 2003; Civil Partnership Act 2004; National Health Service (Consequential Provisions) Act 2006; Mental Health Act 2007.

12ZA Agreement for exercise of approval function: England

(1) The Secretary of State may enter into an agreement with another person for an approval function of the Secretary of State to be exercisable by the Secretary of State concurrently –

(a) with that other person, and
(b) if a requirement under section 12ZB has effect, with the other person by whom the function is exercisable under that requirement.

(2) In this section and sections 12ZB and 12ZC, 'approval function' means –

(a) the function under section 12(2), or
(b) the function of approving persons as approved clinicians.

(3) An agreement under this section may, in particular, provide for an approval function to be exercisable by the other party –

(a) in all circumstances or only in specified circumstances;
(b) in all areas or only in specified areas.

(4) An agreement under this section may provide for an approval function to be exercisable by the other party –

(a) for a period specified in the agreement, or
(b) for a period determined in accordance with the agreement.

(5) The other party to an agreement under this section must comply with such instructions as the Secretary of State may give with respect to the exercise of the approval function.

(6) An instruction under subsection (5) may require the other party to cease to exercise the function to such extent as the instruction specifies.

(7) The agreement may provide for the Secretary of State to pay compensation to the other party in the event of an instruction such as is mentioned in subsection (6) being given.

(8) An instruction under subsection (5) may be given in such form as the Secretary of State may determine.

(9) The Secretary of State must publish instructions under subsection (5) in such form as the Secretary of State may determine; but that does not apply to an instruction such as is mentioned in subsection (6).

(10) An agreement under this section may provide for the Secretary of State to make payments to the other party; and the Secretary of State may make payments to other persons in connection with the exercise of an approval function by virtue of this section.

Amendments: Inserted by the Health and Social Care Act 2012.

12ZB Requirement to exercise approval functions: England

(1) The Secretary of State may impose a requirement on the National Health Service Commissioning Board ('the Board') or a Special Health Authority for an approval function of the Secretary of State to be exercisable by the Secretary of State concurrently –

(a) with the Board or (as the case may be) Special Health Authority, and
(b) if an agreement under section 12ZA has effect, with the other person by whom the function is exercisable under that agreement.

(2) The Secretary of State may, in particular, require the body concerned to exercise an approval function –

(a) in all circumstances or only in specified circumstances;
(b) in all areas or only in specified areas.

(3) The Secretary of State may require the body concerned to exercise an approval function –

(a) for a period specified in the requirement, or
(b) for a period determined in accordance with the requirement.

(4) Where a requirement under subsection (1) is imposed, the Board or (as the case may be) Special Health Authority must comply with such instructions as the Secretary of State may give with respect to the exercise of the approval function.

(5) An instruction under subsection (4) may be given in such form as the Secretary of State may determine.

(6) The Secretary of State must publish instructions under subsection (4) in such form as the Secretary of State may determine.

(7) Where the Board or a Special Health Authority has an approval function by virtue of this section, the function is to be treated for the purposes of the National Health Service Act 2006 as a function that it has under that Act.

(8) The Secretary of State may make payments in connection with the exercise of an approval function by virtue of this section.

Amendments: Inserted by the Health and Social Care Act 2012.

12ZC Provision of information for the purposes of section 12ZA or 12ZB

(1) A relevant person may provide another person with such information as the relevant person considers necessary or appropriate for or in connection with –

(a) the exercise of an approval function; or
(b) the exercise by the Secretary of State of the power –
 (i) to enter into an agreement under section 12ZA;
 (ii) to impose a requirement under section 12ZB; or
 (iii) to give an instruction under section 12ZA(5) or 12ZB(4).

(2) The relevant persons are –

(a) the Secretary of State;
(b) a person who is a party to an agreement under section 12ZA; or
(c) if the Secretary of State imposes a requirement under section 12ZB on the National Health Service Commissioning Board or a Special Health Authority, the Board or (as the case may be) Special Health Authority.

(3) This section, in so far as it authorises the provision of information by one relevant person to another relevant person, has effect notwithstanding any rule of common law which would otherwise prohibit or restrict the provision.

(4) In this section, 'information' includes documents and records.

Amendments: Inserted by the Health and Social Care Act 2012.

12A Conflicts of interest

(1) The appropriate national authority may make regulations as to the circumstances in which there would be a potential conflict of interest such that –

- (a) an approved mental health professional shall not make an application mentioned in section 11(1) above;
- (b) a registered medical practitioner shall not give a recommendation for the purposes of an application mentioned in section 12(1) above.

(2) Regulations under subsection (1) above may make –

- (a) provision for the prohibitions in paragraphs (a) and (b) of that subsection to be subject to specified exceptions;
- (b) different provision for different cases; and
- (c) transitional, consequential, incidental or supplemental provision.

(3) In subsection (1) above, 'the appropriate national authority' means –

- (a) in relation to applications in which admission is sought to a hospital in England or to guardianship applications in respect of which the area of the relevant local social services authority is in England, the Secretary of State;
- (b) in relation to applications in which admission is sought to a hospital in Wales or to guardianship applications in respect of which the area of the relevant local social services authority is in Wales, the Welsh Ministers.

(4) References in this section to the relevant local social services authority, in relation to a guardianship application, are references to the local social services authority named in the application as guardian or (as the case may be) the local social services authority for the area in which the person so named resides.

Amendments: Inserted by Mental Health Act 2007.

13 Duty of approved mental health professionals to make applications for admission or guardianship

(1) If a local social services authority have reason to think that an application for admission to hospital or a guardianship application may need to be made in respect of a patient within their area, they shall make arrangements for an approved mental health professional to consider the patient's case on their behalf.

(1A) If that professional is –

- (a) satisfied that such an application ought to be made in respect of the patient; and
- (b) of the opinion, having regard to any wishes expressed by relatives of the patient or any other relevant circumstances, that it is necessary or proper for the application to be made by him,

he shall make the application.

(1B) Subsection (1C) below applies where –

(a) a local social services authority makes arrangements under subsection (1) above in respect of a patient;
(b) an application for admission for assessment is made under subsection (1A) above in respect of the patient;
(c) while the patient is liable to be detained in pursuance of that application, the authority have reason to think that an application for admission for treatment may need to be made in respect of the patient; and
(d) the patient is not within the area of the authority.

(1C) Where this subsection applies, subsection (1) above shall be construed as requiring the authority to make arrangements under that subsection in place of the authority mentioned there.

(2) Before making an application for the admission of a patient to hospital an approved mental health professional shall interview the patient in a suitable manner and satisfy himself that detention in a hospital is in all the circumstances of the case the most appropriate way of providing the care and medical treatment of which the patient stands in need.

(3) An application under subsection (1A) above may be made outside the area of the local social services authority on whose behalf the approved mental health professional is considering the patient's case.

(4) It shall be the duty of a local social services authority, if so required by the nearest relative of a patient residing in their area, to make arrangements under subsection (1) above for an approved mental health professional to consider the patient's case with a view to making an application for his admission to hospital; and if in any such case that professional decides not to make an application he shall inform the nearest relative of his reasons in writing.

(5) Nothing in this section shall be construed as authorising or requiring an application to be made by an approved mental health professional in contravention of the provisions of section 11(4) above or of regulations under section 12A above, or as restricting the power of a local social services authority to make arrangements with an approved mental health professional to consider a patient's case or of an approved mental health professional to make any application under this Act.

Amendments: Mental Health Act 2007.

14 Social reports

Where a patient is admitted to a hospital in pursuance of an application (other than an emergency application) made under this Part of this Act by his nearest relative, the managers of the hospital shall as soon as practicable give notice of that fact to the local social services authority for the area in which the patient resided immediately before his admission; and that authority shall as soon as practicable arrange for an approved mental health professional to interview the patient and provide the managers with a report on his social circumstances.

Amendments: Children Act 2004; Mental Health Act 2007.

15 Rectification of applications and recommendations

(1) If within the period of 14 days beginning with the day on which a patient has been admitted to a hospital in pursuance of an application for admission for assessment or for

treatment the application, or any medical recommendation given for the purposes of the application, is found to be in any respect incorrect or defective, the application or recommendation may, within that period and with the consent of the managers of the hospital, be amended by the person by whom it was signed; and upon such amendment being made the application or recommendation shall have effect and shall be deemed to have had effect as if it had been originally made as so amended.

(2) Without prejudice to subsection (1) above, if within the period mentioned in that subsection it appears to the managers of the hospital that one of the two medical recommendations on which an application for the admission of a patient is founded is insufficient to warrant the detention of the patient in pursuance of the application, they may, within that period, give notice in writing to that effect to the applicant; and where any such notice is given in respect of a medical recommendation, that recommendation shall be disregarded, but the application shall be, and shall be deemed always to have been, sufficient if–

(a) a fresh medical recommendation complying with the relevant provisions of this Part of this Act (other than the provisions relating to the time of signature and the interval between examinations) is furnished to the managers within that period; and

(b) that recommendation, and the other recommendation on which the application is founded, together comply with those provisions.

(3) Where the medical recommendations upon which an application for admission is founded are, taken together, insufficient to warrant the detention of the patient in pursuance of the application, a notice under subsection (2) above may be given in respect of either of those recommendations.

(4) Nothing in this section shall be construed as authorising the giving of notice in respect of an application made as an emergency application, or the detention of a patient admitted in pursuance of such an application, after the period of 72 hours referred to in section 4(4) above, unless the conditions set out in paragraphs (a) and (b) of that section are complied with or would be complied with apart from any error or defect to which this section applies.

Amendments: Mental Health Act 2007.

16 Position of patients subject to detention or guardianship

(*repealed*)

Amendments: Repealed by Mental Health Act 2007.

17 Leave of absence from hospital

(1) The responsible clinician may grant to any patient who is for the time being liable to be detained in a hospital under this Part of this Act leave to be absent from the hospital subject to such conditions (if any) as that clinician considers necessary in the interests of the patient or for the protection of other persons.

(2) Leave of absence may be granted to a patient under this section either indefinitely or on specified occasions or for any specified period; and where leave is so granted for a specified period, that period may be extended by further leave granted in the absence of the patient.

(2A) But longer-term leave may not be granted to a patient unless the responsible clinician first considers whether the patient should be dealt with under section 17A instead.

(2B) For these purposes, longer-term leave is granted to a patient if –

(a) leave of absence is granted to him under this section either indefinitely or for a specified period of more than seven consecutive days; or

(b) a specified period is extended under this section such that the total period for which leave of absence will have been granted to him under this section exceeds seven consecutive days.

(3) Where it appears to the responsible clinician that it is necessary so to do in the interests of the patient or for the protection of other persons, he may, upon granting leave of absence under this section, direct that the patient remain in custody during his absence; and where leave of absence is so granted the patient may be kept in the custody of any officer on the staff of the hospital, or of any other person authorised in writing by the managers of the hospital or, if the patient is required in accordance with conditions imposed on the grant of leave of absence to reside in another hospital, of any officer on the staff of that other hospital.

(4) In any case where a patient is absent from a hospital in pursuance of leave of absence granted under this section, and it appears to the responsible clinician that it is necessary so to do in the interests of the patient's health or safety or for the protection of other persons, that clinician may, subject to subsection (5) below, by notice in writing given to the patient or to the person for the time being in charge of the patient, revoke the leave of absence and recall the patient to the hospital.

(5) A patient to whom leave of absence is granted under this section shall not be recalled under subsection (4) above after he has ceased to be liable to be detained under this Part of this Act.

(6) Subsection (7) below applies to a person who is granted leave by or by virtue of a provision –

(a) in force in Scotland, Northern Ireland, any of the Channel Islands or the Isle of Man; and

(b) corresponding to subsection (1) above.

(7) For the purpose of giving effect to a direction or condition imposed by virtue of a provision corresponding to subsection (3) above, the person may be conveyed to a place in, or kept in custody or detained at a place of safety in, England and Wales by a person authorised in that behalf by the direction or condition.

Amendments: Mental Health (Patients in the Community) Act 1995; Mental Health Act 2007.

17A Community treatment orders

(1) The responsible clinician may by order in writing discharge a detained patient from hospital subject to his being liable to recall in accordance with section 17E below.

(2) A detained patient is a patient who is liable to be detained in a hospital in pursuance of an application for admission for treatment.

(3) An order under subsection (1) above is referred to in this Act as a "community treatment order".

(4) The responsible clinician may not make a community treatment order unless –

(a) in his opinion, the relevant criteria are met; and
(b) an approved mental health professional states in writing –
  (i) that he agrees with that opinion; and
  (ii) that it is appropriate to make the order.

(5) The relevant criteria are –

(a) the patient is suffering from mental disorder of a nature or degree which makes it appropriate for him to receive medical treatment;
(b) it is necessary for his health or safety or for the protection of other persons that he should receive such treatment;
(c) subject to his being liable to be recalled as mentioned in paragraph (d) below, such treatment can be provided without his continuing to be detained in a hospital;
(d) it is necessary that the responsible clinician should be able to exercise the power under section 17E(1) below to recall the patient to hospital; and
(e) appropriate medical treatment is available for him.

(6) In determining whether the criterion in subsection (5)(d) above is met, the responsible clinician shall, in particular, consider, having regard to the patient's history of mental disorder and any other relevant factors, what risk there would be of a deterioration of the patient's condition if he were not detained in a hospital (as a result, for example, of his refusing or neglecting to receive the medical treatment he requires for his mental disorder).

(7) In this Act –

"community patient" means a patient in respect of whom a community treatment order is in force;
"the community treatment order", in relation to such a patient, means the community treatment order in force in respect of him; and
"the responsible hospital", in relation to such a patient, means the hospital in which he was liable to be detained immediately before the community treatment order was made, subject to section 19A below.

Amendments: Mental Health Act 2007.

17B Conditions

(1) A community treatment order shall specify conditions to which the patient is to be subject while the order remains in force.

(2) But, subject to subsection (3) below, the order may specify conditions only if the responsible clinician, with the agreement of the approved mental health professional mentioned in section 17A(4)(b) above, thinks them necessary or appropriate for one or more of the following purposes –

(a) ensuring that the patient receives medical treatment;
(b) preventing risk of harm to the patient's health or safety;
(c) protecting other persons.

(3) The order shall specify –

(a) a condition that the patient make himself available for examination under section 20A below; and

(b) a condition that, if it is proposed to give a certificate under Part 4A of this Act that falls within section 64C(4) below in his case, he make himself available for examination so as to enable the certificate to be given.

(4) The responsible clinician may from time to time by order in writing vary the condition specified in a community treatment order.

(5) He may also suspend any conditions specified in a community treatment order.

(6) If a community patient fails to comply with a condition specified in the community treatment order by virtue of subsection (2) above, that fact may be taken into account for the purposes of exercising the power of recall under section 17E(1) below.

(7) But nothing in this section restricts the exercise of that power to cases where there is such a failure.

Amendments: Mental Health Act 2007; Health and Social Care Act 2012.

17C Duration of community treatment order

A community treatment order shall remain in force until –

(a) the period mentioned in section 20A(1) below (as extended under any provision of this Act) expires, but this is subject to sections 21 and 22 below;
(b) the patient is discharged in pursuance of an order under section 23 below or a direction under section 72 below;
(c) the application for admission for treatment in respect of the patient otherwise ceases to have effect; or
(d) the order is revoked under section 17F below, whichever occurs first.

Amendments: Mental Health Act 2007.

17D Effect of community treatment order

(1) The application for admission for treatment in respect of a patient shall not cease to have effect by virtue of his becoming a community patient.

(2) But while he remains a community patient –

(a) the authority of the managers to detain him under section 6(2) above in pursuance of that application shall be suspended; and
(b) reference (however expressed) in this or any other Act, or in any subordinate legislation (within the meaning of the Interpretation Act 1978), to patients liable to be detained, or detained, under this Act shall not include him.

(3) And section 20 below shall not apply to him while he remains a community patient.

(4) Accordingly, authority for his detention shall not expire during any period in which that authority is suspended by virtue of subsection (2)(a) above.

Amendments: Mental Health Act 2007.

17E Power to recall to hospital

(1) The responsible clinician may recall a community patient to hospital if in his opinion –

(a) the patient requires medical treatment in hospital for his mental disorder; and
(b) there would be a risk of harm to the health or safety of the patient or to other persons if the patient were not recalled to hospital for that purpose.

(2) The responsible clinician may also recall a community patient to hospital if the patient fails to comply with a condition specified under section 17B(3) above.

(3) The hospital to which a patient is recalled need not be the responsible hospital.

(4) Nothing in this section prevents a patient from being recalled to a hospital even though he is already in the hospital at the time when the power of recall is exercised; references to recalling him shall be construed accordingly.

(5) The power of recall under subsections (1) and (2) above shall be exercisable by notice in writing to the patient.

(6) A notice under this section recalling a patient to hospital shall be sufficient authority for the managers of that hospital to detain the patient there in accordance with the provisions of this Act.

Amendments: Mental Health Act 2007.

17F Powers in respect of recalled patients

(1) This section applies to a community patient who is detained in a hospital by virtue of a notice recalling him there under section 17E above.

(2) The patient may be transferred to another hospital in such circumstances and subject to such conditions as may be prescribed in regulations made by the Secretary of State (if the hospital in which the patient is detained is in England) or the Welsh Ministers (if that hospital is in Wales).

(3) If he is so transferred to another hospital, he shall be treated for the purposes of this section (and section 17E above) as if the notice under that section were a notice recalling him to that other hospital and as if he had been detained there from the time when his detention in hospital by virtue of the notice first began.

(4) The responsible clinician may by order in writing revoke the community treatment order if –

- (a) in his opinion, the conditions mentioned in section 3(2) above are satisfied in respect of the patient; and
- (b) an approved mental health professional states in writing –
  - (i) that he agrees with that opinion; and
  - (ii) that it is appropriate to revoke the order.

(5) The responsible clinician may at any time release the patient under this section, but not after the community treatment order has been revoked.

(6) If the patient has not been released, nor the community treatment order revoked, by the end of the period of 72 hours, he shall then be released.

(7) But a patient who is released under this section remains subject to the community treatment order.

(8) In this section –

- (a) "the period of 72 hours" means the period of 72 hours beginning with the time when the patient's detention in hospital by virtue of the notice under section 17E above begins; and
- (b) references to being released shall be construed as references to being released from that detention (and accordingly from being recalled to hospital).

Amendments: Mental Health Act 2007.

17G Effect of revoking community treatment order

(1) This section applies if a community treatment order is revoked under section 17F above in respect of a patient.

(2) Section 6(2) above shall have effect as if the patient had never been discharged from hospital by virtue of the community treatment order.

(3) The provisions of this or any other Act relating to patients liable to be detained (or detained) in pursuance of an application for admission for treatment shall apply to the patient as they did before the community treatment order was made, unless otherwise provided.

(4) If, when the order is revoked, the patient is being detained in a hospital other than the responsible hospital, the provisions of this Part of this Act shall have effect as if –

- (a) the application for admission for treatment in respect of him were an application for admission to that other hospital; and
- (b) he had been admitted to that other hospital at the time when he was originally admitted in pursuance of the application.

(5) But, in any case, section 20 below shall have effect as if the patient had been admitted to hospital in pursuance of the application for admission for treatment on the day on which the order is revoked.

Amendments: Mental Health Act 2007.

18 Return and readmission of patients absent

(1) Where a patient who is for the time being liable to be detained under this Part of this Act in a hospital –

- (a) absents himself from the hospital without leave granted under section 17 above; or
- (b) fails to return to the hospital on any occasion on which, or at the expiration of any period for which, leave of absence was granted to him under that section, or upon being recalled under that section; or
- (c) absents himself without permission from any place where he is required to reside in accordance with conditions imposed on the grant of leave of absence under that section, he may, subject to the provisions of this section, be taken into custody and returned to the hospital or place by any approved mental health professional, by any officer on the staff of the hospital, by any constable, or by any person authorised in writing by the managers of the hospital.

(2) Where the place referred to in paragraph (c) of subsection (1) above is a hospital other than the one in which the patient is for the time being liable to be detained, the references in that subsection to an officer on the staff of the hospital and the managers of the hospital shall respectively include references to an officer on the staff of the first-mentioned hospital and the managers of that hospital.

(2A) Where a community patient is at any time absent from a hospital to which he is recalled under section 17E above, he may, subject to the provisions of this section, be taken into custody and returned to the hospital by any approved mental health professional, by any officer on the staff of the hospital, by any constable, or by any person authorised in writing by the responsible clinician or the managers of the hospital.

(3) Where a patient who is for the time being subject to guardianship under this Part of this Act absents himself without the leave of the guardian from the place at which he is required by the guardian to reside, he may, subject to the provisions of this section, be taken into custody and returned to that place by any officer on the staff of a local social services authority, by any constable, or by any person authorised in writing by the guardian or a local social services authority.

(4) patient shall not be taken into custody under this section after the later of –

(a) the end of the period of six months beginning with the first day of his absence without leave; and

(b) the end of the period for which (apart from section 21 below) he is liable to be detained or subject to guardianship or, in the case of a community patient, the community treatment order is in force;

(4A) In determining for the purposes of subsection (4)(b) above or any other provision of this Act whether a person who is or has been absent without leave is at any time liable to be detained or subject to guardianship, a report furnished under section 20 or 21B below before the first day of his absence without leave shall not be taken to have renewed the authority for his detention or guardianship unless the period of renewal began before that day.

(4B) Similarly, in determining for those purposes whether a community treatment order is at any time in force in respect of a person who is or has been absent without leave, a report furnished under section 20A or 21B below before the first day of his absence without leave shall not be taken to have extended the community treatment period unless the extension began before that day.

(5) A patient shall not be taken into custody under this section if the period for which he is liable to be detained is that specified in section 2(4), 4(4) or 5(2) or (4) above and that period has expired.

(6) In this Act "absent without leave" means absent from any hospital or other place and liable to be taken into custody and returned under this section, and related expressions shall be construed accordingly.

(7) In relation to a patient who has yet to comply with a requirement imposed by virtue of this Act to be in a hospital or place, references in this Act to his liability to be returned to the hospital or place shall include his liability to be taken to that hospital or place; and related expressions shall be construed accordingly.

Amendments: Mental Health (Patients in the Community) Act 1995; Mental Health Act 2007.

19 Regulations as to transfer of patients

(1) In such circumstances and subject to such conditions as may be prescribed by regulations made by the Secretary of State –

(a) a patient who is for the time being liable to be detained in a hospital by virtue of an application under this Part of this Act may be transferred to another hospital or into the guardianship of a local social services authority or of any person approved by such an authority;

(b) a patient who is for the time being subject to the guardianship of a local social services authority or other person by virtue of an application under this Part of this Act may be transferred into the guardianship of another local social services authority or person, or be transferred to a hospital.

(2) Where a patient is transferred in pursuance of regulations under this section, the provisions of this Part of this Act (including this subsection) shall apply to him as follows, that is to say –

(a) in the case of a patient who is liable to be detained in a hospital by virtue of an application for admission for assessment or for treatment and is transferred to another hospital, as if the application were an application for admission to that other hospital and as if the patient had been admitted to that other hospital at the time when he was originally admitted in pursuance of the application;
(b) in the case of a patient who is liable to be detained in a hospital by virtue of such an application and is transferred into guardianship, as if the application were a guardianship application duly accepted at the said time;
(c) in the case of a patient who is subject to guardianship by virtue of a guardianship application and is transferred into the guardianship of another authority or person, as if the application were for his reception into the guardianship of that authority or person and had been accepted at the time when it was originally accepted;
(d) in the case of a patient who is subject to guardianship by virtue of a guardianship application and is transferred to a hospital, as if the guardianship application were an application for admission to that hospital for treatment and as if the patient had been admitted to the hospital at the time when the application was originally accepted.

(3) Without prejudice to subsections (1) and (2) above, any patient who is for the time being liable to be detained under this Part of this Act in a hospital vested in the Secretary of State for the purposes of his functions under the National Health Service Act 2006, in a hospital vested in the Welsh Ministers for the purposes of their functions under the National Health Service (Wales) Act 2006, in any accommodation used under either of those Acts by the managers of such a hospital or in a hospital vested in a National Health Service trust, NHS foundation trust or Local Health Board, may at any time be removed to any other such hospital or accommodation which is managed by the managers of, or is vested in the National Health Service trust, NHS foundation trust or Local Health Board for, the first-mentioned hospital; and paragraph (a) of subsection (2) above shall apply in relation to a patient so removed as it applies in relation to a patient transferred in pursuance of regulations made under this section.

(4) Regulations made under this section may make provision for regulating the conveyance to their destination of patients authorised to be transferred or removed in pursuance of the regulations or under subsection (3) above.

Amendments: National Health Service and Community Care Act 1990; Health and Social Care (Community Health and Standards) Act 2003; National Health Service (Consequential Provisions) Act 2006; Mental Health Act 2007; Health and Social Care Act 2012; SI 2000/90.

19A Regulations as to assignment of responsibility for community patients

(1) Responsibility for a community patient may be assigned to another hospital in such circumstances and subject to such conditions as may be prescribed by regulations made by the Secretary of State (if the responsible hospital is in England) or the Welsh Ministers (if that hospital is in Wales).

(2) If responsibility for a community patient is assigned to another hospital –

(a) the application for admission for treatment in respect of the patient shall have effect (subject to section 17D above) as if it had always specified that other hospital;

(b) the patient shall be treated as if he had been admitted to that other hospital at the time when he was originally admitted in pursuance of the application (and as if he had subsequently been discharged under section 17A above from there); and

(c) that other hospital shall become "the responsible hospital" in relation to the patient for the purposes of this Act.

Amendments: Mental Health Act 2007.

Duration of authority and discharge

20 Duration of authority

(1) Subject to the following provisions of this Part of this Act, a patient admitted to hospital in pursuance of an application for admission for treatment, and a patient placed under guardianship in pursuance of a guardianship application, may be detained in a hospital or kept under guardianship for a period not exceeding six months beginning with the day on which he was so admitted, or the day on which the guardianship application was accepted, as the case may be, but shall not be so detained or kept for any longer period unless the authority for his detention or guardianship is renewed under this section.

(2) Authority for the detention or guardianship of a patient may, unless the patient has previously been discharged under section 23 below, be renewed –

(a) from the expiration of the period referred to in subsection (1) above, for a further period of six months;

(b) from the expiration of any period of renewal under paragraph (a) above, for a further period of one year, and so on for periods of one year at a time.

(3) Within the period of two months ending on the day on which a patient who is liable to be detained in pursuance of an application for admission for treatment would cease under this section to be so liable in default of the renewal of the authority for his detention, it shall be the duty of the responsible clinician –

(a) to examine the patient; and

(b) if it appears to him that the conditions set out in subsection (4) below are satisfied, to furnish to the managers of the hospital where the patient is detained a report to that effect in the prescribed form; and where such a report is furnished in respect of a patient the managers shall, unless they discharge the patient under section 23 below, cause him to be informed.

(4) The conditions referred to in subsection (3) above are that –

(a) the patient is suffering from mental disorder of a nature or degree which makes it appropriate for him to receive medical treatment in a hospital; and

(b) ...

(c) it is necessary for the health or safety of the patient or for the protection of other persons that he should receive such treatment and that it cannot be provided unless he continues to be detained; and

(d) appropriate medical treatment is available for him

(5) Before furnishing a report under subsection (3) above the responsible clinician shall consult one or more other persons who have been professionally concerned with the patient's medical treatment.

(5A) But the responsible clinician may not furnish a report under subsection (3) above unless a person –

- (a) who has been professionally concerned with the patient's medical treatment; but
- (b) who belongs to a profession other than that to which the responsible clinician belongs, states in writing that he agrees that the conditions set out in subsection (4) above are satisfied.

(6) Within the period of two months ending with the day on which a patient who is subject to guardianship under this Part of this Act would cease under this section to be so liable in default of the renewal of the authority for his guardianship, it shall be the duty of the appropriate practitioner –

- (a) to examine the patient; and
- (b) if it appears to him that the conditions set out in subsection (7) below are satisfied, to furnish to the guardian and, where the guardian is a person other than a local social services authority, to the responsible local social services authority a report to that effect in the prescribed form; and where such a report is furnished in respect of a patient, the local social services authority shall, unless they discharge the patient under section 23 below, cause him to be informed.

(7) The conditions referred to in subsection (6) above are that –

- (a) the patient is suffering from mental disorder of a nature or degree which warrants his reception into guardianship; and
- (b) it is necessary in the interests of the welfare of the patient or for the protection of other persons that the patient should remain under guardianship.

(8) Where a report is duly furnished under subsection (3) or (6) above, the authority for the detention or guardianship of the patient shall be thereby renewed for the period prescribed in that case by subsection (2) above.

(9) (*repealed*)

(10) (*repealed*)

Amendments: Mental Health Act 2007.

20A Community treatment period

(1) Subject to the provisions of this Part of this Act, a community treatment order shall cease to be in force on expiry of the period of six months beginning with the day on which it was made.

(2) That period is referred to in this Act as "the community treatment period".

(3) The community treatment period may, unless the order has previously ceased to be in force, be extended –

- (a) from its expiration for a period of six months;
- (b) from the expiration of any period of extension under paragraph (a) above for a further period of one year, and so on for periods of one year at a time.

(4) Within the period of two months ending on the day on which the order would cease to be in force in default of an extension under this section, it shall be the duty of the responsible clinician –

(a) to examine the patient; and
(b) if it appears to him that the conditions set out in subsection (6) below are satisfied and if a statement under subsection (8) below is made, to furnish to the managers of the responsible hospital a report to that effect in the prescribed form.

(5) Where such a report is furnished in respect of the patient, the managers shall, unless they discharge him under section 23 below, cause him to be informed.

(6) The conditions referred to in subsection (4) above are that –

(a) the patient is suffering from mental disorder of a nature or degree which makes it appropriate for him to receive medical treatment;
(b) it is necessary for his health or safety or for the protection of other persons that he should receive such treatment;
(c) subject to his continuing to be liable to be recalled as mentioned in paragraph (d) below, such treatment can be provided without his being detained in a hospital;
(d) it is necessary that the responsible clinician should continue to be able to exercise the power under section 17E(1) above to recall the patient to hospital; and
(e) appropriate medical treatment is available for him.

(7) In determining whether the criterion in subsection (6)(d) above is met, the responsible clinician shall, in particular, consider, having regard to the patient's history of mental disorder and any other relevant factors, what risk there would be of a deterioration of the patient's condition if he were to continue not to be detained in a hospital (as a result, for example, of his refusing or neglecting to receive the medical treatment he requires for his mental disorder).

(8) The statement referred to in subsection (4) above is a statement in writing by an approved mental health professional –

(a) that it appears to him that the conditions set out in subsection (6) above are satisfied; and
(b) that it is appropriate to extend the community treatment period.

(9) Before furnishing a report under subsection (4) above the responsible clinician shall consult one or more other persons who have been professionally concerned with the patient's medical treatment.

(10) Where a report is duly furnished under subsection (4) above, the community treatment period shall be thereby extended for the period prescribed in that case by subsection (3) above.

Amendments: Mental Health Act 2007.

20B Effect of expiry of community treatment order

(1) A community patient shall be deemed to be discharged absolutely from liability to recall under this Part of this Act, and the application for admission for treatment cease to have effect, on expiry of the community treatment order, if the order has not previously ceased to be in force.

(2) For the purposes of subsection (1) above, a community treatment order expires on expiry of the community treatment period as extended under this Part of this Act, but this is subject to sections 21 and 22 below.

Amendments: Mental Health Act 2007.

21 Special provisions as to patients absent without leave

(1) Where a patient is absent without leave –

(a) on the day on which (apart from this section) he would cease to be liable to be detained or subject to guardianship under this Part of this Act or, in the case of a community patient, the community treatment order would cease to be in force; or

(b) within the period of one week ending with that day, he shall not cease to be so liable or subject, or the order shall not cease to be in force, until the relevant time.

(2) For the purposes of subsection (1) above the relevant time –

(a) where the patient is taken into custody under section 18 above, is the end of the period of one week beginning with the day on which he is returned to the hospital or place where he ought to be;

(b) where the patient returns himself to the hospital or place where he ought to be within the period during which he can be taken into custody under section 18 above, is the end of the period of one week beginning with the day on which he so returns himself; and

(c) otherwise, is the end of the period during which he can be taken into custody under section 18 above.

(3) Where a patient is absent without leave on the day on which (apart from this section) the managers would be required under section 68 below to refer the patient's case to the appropriate tribunal, that requirement shall not apply unless and until –

(a) the patient is taken into custody under section 18 above and returned to the hospital where he ought to be; or

(b) the patient returns himself to the hospital where he ought to be within the period during which he can be taken into custody under section 18 above.

(4) Where a community patient is absent without leave on the day on which (apart from this section) the 72-hour period mentioned in section 17F above would expire, that period shall not expire until the end of the period of 72 hours beginning with the time when –

(a) the patient is taken into custody under section 18 above and returned to the hospital where he ought to be; or

(b) the patient returns himself to the hospital where he ought to be within the period during which he can be taken into custody under section 18 above.

(5) Any reference in this section, or in sections 21A to 22 below, to the time when a community treatment order would cease, or would have ceased, to be in force shall be construed as a reference to the time when it would cease, or would have ceased, to be in force by reason only of the passage of time.

Amendments: Substituted, together with ss 21A, 21B, for s 21 as originally enacted, by the Mental Health (Patients in the Community) Act 1995, s 2(2); Mental Health Act 2007; SI 2008/2833.

21A Patients who are taken into custody or return within 28 days

(1) This section applies where a patient who is absent without leave is taken into custody under section 18 above, or returns himself to the hospital or place where he ought to be, not later than the end of the period of 28 days beginning with the first day of his absence without leave.

(2) Where the period for which the patient is liable to be detained or subject to guardianship is extended by section 21 above, any examination and report to be made and furnished in respect of the patient under section 20(3) or (6) above may be made and furnished within the period as so extended.

(3) Where the authority for the detention or guardianship of the patient is renewed by virtue of subsection (2) above after the day on which (apart from section 21 above) that authority would have expired, the renewal shall take effect as from that day.

(4) In the case of a community patient, where the period for which the community treatment order is in force is extended by section 21 above, any examination and report to be made and furnished in respect of the patient under section 20A(4) above may be made and furnished within the period as so extended.

(5) Where the community treatment period is extended by virtue of subsection (4) above after the day on which (apart from section 21 above) the order would have ceased to be in force, the extension shall take effect as from that day.

Amendments Substituted, together with ss 21, 21B, for s 21 as originally enacted, by the Mental Health (Patients in the Community) Act 1995, s 2(2); Mental Health Act 2007.

21B Patients who are taken into custody or return after more than 28 days

(1) This section applies where a patient who is absent without leave is taken into custody under section 18 above, or returns himself to the hospital or place where he ought to be, later than the end of the period of 28 days beginning with the first day of his absence without leave.

(2) It shall be the duty of the appropriate practitioner, within the period of one week beginning with the day on which the patient is returned or returns himself to the hospital or place where he ought to be (his "return day") –

- (a) to examine the patient; and
- (b) if it appears to him that the relevant conditions are satisfied, to furnish to the appropriate body a report to that effect in the prescribed form; and where such a report is furnished in respect of the patient the appropriate body shall cause him to be informed.

(3) Where the patient is liable to be detained or is a community patient (as opposed to subject to guardianship), the appropriate practitioner shall, before furnishing a report under subsection (2) above, consult –

- (a) one or more other persons who have been professionally concerned with the patient's medical treatment; and
- (b) an approved mental health professional.

(4) Where –

- (a) the patient would (apart from any renewal of the authority for his detention or guardianship on or after his return day) be liable to be detained or subject to guardianship after the end of the period of one week beginning with that day; or

(b) in the case of a community patient, the community treatment order would (apart from any extension of the community treatment period on or after that day) be in force after the end of that period, he shall cease to be so liable or subject, or the community treatment period shall be deemed to expire, at the end of that period unless a report is duly furnished in respect of him under subsection (2) above.

(4A) If, in the case of a community patient, the community treatment order is revoked under section 17F above during the period of one week beginning with his return day –

(a) subsections (2) and (4) above shall not apply; and
(b) any report already furnished in respect of him under subsection (2) above shall be of no effect.

(5) Where the patient would (apart from section 21 above) have ceased to be liable to be detained or subject to guardianship on or before the day on which a report is duly furnished in respect of him under subsection (2) above, the report shall renew the authority for his detention or guardianship for the period prescribed in that case by section 20(2) above.

(6) Where the authority for the detention or guardianship of the patient is renewed by virtue of subsection (5) above –

(a) the renewal shall take effect as from the day on which (apart from section 21 above and that subsection) the authority would have expired; and
(b) if (apart from this paragraph) the renewed authority would expire on or before the day on which the report is furnished, the report shall further renew the authority, as from the day on which it would expire, for the period prescribed in that case by section 20(2) above.

(6A) In the case of a community patient, where the community treatment order would (apart from section 21 above) have ceased to be in force on or before the day on which a report is duly furnished in respect of him under subsection (2) above, the report shall extend the community treatment period for the period prescribed in that case by section 20A(3) above.

(6B) Where the community treatment period is extended by virtue of subsection (6A) above –

(a) the extension shall take effect as from the day on which (apart from section 21 above and that subsection) the order would have ceased to be in force; and
(b) if (apart from this paragraph) the period as so extended would expire on or before the day on which the report is furnished, the report shall further extend that period, as from the day on which it would expire, for the period prescribed in that case by section 20A(3) above.

(7) Where the authority for the detention or guardianship of the patient would expire within the period of two months beginning with the day on which a report is duly furnished in respect of him under subsection (2) above, the report shall, if it so provides, have effect also as a report duly furnished under section 20(3) or (6) above; and the reference in this subsection to authority includes any authority renewed under subsection (5) above by the report.

(7A) In the case of a community patient, where the community treatment order would (taking account of any extension under subsection (6A) above) cease to be in force within the period of two months beginning with the day on which a report is duly furnished in respect of him under subsection (2) above, the report shall, if it so provides, have effect also as a report duly furnished under section 20A(4) above.

(8) (*repealed*)

(9) (*repealed*)

(10) In this section –

"the appropriate body" means –

- (a) in relation to a patient who is liable to be detained in a hospital, the managers of the hospital;
- (b) in relation to a patient who is subject to guardianship, the responsible local social services authority;
- (c) in relation to a community patient, the managers of the responsible hospital; and

"the relevant conditions" means –

- (a) in relation to a patient who is liable to be detained in a hospital, the conditions set out in subsection (4) of section 20 above;
- (b) in relation to a patient who is subject to guardianship, the conditions set out in subsection (7) of that section;
- (c) in relation to a community patient, the conditions set out in section 20A(6) above.

Amendments Substituted, together with ss 21, 21A, for s 21 as originally enacted, by the Mental Health (Patients in the Community) Act 1995; Mental Health Act 2007.

22 Special provisions as to patients sentenced to imprisonment, etc

(1) If –

- (a) a qualifying patient is detained in custody in pursuance of any sentence or order passed or made by a court in the United Kingdom (including an order committing or remanding him in custody); and
- (b) he is so detained for a period exceeding, or for successive periods exceeding in the aggregate, six months, the relevant application shall cease to have effect on expiry of that period.

(2) A patient is a qualifying patient for the purposes of this section if –

- (a) he is liable to be detained by virtue of an application for admission for treatment;
- (b) he is subject to guardianship by virtue of a guardianship application; or
- (c) he is a community patient.

(3) "The relevant application", in relation to a qualifying patient, means –

- (a) in the case of a patient who is subject to guardianship, the guardianship application in respect of him;
- (b) in any other case, the application for admission for treatment in respect of him.

(4) The remaining subsections of this section shall apply if a qualifying patient is detained incustody as mentioned in subsection (1)(a) above but for a period not exceeding, or for successiveperiods not exceeding in the aggregate, six months.

(5) If apart from this subsection –

(a) the patient would have ceased to be liable to be detained or subject to guardianship by virtue of the relevant application on or before the day on which he is discharged from custody; or
(b) in the case of a community patient, the community treatment order would have ceased to be in force on or before that day, he shall not cease and shall be deemed not to have ceased to be so liable or subject, or the order shall not cease and shall be deemed not to have ceased to be in force, until the end of that day.

(6) In any case (except as provided in subsection (8) below), sections 18, 21 and 21A above shall apply in relation to the patient as if he had absented himself without leave on that day.

(7) In its application by virtue of subsection (6) above section 18 above shall have effect as if –

(a) in subsection (4) for the words from "later of" to the end there were substituted "end of the period of 28 days beginning with the first day of his absence without leave"; and
(b) subsections (4A) and (4B) were omitted.

(8) In relation to a community patient who was not recalled to hospital under section 17E above at the time when his detention in custody began –

(a) section 18 above shall not apply; but
(b) sections 21 and 21A above shall apply as if he had absented himself without leave on the day on which he is discharged from custody and had returned himself as provided in those sections on the last day of the period of 28 days beginning with that day.

Amendments Mental Health Act 2007.

23 Discharge of patients

(1) Subject to the provisions of this section and section 25 below, a patient who is for the time being liable to be detained or subject to guardianship under this Part of this Act shall cease to be so liable or subject if an order in writing discharging him absolutely from detention or guardianship is made in accordance with this section.

(1A) Subject to the provisions of this section and section 25 below, a community patient shall cease to be liable to recall under this Part of this Act, and the application for admission for treatment cease to have effect, if an order in writing discharging him from such liability is made in accordance with this section.

(1B) An order under subsection (1) or (1A) above shall be referred to in this Act as "an order for discharge".

(2) An order for discharge may be made in respect of a patient –

(a) where the patient is liable to be detained in a hospital in pursuance of an application for admission for assessment or for treatment by the responsible clinician, by the managers or by the nearest relative of the patient;
(b) where the patient is subject to guardianship, by the responsible clinician, by the responsible local social services authority or by the nearest relative of the patient;
(c) where the patient is a community patient, by the responsible clinician, by the managers of the responsible hospital or by the nearest relative of the patient.

(3) *(repealed)*

(3A) *(repealed)*

(4) The powers conferred by this section on any authority trust, board (other than an NHS foundation trust) or body of persons may be exercised subject to subsection (3) below by any three or more members of that authority trust, board or body authorised by them in that behalf or by three or more members of a committee or sub-committee of that authority trust, board or body which has been authorised by them in that behalf.

(5) The reference in subsection (4) above to the members of an authority, trust, board or body or the members of a committee or sub-committee of an authority, trust, board or body, –

(a) in the case of a Local Health Board or Special Health Authority or a committee or sub-committee of a Local Health Board or Special Health Authority is a reference only to the chairman of the authority or board and such members (of the authority, board, committee or sub-committee, as the case may be) as are not also officers of the authority.or board within the meaning of the National Health Service Act 2006 or the National Health Service (Wales) Act 2006; and

(b) in the case of a National Health Service trust or a committee or sub-committee of such a trust, is a reference only to the chairman of the trust and such directors or (in the case of a committee or sub-committee) members as are not also employees of the trust.

(6) The powers conferred by this section on any NHS foundation trust may be exercised by any three or more persons authorised by the board of the trust in that behalf each of whom is neither an executive director of the board nor an employee of the trust.

Amendments: National Health Service and Community Care Act 1990; Health and Social Care (Community Health and Standards) Act 2003; National Health Service (Consequential Provisions) Act 2006; Mental Health Act 2007; Health and Social Care Act 2012; SI 2000/90; SI 2007/961.

24 Visiting and examination of patients

(1) For the purpose of advising as to the exercise by the nearest relative of a patient who is liable to be detained or subject to guardianship under this Part of this Act, or who is a community patient, of any power to order his discharge, any registered medical practitioner or approved clinician authorised by or on behalf of the nearest relative of the patient may, at any reasonable time, visit the patient and examine him in private.

(2) Any registered medical practitioner or approved clinician authorised for the purposes of subsection (1) above to visit and examine a patient may require the production of and inspect any records relating to the detention or treatment of the patient in any hospital or to any after-care services provided for the patient under section 117 below.

(3) *(repealed)*

(4) *(repealed)*

Amendments: Mental Health (Patients in the Community) Act 1995; Mental Health Act 2007; Health and Social Care Act 2012.

25 Restrictions on discharge by nearest relative

(1) An order for the discharge of a patient who is liable to be detained in a hospital shall not be made under section 23 above by his nearest relative except after giving not less

than 72 hours' notice in writing to the managers of the hospital; and if, within 72 hours after such notice has been given, the responsible clinician furnishes to the managers a report certifying that in the opinion of that clinician the patient, if discharged, would be likely to act in a manner dangerous to other persons or to himself, –

- (a) any order for the discharge of the patient made by that relative in pursuance of the notice shall be of no effect; and
- (b) no further order for the discharge of the patient shall be made by that relative during the period of six months beginning with the date of the report.

(1A) Subsection (1) above shall apply to an order for the discharge of a community patient as it applies to an order for the discharge of a patient who is liable to be detained in a hospital, but with the reference to the managers of the hospital being read as a reference to the managers of the responsible hospital.

(2) In any case where a report under subsection (1) above is furnished in respect of a patient who is liable to be detained in pursuance of an application for admission for treatment, or in respect of a community patient, the managers shall cause the nearest relative of the patient to be informed.

Amendments: Mental Health Act 2007.

Functions of relatives of patients

26 Definition of "relative" and "nearest relative"

(1) In this Part of this Act "relative" means any of the following persons: –

- (a) husband or wife or civil partner;
- (b) son or daughter;
- (c) father or mother;
- (d) brother or sister;
- (e) grandparent;
- (f) grandchild;
- (g) uncle or aunt;
- (h) nephew or niece.

(2) In deducing relationships for the purposes of this section, any relationship of the halfblood shall be treated as a relationship of the whole blood, and an illegitimate person shall be treated as the legitimate child of

- (a) his mother, and
- (b) if his father has parental responsibility for him within the meaning of section 3 of the Children Act 1989, his father.

(3) In this Part of this Act, subject to the provisions of this section and to the following provisions of this Part of this Act, the "nearest relative" means the person first described in subsection (1) above who is for the time being surviving, relatives of the whole blood being preferred to relatives of the same description of the half-blood and the elder or eldest of two or more relatives described in any paragraph of that subsection being preferred to the other or others of those relatives, regardless of sex.

(4) Subject to the provisions of this section and to the following provisions of this Part of this Act, where the patient ordinarily resides with or is cared for by one or more of his relatives (or, if he is for the time being an in-patient in a hospital, he last ordinarily resided with or was cared for by one or more of his relatives) his nearest relative shall be determined –

(a) by giving preference to that relative or those relatives over the other or others; and
(b) as between two or more such relatives, in accordance with subsection (3) above.

(5) Where the person who, under subsection (3) or (4) above, would be the nearest relative of a patient –

(a) in the case of a patient ordinarily resident in the United Kingdom, the Channel Islands or the Isle of Man, is not so resident; or
(b) is the husband or wife or civil partner of the patient, but is permanently separated from the patient, either by agreement or under an order of a court, or has deserted or has been deserted by the patient for a period which has not come to an end; or
(c) is a person other than the husband, wife, civil partner, father or mother of the patient, and is for the time being under 18 years of age;
(d) …

the nearest relative of the patient shall be ascertained as if that person were dead.

(6) In this section "husband", "wife" and "civil partner" include a person who is living with the patient as the patient's husband or wife or as if they were civil partners, as the case may be (or, if the patient is for the time being an in-patient in a hospital, was so living until the patient was admitted), and has been or had been so living for a period of not less than six months; but a person shall not be treated by virtue of this subsection as the nearest relative of a married patient or a patient in a civil partnership unless the husband, wife or civil partner of the patient is disregarded by virtue of paragraph (b) of subsection (5) above.

(7) A person, other than a relative, with whom the patient ordinarily resides (or, if the patient is for the time being an in-patient in a hospital, last ordinarily resided before he was admitted), and with whom he has or had been ordinarily residing for a period of not less than five years, shall be treated for the purposes of this Part of this Act as if he were a relative but –

(a) shall be treated for the purposes of subsection (3) above as if mentioned last in subsection (1) above; and
(b) shall not be treated by virtue of this subsection as the nearest relative of a married patient or a patient in a civil partnership unless the husband, wife or civil partner of the patient is disregarded by virtue of paragraph (b) of subsection (5) above.

Amendments:; Children Act 1989; Mental Health Act 2007; SI 1991/1881.

27 Children and young persons in care

Where –

(a) a patient who is a child or young person is in the care of a local authority by virtue of a care order within the meaning of the Children Act 1989; or
(b) the rights and powers of a parent of a patient who is a child or young person are vested in a local authority by virtue of section 16 of the Social Work (Scotland) Act 1968, the authority shall be deemed to be the nearest relative of the patient in preference to any person except the patient's husband or wife or civil partner (if any).

Amendments: Children Act 1989; Mental Health Act 2007.

28 Nearest relative of minor under guardianship, etc

(1) Where –

- (a) a guardian has been appointed for a person who has not attained the age of eighteen years; or
- (b) a residence order (as defined by section 8 of the Children Act 1989) is in force with respect to such a person,

the guardian (or guardians, where there is more than one) or the person named in the residence order shall, to the exclusion of any other person, be deemed to be his nearest relative.

(2) Subsection (5) of section 26 above shall apply in relation to a person who is, or who is one of the persons, deemed to be the nearest relative of a patient by virtue of this section as it applies in relation to a person who would be the nearest relative under subsection (3) of that section.

(3) In this section "guardian" includes a special guardian (within the meaning of the Children Act 1989), but does not include a guardian under this Part of this Act.

(4) In this section "court" includes a court in Scotland or Northern Ireland, and "enactment" includes an enactment of the Parliament of Northern Ireland, a Measure of the Northern Ireland Assembly and an Order in Council under Schedule 1 of the Northern Ireland Act 1974.

Amendments: Children Act 1989; Adoption and Children Act 2002.

29 Appointment by court of acting nearest relative

(1) The county court may, upon application made in accordance with the provisions of this section in respect of a patient, by order direct that the functions of the nearest relative of the patient under this Part of this Act and sections 66 and 69 below shall, during the continuance in force of the order, be exercisable by the person specified in the order.

(1A) If the court decides to make an order on an application under subsection (1) above, the following rules have effect for the purposes of specifying a person in the order –

- (a) if a person is nominated in the application to act as the patient's nearest relative and that person is, in the opinion of the court, a suitable person to act as such and is willing to do so, the court shall specify that person (or, if there are two or more such persons, such one of them as the court thinks fit);
- (b) otherwise, the court shall specify such person as is, in its opinion, a suitable person to act as the patient's nearest relative and is willing to do so.

(2) An order under this section may be made on the application of –

- (za) the patient;
- (a) any relative of the patient;
- (b) any other person with whom the patient is residing (or, if the patient is then an inpatient in a hospital, was last residing before he was admitted); or
- (c) an approved mental health professional;

(3) An application for an order under this section may be made upon any of the following grounds, that is to say –

(a) that the patient has no nearest relative within the meaning of this Act, or that it is not reasonably practicable to ascertain whether he has such a relative, or who that relative is;
(b) that the nearest relative of the patient is incapable of acting as such by reason of mental disorder or other illness;
(c) that the nearest relative of the patient unreasonably objects to the making of an application for admission for treatment or a guardianship application in respect of the patient;
(d) that the nearest relative of the patient has exercised without due regard to the welfare of the patient or the interests of the public his power to discharge the patient under this Part of this Act, or is likely to do so; or
(e) that the nearest relative of the patient is otherwise not a suitable person to act as such.

(4) If, immediately before the expiration of the period for which a patient is liable to be detained by virtue of an application for admission for assessment, an application under this section, which is an application made on the ground specified in subsection (3)(c) or (d) above, is pending in respect of the patient, that period shall be extended –

(a) in any case, until the application under this section has been finally disposed of; and
(b) if an order is made in pursuance of the application under this section, for a further period of seven days;

and for the purposes of this subsection an application under this section shall be deemed to have been finally disposed of at the expiration of the time allowed for appealing from the decision of the court or, if notice of appeal has been given within that time, when the appeal has been heard or withdrawn, and "pending" shall be construed accordingly.

(5) An order made on the ground specified in subsection (3)(a), (b) or (e) above may specify a period for which it is to continue in force unless previously discharged under section 30 below.

(6) While an order made under this section is in force, the provisions of this Part of this Act (other than this section and section 30 below) and sections 66, 69, 132(4) and 133 below shall apply in relation to the patient as if for any reference to the nearest relative of the patient there were substituted a reference to the person having the functions of that relative and (without prejudice to section 30 below) shall so apply notwithstanding that the person who was the patient's nearest relative when the order was made is no longer his nearest relative; but this subsection shall not apply to section 66 below in the case mentioned in paragraph (h) of subsection (1) of that section.

Amendments: Mental Health Act 2007.

30 Discharge and variation of orders under s 29

(1) An order made under section 29 above in respect of a patient may be discharged by the county court upon application made –

(a) in any case, by the patient or the person having the functions of the nearest relative of the patient by virtue of the order;
(b) where the order was made on the ground specified in paragraph (a), (b) or (e) of section 29(3) above, or where the person who was the nearest relative of the patient when the order was made has ceased to be his nearest relative, on the application of the nearest relative of the patient.

(1A) But, in the case of an order made on the ground specified in paragraph (e) of section 29(3) above, an application may not be made under subsection (1)(b) above by the person who was the nearest relative of the patient when the order was made except with leave of the county court.

(2) An order made under section 29 above in respect of a patient may be varied by the county court, on the application of the patient or of the person having the functions of the nearest relative by virtue of the order or on the application of an approved mental health professional, by substituting another person for the person having those functions.

(2A) If the court decides to vary an order on an application under subsection (2) above, the following rules have effect for the purposes of substituting another person –

(a) if a person is nominated in the application to act as the patient's nearest relative and that person is, in the opinion of the court, a suitable person to act as such and is willing to do so, the court shall specify that person (or, if there are two or more such persons, such one of them as the court thinks fit);
(b) otherwise, the court shall specify such person as is, in its opinion, a suitable person to act as the patient's nearest relative and is willing to do so.

(3) If the person having the functions of the nearest relative of a patient by virtue of an order under section 29 above dies –

(a) subsections (1) and (2) above shall apply as if for any reference to that person there were substituted a reference to any relative of the patient, and
(b) until the order is discharged or varied under those provisions the functions of the nearest relative under this Part of this Act and sections 66 and 69 below shall not be exercisable by any person.

(4) An order made on the ground specified in paragraph (c) or (d) of section 29(3) above shall, unless previously discharged under subsection (1) above, cease to have effect as follows –

(a) if –
    (i) on the date of the order the patient was liable to be detained or subject to guardianship by virtue of a relevant application, order or direction; or
    (ii) he becomes so liable or subject within the period of three months beginning with that date; or
    (iii) he was a community patient on the date of the order, it shall cease to have effect when he is discharged under section 23 above or 72 below or the relevant application, order or direction otherwise ceases to have effect (except as a result of his being transferred in pursuance of regulations under section 19 above);
(b) otherwise, it shall cease to have effect at the end of the period of three months beginning with the date of the order.

(4A) In subsection (4) above, reference to a relevant application, order or direction is to any of the following –

(a) an application for admission for treatment;
(b) a guardianship application;
(c) an order or direction under Part 3 of this Act (other than under section 35, 36 or 38).

(4B) An order made on the ground specified in paragraph (a), (b) or (e) of section 29(3) above shall –

(a) if a period was specified under section 29(5) above, cease to have effect on expiry of that period, unless previously discharged under subsection (1) above;
(b) if no such period was specified, remain in force until it is discharged under subsection (1) above.

(5) The discharge or variation under this section of an order made under section 29 above shall not affect the validity of anything previously done in pursuance of the order.

Amendments: Mental Health Act 2007.

Supplemental

31 Procedure on applications to county court

County court rules [Rules of court] which relate to applications authorised by this Part of this Act to be made to a *county court* [the county court] may make provision –

(a) for the hearing and determination of such applications otherwise than in open court;
(b) for the admission on the hearing of such applications of evidence of such descriptions as may be specified in the rules notwithstanding anything to the contrary in any enactment or rule of law relating to the admissibility of evidence;
(c) for the visiting and interviewing of patients in private by or under the directions of the court.

Prospective Amendment: Words in italics prospectively repealed and subsequent words in square brackets prospectively substituted by the Crime and Courts Act 2013 with effect from a date to be appointed.

32 Regulations for purposes of Part II

(1) The Secretary of State may make regulations for prescribing anything which, under this Part of this Act, is required or authorised to be prescribed, and otherwise for carrying this Part of this Act into full effect.

(2) Regulations under this section may in particular make provision –

(a) for prescribing the form of any application, recommendation, report, order, notice or other document to be made or given under this Part of this Act;
(b) for prescribing the manner in which any such application, recommendation, report, order, notice or other document may be proved, and for regulating the service of any such application, report, order or notice;
(c) for requiring such bodies as may be prescribed by the regulations to keep such registers or other records as may be so prescribed in respect of patients liable to be detained or subject to guardianship under this Part of this Act or community patients, and to furnish or make available to those patients, and their relatives, such written statements of their rights and powers under this Act as may be so prescribed;
(d) for the determination in accordance with the regulations of the age of any person whose exact age cannot be ascertained by reference to the registers kept under the Births and Deaths Registration Act 1953; and
(e) for enabling the functions under this Part of this Act of the nearest relative of a patient to be performed, in such circumstances and subject to such conditions (if any) as may be prescribed by the regulations, by any person authorised in that behalf by that relative; and for the purposes of this Part of this Act any application, report or notice the service of which is regulated under paragraph (b) above shall be deemed to have been received by or furnished to the

authority or person to whom it is authorised or required to be furnished, addressed or given if it is duly served in accordance with the regulations.

(3) Without prejudice to subsections (1) and (2) above, but subject to section 23(4) and (6) above, regulations under this section may determine the manner in which functions under this Part of this Act of the managers of hospitals, local social services authorities, Local Health Board, Special Health Authorities, National Health Service trusts or NHS foundation trusts are to be exercised, and such regulations may in particular specify the circumstances in which, and the conditions subject to which, any such functions may be performed by officers of or other persons acting on behalf of those managers, boards, authorities and trusts.

Amendments National Health Service and Community Care Act 1990; Mental Health (Patients in the Community) Act 1995; Health Authorities Act 1995; Health and Social Care (Community Health and Standards) Act 2003; Mental Health Act 2007; Health and Social Care Act 2012; SI 2007/961; SI 2000/90.

33 Special provisions as to wards of court

(1) An application for the admission to hospital of a minor who is a ward of court may be made under this Part of this Act with the leave of the court; and section 11(4) above shall not apply in relation to an application so made.

(2) Where a minor who is a ward of court is liable to be detained in a hospital by virtue of an application for admission under this Part of this Act or is a community patient, any power exercisable under this Part of this Act or under section 66 below in relation to the patient by his nearest relative shall be exercisable by or with the leave of the court.

(3) Nothing in this Part of this Act shall be construed as authorising the making of a guardianship application in respect of a minor who is a ward of court, or the transfer into guardianship of any such minor.

(4) Where a community treatment order has been made in respect of a minor who is a ward of court, the provisions of this Part of this Act relating to community treatment orders and community patients have effect in relation to the minor subject to any order which the court makes in the exercise of its wardship jurisdiction; but this does not apply as regards any period when the minor is recalled to hospital under section 17E above.

Amendments: Mental Health Act 2007; Mental Health (Patients in the Community) Act 1995.

34 Interpretation of Part II

(1) In this Part of this Act –

"the appropriate practitioner" means –

(a) in the case of a patient who is subject to the guardianship of a person other than a local social services authority, the nominated medical attendant of the patient; and

(b) in any other case, the responsible clinician;

"the nominated medical attendant", in relation to a patient who is subject to the guardianship of a person other than a local social services authority, means the person appointed in pursuance of regulations made under section 9(2) above to act as the medical attendant of the patient;

"registered establishment" means an establishment which would not, apart from subsection (2) below, be a hospital for the purposes of this Part and which –

(a) in England, is a hospital as defined by section 275 of the National Health Service Act 2006 that is used for the carrying on of a regulated activity, within the meaning of Part 1 of the Health and Social Care Act 2008, which relates to the assessment or medical treatment of mental disorder and in respect of which a person is registered under Chapter 2 of that Part; and

(b) in Wales, is an establishment in respect of which a person is registered under Part 2 of the Care Standards Act 2000 as an independent hospital in which treatment or nursing (or both) are provided for persons liable to be detained under this Act;

"the responsible clinician" means –

(a) in relation to a patient liable to be detained by virtue of an application for admission for assessment or an application for admission for treatment, or a community patient, the approved clinician with overall responsibility for the patient's case;

(b) in relation to a patient subject to guardianship, the approved clinician authorised by the responsible local social services authority to act (either generally or in any particular case or for any particular purpose) as the responsible clinician;

(1A) (*repealed*)

(2) Except where otherwise expressly provided, this Part of this Act applies in relation to a registered establishment, as it applies in relation to a hospital, and references in this Part of this Act to a hospital, and any reference in this Act to a hospital to which this Part of this Act applies, shall be construed accordingly.

(3) In relation to a patient who is subject to guardianship in pursuance of a guardianship application, any reference in this Part of this Act to the responsible local social services authority is a reference –

(a) where the patient is subject to the guardianship of a local social services authority, to that authority;

(b) where the patient is subject to the guardianship of a person other than a local social services authority, to the local social services authority for the area in which that person resides.

Amendment: Mental Health (Patients in the Community) Act 1995; Care Standards Act 2000; Mental Health Act 2007; SI 2010/813.

****

PART IV
CONSENT TO TREATMENT

56 Patients to whom Part 4 applies

(1) Section 57 and, so far as relevant to that section, sections 59 to 62 below apply to any patient.

(2) Subject to that and to subsection (5) below, this Part of this Act applies to a patient only if he falls within subsection (3) or (4) below.

(3) A patient falls within this subsection if he is liable to be detained under this Act but not if –

(a) he is so liable by virtue of an emergency application and the second medical recommendation referred to in section 4(4)(a) above has not been given and received;
(b) he is so liable by virtue of section 5(2) or (4) or 35 above or section 135 or 136 below or by virtue of a direction for his detention in a place of safety under section 37(4) or 45A(5) above; or
(c) he has been conditionally discharged under section 42(2) above or section 73 or 74 below and he is not recalled to hospital.

(4) A patient falls within this subsection if –

(a) he is a community patient; and
(b) he is recalled to hospital under section 17E above.

(5) Section 58A and, so far as relevant to that section, sections 59 to 62 below also apply to any patient who –

(a) does not fall within subsection (3) above;
(b) is not a community patient; and
(c) has not attained the age of 18 years.

Amendments: Mental Health Act 2007.

57 Treatment requiring consent and a second opinion

(1) This section applies to the following forms of medical treatment for mental disorder –

(a) any surgical operation for destroying brain tissue or for destroying the functioning of brain tissue; and
(b) such other forms of treatment as may be specified for the purposes of this section by regulations made by the Secretary of State.

(2) Subject to section 62 below, a patient shall not be given any form of treatment to which this section applies unless he has consented to it and –

(a) a registered medical practitioner appointed for the purposes of this Part of this Act by the regulatory authority (not being the responsible clinician (if there is one) or the person in charge of the treatment in question) and two other persons appointed for the purposes of this paragraph by the regulatory authority (not being registered medical practitioners) have certified in writing that the patient is capable of understanding the nature, purpose and likely effects of the treatment in question and has consented to it; and
(b) the registered medical practitioner referred to in paragraph (a) above has certified in writing that it is appropriate for the treatment to be given.

(3) Before giving a certificate under subsection (2)(b) above the registered medical practitioner concerned shall consult two other persons who have been professionally concerned with the patient's medical treatment but, of those persons –

(a) one shall be a nurse and the other shall be neither a nurse nor a registered medical practitioner; and
(b) neither shall be the responsible clinician (if there is one) or the person in charge of the treatment in question.

(4) Before making any regulations for the purpose of this section the Secretary of State shall consult such bodies as appear to him to be concerned

Amendment: Mental Health Act 2007; Health and Social Care Act 2008.

58 Treatment requiring consent or a second opinion

(1) This section applies to the following forms of medical treatment for mental disorder –

(a) such forms of treatment as may be specified for the purposes of this section by regulations made by the Secretary of State;

(b) the administration of medicine to a patient by any means (not being a form of treatment specified under paragraph (a) above or section 57 above or section 58A(1)(b) below) at any time during a period for which he is liable to be detained as a patient to whom this Part of this Act applies if three months or more have elapsed since the first occasion in that period when medicine was administered to him by any means for his mental disorder.

(2) The Secretary of State may by order vary the length of the period mentioned in subsection (1)(b) above.

(3) Subject to section 62 below, a patient shall not be given any form of treatment to which this section applies unless –

(a) he has consented to that treatment and either the approved clinician in charge of it or a registered medical practitioner appointed for the purposes of this Part of this Act by the regulatory authority has certified in writing that the patient is capable of understanding its nature, purpose and likely effects and has consented to it; or

(b) a registered medical practitioner appointed as aforesaid (not being the responsible clinician or the approved clinician in charge of the treatment in question) has certified in writing that the patient is not capable of understanding the nature, purpose and likely effects of that treatment or being so capable has not consented to it but that it is appropriate for the treatment to be given.

(4) Before giving a certificate under subsection (3)(b) above the registered medical practitioner concerned shall consult two other persons who have been professionally concerned with the patient's medical treatment but, of those persons –

(a) one shall be a nurse and the other shall be neither a nurse nor a registered medical practitioner; and

(b) neither shall be the responsible clinician or the approved clinician in charge of the treatment in question.

(5) Before making any regulations for the purposes of this section the Secretary of State shall consult such bodies as appear to him to be concerned.

Amendments: Mental Health Act 2007; Health and Social Care Act 2008.

58A Electro-convulsive therapy, etc

(1) This section applies to the following forms of medical treatment for mental disorder –

(a) electro-convulsive therapy; and

(b) such other forms of treatment as may be specified for the purposes of this section by regulations made by the appropriate national authority.

(2) Subject to section 62 below, a patient shall be not be given any form of treatment to which this section applies unless he falls within subsection (3), (4) or (5) below.

(3) A patient falls within this subsection if –

(a) he has attained the age of 18 years;
(b) he has consented to the treatment in question; and
(c) either the approved clinician in charge of it or a registered medical practitioner appointed as mentioned in section 58(3) above has certified in writing that the patient is capable of understanding the nature, purpose and likely effects of the treatment and has consented to it.

(4) A patient falls within this subsection if –

(a) he has not attained the age of 18 years; but
(b) he has consented to the treatment in question; and
(c) a registered medical practitioner appointed as aforesaid (not being the approved clinician in charge of the treatment) has certified in writing –
    (i) that the patient is capable of understanding the nature, purpose and likely effects of the treatment and has consented to it; and
    (ii) that it is appropriate for the treatment to be given.

(5) A patient falls within this subsection if a registered medical practitioner appointed as aforesaid (not being the responsible clinician (if there is one) or the approved clinician in charge of the treatment in question) has certified in writing –

(a) that the patient is not capable of understanding the nature, purpose and likely effects of the treatment; but
(b) that it is appropriate for the treatment to be given; and
(c) that giving him the treatment would not conflict with –
    (i) an advance decision which the registered medical practitioner concerned is satisfied is valid and applicable; or
    (ii) a decision made by a donee or deputy or by the Court of Protection.

(6) Before giving a certificate under subsection (5) above the registered medical practitioner concerned shall consult two other persons who have been professionally concerned with the patient's medical treatment but, of those persons –

(a) one shall be a nurse and the other shall be neither a nurse nor a registered medical practitioner; and
(b) neither shall be the responsible clinician (if there is one) or the approved clinician in charge of the treatment in question.

(7) This section shall not by itself confer sufficient authority for a patient who falls within section 56(5) above to be given a form of treatment to which this section applies if he is not capable of understanding the nature, purpose and likely effects of the treatment (and cannot therefore consent to it).

(8) Before making any regulations for the purposes of this section, the appropriate national authority shall consult such bodies as appear to it to be concerned.

(9) In this section –

(a) a reference to an advance decision is to an advance decision (within the meaning of the Mental Capacity Act 2005) made by the patient;
(b) "valid and applicable", in relation to such a decision, means valid and applicable to the treatment in question in accordance with section 25 of that Act;

(c) a reference to a donee is to a donee of a lasting power of attorney (within the meaning of section 9 of that Act) created by the patient, where the donee is acting within the scope of his authority and in accordance with that Act; and

(d) a reference to a deputy is to a deputy appointed for the patient by the Court of Protection under section 16 of that Act, where the deputy is acting within the scope of his authority and in accordance with that Act.

(10) In this section, "the appropriate national authority" means –

(a) in a case where the treatment in question would, if given, be given in England, the Secretary of State;

(b) in a case where the treatment in question would, if given, be given in Wales, the Welsh Ministers.

Amendments: Inserted by Mental Health Act 2007.

59 Plans of treatment

Any consent or certificate under section 57, 58 or 58A above may relate to a plan of treatment under which the patient is to be given (whether within a specified period or otherwise) one or more of the forms of treatment to which that section applies

Amendments: Mental Health Act 2007.

60 Withdrawal of consent

(1) Where the consent of a patient to any treatment has been given for the purposes of section 57, 58 or 58A above, the patient may, subject to section 62 below, at any time before the completion of the treatment withdraw his consent, and those sections shall then apply as if the remainder of the treatment were a separate form of treatment.

(1A) Subsection (1B) below applies where –

(a) the consent of a patient to any treatment has been given for the purposes of section 57, 58 or 58A above; but

(b) before the completion of the treatment, the patient ceases to be capable of understanding its nature, purpose and likely effects.

(1B) The patient shall, subject to section 62 below, be treated as having withdrawn his consent, and those sections shall then apply as if the remainder of the treatment were a separate form of treatment.

(1C) Subsection (1D) below applies where –

(a) a certificate has been given under section 58 or 58A above that a patient is not capable of understanding the nature, purpose and likely effects of the treatment to which the certificate applies; but

(b) before the completion of the treatment, the patient becomes capable of understanding its nature, purpose and likely effects.

(1D) The certificate shall, subject to section 62 below, cease to apply to the treatment and those sections shall then apply as if the remainder of the treatment were a separate form of treatment.

(2) Without prejudice to the application of subsections (1) to (1D) above to any treatment given under the plan of treatment to which a patient has consented, a patient

who has consented to such a plan may, subject to section 62 below, at any time withdraw his consent to further treatment, or to further treatment of any description, under the plan.

Amendment: Inserted by Mental Health Act 2007.

61 Review of treatment

(1) Where a patient is given treatment in accordance with section 57(2), 58(3)(b) or 58A(4) or (5) above, or by virtue of section 62A below in accordance with a Part 4A certificate (within the meaning of that section) that falls within section 64C(4) below, a report on the treatment and the patient's condition shall be given by the approved clinician in charge of the treatment to the regulatory authority –

- (a) on the next occasion on which the responsible clinician furnishes a report under section 20(3), 20A(4) or 21B(2) above in respect of the patient; and
- (b) at any other time if so required by the regulatory authority.

(2) In relation to a patient who is subject to a restriction order, limitation direction or restriction direction subsection (1) above shall have effect as if paragraph (a) required the report to be made –

- (a) in the case of treatment in the period of six months beginning with the date of the order or direction, at the end of that period;
- (b) in the case of treatment at any subsequent time, on the next occasion on which the responsible clinician makes a report in respect of the patient under section 41(6), 45B(3) or 49(3) above.

(3) The regulatory authority may at any time give notice directing that, subject to section 62 below, a certificate given in respect of a patient under section 57(2), 58(3)(b) or 58A(4) or (5) above shall not apply to treatment given to him (whether in England or Wales) after a date specified in the notice and sections 57, 58 and 58A above shall then apply to any such treatment as if that certificate had not been given.

(3A) The notice under subsection (3) above shall be given to the approved clinician in charge of the treatment.

Amendments: Crime (Sentences) Act 1997; Mental Health Act 2007; Health and Social Care Act 2008; Health and Social Care Act 2012.

62 Urgent treatment

(1) Sections 57 and 58 above shall not apply to any treatment –

- (a) which is immediately necessary to save the patient's life; or
- (b) which (not being irreversible) is immediately necessary to prevent a serious deterioration of his condition; or
- (c) which (not being irreversible or hazardous) is immediately necessary to alleviate serious suffering by the patient; or
- (d) which (not being irreversible or hazardous) is immediately necessary and represents the minimum interference necessary to prevent the patient from behaving violently or being a danger to himself or to others.

(1A) Section 58A above, in so far as it relates to electro-convulsive therapy by virtue of subsection (1)(a) of that section, shall not apply to any treatment which falls within paragraph (a) or (b) of subsection (1) above.

(1B) Section 58A above, in so far as it relates to a form of treatment specified by virtue of subsection (1)(b) of that section, shall not apply to any treatment which falls within such of paragraphs (a) to (d) of subsection (1) above as may be specified in regulations under that section.

(1C) For the purposes of subsection (1B) above, the regulations –

(a) may make different provision for different cases (and may, in particular, make different provision for different forms of treatment);
(b) may make provision which applies subject to specified exceptions; and
(c) may include transitional, consequential, incidental or supplemental provision.

(2) Sections 60 and 61(3) above shall not preclude the continuation of any treatment or of treatment under any plan pending compliance with section 57, 58 or 58A above if the approved clinician in charge of the treatment considers that the discontinuance of the treatment or of treatment under the plan would cause serious suffering to the patient.

(3) For the purposes of this section treatment is irreversible if it has unfavourable irreversible physical or psychological consequences and hazardous if it entails significant physical hazard.

This section derived from the Mental Health (Amendment) Act 1982, s 48.

Amendments: Mental Health Act 2007.

62A Treatment on recall of community patient or revocation of order

(1) This section applies where –

(a) a community patient is recalled to hospital under section 17E above; or
(b) a patient is liable to be detained under this Act following the revocation of a community treatment order under section 17F above in respect of him.

(2) For the purposes of section 58(1)(b) above, the patient is to be treated as if he had remained liable to be detained since the making of the community treatment order.

(3) But section 58 above does not apply to treatment given to the patient if –

(a) the certificate requirement is met for the purposes of section 64C or 64E below; or
(b) as a result of section 64B(4) or 64E(4) below, the certificate requirement would not apply (were the patient a community patient not recalled to hospital under section 17E above).

(4) Section 58A above does not apply to treatment given to the patient if there is authority to give the treatment, and the certificate requirement is met, for the purposes of section 64C or 64E below.

(5) In a case where this section applies and the Part 4A certificate falls within section 64C(4) below, the certificate requirement is met only in so far as –

(a) the Part 4A certificate expressly provides that it is appropriate for one or more specified forms of treatment to be given to the patient in that case (subject to such conditions as may be specified); or
(b) a notice having been given under subsection (5) of section 64H below, treatment is authorised by virtue of subsection (8) of that section.

(6) Subsection (5) above shall not preclude the continuation of any treatment, or of treatment under any plan, pending compliance with section 58 or 58A above or 64B or

64E below if the approved clinician in charge of the treatment considers that the discontinuance of the treatment, or of the treatment under the plan, would cause serious suffering to the patient.

(6A) In a case where this section applies and the certificate requirement is no longer met for the purposes of section 64C(4A) below, the continuation of any treatment, or of treatment under any plan, pending compliance with section 58 or 58A above or 64B or 64E below shall not be precluded if the approved clinician in charge of the treatment considers that the discontinuance of the treatment, or of treatment under the plan, would cause serious suffering to the patient.

(7) In a case where subsection (1)(b) above applies, subsection (3) above only applies pending compliance with section 58 above.

(8) In subsection (5) above –

"Part 4A certificate" has the meaning given in section 64H below; and
"specified", in relation to a Part 4A certificate, means specified in the certificate.

Amendments: Mental Health Act 2007; Health and Social Care Act 2012.

63 Treatment not requiring consent

The consent of a patient shall not be required for any medical treatment given to him for the mental disorder from which he is suffering, not being a form of treatment to which section 57, 58 or 58A above applies, if the treatment is given by or under the direction of the approved clinician in charge of the treatment.

Amendments: Mental Health Act 2007.

64 Supplementary provisions for Part IV

(1) In this Part of this Act "the responsible clinician" means the approved clinician with overall responsibility for the case of the patient in question and "hospital" includes a registered establishment.

(1A) References in this Part of this Act to the approved clinician in charge of a patient's treatment shall, where the treatment in question is a form of treatment to which section 57 above applies, be construed as references to the person in charge of the treatment.

(1B) References in this Part of this Act to the approved clinician in charge of a patient's treatment shall, where the treatment in question is a form of treatment to which section 58A above applies and the patient falls within section 56(5) above, be construed as references to the person in charge of the treatment.

(1C) Regulations made by virtue of section 32(2)(d) above apply for the purposes of this Part as they apply for the purposes of Part 2 of this Act.

(2) Any certificate for the purposes of this Part of this Act shall be in such form as may be prescribed by regulations made by the Secretary of State.

(3) For the purposes of this Part of this Act, it is appropriate for treatment to be given to a patient if the treatment is appropriate in his case, taking into account the nature and degree of the mental disorder from which he is suffering and all other circumstances of his case.

Amendments: Mental Health Act 2007; Care Standards Act 2000.

PART 4A
TREATMENT OF COMMUNITY PATIENTS NOT RECALLED TO HOSPITAL

Amendments: Inserted by the Mental Health Act 2007.

64A Meaning of "relevant treatment"

In this Part of this Act "relevant treatment", in relation to a patient, means medical treatment which –

(a) is for the mental disorder from which the patient is suffering; and
(b) is not a form of treatment to which section 57 above applies.

Amendments: Inserted by the Mental Health Act 2007

64B Adult community patients

(1) This section applies to the giving of relevant treatment to a community patient who –

(a) is not recalled to hospital under section 17E above; and
(b) has attained the age of 16 years.

(2) The treatment may not be given to the patient unless –

(a) there is authority to give it to him; and
(b) if it is section 58 type treatment or section 58A type treatment, the certificate requirement is met.

(3) But the certificate requirement does not apply if –

(a) giving the treatment to the patient is authorised in accordance with section 64G below; or
(b) the treatment is immediately necessary and –
    (i) the patient has capacity to consent to it and does consent to it; or
    (ii) a donee or deputy or the Court of Protection consents to the treatment on the patient's behalf.

(4) Nor does the certificate requirement apply in so far as the administration of medicine to the patient at any time during the period of one month beginning with the day on which the community treatment order is made is section 58 type treatment.

(5) The reference in subsection (4) above to the administration of medicine does not include any form of treatment specified under 58(1)(a) above.

Amendments: Inserted by the Mental Health Act 2007

64C Section 64B: supplemental

(1) This section has effect for the purposes of section 64B above.

(2) There is authority to give treatment to a patient if –

(a) he has capacity to consent to it and does consent to it;
(b) a donee or deputy or the Court of Protection consents to it on his behalf; or
(c) giving it to him is authorised in accordance with section 64D or 64G below.

(3) Relevant treatment is section 58 type treatment or section 58A type treatment if, at the time when it is given to the patient, section 58 or 58A above (respectively) would have applied to it, had the patient remained liable to be detained at that time (rather than being a community patient).

(4) The certificate requirement is met in respect of treatment to be given to a patient if –

(a) a registered medical practitioner appointed for the purposes of Part 4 of this Act (not being the responsible clinician or the person in charge of the treatment) has certified in writing that it is appropriate for the treatment to be given or for the treatment to be given subject to such conditions as may be specified in the certificate; and

(b) if conditions are so specified, the conditions are satisfied.

(4A) Where there is authority to give treatment by virtue of subsection (2)(a), the certificate requirement is also met in respect of the treatment if the approved clinician in charge of the treatment has certified in writing that the patient has capacity to consent to the treatment and has consented to it.

(4B) But, if the patient has not attained the age of 18, subsection (4A) does not apply to section 58A type treatment.

(5) In a case where the treatment is section 58 type treatment, treatment is immediately necessary if –

(a) it is immediately necessary to save the patient's life; or

(b) it is immediately necessary to prevent a serious deterioration of the patient's condition and is not irreversible; or

(c) it is immediately necessary to alleviate serious suffering by the patient and is not irreversible or hazardous; or

(d) it is immediately necessary, represents the minimum interference necessary to prevent the patient from behaving violently or being a danger to himself or others and is not irreversible or hazardous.

(6) In a case where the treatment is section 58A type treatment by virtue of subsection (1)(a) of that section, treatment is immediately necessary if it falls within paragraph (a) or (b) of subsection (5) above.

(7) In a case where the treatment is section 58A type treatment by virtue of subsection (1)(b) of that section, treatment is immediately necessary if it falls within such of paragraphs (a) to (d) of subsection (5) above as may be specified in regulations under that section.

(8) For the purposes of subsection (7) above, the regulations –

(a) may make different provision for different cases (and may, in particular, make different provision for different forms of treatment);

(b) may make provision which applies subject to specified exceptions; and

(c) may include transitional, consequential, incidental or supplemental provision.

(9) Subsection (3) of section 62 above applies for the purposes of this section as it applies for the purposes of that section.

Amendments: Inserted by the Mental Health Act 2007.

64D Adult community patients lacking capacity

(1) A person is authorised to give relevant treatment to a patient as mentioned in section 64C(2)(c) above if the conditions in subsections (2) to (6) below are met.

(2) The first condition is that, before giving the treatment, the person takes reasonable steps to establish whether the patient lacks capacity to consent to the treatment.

(3) The second condition is that, when giving the treatment, he reasonably believes that the patient lacks capacity to consent to it.

(4) The third condition is that –

- (a) he has no reason to believe that the patient objects to being given the treatment; or
- (b) he does have reason to believe that the patient so objects, but it is not necessary to use force against the patient in order to give the treatment.

(5) The fourth condition is that –

- (a) he is the person in charge of the treatment and an approved clinician; or
- (b) the treatment is given under the direction of that clinician.

(6) The fifth condition is that giving the treatment does not conflict with –

- (a) an advance decision which he is satisfied is valid and applicable; or
- (b) a decision made by a donee or deputy or the Court of Protection.

(7) In this section –

- (a) reference to an advance decision is to an advance decision (within the meaning of the Mental Capacity Act 2005) made by the patient; and
- (b) "valid and applicable", in relation to such a decision, means valid and applicable to the treatment in question in accordance with section 25 of that Act.

Amendments Inserted by the Mental Health Act 2007.

64E Child community patients

(1) This section applies to the giving of relevant treatment to a community patient who –

- (a) is not recalled to hospital under section 17E above; and
- (b) has not attained the age of 16 years.

(2) The treatment may not be given to the patient unless –

- (a) there is authority to give it to him; and
- (b) if it is section 58 type treatment or section 58A type treatment, the certificate requirement is met.

(3) But the certificate requirement does not apply if –

- (a) giving the treatment to the patient is authorised in accordance with section 64G below; or
- (b) in a case where the patient is competent to consent to the treatment and does consent to it, the treatment is immediately necessary.

(4) Nor does the certificate requirement apply in so far as the administration of medicine to the patient at any time during the period of one month beginning with the day on which the community treatment order is made is section 58 type treatment.

(5) The reference in subsection (4) above to the administration of medicine does not include any form of treatment specified under section 58(1)(a) above.

(6) For the purposes of subsection (2)(a) above, there is authority to give treatment to a patient if –

(a) he is competent to consent to it and he does consent to it; or
(b) giving it to him is authorised in accordance with section 64F or 64G below.

(7) Subsections (3) to (4A) and (5) to (9) of section 64C above have effect for the purposes of this section as they have effect for the purposes of section 64B above; and for the purpose of this subsection, subsection (4A) of section 64C above has effect as if –

(a) the references to treatment were references only to section 58 type treatment,
(b) the reference to subsection (2)(a) of section 64C were a reference to subsection (6)(a) of this section, and
(c) the reference to capacity to consent were a reference to competence to consent.

(8) Regulations made by virtue of section 32(2)(d) above apply for the purposes of this section as they apply for the purposes of Part 2 of this Act.

Amendments: Mental Health Act 2007; Health and Social Care Act 2012.

64F Child community patients lacking competence

(1) A person is authorised to give relevant treatment to a patient as mentioned in section 64E(6)(b) above if the conditions in subsections (2) to (5) below are met.

(2) The first condition is that, before giving the treatment, the person takes reasonable steps to establish whether the patient is competent to consent to the treatment.

(3) The second condition is that, when giving the treatment, he reasonably believes that the patient is not competent to consent to it.

(4) The third condition is that –

(a) he has no reason to believe that the patient objects to being given the treatment; or
(b) he does have reason to believe that the patient so objects, but it is not necessary to use force against the patient in order to give the treatment.

(5) The fourth condition is that –

(a) he is the person in charge of the treatment and an approved clinician; or
(b) the treatment is given under the direction of that clinician.

Amendments: Inserted by Mental Health Act 2007.

64FA Withdrawal of consent

(1) Where the consent of a patient to any treatment has been given as mentioned in section 64C(2)(a) above for the purposes of section 64B or 64E above, the patient may at any time before the completion of the treatment withdraw his consent, and those sections shall then apply as if the remainder of the treatment were a separate form of treatment.

(2) Subsection (3) below applies where –

(a) the consent of a patient to any treatment has been given as mentioned in section 64C(2)(a) above for the purposes of section 64B or 64E above; but
(b) before the completion of the treatment, the patient loses capacity or (as the case may be) competence to consent to the treatment.

(3) The patient shall be treated as having withdrawn his consent and section 64B or (as the case may be) section 64E above shall then apply as if the remainder of the treatment were a separate form of treatment.

(4) Without prejudice to the application of subsections (1) to (3) above to any treatment given under the plan of treatment to which a patient has consented, a patient who has consented to such a plan may at any time withdraw his consent to further treatment, or to further treatment of any description, under the plan.

(5) This section shall not preclude the continuation of any treatment, or of treatment under any plan, pending compliance with section 58, 58A, 64B or 64E above if the approved clinician in charge of the treatment considers that the discontinuance of the treatment, or of treatment under the plan, would cause serious suffering to the patient.

Amendment: Inserted by Health and Social Care Act 2012.

64G Emergency treatment for patients lacking capacity or competence

(1) A person is also authorised to give relevant treatment to a patient as mentioned in section 64C(2)(c) or 64E(6)(b) above if the conditions in subsections (2) to (4) below are met.

(2) The first condition is that, when giving the treatment, the person reasonably believes that the patient lacks capacity to consent to it or, as the case may be, is not competent to consent to it.

(3) The second condition is that the treatment is immediately necessary.

(4) The third condition is that if it is necessary to use force against the patient in order to give the treatment –

(a) the treatment needs to be given in order to prevent harm to the patient; and
(b) the use of such force is a proportionate response to the likelihood of the patient's suffering harm, and to the seriousness of that harm.

(5) Subject to subsections (6) to (8) below, treatment is immediately necessary if –

(a) it is immediately necessary to save the patient's life; or
(b) it is immediately necessary to prevent a serious deterioration of the patient's condition and is not irreversible; or
(c) it is immediately necessary to alleviate serious suffering by the patient and is not irreversible or hazardous; or
(d) it is immediately necessary, represents the minimum interference necessary to prevent the patient from behaving violently or being a danger to himself or others and is not irreversible or hazardous.

(6) Where the treatment is section 58A type treatment by virtue of subsection (1)(a) of that section, treatment is immediately necessary if it falls within paragraph (a) or (b) of subsection (5) above.

(7) Where the treatment is section 58A type treatment by virtue of subsection (1)(b) of that section, treatment is immediately necessary if it falls within such of paragraphs (a) to (d) of subsection (5) above as may be specified in regulations under section 58A above.

(8) For the purposes of subsection (7) above, the regulations –

(a) may make different provision for different cases (and may, in particular, make different provision for different forms of treatment);
(b) may make provision which applies subject to specified exceptions; and
(c) may include transitional, consequential, incidental or supplemental provision.

(9) Subsection (3) of section 62 above applies for the purposes of this section as it applies for the purposes of that section.

Amendments: Inserted by Mental Health Act 2007.

64H Certificates: supplementary provisions

(1) A certificate under section 64B(2)(b) or 64E(2)(b) above (a "Part 4A certificate") may relate to a plan of treatment under which the patient is to be given (whether within a specified period or otherwise) one or more forms of section 58 type treatment or section 58A type treatment.

(2) A Part 4A certificate shall be in such form as may be prescribed by regulations made by the appropriate national authority; and the regulations may make different provision for the different descriptions of Part 4A certificate.

(3) Before giving a Part 4A certificate that falls within section 64C(4) above, the registered medical practitioner concerned shall consult two other persons who have been professionally concerned with the patient's medical treatment but, of those persons –

(a) at least one shall be a person who is not a registered medical practitioner; and
(b) neither shall be the patient's responsible clinician or the person in charge of the treatment in question.

(4) Where a patient is given treatment in accordance with a Part 4A certificate that falls within section 64C(4) above, a report on the treatment and the patient's condition shall be given by the person in charge of the treatment to the regulatory authority if required by that authority.

(5) The regulatory authority may at any time give notice directing that a Part 4A certificate that falls within section 64C(4) above shall not apply to treatment given to a patient after a date specified in the notice, and the relevant section shall then apply to any such treatment as if that certificate had not been given.

(6) The relevant section is –

(a) if the patient is not recalled to hospital in accordance with section 17E above, section 64B or 64E above;
(b) if the patient is so recalled or is liable to be detained under this Act following revocation of the community treatment order under section 17F above –
    (i) section 58 above, in the case of section 58 type treatment;
    (ii) section 58A above, in the case of section 58A type treatment;

(subject to section 62A(2) above).

(7) The notice under subsection (5) above shall be given to the person in charge of the treatment in question.

(8) Subsection (5) above shall not preclude the continuation of any treatment or of treatment under any plan pending compliance with the relevant section if the person in charge of the treatment considers that the discontinuance of the treatment or of treatment under the plan would cause serious suffering to the patient.

(9) In this section, "the appropriate national authority" means –

(a) in relation to community patients in respect of whom the responsible hospital is in England, the Secretary of State;
(b) in relation to community patients in respect of whom the responsible hospital is in Wales, the Welsh Ministers.

Amendments: Mental Health Act 2007; Health and Social Care Act 2012.

64I Liability for negligence

Nothing in section 64D, 64F or 64G above excludes a person's civil liability for loss or damage, or his criminal liability, resulting from his negligence in doing anything authorised to be done by that section.

Amendments: Mental Health Act 2007.

64J Factors to be considered in determining whether patient objects to treatment

(1) In assessing for the purposes of this Part whether he has reason to believe that a patient objects to treatment, a person shall consider all the circumstances so far as they are reasonably ascertainable, including the patient's behaviour, wishes, feelings, views, beliefs and values.

(2) But circumstances from the past shall be considered only so far as it is still appropriate to consider them.

Amendments: Mental Health Act 2007.

64K Interpretation of Part 4A

(1) This Part of this Act is to be construed as follows.

(2) References to a patient who lacks capacity are to a patient who lacks capacity within the meaning of the Mental Capacity Act 2005.

(3) References to a patient who has capacity are to be read accordingly.

(4) References to a donee are to a donee of a lasting power of attorney (within the meaning of section 9 of the Mental Capacity Act 2005) created by the patient, where the donee is acting within the scope of his authority and in accordance with that Act.

(5) References to a deputy are to a deputy appointed for the patient by the Court of Protection under section 16 of the Mental Capacity Act 2005, where the deputy is acting within the scope of his authority and in accordance with that Act.

(6) Reference to the responsible clinician shall be construed as a reference to the responsible clinician within the meaning of Part 2 of this Act.

(7) References to a hospital include a registered establishment.

(8) Section 64(3) above applies for the purposes of this Part of this Act as it applies for the purposes of Part 4 of this Act.

Amendments: Mental Health Act 2007.

PART V
MENTAL HEALTH REVIEW TRIBUNALS

Constitution etc

65 Mental Health Review Tribunals for Wales

(1) There shall be a Mental Health Review Tribunal for Wales.

(1A) The purpose of that tribunal is to deal with applications and references by and in respect of patients under the provisions of this Act.

(2) The provisions of Schedule 2 to this Act shall have effect with respect to the constitution of the Mental Health Review Tribunal for Wales.

(3) Subject to the provisions of Schedule 2 to this Act, and to rules made by the Lord Chancellor under this Act, the jurisdiction of the Mental Health Review Tribunal for Wales may be exercised by any three or more of its members, and references in this Act to the Mental Health Review Tribunal for Wales shall be construed accordingly.

(4) The Welsh Ministers may pay to the members of the Mental Health Review Tribunal for Wales such remuneration and allowances as they may determine, and defray the expenses of that tribunal to such amount as they may determine, and may provide for that tribunal such officers and servants, and such accommodation, as that tribunal may require.

Amendments: Health Authorities Act 1995; Mental Health Act 2007; SI 2008/2833.

Applications and references concerning Part II patients

66 Applications to tribunals

(1) Where –

- (a) a patient is admitted to a hospital in pursuance of an application for admission for assessment; or
- (b) a patient is admitted to a hospital in pursuance of an application for admission for treatment; or
- (c) a patient is received into guardianship in pursuance of a guardianship application; or
- (ca) a community treatment order is made in respect of a patient; or
- (cb) a community treatment order is revoked under section 17F above in respect of a patient; or
- (d) …
- (e) a patient is transferred from guardianship to a hospital in pursuance of regulations made under section 19 above; or
- (f) a report is furnished under section 20 above in respect of a patient and the patient is not discharged under section 23 above; or
- (fza) a report is furnished under section 20A above in respect of a patient and the patient is not discharged under section 23 above; or
- (fa) a report is furnished under subsection (2) of section 21B above in respect of a patient and subsection (5) of that section applies (or subsections (5) and (6)(b) of that section apply) in the case of the report; or
- (faa) a report is furnished under subsection (2) of section 21B above in respect of a community patient and subsection (6A) of that section applies (or subsections (6A) and (6B)(b) of that section apply) in the case of the report; or
- (fb) …

(g) a report is furnished under section 25 above in respect of a patient who is detained in pursuance of an application for admission for treatment or a community patient; or

(ga) …

(gb) …

(gc) …

(h) an order is made under section 29 above on the ground specified in paragraph (c) or (d) of subsection (3) of that section in respect of a patient who is or subsequently becomes liable to be detained or subject to guardianship under Part II of this Act or who is a community patient,

an application may be made to the appropriate tribunal within the relevant period –

(i) by the patient (except in the cases mentioned in paragraphs (g) and (h) above), and

(ii) in the cases mentioned in paragraphs (g) and (h) above, by his nearest relative.

(2) In subsection (1) above "the relevant period" means –

(a) in the case mentioned in paragraph (a) of that subsection, 14 days beginning with the day on which the patient is admitted as so mentioned;

(b) in the case mentioned in paragraph (b) of that subsection, six months beginning with the day on which the patient is admitted as so mentioned;

(c) in the case mentioned in paragraph (c) of that subsection, six months beginning with the day on which the application is accepted;

(ca) in the case mentioned in paragraph (ca) of that subsection, six months beginning with the day on which the community treatment order is made;

(cb) in the case mentioned in paragraph (cb) of that subsection, six months beginning with the day on which the community treatment order is revoked;

(d) in the case mentioned in paragraph (g) of that subsection, 28 days beginning with the day on which the applicant is informed that the report has been furnished;

(e) in the case mentioned in paragraph (e) of that subsection, six months beginning with the day on which the patient is transferred;

(f) in the case mentioned in paragraph (f) or (fa) of that subsection, the period or periods for which authority for the patient's detention or guardianship is renewed by virtue of the report;

(fza) in the cases mentioned in paragraphs (fza) and (faa) of that subsection, the period or periods for which the community treatment period is extended by virtue of the report;

(fa) …

(g) in the case mentioned in paragraph (h) of that subsection, 12 months beginning with the date of the order, and in any subsequent period of 12 months during which the order continues in force.

(2A) Nothing in subsection (1)(b) above entitles a community patient to make an application by virtue of that provision even if he is admitted to a hospital on being recalled there under section 17E above.

(3) Section 32 above shall apply for the purposes of this section as it applies for the purposes of Part II of this Act.

(4) In this Act "the appropriate tribunal" means the First-tier Tribunal or the Mental Health Review Tribunal for Wales.

(5) For provision determining to which of those tribunals applications by or in respect of a patient under this Act shall be made, see section 77(3) and (4) below.

Amendments: Mental Health (Patients in the Community) Act 1995; Mental Health Act 2007; SI 2008/2833.

67 References to tribunals by Secretary of State concerning Part II patients

(1) The Secretary of State may, if he thinks fit, at any time refer to the appropriate tribunal the case of any patient who is liable to be detained or subject to guardianship under Part II of this Act or of any community patient.

(2) For the purpose of furnishing information for the purposes of a reference under subsection (1) above any registered medical practitioner or approved clinician authorised by or on behalf of the patient may, at any reasonable time, visit the patient and examine him in private and require the production of and inspect any records relating to the detention or treatment of the patient in any hospital or to any after-care services provided for the patient under section 117 below.

(3) Section 32 above shall apply for the purposes of this section as it applies for the purposes of Part II of this Act.

Amendments: Mental Health (Patients in the Community) Act 1995; Mental Health Act 2007; SI 2008/2833.

68 Duty of managers of hospitals to refer cases to tribunal

(1) This section applies in respect of the following patients –

- (a) a patient who is admitted to a hospital in pursuance of an application for admission for assessment;
- (b) a patient who is admitted to a hospital in pursuance of an application for admission for treatment;
- (c) a community patient;
- (d) a patient whose community treatment order is revoked under section 17F above;
- (e) a patient who is transferred from guardianship to a hospital in pursuance of regulations made under section 19 above.

(2) On expiry of the period of six months beginning with the applicable day, the managers of the hospital shall refer the patient's case to the appropriate tribunal.

(3) But they shall not do so if during that period –

- (a) any right has been exercised by or in respect of the patient by virtue of any of paragraphs (b), (ca), (cb), (e), (g) and (h) of section 66(1) above;
- (b) a reference has been made in respect of the patient under section 67(1) above, not being a reference made while the patient is or was liable to be detained in pursuance of an application for admission for assessment; or
- (c) a reference has been made in respect of the patient under subsection (7) below.

(4) A person who applies to a tribunal but subsequently withdraws his application shall be treated for these purposes as not having exercised his right to apply, and if he withdraws his application on a date after expiry of the period mentioned in subsection (2) above, the managers shall refer the patient's case as soon as possible after that date.

(5) In subsection (2) above, "the applicable day" means –

(a) in the case of a patient who is admitted to a hospital in pursuance of an application for admission for assessment, the day on which the patient was so admitted;

(b) in the case of a patient who is admitted to a hospital in pursuance of an application for admission for treatment –

(i) the day on which the patient was so admitted; or

(ii) if, when he was so admitted, he was already liable to be detained in pursuance of an application for admission for assessment, the day on which he was originally admitted in pursuance of the application for admission for assessment;

(c) in the case of a community patient or a patient whose community treatment order is revoked under section 17F above, the day mentioned in sub-paragraph (i) or (ii), as the case may be, of paragraph (b) above;

(d) in the case of a patient who is transferred from guardianship to a hospital, the day on which he was so transferred.

(6) The managers of the hospital shall also refer the patient's case to the appropriate tribunal if a period of more than three years (or, if the patient has not attained the age of 18 years, one year) has elapsed since his case was last considered by such a tribunal, whether on his own application or otherwise.

(7) If, in the case of a community patient, the community treatment order is revoked under section 17F above, the managers of the hospital shall also refer the patient's case to the appropriate tribunal as soon as possible after the order is revoked.

(8) For the purposes of furnishing information for the purposes of a reference under this section, a registered medical practitioner or approved clinician authorised by or on behalf of the patient may at any reasonable time –

(a) visit and examine the patient in private; and

(b) require the production of and inspect any records relating to the detention or treatment of the patient in any hospital or any after-care services provided for him under section 117 below.

(9) Reference in this section to the managers of the hospital –

(a) in relation to a community patient, is to the managers of the responsible hospital;

(b) in relation to any other patient, is to the managers of the hospital in which he is liable to be detained.

Amendments: Mental Health Act 2007; SI 2008/2833.

68A Power to reduce periods under section 68

(1) The appropriate national authority may from time to time by order amend subsection (2) or (6) of section 68 above so as to substitute for a period mentioned there such shorter period as is specified in the order.

(2) The order may include such transitional, consequential, incidental or supplemental provision as the appropriate national authority thinks fit.

(3) The order may, in particular, make provision for a case where –

(a) a patient in respect of whom subsection (1) of section 68 above applies is, or is about to be, transferred from England to Wales or from Wales to England; and

(b) the period by reference to which subsection (2) or (6) of that section operates for the purposes of the patient's case is not the same in one territory as it is in the other.

(4) A patient is transferred from one territory to the other if –

(a) he is transferred from a hospital, or from guardianship, in one territory to a hospital in the other in pursuance of regulations made under section 19 above;
(b) he is removed under subsection (3) of that section from a hospital or accommodation in one territory to a hospital or accommodation in the other;
(c) he is a community patient responsibility for whom is assigned from a hospital in one territory to a hospital in the other in pursuance of regulations made under section 19A above; or
(d) on the revocation of a community treatment order in respect of him under section 17F above he is detained in a hospital in the territory other than the one in which the responsible hospital was situated;
(e) …

(5) Provision made by virtue of subsection (3) above may require or authorise the managers of a hospital determined in accordance with the order to refer the patient's case to the appropriate tribunal.

(6) In so far as making provision by virtue of subsection (3) above, the order –

(a) may make different provision for different cases;
(b) may make provision which applies subject to specified exceptions.

(7) Where the appropriate national authority for one territory makes an order under subsection (1) above, the appropriate national authority for the other territory may by order make such provision in consequence of the order as it thinks fit.

(8) An order made under subsection (7) above may, in particular, make provision for a case within subsection (3) above (and subsections (4) to (6) above shall apply accordingly).

(9) In this section, "the appropriate national authority" means –

(a) in relation to a hospital in England, the Secretary of State;
(b) in relation to a hospital in Wales, the Welsh Ministers.

Amendments: Mental Health Act 2007; Health and Social Care Act 2012; SI 2008/2833.

Applications and references concerning Part III patients

69 Applications to tribunals concerning patients subject to hospital and guardianship orders

(1) Without prejudice to any provision of section 66(1) above as applied by section 40(4) above, an application to the appropriate tribunal may also be made –

(a) in respect of a patient liable to be detained in pursuance of a hospital order or a community patient who was so liable immediately before he became a community patient, by the nearest relative of the patient in any period in which an application may be made by the patient under any such provision as so applied; and
(b) in respect of a patient placed under guardianship by a guardianship order –
   (i) by the patient, within the period of six months beginning with the date of the order;

(ii) by the nearest relative of the patient, within the period of 12 months beginning with the date of the order and in any subsequent period of 12 months.

(2) Where a person detained in a hospital –

(a) is treated as subject to a hospital order, hospital direction or transfer direction by virtue of section 41(5) above or section 80B(2), 82(2) or 85(2) below; or
(b) is subject to a direction having the same effect as a hospital order by virtue of section 47(3) or 48(3) above,

then, without prejudice to any provision of Part II of this Act as applied by section 40 above, that person may make an application to the appropriate tribunal in the period of six months beginning with the date of the order or direction mentioned in paragraph (a) above or, as the case may be, the date of the direction mentioned in paragraph (b) above.

(3) The provisions of section 66 above as applied by section 40(4) above are subject to subsection (4) below.

(4) If the initial detention period has not elapsed when the relevant application period begins, the right of a hospital order patient to make an application by virtue of paragraph (ca) or (cb) of section 66(1) above shall be exercisable only during whatever remains of the relevant application period after the initial detention period has elapsed.

(5) In subsection (4) above –

(a) "hospital order patient" means a patient who is subject to a hospital order, excluding a patient of a kind mentioned in paragraph (a) or (b) of subsection (2) above;
(b) "the initial detention period", in relation to a hospital order patient, means the period of six months beginning with the date of the hospital order; and
(c) "the relevant application period" means the relevant period mentioned in paragraph (ca) or (cb), as the case may be, of section 66(2) above.

Amendments: Crime (Sentences) Act 1997; Mental Health Act 2007; SI 2008/2833.

70 Applications to tribunals concerning restricted patients

A patient who is a restricted patient within the meaning of section 79 below and is detained in a hospital may apply to the appropriate tribunal –

(a) in the period between the expiration of six months and the expiration of 12 months beginning with the date of the relevant hospital order, hospital direction or transfer direction; and
(b) in any subsequent period of 12 months.

Amendments: Crime (Sentences) Act 1997; SI 2008/2833.

71 References by Secretary of State concerning restricted patients

(1) The Secretary of State may at any time refer the case of a restricted patient to the appropriate tribunal.

(2) The Secretary of State shall refer to the appropriate tribunal the case of any restricted patient detained in a hospital whose case has not been considered by such a tribunal, whether on his own application or otherwise, within the last three years.

(3) The Secretary of State may by order vary the length of the period mentioned in subsection (2) above.

(3A) An order under subsection (3) above may include such transitional, consequential, incidental or supplemental provision as the Secretary of State thinks fit.

(4) Any reference under subsection (1) above in respect of a patient who has been conditionally discharged and not recalled to hospital shall be made to the tribunal for the area in which the patient resides.

(5) *(repealed)*

(6) *(repealed)*

Amendments: Domestic Violence, Crime and Victims Act 2004; Mental Health Act 2007; SI 2008/2833.

Discharge of patients

72 Powers of tribunals

(1) Where application is made to the appropriate tribunal by or in respect of a patient who is liable to be detained under this Act or is a community patient, the tribunal may in any case direct that the patient be discharged, and –

- (a) the tribunal shall direct the discharge of a patient liable to be detained under section 2 above if it is not satisfied –
  - (i) that he is then suffering from mental disorder or from mental disorder of a nature or degree which warrants his detention in a hospital for assessment (or for assessment followed by medical treatment) for at least a limited period; or
  - (ii) that his detention as aforesaid is justified in the interests of his own health or safety or with a view to the protection of other persons;
- (b) the tribunal shall direct the discharge of a patient liable to be detained otherwise than under section 2 above if it is not satisfied –
  - (i) that he is then suffering from mental disorder or from mental disorder of a nature or degree which makes it appropriate for him to be liable to be detained in a hospital for medical treatment; or
  - (ii) that it is necessary for the health of safety of the patient or for the protection of other persons that he should receive such treatment; or
  - (iia) that appropriate medical treatment is available for him; or
  - (iii) in the case of an application by virtue of paragraph (g) of section 66(1) above, that the patient, if released, would be likely to act in a manner dangerous to other persons or to himself;
- (c) the tribunal shall direct the discharge of a community patient if it is not satisfied –
  - (i) that he is then suffering from mental disorder or mental disorder of a nature or degree which makes it appropriate for him to receive medical treatment; or
  - (ii) that it is necessary for his health or safety or for the protection of other persons that he should receive such treatment; or
  - (iii) that it is necessary that the responsible clinician should be able to exercise the power under section 17E(1) above to recall the patient to hospital; or
  - (iv) that appropriate medical treatment is available for him; or
  - (v) in the case of an application by virtue of paragraph (g) of section 66(1) above, that the patient, if discharged, would be likely to act in a manner dangerous to other persons or to himself.

(1A) In determining whether the criterion in subsection (1)(c)(iii) above is met, the tribunal shall, in particular, consider, having regard to the patient's history of mental disorder and any other relevant factors, what risk there would be of a deterioration of the patient's condition if he were to continue not to be detained in a hospital (as a result, for example, of his refusing or neglecting to receive the medical treatment he requires for his mental disorder).

(2) ...

(3) A tribunal may under subsection (1) above direct the discharge of a patient on a future date specified in the direction; and where a tribunal does not direct the discharge of a patient under that subsection the tribunal may –

(a) with a view to facilitating his discharge on a future date, recommend that he be granted leave of absence or transferred to another hospital or into guardianship; and
(b) further consider his case in the event of any such recommendation not being complied with.

(3A) Subsection (1) above does not require a tribunal to direct the discharge of a patient just because it thinks it might be appropriate for the patient to be discharged (subject to the possibility of recall) under a community treatment order; and a tribunal –

(a) may recommend that the responsible clinician consider whether to make a community treatment order; and
(b) may (but need not) further consider the patient's case if the responsible clinician does not make an order.

(4) Where application is made to the appropriate tribunal by or in respect of a patient who is subject to guardianship under this Act, the tribunal may in any case direct that the patient be discharged, and shall so direct if it is satisfied –

(a) that he is not then suffering from mental disorder; or
(b) that it is not necessary in the interests of the welfare of the patient, or for the protection of other persons, that the patient should remain under such guardianship.

(4A) (*repealed*)

(5) (*repealed*)

(6) Subsections (1) to (4) above apply in relation to references to a the appropriate tribunal as they apply in relation to applications made to the appropriate tribunal by or in respect of a patient.

(7) Subsection (1) above shall not apply in the case of a restricted patient except as provided in sections 73 and 74 below.

Amendments: Mental Health (Patients in the Community) Act 1995; Mental Health Act 2007; SI 2001/3712; SI 2008/2833.

73 Power to discharge restricted patients

(1) Where an application to the appropriate tribunal is made by a restricted patient who is subject to a restriction order, or where the case of such a patient is referred to the appropriate tribunal, the tribunal shall direct the absolute discharge of the patient if –

(a) the tribunal is not satisfied as to the matters mentioned in paragraph (b)(i), (ii) or (iia) of section 72(1) above; and

(b) the tribunal is satisfied that it is not appropriate for the patient to remain liable to be recalled to hospital for further treatment.

(2) Where in the case of any such patient as is mentioned in subsection (1) above –

(a) paragraph (a) of that subsection applies; but
(b) paragraph (b) of that subsection does not apply,

the tribunal shall direct the conditional discharge of the patient.

(3) Where a patient is absolutely discharged under this section he shall thereupon cease to be liable to be detained by virtue of the relevant hospital order, and the restriction order shall cease to have effect accordingly.

(4) Where a patient is conditionally discharged under this section –

(a) he may be recalled by the Secretary of State under subsection (3) of section 42 above as if he had been conditionally discharged under subsection (2) of that section; and
(b) the patient shall comply with such conditions (if any) as may be imposed at the time of discharge by the tribunal or at any subsequent time by the Secretary of State.

(5) The Secretary of State may from time to time vary any condition imposed (whether by the tribunal or by him) under subsection (4) above.

(6) Where a restriction order in respect of a patient ceases to have effect after he has been conditionally discharged under this section the patient shall, unless previously recalled, be deemed to be absolutely discharged on the date when the order ceases to have effect and shall cease to be liable to be detained by virtue of the relevant hospital order.

(7) A tribunal may defer a direction for the conditional discharge of a patient until such arrangements as appear to the tribunal to be necessary for that purpose have been made to its satisfaction; and where by virtue of any such deferment no direction has been given on an application or reference before the time when the patient's case comes before the tribunal on a subsequent application or reference, the previous application or reference shall be treated as one on which no direction under this section can be given.

(8) This section is without prejudice to section 42 above.

Amendments: Mental Health Act 2007; SI 2001/3712; SI 2008/2833.

74 Restricted patients subject to restriction directions

(1) Where an application to the appropriate tribunal is made by a restricted patient who is subject to a limitation direction or restriction direction, or where the case of such a patient is referred to the appropriate tribunal the tribunal –

(a) shall notify the Secretary of State whether, in its opinion, the patient would, if subject to a restriction order, be entitled to be absolutely or conditionally discharged under section 73 above; and
(b) if the tribunal notifies him that the patient would be entitled to be conditionally discharged, may recommend that in the event of his not being discharged under this section he should continue to be detained in hospital.

(2) If in the case of a patient not falling within subsection (4) below –

(a) the tribunal notifies the Secretary of State that the patient would be entitled to be absolutely or conditionally discharged; and
(b) within the period of 90 days beginning with the date of that notification the Secretary of State gives notice to the tribunal that the patient may be so discharged,

the tribunal shall direct the absolute or, as the case may be, the conditional discharge of the patient.

(3) Where a patient continues to be liable to be detained in a hospital at the end of the period referred to in subsection (2)(b) above because the Secretary of State has not given the notice there mentioned, the managers of the hospital shall, unless the tribunal has made a recommendation under subsection (1)(b) above, transfer the patient to a prison or other institution in which he might have been detained if he had not been removed to hospital, there to be dealt with as if he had not been so removed.

(4) If, in the case of a patient who is subject to a transfer direction under section 48 above, the tribunal notifies the Secretary of State that the patient would be entitled to be absolutely or conditionally discharged, the Secretary of State shall, unless the tribunal has made a recommendation under subsection (1)(b) above, by warrant direct that the patient be remitted to a prison or other institution in which he might have been detained if he had not been removed to hospital, there to be dealt with as if he had not been so removed.

(5) Where a patient is transferred or remitted under subsection (3) or (4) above the relevant hospital direction and the limitation direction or, as the case may be, the relevant transfer direction and the restriction direction shall cease to have effect on his arrival in the prison or other institution.

(5A) Where the tribunal has made a recommendation under subsection (1)(b) above in the case of a patient who is subject to a restriction direction or a limitation direction –

(a) the fact that the restriction direction or limitation direction remains in force does not prevent the making of any application or reference to the Parole Board by or in respect of him or the exercise by him of any power to require the Secretary of State to refer his case to the Parole Board, and
(b) if the Parole Board make a direction or recommendation by virtue of which the patient would become entitled to be released (whether unconditionally or on licence) from any prison or other institution in which he might have been detained if he had not been removed to hospital, the restriction direction or limitation direction shall cease to have effect at the time when he would become entitled to be so released.

(6) Subsections (3) to (8) of section 73 above shall have effect in relation to this section as they have effect in relation to that section, taking references to the relevant hospital order and the restriction order as references to the hospital direction and the limitation direction or, as the case may be, to the transfer direction and the restriction direction.

(7) This section is without prejudice to sections 50 to 53 above in their application to patients who are not discharged under this section.

Amendments: Crime (Sentences) Act 1997; Criminal Justice Act 2003; SI 2008/2833.

75 Applications and references concerning conditionally discharged restricted patients

(1) Where a restricted patient has been conditionally discharged under section 42(2), 73 or 74 above and is subsequently recalled to hospital –

(a) the Secretary of State shall, within one month of the day on which the patient returns or is returned to hospital, refer his case to the appropriate tribunal; and
(b) section 70 above shall apply to the patient as if the relevant hospital order, hospital direction or transfer direction had been made on that day.

(2) Where a restricted patient has been conditionally discharged as aforesaid but has not been recalled to hospital he may apply to the appropriate tribunal –

(a) in the period between the expiration of 12 months and the expiration of two years beginning with the date on which he was conditionally discharged; and
(b) in any subsequent period of two years.

(3) Sections 73 and 74 above shall not apply to an application under subsection (2) above but on any such application the tribunal may –

(a) vary any condition to which the patient is subject in connection with his discharge or impose any condition which might have been imposed in connection therewith; or
(b) direct that the restriction order, limitation direction or restriction direction to which he is subject shall cease to have effect;

and if the tribunal gives a direction under paragraph (b) above the patient shall cease to be liable to be detained by virtue of the relevant hospital order, hospital direction or transfer direction.

Amendments: Crime (Sentences) Act 1997; Mental Health Act 2007; SI 2008/2833.

General

76 Visiting and examination of patients

(1) For the purpose of advising whether an application to the appropriate tribunal should be made by or in respect of a patient who is liable to be detained or subject to guardianship under Part II of this Act or a community patient, or of furnishing information as to the condition of a patient for the purposes of such an application, any registered medical practitioner or approved clinician authorised by or on behalf of the patient or other person who is entitled to make or has made the application –

(a) may at any reasonable time visit the patient and examine him in private, and
(b) may require the production of and inspect any records relating to the detention or treatment of the patient in any hospital or to any after-care services provided for the patient under section 117 below.

(2) Section 32 above shall apply for the purposes of this section as it applies for the purposes of Part II of this Act.

Amendments: Mental Health (Patients in the Community) Act 1995; Mental Health Act 2007; SI 2008/2833.

77 General provisions concerning tribunal applications

(1) No application shall be made to the appropriate tribunal by or in respect of a patient under this Act except in such cases and at such times as are expressly provided by this Act.

(2) Where under this Act any person is authorised to make an application to the appropriate tribunal within a specified period, not more than one such application shall be made by that person within that period but for that purpose there shall be

disregarded any application which is withdrawn in accordance with Tribunal Procedure Rules or rules made under section 78 below.

(3) Subject to subsection (4) below an application to a tribunal authorised to be made by or in respect of a patient under this Act shall be made by notice in writing addressed –

(a) in the case of a patient who is liable to be detained in a hospital, to the First-tier Tribunal where that hospital is in England and to the Mental Health Review Tribunal for Wales where that hospital is in Wales;

(b) in the case of a community patient, to the First-tier Tribunal where the responsible hospital is in England and to the Mental Health Review Tribunal for Wales where that hospital is in Wales;

(c) in the case of a patient subject to guardianship, to the First-tier Tribunal where the patient resides in England and to the Mental Health Review Tribunal for Wales where the patient resides in Wales.

(4) Any application under section 75(2) above shall be made to the First-tier Tribunal where the patient resides in England and to the Mental Health Review Tribunal for Wales where the patient resides in Wales.

Amendments: Mental Health Act 2007; SI 2008/2833; SI 2009/1307.

78 Procedure of Mental Health Review Tribunal for Wales

(1) The Lord Chancellor may make rules with respect to the making of applications to the Mental Health Review Tribunal for Wales and with respect to the proceedings of that tribunal and matters incidental to or consequential on such proceedings.

(2) Rules made under this section may in particular make provision –

(a) for enabling the tribunal, or the *chairman* [President] of the tribunal, to postpone the consideration of any application by or in respect of a patient, or of any such application of any specified class, until the expiration of such period (not exceeding 12 months) as may be specified in the rules from the date on which an application by or in respect of the same patient was last considered and determined under this Act by the tribunal or the First-tier Tribunal;

(b) for the transfer of proceedings to or from the Mental Health Review Tribunal for Wales in any case where, after the making of the application, the patient is moved into or out of Wales;

(c) for restricting the persons qualified to serve as members of the tribunal for the consideration of any application, or of an application of any specified class;

(d) for enabling the tribunal to dispose of an application without a formal hearing where such a hearing is not requested by the applicant or it appears to the tribunal that such a hearing would be detrimental to the health of the patient;

(e) for enabling the tribunal to exclude members of the public, or any specified class of members of the public, from any proceedings of the tribunal, or to prohibit the publication of reports of any such proceedings or the names of any persons concerned in such proceedings;

(f) for regulating the circumstances in which, and the persons by whom, applicants and patients in respect of whom applications are made to the tribunal may, if not desiring to conduct their own case, be represented for the purposes of those applications;

(g) for regulating the methods by which information relevant to an application may be obtained by or furnished to the tribunal, and in particular for authorising the members of the tribunal, or any one or more of them, to visit and interview in private any patient by or in respect of whom an application has been made;

(h) for making available to any applicant, and to any patient in respect of whom an application is made to the tribunal, copies of any documents obtained by or furnished to the tribunal in connection with the application, and a statement of the substance of any oral information so obtained or furnished except where the tribunal considers it undesirable in the interests of the patient or for other special reasons;

(i) for requiring the tribunal, if so requested in accordance with the rules, to furnish such statements of the reasons for any decision given by the tribunal as may be prescribed by the rules, subject to any provision made by the rules for withholding such a statement from a patient or any other person in cases where the tribunal considers that furnishing it would be undesirable in the interests of the patient or for other special reasons;

(j) for conferring on the tribunal such ancillary powers as the Lord Chancellor thinks necessary for the purposes of the exercise of its functions under this Act;

(k) for enabling any functions of the tribunal which relate to matters preliminary or incidental to an application to be performed by the *chairman* [President] of the tribunal.

(3) Subsections (1) and (2) above apply in relation to references to the Mental Health Review Tribunal for Wales as they apply in relation to applications to that tribunal by or in respect of patients.

(4) Rules under this section may make provision as to the procedure to be adopted in cases concerning restricted patients and, in particular –

(a) for restricting the persons qualified to serve as *president* [chairman] of the tribunal for the consideration of an application or reference relating to a restricted patient;

(b) for the transfer of proceedings to or from the tribunal in any case where, after the making of a reference or application in accordance with section 71(4) or 77(4) above, the patient begins or ceases to reside in Wales.

(5) Rules under this section may be so framed as to apply to all applications or references or to applications or references of any specified class and may make different provision in relation to different cases.

(6) Any functions conferred on the *chairman* [President] of the Mental Health Review Tribunal for Wales by rules under this section may be exercised by another member of that tribunal appointed by him for the purpose.

(7) The Mental Health Review Tribunal for Wales may pay allowances in respect of travelling expenses, subsistence and loss of earnings to any person attending the tribunal as an applicant or witness, to the patient who is the subject of the proceedings if he attends otherwise than as the applicant or a witness and to any person (other than an authorised person (within the meaning of Part 3)) who attends as the representative of an applicant.

(8) (*repealed*)

(9) Part I of the Arbitration Act 1996 shall not apply to any proceedings before the Mental Health Review Tribunal for Wales except so far as any provisions of that Act may be applied, with or without modifications, by rules made under this section.

Amendments: Mental Health Act 2007; SI 2008/2833

Prospective Amendments: Words in italics prospectively repealed and subsequent words in square brackets prospectively substituted by the Mental Health Act 2007, s 38(1), (3)(a) with effect from a date to be appointed.

78A Appeal from the Mental Health Review Tribunal for Wales to the Upper Tribunal

(1) A party to any proceedings before the Mental Health Review Tribunal for Wales may appeal to the Upper Tribunal on any point of law arising from a decision made by the Mental Health Review Tribunal for Wales in those proceedings.

(2) An appeal may be brought under subsection (1) above only if, on an application made by the party concerned, the Mental Health Review Tribunal for Wales or the Upper Tribunal has given its permission for the appeal to be brought.

(3) Section 12 of the Tribunals, Courts and Enforcement Act 2007 (proceedings on appeal to the Upper Tribunal) applies in relation to appeals to the Upper Tribunal under this section as it applies in relation to appeals to it under section 11 of that Act, but as if references to the First-tier Tribunal were references to the Mental Health Review Tribunal for Wales.

Amendments: SI 2008/2833.

79 Interpretation of Part V

(1) In this Part of this Act "restricted patient" means a patient who is subject to a restriction order, limitation direction or restriction direction and this Part of this Act shall, subject to the provisions of this section, have effect in relation to any person who –

- (a) is treated by virtue of any enactment as subject to a hospital order and a restriction order; or
- (b) ...
- (c) is treated as subject to a hospital order and a restriction order, or to a hospital direction and a limitation direction, or to a transfer direction and a restriction direction, by virtue of any provision of Part 6 of this Act (except section 80D(3), 82A(2) or 85A(2) below),

as it has effect in relation to a restricted patient.

(2) Subject to the following provisions of this section, in this Part of this Act "the relevant hospital order", "the relevant hospital direction" and "the relevant transfer direction", in relation to a restricted patient, mean the hospital order, the hospital direction or transfer direction by virtue of which he is liable to be detained in a hospital.

(3) In the case of a person within paragraph (a) of subsection (1) above, references in this Part of this Act to the relevant hospital order or restriction order shall be construed as references to the direction referred to in that paragraph.

(4) In the case of a person within paragraph (b) of subsection (1) above, references in this Part of this Act to the relevant hospital order or restriction order shall be construed as references to the order under the provisions mentioned in that paragraph.

(5) In the case of a person within paragraph (c) of subsection (1) above, references in this Part of this Act to the relevant hospital order, the relevant hospital direction, the relevant transfer direction, the restriction order, the limitation direction or the restriction direction or to a transfer direction under section 48 above shall be construed as references to the hospital order, hospital direction, transfer direction, restriction order,

limitation direction, restriction direction or transfer direction under that section to which that person is treated as subject by virtue of the provisions mentioned in that paragraph.

(5A) Section 75 above shall, subject to the modifications in subsection (5C) below, have effect in relation to a qualifying patient as it has effect in relation to a restricted patient who is conditionally discharged under section 42(2), 73 or 74 above.

(5B) A patient is a qualifying patient if he is treated by virtue of section 80D(3), 82A(2) or 85A(2) below as if he had been conditionally discharged and were subject to a hospital order and a restriction order, or to a hospital direction and a limitation direction, or to a transfer direction and a restriction direction.

(5C) The modifications mentioned in subsection (5A) above are –

(a) references to the relevant hospital order, hospital direction or transfer direction, or to the restriction order, limitation direction or restriction direction to which the patient is subject, shall be construed as references to the hospital order, hospital direction or transfer direction, or restriction order, limitation direction or restriction direction, to which the patient is treated as subject by virtue of section 80D(3), 82A(2) or 85A(2) below; and

(b) the reference to the date on which the patient was conditionally discharged shall be construed as a reference to the date on which he was treated as conditionally discharged by virtue of a provision mentioned in paragraph (a) above.

(6) In this Part of this Act, unless the context otherwise requires, "hospital" means a hospital, and "the responsible clinician" means the responsible clinician, within the meaning of Part II of this Act.

(7) (*repealed*)

Amendments: Health Authorities Act 1995; Crime (Sentences) Act 1997; Domestic Violence, Crime and Victims Act 2004; Mental Health Act 2007; SI 2008/2833.

****

PART VIII
MISCELLANEOUS FUNCTIONS OF LOCAL AUTHORITIES AND THE SECRETARY OF STATE

Approved mental health professionals

114 Approval by local social services authority

(1) A local social services authority may approve a person to act as an approved mental health professional for the purposes of this Act.

(2) But a local social services authority may not approve a registered medical practitioner to act as an approved mental health professional.

(3) Before approving a person under subsection (1) above, a local social services authority shall be satisfied that he has appropriate competence in dealing with persons who are suffering from mental disorder.

(4) The appropriate national authority may by regulations make provision in connection with the giving of approvals under subsection (1) above.

(5) The provision which may be made by regulations under subsection (4) above includes, in particular, provision as to –

(a) the period for which approvals under subsection (1) above have effect;
(b) the courses to be undertaken by persons before such approvals are to be given and during the period for which such approvals have effect;
(c) the conditions subject to which such approvals are to be given; and
(d) the factors to be taken into account in determining whether persons have appropriate competence as mentioned in subsection (3) above.

(6) Provision made by virtue of subsection (5)(b) above may relate to courses approved or provided by such person as may be specified in the regulations (as well as to courses approved under section 114ZA or 114A below).

(7) An approval by virtue of subsection (6) above may be in respect of a course in general or in respect of a course in relation to a particular person.

(8) The power to make regulations under subsection (4) above includes power to make different provision for different cases or areas.

(9) In this section "the appropriate national authority" means –

(a) in relation to persons who are or wish to become approved to act as approved mental health professionals by a local social services authority whose area is in England, the Secretary of State;
(b) in relation to persons who are or wish to become approved to act as approved mental health professionals by a local social services authority whose area is in Wales, the Welsh Ministers.

(10) In this Act "approved mental health professional" means –

(a) in relation to acting on behalf of a local social services authority whose area is in England, a person approved under subsection (1) above by any local social services authority whose area is in England, and
(b) in relation to acting on behalf of a local social services authority whose area is in Wales, a person approved under that subsection by any local social services authority whose area is in Wales.

Amendments: Mental Health Act 2007; Health and Social Care Act 2012.

114ZA Approval of courses: England

(1) The Health and Care Professions Council may approve courses for persons who are, or wish to become, approved to act as approved mental health professionals by a local social services authority whose area is in England.

(2) The Council must publish a list of –

(a) the courses which are approved under this section, and
(b) the courses which have been, but are no longer, approved under this section and the periods for which they were so approved.

(3) The functions of an approved mental health professional are not to be considered to be relevant social work for the purposes of Part 4 of the Care Standards Act 2000.

(4) Where the function under subsection (1) is, in accordance with the Health and Social Work Professions Order 2001, exercisable by a committee of the Council, the committee may arrange for another person to exercise the function on the Council's behalf.

Amendments: Health and Social Care Act 2012.

114A Approval of courses: Wales

(1) The Care Council for Wales may, in accordance with rules made by it, approve courses for persons who are, or wish to become, approved to act as approved mental health professionals by a local social services authority whose area is in Wales.

(2) For that purpose –

- (a) subsections (2) to (4)(a) and (7) of section 63 of the Care Standards Act 2000 apply as they apply to approvals given, rules made and courses approved under that section; and
- (b) sections 66 and 71 of that Act apply accordingly.

(3) (*repealed*)

(4) The functions of an approved mental health professional shall not be considered to be relevant social work for the purposes of Part 4 of the Care Standards Act 2000.

(5) The Care Council for Wales may also carry out, or assist other persons in carrying out, research into matters relevant to training for approved mental health professionals.

Amendments: Mental Health Act 2007; Health and Social Care Act 2012.

115 Powers of entry and inspection

(1) An approved mental health professional may at all reasonable times enter and inspect any premises (other than a hospital) in which a mentally disordered patient is living, if he has reasonable cause to believe that the patient is not under proper care.

(2) The power under subsection (1) above shall be exercisable only after the professional has produced, if asked to do so, some duly authenticated document showing that he is an approved mental health professional.

Amendments: Mental Health Act 2007.

Visiting patients

116 Welfare of certain hospital patients

(1) Where a patient to whom this section applies is admitted to a hospital[, independent hospital or care home in England and Wales (whether for treatment for mental disorder or for any other reason) then, without prejudice to their duties in relation to the patient apart from the provisions of this section, the authority shall arrange for visits to be made to him on behalf of the authority, and shall take such other steps in relation to the patient while in the hospital, independent hospital or care home as would be expected to be taken by his parents.

(2) This section applies to –

- (a) a child or young person –
  - (i) who is in the care of a local authority by virtue of a care order within the meaning of the Children Act 1989, or
  - (ii) in respect of whom the rights and powers of a parent are vested in a local authority by virtue of section 16 of the Social Work (Scotland) Act 1968;
- (b) a person who is subject to the guardianship of a local social services authority under the provisions of this Act; or

(c) a person the functions of whose nearest relative under this Act are for the time being transferred to a local social services authority.

Amendments: Courts and Legal Services Act 1990; Care Standards Act 2000; SI 2005/2078.

After-care

117 After-care

(1) This section applies to persons who are detained under section 3 above, or admitted to a hospital in pursuance of a hospital order made under section 37 above, or transferred to a hospital in pursuance of a hospital direction made under section 45A above or a transfer direction made under section 47 or 48 above, and then cease to be detained and (whether or not immediately after so ceasing) leave hospital.

(2) It shall be the duty of the clinical commissioning group or Local Health Board and of the local social services authority to provide, in co-operation with relevant voluntary agencies, after-care services for any person to whom this section applies until such time as the clinical commissioning group or Local Health Board and the local social services authority are satisfied that the person concerned is no longer in need of such services; but they shall not be so satisfied in the case of a community patient while he remains such a patient.

(2A) (*repealed*)

(2B) Section 32 above shall apply for the purposes of this section as it applies for the purposes of Part II of this Act.

(2C) References in this Act to after-care services provided for a patient under this section include references to services provided for the patient –

(a) in respect of which direct payments are made under regulations under section 57 of the Health and Social Care Act 2001 or section 12A(4) of the National Health Service Act 2006, and
(b) which would be provided under this section apart from the regulations.

(2D) Subsection (2), in its application to the clinical commissioning group, has effect as if for "to provide" there were substituted "to arrange for the provision of".

(2E) The Secretary of State may by regulations provide that the duty imposed on the clinical commissioning group by subsection (2) is, in the circumstances or to the extent prescribed by the regulations, to be imposed instead on another clinical commissioning group or the National Health Service Commissioning Board.

(2F) Where regulations under subsection (2E) provide that the duty imposed by subsection (2) is to be imposed on the National Health Service Commissioning Board, subsection (2D) has effect as if the reference to the clinical commissioning group were a reference to the National Health Service Commissioning Board.

(2G) Section 272(7) and (8) of the National Health Service Act 2006 applies to the power to make regulations under subsection (2E) as it applies to a power to make regulations under that Act.

(3) In this section "the clinical commissioning group or Local Health Board" means the clinical commissioning group or Local Health Board, and "the local social services authority" means the local social services authority, for the area in which the person

concerned is resident or to which he is sent on discharge by the hospital in which the person concerned is resident or to which he is sent on discharge by the hospital in which he was detained.

Amendments: Mental Health (Patients in the Community) Act 1995; Health Authorities Act 1995; Crime (Sentences) Act 1997; National Health Service Reform and Health Care Professions Act 2002; Mental Health Act 2007; Health Act 2009; Health and Social Care Act 2012; SI 2007/961.

Functions of the Secretary of State

118 Code of practice

(1) The Secretary of State shall prepare, and from time to time revise, a code of practice –

- (a) for the guidance of registered medical practitioners, approved clinicians, managers and staff of hospitals, independent hospitals and care homes and approved mental health professionals in relation to the admission of patients to hospitals and registered establishments under this Act and to guardianship and community patients under this Act; and
- (b) for the guidance of registered medical practitioners and members of other professions in relation to the medical treatment of patients suffering from mental disorder.

(1A) The Code which must be prepared, and from time to time revised, in relation to Wales shall also be for the guidance of independent mental health advocates appointed under arrangements made under section 130E below.

(2) The code shall, in particular, specify forms of medical treatment in addition to any specified by regulations made for the purposes of section 57 above which in the opinion of the Secretary of State give rise to special concern and which should accordingly not be given by a registered medical practitioner unless the patient has consented to the treatment (or to a plan of treatment including that treatment) and a certificate in writing as to the matters mentioned in subsection (2)(a) and (b) of that section has been given by another registered medical practitioner, being a practitioner appointed for the purposes of this section by the regulatory authority.

(2A) The code shall include a statement of the principles which the Secretary of State thinks should inform decisions under this Act.

(2B) In preparing the statement of principles the Secretary of State shall, in particular, ensure that each of the following matters is addressed –

- (a) respect for patients' past and present wishes and feelings,
- (b) respect for diversity generally including, in particular, diversity of religion, culture and sexual orientation (within the meaning of section 35 of the Equality Act 2006),
- (c) minimising restrictions on liberty,
- (d) involvement of patients in planning, developing and delivering care and treatment appropriate to them,
- (e) avoidance of unlawful discrimination,
- (f) effectiveness of treatment,
- (g) views of carers and other interested parties,
- (h) patient wellbeing and safety, and
- (i) public safety.

(2C) The Secretary of State shall also have regard to the desirability of ensuring –

(a) the efficient use of resources, and
(b) the equitable distribution of services.

(2D) In performing functions under this Act persons mentioned in subsection (1)(a) or (b) and subsection (1A) shall have regard to the code.

(3) Before preparing the code or making any alteration in it the Secretary of State shall consult such bodies as appear to him to be concerned.

(4) The Secretary of State shall lay copies of the code and of any alteration in the code before Parliament; and if either House of Parliament passes a resolution requiring the code or any alteration in it to be withdrawn the Secretary of State shall withdraw the code or alteration and, where he withdraws the code, shall prepare a code in substitution for the one which is withdrawn.

(5) No resolution shall be passed by either House of Parliament under subsection (4) above in respect of a code or alteration after the expiration of the period of 40 days beginning with the day on which a copy of the code or alteration was laid before that House; but for the purposes of this subsection no account shall be taken of any time during which Parliament is dissolved or prorogued or during which both Houses are adjourned for more than four days.

(6) The Secretary of State shall publish the code as for the time being in force.

(7) The Care Quality Commission may at any time make proposals to the Secretary of State as to the content of the code of practice which the Secretary of State must prepare, and from time to time revise, under this section in relation to England.

Amendments: Mental Health (Patients in the Community) Act 1995; Care Standards Act 2000; Mental Health Act 2007; Health and Social Care Act 2008; Mental Health (Wales) Measure 2010.

119 Practitioners approved for Part IV and s 118

(1) The regulatory authority may make such provision as it may with the approval of the Treasury determine for the payment of remuneration, allowances, pensions or gratuities to or in respect of registered medical practitioners appointed by the authority for the purposes of Part IV of this Act and section 118 above and to or in respect of other persons appointed for the purposes of section 57(2)(a) above.

(2) A registered medical practitioner or other person appointed for the purposes of the provisions mentioned in subsection (1) above may, for the purpose of exercising his functions under those provisions or under Part 4A of this Act, at any reasonable time –

(a) visit and interview and, in the case of a registered medical practitioner, examine in private any patient detained in a hospital or registered establishment or any community patient in a hospital or regulated establishment (other than a hospital) or (if access is granted) other place; and
(b) require the production of and inspect any records relating to the treatment of the patient there.

(3) In this section "regulated establishment" means –

(a) an establishment in respect of which a person is registered under Part 2 of the Care Standards Act 2000; or
(b) premises used for the carrying on of a regulated activity, within the meaning of Part 1 of the Health and Social Care Act 2008, in respect of which a person is registered under Chapter 2 of that Part.

Amendments: Mental Health Act 2007; Health and Social Care Act 2008; SI 2010/813.

120 General protection of relevant patients

(1) The regulatory authority must keep under review and, where appropriate, investigate the exercise of the powers and the discharge of the duties conferred or imposed by this Act so far as relating to the detention of patients or their reception into guardianship or to relevant patients.

(2) Relevant patients are –

(a) patients liable to be detained under this Act,
(b) community patients, and
(c) patients subject to guardianship.

(3) The regulatory authority must make arrangements for persons authorised by it to visit and interview relevant patients in private –

(a) in the case of relevant patients detained under this Act, in the place where they are detained, and
(b) in the case of other relevant patients, in hospitals and regulated establishments and, if access is granted, other places.

(4) The regulatory authority must also make arrangements for persons authorised by it to investigate any complaint as to the exercise of the powers or the discharge of the duties conferred or imposed by this Act in respect of a patient who is or has been detained under this Act or who is or has been a relevant patient.

(5) The arrangements made under subsection (4) –

(a) may exclude matters from investigation in specified circumstances, and
(b) do not require any person exercising functions under the arrangements to undertake or continue with any investigation where the person does not consider it appropriate to do so.

(6) Where any such complaint as is mentioned in subsection (4) is made by a Member of Parliament or a member of the National Assembly for Wales, the results of the investigation must be reported to the Member of Parliament or member of the Assembly.

(7) For the purposes of a review or investigation under subsection (1) or the exercise of functions under arrangements made under this section, a person authorised by the regulatory authority may at any reasonable time –

(a) visit and interview in private any patient in a hospital or regulated establishment,
(b) if the authorised person is a registered medical practitioner or approved clinician, examine the patient in private there, and
(c) require the production of and inspect any records relating to the detention or treatment of any person who is or has been detained under this Act or who is or has been a community patient or a patient subject to guardianship.

(8) The regulatory authority may make provision for the payment of remuneration, allowances, pensions or gratuities to or in respect of persons exercising functions in relation to any review or investigation for which it is responsible under subsection (1) or functions under arrangements made by it under this section.

(9) In this section "regulated establishment" means –

(a) an establishment in respect of which a person is registered under Part 2 of the Care Standards Act 2000, or

(b) premises used for the carrying on of a regulated activity (within the meaning of Part 1 of the Health and Social Care Act 2008) in respect of which a person is registered under Chapter 2 of that Part.

Amendments: Health and Social Care Act 2008; Sub-s (5): repealed by the Registered Homes Act 1984, s 57, Sch 3.

120A Investigation reports

(1) The regulatory authority may publish a report of a review or investigation carried out by it under section 120(1).

(2) The Secretary of State may by regulations make provision as to the procedure to be followed in respect of the making of representations to the Care Quality Commission before the publication of a report by the Commission under subsection (1).

(3) The Secretary of State must consult the Care Quality Commission before making any such regulations.

(4) The Welsh Ministers may by regulations make provision as to the procedure to be followed in respect of the making of representations to them before the publication of a report by them under subsection (1).

Amendments: Inserted by the Health and Social Care Act 2008.

120B Action statements

(1) The regulatory authority may direct a person mentioned in subsection (2) to publish a statement as to the action the person proposes to take as a result of a review or investigation under section 120(1).

(2) The persons are –

(a) the managers of a hospital within the meaning of Part 2 of this Act;
(b) a local social services authority;
(c) persons of any other description prescribed in regulations.

(3) Regulations may make further provision about the content and publication of statements under this section.

(4) "Regulations" means regulations made –

(a) by the Secretary of State, in relation to England;
(b) by the Welsh Ministers, in relation to Wales.

Amendments: Inserted by the Health and Social Care Act 2008.

120C Provision of information

(1) This section applies to the following persons –

(a) the managers of a hospital within the meaning of Part 2 of this Act;
(b) a local social services authority;
(c) persons of any other description prescribed in regulations.

(2) A person to whom this section applies must provide the regulatory authority with such information as the authority may reasonably request for or in connection with the exercise of its functions under section 120.

(3) A person to whom this section applies must provide a person authorised under section 120 with such information as the person so authorised may reasonably request for or in connection with the exercise of functions under arrangements made under that section.

(4) This section is in addition to the requirements of section 120(7)(c).

(5) "Information" includes documents and records.

(6) "Regulations" means regulations made –

(a) by the Secretary of State, in relation to England;
(b) by the Welsh Ministers, in relation to Wales.

Amendments: Inserted by the Health and Social Care Act 2008.

120D Annual reports

(1) The regulatory authority must publish an annual report on its activities in the exercise of its functions under this Act.

(2) The report must be published as soon as possible after the end of each financial year.

(3) The Care Quality Commission must send a copy of its annual report to the Secretary of State who must lay the copy before Parliament.

(4) The Welsh Ministers must lay a copy of their annual report before the National Assembly for Wales.

(5) In this section "financial year" means –

(a) the period beginning with the date on which section 52 of the Health and Social Care Act 2008 comes into force and ending with the next 31 March following that date, and
(b) each successive period of 12 months ending with 31 March.

Amendments: Inserted by the Health and Social Care Act 2008.

121 (*repealed*)

Amendments: Repealed by the Health and Social Care Act 2008.

122 Provision of pocket money for in-patients in hospital

(1) The Welsh Ministers may (in relation to Wales) pay to persons who are receiving treatment as in-patients (whether liable to be detained or not) in *special hospitals or other hospitals being* hospitals wholly or mainly used for the treatment of persons suffering from mental disorder, such amounts as the Welsh Ministers think fit in respect of those persons occasional personal expenses where it appears to the Welsh Ministers that those persons would otherwise be without resources to meet those expenses.

(2) For the purposes of the the National Health Service (Wales) Act 2006, the making of payments under this section to persons for whom hospital services are provided under that Act shall be treated as included among those services.

Amendments: National Health Service (Consequential Provisions) Act 2006; Health and Social Care Act 2008.

Prospective Amendment: Sub-s (1): words in italics prospectively repealed by the Health Act 1999, s 65, Sch 4, paras 65, 66, Sch 5 (in force in relation to England and Wales; date in force in relation to Scotland to be appointed).

123 *(repealed)*

Amendments: Repealed by the Health and Social Care Act 2008.

124 *(repealed)*

Amendments: Repealed by the National Health Service and Community Care Act 1990.

125 *(repealed)*

Amendments: Repealed by the Inquiries Act 2005.

****

135 Warrant to search for and remove patients

(1) If it appears to a justice of the peace, on information on oath laid by an approved mental health professional, that there is reasonable cause to suspect that a person believed to be suffering from mental disorder –

(a) has been, or is being, ill-treated, neglected or kept otherwise than under proper control, in any place within the jurisdiction of the justice, or
(b) being unable to care for himself, is living alone in any such place,

the justice may issue a warrant authorising any constable to enter, if need be by force, any premises specified in the warrant in which that person is believed to be, and, if thought fit, to remove him to a place of safety with a view to the making of an application in respect of him under Part II of this Act, or of other arrangements for his treatment or care.

(2) If it appears to a justice of the peace, on information on oath laid by any constable or other person who is authorised by or under this Act or under article 8 of the Mental Health (Care and Treatment) (Scotland) Act 2003 (Consequential Provisions) Order 2005 to take a patient to any place, or to take into custody or retake a patient who is liable under this Act or under the said article 8 to be so taken or retaken –

(a) that there is reasonable cause to believe that the patient is to be found on premises within the jurisdiction of the justice; and
(b) that admission to the premises has been refused or that a refusal of such admission is apprehended,

the justice may issue a warrant authorising any constable to enter the premises, if need be by force, and remove the patient.

(3) A patient who is removed to a place of safety in the execution of a warrant issued under this section may be detained there for a period not exceeding 72 hours.

(3A) A constable, an approved mental health professional or a person authorised by either of them for the purposes of this subsection may, before the end of the period of 72 hours mentioned in subsection (3) above, take a person detained in a place of safety under that subsection to one or more other places of safety.

(3B) A person taken to a place of safety under subsection (3A) above may be detained there for a period ending no later than the end of the period of 72 hours mentioned in subsection (3) above.

(4) In the execution of a warrant issued under subsection (1) above, a constable shall be accompanied by an approved mental health professional and by a registered medical practitioner, and in the execution of a warrant issued under subsection (2) above a constable may be accompanied –

(a) by a registered medical practitioner;
(b) by any person authorised by or under this Act or under article 8 of the Mental Health (Care and Treatment) (Scotland) Act 2003 (Consequential Provisions) Order 2005 to take or retake the patient.

(5) It shall not be necessary in any information or warrant under subsection (1) above to name the patient concerned.

(6) In this section "place of safety" means residential accommodation provided by a local social services authority under Part III of the National Assistance Act 1948, a hospital as defined by this Act, a police station, an independent hospital or care home for mentally disordered persons or any other suitable place the occupier of which is willing temporarily to receive the patient.

Amendments: Mental Health Act 2007; Police and Criminal Evidence Act 1984; Mental Health (Scotland) Act 1984; National Health Service and Community Care Act 1990; Care Standards Act 2000; SI 2005/2078.

NATIONAL ASSISTANCE ACT 1948

PART III
LOCAL AUTHORITY SERVICES PROVISION OF ACCOMMODATION

****

21 Duty of local authorities to provide accommodation

(1) Subject to and in accordance with the provisions of this Part of this Act, a local authority may with the approval of the Secretary of State, and to such extent as he may direct shall, make arrangements for providing –

(a) residential accommodation for persons aged eighteen or over who by reason of age, illness, disability or any other circumstances are in need of care and attention which is not otherwise available to them; and
(aa) residential accommodation for expectant and nursing mothers who are in need of care and attention which is not otherwise available to them.
(b) ...

(1A) A person to whom section 115 of the Immigration and Asylum Act 1999 (exclusion from benefits) applies may not be provided with residential accommodation under subsection (1)(a) if his need for care and attention has arisen solely –

(a) because he is destitute; or
(b) because of the physical effects, or anticipated physical effects, of his being destitute.

(1B) Subsections (3) and (5) to (8) of section 95 of the Immigration and Asylum Act 1999, and paragraph 2 of Schedule 8 to that Act, apply for the purposes of subsection (1A) as they apply for the purposes of that section, but for the references in subsections (5) and (7) of that section and in that paragraph to the Secretary of State substitute references to a local authority.

(1B) Section 95(2) to (7) of that Act shall apply for the purposes of subsection (1A) above; and for that purpose a reference to the Secretary of State in section 95(4) or (5) shall be treated as a reference to a local authority.

(2) In making any such arrangements a local authority shall have regard to the welfare of all persons for whom accommodation is provided, and in particular to the need for providing accommodation of different descriptions suited to different descriptions of such persons as are mentioned in the last foregoing subsection.

(2A) In determining for the purposes of paragraph (a) or (aa) of subsection (1) of this section whether care and attention are otherwise available to a person, a local authority shall disregard so much of the person's resources as may be specified in, or determined in accordance with, regulations made by the Secretary of State for the purposes of this subsection.

(2B) In subsection (2A) of this section the reference to a person's resources is a reference to his resources within the meaning of regulations made for the purposes of that subsection.

(3) (*repealed*)

(4) Subject to the provisions of section 26 of this Act accommodation provided by a local authority in the exercise of their functions under this section shall be provided in premises managed by the authority or, to such extent as may be determined in accordance with the arrangements under this section, in such premises managed by another local authority as may be agreed between the two authorities and on such terms, including terms as to the reimbursement of expenditure incurred by the said other authority, as may be so agreed.

(5) References in this Act to accommodation provided under this Part thereof shall be construed as references to accommodation provided in accordance with this and the five next following sections, and as including references to board and other services, amenities and requisites provided in connection with the accommodation except where in the opinion of the authority managing the premises their provision is unnecessary.

(6) References in this Act to a local authority providing accommodation shall be construed, in any case where a local authority agree with another local authority for the provision of accommodation in premises managed by the said other authority, as references to the first-mentioned local authority.

(7) Without prejudice to the generality of the foregoing provisions of this section, a local authority may –

(a) provide, in such cases as they may consider appropriate, for the conveyance of persons to and from premises in which accommodation is provided for them under this Part of the Act;

(b) make arrangements for the provision on the premises in which accommodation is being provided of such other services as appear to the authority to be required.

(8) nothing in this section shall authorise or require a local authority to make any provision authorised or required to be made (whether by that or by any other authority) by or under any enactment not contained in this Part of this Act or authorised or required to be provided under the National Health Service Act 2006 or the National Health Service (Wales) Act 2006.

Amendments: Social Work (Scotland) Act 1968; Local Government Act 1972; Children Act 1989; National Health Service and Community Care Act 1990; Immigration and Asylum Act 1999.

Prospective Amendments: Sub-s (1B) in italics prospectively substituted for Sub-s (1B) in square brackets by the Nationality, Immigration and Asylum Act 2002, s 45(5) with effect from a date to be appointed.

22 Charges to be made for accommodation

(1) Subject to section 26 of this Act, where a person is provided with accommodation under this Part of this Act the local authority providing the accommodation shall recover from him the amount of the payment which he is liable to make in accordance with the following provisions of this section.

(2) Subject to the following provisions of this section, the payment which a person is liable to make for any such accommodation shall be in accordance with a standard rate fixed for that accommodation by the authority managing the premises in which it is provided and that standard rate shall represent the full cost to the authority of providing that accommodation.

(3) Where a person for whom accommodation in premises managed by any local authority is provided, or proposed to be provided, under this Part of this Act satisfies the local authority that he is unable to pay therefor at the standard rate, the authority shall assess his ability to pay and accordingly determine at what lower rate he shall be liable to pay for the accommodation:

(4) In assessing for the purposes of the last foregoing subsection a person's ability to pay, a local authority shall assume that he will need for his personal requirements such sum per week as may be prescribed by the Minister, or such other sum as in special circumstances the authority may consider appropriate.

(4A) Regulations made for the purposes of subsection (4) of this section may prescribe different sums for different circumstances.

(5) In assessing as aforesaid a person's ability to pay, a local authority shall give effect to regulations made by the Secretary of State for the purposes of this subsection except that, until the first such regulations come into force, a local authority shall give effect to Part III of Schedule 1 to the Supplementary Benefits Act 1976, as it had effect immediately before the amendments made by Schedule 2 to the Social Security Act 1980.

(5A) If they think fit, an authority managing premises in which accommodation is provided for a person shall have power on each occasion when they provide accommodation for him, irrespective of his means, to limit to such amount as appears to them reasonable for him to pay the payments required from him for his accommodation during a period commencing when they begin to provide the accommodation for him and ending not more than eight weeks after that.

(6)–(7) (*repealed*)

(8) Where accommodation is provided by a local authority in premises managed by another local authority, the payment therefor under this section shall be made to the authority managing the premises and not to the authority providing accommodation, but the authority managing the premises shall account for the payment to the authority providing the accommodation.

(8A) This section shall have effect subject to any regulations under section 15 [or 16] of the Community Care (Delayed Discharges etc) Act 2003 (power to require certain community care services and services for carers to be provided free of charge).

(9) (*repealed*)

Amendments: Social Security Act 1980; Social Security Act 1986; National Health Service and Community Care Act 1990; Community Care (Delayed Discharges etc) Act 2003.

Prospective Amendments: Sub s (8A) words in square brackets prospectively inserted by Personal Care at Home Act 2010 with effect from a date to be appointed.

23 Management of premises in which accommodation provided

(1) Subject to the provisions of this Part of this Act, a local authority may make rules as to the conduct of premises under their management in which accommodation is provided under this Part of this Act and as to the preservation of order in the premises.

(2) Rules under this section may provide that where by reason of any change in a person's circumstances he is no longer qualified to receive accommodation under this Part of this Act or where a person has otherwise become unsuitable therefor, he may be required by the local authority managing the premises to leave the premises in which the accommodation is provided.

(3) Rules under this section may provide for the waiving of part of the payments due under the last foregoing section where in compliance with the rules persons for whom accommodation is provided assist in the running of the premises.

Amendments: Repealed in relation to Scotland by the Social Work (Scotland) Act 1968.

24 Authority liable for provision of accommodation

(1) The local authority empowered under this Part of this Act to provide residential accommodation for any person shall subject to the following provisions of this Part of this Act be the authority in whose area the person is ordinarily resident.

(2) (*repealed*)

(3) Where a person in the area of a local authority –

(a) is a person with no settled residence, or
(b) not being ordinarily resident in the area of the local authority, is in urgent need of residential accommodation under this Part of this Act,

the authority shall have the like power to provide residential accommodation for him as if he were ordinarily resident in their area.

(4) Subject to and in accordance with the arrangements under section twenty-one of this Act, a local authority shall have power, as respects a person ordinarily resident in the area of another local authority, with the consent of that other authority to provide residential accommodation for him in any case where the authority would have a duty to provide such accommodation if he were ordinarily resident in their area.

(5) Where a person is provided with residential accommodation under this Part of this Act, he shall be deemed for the purposes of this Act to continue to be ordinarily resident in the area in which he was ordinarily resident immediately before the residential accommodation was provided for him.

(6) For the purposes of the provision of residential accommodation under this Part, a patient ("P") for whom NHS accommodation is provided shall be deemed to be ordinarily resident in the area, if any, in which P was resident before the NHS accommodation was provided for P, whether or not P in fact continues to be ordinarily resident in that area.

(6A) In subsection (6) "NHS accommodation" means –

(a) accommodation (at a hospital or elsewhere) provided under the National Health Service Act 2006 or the National Health Service (Wales) Act 2006, or
(b) accommodation provided under section 117 of the Mental Health Act 1983 by a clinical commissioning group or Local Health Board, other than accommodation so provided jointly with a local authority.

(6B) The reference in subsection (6A)(b) to accommodation provided by a clinical commissioning group includes a reference to accommodation –

(a) in respect of which direct payments are made under regulations under section 12A(4) of the National Health Service Act 2006, and
(b) which would be provided under section 117 of the Mental Health Act 1983 apart from the regulations.

(6C) The references in subsections (6A) and (6B) to a clinical commissioning group are, so far as necessary for the purposes of regulations under section 117(2E) of the Mental Health Act 1983, to be read as references to the National Health Service Commissioning Board.

Amendments: Local Government Act 1972; Housing (Homeless Persons) Act 1977; Health and Social Care Act 2008; Health Act 2009; Health and Social Care Act 2012.

26 Provision of accommodation in premises maintained by voluntary organisations

(1) Subject to subsections (1A) and (1C) below, arrangements under section 21 of this Act may include arrangements made with a voluntary organisation or with any other person who is not a local authority where –

(a) that organisation or person manages premises which provide for reward accommodation falling within subsection (1)(a) or (aa) of that section, and
(b) the arrangements are for the provision of such accommodation in those premises.

(1A) Arrangements must not be made by virtue of this section for the provision of accommodation together with nursing or personal care for persons such as are mentioned in section 3(2) of the Care Standards Act 2000 (care homes) unless –

(a) the accommodation is to be provided, under the arrangements, in a care home (within the meaning of that Act) which is managed by the organisation or person in question; and
(b) that organisation or person –
    (i) in the case of a home in England, is registered under Chapter 2 of Part 1 of the Health and Social Care Act 2008 in respect of a regulated activity (within the meaning of that Part) carried on in the home, or
    (ii) in the case of a home in Wales, is registered under Part 2 of the Care Standards Act 2000 in respect of the home.

(1C) Subject to subsection (1D) below, no arrangements may be made by virtue of this section for the provision of accommodation together with nursing without the consent of such clinical commissioning group or Local Health Board as may be determined in accordance with regulations.

(1D) Subsection (1C) above does not apply to the making by an authority of temporary arrangements for the accommodation of any person as a matter of urgency; but, as soon as practicable after any such temporary arrangements have been made, the authority shall seek the consent required by subsection (1C) above to the making of appropriate arrangements for the accommodation of the person concerned.

(1E) (*repealed*)

(2) Any arrangements made by virtue of this section shall provide for the making by the local authority to the other party thereto of payments in respect of the accommodation provided at such rates as may be determined by or under the arrangements and subject to subsection (3A) below the local authority shall recover from each person for whom accommodation is provided under the arrangements the amount of the refund which he is liable to make in accordance with the following provisions of this section.

(3) Subject to subsection (3A) below a person for whom accommodation is provided under any such arrangements shall, in lieu of being liable to make payment therefor in accordance with section twenty-two of this Act, refund to the local authority any payments made in respect of him under the last foregoing subsection:

Provided that where a person for whom accommodation is provided, or proposed to be provided, under any such arrangements satisfies the local authority that he is unable to make a refund at the full rate determined under that subsection, subsections (3) to (5) of section twenty-two of this Act shall, with the necessary modifications, apply as they apply where a person satisfies the local authority of his inability to pay at the standard rate as mentioned in the said subsection (3).

(3A) Where accommodation in any premises is provided for any person under arrangements made by virtue of this section and the local authority, the person concerned and the voluntary organisation or other person managing the premises (in this subsection referred to as "the provider") agree that this subsection shall apply –

(a) so long as the person concerned makes the payments for which he is liable under paragraph (b) below, he shall not be liable to make any refund under subsection (3) above and the local authority shall not be liable to make any payment under subsection (2) above in respect of the accommodation provided for him;
(b) the person concerned shall be liable to pay to the provider such sums as he would otherwise (under subsection (3) above) be liable to pay by way of refund to the local authority; and
(c) the local authority shall be liable to pay to the provider the difference between the sums paid by virtue of paragraph (b) above and the payments which, but for paragraph (a) above, the authority would be liable to pay under subsection (2) above.

(4) *Subsections (5A) (7) and (9)* Subsection (5A) of the said section twenty-two shall, with the necessary modifications, apply for the purposes of the last foregoing subsection as *they apply* it applies for the purposes of the said section twenty-two.

(4AA) Subsections (2) to (4) shall have effect subject to any regulations under section 15 [or 16] of the Community Care (Delayed Discharges etc) Act 2003 (power to require certain community care services and services for carers to be free of charge).

(4A) Section 21(5) of this Act shall have effect as respects accommodation provided under arrangements made by virtue of this section with the substitution for the reference to the authority managing the premises of a reference to the authority making the arrangements.

(5) Where in any premises accommodation is being provided under this section in accordance with arrangements made by any local authority, any person authorised in that behalf by the authority may at all reasonable times enter and inspect the premises.

(6) (*repealed*)

(7) In this section the expression "voluntary organisation" includes any association which is a housing association for the purposes of the Housing Act 1936 and "exempt body" means an authority or body constituted by an Act of Parliament or incorporated by Royal Charter.

Amendments: Local Government Act 1972; Health Services and Public Health Act 1968; Health and Social Services and Social Security Adjudications Act 1983, s 20(1); National Health Service and Community Care Act 1990; Community Care (Residential Accommodation) Act 1992; Care Standards Act 2000; National Health Service Reform and Health Care Professions Act 2002; Health and Social Care Act 2012; SI 2007/961; SI 2010/813.

Prospective Amendments: Sub-s (4): words "Subsections (5A), (7) and (9)" in italics prospectively repealed and subsequent words in square brackets prospectively substituted, in relation to Scotland; Sub-s (4): words "they apply" in italics prospectively repealed and subsequent words in square brackets prospectively substituted, in relation to Scotland, by the Adult Support and Protection (Scotland) Act 2007, s 77(1), Sch 1, para 1(a)(ii); Sub-s (4AA) words "or 16" in square brackets prospectively inserted, in relation to England and Wales, by the Personal Care at Home Act 2010 with effect from a date to be appointed.

Welfare Services

29 Welfare arrangements for blind, deaf, dumb and crippled persons, etc

(1) A local authority may, with the approval of the Secretary of State, and to such extent as he may direct in relation to persons ordinarily resident in the area of the local authority shall make arrangements for promoting the welfare of persons to whom this section applies, that is to say persons aged eighteen or over who are blind, deaf or dumb or who suffer from mental disorder of any description, and other persons aged eighteen or over who are substantially and permanently handicapped by illness, injury, or congenital deformity or such other disabilities as may be prescribed by the Minister.

(2), (3) *(repealed)*

(4) Without prejudice to the generality of the provisions of subsection (1) of this section, arrangements may be made thereunder –

- (a) for informing persons to whom arrangements under that subsection relate of the services available for them thereunder;
- (b) for giving such persons instruction in their own homes or elsewhere in methods of overcoming the effects of their disabilities;
- (c) for providing workshops where such persons may be engaged (whether under a contract of service or otherwise) in suitable work, and hostels where persons engaged in the workshops, and other persons to whom arrangements under subsection (1) of this section relate and for whom work or training is being provided in pursuance of the Disabled Persons (Employment) Act 1944 or the Employment and Training Act 1973 may live;
- (d) for providing persons to whom arrangements under subsection (1) of this section relate with suitable work (whether under a contract of service or otherwise) in their own homes or elsewhere;
- (e) for helping such persons in disposing of the produce of their work;
- (f) for providing such persons with recreational facilities in their own homes or elsewhere;
- (g) for compiling and maintaining classified registers of the persons to whom arrangements under subsection (1) of this section relate.

(4A) Where accommodation in a hostel is provided under paragraph (c) of subsection (4) of this section –

(a) if the hostel is managed by a local authority, section 22 of this Act shall apply as it applies where accommodation is provided under section 21;
(b) if the accommodation is provided in a hostel managed by a person other than a local authority under arrangements made with that person, subsections (2) to (4A) of section 26 of this Act shall apply as they apply where accommodation is provided under arrangements made by virtue of that section; and
(c) section 32 shall apply as it applies where accommodation is provided under sections 21 to 26;

and in this subsection references to "accommodation" include references to board and other services, amenities and requisites provided in connection with the accommodation, except where in the opinion of the authority managing the premises or, in the case mentioned in paragraph (b) above, the authority making the arrangements their provision is unnecessary.

(5) *(repealed)*

(6) Nothing in the foregoing provisions of this section shall authorise or require –

(a) the payment of money to persons to whom this section applies, other than persons for whom work is provided under arrangements made by virtue of paragraph (c) or paragraph (d) of subsection (4) of this section or who are engaged in work which they are enabled to perform in consequence of anything done in pursuance of arrangements made under this section; or
(b) the provision of any accommodation or services required to be provided under the National Health Service Act 2006 or the National Health Service (Wales) Act 2006.

(7) A person engaged in work in a workshop provided under paragraph (c) of subsection (4) of this section, or a person in receipt of a superannuation allowance granted on his retirement from engagement in any such workshop, shall be deemed for the purposes of this Act to continue to be ordinarily resident in the area in which he was ordinarily resident immediately before he was accepted for work in that workshop; and for the purposes of this subsection a course of training in such a workshop shall be deemed to be work in that workshop.

Amendments: Local Government Act 1972; Employment and Training Act 1973; Health and Social Services and Social Security Adjudications Act 1983; National Health Service and Community Care Act 1990.

30 Voluntary organisations for disabled persons' welfare

(1) A local authority may, in accordance with arrangements made under section 29 of this Act, employ as their agent for the purposes of that section any voluntary organisation or any person carrying on, professionally or by way of trade or business, activities which consist of or include the provision of services for any of the persons to whom section 29 above applies, being an organisation or person appearing to the authority to be capable of providing the service to which the arrangements apply.

(2)–(3) *(repealed)*

Amendments: Repealed in relation to Scotland by the Social Work (Scotland) Act 1968, s 95(2), Sch 9, Part I; amended by Statute Law Revision Act 1953; Health Services and Public Health Act 1968; Local Government Act 1972; National Health Service and Community Care Act 1990

30A Research

Without prejudice to any powers conferred on them by any other Act, –

(a) the Secretary of State may promote research into any matter relating to the functions of local authorities under this Part of this Act, and, in particular, may participate with or assist other persons in conducting such research; and
(b) a local authority may conduct or assist other persons in conducting research into any matter relating to the functions of local authorities under this Part of this Act.

Amendments: Inserted by the Health and Social Services and Social Security Adjudications Act 1983.

Financial adjustments between Local Authorities

32 Adjustments between authority providing accommodation, etc, and authority of area of residence

(1) Any expenditure which apart from this section would fall to be borne by a local authority –

(a) in the provision under this Part of this Act of accommodation for a person ordinarily resident in the area of another local authority, or
(b) in the provision under section twenty-nine of this Act of services for a person ordinarily so resident, or
(c) in providing under paragraph (a) of subsection (7) of section twenty-one of this Act for the conveyance of a person ordinarily resident as aforesaid,

shall be recoverable from the said other local authority, and in this subsection any reference to another local authority includes a reference to a local authority in Scotland.

(2) For the purposes of paragraph (a) of the last foregoing subsection it shall be assumed that the expenditure incurred by a local authority in providing accommodation for any person is, as respects accommodation provided in premises managed by a local authority, at the rate for the time being fixed for that accommodation under subsection (2) of section twenty-two of this Act, and, as respects accommodation provided pursuant to an arrangement made under section twenty-six of this Act, at the rate referred to in subsection (2) of that section.

(3) Any question arising under this Part as to a person's ordinary residence shall be determined by the Secretary of State or by the Welsh Ministers.

(4) The Secretary of State and the Welsh Ministers shall make and publish arrangements for determining which cases are to be dealt with by the Secretary of State and which are to be dealt with by the Welsh Ministers.

(5) Those arrangements may include provision for the Secretary of State and the Welsh Ministers to agree, in relation to any question that has arisen, which of them is to deal with the case.

Amendment: Repealed in relation to Scotland by the Social Work (Scotland) Act 1968, s 95(2), Sch 9, Part I; amended by Social Work (Scotland) Act 1968; Health and Social Care Act 2008.

Local and Central Authorities

33 Local Authorities for purposes of Part III

(1) In this Part of this Act the expression "local authority" means a council which is a local authority for the purposes of the Local Authority Social Services Act 1970 in England or Wales, and a council constituted under section 2 of the Local Government etc (Scotland) Act 1994 in Scotland:

(2) *(repealed)*

Amendments: Local Government Act 1972; Local Government (Scotland) Act 1973; Local Authority Social Services Act 1970; Local Government etc (Scotland) Act 1994.

35 Central Authority for purposes of Part III

(1) For the purposes of this Part of this Act the expression "the Minister" means the Minister of Health.

(2)–(3) *(repealed)*

Amendments: Repealed in relation to Scotland by the Social Work (Scotland) Act 1968, s 95(2), Sch 9, Part I; amended by Social Work (Scotland) Act 1968; National Health Service and Community Care Act 1990.

47 Removal to suitable premises of persons in need of care and attention

(1) The following provisions of this section shall have effect for the purposes of securing the necessary care and attention for persons who—

(a) are suffering from grave chronic disease or, being aged, infirm or physically incapacitated, are living in insanitary conditions, and
(b) are unable to devote to themselves, and are not receiving from other persons, proper care and attention.

(1A) But this section does not apply to a person ("P") in either of the following cases.

(1B) The first case is where an order of the Court of Protection authorises the managing authority of a hospital or care home (within the meaning of Schedule A1 to the Mental Capacity Act 2005) to provide P with proper care and attention.

(1C) The second case is where—

(a) an authorisation under Schedule A1 to the Mental Capacity Act 2005 is in force, or
(b) the managing authority of a hospital or care home are under a duty under paragraph 24 of that Schedule to request a standard authorisation, and

P is, or would be, the relevant person in relation to the authorisation.

(2) If the medical officer of health certifies in writing to the appropriate authority that he is satisfied after thorough inquiry and consideration that in the interests of any such person as aforesaid residing in the area of the authority, or for preventing injury to the health of, or serious nuisance to, other persons, it is necessary to remove any such person as aforesaid from the premises in which he is residing, the appropriate authority may apply to a court of summary jurisdiction having jurisdiction in the place where the premises are situated for an order the next following subsection.

(3) On any such application the court may, if satisfied on oral evidence of the allegations in the certificate, and that it is expedient so to do, order the removal of the person to whom the application relates, by such officer of the appropriate authority as may be specified in the order, to a suitable hospital or other place in, or within convenient distance of, the area of the appropriate authority, and his detention 5and maintenance therein:

Provided that the court shall not order the removal of a person to any premises, unless either the person managing the premises has been heard in the proceedings or seven clear days' notice has been given to him of the intended application and of the time and place at which it is proposed to be made.

(4) An order under the last foregoing subsection may be made so as to authorise a person's detention for any period not exceeding three months, and the court may from time to time by order extend that period for such further period, not exceeding three months, as the court may determine.

(5) An order under subsection (3) of this section may be varied by an order of the court so as to substitute for the place referred to in that subsection such other suitable place in, or within convenient distance of, the area of the appropriate authority as the court may determine, so however that the proviso to the said subsection (3) shall with the necessary modification apply to any proceedings under this subsection.

(6) At any time after the expiration of six clear weeks from the making of an order under subsection (3) or (4) of this section an application may be made to the court by or on behalf of the person in respect of whom the order was made, and on any such application the court may, if in the circumstances it appears expedient so to do, revoke the order.

(7) No application under this section shall be entertained by the court unless, seven clear days before the making of the application, notice has been given of the intended application and of the time and place at which it is proposed to be made –

(a) where the application is for an order under subsection (3) or (4) of this section, to the person in respect of whom the application is made or to some person in charge of him;
(b) where the application is for the revocation of such an order, to the medical officer of health

(8) Where in pursuance of an order under this section a person is maintained neither in hospital accommodation provided by the Minister of Health under the National Health Service Act 2006 or the National Health Service (Wales) Act 2006, or by the Secretary of State under the National Health Service (Scotland) Act 1947, nor in premises where accommodation is provided by, or by arrangement with, a local authority under Part III of this Act, the cost of his maintenance shall be borne by the appropriate authority.

(9) Any expenditure incurred under the last foregoing subsection shall be recoverable from the person maintained; and any expenditure incurred by virtue of this section in connection with the maintenance of a person in premises where accommodation is provided under Part III of this Act shall be recoverable in like manner as expenditure incurred in providing accommodation under the said Part III.

(10) (*repealed*)

(11) Any person who wilfully disobeys, or obstructs the execution of, an order under this section shall be guilty of an offence and liable on summary conviction to a fine not exceeding level 1 on the standard scale.

(12) For the purposes of this section, the appropriate authorities shall be the councils of districts and London Boroughs and the Common Council of the City of London, in Wales the councils of counties and county boroughs and in Scotland the councils constituted under section 2 of the Local Government etc (Scotland) Act 1994.

(12A) In this section, "the court"—

(a) in England and Wales, means a magistrates' court acting in the local justice area where the premises are situated;
(b) in Scotland, means the sheriff having jurisdiction in the place where the premises are situated.

(13) The foregoing provisions of this section shall have effect in substitution for any provisions for the like purposes contained in, or having effect under, any public general or local Act passed before the passing of this Act:

Provided that nothing in this subsection shall be construed as affecting any enactment providing for the removal to, or detention in, hospital of persons suffering from notifiable or infectious diseases.

(14) Any notice under this section may be served by post.

Amendments: London Government Act 1963; Local Government (Wales) Act 1994; Local Government Act 1972; Criminal Law Act 1977; Criminal Justice Act 1982; National Health Service Reorganisation Act 1973; Mental Health Act 2007; Courts Act 2003; National Health Service (Consequential Provisions) Act 2006; Health and Social Care Act 2008.

APPENDIX 2

WHERE TO FIND OTHER LEGISLATION AND GUIDANCE

The Court of Protection Rules 2007 are available from http://www.justice.gov.uk/courts/rcj-rolls-building/court-of-protection.

The Civil Procedure Rules are available from http://www.justice.gov.uk/courts/procedure-rules/civil/rules.

Other legislation (such as Acts of Parliament, Regulations and Orders) is available from www.legislation.gov.uk.

Most of the guidance referred to in this book is available on the Internet. The links in the table were checked at the time of publication.

Mental Capacity Act 2005 Code of Practice	http://www.justice.gov.uk/downloads/protecting-the-vulnerable/mca/mca-code-practice-0509.pdf
Mental Health Act Code of Practice 2008 (England)	http://webarchive.nationalarchives.gov.uk/20130107105354/http://www.dh.gov.uk/prod_consum_dh/groups/dh_digitalassets/@dh/@en/documents/digitalasset/dh_087073.pdf
Mental Health Act Code of Practice for Wales	http://www.wales.nhs.uk/sites3/Documents/816/Mental%20Health%20Act%201983%20Code%20of%20Practice%20for%20Wales.pdf
Alzheimer's Society: Position Statements	http://www.alzheimers.org.uk/site/scripts/documents_info.php?documentID=1034
Guidance for access to health records and requests (2010)	http://webarchive.nationalarchives.gov.uk/20130107105354/http://www.dh.gov.uk/en/Publicationsandstatistics/Publications/PublicationsPolicyAndGuidance/DH_112916
Confidentiality NHS Code of Practice (2003)	https://www.gov.uk/government/publications/confidentiality-nhs-code-of-practice

At a glance: Guide to the current Medical Standards of Fitness to Drive (April 2013)	https://www.gov.uk/government/publications/at-a-glance
GMC – Confidentiality: reporting concerns about patients to the DVLA or the DVA	http://www.gmc-uk.org/Confidentiality_reporting_concerns_DVLA_2009.pdf_27494214.pdf
Guide to Data Protection, Information Commissioner's Office	http://www.ico.org.uk/for_organisations/data_protection/the_guide
Subject Access Code of Practice: Dealing with requests for personal information	http://www.ico.org.uk/for_organisations/data_protection/the_guide/principle_6/access_to_personal_data#others
Data Protection Act 1998 Guidance for Social Services (2000)	http://webarchive.nationalarchives.gov.uk/+/www.dh.gov.uk/en/publicationsandstatistics/publications/publicationslegislation/dh_4010391
Prioritising need in the context of Putting People First: A whole system approach to eligibility for social care (Guidance on Eligibility Criteria for Adult Social Care, England 2010)	http://webarchive.nationalarchives.gov.uk/20130107105354/http:/www.dh.gov.uk/en/Publicationsandstatistics/Publications/PublicationsPolicyAndGuidance/DH_113154
Creating a Unified and Fair System for Assessing and Managing Care	www.wales.gov.uk/subisocialpolicysocialservices/content/mangingcircular-e.htm
National Framework for NHS Continuing Healthcare and NHS-funded Nursing Care	https://www.gov.uk/government/publications/national-framework-for-nhs-continuing-healthcare-and-nhs-funded-nursing-care
Decision Support Tool for NHS Continuing Healthcare (November 2012)(Revised)	https://www.gov.uk/government/uploads/system/uploads/attachment_data/file/213139/Decision-Support-Tool-for-NHS-Continuing-Healthcare.pdf
NHS Continuing Healthcare Checklist (November 2012)	https://www.gov.uk/government/uploads/system/uploads/attachment_data/file/213138/NHS-CHC-Checklist-FINAL.pdf
Continuing NHS Healthcare: The National Framework for Implementation in Wales (EH/ML/018/10 Welsh Assembly Government Circular: 015/2010)	http://wales.gov.uk/docs/dhss/publications/100614chcframeworken.pdf

No Secrets' guidance on developing and implementing multi-agency policies and procedures to protect vulnerable adults from abuse	https://www.gov.uk/government/uploads/system/uploads/attachment_data/file/194272/No_secrets__guidance_on_developing_and_implementing_multi-agency_policies_and_procedures_to_protect_vulnerable_adults_from_abuse.pdf
Who Pays? Determining responsibility for payments to providers, August 2013	http://www.england.nhs.uk/wp-content/uploads/2013/08/who-pays-aug13.pdf
NHS-funded Nursing Care Practice Guide, July 2013 (Revised)	https://www.gov.uk/government/uploads/system/uploads/attachment_data/file/211256/NHS-funded_Nursing_Care_Best_Practice_Guidance.pdf
Refocusing the Care Programme Approach, Policy and Positive Practice Guidance, March 2008	http://webarchive.nationalarchives.gov.uk/20130107105354/http:/www.dh.gov.uk/prod_consum_dh/groups/dh_digitalassets/@dh/@en/documents/digitalasset/dh_083649.pdf
NICE clinical guideline 42, Dementia – Supporting people with dementia and their carers in health and social care, November 2006	http://www.nice.org.uk/nicemedia/live/10998/30318/30318.pdf
Fair Access to Care Services Practice Guidance: Implementation Questions and Answer	http://webarchive.nationalarchives.gov.uk/20130107105354/http://www.dh.gov.uk/prod_consum_dh/groups/dh_digitalassets/@dh/@en/documents/digitalasset/dh_4019734.pdf
Fairer Charging Policies for Home Care and Other non-residential Social Service	https://www.gov.uk/government/uploads/system/uploads/attachment_data/file/208323/Fairer_Charging_Guidance_final_2013-06-20_rc.pdf
Introducing More Consistency in Local Authorities' Charging for Non-Residential Social Services	http://wales.gov.uk/docs/dhss/publications/110615chargingen.pdf
Guidance on Direct Payments England	http://webarchive.nationalarchives.gov.uk/20130107105354/http://www.dh.gov.uk/prod_consum_dh/groups/dh_digitalassets/@dh/@en/@ps/documents/digitalasset/dh_121131.pdf
Direct Payments Guidance Wales	http://wales.gov.uk/docs/dhss/publications/110801payentsen.pdf

Fairer Contributions Guidance 2010: Calculating an Individual's Contribution to their Personal Budget	https://www.gov.uk/government/uploads/system/uploads/attachment_data/file/215974/dh_121223.pdf
Charging for Residential Accommodation Guide (England)	https://www.gov.uk/government/uploads/system/uploads/attachment_data/file/208532/CRAG_guidance_web_publishing_2013_-_06-20rc_1_.pdf
Welsh Assembly Government Charging for Residential Accommodation Guide	http://wales.gov.uk/docs/dhss/publications/110803crag2011en.doc
LAC (98) 19	http://webarchive.nationalarchives.gov.uk/20130107105354/http://www.dh.gov.uk/prod_consum_dh/groups/dh_digitalassets/@dh/@en/documents/digitalasset/dh_4012554.pdf
LAC (2003) 14	http://webarchive.nationalarchives.gov.uk/20130107105354/http://www.dh.gov.uk/prod_consum_dh/groups/dh_digitalassets/@dh/@en/documents/digitalasset/dh_4012833.pdf
LAC (2001) 25	http://webarchive.nationalarchives.gov.uk/20130107105354/http://www.dh.gov.uk/prod_consum_dh/groups/dh_digitalassets/@dh/@en/documents/digitalasset/dh_4077806.pdf
Equality and Human Rights Commission Codes of Practice and Guidance	http://www.equalityhumanrights.com/legal-and-policy/equality-act/equality-act-codes-of-practice-and-technical-guidance

INDEX

References are to paragraph numbers.